Value and Vulnerability

VALUE AND VULNERABILITY

An Interfaith Dialogue on Human Dignity

EDITED BY

Matthew R. Petrusek and Jonathan Rothchild

University of Notre Dame Press

Notre Dame, Indiana

University of Notre Dame Press
Notre Dame, Indiana 46556
undpress.nd.edu

Published in the United States of America

Library of Congress Control Number: 2020937031

ISBN: 978-0-268-10665-2 (Hardback)
ISBN: 978-0-268-10667-6 (WebPDF)
ISBN: 978-0-268-10668-3 (Epub)

M.P.: To Maria Nieves, Mateo, Solana, and Julieta
J.R.: To Charlotte, Theo, and Max

Contents

Acknowledgments

This volume was made possible through collaboration of contributors, editors, and the University of Notre Dame Press. The editors are grateful to the contributors for their nuanced arguments and responsiveness to deadlines and to members of the press, particularly Stephen Little, acquisitions editor, for their professionalism and stewardship of the project. Comments from the three anonymous external reviewers helped clarify the structure and flow of the volume. We also wish to thank the Huffington Ecumenical Institute at Loyola Marymount University and the Dean's Office of Bellarmine College of Liberal Arts for their financial support. Thanks also to colleagues in the Theological Studies Department at LMU for their collegiality and intellectual community.

INTRODUCTION

Matthew R. Petrusek and Jonathan Rothchild

The word "dignity" is frequently invoked in courtrooms, hospital rooms, places of worship, and on battlefields. Laws are designed to protect and promote dignity in terms of prohibitions, such as against torture and genocide, and in terms of positive freedoms, such as the right to work and to exercise conscience. There may be general consensus about the importance of dignity as a basis for modern human rights, but the complexities of individual, communal, institutional, and global contexts and competing and conflicting goods, values, and interests often problematize straightforward implementation of policies and practices rooted in human dignity. Dimensions of power, oppressive social structures (social sin), and various forms of injustice further exacerbate violations of human rights, which are necessary for the full realization of human dignity. In the face of dehumanizing systems and forces, can theological, philosophical, and legal frameworks provide conceptual clarity regarding universally accepted meanings of dignity and encourage practical strategies that address contexts and lived experiences of diminished dignity?

In response to these issues, contemporary scholarship on human dignity has appeared to reach two firm, if problematic, conclusions: (1) the appeal to dignity as a foundational moral principle is widespread in moral discourse in a vast number of fields (e.g., law, medicine, education, politics) and on numerous issues (e.g., abortion, euthanasia, torture, immigration, marriage equality), and it does not show any signs of abating; (2) there is nothing close to a widespread consensus on how to define dignity or on what specific actions dignity prohibits or requires. Like "equality," "freedom," or "fairness," "dignity" appears to be one of those ideas that most everybody agrees on until someone starts making claims about what it might mean and asserts it as a warrant for specific ethical judgments.

The fact that advocates on both sides of hotly contested issues frequently draw on dignity in order to demonstrate the error, if not moral depravity, of the opposing side—as we see, for example, in debates on assisted suicide, abortion, and, more recently, religious freedom—raises the question of whether dignity has any fixed meaning at all. Add to this the complexity of the philosophical and theological disagreement lying beneath the different conceptions of dignity and the question becomes even sharper: Is dignity destined to fail as a coherent and useful moral principle? Is there any unity to dignity's diversity beyond an appeal to the same word? Or, as Christopher McCrudden, editor of *Understanding Human Dignity*, has put it, "Are we all singing from the same hymn sheet when we use the concept of human dignity, and is it a problem if we are not?"[1]

Given dignity's prevalence in theological and secular discourse and the many contexts in which it appears as the basis for moral judgment, these questions have more than theoretical importance. If dignity is going to continue to function as more than an evocative but otherwise vacuously malleable principle in contemporary moral discourse, more work needs to be done both to identify and analyze dignity's meaning in different religious and secular traditions, and to demonstrate how these meanings can help address concrete moral problems. Despite a growing scholarly interest in the definition and application of dignity,[2] this interpretive, comparative, and normative work on the problem of human worth still stands as one of the most important tasks in contemporary ethics. And it is precisely this task to which this book seeks to make a fresh contribution.

The collection of essays in this volume approaches the question of dignity from three interrelated perspectives: systematically, comparatively, and practically. First, the chapters in part I offer a sustained and nuanced conceptual examination of the definition of dignity from diverse religious and philosophical traditions. We have already noted that there has been some important theological and philosophical work on defining dignity recently. However, despite the growing prevalence of dignity in popular and academic discourses, scholarly literature on the topic has still not sufficiently examined dignity's normative meaning and its grounding from a systematic perspective, especially in relation to these kinds of fundamental questions: What is dignity and on what grounds do humans possess it? Does dignity require being ontologically grounded in the transcendent in order to provide a coherent explanation for its existence? What, if anything, is unique about dignity? Is it universal and equal? Is it inherent or attained? Can it be lost or diminished, that is, is it vulnerable to harm?

Epistemologically, how can one *know* that humans have dignity, particularly if one seeks to make appeals to sacred texts to establish its existence and moral relevance? Part I addresses these and related questions from the perspectives of eight distinct traditions: Catholicism, Protestantism, Eastern Orthodoxy, Judaism, Islam, Hinduism, Buddhism, and humanism.

Second, and related, the book places these perspectives in constructive comparison. In addition to its systematic analysis of dignity, part I also provides responses that critically analyze two traditions from a different viewpoint, highlighting similarities, differences, and points of interest and concern (so, for example, there is a Catholic response to the chapters on Judaism and Orthodoxy; Jewish and Hindu responses to each other's chapters, etc.). These responses seek to expand and deepen each tradition's respective conception of dignity while also serving the mutually illuminating purpose of demonstrating where there is—and is not—substantive agreement or overlapping consensus. The respective systematic conceptions of dignity thus do not stand in isolation; placed in constructive comparison, they provide a framework for interreligious and ecumenical conversation on the normative understanding and application of dignity.

Third, the book demonstrates how dignity can be applied in practice in different contexts, particularly in situations of conflict broadly defined. In part I, many chapters identify central themes and also differing strands of thought within a tradition shaped by contexts and conflicts of interpretations. These chapters conclude by reflecting on the ways that understandings of dignity can be applied to contested contemporary moral issues. Moreover, part II provides a more sustained case study analysis of the role dignity can and should play in adjudicating diverse situations of conflict, including gendered violence, religiously based disputes, race and racism, immigration, peacebuilding, ecology, and criminal justice. In short, the chapters in both parts I and II seek to demonstrate how the otherwise potentially abstract conceptions of human worth can provide concrete norms for protecting and advancing individual and communal flourishing amidst violence and other forms of moral harm.

Ultimately, our overriding goal is to provide greater illumination on what has emerged as an indispensable, if still unclearly defined, concept in contemporary theological and philosophical moral discourse. In the process, without collapsing differences between and within traditions, the contributors also seek to identify and establish common ground among differing conceptions of God and the human good.

A COMPARATIVE ANALYSIS: CONCEPTUAL SIMILARITIES AND DIFFERENCES IN RESPONSE TO SEVEN INTERRELATED QUESTIONS

A common theme that emerges from the chapters herein comes in the form of a response to the question, posed above, of whether there is any unity to the diversity of dignity's respective formulations and applications. In short, yes: although dignity may not be "universal" in an empirical sense, meaning that we can point to some conception of it in *every* theological and philosophical tradition, the sustained analysis of dignity in these pages demonstrates that there is, indeed, some foundational conception of human worth within many of the world's major traditions. That, by itself, is a vitally important conclusion: dignity may be flexible, but it does not appear to be formless. The book confirms that there is, indeed, a "there" there after all, one that we have good reason to draw on in order to address local and global issues. Dignity provides an important bridge concept for interfaith dialogue.

Yet given the different moral systems the traditions affirm, each based on a different conception of ultimate reality and shaped by unique historical, cultural, and sociopolitical factors, how can we speak about these similarities cogently while also identifying and understanding their relevant differences? Within the discourse of dignity in the West, in particular, several key terms have emerged as central to defining and normatively applying dignity as a practical moral principle. These include "freedom," "autonomy," "rationality," "personhood," "individuality," and "uniqueness," among others. These and related terms remain important to the contemporary discussion of dignity, but the diversity of religious and philosophical perspectives in this book quickly reveals that they are not universal, nor do they have univocal meanings within the different traditions that employ them. For example, both Catholicism and humanism may describe human beings as "free" and even identify freedom as an essential characteristic of what it means to possess dignity. However, "freedom" from a Catholic perspective could be defined as the capacity to conform one's whole being to Christ in and through living according to the natural law and the theological and moral teachings of the magisterium, but "freedom" from a humanistic perspective could be defined as a capacity to choose among morally licit but otherwise amoral ends (which may or may not include any conception of conforming one's being to the divine) within a paradigm of dignity conceived of as "autonomy" (that is, being a law unto oneself). In this case, stating that "both Catholicism and humanism locate freedom at the center of their conceptions of dignity," even if descriptively accurate, would obfuscate as much as it clarifies, given the profoundly different definitions of freedom operating within each tradition.

Another example is the concept of personhood. The idea of the non-self of all conditioned beings in Buddhist traditions provides a basis for challenging the normativity implied by human dignity. Other traditions locate personhood within human nature, whereas still others describe personhood as freedom from nature. Seeking to establish fixed substantive meanings to key terms often associated with discourses on dignity is problematic in a comparative context, something that will become even more apparent in subsequent chapters.

However, recognizing this complexity does not mean that we cannot identify a shared foundation for comparison. Indeed, one answer to the question of how to speak cogently about the similarities and differences among the different traditions represented in this book takes the form of the concept of dignity itself. The recognition that each tradition contains something like the affirmation that human beings qua human beings have value provides the grounds for a coherent comparison. Each tradition provides distinctive accounts of what specifically defines the "human" and distinctive accounts of what, specifically, gives human beings "worth," but each *different* conception answers the *same* basic questions about the existence and nature of dignity. Moreover, the answers the traditions provide to these questions tend to fall into another set of basic conceptual categories. These questions, and corresponding answers, provide the basis for comparison among the differing traditions (and strands within these traditions) while also helping to clarify each tradition's internal understanding of its own conception of dignity.

Below we have posted seven basic conceptual questions, along with categories of possible answers, which define conceptions of dignity in this book. In our introduction to part I, we provide brief summaries of the chapters, but here we use the seven conceptual questions as lenses for comparative analysis of the traditions. These questions, it is important to note, do not seek to capture the substantive nuances of each tradition's conception of dignity, nor do they seek to provide an exhaustive descriptive account of each tradition (and its internal methodological debates and conflicts of interpretations) more broadly (e.g., a definition of "Catholicism," "Judaism," or "Hinduism," as such), either in terms of how a tradition understands itself or how it may be understood by other traditions. The scope of consideration is deliberately limited to the conceptions of dignity as each contributor portrays them. Within that arena, however, we believe that the following questions and answers provide coherent and illuminating grounds for identifying and conceptually organizing each tradition's conception of dignity, both individually and in relation to the other traditions, while also continuing to allow each tradition to speak for itself.

Question One: What sources justify dignity's existence, nature, and purpose?

Each tradition's conception of dignity not only makes claims about its distinctive understanding of why and how human beings have value as humans, but each also provides an account of *why* that is the case, including identifying and defending the source or sources of its particular conceptions. Again, there is substantive diversity among the traditions on the specific content of the sources each draws upon in constructing its account of dignity, but they all fall *primarily* into one or more of the four categories of sources we list below. Each source is followed by a brief definition:

1. *Sacred Texts and Revelation.* Conceptions of dignity in this category appeal to some form of sacred, canonical text in order to define *why* humans have dignity and what defines dignity. The basic defining feature of conceptions of dignity in this category is the implied epistemological and practical limitation on dignity's existence and nature: one must recognize the authority of the sacred text and its particular interpretation in order to know both (a) what fully defines dignity and (b) why dignity ought to serve as a morally obligatory guide for human action. Presumably, those who deny the authority of such texts, or are not otherwise aware of their content, would not have access to the unique claims about dignity that such texts affirm. Moreover, unlike the "Ecclesial Structures and Tradition" category (see no. 4, below), this category does not emphasize the necessity of an institutional authority to establish the normative interpretation of the sacred text.
2. *Reason and Empirical Observation.* Conceptions of dignity in this category seek to locate the grounds of human worth within some claim or set of claims that is accessible to all human beings otherwise identified as "rational." Unlike appeals to sacred texts or revelation, rational conceptions of dignity do not presume the authority of revealed truth in order to demonstrate the validity of their conception of dignity. Also, unlike the following two categories (3 and 4, below), they also do not presuppose any specific kind of personal or cultural experience or the mediating presence of

an institution or intellectual tradition. Dignity from this perspective seeks to be understood as "self-evident," meaning, in this context, that all rational persons, doing an authentic analysis of existence, including human existence, should be able to identify the same conception of dignity and the moral obligations that emanate from it without the aid of revelation or an ecclesial structure.

3. *Personal/Interpersonal Experience and Culture.* Conceptions of dignity in this category locate dignity within some kind of personal and/or interpersonal experience, including socialized and normatized experiences in the form of culture. In this category, the locus for understanding the existence and nature of dignity is not the observation of some "objective" phenomena or state of affairs, which would place it more in the "rational" category (no. 2, above); rather, it is a focus on the lived experiences of individuals and groups—including experiences of the divine—that may or may not be presumed to be universally applicable to all human beings. The experience of "shame," for example, is prominent in this category—dignity, from this perspective, is related to avoiding actions that cause shame, and in order to know what constitutes such possible shameful actions, one must consult cultural norms and/or individual experience.
4. *Ecclesial Structures and Tradition.* Conceptions of dignity in this category rely on some kind of mediating institution, such as the teaching authority of a church, to provide an account for dignity's existence and purpose. This category is distinct from the "Sacred Texts and Revelation" category because it presumes that such texts cannot and do not interpret themselves on the question of dignity; there must be some kind of authoritative body, in the form of a church hierarchy and/or church councils, that provides the fullest and most authentic interpretation of the text's meaning. Rationality, experience, and culture may be included as part of the theological deliberation of the authoritative body from this point of view, but ultimately this category maintains that the full truth about dignity is not only revealed but revealed through an institutional structure, and, therefore, one must accept the authority of the institution in order to fully comprehend and apply its teachings on human dignity.

To be sure, one could argue that each tradition discussed in this book, depending on its *specific* interpretation, falls into more than one of the above categories. Yet it remains the case that each tradition is defined within the contours of primarily *one* of the categories. For example, the Jewish, Protestant, and Islamic conceptions of dignity, notwithstanding their profound substantive differences, even with their shared Abrahamic lineage, fall primarily into the "Sacred Texts and Revelation" category: though they appeal to different sacred texts, it is primarily the content and authority of the texts themselves that identify the existence, nature, and purpose of human worth. The Hindu conception, in turn, primarily falls into the "Personal/Interpersonal Experience and Culture" category insofar as cultural norms (which are related, but not reducible, to sacred texts) and the experience of individuals within culture dictate the nature and application of dignity. In turn, both the Buddhist and humanistic understandings of dignity fall into the "Reason and Empirical Observation" category: although they appeal to profoundly different understandings of rationality, both identify conceptions of dignity that seek to be independent of any sacred text or membership in a particular cultural group. Instead, each bases its claims on forms of knowing that are presumably available to all human beings otherwise considered "rational." The Catholic and Orthodox conceptions, in turn, fall primarily into the "Ecclesial Structures and Tradition" category. Like the other traditions, both Catholicism and Eastern Orthodoxy contain elements from the other categories, but they ultimately recognize that it is the teaching authority of the Church—the magisterium in the case of Catholicism, and authoritative Church councils in the case of Orthodoxy—that has final authority over the meaning and normative use of dignity as a moral principle.

In short, each tradition *privileges* one of the four sources of dignity. In making this observation, we can establish both similarities and differences among the traditions at the conceptual level. Despite caveats and provisos, we can point to general conclusions. For example, with regard to the question of what kind of sources justify dignity's existence and purpose, Buddhism appears to be closer to humanism than to any of the "religious" traditions, and Judaism seems closer to Islam and Protestantism than to Catholicism or Eastern Orthodoxy. Hinduism, in contrast, appears to stand apart from all the other traditions, at least in the sense that it privileges interpersonal experience and culture as the primary interpretative lens. Overall, these categories help demonstrate in this context that traditions—that otherwise have very different substantive content (e.g., different names and definitions for the divine) and have been influenced by unique historical, cultural, and political contexts—nevertheless tend to draw on the *same kinds* of sources in order to explain their respective conceptions of dignity.

Question Two: What is the relationship between the divine and human dignity?

This question, in turn, can be divided into two subquestions: (1) Does the tradition ground its conception of dignity in some conception of the divine at all? (2) If the tradition *does* ground its conception of dignity in the divine, what is the specific nature of the relationship between the divine and dignity: (a) ontological, (b) relational, or (c) both relational and ontological?

Each tradition can and does fit into more than one category in relation to this question. However, each tradition is defined *primarily* by one category. For example, Buddhism and humanism seek to establish their conceptions of dignity independently of an appeal to "God," at least "God" conceived of as a transcendent, personal being who, by an act of divine will, creates and chooses to be in relationship with human beings (though, it is important to note, chapter 11 on humanism ultimately advances a version of "theological humanism," which complicates its placement in this category).

Islam and Judaism, in contrast, locate their conception of dignity within the divine, but do so primarily in the form of recognizing that dignity is a result of God having created human beings in a particular way. This takes the form of the *imago Dei* in Jewish thought and the recognition of human beings as the "vicegerent" of creation in Islamic thought. The value that humans qua humans bear in these traditions is ontological and inherent; it is not primarily something that God establishes by coming into personal relationship with human beings "after the fact" of creation.

The Protestant conception of dignity, in turn, also recognizes dignity as grounded in the divine. However, unlike Jewish and Islamic thought, it tends to understand dignity not primarily in an ontological sense, but rather as the result of God choosing to establish a personal, redemptive relationship with the individual in and through Jesus Christ. Although the Protestant account recognizes that God created human beings in God's image and likeness (*imago Dei*), it tends to understand human sin as having blotted out humanity's original goodness; consequently, any value that human beings "possess" after the Fall must be imputed to them by God in and through an ongoing relationship.

The Eastern Orthodox and Catholic traditions, in contrast, also locate dignity in the divine, but do so in a way that is both ontological and relational: human beings have dignity by virtue of being human beings made in the image and likeness of God (ontological), but because of human sin—which these traditions tend to interpret as degrading but not eradicating humanity's original goodness—that dignity can only be fully realized by God's redemptive action in and through Jesus Christ and the Holy Spirit (relational), which more specifically takes some form of sanctification.

Finally, Hinduism, too, locates its conception of dignity within the divine, though its recognition of multiple gods complicates the precise role the divine plays in dignity's existence and purpose. Notwithstanding this complexity, however, dignity in Hindu thought, similar in this respect to Judaism and Islam, appears to take a more ontological (dignity as inherent) rather than relational form.

In sum, on the question of the relationship between the dignity and the divine, Buddhism and humanism stand apart from the other traditions insofar as they do not explicitly derive their conceptions of dignity from the existence of a personal God or gods. All of the other traditions, in contrast, do recognize the necessity of the divine in order to establish the existence and purpose of dignity, but they do so in substantially different ways: Islam, Judaism, and Hinduism emphasize dignity as ontological, Protestantism emphasizes dignity as relational, and Eastern Orthodoxy and Catholicism recognize dignity as both ontological and relational (though we will also see that Orthodoxy's specific account of God's relationship with human beings has some affinities with the Protestant account of relationality).

Question Three: What is the relationship between dignity and the human body?

The relation between human dignity and the human body—understood, in this context, as the unique, material, corporal reality of each person that is distinct from his or her "soul"—is complex in each tradition. All of the traditions, however, share two foundational similarities on the question: (1) possessing dignity as a human being is profoundly related to having a human body in an ontological and moral sense, so that, for example, harming the human body can be defined as a *violation* of human dignity in each tradition; and (2) human dignity, in each tradition, is not *reducible* to the human body, so that, for example, each tradition can claim in different ways that biological death does not annihilate dignity.

This is another way of recognizing that none of the conceptions of dignity presented here is materialistic in the sense of *only* recognizing that which is made of matter, and that which is empirically observable, as the only substance in existence that is "real" and, consequently, morally relevant. Although each tradition differs, sometimes profoundly, on what defines a human "soul" in relation to dignity, all of them recognize the reality of some kind of nonempirical spiritual substance in human beings that is closely related not only to the definition of the human being as such (i.e., human beings are beings that have bodies *and* souls) but also to the *moral* definition of human beings (i.e., because human beings are beings that have bodies and souls, they therefore have moral value).

At the same time, each tradition, in its own way, seeks to recognize that that reality of a soul does not mean that the body is morally unimportant; in other words, none of the traditions embrace a Platonic or Gnostic understanding of the human being in which the body is negatively interpreted as a "prison" or some other kind of detriment to one's authentic humanity that must be "escaped." Every tradition, in short, affirms human beings as bearers of both body and soul and recognizes that *both* contribute to human beings having dignity, and thus both are morally relevant in considering what it means to treat a human being as dignified.

The differences among the traditions lie in the specific formulations within each tradition of what defines the soul, what defines the particular relationship between the soul and the body (e.g., the belief that a soul can be reincarnated in contrast with the belief that souls are embodied in individuals only once), and the *degree* to which the good of the body is indexed to the good of the soul in relation to human dignity. For example, the humanistic account of dignity does not appeal to any form of materialism, but it primarily conceives of dignity in terms of the integrity of all life, especially including human life, bodily understood. In contrast, Buddhism and Hinduism tend to mark a greater separation between the good of the body and the good of the soul in relation to dignity than do humanism and the other religious traditions, especially in their emphasis on ascetic practices and the overcoming of human desire as necessary for the attainment of one's full humanity. Islam, Judaism, Catholicism, and Eastern Orthodoxy, in turn, take a more moderate approach to the relative good of the body in relation to the soul, perhaps because each tradition recognizes, in its own way, that to be created by God means that one reflects the divine in one's bodily and spiritual existences. The belief in the Incarnation—the affirmation that God became fully human while remaining fully divine in the person of Jesus Christ—also heightens the moral value of the body in the Christian traditions in ways that distinguish them from the other traditions.

None of our contributors provide an exhaustive theological anthropology, but their respective descriptions of the human being as being both body and soul highlight the moral implications of the relative value of each in relation to dignity. For example, emphasizing the body as the primary category for defining dignity, as, for example, we especially see in humanism, may help clearly identify how dignity is vulnerable and in need of protection insofar as harm to one's body can be interpreted as harm to one's dignity. However, too closely aligning human dignity with the body may also undermine any claim that dignity is "transcendent" or "unconditional," two characteristics that may be conceptually necessary to claim that dignity is universal and equal (see question six below). Also, identifying dignity with the body complicates the claim that self-sacrificial love, including giving's one's life, can represent the fullest expression of what it means to have dignity (think, for example, of John 15:13: "Greater love has no man than this, that he lay down his life for his friends").

Conversely, emphasizing the soul as the primary category for defining dignity, as we see in the various religious traditions, may provide the conceptual ground for affirming dignity as equal, universal, and unconditional, and therefore not dependent on any action (or failure to act) for its existence. However, if one's dignity primarily resides in one's soul, then actions or historical-cultural environments that potentially harm the body may not be seen as morally problematic or urgent. If, for example, such a position were to uphold that it is possible to harm a body without harming a soul, then such a position would also would appear to imply that one's dignity can and does remain intact no matter what is done (or not done) to one's body. Framing the relationship between and among the soul, body, and dignity in this way may be beneficial in the sense that it potentially provides the grounds for claiming that no one or no thing can strip an individual of her or his dignity. However, it may also be morally problematic for the same reason: If dignity is invulnerable to any harm that may be done to the body, does that mean that the integrity of the body is morally unimportant?

This tension between the body and the soul is present in all the traditions we examine. Indeed, the normative relationship between the body and the soul as relates to human dignity remains a contested question both within each tradition and, comparatively, among them. No tradition in this context ultimately provides a definitive answer on how to resolve this tension, but all share a concern for highlighting the importance of both the material and spiritual dimensions of humanity in explaining why humans have dignity and what it means to treat individuals in accordance with that dignity.

Question Four: Is dignity vulnerable or invulnerable to moral harm?

This question, in turn, can be divided into two subquestions: (1) Is dignity vulnerable to moral harm *at all*? (2) If dignity *is* vulnerable to moral harm, is it vulnerable to (a) personal moral harm, (b) interpersonal moral harm, or (c) both? Before discussing each tradition in relation to these categories, it is important to flesh out what this question and related subquestions mean. To say that dignity is "invulnerable" in this context (responding "no" to subquestion "1") is to affirm that nothing—no action, no culture, no disease, no tragedy, no natural disaster—can harm dignity in the form of diminishing it or destroying it. Dignity defined as such is immune to any and every threat to its integrity. It is important to recognize, again, that attributing this kind of invulnerability to dignity appears to be necessary for defining dignity as both universal and equal (see question six below). In order for any tradition to claim that dignity applies to *all* human beings (universality) in the same measure and degree (equality), it must somehow explain how and why dignity can neither be extirpated or otherwise diminished by human action or anything else; for to recognize the possibility of extirpation or diminishment implies that there are some instances in which humans could either lose their dignity or have less dignity than others, which would directly contradict dignity's universality and/or equality. Describing dignity as invulnerable to moral harm is thus not only potentially one away to think of dignity among others, but it also seems to be a conceptual requisite to speak about *human* dignity at all, if, by "human," we mean *every* member of the human species.

To say that dignity is "vulnerable," in contrast (responding to subquestion "2"), is to recognize that dignity *is* vulnerable to harm. Although vulnerability, as a category, can recognize that dignity can be harmed by events and conditions outside of human control (e.g., disease, disability, natural disasters, etc.), the focus of vulnerability in this context is what is under human control, namely, human action. Human action, in turn, can be divided into two different types that are relevant for evaluating dignity's vulnerability: (a) personal action, and (b) interpersonal action and social structures. Personal action is defined as any action an individual commits, or fails to commit, in relation to oneself. The defining characteristic of such action is that one voluntarily chooses to perform such action specifically in relation to oneself. All other things being equal, for example, a paradigmatic example of personal action would be an individual's choice to try a recreational drug for the first time; even though subsequent uses of the drug may or may not be fully voluntary, the first time likely is: one is purposefully choosing to do something to oneself. Likewise, again, all other factors being equal, one could voluntarily choose never to exercise; though one is choosing *not* to do something, refraining from acting in this instance is also specifically in relation to oneself. To be sure, there are philosophical and theological positions that deny any action is "voluntary" because they locate the efficient cause of an individual's act ultimately outside her reason and will (e.g., in a chemical reaction in the brain or in God's omnipotence). However, insofar as any tradition is willing to recognize the existence of voluntary action at all, *personal* action, in this context, is defined as action that one chooses to commit in relation to oneself and, consequently, in this context, in relation to one's own dignity. Thus, to claim that dignity is personally vulnerable is to claim that the integrity of one's own dignity is vulnerable to how one acts, or fails to act, in relation to oneself. It is important to add that "thoughts" and "beliefs" can constitute personal actions defined in this way because they can potentially have an effect on an individual's dignity even if there is no corresponding external action (e.g., believing oneself to be "worthless" while continuing to act "normally").

To claim that dignity is interpersonally vulnerable, on the other hand, is to recognize that the integrity of dignity is vulnerable to the actions of *others* and/or their failure to act. Given that we cannot know what others' thoughts and beliefs are without some external manifestation of them (e.g., speaking, looking askance, refusing to serve, etc.), actions in this category do not include thoughts and beliefs. Rather, interpersonal vulnerability focuses on how others' *treatment* of an individual can potentially affect the integrity of that individual's dignity.

Interpersonal vulnerability recognizes that this treatment can take more than one form. It is not limited only to individuals acting in relation to other individuals. For example, being mugged, sexually assaulted, or tortured would certainly constitute examples of interpersonal action that can harm an individual's dignity. However, actions that cannot clearly be traced back to one person or a specific group of people—for example, cultural attitudes, economic systems, prejudicial hiring practices or sentencing guidelines—can also potentially undermine an individual's dignity, and so also fall within the gamut of interpersonal action and, hence, interpersonal vulnerability. Extending further, one can argue that forms of social sin such as racism, sexism, and classism also pertain to personal vulnerability in that they limit and erode an individual's free choice to pursue the good. In sum, whether the source of the action is another individual or an entire "system," interpersonal vulnerability recognizes that dignity is vulnerable both to what others do and fail to do (e.g., not providing an education or police protection).

As with defining dignity as *in*vulnerable, defining dignity as *vulnerable* in this way has important moral implications. In particular, attributing vulnerability to dignity may be necessary for explaining how dignity can function as a practical moral principle, that is, a principle that can coherently prohibit and prescribe certain kinds of actions. If, for example, a tradition were only to define dignity as invulnerable in the sense described above, it may be able to account for why and how dignity is universal and equal. However, it would be unclear what moral work dignity would do as a moral principle; for why would one need to protect something that, by definition, could not be protected? What would be the purpose of proclaiming that all humans have equal value while concurrently affirming that there is nothing we can do to safeguard that value because, again, it is defined as something that does not need safeguarding? In short, attributing some form of vulnerability to dignity appears necessary for explaining how dignity can help identify actions that protect dignity (and thus ought to be performed) and actions that harm dignity (and thus ought not be performed). It is not clear how a definition of dignity as exclusively invulnerable could function in this way.

Moreover, describing dignity as interpersonally *and* personally vulnerable to action more specifically also seems necessary in order to define it as a coherent and actionable moral principle. Think, for example, of a definition of dignity that could be derived from a conception of moral worth similar to the one in St. John Chrysostom's classic text *No One Can Harm the Man Who Does Not Harm Himself*, which, in turn, has roots in Socrates's response to his death sentence in the *Apology*: "A good man cannot be harmed either in life or in death, and . . . his affairs are not neglected by the gods."[3] Both Chrysostom and Socrates affirm that one's authentic value as a human being, one's "goodness," is only vulnerable to one's own action, not to the actions of others. That is, one *can* morally harm oneself, but one *cannot* morally harm other persons, at least without their consent. Applied to a conception of dignity, this would mean that dignity is personally vulnerable but not interpersonally vulnerable: I can violate my own dignity and you can violate yours, but we cannot violate each other's. The potential problem of defining dignity in this way, however, is that it seems to render the protection of dignity moot; if I cannot harm your dignity and you cannot harm mine, then what practical value does dignity have beyond instructing individuals how they ought to treat themselves? Like defining dignity as invulnerable to all action, it is not clear how defining dignity as vulnerable only to *self-referential* action helps provide a guide for how dignity ought to direct action towards *others*.

Defining dignity as only interpersonally vulnerable, on the other hand, would have its own problematic implications. To claim that you can harm my dignity and I can harm your dignity, but we cannot harm our own dignity—which is what an exclusively interpersonal conception of dignity would uphold—appears to be contradictory. If, for example, I claim that I ought not to physically harm you and you ought not to physically harm me because such harm constitutes a violation of our dignity as human beings, how could I claim that *self*-inflicted harm would not also constitute such a violation? Upholding this position requires maintaining there is *nothing* one can do to oneself that could constitute a violation of dignity, even if doing the exact same thing to another person would constitute a violation.[4] It is not clear how such a conception of vulnerability is internally consistent. If one can harm others' dignity, it seems necessary to conclude that one can harm one's own dignity. Avoiding the problematic implications of defining dignity as only personally vulnerable or only interpersonally vulnerable thus requires conceiving of vulnerability in relation to dignity as both personally and interpersonally vulnerable.

This brief discussion of invulnerability and vulnerability as it relates to dignity points towards another potentially problematic issue for any tradition seeking to offer its own account of dignity. On the one hand, if a tradition wants to define dignity as universal and equal, then it appears that it must somehow explain how dignity is invulnerable to human action and any other influence. On the other hand, if a tradition wants to explain how and why dignity needs to be protected, then it must somehow explain how the same conception of dignity is also vulnerable to human action, and vulnerable to both personal and interpersonal action more specifically. In other words, it appears that a tradition must define dignity as both invulnerable and vulnerable if the tradition wants to uphold the claims that dignity applies equally to all humans and that dignity needs to be protected.

How do the traditions explained in this book address this apparent paradox of (in)vulnerability? Although no tradition provides a systematic explanation for how its particular conception of dignity is both invulnerable and vulnerable, it is important to recognize that *all* of them, in different ways, recognize the conceptual necessity of attributing both characteristics to dignity. That is, each tradition, in its own way, portrays dignity as applying to all humans in equal measure (and thus, presumably, invulnerable to human action) and yet also something that needs to be protected (and thus, presumably, vulnerable to human action). Moreover, each tradition also appears to recognize that dignity's vulnerability is limited not only to others' actions or one's own actions but to both; in other words, every tradition seems to recognize that dignity is both personally and interpersonally vulnerable.

However, it is also important to note that the specific relationship between dignity's vulnerability and invulnerability—similar to the specific relationship between the body and the soul—often remains ambiguous and a point of ongoing debate within each tradition. Much of this ambiguity emerges from each tradition's conception of the relationship between conceiving of dignity as inherent and conceiving of dignity as something that is attained (see question five below). What remains clear, however, is that every tradition we examine seeks to advance a vision of dignity that applies to all humanity and yet is in danger of being harmed by how one acts in relation to oneself and how one acts in relation to others. We ask of each tradition whether and how it has the conceptual resources to account for both sets of these characteristics.

Question Five: Is dignity inherent or attained?

The question of whether dignity is inherent in the sense of being constitutive of the human being qua human being, or whether it is something that humans attain in the sense of becoming more "fully human" is, like the question of dignity's vulnerability and invulnerability, a complex issue in each tradition. There are profound moral implications at stake here. For example, defining dignity as inherent implies that nothing must be done, or not done, in order for human beings to have dignity. They must only *be* human; that is the *only* condition. However, this claim, like the question of invulnerability, raises questions about the moral purpose of dignity; if humans have dignity simply by virtue of existing, then it is not clear what role human action, either one's own action or the actions of others, has in relation to dignity. If dignity is ontologically fixed in this way, then what does it mean to "violate" dignity if no "violation" has any effect on an individual's dignity? One response may be to recognize that inherent dignity could be defined as vulnerable to human action in the sense that it could be "lost." However, defining dignity in this way seems to suggest that those who "lose" their dignity would have less dignity than other human beings who have not lost it, which, in turn appears to contradict the claim that the only condition for having dignity is being human—that is, the claim that dignity is inherent. If dignity is inherent, in other words, it is not clear how it can also be conditional based on any other characteristic than being human and thus not clear how it could be "lost"; and if dignity is unconditional, it is not clear how it can be violated and is thus in need of protection.

Conversely, defining dignity as attained may provide the grounds for concretely identifying what "violating" dignity would mean; since from this point of view it is presumably possible for an individual *not* to attain her or his dignity, then any personal or interpersonal action that prevents an individual from realizing the full potential of her or his dignity could be defined as a "violation" of dignity and, thus, morally prohibited. However, like the question of vulnerability, describing dignity as dynamic and teleological in this way raises questions about dignity's universality and equality. If dignity is attained, for example, do those who fail to attain it, for whatever reason, have *less* dignity than others, and does that, in turn, mean that they are less than fully human in a moral sense? If dignity is defined as a potential that individuals can realize or fail to realize, the answer would seem to have to be "yes": the integrity of your dignity, how "much" you have in a qualitative sense, would depend on whether or not you are realizing its potential. Conceiving of dignity in this way also raises the necessity for providing a dual definition of what constitutes normative realized dignity, identifying both (1) what defines dignity in the form of unrealized potential and (2) what defines dignity in the form of realized potential.

In short, it thus appears that dignity must be defined as inherent in order for it to be universally equal, and as attained in order for it to be able to explain how human action makes a difference for dignity. This paradox, like the paradox of vulnerability and invulnerability, is one each tradition addresses in different ways. First, it is important to highlight that each tradition, notwithstanding it own substantive differences, affirms that dignity is in some way inherent in human beings. Eastern Orthodoxy, Catholicism, and Judaism, for example, appeal to the *imago Dei* as the grounds for inherent dignity. Islam, with its emphasis on God creating human beings as vice-regents makes a similar claim to intrinsic worth, though its account of creation is significantly different from the account in Genesis.

Interestingly, the Protestant conception of dignity, though sharing the same biblical resources, tends not to define dignity as "inherent" in the same way as Judaism, Orthodoxy, and Catholicism; because of the severity of sin after the Fall, the Protestant perspective maintains that dignity is only "inherent" in humans in the sense that it is *imputed* by God in and through Jesus Christ establishing a personal relationship with the individual. Nevertheless, insofar as it is God who establishes value in human beings, humans have dignity in this paradigm independently of how they act either in relation to themselves or towards each other, making dignity a feature of human beings as such and thus still "inherent" in the sense described above.

Hinduism, in turn, though it does not identify an *imago Dei* in a Judeo-Christian sense, speaks of the human being's inner self (*ātman*) as constitutively connected to the divine presence in all reality, or Brahman. Buddhism, in contrast, does not identify a "self" in the same way as do other religious traditions (either an "inner self" or a self created in the image and likeness of God), yet it still recognizes the presence of what it identifies as sentience, or *sattva/satta*, in all human beings (and all other life), which grounds dignity within humans as such. Humanism, in turn, emphasizes the irreducible distinctiveness of the human person, different from everything else in existence, and, more specifically, the individual's capacity to be an "I" and to be able to recognize a "you" and a "they" as constitutive of individual dignity. In short, notwithstanding the profoundly different formulations of dignity as inherent, each tradition seeks to locate dignity in some form of human *being* rather than human doing.

There is also a sense in which the traditions recognize dignity as attained. The Christian traditions, albeit in very different ways, understand dignity in relation to some form of sanctification: to be fully human in a normative sense and to fulfill the value one has as a human being created in the image and likeness of God is ultimately to seek to become Christlike. Judaism and Islam do not have a conception of sanctification in this sense, though both affirm that having dignity requires human beings to act in accordance with God's will with respect to their treatment of others and of themselves, and a failure to follow God's will is to *degrade* one's dignity. The Hindu perspective, in turn, emphasizes that one must embrace four principles in order to advance and live in harmony with one's dignity: material sufficiency (*artha*), pleasure (*kāma*), community participation (*dharma*), and a sense of spiritual purpose and accomplishment (*mokṣa*). The aim of dignity from the Buddhist perspective, in turn, is to achieve *arahant*, or "liberation," by freeing oneself from greed, hatred, and delusion. Finally, the humanistic conception of dignity calls the individual to *exercise* her distinctive human capacities to enhance the integrity of all life, including but not limited to human life, by seeking the flourishing of self and other. It is important to note that in all the traditions, the attainment of dignity is vulnerable to both personal and interpersonal action.

In sum, despite disagreeing on the content of what defines dignity in both its unrealized and realized forms, every tradition we examine defines dignity as *both* inherent *and* attained. At least from a conceptual perspective, every tradition thus has the resources for accounting for how dignity is universally equal and vulnerable and thus in need of protection. The question for each tradition, similar to the question of dignity as it relates to vulnerability and invulnerability, is how to coherently relate dignity's dual nature as inherent and acquired and how to coherently explain how something that is inherent is, at the same time, something that can also be attained—or not.

Question Six: Is dignity universal and equal?

The discussion of the previous questions has already indicated the importance of both universality and equality in each tradition's conception of dignity. Each tradition, in its own way, seeks to describe dignity as something that applies to all human beings (universality) and something that applies to human beings in the same way to the same degree (equality). Each tradition contains the conceptual resources to speak about dignity as invulnerable to human action and as inherent, which are both necessary in order to define dignity as universal and equal. However, as the discussion of the previous questions has already indicated, each tradition also has the challenge of explaining how all of the other elements of its conceptions of dignity relate to its respective claims about dignity's universality and equality. For example, if dignity is derived from a human capacity, as it appears to be in humanism, can one coherently claim that dignity is universal when, empirically, it does not appear to be the case that all humans have the same capacities or the same possibilities to exercise those capacities to their full potential? Likewise, insofar as any conception of dignity is tied to a conception of the *imago Dei* or otherwise infused with unique value by the divine, how can one speak about that dignity as universal and equal if it is, at least in some way, (1) dependent on divine revelation and/or recognizing the authority of a sacred text and/or ecclesial institution? or (2) dependent on accepting the authority of particular cultural and social practices? Can dignity be universal and equal, in other words, if it is epistemologically based on revelation and/or cultural experiences that are not universal and equal? These questions pose a challenge to all three of the Christian conceptions of dignity, and to the Jewish, Islamic, and Hindu conceptions. Likewise, insofar as the Buddhist understanding of dignity appears to be based on exercising a particular set of capacities—namely, the capacities to overcome greed, hatred, and delusion—it, too, may run into the question of how it can affirm universally equal dignity while recognizing the apparently empirical truth that not all humans possess these capacities in equal measure. If, in response, Buddhism points to its affirmation of sentience as the ground of dignity, which may, indeed, apply to all human beings in some sense, how can it account for uniquely *human* dignity if this sentience is also shared by nonhuman life?

A close reading of each tradition generates many more questions along similar lines. However we might formulate these questions, it is important to keep in mind that merely affirming that dignity is universal and equal, which every tradition we examine seeks to do, is not sufficient for making it so. Ultimately, each has to provide an explanation and justification for how it can support the claim that every being we call "human" has the same value in the same measure without any exceptions.

Question Seven: Is dignity practical?

Finally is the question of whether each tradition seeks to define dignity in such a way that it can serve as a moral principle to guide action. The answer, as the discussion in the previous questions demonstrate, is "yes": every tradition we treat in this book affirms that dignity ought to generate particular kinds of moral responses, creating obligations both to refrain from doing certain actions (e.g., torturing) and to perform certain kinds of actions (e.g., providing assistance to the vulnerable). At the foundation of this shared recognition of dignity's practicality is another shared recognition of dignity's vulnerability: each tradition recognizes that there are real and urgent threats to dignity's integrity and, perhaps in some form, to dignity's very existence itself. Each tradition, in other words, affirms that dignity is ultimately not merely a question for theoretical debate but rather a reality that can and must be protected right now in all of its different contexts.

These traditions express ontological, anthropological, axiological, and normative claims that have significance for public discourse and debate. Insights from these traditions cannot be restricted to the margins and background of public discussions about the meaning of dignity and the duties and obligations that emerge out of those meanings. Dismissing religious traditions as legitimate sources for public debate about dignity has at least two deleterious effects. First, it reduces conceptions of dignity to almost exclusively legalistic and secular understandings.[5] Second, it tends to reduce the human moral imagination to the purview of rights. To be sure, as the authors in this volume demonstrate, the relationship between dignity and rights is an inherently generative one;[6] however, the language of rights does not fully capture the depths and scope of human dignity. Moreover, legal structures and rights-based political frameworks may fail through their own strictures to protect human dignity. As legal theorist Catherine Dauvergne observes, "The power of the law is implicated in the failure of human rights norms to reach those who are most marginalized because of the tyranny of jurisdiction."[7] This tyranny of jurisdiction has not only resulted in political actors abandoning some of the most vulnerable persons, but it has also failed to protect displaced persons from capricious exercises of power (e.g., arbitrary detention) and structural oppression (e.g., discrimination and sexual and gender-based violence).

Religious thought, discourse, and practices are certainly not immune from critiques regarding versions of the "tyranny of jurisdiction" and other challenging aspects of traditions that have done violence to human dignity and flourishing. However, religious traditions also account for the kinds of conceptual questions we've noted in ways that purely legalistic or secular models cannot always satisfactorily answer. Religious traditions provide "thick" accounts of human goodness, sin, agency, responsibility, and community that can prophetically confront violations of human dignity and augment, disabuse, and complement legal, cultural, and political models.[8] In defending the relevance and importance of religious discourse and symbols in the public sphere, our book also cautions against temptations to reduce the differences of these traditions into one unified perspective or to translate these religious traditions into one common secular message. In other words, we hope that these traditions can speak for themselves but also become embedded within ecumenical and interreligious frameworks and wider public conversations with secular conceptions of dignity that have difficulty in providing a comprehensive account of dignity.

Part of those wider public conversations involves our shared political, economic, legal, and cultural lives, including conflicts over conceptions of basic values, goods, and duties. In part II of the book, authors take up seven case studies—on gendered violence, religious violence, racial violence, criminal justice, immigration, ecology, and religious peacebuilding. These case studies function as tests for the questions we have raised above with respect to the interpretation of dignity and its application. Putting religious traditions in interdisciplinary conversation with a number of sources, contexts, and conversation partners, these chapters address dignity historically, critically, and constructively.

The chapters of part I ("Traditions") and part II ("Case Studies") further demonstrate the widespread appeal to dignity as a foundational moral principle. But there are diverse perspectives on dignity within and among the traditions, so we must observe two significant characteristics about those traditions. First, there are resources within each tradition that similarly point to dignity as a foundational principle for moral reasoning. Second, these traditions agree on substantive considerations of the existence, nature, and application of dignity. These substantive agreements may appear to be surprising given the profound theological differences, but they also offer reason to believe that consensus may be possible amidst ongoing domestic and global conflicts and threats to human dignity. Religious traditions need not think of themselves as talking past each other on issues of dignity, because they can engage in authentic conversations that have theoretical and practical import and can clarify their own internal understandings of dignity and how they relate to each other. As the case study chapters in particular show, the recognition of dignity is an indispensable moral principle. It is nearly impossible to confront the complexity of, say, gendered violence or racial violence without a sustained and critical appeal to human worth. Other conceptions, such as autonomy, agency, status, utility, or well-being, fall short in their attempt to reduce humanity to a set of capacities or set of affairs. However we might define dignity, the concept seeks to express the full complexity, depth, diversity, and unity of what it means to be human.

NOTES

1. Christopher M. McCrudden, "In Pursuit of Human Dignity: An Introduction to Current Debates," in *Understanding Human Dignity*, ed. Christopher M. McCrudden (Oxford: Oxford University Press, 2013), 1.

2. Recent literature includes a broad range of theological, philosophical, legal, and political perspectives: George Kateb, *Human Dignity* (Cambridge, MA: Belknap Press of Harvard University Press, 2011); Jeremy Waldron, *Dignity, Rank, and Rights* (Oxford: Oxford University Press, 2012); Gilbert Meilaender, *Neither Beast Nor God: The Dignity of the Human Person* (New York: Encounter, 2009); Mark P. Lagon and Anthony Clark Arend, eds., *Human Dignity and the Future of Global Institutions* (Washington, DC: Georgetown University Press, 2014); Michael Rosen, *Dignity: Its History and Meaning* (Cambridge, MA: Harvard University Press, 2012); Gaymon Bennett, *Technicians of Human Dignity: Bodies, Souls, and the Making of Intrinsic Worth* (New York: Fordham University Press, 2016); R. Kendall Soulen and Linda Woodhead, eds., *God and Human Dignity* (Grand Rapids, MI: Wm. B. Eerdmans, 2006).

3. Plato, *Five Dialogues* (Indianapolis: Hackett, 2002), 42.

4. Raising the question of vulnerability in this way invites the question of whether or not a conception of dignity based exclusively on consent might be able to explain how one could claim that dignity is interpersonally vulnerable but not personally vulnerable. So long as both parties fully and freely consent to the action that is performed, then, by definition the act could not be deemed as morally harmful no matter what its objective content. Using this reasoning, anything I do to myself would, presumably, involve my own consent, and so I could claim that I may be able to harm others' dignity because it is possible for me to do things against their will, but could never harm my own dignity because, barring some form of mental illness or intoxication, self-referential actions must necessarily imply my consent.

Although this may be one way to formulate a conception of dignity that is interpersonally vulnerable but not personally vulnerable, no tradition examined in this volume seeks to define dignity exclusively in terms of consent, and so recognizing consent as a possible basis for dignity is not necessary in this context. It should be noted, however, that "consent" is not necessarily the same as "autonomy," and that Immanuel Kant—perhaps the most paradigmatic example of what dignity founded exclusively on autonomy looks like—very clearly affirms that *one must also treat oneself as an end in itself*, which prohibits certain kinds of actions because they violate dignity whether or not one "consents" to them. This applies to self-referential action *and* action in relation to others.

5. See, for example, Waldron, *Dignity, Rank, and Rights*.

6. See also, for example, Jürgen Moltmann, *On Human Dignity: Political Theology and Ethics* (Philadelphia: Fortress, 1984), where the first part has essays addressing human rights.

7. Catherine Dauvergne, *Making People Illegal: What Globalization Means for Migration and Law* (Cambridge: Cambridge University Press, 2008), 17.

8. Lisa Sowle Cahill problematizes interpretations of Christian theological symbols and parables of "thick" in contrast to the "thin" accounts provided by the market, science, and liberalism; see Cahill, *Theological Bioethics: Participation, Justice, Change* (Washington, DC: Georgetown University Press, 2005).

Part I

TRADITIONS

INTRODUCTION TO PART I

The contributors in part I examine human dignity from the lenses of eight traditions. Each represents an interpretation of a tradition, but all the authors engage key concepts, themes, and thinkers that have shaped that tradition's conception of dignity. Some treatments chart typologies or trajectories of thought, and others include practical applications and case studies. Traditions are compared by twos, and there is a response for each pair that comparatively addresses and analyzes the pairing with an eye to conceptual and methodological similarities and differences.

In "Dignity: A Catholic Perspective," Darlene Fozard Weaver draws on major papal encyclicals and contemporary theologians to describe and analyze a fourfold meaning of dignity: affirmation of human worth, encapsulation of the human good, moral criterion that constrains and entitles, and moral expression of Christian humanism. She views dignity as a value commitment of inclusive regard for the equal moral worth of fellow beings and a corresponding responsibility to dignify our own and others' lives. Unpacking anthropological, practical, and revelatory dimensions of dignity and their dynamic connections to sin and grace, she argues that Catholic perspectives seek to defend dignity and all stages of life and to bring together prophetic resistance and moral consensus. Weaver notes certain tensions within Catholic perspectives (e.g., regarding human capacities, the role of experience in moral judgments), and she identifies Catholic and philosophical critiques of various expressions of human dignity. She concludes that a relational understanding of the *imago Dei* captures a broader range of thinking about dignity than the more substantialist account, which is capacity-based.

In "Dignity: A Buddhist Perspective," Kristin Scheible systematically addresses the challenges of describing a Buddhist conception of dignity in light of Buddhism's foundational rejection of the existence of a permanent "self" and the existence of, in Scheible's words, a "creator/adjudicator" God. In seeking to identify conceptual resources for comparison with other religious and philosophical traditions on the question of dignity's existence and nature, Scheible identifies a number of possibilities, including *priya/piya* (what is most dear), *sattva/satta* (sentience, or sentient being), *anātman/anattā* (no-self), *pratītyasamutpāda* (interconnectedness), and *pāramitā/pārami* (perfections or virtues), among others. Scheible concludes that although "dignity" as it is typically conceived in Western theological and philosophical thought may not be native to Buddhism, it is not entirely foreign, either. Moreover, she argues that the vulnerability inherent in the distinctively Buddhist conception of "self-less dignity" provides a promising possibility not only for (re)defining dignity but also for demonstrating how and why dignity urgently needs protection and nourishment.

In "Catholic and Buddhist Perspectives on Dignity: A Response," comparative theologian Karen Enriquez examines their analogous descriptions of being human, including a distinctive value or worth to being human that is tied to some innate capacity or potential to fulfill what is seen as the "good" in each of the two traditions. She also puts their differences in constructive dialogue; she asserts, for example, that Weaver's discussion of the role of perception could be complemented by dialogue with Buddhism and its analysis of the human condition in terms of ignorance or mis-knowing. Enriquez contends that exchanges regarding spiritual practices are a fruitful activity for Buddhist–Catholic dialogue.

In "Dignity: A Jewish Perspective," Elliot Dorff and Daniel Nevins provide a close textual analysis of Hebrew scripture and various classical and contemporary rabbinic writings to demonstrate how central the principle of dignity—ultimately grounded in the affirmation of the *imago Dei* present in each human being—is to Jewish moral reasoning. Indeed, Dorff and Nevins highlight how considerations of dignity can frequently allow for actions that might otherwise "violate" rabbinic law, especially to avoid situations of potential humiliation. Though "divine dignity," as Dorff and Nevins describe it, always supersedes human dignity, they argue that the tradition has made it clear that humans must never be treated as if they only had instrumental value, especially the most vulnerable. Dorff and Nevins conclude the chapter by identifying how this conception of dignity informs Jewish moral thinking on questions of war, domestic abuse, abortion, homosexuality and gender identity, and genetic engineering.

In "Dignity: A Hindu Perspective," Chris Chapple provides a broad overview of classical and contemporary sources to highlight the various meanings of dignity within the Hindu tradition. Hinduism, Chapple explains, identifies inherent value within each individual, yet, unlike many more Western conceptions of dignity, locates that value in relationship to other individuals, often within a complex and sometimes hierarchical web of social, culturally mediated relations. Above all, he emphasizes, Hinduism conceives of dignity as the state of being in which the "self" is freed from false identities and worldly attractions. In light of his analysis of the *Bhagavad Gītā*, the practices of yoga, and the theology of Mahatma Gandhi and his contemporary followers, Chapple demonstrates the promise—and limitations—of the Hindu conception of dignity for helping us address many of the conflictual issues that Western understandings of dignity have helped generate—for example, the modern economy (and its excesses), technology, and the definition of "medicine."

Chapter 6, "Jewish and Hindu Perspectives on Dignity: Responses," consists of responses by Elliot Dorff and Chris Chapple to one another's chapters. In his response, Dorff suggests that putative differences between Hinduism and Judaism may not be as clear-cut as imagined. Dorff outlines areas of divergence and convergence between the two traditions with respect to a wide range of issues. He undertakes detailed comparative analysis involving Hindu and Jewish conceptions of the uniqueness of identity, work, medicine, education, law, character education, marriage, endogamy, infertility, children, groups within the community, changing social status, and humans and other animals. In his own response, Chapple similarly explores the similarities and differences between Judaism and Hinduism. He focuses on historical developments, distinct sources, and theological assumptions that inform the two traditions' understandings of dignity. Chapple comparatively discusses the practical cases of war, domestic violence, marital and family patterns, abortion, sexual orientation, and genetic engineering.

In "Dignity: A Protestant Perspective," David Gushee takes as his point of departure that dignity is linked to the central claim that life is sacred, which he locates in the nexus of the biblical faiths of Judaism and Christianity. He addresses questions of agency and justification in order to develop a warrant for human dignity. Contrasting his position with approaches in Catholicism, social constructionism, and the UN Universal Declaration of Human Rights (1948), Gushee grounds his warrant for human dignity in a theocentric account of divine freedom and the incarnate Christ whereby humans cannot forfeit their dignity. In revisiting his earlier normative account of dignity in *The Sacredness of Human Life*,[1] Gushee considers the case studies of torture and LGBT rights in light of his divine revelation–based account of dignity. As he wrestles with ideas about theological warrants, he concludes that the robust conception of human dignity and sacredness of life is only the beginning of moral inquiry and action.

In "Dignity: An Orthodox Perspective," Aristotle Papanikolaou critically analyzes the construal of dignity in an official document—*The Russian Orthodox Church's Basic Teaching on Human Dignity, Freedom and Rights*—on human rights issued in 2008 by the Russian Orthodox Church (ROC). The document critiques Western, liberal understandings and secularized standards of human rights and dignity. Papanikolaou argues that the document attempts to define a morally homogenous account of the person that distinguishes it from the West's account; moreover, he disagrees with the ROC's Orthodox notion of human rights. He marshals arguments regarding the Orthodox theology of personhood, drawing on the work of Lossky and Zizioulas and examining the distinction between image and likeness in Orthodox theology. He assesses whether or not the ROC's conclusions are the inevitable result of Orthodox understandings of the human person in terms of equal worth and irreducible particularity. He determines that the ROC's mistake is in eliding the ecclesial and the political and seeing the latter as that whose purpose is to facilitate divine–human communion.

In "Protestant and Orthodox Perspectives on Dignity: A Response," Matthew Petrusek argues that dignity offers an excellent heuristic for identifying the two traditions' underlying theological similarities and differences while demonstrating, more broadly, how much theology makes a difference for ethics. He contrasts Gushee's appeal to the image and likeness of God with Papanikolaou's differentiation between image and likeness to assert that Gushee appears to advance a "relational" conception of dignity, while Papanikolaou advances one that is both "relational" and "inherent." Through a detailed analysis of the arguments developed by Gushee and Papanikolaou, Petrusek notes subtle features that challenge facile assumptions about these traditions.

In "Dignity: An Islamic Perspective," Zeki Saritoprak appeals to classical Islamic sources, especially commentaries on the Qur'an, to express dignity as supplication to and relationship with the divine and as the superiority of human beings over other creatures. Concepts such as *al-ins* (humankind, but also intimate friend), *khalifa* (God's representative on earth or God's vicegerents), and the children of Adam convey a rich anthropology whereby human beings strive toward perfection, use reason to distinguish between right and wrong, and deserve—both believers and nonbelievers, as illustrated by the Prophet's concern for the other—respect and honor. Human dignity is dynamic because it is linked to learning and freely developing one's capacities, yet it is also vulnerable because of

Satan and the dualistic nature of humanity (angelic and satanic). Saritoprak notes passages in the Qur'an where human beings remain accountable to God, fellow human beings, and the environment. Respect for dignity must be universal; the Qur'an repudiates claims of superiority through ancestors or tribes.

In "Dignity: A Humanistic Perspective," William Schweiker situates the idea of human dignity within the networks of thought and life broadly called "humanistic," including religious, secular, and "antihumanistic" forms. He maps a typology of humanistic positions with respect to whether dignity is a term of "status" or "constitutive" of the human being and conjointly whether it is conceived in religious or nonreligious terms. Schweiker argues that what is distinctive about a humanist conception of dignity is the framework of convictions that motivate a life dedicated to respecting and enhancing the dignity of human lives. Engaging conceptual and social paradoxes related to dignity, Schweiker charts ways in which humanists affirm responsibility for the integrity of life as basic mode. He describes the ontological, epistemological, existential, and axiological convictions shared by humanists, and he concludes by advocating for a form of humanism that interrelates human dignity with the worth of nonhuman life.

In "Islamic and Humanist Perspectives on Dignity: A Response," Jonathan Rothchild thinks that the accounts of Schweiker and Saritoprak similarly uphold two central assumptions: (1) dignity is intrinsic but vulnerable, and (2) upholding dignity requires attending to personal aspects (cultivating virtue) and interpersonal aspects (granting respect and undertaking responsibility). He then assesses the ethical implications of these assumptions in light of Protestant perspectives on disability. He explores the history of Islamic humanism and contemporary debates about human rights. Rothchild contends that a conversation between humanism and Islam is needed in our contemporary context for at least two important reasons: it can help mediate current disagreements between Islamic thinkers and Western, liberal thinkers on the nature and status of human rights, and it can challenge long-standing, Eurocentric biases embedded in Western humanistic accounts of dignity.

NOTE

1. David Gushee, *The Sacredness of Human Life* (Grand Rapids, MI: Eerdmans, 2013).

one

DIGNITY

A Catholic Perspective

Darlene Fozard Weaver

Every day and across the globe, human life and well-being are violated on a massive scale. As many as 1.6 billion people live in poverty, many of them children.[1] More than 11 million Syrians have been killed or forced to flee their homeland; many refugees who survive their journey face considerable challenges in camps or in receiving countries.[2] Millions of people face unimaginable horrors from racism, homophobia, violence, and human trafficking. In the United States alone someone is sexually assaulted every two minutes.[3] Appeals to human dignity are meant to respond to such atrocities, to exhort our consciences, and to ground moral understanding of and solutions for social problems. In the face of so many complex and seemingly intractable problems, it can appear that the concept of dignity is not adequate to moral reality. Critics of dignity argue that the grounds of dignity are either problematic or overly particular, that dignity is ineffective as a moral concept, and that appeals to dignity impose one group's cultural or religious convictions on others.

Nevertheless, the concept of human dignity can assist with the important work of building and sustaining consensus and collaborative problem-solving. Here I offer a generally appreciative account of Catholic thinking about human dignity as an important resource for such work. Catholic tradition is not monolithic, and my account does not pretend to be exhaustive. Rather, I explicate the general understanding of dignity found in magisterial texts (official documents from the teaching office of the Church). We'll see that dignity has a fourfold meaning in Catholic tradition: dignity is (1) an affirmation of human worth, (2) an encapsulation of the human good, (3) a moral criterion that constrains and entitles, and (4) a moral expression of Christian humanism. I argue that the fourfold account of dignity delineated at the outset includes resources to respond to critics of dignity, but that Catholic understanding of and appeals to dignity would be strengthened by more reflection on the perceptual character of dignity within the dynamics of sin and grace. Dignity is then better understood as a value commitment of inclusive regard for the equal moral worth of fellow human beings and a corresponding responsibility to dignify our own and others' lives, especially the most vulnerable, by cultivating the human and common good.

THE MEANING OF DIGNITY

Human dignity is arguably a bedrock principle of Catholic social thought, the body of social teaching developed and deployed by popes, bishops, theologians, and ethicists. The meaning of human dignity develops across Catholic tradition and displays cultural variations, but its basic content is linked to a broadly humanistic understanding of the good and to the revelation of humanity in Jesus Christ. Human dignity figures prominently in Catholic moral reflection on health care, sexual ethics, criminal justice, immigration, the economy, and other moral matters. It posits a right to health care, for example, and offers principles that limit burdensome medical treatments.[4] With regard to criminal justice, human dignity entails both an insistence on holding offenders responsible for criminal wrongdoing and an emphasis on restoring them to community whenever possible.[5] Human dignity also underlies and informs other principles, such as the common good and respect for life. Indeed, Catholic tradition offers a rich body of reflection on human dignity that can orient and inform moral inquiry and collaborative problem-solving among a wide array of interlocutors and on a broad range of social issues.

Human Worth

In the Catholic tradition, the principle of human dignity designates the moral status of human beings qua human. Human beings have inherent, noncontingent worth. As an inherent worth, dignity belongs to them irrespective of their particular aptitudes, accomplishments, social status, or actions. Dignity therefore operates in a democratizing fashion, stipulating a kind of equality among all human beings that endures despite forms of inequality in abilities, accomplishments, or assets.[6] As an inherent worth, dignity affirms the noninstrumental value of human beings, which matters greatly with regard to the entitlements that dignity founds.[7] Human beings do not need to demonstrate some measure of social utility, for example, as a prerequisite for respect, nor can human beings be objectified or treated as means to others' ends. There is more to say about dignity as inherent worth, but it is important to note two implications at the outset. First, Catholic tradition tends to construe dignity as an attribute or possession of human beings. Dignity is something humans have. Moreover, as inherent, dignity cannot be lost.[8] Terrorists and traffickers do not relinquish their own dignity, even though they behave in a manner that is profoundly at odds with it, and thus they betray their own dignity and that of their victims. The point is that the concept of dignity encapsulates a fundamentally intrinsic and equal moral status of human beings qua human as a standing feature of humanity. Second, to construe dignity as an inherent possession or attribute of humans is to raise rather than answer questions regarding the grounds for that worth. What is it about human beings that endows them with a worth that distinguishes them from other creatures?[9] Catholic tradition has supplied different answers to this question, pointing sometimes to rationality, sometimes to freedom (particularly purposive freedom to direct ourselves in pursuit of the good), sometimes to transcendence, and at other times to human capacities for relationality.[10]

Often the claim that human beings are the *imago Dei*, created in the image of God, is used to express these answers or as an answer in its own right. The stipulation that human beings have inherent worth raises rather than answers questions about the grounds for such an assertion. The claim that human beings are the *imago Dei* provides a theological response to that question. David Hollenbach rightly notes that Catholic tradition includes both "substantialist" and "relational or functional" interpretations of the *imago Dei*.[11] The former link human likeness to God to "aspects of the very substance of the person," such as transcendence, reason, or freedom.[12] Substantialist interpretations of the *imago Dei* look to validate intrinsic human worth by pointing to human qualities or capacities. Functional or relational interpretations of the *imago Dei* construe dignity in more teleological terms. Some approaches emphasize the actualization of dignity in more functional terms. Other approaches, such as those arising from disability ethics, worry that functional construals of dignity risk excluding people in ways that are similar to substantialist, capacity-based concepts of dignity.[13] Relational approaches assert that dignity "can only be achieved when persons enter into fraternity and solidarity with each other."[14] Dignity is here understood as a praxis; relationships marked by solidarity are dignifying for those involved.[15] Relational accounts of dignity are more in keeping with the second meaning of dignity that we explore below.

Importantly, Catholic tradition affirms the dignity of human beings at all stages of life, from the moment of conception to the moment of natural death.[16] Dignity is therefore linked intimately to respect for life. Appeals to human dignity are essential to Catholic moral arguments regarding abortion, euthanasia, physician-assisted suicide, embryonic stem cell research, assisted reproductive technologies, and artificial nutrition and hydration. In its best moments, Catholic tradition demonstrates a so-called consistent ethic of life, a moral stance that refuses to limit respect for life to reproductive and end-of-life ethics.[17] In a consistent ethic of life, issues such as poverty, violence, education, racism, and environmental sustainability matter equally, and the dignity of immigrants, the disabled, the incarcerated, and the poor matter as much as that of the unborn, the vegetative, and the dying.[18] Accordingly, the U.S. bishops insist that "any politics of human dignity must seriously address issues of racism, poverty, hunger, employment, education, housing and health care."[19]

The presence of dignity across the natural human lifespan highlights a distinction between human beings and persons.[20] Twentieth-century Catholic theological anthropology is deeply indebted to the personalism of thinkers such as Jacques Maritain and Pope St. John Paul II, and magisterial teaching readily employs the language of personhood, but dignity belongs to all human beings and not only to those who display particular indicators of personhood. Embryonic human life has potential for rationality, freedom, memory, and other capacities that typically attend the concept of personhood.[21] For human patients in comas or persistent vegetative states, these same capacities are indefinitely suspended or perhaps irretrievably lost. In both cases, Catholic tradition affirms the inherent worth of these human beings and the moral claims that attend it.[22] Nevertheless, Catholic theological anthropology does emphasize human reason, freedom, transcendence, and relationality in extolling the distinctive place human beings occupy among God's creation.

Given the tendency to view dignity as an attribute belonging to human beings, an emphasis on these qualities or capacities creates some internal tensions within Catholic tradition. If these qualities illustrate, explain, or ground human dignity, what do we make of human lives that appear to lack them because of developmental prematurity, decline, disability, or trauma? It may appear that in Catholicism the principle of human dignity amounts to biologism or speciesism. Biologism is the position that biological life is an absolute value. Catholic tradition rejects biologism.[23] Human life is good without qualification but is not an absolute value. For this reason Catholic tradition has always permitted the use of force, even lethal force, against other human beings under certain moral conditions. The refusal to treat life as an absolute value is also reflected in the Catholic defense of a patient's right to refuse burdensome life-sustaining medical therapies. Speciesism refers to the position that only the human species has dignity. Catholic tradition is more susceptible to this charge, but Catholic environmental ethics is gradually offering more explicit affirmations of the intrinsic worth of nonhuman animals.[24] In Catholic tradition, dignity warrants respect for human beings across their lifespan, and life is considered to be intrinsically good. Nevertheless, death may be welcomed (for instance, by refusing burdensome life-extending treatments), and human life may licitly be taken under certain circumstances (for example, by killing enemy combatants in a just war).

Normative Ideal

Thus far we have focused on dignity as an affirmation of inherent human worth. In Catholic tradition, dignity also operates as a shorthand for a Catholic understanding of the human good. Consider, for example, the rich description of dignity found in the *Catechism of the Catholic Church*, which states that "the dignity of the human person is rooted in his creation in the image and likeness of God," "is fulfilled in his vocation to divine beatitude," and is keyed to the "essential" human capacity "freely to direct himself to this fulfillment."[25] This description includes the notion of dignity as an attribute of the human being, but it extends the concept of dignity by describing this attribute as a potential capable of fulfillment. This much is echoed in magisterial documents that speak of human dignity as though it could be diminished or forsaken. The Vatican II document *Gaudium et spes*, for example, states that human "dignity demands that [one] act according to a knowing and free choice that is personally motivated and prompted from within, not under blind impulse nor by mere external pressure," thereby expressing dignity as somehow residing within the human being and linking it to a capacity for free and purposeful action. Yet the very next sentence describes dignity as something to be attained: one "achieves such dignity when . . . [one] pursues [one's] goal in a spontaneous choice of what is good."[26] Here human dignity appears more dynamic. It designates a normative ideal, a eudaimonistic marker of flourishing. For example, in his encyclical on the environment, Pope Francis recognizes that technology can affect our lives in ways that permit us to live with more or with less dignity, thereby construing dignity as a qualitative feature of our lives that can wax or wane.[27]

Dignity is not simply a standing worth that we have but an ideal we may realize. Dignity names a potential we may actualize or enact in directing ourselves toward that end through purposeful action. This more dynamic understanding of dignity, however, still rests upon the prior notion of dignity as inherent worth, as an attribute or possession. A dignified manner of life derives its normative weight and general shape from dignity understood as worth. Indeed, reflection on the moral quality of particular ways of life is answerable to the notion of dignity as worth. Human dignity, then, is not only a principled stipulation of human worth or a fixed attribute linked to our creaturely status or specific capacities. Dignity is the measure of our lives.

In Catholic tradition, the human good is understood as intrinsic. It does not consist in an external divine verdict about the person, or by attaining a standard that is foreign to human nature. Rather, the good is the perfection and fulfillment of our being.[28] Experience therefore plays an important role in testifying to whether actions and relations are conducive to the human good and therefore consistent with human dignity, and when they violate this dignity. When actions, relationships, or particular social systems are contrary to the human and common good, we experience this dissonance and contradiction in our very being.[29] By the same token, when our choices, relationships, or manner of life are consistent with our good, we experience this consonance. Catholic appeals to human dignity in social ethical analysis therefore depend in part on the testimony of experience. Experience, of course, is not a straightforward or foolproof source for moral reasoning. Experience can provide "false" testimony as to whether a behavior, relationship, or manner of life is conducive to our flourishing. We can love what is destructive, lack sufficient consciousness to recognize the toxicity of a particular situation, or be motivated by self-interest, fear, or bias into complicit support for systems at odds with our flourishing. Indeed, liberation theologies appeal to the experience of particular populations, such as African Americans, the disabled, or the poor, to provide a corrective to the privilege encoded in cultural systems, including the dominant structures and theologies of Catholicism. Perspectives from "the margins" can illuminate the provincialism, violence, and self-protection expressed in judgments about human nature and the human good.[30] As an encapsulation of the human good, Catholic treatment of dignity suggests that there are objective markers of human well-being—such as ready access to resources necessary for sustaining life, friendships, physical safety in one's personal relationships, community, and workplace, and so forth. These markers can be ambiguous, and human beings can fashion lives of meaning, joy, and value under various conditions of deprivation or in the context of suffering. Moreover, objective markers of human well-being can become confused or conflated within economic, racial, and class systems that distort our perceptions of human well-being with problematic visions of the good life. Even so, Catholic tradition's use of dignity as a normative ideal that encapsulates the human good suggests that the "relational or functional" understandings of the *imago Dei* capture a broader range of Catholic thinking about dignity than the more "substantialist" accounts.

Moral Criterion

Human dignity also operates as a criterion that assists the work of moral judgment. For example, the U.S. Catholic bishops' pastoral letter on the economy, *Economic Justice for All*, states, "The dignity of the human person, realized in community with others, is the criterion against which all aspects of economic life must be measured. All human beings, therefore, are ends to be served by the institutions that make up the economy, not means to be exploited for more narrowly defined goals."[31] At the outset of the letter the bishops pose three questions: "What does the economy do for people? What does it do to people? And how do people participate in it?"[32] These questions structure moral assessment of economic policies around the dignity of the person. As a moral criterion, human dignity applies to particular actions or practices and to social conditions and systems. *Gaudium et spes* observes:

> Whatever is opposed to life itself, such as any type of murder, genocide, abortion, euthanasia or willful self-destruction, whatever violates the integrity of the human person, such as mutilation, torments inflicted on body or mind, attempts to coerce the will itself; whatever insults human dignity, such as subhuman living conditions, arbitrary imprisonment, deportation,

> slavery, prostitution, the selling of human beings; as well as disgraceful working conditions, where human beings are treated as mere tools for profit, rather than as free and responsible persons; all these things and others of their like are infamies indeed. They poison human society, but they do more harm to those who practice them than those who suffer from the injury.[33]

Gaudium et spes here uses the first two senses of dignity so that dignity provides a criterion that constrains the choices morally available to us. Attacks on human life and integrity violate dignity as inherent moral worth. Conditions that do not permit human beings to live in a manner consonant with their dignity, and practices and systems that objectify human beings, also undermine the second sense of dignity as a potential for actualizing the human good. Violations of dignity are contrary not only to the dignity of those who suffer them but also to the dignity of perpetrators and complicit bystanders.[34] They also undermine the common good, because behavior and conditions that are contrary to the inherent worth of others are contrary to our own worth and to our prospects for mutual flourishing. Human dignity sets a moral limit on the exercise of our freedom.

Dignity also entitles human beings to the conditions necessary for a manner of life consistent with that dignity, what *Gaudium et spes* calls "a genuinely human life": "There must be available to all people everything necessary for leading a life truly human, such as food, clothing, and shelter; the right to choose a state of life freely and to found a family, the right to education, to employment, to a good reputation, to respect, to appropriate information, to activity in accord with the upright norm of one's own conscience, to protection of privacy and rightful freedom even in matters religious."[35] Of course, the practical challenge of enacting respect for human dignity remains an open and vexing question. Catholic moral theologians disagree regarding moral norms, the relationship between objective and subjective dimensions of morality, and specific moral issues. Moreover, in many areas of social ethics, the moral teaching of Catholic tradition is substantive but general. Catholic tradition, for example, offers a vision of political life and the governments and moral principles that inform political theology, but does not endorse a particular economic or political system.[36] The work of forging conditions conducive to dignified lives for ourselves and others can and should play out in ways that are appropriate to local contexts. Take access to potable water, for example.[37] Limited access is already a problem for significant numbers of human beings. Pollution, depletion of aquifers, population growth, and climate change will further exacerbate this problem. If access to potable water is arguably a human right, there remain many unresolved ethical questions regarding how to respect and realize this right. What ought we to make of human choices to farm in ecosystems that are not suitable for such an undertaking? In this and many circumstances, appeals to human dignity do not translate into clear policy directives. A right to clean water—a necessary condition for sustaining life—may be clear, but there may be considerable practical and moral disagreement over how to ensure this right and balance practical mechanisms in relation to other moral claims.

The principle of human dignity is related to other features of Catholic tradition and to other principles of Catholic social thought. It is connected to a larger worldview and to practices of Catholic faith. When James Hanvey makes this argument he is suggesting that a Catholic conception of dignity is distinctive and cannot fully be understood without reference to a larger metaphysic.[38] A stringent version of Hanvey's claim would heighten the particularity of Catholic tradition and construe the broad humanism of Catholic tradition as a more sectarian theological anthropology. A more modest version simply links the full meaning of dignity to the larger ecology of beliefs, sources, principles, and practices that make up Catholic tradition. To understand a Catholic account of human dignity it is necessary to understand other elements of Catholic tradition. In Catholic social thought, the principle of human dignity is closely related to several other principles, including participation, the common good, a preferential option for the poor and vulnerable, subsidiarity, and solidarity.[39] Just as dignity derives some of its meaning from larger Catholic tradition, so too do Catholic moral principles generally rely on dignity understood as an inherent moral worth, and those principles work together to flesh out a notion of dignity as a potentiality that is actualized in a certain manner of life (the human good). The principle of participation, for example, identifies the importance of participation in social, political, economic, and cultural life, and it is a crucial condition for the actualization of a dignified manner of life.[40] Through participation human beings can contribute their gifts and talents to society and strive to meet their own needs. Limiting someone's ability to participate, for example through politically self-interested gerrymandering or unduly restrictive voter registration laws, violates their dignity as inherent worth because it hinders their ability to actualize dignity as a manner of life consistent with that worth.[41]

Christian Humanism

The work of discerning whether a manner of life or aspect thereof is consistent with dignity as inherent worth is mediated by a robust theological ethical anthropology. A Catholic conception of dignity is also humanistic in its attentiveness to features of human existence and in its rejection of reductionistic views of humanity. Catholic theological anthropology is deeply indebted to the Aristotelian-Thomistic intellectual tradition. The larger meaning of dignity in Catholic thought relies on an understanding of the person as a composite creature, embodied and ensouled, rational and appetitive, profoundly social but ultimately responsible for oneself.[42] Such features of human existence both warrant and give content to dignity as a universal human attribute and a cross-cultural moral principle. As embodied creatures, human beings have shared physical needs, such as a need for food and shelter. Human beings also share experiences, such as sexual desire, kinship relations, hunger, and play. To be sure, these needs, capacities, and experiences are interpreted and met in historically and culturally diverse ways. However, the fact of common needs and experiences has normative significance. Catholic tradition is characteristically confident that, through critical reflection on experience, people of good will can discern the moral good, forge moral consensus, and engage in responsible moral criticism while also cultivating respect for diverse ways of human life. In the best moments of the Catholic tradition, the articulation and application of human dignity unfolds as a collaborative effort to discern and promote the human good within the concrete circumstances of life. The humanism of Catholic tradition is an important source of resistance to intellectual traditions and cultural movements that view humanity in reductionistic terms. Catholic appreciation for human freedom and transcendence challenges anthropologies that emphasize human social formation to the point of determinism. Catholic appreciation for imagination and sociality challenges anthropologies that reduce human beings to neurobiological processes.

The meaning of human dignity also draws from revelation, specifically from the person and work of Jesus Christ. In his 1993 encyclical, *Veritatis splendor*, John Paul II states, "The decisive answer to every one of man's questions, his religious and moral questions in particular, is given by Jesus Christ, or rather is Jesus Christ himself."[43] We can learn more about human dignity by reflecting on Jesus. Jesus discloses the purpose of and possibilities for human life. The purpose of human life is loving communion with God and neighbor.

In reflecting on the person and work of Jesus we also discover possibilities for human life, that forms of human misery can be redeemed, that freedom, solidarity, joy, self-giving, and fulfillment are possible in degrees or in aspects of life that are new to us. Revelation does not displace the humanistic content of dignity. The purposes and possibilities disclosed in Jesus are not alien to human nature. As Thomas Aquinas observed, grace perfects nature. Faith in Christ empowers us to live fully human and humane lives. In the light of Christian revelation, dignity still appears as something we have, though qualities such as transcendence, freedom, reason, and relationality may be subsumed into a general capacity for or fitness to relationship with God and neighbor. Dignity here is less static. Rather than a fixed attribute, it is a vocation. Importantly, in the light of revelation, our dignity is linked to the work of dignifying our lives in solidarity with others. God's revelation in Jesus Christ warrants relational understandings of human dignity as worth, and in that way revelation points to the second sense of dignity as a command to dignify our own and others' lives through justice and love. Jesus's own life and death clarify dignity as a moral criterion, yoking it to inclusivity, mercy, and a preferential option for vulnerable human beings. Christian revelation therefore also provides a critical reference point for evaluating the tradition by these insights. We will return to this point below.

A Catholic conception of the human good aligns with the consensus of other religious traditions and with much of secular humanism, particularly in human rights discourse. The 1963 encyclical *Pacem in terris* enumerates a set of human rights that closely resembles the rights identified in the UN Universal Declaration of Human Rights.[44] The alignment between a Catholic understanding of dignity and other accounts indicates consensus that can be leveraged in collaborative problem-solving. Yet, a Catholic conception of the human good is also countercultural. Human dignity grounds arguments against embryonic stem cell research, direct abortion, methods of assisted reproduction that involve conception apart from the conjugal act, physician-assisted suicide, and euthanasia; each of these practices enjoys wide support in Western cultures, albeit to varying degrees. Appeals to human dignity also figure in calls to welcome refugees, immigrant-friendly policies, support for universal health care, environmental regulations, and stances on a range of other contested issues. Catholic conceptions of dignity arguably anchor a necessary mediation between prophetic forms of moral witness and resistance, on the one hand, and moral consensus and collaboration with secular organizations and other faith traditions, on the other.[45]

The humanism of a Catholic understanding of dignity signals and contributes to considerable moral consensus across religious and secular traditions. The particularity of Christian revelation provides a vital insight that links dignity to our dignifying work in solidarity with others. We now turn to criticisms of dignity in general and Catholic thinking about dignity more particularly.

THE PROBLEM WITH DIGNITY

Although the concept of human dignity figures prominently in political thought and policy around the globe, dignity has its detractors. Some criticize the concept as vague and imprecise. Steven Pinker claims that "'dignity' is a squishy, subjective notion, hardly up to the heavyweight moral demands assigned to it."[46] Ruth Macklin argues that dignity is useless because it is superfluous.[47] For Macklin, dignity means nothing other than respect for one's autonomy. Samuel Moyn argues that the concept of dignity is not useless in principle but has become so in practice, because various religious and political communities have claimed and deployed the concept in service of divergent and contradictory agendas.[48] Moyn and others note that dignity can be enlisted to argue for or against contradictory positions. For example, one can appeal to human dignity to argue for the wrongness of abortion or to argue for its necessity to secure women's social equality.

The Catholic account of dignity we presented in the last section shows that dignity is a complex idea capable of informing practical moral reflection. Contrary to Macklin, dignity, at least a Catholic conception of it, cannot be reduced to respect for autonomy. Other intellectual traditions—secular and religious—also offer accounts of human dignity that are richer and normatively more fruitful than accounts of respect for autonomy. Human worth needs to be affirmed in complex situations in which one person's interests appear to conflict with others, or in which various material or moral goods are in tension. The fact that dignity can be invoked in support of divergent moral judgments regarding practical matters neither invalidates the principle of human dignity nor renders it useless for the ongoing task of discerning how to respect and promote human well-being. Nevertheless, concerns that dignity is too anemic to work properly really signal a deeper set of problems. What are the grounds for asserting the dignity of human beings in a religiously and culturally diverse world? What distinctive work can dignity undertake compared with other moral principles like autonomy?

The humanism expressed in Catholic thinking about dignity is an asset here, at least in its broad features. Catholic understanding of humanity as embodied, social, rational, free, and transcendent affirms shared features of humanity as cross-cultural bases for normative reflection on the human good. A Catholic account of dignity does normative work that extends beyond that of autonomy because the humanism expressed in it encompasses features that are material to a conception of the human good. In the terms we used earlier, dignity in Catholic tradition is an encapsulation of the human good and a criterion for judging human efforts to support, actualize, and protect it. Catholic thinking about dignity provides nonsectarian insights for the project of understanding, articulating, and realizing human well-being.

However, the question remains why the human being so understood possesses inherent and irreducible moral value. The humanism expressed in a Catholic account of dignity grounds the normative work of dignity but still depends on a prior stipulation of moral worth. Catholic thinkers find the grounds for this stipulation in the claim that human beings are the *imago Dei* or by looking to particular features or capacities humans have. The latter still requires a decision to regard a given capacity as endowing human beings with moral worth. The former is a theological claim that some persons reject. Granted, human dignity can have its source in God whether or not others believe it does. However, since many criticisms of dignity essentially concern whether dignity can accomplish the normative work it is expected to perform, if the efficacy of a Catholic account of dignity requires assent to the theological claim that God endows humans with their moral status, the usefulness of the account beyond certain theistic communities seems compromised.

Moreover, as the broad features of Catholic humanism are rendered in more specific claims, other criticisms emerge. For example, a prominent feature of Catholic humanism is the notion of gender complementarity. In Catholic magisterial teaching, humankind is sexually differentiated and this sexual differentiation aligns firmly with a binary conception of gender. Male and female gender identities are different yet complementary. For instance, the theology of the body developed by John Paul II describes this complementarity in nuptial terms.[49] Men and women alike are called to mutual self-gifting but also to share themselves in characteristically gendered ways. Women's dignity appears in their special "genius" for receiving others and nurturing them.[50] The gender essentialism is part of a larger Catholic affirmation of embodiment and Catholic readiness to cull normative judgments from reflection on embodiment. But, as some Catholic and non-Catholic critics note, Catholic tradition is insufficiently attentive to the influence of patriarchy and sexism in understanding and evaluating women's embodiment. Celebrating women's special aptitude for the traditionally female labor of caregiving arguably reinforces rather than mitigates patterns of yoking women's value to their sexual and reproductive capacities.

The example of gender essentialism illustrates a wider worry about Catholic accounts of human dignity and the concept of dignity more generally. Indeed, a significant concern is that appeals to and policies based on dignity are a form of cultural or religious imperialism. Human dignity has been closely allied to the articulation and defense of human rights. Critics of both argue that the concept of dignity and human rights agendas are indebted to the liberalism and individualism of Western modernity.[51] For critics, the emergence of dignity as a central feature of international declarations and development plans represents a fresh wave of Western colonialism. Others consider the prominence of dignity in contemporary bioethics and discern undue religious influence. Pinker's brief but much-discussed article "The Stupidity of Dignity" argues that in bioethics the concept of dignity is used to "impose a Catholic agenda on a secular democracy."[52] According to Pinker, "An alleged breach of dignity provides a way for third parties to pass judgment on actions that are knowingly and willingly chosen by the affected individuals. It thus offers a moralistic justification for expanded government regulation of science, medicine, and private life. And the Church's franchise to guide people in the most profound events of their lives—birth, death, and reproduction—is in danger of being undermined when biomedicine scrambles the rules."[53] Similarly, Michael Rosen calls dignity a "Trojan horse for religiously inspired attacks on equality."[54] But Rosen's understanding of Catholic conceptions of dignity is seriously flawed. Still, Pinker and Rosen do raise an important issue. Appeals to and applications of human dignity are subject to personal and communal interests, power dynamics, and systemic distortion. They assume shared beliefs and associated value commitments that are far from universal. How can appeals to dignity mitigate the risk of imperialism?

The problem of dignity is that our inevitably particular or perspectival accounts of human being, human worth, and the human good all reflect dynamics of power and powerlessness, selective interests, and exclusion. How do we validate and improve these accounts, especially in relation to vulnerable populations? How do we foster ongoing efforts to understand dignity and to do the work of dignifying in ever-more inclusive and just ways? The challenge is, first, to ground human dignity in a manner that is not merely taxonomic but also recognizes the ineradicable character of dignity as a phenomenon of human perception, or as unavoidably a value commitment; second, to show the content of dignity is distinctive and robust enough to inform normative work but also permits respect for religious and moral diversity as a standing feature or irreplaceable condition for the actualization of dignity; and third, to construe dignity in a manner that is attentive to systems of power that operate even (especially) in ostensibly universal descriptions and defenses of human well-being. To meet this challenge, Catholic approaches to dignity need to be more attentive to the perceptual character of dignity within dynamics of sin and grace.

PERCEPTION OF WORTH

To capitalize on the strengths of a Catholic account of dignity and mitigate its weaknesses it is important to grapple with the perceptual character of human dignity. Pinker points out that "dignity is a phenomenon of human perception. Certain signals from the world trigger an attribution in the mind of a perceiver."[55] Here Pinker construes dignity as a perception of status, and the status he has in mind is broader than moral worth. Things such as clothing, speech patterns, and personal possessions can trigger attributions of status. However, Pinker does appreciate what is morally at stake in dignity. The phenomenon of perceiving another's status "explains why dignity is morally significant: We should not ignore a phenomenon that causes one person to respect the rights and interests of another."[56] Nevertheless, for Pinker the perceptual character of dignity makes dignity dangerous. As a phenomenon of human perception, dignity is unreliable. We may fail to see it where we ought, or be mistaken by superficial or counterfeit indicators of merit. To recognize dignity as a phenomenon of human perception seems to challenge the claim that dignity is inherent, that it is a moral status human beings have. The perceptual character of dignity instead implies that dignity is a subjective, idiosyncratic, and partisan regard for some and a corresponding neglect or dehumanization of others. For these reasons, Pinker thinks autonomy and respect for persons are more reliable grounds for attributing and protecting human worth. For our purposes, Pinker's reflection highlights an important insight: dignity concerns the recognition or misrecognition of human moral status within dynamics of vulnerability, power, deception, and truthfulness.

These dynamics become clearer in light of Christian reflection on sin and grace. Sin designates the disruption of a proper relationship with God and others.[57] Sin in all its forms undermines our recognition of others' dignity. Original sin names the distorted ecology of relationships that we inherit, that warp our reason, will, and affective capacities from their earliest development. Our personal sinful attitudes and choices reflect and contribute to this disruption. Social sin designates the systemic manifestation of sinful dynamics, expressing the reality that organizations, policies, traditions, and systems reflect and exacerbate the havoc and harm we visit upon one another. Sin corrupts our capacities to perceive and respect the dignity of others, to discern how to translate dignity into concrete moral judgments, particular sorts of behaviors, and social policies. Sin erodes our willingness to promote the conditions necessary for others to live lives that are consistent with that dignity. Importantly, sin may also operate in defenses of dignity, influencing the way we understand what it means to be human, what we value about human existence, and how we envision the human good and identify departures from it. This insight is at stake in criticisms of dignity as a form of cultural or religious imperialism.

It is helpful to invoke the language of sin precisely because it is a theological language. The theological referent of sin captures the depths of this distortion in the very capacities that make us human agents: our capacities to know, to value, and to will. As a theological language, sin is more than a linguistic embellishment for speaking about the disruption of proper relationships. In relation to human dignity, attention to dynamics of sin keeps us mindful that appeals to human dignity are always ultimately calls to conversion. We must stipulate that human beings have equal moral status because every day and across the world we performatively declare that they do not. Moreover, attention to the perceptual character of dignity in light of sin may also keep us mindful that we cannot simply muster and faithfully abide in commitments to regard our fellow human beings as inherently morally worthy. The conversion we require is an ongoing process.

Grace is the name for the dynamics of right relationship. Given sin's distortion of our capacities as moral agents and the corresponding disruption of our ecology of relationships, we need to be empowered to see one another truthfully and to be disposed for right relationship. In Catholic tradition, grace is an unmerited gift. In the context of appeals to human dignity, linking the perception of others' moral status to unmerited grace could construe dignity either as a conferral of worth that is undeserved or as more a matter of justice than grace. Yet, Catholic tradition also understands grace as a share in God's own life. Understood thus, grace is the power for inclusive recognition of others as equal in worth and for the will to cultivate the conditions necessary for a manner of life consistent with that dignity. As a share in God's own life, grace also points toward a more functional or relational understanding of what it means to be the *imago Dei* than a substantialist one. Whereas substantialist conceptions of the *imago Dei* emphasize possession of certain features or capacities as essential to human nature, a relational or functional interpretation of the *imago Dei* stresses our active self-disposal. The *imago Dei* is as much something we are called to enact as it is something we already are. We image God when we perceive finite life as good and commit ourselves to be persons whose character is known by our inclusive regard and solicitous action on behalf of others, especially vulnerable populations.

The defense of human dignity as an inherent moral worth is compatible with reflection on the perceptual character of dignity in the context of dynamics of sin and grace. To better appreciate why, let us consider the way Daniel Sulmasy describes various meanings of dignity in relation to Catholic tradition. Sulmasy, a physician, ethicist, and Franciscan, distinguishes three historical uses of dignity. (1) *Attributed* dignity is "worth or value that human beings confer upon others by acts of attribution. The act of conferring this worth or value may be accomplished individually or communally, but it always involves a choice. Attributed dignity is, in a sense, created. It constitutes a conventional form of value."[58] Attributed dignity is generally not the sort of dignity considered in Catholic tradition. It represents a decision to confer worth and therefore appears more capricious and more subject to bias or self-interest. Given a human propensity to love the wrong things or to love the right things in the wrong measure, attributed dignity is more likely an object of moral critique than a basis for morality. By contrast, (2) *intrinsic* dignity is "that worth or value that people have simply because they are human, not by virtue of any social standing, ability to evoke admiration, or any particular set of talents, skills, or powers. Intrinsic dignity is the value that human beings have simply by virtue of the fact that they are human beings. . . . [It] is prior to human attribution."[59] As we have seen, this is the primary meaning of dignity in Catholic tradition and is the first sense (human worth) of dignity identified in our fourfold account. Sulmasy argues that it is morally foundational.[60] (3) *Inflorescent* dignity refers to "the value of a state of affairs by which an individual expresses human excellence. In other words, inflorescent dignity is used to refer to individuals who are flourishing as human beings—living lives that are consistent with and expressive of the intrinsic dignity of the human."[61] Inflorescent dignity is akin to the second sense of dignity (normative ideal) in our fourfold account. Sulmasy notes that inflorescent dignity entails the notion of intrinsic dignity.

For Sulmasy, Catholic teaching about dignity eschews attributed dignity. However, when we pay attention to the perceptual character of dignity in the context of dynamics of sin and grace, we realize that the three meanings of dignity Sulmasy describes are interdependent. Sin, as the disruption of proper relationships with God and neighbor, encompasses the misrecognition of others' moral worth, our contributions to systems that facilitate and warrant this misrecognition, and the consequences of such misrecognition in an ecology of relationships that is at odds with our dignity and theirs. The dynamics of grace are dynamics for right relationship, in which we come to perceive the moral worth of others and enact respect and support for its full realization in our behaviors, relationships, and social systems. In short, what Sulmasy calls inflorescent dignity can only be fully realized in conditions of inclusive regard for intrinsic dignity, which in turn depends on our being converted so that we more truthfully attribute dignity to others in contexts that distort our perception and our will. Our commitment to perceive human worth is efficacious. Our excellence as human beings (our inflorescent dignity/the human good) appears as we nurture relationships of inclusive regard for the inherent dignity of others and cultivate the common good.

Attending to the perceptual character of dignity also clarifies how theological claims regarding human moral worth are not prerequisite convictions upon which the normative efficacy of dignity depends, but they are interpretive resources that enable us to discover and endorse the moral worth of others more inclusively. To be clear, the fact of their interpretive quality does not mean they are not true. Theological discourse affirms God as the Creator and as the source of all that is good. Just so, theological discourse is a language that expresses resistance to the notion that we are the only source of value, that all worth is merely attributed. It interprets life through the conviction that creation has value independent of our making. At the same time, in its recognition of sin and grace, theological discourse situates human agency within dynamics that warp or empower our capacities to perceive this value and to endorse it in our actions and relations. Put differently, the truthfulness of Christian theological claims is indexed to their participation in the divine work of creation, reconciliation, and sanctification.

What does the perceptual character of dignity mean for the challenge posed by criticisms of dignity? Recall that the first task was to ground human dignity in a manner that is not merely stipulative but also recognizes the ineradicable character of dignity as a phenomenon of human perception, or as unavoidably a value commitment. I have argued that dignity as inherent worth is compatible with dignity as a subjective perception. The point is not that human beings only have worth if we attribute it to them, but that there is no escaping the phenomenon of perception amidst dynamics that profoundly distort or alternatively empower human apprehension of the worth of fellow human beings. Defenses of human dignity are unavoidably calls to adopt a value commitment of inclusive regard for the equal moral worth of human beings. So, the question about grounds for dignity is a bit misleading. It implies that there must be a stipulative claim universally regarded as valid, and therefore efficacious enough to motivate hearts and settle our normative and practical disputes. Otherwise, according to critics of dignity, dignity is not a valid concept. Instead, appeals to dignity are moral exhortations.

The second task was to show that the content of dignity is distinctive and robust enough to inform normative work but that it also permits respect for religious and moral diversity as a standing feature or irreplaceable condition for the actualization of dignity. The fourfold account of dignity presented at the outset marshals a rich anthropology, orients and informs deliberation on practical issues, and offers more fodder for normative reflection and boundary-spanning collaboration than concepts such as "autonomy" or "respect." Moreover, consideration for the perceptual character of dignity indicates that appeals to human dignity are essentially exhortations to make a value commitment. To attribute dignity to all human beings qua human is to participate in the dignifying work necessary to realize the human and common good. Arguments for inherent human worth can warrant commitments to ensuring religious and moral diversity when they are accompanied by an anthropology that esteems human freedom, is duly attentive to the realities of inculturation, and is developed with intellectual humility. Of course, arguments for inherent human worth can also be forms of cultural imperialism or structural violence/social sin.

Thus, the third task was to construe dignity in a manner that is attentive to systems of power that operate even (especially) in ostensibly universal descriptions and defenses of human well-being. Catholic treatment of dignity does rely too heavily on a taxonomic or stipulative assertion of human moral worth and pays insufficient attention to sin as a reality that can influence and operate in conceptualizations of human beings, human worth, and the human good.[62] By considering dignity as a phenomenon of human perception we can retain the moral realism and universalism that attends the broad humanism of a Catholic conception of dignity while also regarding with greater sensitivity and humility the potential limitations of more specific aspects of that humanism.

In Catholic tradition, dignity also takes its meaning from the revelation of humanity in Jesus Christ. Revelation can further direct the normative explication and application of human dignity. God's revelation in Jesus Christ discloses the importance of solidarity with others, especially the most vulnerable. This point bears on the essentializing tendencies of Catholic approaches to dignity and underscores the importance of describing and defending human dignity in a manner that is deeply informed by the experiences of those whose dignity is routinely denied or violated. Of course, revelation must always be interpreted, and it can be interpreted in a fashion that serves the maldistribution of power and of conditions for well-being. For this reason we return to the claim that dignity is a value commitment to attribute equal moral worth to our fellow human beings. Doing so is a necessary aspect of discerning their inherent value, an indispensable condition for realizing the human good that Catholic talk of dignity encapsulates, for applying dignity as a moral criterion, and for modulating the humanism of Catholic tradition so that it participates more fully in the work of dignifying human lives.

CONCLUSION

Appeals to human dignity are an important element in Catholic teaching and practice. Catholic understanding of human dignity is a rich resource that can facilitate consensus-building and collaboration with other faith traditions and secular efforts to respond to social problems. Catholic teaching about human dignity does tend to emphasize more stipulative assertions of human worth that are subsequently fleshed out in an essentialist anthropology and a vision of the human good. Reflection on the perceptual character of dignity suggests that dignity is helpfully construed as a value commitment of inclusive regard for the equal worth of all human beings, and as a responsibility to dignify our own and others' lives.

NOTES

1. See Tanya Basu, "How Many People in the World Are Actually Poor?," *The Atlantic*, June 19, 2014, http://www.theatlantic.com/business/archive/2014/06/weve-been-measuring-the-number-of-poor-people-in-the-world-wrong/373073/.

2. See the website Syrian Refugees, http://syrianrefugees.eu.

3. See "Victims of Sexual Violence: Statistics," https://www.rainn.org/statistics/victims-sexual-violence.

4. United States Conference of Catholic Bishops [USCCB], *Ethical and Religious Directives for Catholic Health Care Services*, 5th ed. (Washington, DC: USCCB, 2009).

5. USCCB, *Responsibility, Rehabilitation, and Restoration: A Catholic Perspective on Crime and Criminal Justice* (Washington, DC: USCCB, 2000).

6. John XXIII, *Pacem in terris* (1963), no. 89, http://w2.vatican.va/content/john-xxiii/en/encyclicals/documents/hf_j-xxiii_enc_11041963_pacem.html.

7. Benedict XVI, *Message for the Celebration of the World Day of Peace*, January 1, 2007, http://w2.vatican.va/content/benedict-xvi/en/messages/peace/documents/hf_ben-xvi_mes_20061208_xl-world-day-peace.html.

8. *Gaudium et spes* (*Pastoral Constitution on the Church in the Modern World*), no. 29, http://www.vatican.va/archive/hist_councils/ii_vatican_council/documents/vat-ii_const_19651207_gaudium-et-spes_en.html.

9. For a critique of Christianity as anthropocentric, see the classic essay by Lynn White Jr., "The Historical Roots of Our Ecologic Crisis," *Science* 155, no. 3767 (1967): 1203–7.

10. See, for example, Janet Soskice, *Imago Dei and Sexual Difference: Toward an Eschatological Anthropology* (Grand Rapids, MI: William B. Eerdmans, 2011).

11. David Hollenbach, "Human Dignity in Catholic Thought," in *The Cambridge Handbook of Human Dignity: Interdisciplinary Perspectives*, ed. Marcus Düwell, Jens Braarvig, Roher Brownsword, and Dietmar Mieth (Cambridge: Cambridge University Press, 2014), 250–59.

12. Ibid., 253.

13. Molly Haslam, *A Constructive Theology of Intellectual Disability* (New York: Fordham University Press, 2012); Hans S. Reinders, *Receiving the Gift of Friendship: Profound Disability, Theological Anthropological, and Ethics* (Grand Rapids, MI: Eerdmans, 2008); Michelle A. Gonzalez, *Created in God's Image: An Introduction to Feminist Theological Anthropology* (Maryknoll, NY: Orbis, 2007); David Brion Davis, *In the Image of God: Religion, Moral Values, and Our Heritage of Slavery* (New Haven, CT: Yale University Press, 2001). See also Bryan N. Massingale, *Racial Justice and the Catholic Church* (Maryknoll, NY: Orbis, 2014).

14. Hollenbach, "Human Dignity in Catholic Thought," 254.

15. Stanley Grenz, *The Social God and the Relational Self: A Trinitarian Theology of the* Imago Dei (Louisville, KY: Westminster/John Knox Press, 2001); Daniel Louw, "Identity and Dignity within the Human Rights Discourse: An Anthropological and Praxis Approach," *Verbum et Ecclesia* 35, no. 2 (2014): 1–9.

16. John Paul II, *Evangelium vitae* (Washington, DC: United States Catholic Conference, 1995).

17. Joseph Cardinal Bernadin, *Consistent Ethic of Life* (Kansas City, MO: Sheed & Ward, 1988).

18. All human beings have equal moral worth, yet decisions sometimes must be made regarding moral priorities and the allocation of limited resources. Moral considerations such as a preferential option for the poor and vulnerable help in the task of adjudicating these decisions.

19. USCCB, *Living the Gospel of Life: A Challenge to American Catholics* (Washington, DC: USCCB, 1998), no. 23.

20. Stanley Rudman, *Concepts of Persons and Christian Ethics* (Cambridge: Cambridge University Press, 2008). See also Joseph Fletcher, "Four Indicators of Humanhood: The Enquiry Matures," in *On Moral Medicine: Theological Perspectives*, 3rd ed., ed. Therese Lysaught and Joseph Kotva (Grand Rapids, MI: William B. Eerdmans, 2012), 334–37, and Oliver O'Donovan, "Again, Who Is a Person?," in ibid., 367–71.

21. Christopher Tollefsen, "A Catholic Perspective on Human Dignity," in *Human Dignity in Bioethics: From Worldviews to the Public Square*, ed. Stephen Dilley and Nathan J. Palpant (New York: Routledge, 2015).

22. Christopher Tollefsen, ed., *Artificial Nutrition and Hydration: The New Catholic Debate* (Dordrecht: Springer, 2008).

23. Helen Watt, "Life and Health: A Value in Itself for Human Beings?" *HEC Forum* 27, no. 3 (2015): 207–28. See also Richard A. McCormick, *Corrective Vision* (Lanham, MD: Rowman and Littlefield, 1994), 212, and David Kelly, Gerard Magill, and Henk ten Have, *Contemporary Catholic Health Care Ethics*, 2nd ed. (Washington, DC: Georgetown University Press, 2013).

24. John Berkman, "From Theological Speciesism to a Theological Ethology: Where Catholic Theology Needs to Go," *Journal of Moral Theology* 3, no. 2 (2014): 11–34.

25. *The Catechism of the Catholic Church*, 2nd ed. (Washington, DC: USCCB, 2000), no. 1700.

26. *Gaudium et spes*, no. 17.

27. Pope Francis, *Laudato Si'* (*On Care for Our Common Home*) (2015), no. 112, http://w2.vatican.va/content/francesco/en/encyclicals/documents/papa-francesco_20150524_enciclica-laudato-si.html.

28. New natural law thinkers such as Germain Grisez and John Finnis argue that several self-evident goods are constitutive of the human good, including life and health, friendship, and knowledge. In human action, agents willingly take up some relation to these objective goods. New natural law thinkers, sometimes also called basic goods theorists, argue that it is wrong to violate these goods. See, for example, Germain Grisez, *The Way of the Lord Jesus*, vol. 1, *Christian Moral Principles* (Chicago: Franciscan Herald Press, 1983); John Finnis, *Moral Absolutes: Tradition, Revision, and Truth* (Washington, DC: Catholic University of America Press, 1991). Revisionist moral theologians argue that this approach risks a "physicalism" that conflates the moral quality of an action with

the performance of it. Revisionists contend that the agent's intention and the circumstances surrounding the action must be considered in morally evaluating it. See Bernard Hoose, *Proportionalism: The American Debate and Its European Roots* (Washington, DC: Georgetown University Press, 1983).

29. Darlene Fozard Weaver, *The Acting Person and Christian Moral Life* (Washington, DC: Georgetown University Press, 2011).

30. Russell B. Connors and Patrick T. McCormick, *Character, Choices, and Community: The Three Faces of Christian Ethics* (New York: Paulist Press, 1998).

31. USCCB, *Economic Justice for All: Pastoral Letter on Catholic Social Teaching and the Economy* (Washington, DC: USCCB, 1986), no. 28.

32. Ibid., no. 1

33. *Gaudium et spes*, no. 27.

34. Elisabeth Vasko, *Beyond Apathy: A Theology for Bystanders* (Minneapolis: Fortress, 2015).

35. *Gaudium et spes*, no. 26.

36. John Paul II, *Sollicitudo rei socialis* (Washington, DC: USCCB, 1988), no. 41.

37. Christiana Peppard, *Just Water: Theology, Ethics, and the Global Water Crisis* (Maryknoll, NY: Orbis, 2013).

38. James Hanvey, "Dignity, Person, and *Imago Trinitatis*," in *Understanding Human Dignity*, ed. Christopher McCrudden (Oxford: Oxford University Press, 2013), 210–12.

39. William J. Byron, "Ten Building Blocks of Catholic Social Teaching," *America*, October 31, 1998, 9–12.

40. Julia Fleming, "The Right to Reputation and the Preferential Option for the Poor," *Journal of the Society of Christian Ethics* 24, no. 1 (2004): 73–87.

41. USCCB, *Forming Consciences for Faithful Citizenship*, 2015, http://www.usccb.org/issues-and-action/faithful-citizenship/forming-consciences-for-faithful-citizenship-title.cfm.

42. *Gaudium et spes*, no. 14.

43. John Paul II, *Veritatis splendor* (Boston: St. Paul Books and Media, 1993), no. 2.

44. John XXIII, *Pacem in terris*, nos. 11–27.

45. I am grateful to Jonathan Rothchild and Matthew Petrusek for suggesting this insight.

46. Steven Pinker, "The Stupidity of Dignity," *The New Republic*, May 28, 2008, https://newrepublic.com/article/64674/the-stupidity-dignity.

47. Ruth Macklin, "Dignity Is a Useless Concept," *British Medical Journal* 327 (2003): 1419–20, http://www.bmj.com/content/327/7429/1419.

48. Samuel Moyn, "The Secret History of Constitutional Dignity," in McCrudden, ed., *Understanding Human Dignity*, 111.

49. John Paul II, *The Theology of the Body: Human Love in the Divine Plan* (Boston: Pauline Books and Media, 1997).

50. John Paul II, *Letter to Women*, no. 10, https://w2.vatican.va/content/john-paul-ii/en/letters/1995/documents/hf_jp-ii_let_29061995_women.html.

51. U. Schuklenk and W. Landman, "From the Editors: UNESCO 'Declares' Universals in Bioethics and Human Rights—Many Unexpected Universal Truths Unearthed by UN Body," *Developing World Bioethics* 5, no. 3 (2005): iii–iv.

52. Pinker, "The Stupidity of Dignity."

53. Ibid.

54. Michael Rosen, "Dignity: The Case Against," in McCrudden, ed., *Understanding Human Dignity*, 147.

55. Pinker, "The Stupidity of Dignity."

56. Ibid.

57. Weaver, *The Acting Person*, 31–60.

58. Daniel P. Sulmasy, O. F. M., "Dignity and Bioethics: History, Theory, and Selected Applications," in *Human Dignity and Bioethics*, ed. Edmund D. Pellegrino, Adan Schulman, and Thomas W. Merrill (Notre Dame, IN: University of Notre Dame Press, 2009), 473.

59. Ibid.

60. Ibid., 474.

61. Ibid., 473.

62. Alistair McFadyen makes a similar argument in his article on the *imago Dei*. See McFadyen, "Redeeming the Image," *International Journal for the Study of the Christian Church* 16, no. 2 (2016): 108–25.

two

DIGNITY

A Buddhist Perspective

Kristin Scheible

Does dignity have a normative meaning and is "dignity" justificatory grounding for human worth in Buddhist thought and practice? In his survey of current debates, Christopher McCrudden wonders if we are "all singing from the same hymn sheet" in understanding dignity as the command to all "that we (individually and collectively) should value the human person, simply because he or she is human."[1] His choice of idiom is telling, because much recent scholarship on dignity relies on discourse firmly rooted in Christian traditions and understandings, such as the biblical basis of *imago Dei* established in Genesis. There is perhaps no way around the feeling of discordance when expanding the chorus to include traditions such as Buddhism that maintain fundamentally different conceptions of what constitutes a "human person" in the first place (and given the nature of *saṃsāra*,[2] the cycle of birth-life-death-repeat, or metempsychosis, we might say first place, second, third, etc.). How might a Buddhist chime in?

With the wide range of meaning invoked by "dignity" in mind, I will consider possible analogues in Buddhist thought and ask a series of interrelated questions. What might constitute dignity in Buddhist thought and practice? In Buddhist thought, is the concept of dignity universal, natural, and equally palpable in all humans, an ontological lowest common denominator? Or do some beings have more than others? Can it be measured? Is it an innate and natural value or an acquired and cultivated virtue? Is one's dignity vulnerable to change over time and experience? Can it be nurtured and enhanced? In the absence of a transcendent moral authority, such as a creator/adjudicator god, is there a coherent explanation for human dignity?

The attempted answers I outline will reflect on and harmonize classical and canonical sources held as authoritative in all schools of Buddhist thought, focusing on some particularly salient texts for Theravāda and on the expressions of particularly notable contemporary Buddhists. To elucidate *the* Buddhist understanding of dignity is a daunting task, and I am attentive to the near impossibility because of the vastness of scope: varied traditions aligned with what we call "Buddhism" have thrived for 2,500 years, through many iterations, materials, practices, beliefs, traditions, understandings, and frequently in theoretical and physical conflict with each other. Traditionally conceived Buddhist analogues to what Western twenty-first-century scholars may call "dignity" exist, but human dignity is a modern concept, deeply interconnected with modern understandings of human rights, replete with a multitude of manifestations and interpretations in religious, legal, and political institutions. There is no way to easily resolve the tension between the normative claims implied by the concepts "human dignity" and "human rights" and the various culturally constituted comprehensions of just what being human entails. What Damien Keown has said about balancing the particularities of cultural forms while maintaining the universal applicability of doctrines rings true even if we were to replace "human rights" with "human dignity":

> The essence of any doctrine of human rights is its unrestricted scope, and it would be strange to have distinct "Theravāda," "Tibetan" and "Zen" doctrines of human rights as it would be to have "Catholic," "Protestant" and "Eastern Orthodox" ones. To insist on the priority of cultural and historical circumstances would be tantamount to denying the validity of human rights as a concept.[3]

Yet the utility of the concept of dignity surely fluctuates with the varied ontologies and metaphysics espoused by religious traditions.

Dignity thus evades singular, direct translation or correlation within Buddhist texts, but there is utility in employing the term nonetheless. In Mahāyāna Buddhist thought there is a concept called *upāya kauśalya*, "expedient means" or "skillful devices." *Upāya* are tools that may be craftily manipulated for a benefit otherwise difficult to obtain. It may be that employing the term "dignity" is a skillful way to discern something about the value and vulnerability of human life. "Dignity" may not map onto the Buddhist tradition precisely, but it can form an "interpretive bridge" to enable meaningful dialogue with other religious traditions.[4] "Dignity" resists a solid definition and maintains a "know-it-when-you-see-it"[5] quality that makes it a malleable and resilient bridge. Doron Shultziner observes "a twofold feature of human dignity as it is used as a justification for rights and duties in legal documents: symbolic-representation and a lack of a fixed content."[6] Referring to the tack taken by the framers of the Universal Declaration of Human Rights (UDHR), he considers the advantage of symbolic representation:

> For the abstention from a *philosophical* decision regarding the source and cause for rights and duties paves the way for a *political* consent concerning the specific rights and duties that *ought* to be legislated and enforced *in practice* without waiving or compromising basic principles of belief. Thus, the different parties that take part in a constitutive act can conceive human dignity as representing their particular set of values and worldview. In other words, human dignity is used as a linguistic-symbol that can represent different outlooks, thereby justifying a concrete political agreement on a seemingly shared ground.[7]

Citing the above passage, Christopher McCrudden notes, "This is not to imply that dignity has no content at all. Unlike in linguistics, where a placeholder carries no semantic information, dignity carries an enormous amount of content, but different content for different people. As we have seen, human dignity was a rallying cry in intellectual debate across the political and philosophical spectrum."[8] That "different content for different people" is embedded within the operative concept "human dignity" accords with Buddhist understandings about the variability of human experience.

My project will be to problematize the operative category "dignity" and to probe its utility, not as a translation of a particular value in Buddhist thought, but as a linguistic symbol that is a place connector rather than placeholder—"dignity" is a useful interpretive bridge for interfaith dialogue. Before crossing, we need to get a sense of the conceptual terrain, at once firmly established and venerable (the Buddhist tradition is old, vast, complicated, nuanced, lived, and diverse) and shifty. I will remain tethered to the Theravāda tradition that is for me most familiar ground, but I will enlist thinkers and particularly iconic teachers in other traditions to articulate meaningful connections with conceptions of dignity held by other religious traditions and framed legally and politically by documents such as the UDHR. I suggest there is stability, or at least continuity and shared ground, within the traditions within the complex we call Buddhism, even if the Buddhist moorings of this shared ground challenge the normativity implied by "human dignity."

DIGNITY IN BUDDHIST THOUGHT AND PRACTICE

Before searching for a salient Buddhist analogue, we must ask, What is the root meaning of dignity? In Latin, *dignitas* literally means "a being worthy," "worth," "worthiness," and "merit"; this meaning amplifies to dignity, greatness, grandeur, authority, and rank. Early usage connects it to rank and status; within the definition are many references to office and honorable employment, and *dignitas* can even extend to inanimate things to denote value and excellence.[9] The word and discursive weight of "dignity" seems to have expanded its meaning through time; through recent political and human rights discourse, it has come to mean something like "soul," some ubiquitous, innate quality that can be found in any human and that is at once inviolable and vulnerable, deserving protection. As the term has been increasingly used in legal and political domains, it has become even more expansive and inclusive. The Preamble to the Charter of the United Nations, for example, finds its foundation in the "faith in fundamental human rights, in the dignity and worth of the human person."[10] Within the UDHR, adopted by the UN General Assembly on December 10, 1948, dignity dominates the very first line of the preamble, the first value to be enshrined, albeit yoked to the comparable concept of rights: "Whereas recognition of the inherent dignity and of the equal and inalienable rights of all members of the human family is the foundation of freedom, justice, and peace in the world"; and again further into the document as article 1, "All human beings are born free and equal in dignity and rights. They are endowed with reason and conscience and should act towards one another in a spirit of brotherhood."[11] Dignity is expansive, inclusive, innate, universal, natural, presumed, and foundational, at least in the UDHR. But what if a particular religious tradition maintains a less concrete and enduring sense of what it means to be a "human person" in the first place?

There is a challenge in translation, not just of words' meanings but of the nuanced and context-specific semantic fields they conjure. Dignity is not always the same as respect, agency, or autonomy, and a universal sense of dignity cannot be bound to metaphysics because there is radical diversity among and within religious traditions. Translating to Buddhist concepts, if dignity is an innate and universal aspect of a life, it could possibly be analogous to *sattva/satta*, "sentience" or "sentient being."[12] But in Buddhist thought, sentience exceeds the human condition and is not an exclusive value of humanity. In the perspectives of other traditions, do beings other than humans have dignity? Buddhist cosmology maintains possible previous and future rebirth in any number of birth forms, including animals, hungry ghosts, hell beings, even gods, and it also posits instability (*anitya/anicca*) as a fundamental truth of all life. Who—or what—would not have dignity? Dignity might mean "that which is most dear (*priyam/piyam*)," which we will see equated to the basest element of human nature, a universal experience. And regarding dignity, one might be inspired to nonharm (*ahiṃsa*), which, in turn, reflects the dignity of the nonharmer.

DIGNITY AS LOWEST COMMON DENOMINATOR

In Buddhist thought, is something like dignity universal, natural, and equally palpable in all humans? The integrally linked, so-called three marks of existence (*duḥkha/dukkha*, "suffering," or dis-ease of all conditioned things; *anitya/anicca*, "impermanence" of all conditioned things; and *anātman/anattā*, "non-self" of all conditioned things) are universal, natural, and palpable. The foundational doctrine of *anātman/anattā*, literally, "no-self" or "no-soul," means that each "self" is understood to be a construct, an amalgamation of physiological and psychological elements that together constitute a person. Buddhists understand personhood as a construct of five *skandhas/khandhas* (aggregates): (1) materiality, form (*rūpa*), (2) feelings, sensations (*vedanā*), (3) perceptions, discernments (*saṃjñā/saññā*), (4) volitions, constructing activities (*saṃskāra/sankhāra*; one salient example for us is *cetanā*, which can be translated as "intention," "will," or "volition"), (5) consciousness (*vijñāna/viññāṇa*).[13] In other words, what we conventionally refer to as "self" is not stable or enduring; the self is only a heuristically useful designation for a being in time, experiencing personally dis-ease (*duḥkha/dukkha*) and impermanence (*anitya/anicca*) of all things, "self" included.

A "self" changes not only through one lifetime, but through many, and the course of metempsychosis is determined by one's *karma/kamma* (actions) through time. The whole process is known as *saṃsāra*, the "wandering on" cycle of birth-life-death that repeats with variation until final release forms the cycle that is *nirvāṇa/nibbāna* ("blowing out," unbinding), the ultimate goal.[14] Within *saṃsāra*, rounds of rebirths, incarnations of new "selves," occur because of *karma*, literally, "action," which is understood to be a natural law based on actions (words, thoughts, and deeds).

As individuals move through the rounds of rebirth, they meet with multiple opportunities to cultivate merit or accrue demerit through their actions. Moral actions are skillful, unskillful, or neutral, and they yield concomitant karmic weight. Skillful moral actions earn merit, or *puṇya/puñña*, while negative or unskillful actions result in demerit, *pāpa*. One's actions have effects, and even though one cannot control when or how the effects will come to be (*karmaphala vipāka*, literally, "the fruit of karma ripens"), one has the ability to exert agency in determining the moral weight of one's effects by intending to do good things and by doing them. The Buddha purportedly articulated this relationship between moral actions and intention: "It is intention [*cetanā*], O monks, that I call Karma; having willed one acts through body, speech, or mind."[15]

Selves are woven together in a matrix of karmic relationships through time, as individuals have repeated experiences as each other's mothers, sons, friends, and enemies. Pulling back one's focus from this lifetime, and contextualizing the "self" as but another fleeting aspect of *saṃsāra*, the distinction between the self and another is blurred. When one, therefore, comes into contact with another, Buddhist thought and practice encourages recognition of this complex social web. As I have framed it elsewhere, "The self and the other do not inhabit conflicting, but rather conflated moral universes. In other words, when each and every 'other' might have been your mother in a past life or might be your mother in a future one, what you do in this life that you have now matters."[16]

Experiencing life as a human self is challenging, but it is also an opportunity. A human birth, says the tradition, is rare and special because it presents the opportunity for a self to do good and make progress on the path toward enlightenment. Bhikkhu Bodhi, the American Theravāda monk, translator, exegete, and dharma teacher, explains:

> This moral complexity can make of human life a painful struggle indeed, but it also renders the human realm the most fertile ground for sowing the seeds of enlightenment. It is at this tauntingly ambiguous crossroads in the long journey of being that we can either rise to the heights of spiritual greatness or fall to degrading depths. The two alternatives branch out from each present moment, and which one we take depends on ourselves.[17]

The "moral complexity" does make it rather difficult to determine in what "self" dignity might be perceived. As selfhood itself is shifty terrain, the agent fluctuates. How might one land on a sense of "dignity" within this instability?

Because human dignity and human rights are mutually constitutive concepts, a self-less sense of dignity has practical implications more generally. Śantipala Stephen Evans has explained the practical, social, and political complexities of the self-less self for human rights discourse:

> In the language of human rights the person is an invariant bundle of rights and duties; invariant not only over time but also among distinct individuals. We become abstract units in the machinery of the state. This abstraction may be necessary in order to formulate legalisms through which real human beings are protected, but it misses the richness of human existence. In Buddhist terms it violates *anattā* (non-self) and *anicca* (impermanence). Buddhism *may* recognize invariant laws by which the person develops, but the bundle of possibilities, limitations, habits, and so forth, which "person" stands in for is in flux, lacking even a sacred core of being to which the rights and duties may apply.[18]

The problem is framed another way in Mahāyāna Buddhist thought, where no-self is a manifestation of *śūnyatā* (emptiness), the fundamental understanding of ultimate reality. Bernard Faure reminds us of the metaphysical complication:

> Indeed, how can one kill another person when, according to good Buddhist orthodoxy, all is emptiness? The man who kills with full knowledge of the facts kills no one because he realizes that all is but illusion, himself as well as the other person. He can kill, because he does not actually kill anyone. One cannot kill emptiness, nor destroy the wind.[19]

Canonically, running through all Buddhist traditions is the doctrine of interconnectedness. No-self (*anātman/anattā*) enables (perhaps) an appreciation of a natural, universal, and equally palpable and present dignity in all humans, in fact, in all life. Interconnectedness is articulated in the doctrine of dependent co-origination, (*pratītyasamutpāda/paṭiccasamuppāda*) a twelve-point chain of causation that is enshrined in this brief formula:

When this is, that is.
From the arising of this comes the arising of that.
When this isn't, that isn't.
From the cessation of this comes the cessation of that.[20]

Establishing his Order of Interbeing (*Tiếp Hiện*), Thích Nhất Hạnh, the Vietnamese Zen monk, dharma teacher, and peace activist, has expressively woven together a profound understanding of no-self (*anātman*), emptiness (*śūnyatā*), and dependent co-arising (*pratītyasamutpāda*). In Buddhist Studies classrooms, many of us teach his poem "Please Call Me by My True Names" because it illustrates interconnectedness in a poignant way. In it, barriers between self and other are broken, so a shared identity (what might be called dignity) reveals itself. Thích Nhất Hạnh has written that the poem was inspired by a letter he had received recounting the plight of refugees, boat people, in Southeast Asia, who were often victims not only of circumstance, political trauma, and displacement, but of piracy on the seas. The inspiration for the poem was the story of a clear violation of human dignity, a rape and subsequent suicide of one particular twelve-year-old girl.[21] Beyond the natural identification with, and sympathy for, the victim denied her dignity, Thích Nhất Hạnh also reveals deep sympathy and compassion for the perpetrator. The poem presents a pathway of understanding to begin to redress conflict, a way of expanding one's understanding and compassion, even in accepting some responsibility for being complicit in the circumstances. Amidst political images of exploitation and conflict in the rest of the poem, in the excerpts here we see that the use of nature imagery further enforces a sense of the inner dignity of all as natural law:

I am a mayfly metamorphosing
on the surface of the river.
And I am the bird
that swoops down to swallow the mayfly.
I am a frog swimming happily
in the clear water of a pond,
and I am the grass-snake
that silently feeds itself on the frog . . .
. . . I am the twelve-year-old girl,
refugee on a small boat,
who throws herself into the ocean

> after being raped by a sea pirate.
> And I am the pirate,
> my heart not yet capable
> of seeing and loving.
> . . . .
> Please call me by my true names,
> so I can hear all my cries and laughter at once,
> so I can see that my joy and pain are one.
> Please call me by my true names,
> so I can wake up
> and the door of my heart
> could be left open,
> the door of compassion.[22]

An engaged Buddhist activist, Thích Nhất Hạnh advocates a radical mindfulness, a deeper understanding of no-self, where one moves beyond attention to one's own thoughts and acts in expanding attention to surrounding and interconnecting social situations. The protagonist of the poem is "me" ("call *me* by my true names"); as interconnectedness means mutual constitution and responsibility, once the awareness of a conflict is raised, one is already in a position to take a position. The human birth, recall, is a privileged one where agency (choices, intention, action) means the cultivation of merit. In another context, Śantipala Stephen Evans considers what this agency means, given the Buddhist understanding of no-self (*anātman/anattā*):

> Here is a kind of inviolability. Not that there is a "dignity" resident somehow in every human breast, but that such a dignity, as it were, appears along with the relation between persons: I *am* for you, and you for me, and as soon as I enter into a relationship with you, you become necessary to my being. This "dignity" is inescapable *because* ephemeral, *my* lack of self corresponds to *yours*. If I order your execution, I *am* that death. As a *subject* if I fail to resist known injustice, I am complicit, because "resignation" is a choice.[23]

In line with Buddhist thought, perception of interconnectedness, for humans, reveals shared dignity and ought to lead to compassion and action—it is a motivating force, and an opportunity to make the right choice to make best use of the special human birth. Perception of interconnectedness engenders the first precept:[24] "I undertake the precept to do no harm to living creatures." Dignity, then, extends beyond human boundaries into all life—a position clearly articulated in Thích Nhất Hạnh's poem ("I am the mayfly . . . frog . . . bird . . . grass-snake"). Damien Keown reflects on this rationale for the first precept:

> Abstention from taking life is therefore ideally the result of a compassionate identification with living things, rather than a constraint imposed contrary to natural inclination. To observe the first precept perfectly requires a profound understanding of the relationship between living beings (according to Buddhism, in the long cycle of reincarnation we have all been each others' fathers, mothers, sons, and so forth) coupled with an unswerving disposition of universal benevolence and compassion. Although few have perfected these capacities, in respecting the precepts they habituate themselves to the conduct of one who has, and in so doing come a step closer to enlightenment.[25]

But is the perception of interconnectedness robust enough to be an analogue of, or claim the basis for, human dignity? Elsewhere Keown has problematized the *pratītyasamutpāda* reading of dignity:

> The derivation of human rights from the doctrine of dependent-origination is a conjuring trick. From the premise that we live in "a mutually constituted existential realm" (we all live together) it has "thereby become a fact" that there will be "mutual respect of fellow beings." In the twinkling of an eye, values have appeared from facts like a rabbit out of a hat. However, the fact that human beings live in relationship with one another is not a moral argument about *how they ought to behave.*[26]

Pratītyasamutpāda/paṭiccasamuppāda (dependent co-origination, dependent arising), in other words, is descriptive. Dignity might be something that can be perceived through the awareness of dependent co-origination, or Interbeing in Thích Nhất Hạnh's language. But dignity, a conditioned thing, as a facet of the human condition is unsteady and impermanent. What does the perception of dignity in another activate? What good is dignity if not for the good of humanity?

I have said elsewhere that the Golden Rule–flavored formula in Buddhism is "neither completely positive nor negative, but conditional and relative; moreover, it falls somewhere between a simple observation and a prescriptive command,"[27] between rights and duties. As we will see, in the absence of an enduring sense of self, perhaps dignity is what is dear, *priya/piya*, what is valuable. The idea of value or valuable captures the self-interest involved in recognizing and upholding one's dignity. In a canonical formulation, it is once again the situation of conflict where what is dear (self-interest) becomes perceptible:

> On traversing all directions with the mind
> One finds no one dearer than oneself.
> Likewise everyone holds himself most dear,
> Hence one who loves himself should not harm another.[28]

This moral lesson, delivered by the Buddha, is in many ways a distillation of the dharma (Buddhist teaching), a conceptual bridge between what is personal and particular and what is social and universal, a bridge between the concrete, experiential epistemic tool that is the self and the ethical abstraction of others. Self-interest is simply a fact, and we can deduce that every other individual is similarly self-interested. It is on this basis that one should not harm another, because it would be a violation of another's self-interest. Perhaps self-interest and dignity are in alignment. As in other traditions, Buddhists have written commentaries that reveal how textual communities negotiate interpretation of canonical sources and doctrine. The monastic exegete Dhammapāla explicated the final line ("hence one who loves himself should not harm another") in the *Paramatthadīpanī* (commentary) on the Udāna:

> *Therefore one desiring self should not harm another* (*tasmā na hiṁse paramattakāmo*): since each being holds the self dear in that way, is one desiring happiness for that self, one for whom *dukkha* is repulsive, therefore one desiring self, in wanting well-being of and happiness for that self, should not harm, should not kill, should not even antagonize with the hand, a clod of earth or a stick and so on, another being, upwards from and including even a mere ant or (other) small insect. For when *dukkha* is caused by oneself to some other, that (*dukkha*) is, after an interval of time, observed in one's (own) self, as though it were passing over therefrom. For this is the law of *karma*.[29]

Reflecting a Mahāyāna orientation, Masao Abe asserts that the peremptory nonharm (*ahiṃsā*) extends beyond humankind, and even beyond the ants of the Theravādin commentator: "Under the commandment 'Not to destroy any life,' the rights of animals and plants are as equally recognized as human rights."[30] Several narratives explore the practical extent of nonharm; blind monks accidentally walk on ants, a tongue is used to remove maggots where a finger may do harm, or a monkey gingerly removes bee larvae before honey can be consumed.

Many Buddhist narratives are discursive sites for negotiating the theoretical nuances and practical dimensions of dharma. Stories of conflict are especially salient for ethical negotiations. The commentary on the Pāli Dhammapada, another canonical text, tells of two factions of monks, one older and one younger, who were in conflict over a new dwelling that had been built by the younger monks. The older monks assumed that on the basis of their status (perhaps with a sense of their own *dignitas*), they deserved to reside in the new dwelling, and even the conflict that arose was perceived as a slight to their dignity, authority, and status. The two conflicting factions would surely come to blows, an urgent situation provoking the verse uttered by the Buddha, their teacher/adjudicator:

> All tremble before violence.
> All fear death.
> Having done the same yourself,
> you should neither harm nor kill.
> All tremble before violence.
> Life is held dear by all.
> Having done the same yourself,
> you should neither harm nor kill.
> Whoever, through violence, does harm
> to living beings desiring ease,
> hoping for such ease himself,
> will not, when he dies, realize ease.
> Whoever does no harm through violence
> To living beings desiring ease,
> Hoping for such ease himself,
> Will, when he dies, realize ease.[31]

The word translated "ease" here, *sukha,* also means "happiness," "contentedness," "well-being." It is the opposite of *dukkha,* "suffering," "unease," and "disease," which is at once the primary mark of all existence and the goal for eradication. *Sukha* could be analogous to dignity: vulnerable in the face of conflict and force, but an innate and desirable characteristic, worthy of amplification and augmentation. And as the spiritual leader of the Tibetan people, His Holiness the Dalai Lama, has said, "Brute force, no matter how strongly applied, can never subdue the basic human desire for freedom and dignity."[32] As a basic human desire, *sukha*—and dignity—is a universal.

DIGNITY MEASURED

All beings may eschew harm and desire ease, freedom, and dignity, but some beings seem more clearly in possession of innate or previously cultivated ease, freedom, and dignity. In Mahāyāna Buddhism, the *bodhisattva* ("one whose essence is perfect knowledge," an enlightened being, or one who is set on enlightenment) is one who wishes and acts for the enlightenment of all sentient beings. One on the *bodhisattva* path vows to stay bound in *saṃsāra* to effect this goal. In Theravāda, the eventual goal is to become an enlightened being no longer subject to the bounds of *saṃsāra*, free, which requires the cultivation of ten *pāramitā/pārami* (literally, "perfections," "virtues").[33] An *arhat/arahant* ("one who is worthy") is one who has destroyed the fetters, uprooted the roots (*kleśa/kilesa*; namely, greed, hatred, and delusion) of *dukkha* that keep the "self" bound and captive in *saṃsāra*. The *kleśa/kilesa* are the opposite of dignity and interfere with its appreciation. Greed, hatred, and delusion prevent one from "seeing things as they truly are," namely, through the basic marks of all existence, *duḥkha/dukkha* (suffering or dis-ease), *anitya/anicca* (impermanence), and *anātman/anattā* (non-self). The *kleśa/kilesa* are both natural inclinations and mental afflictions that can be righted and cured. As beings who have eradicated the *kleśa/kilesa*, the worthy ones (*arhat/arahant*) are moral exemplars. To explain the value of such an exemplar to beings who are themselves privileged with a human birth to make the right choices and perform the right actions for self-cultivation, Bhikkhu Bodhi identifies a distinction between what he calls *intrinsic* and *active* dignity:

> While this unique capacity for moral choice and spiritual awakening confers intrinsic dignity on human life, the Buddha does not emphasize this so much as he does our ability to acquire active dignity. This ability is summed up by a word that lends its flavor to the entire teaching, *ariya* or noble. The Buddha's teaching is the *ariyadhamma*, the noble doctrine, and its purpose is

> to change human beings from "ignorant worldlings" into noble disciples resplendent with noble wisdom. The change does not come about through mere faith and devotion but by treading the Buddhist path, which transmutes our frailties into invincible strengths and our ignorance into knowledge. . . . The person who represents the apex of dignity for Buddhism is the arahant, the liberated one, who has reached the pinnacle of spiritual autonomy: release from the dictates of greed, hatred, and delusion. The very word *arahant* suggests this sense of dignity: the word means "worthy one," one who deserves the offerings of gods and humans. Although in our present condition we might still be far from the stature of an arahant, this does not mean we are utterly lost, for the means of reaching the highest goal is already within our reach.[34]

In other words, in a Buddhist inflection, perhaps the human condition confers intrinsic dignity, which is the impetus for cultivating active dignity, perfected and exemplified by the *arahant.*

Some beings, then, clearly can have "more" dignity or augmented dignity. But what about the other end of the spectrum? Might there be human beings deprived or deprivable of dignity? Again, we will appeal to a Buddhist narrative for an example. A nonnormative but highly influential source, held aloft as authoritative, even prescriptive by Sinhalese Theravāda Buddhists, is the fifth-century historical chronicle *Mahāvaṃsa.*[35] An inner conflict, provoked by ruminations on a political conflict, presents the opportunity for the protagonist-hero within the text—and the readers outside the text—to confront the boundaries of the semantic field circumscribed by dignity. Do all sentient beings have dignity, or just human beings, or just Buddhists?

In chapter 25 ("The Victory of Duṭṭhagāmaṇī") of the Pāli *Mahāvaṃsa,* the conqueror-king (and enduring national hero) Duṭṭhagāmaṇī has concluded a murderous battle against the Dāmila outsider Elāra.[36] While at a victory celebration, right when he ought to feel most secure, proud, powerful, and accomplished, Duṭṭhagāmaṇī instead feels remorse at having killed so many people (other beings) in battle. Distraught, he solicits comfort and advice from his adviser monks: "How will there be any comfort for me, venerable sirs, since the slaughter of a great many numbering millions was caused by me?" A Buddhist, Duṭṭhagāmaṇī has violated the first precept (do no harm). But his advisers absolve him of his guilt and responsibility, even the concomitant karmic implications:

> From this act of yours there is no obstacle to the way to heaven. In this world the Lord of Men [Duṭṭhagāmaṇī] has slain only one and a half human beings. One was steadfast in the Refuges [the Buddha, Dhamma (his teachings), and Saṅgha (community of monks); the Triple Refuge is the enunciation of one's being Buddhist], and the other the Five Precepts; the remainder were of bad character and wrong views, considered beasts. But in many ways you will cause the *buddhasāsana*[37] to shine, therefore, Lord of Men, drive out the perplexity from your mind![38]

As the *Mahāvaṃsa* tells it, after killing many people on the battlefield, Duṭṭhagāmaṇī feels guilty and struggles with his worthiness; he is then educated by eight *arahants* (worthy ones) that he is indeed a good person who is destined to do good things.[39] The majority of the beings killed "were of bad character and wrong views, considered beasts," with no innate dignity palpable. There is no sense of an extension of the perception of dignity to non-Buddhists, to other humans, let alone beyond the category of human.

This narrative derives its force from an Aśokan paradigm, though the story of the Buddhist king Aśoka ends with the opposite conclusion, namely, the inherent worth of all beings—even nonhuman. King Aśoka (ca. 274–232 BCE) was a great unifier of the landmass now known as India. But he conquered the land in violent ways, and expressed a great change of heart and extreme remorse and regret:

> The Kaliṅga country was conquered by King Priyadarśī, Beloved of the Gods [Aśoka], in the eighth year of his reign. One hundred and fifty thousand persons were carried away captive, one hundred thousand were slain, and many times that number died. Immediately after the Kaliṅgas had been conquered, King Priyadarśī became intensely devoted to the study of Dharma, to the love of Dharma, and to the inculcation of Dharma. The Beloved of the Gods, conqueror of the Kaliṅgas, is moved to remorse now. For he has felt profound sorrow and regret because the conquest of a people previously unconquered involves slaughter, death, and deportation.[40]

This particular rock edict then reveals that the depth of Aśoka's remorse is magnified by the fact that even those who escaped the calamitous misfortune of falling under Aśoka's sword nonetheless feel suffering (*duḥkha/dukkha*), and "thus all men share in the misfortune, and this weighs on King Priyadarśī's mind."[41] Unlike the self-interested angst experienced by Duṭṭhagāmaṇī, Aśoka's reflection reveals his recognition, perhaps, of the universality of dignity among humankind:

> King Priyadarśī now thinks that even a person who wrongs him must be forgiven for wrongs that can be forgiven. . . . For Priyadarśī desires security, self-control, impartiality, and cheerfulness for all living creatures.[42]

Aśoka's epithet, Priyadarśī, means "seer of what is dear." The "dear" here, *priya*, is the same dear we encountered above in both the Dhammapada verse ("Life is held dear by all") and the Udāna verses ("One finds no one dearer than oneself. Likewise everyone holds himself most dear"). If what we take as "dignity" is "what is dear," it can certainly be perceived and appreciated, recognized as a value, and, in this way, measured.

NATURAL VALUE OR CULTIVATED VIRTUE?

Aśoka's reflection and the Dhammapada and Udāna verses support the understanding that dignity, what is dear, is an innate and universal value. But innateness does not preclude cultivation; the *arahant* and the *bodhisattva* show that it intensifies (through lifetimes in the case of the *arahant*) through intentional cultivation and the attainment of the perfections. The tradition posits the Buddha as the primary exemplar of the cultivation, enshrined in the veneration verse that opens every Buddhist text and ceremony: "Homage to the Blessed One, the Worthy One, the Fully Enlightened One" (*Namo tassa bhagavato arahato sammāsambuddhassa*).

The Buddha is the ultimate manifestation, then, of dignity: that which is most dear is cultivated through many lifetimes, resulting in the most worthy being. The Yogācāra, a prominent school of Mahāyāna Buddhism, understands the potential of perfectibility innate in humankind as *tathāgatagarbha*, literally, the "seed of Tathāgata" ("Thus-come/thus-gone," an epithet of the Buddha), the embryo of Buddhahood in all living beings. Peter Junger, law professor, activist, and Buddhist, identified *tathāgatagarbha* as dignity, and framed it in practical terms: "Of course it would be nice if everyone had work, and not too much of it, if everyone had enough to eat and a roof over their heads, if everyone's dignity—everyone's Buddha nature—were universally recognized."[43] His sentiment presumes the superiority of the Buddhist orientation, an inclusivist maneuver that challenges a universal understanding of human dignity. Śantipala Stephen Evans remarked, "If the potential for enlightenment is the ground for human dignity, where does that leave those who have no interest in realizing that potential?"[44] For the recognition of, and response to, the universality of human dignity, must there be a universal definition? If it is innate and natural in all humanity, whether stable, acquired, or cultivated, the concept of dignity is bound by culturally contextual constraints.

CHANGE, NURTURING, AND ENHANCEMENT

In Buddhist thought, all things are subject to change over time, and as a "thing," dignity would be too. Cultivation of the self is of paramount importance, and conscientiously treading the Noble Eightfold Path, the practical means by which *duḥkha/dukkha* may be alleviated, is the way. No matter the particular school of Buddhist thought, whether an understanding of a "Buddha seed," or *tathāgatagarbha*, is explicitly articulated or not, the human birth is a precious one among countless possible birth stations, and such a birth presents a most salient opportunity for the cultivation of merit and work toward the perfections. The Buddhist tradition has developed a set of practices to generate what is called the *Brahmavihārā* (Divine Abodes), a system of four virtues and concomitant cultivating practices: (1) loving-kindness (*maitrī/mettā*); (2) compassion (*karuṇā*); (3) empathetic joy (*muditā*), defined as the absence of self-interest, taking pure joy in an other; and (4) equanimity (*upekṣā/upekkhā*); perhaps another candidate as a translation of "dignity," *upekkhā* is a superpower form of neutrality, an innate aversion to conflict in a most profound sense, akin to Epicurean *ataraxia*.

The first two qualities in particular, loving-kindness and compassion, affect the cultivation of the self and may improve a Buddhist's ability to recognize and appreciate what is dear—dignity—in another. The two appear almost interchangeable at first glance, though there are significant doctrinal differences in how they are categorized and manifested. In Theravāda, practicing loving-kindness (*mettā*) overcomes conflict. In his *Buddhist Ethics*, Hammalawa Saddhatissa gives a synopsis of the *mettā* meditation practice: first, one pervades oneself with *mettā*; second, one cultivates *mettā* toward one's teacher, considering all the gifts one has received; third, one thinks of, and extends *mettā* to, a dear friend; fourth, one thinks of, and extends *mettā* to, a person toward whom one feels neutral as if they were a dear friend; and fifth, cultivating *mettā*, one regards a hostile person as if neutral (other lists omit the teacher, and end with the fifth stage as generating *mettā* toward all living beings). The reason for this practice is that through the vicissitudes of *saṃsāra* one has been in various relationships with others, and it is useful to pay attention to that perpetual and fluctuating interconnectedness. Canonically grounded, Saddhatissa cites Samyutta Nikaya II.89: "Bhikkhus, it is not easy to find a being who has not formerly been your mother, or your father, your brother, your sister, or your son or daughter."[45] A variation of this practice, a meditation on the exchange of self and other, exists across Buddhist traditions. Its crystallization, a pre-percussion perhaps of the UDHR, is in the *Mettā Sutta*:

> Whatever living beings there be—
> Feeble or strong, tall, stout or medium,
> Short, small or large, without exception—
> Seen or unseen, those dwelling far or near,
> Those who are born or who are to be born,
> May all beings be happy.[46]

Karuṇā (compassion) may be integral to Buddhist thought and practice, but it has been linked by His Holiness the Dalai Lama to a "universal responsibility," what scholar Sallie King notes is "one of the signature themes of his speeches."[47]

> As a Buddhist monk, my concern extends to all members of the human family and, indeed, to all sentient beings who suffer. I believe all suffering is caused by ignorance. People inflict pain on others in the selfish pursuit of their happiness or satisfaction. Yet true happiness comes from a sense of brotherhood and sisterhood. We need to cultivate a universal responsibility for one another and the planet we share. Although I have found my own Buddhist religion helpful in generating love and compassion, even for those we consider our enemies, I am convinced that everyone can develop a good heart and a sense of universal responsibility with or without religion. . . . I pray for all of us, oppressor and friend, that together we succeed in building a better world through human understanding and love, and that in doing so we may reduce the pain and suffering of all sentient beings.[48]

COHERENT EXPLANATION

In Buddhism, dignity is not ontologically grounded in some transcendent authority; dignity is only coherently explained with recourse to the predominant understanding of dharma (*saṃsāra*, *kamma*, *dukkha*, *anicca*, *anattā*). Religions that imagine a creator God responsible for the fashioning of humanity seem to have an advantage in establishing default, innate dignity. The *imago Dei* establishes at the outset of humanity a facsimile that is clear: humans, male and female, are created in the image of God, are blessed, and are charged with dominion over all other livings things, "Let us make humankind in our image, according to our likeness" (Gen. 1:26). Unlike the *imago Dei* articulated in Genesis 1:26 that anchors Christian and Jewish understandings of dignity to a transcendent moral authority, in the Buddhist canon a "creation text" challenges any such authority or moral mooring outside the cultivation of the self.

"In the beginning," Buddhism maintains no creator God, no image to live up to in that way. Within a universe of incessant fluctuation, Buddhism even resists a singular beginning. There is a narrative of a beginning of humanity revealing both etiology and moral topography, but unlike Genesis it is not the threshold of a holy canon, the priming device one encounters at the very outset; the *Aggañña Sutta* is articulated deep within one section of the *Dīgha Nikāya*, which is itself one section of the *sūtras/suttas* within one section of the *Tripiṭaka/Tipiṭaka* (the canon). Its placement in the midst of the teachings rather than at the outset seems to reflect the core nature of Buddhist interconnectedness rather than a structure based on foundations and beginnings. The teaching begins with a frame narrative, a common device in Buddhist moral didactic materials, where the Buddha narrates that "original sin" is greed (one of the *kleśa/kilesa* that keep one bound in *saṃsāra*). To illustrate, the Buddha explains there was a paradise of sorts, in a time many times ago, where beings did not suffer and were self-luminescent beings of light and bliss, incapable of discrimination between male and female, good and evil, and so on. At that time, hovering weightless, one being first desires, then exerts agency, to taste the earth below, which is like a dessert of honey and butter. Greed and curiosity initiate a decline, quite literally a fall, as other beings taste of this earth essence and sink as they get weighty, lose luminosity, and start seeing distinctions such as male and female, good and bad; crime begins because of the discrimination and greed, the beings begin to hoard food and possessions, requiring policing and government. The greed begets all sorts of harmful practices, such as theft, sex, and violence, and the practical result is that the beings decide to submit to an authority, a king and government.[49]

For our developing sense of human dignity in the Buddhist tradition, this story underscores the relationship of actions and existence. The way to stop the devolution is to enter the path toward eventual enlightenment; to apply one's understanding and agency to cultivate through right practices the virtues (perfections), one can potentially reverse moral entropy. To distinguish it from a "transcendent moral authority," Damien Keown articulates the process of self-cultivation as a "transcendent ground":

> The twin axes of human good are knowledge (*prajñā*) and moral concern (*karuṇā*) and on the graph defined by these axes can be plotted the soteriological coordinates of any individual. Through participation in these twin categories of good, human nature progressively transcends its limitations and becomes saturated with nirvanic goodness. Eventually, in post-mortem *nirvāṇa*, this goodness attains a magnitude which can no longer be charted. If a transcendent ground for human rights is desired, this is where it should be sought.[50]

SELF-LESS DIGNITY AS VULNERABLE

To assert that humans are endowed with innate human dignity is to pronounce a normative claim. Locating human dignity as the foundation for human rights privileges a fundamental, foundational, essential, and recognizable quality to human selves. The self, however, in a Buddhist understanding, defies stability. Perhaps to underscore the instability of foundational terms such as "human dignity," throughout this chapter human dignity and human rights have been intertwined. This apparent slipperiness of terms might be especially destabilizing, even problematic, for interfaith dialogue, but in a Buddhist sense the conflation of these concepts reveals their mutual constitution. The apparent slippage between dignity and human rights points to a mutual constructedness that follows a familiar flow in Buddhist thought; recognition of universal human dignity is both cause and result of human rights, and human rights are both inalienable and the cause and effect of dignity.

There are several terms and concepts in Buddhist thought and practice that share the semantic field of "human dignity." If we go with the adjectival *priya/piya*, "what is most dear," dignity is universal, natural, and palpable in all humans. If we go with the sense of worth or nobility implied by *dignitas*, personified by the *arhat/arahant*, some exemplary humans are endowed with more than others, and it can be perceived, measured, comprehended, aspired to, and cultivated. If we understand dignity as *tathāgatagarbha*, the seed of Buddhahood, we see the germ may be innate and latent, but that it must be cultivated for fruition. As all things in *saṃsāra*, dignity is vulnerable to fluctuation, impermanence (*anitya/anicca*). Vulnerability comes in any unstable environment, whether it is a war-torn community, a physical terrain, a mental construction or political position, or a sense of self. A self-less one who engages in the path of self-cultivation recognizes the vulnerability and value of dignity within herself and recognizes the vulnerability and value of dignity in others.

NOTES

1. Christopher McCrudden, "In Pursuit of Human Dignity: An Introduction to Current Debates," in *Understanding Human Dignity*, ed. Christopher McCrudden (New York: Oxford University Press, 2014), 1.

2. Buddhist terms throughout will appear in both Pāli and Sanskrit, unless the term is the same in both languages, as in the case of *saṃsāra*, "the wandering on" cycle of rebirths.

3. Damien Keown, "Are There Human Rights in Buddhism?," in *Buddhism and Human Rights*, ed. Wayne R. Husted, Damien V. Keown, and Charles S. Prebish (New York: Routledge, 2015), 17.

4. Charles Hallisey, "Ethical Particularism in Theravāda Buddhism," *Journal of Buddhist Ethics* 3 (1996): 32–43. He writes, "It is important that we try to fashion terms like 'ethical particularism' into interpretive bridges if we are ever to make the study of Buddhist ethics a part of academic discussions of ethics as well as a concern of Buddhist studies. Such efforts at translation will necessarily be halting and tentative—indeed, many of them will probably fail—but this should not discourage close attention to Buddhist ethical thought as a resource for broader academic discussions about ethics" (43).

5. "We do not find an explicit definition of the expression 'dignity of the human person' in international instruments or (as far as I know) in national law. Its intrinsic meaning has been left to intuitive understanding, conditioned in large measure by cultural factors. When it has been invoked in concrete situations, it has been generally assumed that a violation of human dignity can be recognized even if the abstract term cannot be defined. 'I know it when I see it even if I cannot tell you what it is'"; Oscar Schachter, "Human Dignity as a Normative Concept," *The American Journal of International Law* 77, no. 4 (1983): 849.

6. Doron Shultziner, "Human Dignity: Functions and Meanings," in *Perspectives on Human Dignity*, ed. Jeff Malpas and Norelle Lickiss (Dordrecht: Springer, 2007), 77.

7. Doron Shultziner, "Human Dignity: Functions and Meanings," in *Perspectives on Human Dignity*, ed. Jeff Malpas and Norelle Lickiss (Dordrecht: Springer, 2007), 77–78 (original emphasis); cited in Christopher McCrudden, "Human Dignity and Judicial Interpretation of Human Rights," *The European Journal of International Law* 19, no. 4 (2008): 678.

8. McCrudden, "Human Dignity," 678.

9. Charlton T. Lewis and Charles Short, *A Latin Dictionary* (Oxford: Clarendon, 1879), http://www.perseus.tufts.edu/hopper/text?doc=Perseus%3Atext%3A1999.04.0059%3Aentry%3Ddignitas. Thank you to classicist Jessica Seidman for discussing the semantic field of *dignitas* with me.

10. Preamble, Charter of the United Nations, http://www.un.org/en/sections/un-charter/preamble/index.html.

11. Universal Declaration of Human Rights (UDHR), https://www.un.org/en/universal-declaration-human-rights/, cited in full in Husted, Keown, and Prebish, eds., *Buddhism and Human Rights*, ix. Keown notes the inclusivist response of Perera, a notable Buddhist, in his commentary to the UDHR: "Buddhahood itself is within the reach of all human beings . . . and if all could attain Buddhahood what greater equality in dignity and rights can there be?"; cited in Keown, "Are There Human Rights in Buddhism?," 29.

12. Surveying the conceptual terrain, there are several other words in Sanskrit that may connote "dignity," or begin to reveal it, such as the following: *gāmbhīrya* (gravity, depth, profundity, sobriety, and dignity); *anubhāva* (dignity, authority, power; also the spontaneous expression of innermost being); *virāj* and similar terms connote kingship and honor; *adirājya* (sovereignty, supremacy, dignity); *vīrya*, one of the perfections to cultivate (virility, vitality, power, vigor, heroism, dignity).

13. A helpful and concise introduction can be found in Peter Harvey, *An Introduction to Buddhism: Teachings, History and Practices* (Cambridge: University of Cambridge Press, 1990), 49–53. An excellent, thorough exploration of the idea of self in Theravāda Buddhism can be found in Steven Collins, *Selfless Persons: Imagery and Thought in Theravāda Buddhism* (Cambridge: Cambridge University Press, 1982).

14. "This is peace, this is exquisite—the resolution of all fabrications, the relinquishment of all acquisitions, the ending of craving; dispassion; cessation; Nibbāna" (Anguttara Nikāya 3.32).

15. Anguttara Nikāya, 6.63 (PTS: A iii 410).

16. Kristin Scheible, "The Formulation and Significance of the Golden Rule in Buddhism I," in *The Golden Rule: The Ethics of Reciprocity in World Religions*, ed. Jacob Neusner and Bruce Chilton (London: Continuum, 2008), 117.

17. Bhikkhu Bodhi, "Giving Dignity to Life," Access to Insight (Legacy Edition), June 5, 2010, http://www.accesstoinsight.org/lib/authors/bodhi/bps-essay_38.html.

18. Śantipala Stephen Evans, "Buddhist Resignation and Human Rights," in Husted, Keown, and Prebish, eds., *Buddhism and Human Rights*, 144 (emphasis original).

19. Bernard Faure, "Afterthoughts," in *Buddhist Warfare*, ed. Michael Jerryson and Mark Juergensmeyer (New York: Oxford University Press, 2010), 212.

20. "Bodhi Sutta (Ud 1.3)," translated from the Pāli by Thanissaro Bhikkhu, Access to Insight (Legacy Edition), August 29, 2012, http://www.accesstoinsight.eu/en/tipitaka/sut/kn/ud/ud.1.03.than:

Imasmiṃ sati idaṃ hoti;
imass'uppādā idaṃ uppajjati;
imasmiṃ asati, idaṃ na hoti;
imassa nirodhā imaṃ nirujjhati.

This quintessential formulation of *pratītyasamutpāda* appears in many places throughout the canon, including Samyutta Nikāya 12.61 (PTS: S ii 94), Anguttara Nikāya 10.92 (PTS: A v 182), and Udāna 1.3 (PTS: Ud 3). Alternatively translated by Hammalawa Saddhatissa, *Buddhist Ethics* (Somerville, MA: Wisdom Publications, 1997), 18:

That being thus this comes to be;
From the coming to be of that, this arises;
That being absent, this does not happen;
From the cessation of that, this ceases.

21. Thích Nhất Hạnh, *Being Peace* (Berkeley, CA: Parallax Press, 1987, 2005), 65.

22. *Call Me by My True Names: The Collected Poems of Thich Nhat Hanh* (Berkeley, CA: Parallax Press, 2001), 72–73.

23. Evans, "Buddhist Resignation and Human Rights," 152 (emphasis original).

24. All Buddhist laity undertake the five precepts as an ethical orientation, and they are articulated regularly in devotional practices. They comprise intentions to abstain from killing, taking what is not given (stealing), sexual misconduct, false speech (lying and "idle chatter"), and intoxication. Canonically, Anguttara Nikāya 8.43 articulates the eight precepts to be followed by the virtuosi (both the ordained and the laity who undertake more rigorous practice). In this case, the first precept to not kill is expressed more generally as abstention from causing harm or taking life, human or nonhuman (*ahiṃsa*).

25. Damien Keown, *Buddhist Ethics: A Very Short Introduction* (New York: Oxford University Press, 2005), 12.

26. Keown, "Are There Human Rights in Buddhism?," 27–28 (original emphasis).

27. Kristin Scheible, "The Formulation and Significance of the Golden Rule in Buddhism I," in Neusner and Chilton, eds., *The Golden Rule*, 117.

28. John Ireland, *The Udāna: Inspired Utterances of the Buddha* (Kandy, Sri Lanka: Buddhist Publication Society, 1990), 68.

"Sabbā disā anuparigamma cetasā,
Nevajjhagā piyataramattanā kvaci.
Evaṁ piyo puthu attā paresaṁ,
Tasmā na hiṁse paramattakāmo" ti.

29. *The Udāna Commentary* (*Paramatthadīpanī nāma Udānaṭṭhakathā*), by Dhammapāla, trans. Peter Masefield (Oxford: The Pali Text Society, 1994–95), 731–32. In a footnote, the translator explains that the word in the passage for "kill," *haneyya*, is replaced in some manuscripts with the more general *hileyya*, "show hostility towards" (797n25).

30. Masao Abe, "Religious Tolerance and Human Rights: A Buddhist Perspective," in *Religious Liberty and Human Rights in Nations and in Religions*, ed. Leonard Swidler (Philadelphia: Ecumenical Press, 1986), 205.

31. *Dhammapada* X.129–32: Glenn Wallis, trans., *The Dhammapada: Verses on the Way* (New York: The Modern Library, 2004), 29.

32. His Holiness the XIV Dalai Lama of Tibet, "Human Rights and Universal Responsibility," in Husted, Keown, and Prebish, eds., *Buddhism and Human Rights*, xix.

33. The Theravāda tradition articulates ten perfections (Mahāyāna maintains six): *dāna* (generosity), *sila* (morality), *nekkhamma* (renunciation), *paññā* (wisdom), *viriya* (effort), *khanti* (patience), *sacca* (honesty), *aditthāna* (determination), *mettā* (loving-kindness), *upekkhā* (equanimity).

34. Bhikkhu Bodhi, "Giving Dignity to Life," Access to Insight (Legacy Edition), June 5, 2010, http://www.accesstoinsight.org/lib/authors/bodhi/bps-essay_38.html.

35. For more on the dubiousness of charter status of this text, see Kristin Scheible, *Reading the Mahāvaṃsa: The Literary Aims of a Theravāda Buddhist History* (New York: Columbia University Press, 2016).

36. The text classifies the Dāmila as occupiers of what is rightfully a Buddhist land. Dāmila is often translated as "Tamil," and this particular passage eulogizing the violent victory of Duṭṭhagāmaṇī is still used as justification for the continued violence in contemporary Sri Lanka.

37. The tradition, teachings, and institutions of Buddhism.

38. *Mahāvaṃsa* XXV.108–11.

39. *Mahāvaṃsa* XXV.109–11: *Saggamaggantarāyo ca nātthi te tena kammunā, diyaḍḍ hamanujā vettha ghātitā manujādhipa, saraṇesu ṭhito eko, pañcasīle pi cāparo, micchādiṭṭhī ca dussīlā sesā pasusamā matā. Jotayissasi ceva tvaṃ bahudhā buddhasāsanaṃ, manovilekhaṃ tasmā tvaṃ vinodaya narissara.*

40. Rock Edict XIII, in *The Edicts of Asoka*, ed. N. A. Nikam and Richard McKeon (Chicago: University of Chicago Press, 1959), 27. Aśokan edicts are inscribed on rock faces and pillars throughout his domain.

41. Rock Edict XIII, *The Edicts of Asoka*, 28.

42. Ibid., 28–29.

43. Peter Junger, "Why the Buddha Has No Rights," in Husted, Keown, and Prebish, eds., *Buddhism and Human Rights*, 61.

44. Evans, "Buddhist Resignation and Human Rights," 143.

45. Saddhatissa, *Buddhist Ethics*, 63.

46. *Mettā Sutta* (*Karaṇīyamettā Sutta*) found in the Sutta Nipata (Sn1.8) and Khuddakapātha (Khp 9); cited in Saddhatissa, *Buddhist Ethics*, 63.

47. Sallie King, "Buddhism and Human Rights," in *Religion and Human Rights: An Introduction* (New York: Oxford University Press, 2011), 113.

48. His Holiness the XIV Dalai Lama of Tibet, Nobel Peace Prize Acceptance Speech, University Aula, Oslo, December 10, 1989, http://www.dalailama.com/messages/acceptance-speeches/nobel-peace-prize.

49. I cannot help but playfully imagine that this would then lead to the need for affirmations and politically expedient documents such as the UDHR.

50. Keown, "Are There Human Rights in Buddhism?," 34.

three

CATHOLIC AND BUDDHIST PERSPECTIVES ON DIGNITY

A Response

Karen B. Enriquez

As I read the chapters on Buddhist and Catholic discussions on human dignity and the related discussions of what it means to be human, I was reminded of this phrase in the Philippines, "*madaling maging tao, mahirap magpakatao*" (translation: it is easy to be born human, but it is difficult to live "humanly" or to behave as a human being).[1] The saying reminds us of how we take for granted that we are all human beings, and yet what it means and how we live it out can be difficult and understood very differently. In these two chapters, the authors attempt to answer these questions as they pertain to the question of dignity, including giving definitions of dignity, the source or ground of it, and the obstacles to recognizing dignity in another. In the process, the authors flesh out broad sketches of Buddhist or Catholic theological anthropologies that argue for somewhat of a distinctive character of being human that grounds our dignity and hence the need to perceive, as Scheible writes, the "value and vulnerability of human life" (56). Yet, they do this in divergent ways. Scheible, on self-less dignity focusing on Buddhist traditions, looks at a nontheistic religion and reminds us of the challenge of discussions of human dignity, especially when there are different conceptions of what constitutes a human person. In the case of Buddhism, as Scheible describes, the doctrine of "no-self" (*anātman/anattā*) teaches that the human person is made up of the five aggregates (*skandhas/khandhas*) and that the "self" is an "amalgamation of physiological and psychological elements" (59). On the other hand, Weaver's discussion of the Catholic tradition is rooted in the notion of understanding persons and the dignity of persons as *imago Dei*, including both its substantialist and relational interpretations.

In this response, I will look at the points of intersection in these two discussions; despite seeming contrasts, there are some analogous descriptions of being human, including our innate yet also active (or cultivated) capacity to fulfill the good (or to reach enlightenment). Second, as a comparative theologian, I will also look at the ways that they are different and how a dialogue between the two can deepen their own discussions on the perception of dignity, the conditions necessary to live a life of dignity, and the role of religions in discussions on human dignity.

ON HUMAN DIGNITY AND HUMAN BE-ING

In both chapters, human dignity is tied to a sense of worth that is both innate (inherent) and yet also to be cultivated or to be realized (acquired). In Weaver's discussion of the Catholic tradition, she notes that the Catholic tradition tends to construe dignity as an innate attribute, that is, something we humans have because of the *imago Dei*. At the same time, it is also a capacity for free and purposeful action, "an ideal we may realize. Dignity names a potential we may actualize" (36). The ideal of what it means to be human is revealed through Jesus, who, as Weaver writes, "discloses the purpose of and possibilities for human life" (40). What is revealed by Jesus is that human life is meant to be lived in relationship with God and with each other. Moreover, Jesus does not only reveal this ideal but also empowers us to actualize these possibilities to the fullest. In this way, dignity is not simply static but also active, a command, as Weaver argues, "to dignify our own and others' lives through justice and love" (41). Jesus's own life and death serves as the example and moral criterion for living out our own lives of dignity. One sees how both the substantialist and relational interpretations of *imago Dei* are at work in Weaver's analysis. Substantialist interpretations of *imago Dei*—qualities or attributes that human beings have, such as freedom, reason, transcendence—are not simply possessed by human beings but also must be exercised and activated in pursuit of the good, which entails not simply one's personal well-being but the well-being of others. This then intersects with the relational interpretation of *imago Dei*, where human beings are called to be in relationship with God and with one another, which includes a commitment to ensuring that every person is able to live a life of dignity.

Analogously, in the Buddhist tradition, the teaching on "precious human birth" allows for a distinctive place human beings occupy among all sentient beings. As Scheible notes, this state is rare and special, and only in this state is enlightenment possible. Hence, one could say that only as a human being can one reach that more "dignified" state of an *arhat/arahant*, a *bodhisattva*, and/or a Buddha. And again, as Scheible describes, "the Buddha is the ultimate manifestation, then, of dignity . . . resulting in the most worthy being" (70). To reach enlightenment, one must cultivate the wisdom that understands the Buddhist teaching of "no-self" and its corollary, the teaching on dependent co-origination (*pratītyasamutpāda/paṭiccasamuppāda*), which implies and includes our interconnection with all other beings, which are then seen as not different from oneself. This becomes the motivation for compassion, and, combined with the teaching on the "precious human birth," compels us to act now so as not to waste this special opportunity as a human being.

However, supported by the arguments of Damien Keown, Scheible contends that the teaching on no-self and dependent co-origination is not enough. Rather, another aspect she discusses is the way dignity can be seen as both innate (inherent) and also something that must be cultivated (acquired); this discussion is reinforced by Keown:

> Human rights cannot be derived from any factual non-evaluative analysis of human nature, whether in terms of its psycho-physical constitution (the five "aggregates" which lack a self), its biological nature (needs, urges, drives), or the deep structure of interdependency (*paṭiccasamuppāda*). Instead, the most promising approach will be one which locates human rights and dignity within a comprehensive account of human goodness, and which sees basic rights and freedoms as integrally related to human flourishing and self-realization. This is because *the source of human dignity in Buddhism lies nowhere else than in the literally infinite capacity of human nature for participation in goodness.*[2]

This infinite capacity for goodness, as Keown notes, is found in the Buddhist teaching on Buddha-nature. As Scheible discusses in her chapter, in the Mahāyāna tradition, particularly in Yogācāra, there is the teaching on the *tathāgatagarbha* (embryo of Buddhahood) that states that this capacity for enlightenment is both innate and needs cultivation. It is a potential that needs to be actualized, or, to use Buddhist imagery, it is a seed that has the potential to become a tree or to bear fruit. In that sense, ordinary human beings are not that different from arhats or Buddhas since we all carry this seed, this innate potential in each of us. We all possess Buddha-nature. The only difference is that more advanced beings (arhats, bodhisattvas, and/or Buddhas) have cultivated this potential and serve as exemplars for ordinary beings of what all of us can become. In this way, they are more "dignified" or more worthy because they have cultivated this capacity for goodness, but all of us can be just as worthy if we follow their same path and cultivate that same potential already in each one of us. This path is laid out in various Buddhist teachings. From the earliest teachings, this is laid out in the Third and especially the Fourth Noble Truths (Eightfold Path), and, in the Mahāyāna traditions, this has been reformulated into the six perfections (*pāramitās*) of generosity, morality, patience, effort, concentration, and wisdom. Together, they revolve around the twin axes that Scheible mentions, quoting Keown: knowledge (*prajñā*) and moral concern (*karuṇā*), which are seen as the two wings on the bodhisattva path.

Looking at the Buddhist and Catholic discussions on dignity and what it means to be human, we can see a number of points of intersection between the two traditions. First, in both cases, there is a distinctive value or worth to being human that is tied to some innate capacity or potential to fulfill what is seen as the "good" in each of the traditions, whether it is communion with God or others (Catholic) or reaching enlightenment (Buddhist). In this case, dignity is then seen not simply as something one possesses but something that must be exercised or cultivated in order to live a dignified life. Hence, dignity is not simply static but also must be active, lived out, and experienced in one's life. For Buddhists, as Scheible points out, there is no need for a transcendent God as the ground or source of one's dignity, but simply the realization that the capacity for infinite good, the capacity for the twin axes of wisdom and compassion, already resides within oneself. Second, this dignity—both innate and active—is something to be realized not simply in oneself but also in others, because both traditions emphasize relationality or interconnection as part of what it means to be human. In the Buddhist tradition, this includes recognizing the other as oneself (which becomes the root of compassionate action), and, in the Catholic tradition, seeing the other as possessing the *imago Dei*. Hence, there is also the responsibility to work for the dignity of others and not simply of oneself. Finally, in both, there is also the need for exemplars who not only reveal or remind each of us of this capacity for and responsibility toward the good, but who also somehow empower and make us capable of doing it. In the Buddhist traditions, Scheible discusses the role of these exemplary human beings—arhats, bodhisattvas, and Buddhas. Weaver discusses the role of Jesus Christ, who is more than just an exemplar; as fully human and divine, he reveals both who God is and who we are as human beings.[3]

DEGREES OF DIGNITY

Scheible asks if some have "more" dignity than others (the case of the arhats), or if some have less or even no dignity at all (the case of the barbarians and the story of Duṭṭhagāmaṇī). In that story, it seems that because the majority of those killed were considered "barbarians" (of bad character and wrong views), this mitigated Duṭṭhagāmaṇī's karma (his actions and their consequences). This leads me back to Weaver's discussion about dignity and the perception of worth and how the "perceptual character of dignity makes dignity dangerous" (45). In her case, she looks at the doctrine of sin to show the depths of the distortion of our capacity to recognize the value and worth of each human person, and how such perception affects and directs our action toward the other: "Sin corrupts our capacities to perceive and respect the dignity of others, to discern how to translate dignity into concrete moral judgments, particular sorts of behaviors, and social policies" (46). In the case of Duṭṭhagāmaṇī, we see how labeling those killed as "barbarians" made it easier to justify their killing.

Weaver's discussion of the role of perception could also be complemented by dialogue with Buddhism and its analysis of the human condition in terms of ignorance, or mis-knowing (*avidyā*), understood as the root cause of suffering (Second Noble Truth). This ignorance about the true nature of existence leads to our misperception about self and other, particularly the way we label others (ranging from most "valuable" or "worthy" to least) as "friends," "strangers," or "enemies." These projections then guide and even justify our behavior and actions toward these various groups. What exacerbates these judgments is when society feeds into these misperceptions of the worth that one may have—what has been named "structural or social sin" in the Catholic tradition—which affects our personal decisions and actions. John Makransky describes this tendency in the Buddhist tradition in terms of karma:

> It is extremely hard to break out of the communal maps that project the appearance of a world of intrinsic "friends," "enemies," and "strangers," the maps that organize communal violence here and abroad, precisely because

> such maps are a social construction viewed as real by social consensus. This is an important meaning of the Buddhist term *karma* for our time. *Karma* in classical Buddhist theory refers to the habitual patterns of thought, intention, and reaction through which individuals experience and react to their world. Largely missing in classical Buddhist treatments of this topic is the way that patterns of thought and reaction (*karma*) comprise not just individually conditioned but also socially conditioned and reinforced phenomena. . . . When everyone around me believes that only certain people deserve to be loved while certain other people deserve just to be hated and feared, I become accustomed to seeing and reacting to them in that way and as I treat them that way; I receive the feedback that reinforces the impression, react accordingly, and thereby condition others around me to the same deluded view. Such social patterning of interpretation and reaction (*karma*) is largely subconscious, hard even to notice, and hence hard to change.[4]

From this analysis, there could be a rich and fruitful discussion about Buddhist teachings on karma and ignorance and the Catholic teaching on sin, not simply in terms of free will, but, as Weaver argues, as misrecognition or misperception that distorts our capacity to choose or even recognize that which is good or dignified in another, and how deeply entrenched this tendency is as part of our human condition. This shows the need for practices that not only reveal the depth of this distortion but also move toward recalibrating our perception. At the very least, in the case of Duṭṭhagāmaṇī, one could begin to analyze the label of "barbarian"—to whom has it been given, who has given it, what function does it serve to do so—in order to begin to break free of one's ignorance or misperception that leads to our conceptualization of others and their worth, which then justifies our actions or inaction toward the other. By labeling the other as "barbarian," we perceive them as not having worth. We have deprived them of their dignity.

In the case above, we have analyzed the intersection of our personal capacity to see or recognize dignity in another with social conditions and conditioning that may prevent us from doing so. But there is also another angle to exploring the dignity of the "barbarian": the intersection between the other's personal capacity to see and choose the good and the social conditions that may prevent them from accomplishing that. Weaver talks about this in terms of the conditions necessary in order to live a life of dignity, as part of the ground for the work of justice and solidarity with others, especially those most vulnerable.

In the case of Buddhism, one could argue that if the source of dignity is the capacity for reaching enlightenment or participating in the good, then one must also begin to examine the conditions necessary in order to fulfill this capacity and also look at the obstacles. Through dialogue with the Catholic tradition, this reflection on the interconnection between the personal and social dimensions of reality can strengthen the Buddhist analysis that personal enlightenment (a more dignified state) cannot be achieved without certain social conditions met. The conditions of one's life or living may not be optimal, or one's personal situation may serve as an obstacle to cultivating one's capacity to pursue the good. Compassion then takes the form of helping the other restore the conditions necessary in order to live that life of dignity. In another article, I argued for reinterpreting the "barbarian" in the Buddhist tradition using this social analysis:

> The Buddhist traditions hold eight forms of ease/freedom and ten forms of wealth that are prerequisites for entering the path of Enlightenment. This includes being born human (and not born in the other realms) and being born in a time and place where there is access to Buddhist teachers and practices. However, with the contemporary understanding of the social dimension of the person, could these forms of freedoms and wealth be re-interpreted as the foundation for fighting for more favorable conditions in society in order for spiritual practice and awakening to become possible? For example, one of the eight freedoms includes the freedom to not be born "among barbarians who are ignorant of the teachings and practices of the Buddhadharma." "Barbarians" were traditionally understood as non-Buddhists who had no interest in the Dharma and practiced such things as killing animals or people. One possible re-interpretation of this would then be being subjected today to barbaric conditions and those that perpetrate them that lead to the suffering and death of the poor, that obscure the teachings and practices of the Buddhadharma for both the perpetrator and their victims. How could one even think about practice under such conditions? How does one resist that kind of culture and not be shaped by it?[5]

Through this analysis, one brings together the discussion of dignity as a capacity for fulfilling human potential (in whatever way that is understood) and our responsibility toward the other in helping them to live lives of dignity. Once again, one breaks open the label "barbarian," but this time in terms of a social analysis that looks at what has led to that person living life in "barbaric" conditions or what has caused that person to be seen as a "barbarian" in some way, and hence perceived as having less or no dignity at all. From such analysis then comes the responsibility and commitment to that other in terms of reestablishing the conditions necessary so that they are once again able to live lives of dignity, able to cultivate their potential in order to live life as fully and humanly as possible.

PERCEIVING PERSONS AND THEIR DIGNITY

Weaver argues that reflections on the perceptual character of dignity lead to the exhortation to make a value commitment that attributes dignity to all human beings qua human. At the same time, her own discussions on sin show the difficulty of making such a commitment or assertion. Hence the call to conversion, which cannot simply be intellectual or moral but must also include the spiritual—not merely a change of mind but also of hands and heart. This is another area where Buddhist–Catholic dialogue can be fruitful—an exchange over the spiritual practices needed in order to lead to the kind of conversion that Weaver describes: one that leads us to see the depth of our misperception so that one is able to see clearly the "equal worth of all human beings" and in so doing, lay the foundation for solidarity and action that lead us, as she writes, to "dignify our own and others' lives" (50).

Scheible introduces us to many different Buddhist practices that are meant precisely as an antidote to our misperception of the other by looking more deeply and seeing how others are intimately related and similar to oneself. For example, she offers a description of a meditation on the four divine abodes where the practitioner is instructed to generate loving-kindness, compassion, and such in ever-widening circles: from self to loved ones, to strangers, to enemies, and finally to all beings. She mentions that the practice of loving-kindness (*maitrī/mettā*) is meant to overcome conflict. However, as Sharon Salzberg, a noted Vipassana teacher, explains, it is also a "sneaky wisdom practice": "In the moment of letting go—without any intended development of wisdom—you find wisdom. Ultimately, of course, the most powerful insight that comes from metta practice is the sense of nonseparateness, and that insight comes through opening one's heart, from being inclusive rather than exclusive."[6] Hence, beyond overcoming conflict, loving-kindness practice and meditation on the other abodes are ultimately meant to cultivate the wisdom of "no-self" and dependent co-origination, including the sense of interconnection with all other beings. This helps against the tendency to label others and to think that some are more "worthy" or deserving of love and compassion. In this practice, one cultivates the ability to see all beings as worthy of love instead of our usual judgment of some as more or less worthy.

Moreover, Scheible also examines the poem "Call Me by My True Names" by Thích Nhất Hạnh, which is another way to begin to realize our radical interconnectedness and our responsibility toward each other. Once again, in this poem, there is the challenge of breaking our usual perceptions and the boundaries we set with others. In this case, the challenge is to allow oneself not simply to feel empathy and solidarity with those whom we might identify as "victims" or "sufferers" (and hence we might judge as more "worthy"), but also to learn to identify with perpetrators, or those who cause suffering, and to feel empathy and compassion for them. In this way, one is challenged to cultivate loving-kindness and compassion not simply for loved ones but even for one's enemies so one can begin to see that everyone has equal value; everyone is deserving of love and compassion.

Finally, there are other practices that focus on meditating on the sameness of self and other, which becomes the basis for the practice of exchanging self and other that Scheible mentions. One key text favored especially among Tibetan Buddhist practitioners is from Shantideva's *The Way of the Bodhisattva*, which states:

> Strive at first to meditate
> Upon the sameness of yourself and others.
> In joy and sorrow all are equal.
> Thus be guardian of all, as of yourself.
>
> The hand and other limbs are many and distinct,
> But all are one—one body to be kept and guarded.
> Likewise, different beings in their joys and sorrows,
> Are, like me, all one in wanting happiness.[7]

Meditating in this way, Khenchen Kunzang Palden in his commentary on these verses explains that one begins to realize the nondualism of self and other, to see "I" and "other" as totally unreal and illusory, and "it is no longer possible to make a separation between 'I' and 'other,' and there arises an attitude of wanting to protect others as oneself, to protect all that belongs to them with the same care as if it were one's own."[8] Such insights into wisdom and compassion, as demonstrated by Shantideva, can only happen within meditation.

In looking at these various Buddhist meditation practices that aim to correct ignorance and our misperception of self and other, I begin to think about analogous Catholic spiritual practices that could help support the realization of how deeply entrenched human beings are in sin and badly in need of grace, as Weaver argues. In looking at the passage above by Shantideva, I think about various ways one can meditate on the body of Christ as communion with each other that can become the foundation for our work in dignifying our lives and those of others. What practices help to deepen one's understanding of this image? How does one pray with this image in ways that lead to intellectual, moral, and spiritual conversion? Moreover, what kind of prayer did Thomas Merton do that led him to see the dignity of all human persons as *imago Dei*? In his moving passage about his experience of communion with all humanity, Merton writes:

> Thank God, thank God that I *am* like other men, that I am only a man among others. . . . It is a glorious destiny to be a member of the human race, though it is a race dedicated to many absurdities and one which makes many terrible mistakes: yet, with all that, God Himself gloried in becoming a member of the human race. . . . I have the immense joy of being *man*, a member of a race in which God Himself became incarnate. As if the sorrows and stupidities of the human condition could overwhelm me, now I realize what we all are. . . . There is no way of telling people that they are walking around shining like the sun.[9]

This passage gives us an insight into the movement in prayer that allows for the transformation of the self, which, in turn, leads to solidarity with others and a recognition of their equal dignity. As others have pointed out, these Christian spiritual practices could be complemented by Buddhist meditation practices that (1) examine the labels of "friends" and enemies," (2) extend loving-kindness and compassion to the enemy, (3) perceive ourselves through the eyes of the "enemy" (such as the equalizing and exchanging of self and other), and (4) help us to see ourselves and reality from that perspective and learn from those others. In this way, we can continue to turn our "enemies" into "friends," and Buddhist meditation practices can help us unpack even more how our "enemies" could be "friends." Could we practice the same kind of honesty in the way we view the "enemy" and see them too as having the capacity to function as sacraments of transcendence? In this way, we continually break that habit of assigning dignity based on our perception of the worth of another, and we are constantly reminded to cultivate the perception of the equal worth of all beings and to work toward the fulfillment of such a vision.

In this exploration of Buddhist and Christian spiritual practices, we begin to see how the attribution of dignity to all is not simply an intellectual or moral act, but also that it must be supported by spiritual practices. It is work that entails a critical analysis of the individual and social dimension of persons and communities, but also the hard work of constantly questioning our perceptions and judgments. It is the work of humility and patience, a work of the heart that keeps the conclusions of our intellect tentative and open to being changed and corrected.

FINAL REFLECTIONS

In the end, after the comparison of Catholic and Buddhist traditions, we see the complexity in trying to understand what it means to be human and in how we understand human dignity, including its source and the responsibilities it places on us. At the very least, from these two chapters, we understand how, on a personal level, dignity is something that we have and yet also something that we are called to actualize and exercise. Moreover, on a social or institutional level, we are reminded of forms of oppression and our responsibility to respond in a way that dignifies our lives and the lives of others. And in both traditions, though there is no consensus as to the ground or source of dignity, or even a common understanding of what constitutes a human person, there is still a normative claim to the distinctiveness of human persons and hence to their innate human dignity, which becomes the foundation for active compassion and the work for justice. In both, part of the claim is that there is something more to being human than mere instrumental value, that there is worth beyond what is based on one's own perception/estimation. This is part of the basis of the claim for the dignity of every person. And so, is this part of the role of religions in these discussion, that human beings are more than what we might think or perceive? David Loy muses, for example, whether religions "remain our best hope for challenging the commodification of the world."[10] In the discussions on Buddhist and Catholic spiritual practices, it became clearer for me that maybe part of what these religions provide are not only normative claims or final answers but also the cultivation of an attitude that resists the perception of seeing human beings as just one more thing amidst all the other things of the world. Rather, they also cultivate an attitude of unknowing that seeks to question our certainties and judgment.

NOTES

1. I indicate this difference by using the term "be-ing" (activity of behaving or becoming more human—a more active state) versus "being" (the state of being born human—more static state).

2. Damien Keown, "Are There Human Rights in Buddhism?," in *Buddhism and Human Rights*, ed. Wayne R. Husted, Damien V. Keown, and Charles S. Prebish (Surrey: Curzon, 1998), 29–30 (my emphasis).

3. Though the status of Jesus Christ in the Christian traditions is not the same as the status of bodhisattvas and Buddhas in the Buddhist traditions, there have been many comparisons made of Jesus and bodhisattvas. For example, the Dalai Lama has talked about Jesus as a bodhisattva and has written a book that reflects on Jesus's teachings from a Buddhist perspective. See Dalai Lama, *A Good Heart: A Buddhist Perspective on the Teachings of Jesus*, trans. Geshe Thupten Jinpa (Somerville, MA: Wisdom Publications, 1998). See also Hee-Sung Keel, "Jesus the Bodhisattva: Christology from a Buddhist Perspective," *Buddhist-Christian Studies* 16 (1996): 169–85.

4. John Makransky, "No Real Protection without Authentic Love and Compassion," *Journal of Buddhist Ethics* 12 (2005): 32–33.

5. Karen B. Enriquez, "Expanding the Cultivation and Practice of Love and Compassion in Our Suffering World: Continuing the Dialogue between Liberation Theologians and Engaged Buddhists," *Buddhist-Christian Studies* 36 (2016): 84.

6. Sharon Salzberg, "Metta Practice," in *Radiant Mind: Essential Buddhist Teachings and Texts*, ed. Jean Smith (New York: Riverhead Books, 1999), 174.

7. Shantideva, *The Way of the Bodhisattva: A Translation of the Bodhicaryāvatāra*, trans. Padmakara Translation Group (Boston: Shambhala, 2003), 8.90–91.

8. Ibid., 181.

9. Thomas Merton, *Conjectures of a Guilty Bystander* (Garden City, NY: Doubleday, Image Books, 1968), 157–58 (original emphasis); quoted in Henri Nouwen, *Reaching Out: The Three Movements of the Spiritual Life* (Garden City, NY: Image Books, 1986) 42–43.

10. David Loy, *The Great Awakening: A Buddhist Social Theory* (Boston: Wisdom Publications, 2003), 71. I would also ask how these discussions on human dignity and human be-ing are tied to reflections on our interconnection with the world and how they can address ecological issues tied to the commodification that has led to ecological destruction.

four

DIGNITY

A Jewish Perspective

Elliot N. Dorff and Daniel Nevins

As the biblical and rabbinic sources cited in this chapter will indicate, "dignity" in the Jewish tradition refers to the inherent worth that each person has as someone created in the image of God. People have this status regardless of gender, race, age, level of abilities or disabilities, or even the morality of their actions and their treatment of others, because God has implanted this worth in them. The Jewish tradition certainly distinguishes among groups of people (Jews and non-Jews, men and women, children and adults, young and old), has many rules and models to distinguish good from bad behavior, and presents ideal ways to interact with others in opposition to those that are less so or even wrong and prohibited. But in the end, even those who commit capital crimes must be punished for them in a way that preserves their inherent value as a creature and reflection of God.

Furthermore, the stamp of God in each one of us means that we must treat everyone else with respect. This does not mean that we must like everyone else or approve of their deeds, but it does mean that we may not slander them or denigrate them. So, for example, the Torah (the Five Books of Moses, the primary source of authority in the Jewish tradition—the Jewish Constitution, as it were) not only allows but demands that we give constructive criticism when it is warranted "so that you do not hate someone in your heart"; it prohibits taking revenge or bearing a grudge against another; and it demands that you must "love your neighbor as yourself" (Lev. 19:17–18). Judaism certainly makes moral distinctions among acts and modes of character, and it gives us guidance as to how to put those distinctions into practice. But even the most vile of people, even though warranting punishment for their evil acts, must be recognized as having inherent dignity in the process of doing so.

Within the classical halakhic literature, human dignity is proclaimed to be a "great" value capable of overriding competing normative claims.[1] Dignity concerns generate obligations and also exemptions. Humiliating another person is considered akin to murdering them, if not in body then in social standing, and financial penalties are imposed for offenses to the dignity of another person. In truth, it has been many centuries since rabbinic courts imposed financial penalties for such infractions, but this reflects the changed historical circumstances of rabbinic authority, not any shift in the values taught by Judaism.

As we explore the concept of dignity in the Jewish tradition, readers should be aware of the methodology we are using. As Conservative rabbis, we believe in both the authoritative nature of the tradition for our lives and in the need to understand the tradition in its historical context. We also believe that Jews now must apply the tradition to our own lives using the best of current knowledge available to us, including what the relevant sciences tell us. Therefore, we will cite generously from the classical Jewish tradition as it developed from the Torah to modern times, and we will also invoke what we know from modern sciences in applying that tradition to our lives today.

DIGNITY IN THE TORAH

In its very first chapter, the Torah declares that God created each person in the divine image: "And God created humankind in the divine image, creating it in the image of God, creating them male and female."[2]

Exactly which feature of the human being reflects this divine image is a matter of debate within the Jewish tradition.[3] The Torah itself seems to tie it to humanity's ability to make moral judgments—that is, to distinguish good from bad and right from wrong, to behave accordingly, and to judge one's own actions and those of others on the basis of this moral knowledge.[4] Another human faculty connected to divinity by the Torah and by the later tradition is the ability to speak.[5] Maimonides, a twelfth-century rabbi, physician, and philosopher, claims that the divine image resides in our capacity to think, especially discursively.[6] Locating the divine image within us may also be the Torah's way of acknowledging that we can love, just as God does,[7] or that we are at least partially spiritual and thus share God's spiritual nature.[8]

This doctrine *describes* aspects of our nature, but it also *prescribes* behavior founded on moral imperatives. Specifically, because human beings are created in God's image, we affront God when we insult another person.[9] The Torah even presumes that people convicted of a capital crime have dignity. Thus, it says that when such a person is hanged, his or her body must be removed before nightfall, because a hanging body "is a curse of God."[10] The Rabbis expand this idea in the following story that makes God and human beings so close in identity that they are like twins:

> Rabbi Meir gave a parable: To what is this similar? To two twin brothers who were in a given city. One they [the people of the city] appointed king, and the other became a thief. The king commanded that the thief be hanged, but everyone who saw him said that the king had been hanged. So, the king commanded that he be taken down [from the gallows].[11]

The biblical verse and this story based on it also establish that for the Torah and the Rabbis human dignity is not acquired and cannot be removed by any bad things that a person does; it is, rather, a feature of human beings implanted by God and integral to their nature.

The relationship of human dignity to God is illustrated by another of the Torah's verses. According to Genesis 9:5–6, someone who takes a life, someone else's or one's own, has not only violated the law but has also diminished the image of God in the world. Thus, regardless of age, sex, skin color, religion, mental or physical abilities, and even one's own deeds, each of us is infused with the image of God and therefore has an indestructible source of dignity within him or her.

CLASSICAL RABBINIC LITERATURE

Judaism, however, is not the religion of the Bible alone; the Bible, especially the Torah within it, is the basis of Judaism, but Judaism is defined by how the Rabbis interpreted and applied the Bible, first in the classical rabbinic period of approximately 200 BCE to 600 CE, and then subsequently through rabbinic interpretations and applications of the tradition and through Jewish practice to our own times. In this way, Judaism is like Christianity, which is based on the Bible but shaped by how the Church Fathers and then subsequent authorities interpreted and applied it over the centuries, and by Christians living according to what they understood the Bible and subsequent Christian traditions and customs to demand of them. In the same way, U.S. law is based on the U.S. Constitution but is not limited to it, consisting instead of the laws Congress has created ever since, how the Supreme Court has interpreted those laws and the Constitution itself, and how the American people have acted in practice. In short, Judaism, like Christianity and U.S. law, is a *tradition based on founding texts*, and so one must know not only the founding texts but also the traditions based on them and the practice of the people trying to live by them in order to know what the tradition actually stands for.

The most important classical rabbinic works, whose authors are usually referred to as "the Rabbis" with a capital *R*, are the Mishnah, edited circa 200 CE; the Babylonian Talmud, edited in the sixth century CE; and the Midrash, originating in the same classical period but recorded in books edited over a long period of time, from the fifth to the twelfth century CE.[12] It is to classical rabbinic works and later rabbinic interpretations, and to the actual practices and customs of Jews throughout the ages, that we must then turn to see how Judaism has understood human dignity and its implications for Jewish practice.

Let us begin with some early rabbinic statements:

> Rabbi Eliezer says, "Let your neighbor's dignity be precious to you as your own."[13]

> Rabbi Akiva says, "Beloved is humanity, created in the divine image; even more beloved are human beings by virtue of the fact that they were informed that they were created in the divine image, as the Torah says, 'In the divine image God created them' (Genesis 1:27)."[14]

Human dignity may not be the ultimate value in Judaism (divine dignity has priority), but it is cited frequently in the Talmud as a principle with normative consequences.[15]

For the Rabbis, as for the Bible, each individual has uniqueness and divine worth because all human beings embody the image of God, as the Mishnah says:

> For this reason Adam was created as a single person, to teach you that anyone who destroys one soul is described in Scripture as if he destroyed an entire world, and anyone who sustains one soul is described in Scripture as if he sustained an entire world. . . . And to declare the greatness of the Holy One, praised be He, for a person uses a mold to cast a number of coins, and they

> are all similar to each other, while the Sovereign of all sovereigns, the Holy Blessed One, cast each person in the mold of the first human being and yet none of them is similar to any other. Therefore, each person must say: "For me the world was created."[16]

One practical application of this principle was how the Rabbis determined that we should react to seeing a disabled person. Instead of recoiling from such a person or thanking God for not being similarly disabled, the Rabbis required that we recite this blessing: "Praised are you, Lord our God, *meshaneh ha-briyyot*, who makes different creatures," or "who created us different [from one another]." Judaism thus bids us to embrace the divine image in such people—indeed, to bless God for creating some of us so.[17]

Moreover, the Bible creates a culture of inclusion in which people with frailty or physical disabilities deserve protection, and its heroes often face physical challenges, such as speech impediments (Moses), blindness (Isaac), barrenness (Sarah, Rebecca, Rachel, and Hannah), and small stature (David). In 1 Samuel 16:7, God chides the prophet not to identify leadership potential based on what the eyes perceive, but on the heart. Psalm 118:22 proclaims, "The stone once despised by the builders has become the keystone," and this verse is interpreted as David's vindication. The Rabbis emphasize this point by declaring, "Do not look at the container, but at what it contains."[18]

To see that this Jewish position is not obvious, contrast it with the typical American way of thinking, which is thoroughly pragmatic: a person's value is a function of what that person can *do* for others. One's "net worth" is how much money he or she has accumulated, presumably—but not always—on the basis of having created a good or service that people want or need. It is this view, so deeply ingrained in American culture, that prompts Americans to value those who have unusual abilities and assets, who *succeed*—and, conversely, to devalue those who are poor or disabled in some way, even to question whether someone with severe disabilities should continue to live. In recent years, people have been encouraged to view themselves as a "brand" and to measure their personal influence by the number of people who follow their messages on social media and "like" their posts. This dynamic reinforces self-promotion and undermines virtues, such as humility, that have traditionally been associated with human dignity in Jewish culture. Such utilitarian criteria for judging the value of a given person's life are often embedded in "quality of life" discussions in the United States, not only when others are making the judgment but even when a sick or disabled person is doing so. Only since the enactment in 1990 of the Americans with Disabilities Act have Americans passed laws to help disabled people to function as well as they can, and one suspects that the motivation for that legislation was not only considerations of dignity but also a pragmatic concern for assisting disabled people to do what they can to help society function more smoothly and to improve collective productivity.

The Rabbis went so far as to say that human dignity can supersede the authority that the Torah gives to the Rabbis, when it says that we must follow the instructions of the judges in our generation and act according to how they interpret the Torah and that we not stray from their rulings (Deut. 17:11). The primary text for this topic is in the Talmudic tractate *Berakhot* 19b, where we learn that a Sage must strip off a garment in public should it be found to contain a mixture of woolen and linen threads forbidden by the Torah (Lev. 19:19). Since appearing unclothed in public (even if not fully naked) is considered a great disgrace, this ruling teaches us that human dignity is secondary to divine dignity. In this context, human dignity is associated with appearing clothed appropriately in public. Divine dignity is associated with the respect accorded by the covenanted people to a biblical command, which was issued by God. Were the Sage publicly to ignore the biblical prohibition of wearing wool and linen together, his brazen act would give priority to his own human dignity over divine dignity.[19] For this reason, he must strip off the garment, even in public.

Yet the Talmud continues to describe cases where human dignity does, in fact, override rabbinic and even biblical imperatives. In each case, the Talmud seeks to contextualize and limit the supersession of individual dignity over the established law, but the cumulative effect remains significant. For example, in order to comfort a mourner, a *kohen* (a descendant of Aaron, Moses's brother), whose family officiated in the ancient Temple, may accompany the mourner, even through a field that may have human remains buried within it, which would taint the ritual purity of the *kohen*. The Talmud limits this leniency to a field of doubtful status. In other words, the *kohen* may not ignore the Torah's command that he avoid the ritual impurity caused by proximity to the dead (Lev. 21:1) in order to accompany and thus give dignity to a mourner, but he may ignore the Rabbis' expansion of that ruling to a field that may or may not be a cemetery.

The next case seems even bolder. Rabbi Elazar bar Zadok, who was a *kohen*, recalls, "We used to go skipping across graves to greet the kings of Israel." This would appear to place the dignity of the human king higher than that of God, represented by the biblical verse just mentioned (Lev. 21:1) that prohibits descendants of Aaron from coming into contact with the ritual impurity of the dead. Once again, the Talmud limits the effect of this anecdote, stating that most graves are designed in a way that minimizes the transmission of impurity.[20] Moreover, the Rabbis gave great deference to the king, who represented the entire nation and for whom any shaming would amount to disgracing the whole nation.

Grammatically, Rabbi Elazar bar Zadok's use of the past continuous form of the verb, "We used to . . . ," indicates that this supersession of the law based on the demands of human dignity was "a continuous or repeated action."[21] This Talmudic example, together with more recent Jewish legal applications of the principle of human dignity that we will discuss below, refutes the claims of some that it functions only as an emergency measure and never as a permanent policy.

> Returning to the Talmud's discussion, our general principle is now stated dramatically:
>
> Come and learn: So great is human dignity that it supersedes a negative commandment of the Torah. And why? Do we not say, "There is no wisdom, nor comprehension nor counsel against the Lord" (Proverbs 21:30)? Rav bar Sheba interpreted it thus before Rav Kahana: "[This principle applies only] to the negative commandment of 'Do not stray'" (Deut. 17:11). They [i.e., his colleagues] laughed at him, saying, "'Do not stray' is itself from the Torah!" But Rav Kahana said to them, "When a great man states a matter, do not laugh at it. For all of the words of the Sages are supported by the negative commandment of 'Do not stray,' but for his [any person's] dignity, the Rabbis permitted him [to ignore their ruling]."

In this context, human dignity is associated with the practice of going out to greet the king, who is the most dignified of people. Divine dignity is associated once again with a biblical command, this time the ban on priests coming into contact with the dead. However, the text here creates a middle position—an attenuated form of contact that is not forbidden by biblical authority, but only by rabbinic decree. It therefore serves as a test case for the power of rabbinic authority—is it so great that it requires universal obedience, even at the cost of humiliating the people? This passage establishes that the Sages waived their own dignity (i.e., the power of their precedents), but not the dignity of the Torah, in deference to the dignity of other people. Even though the Sages traced their own authority to Deuteronomy 17:11, they still distinguished between the stature of their rulings, which they themselves said should be superseded, if necessary, in order to preserve someone's dignity, and the laws of the Torah itself, which cannot be superseded even by this fundamental concern of preserving human dignity.

In the hierarchy of Jewish legal values, God's dignity is highest, but human dignity is not far below, as Psalm 8:6 famously declares: "You have made him little less than divine, and adorned him with glory and majesty."[22] Although the Rabbis felt responsible for extending many biblical commands with an extra "fence around the Torah," they understood that the social cost for compliance with these stringencies could become too high. Rather than humiliate the people and thus tempt them to ignore rabbinic authority altogether, they raised up the value of human dignity. In their humble sensitivity to the status of other people, the Rabbis made an important theological point that, as Rabbi Akiva said in what was quoted above, "Beloved is humanity, made in the divine image."

Indeed, the final passage of this Talmudic discussion in *Berakhot* 19b gives an example in which the clear biblical command (Deut. 21:1) to return a lost object (in this case, a stray animal) is waived for an elderly person who found the animal, for in that case, in the Rabbis' judgment, the dignity of the finder would be compromised because of his or her age with respect to the obligation to lead the animal back to its owner. Here the maxim that human dignity supersedes the Torah's commandments applies not only to a rabbinic injunction but even to a biblical command, albeit through the passive mechanism of "Sit and do not act."

This, though, is an exception to the rule, for in other Talmudic contexts, this principle of human dignity superseding a Jewish law is restricted to rabbinic injunctions. For example, in *Shabbat* 81a–b, permission is granted to carry smooth stones up to a roof on the Sabbath to be used for hygienic purposes. Here a form of carrying prohibited on the Sabbath by the Rabbis, but not by the Torah, is permitted in deference to human dignity. A similar case is brought at *Eiruvin* 41b. Likewise in *Shabbat* 94b, Rav Naḥman allowed the removal of a dead body from a house to a semipublic area on the Sabbath despite the rabbinic prohibition of carrying the body from one's private domain to such a semipublic area, out of deference to human dignity.

Another application of our principle comes from *Megillah* 3b. The Rabbis ask which mitzvah takes precedence, reading the book of Esther on the holiday of Purim at its prescribed time, or attending to the burial of an abandoned body? The abandoned body has priority, they say, for "so great is human dignity that it supersedes a negative commandment of the Torah"—in this case, the commandment not to delay the reading of the book of Esther from its proper time.

Moreover, in Talmud *Hagigah* 16b, a story is related in the name of Abba Eliezer of a departure from the policy preventing women from laying hands on the sacrifice in order "to make them feel pleased." This passage does not cite human dignity, but it is an example of rabbinic consideration for the feelings of an excluded population to participate more fully in the public rituals of Judaism.[23]

From this brief survey of the citation of human dignity in Talmudic texts,[24] we learn that this principle is not merely a *soft* value—one that is praised but not incorporated in legal rulings governing behavior—but is also used in *hard* legal applications to override even biblical requirements, such as the law requiring all Israelites to return lost objects. In addition, forms of carrying prohibited by the Rabbis on the Sabbath can be waived for the sake of human dignity.

Even so, there remains a significant restraint on the application of this principle. In the Talmud and the later medieval codes of Jewish law, it applies only to rabbinic prohibitions, despite some Talmudic precedents that release individuals from biblically based monetary obligations (such as returning lost property) in order to preserve human dignity.[25] Even assuming that human dignity can supersede only rabbinic rulings, however, these texts indicate that when the Rabbis of the Mishnah and Talmud claimed to value human dignity, they truly meant it, and they translated this value into normative practice.[26]

The opposite of dignity, disgrace (*boshet*), is a major offense in Jewish law.[27] Of course, there is always a subjective element to the measure of both dignity and disgrace. Some situations are considered to be inherently undignified. Being stripped naked, hit or spat upon, or forced to stand while others sit—these are all conditions that would humiliate any person. The Talmudic sources, though, are sensitive to the different circumstances of people based on age, gender, social class, scholarship, and other factors. Paradoxically, a person of average means might be less wont to suffer humiliation than would be either a much richer or a much poorer person. Likewise, the Sages were sensitive to variations in status in their knowledge economy—the great sage and the illiterate farmer were considered outliers whose sensitivities required attention.

Fear of shaming illiterate individuals led to exempting them from reciting the biblically required firstfruits declaration required in Deuteronomy 26:5–10, allowing the *kohen* to read it on their behalf. The same concern led to the modification of many funeral customs.[28] It also led to the separation of the honor of being called to the Torah during worship from the obligation to chant the actual text; knowing how to recite the blessings before and after the reading, which are much easier to learn and are the same every time the Torah is read, was deemed enough to justify calling people up to the Torah during its reading in public worship so that people who did not know how to read the Torah could nevertheless be publicly honored.

This last example illustrates that shame is also a relative phenomenon. If all people have a benefit and one person or a group of people (in this case, those who cannot read the Torah) does not, he or she is shamed.

Furthermore, the Talmud recognizes that shame could be measured by any of three different criteria: (1) only if the person feels the shame—and so sleeping people, for example, could not collect monetary damages for shame because they did not feel it, at least at the time that the shaming occurred; (2) if the family feels it, so that even if the disgraced person does not feel shame, his or her family could collect monetary damages from those who insulted the member of the family; and (3) if the community considers the person to have been shamed, even if he or she does not feel it.[29]

In Jewish life, these Talmudic distinctions are not intended only for theoretical acuity; they are rather intended to be applied to life as we live it. One example of that, using the three modes of measuring shame just described, is this: One of the authors of this essay, Elliot Dorff, used this Talmudic discussion to guide the Ethics Committee of the Los Angeles Jewish Homes for the Aged. A gerontologist at UCLA Medical Center presented some research showing that residents of nursing homes who are mentally competent and who are assured that whatever they say will not be reported to the staff of the nursing home, so that they need not fear revenge by the staff for negative reports about them, routinely say that they are happy with their care. An objective analysis of how often the residents are taken for a walk so as to avoid bedsores and how often their diapers are changed, however, revealed that in many nursing homes (*not* the Los Angeles Jewish Homes for the Aged) that level of minimally decent care happened only seldom, way below when those services needed to be done to preserve the residents' dignity. This, then, called into question the American value of individual autonomy, for the residents were happy with the care they were receiving even though it was objectively inadequate and sullied their dignity. Using the second and, especially, the third of the Talmud's understandings of when shame takes place, however, clearly established that shame had indeed taken place, for even though the residents had not felt it, their families and the community as a whole recognized it as such. So human dignity, as the Talmud perceptively recognizes, is a familial and communal matter and not just a function of what the victim of insulting behavior feels.

Returning to the Rabbis, another facet of dignity they recognized was related to the value of work and how not being able to work diminishes dignity. Thus they say, "Great is work, for it honors the workmen."[30] It must be so, they reasoned, in part because it is God's intention for us to work, as indicated both by the fact that Adam, even in the garden of Eden, had to till and keep the earth in order to eat, and also that God specifically commands, "Six days shall you work, and on the seventh shall you desist [from work]."[31] In expanding the rabbinic dictum "Love work,"[32] the Rabbis say this:

> Even Adam did not taste food until he had done work; as it is said, "The Lord God took the man and put him into the Garden of Eden to till it and keep it" (Genesis 2:15), after which He said, "Of every tree of the garden you may eat" (Genesis 2:16). Even the Holy Blessed One did not cause his Presence to dwell among the People Israel until they had done work; as it is said, "Let them make for Me a sanctuary that I may dwell among them" (Exodus 25:8). If one is unemployed, what should he do? If he has a courtyard or a field in a state of decay, let him busy himself with it; as it is said, "Six days shall you labor and do all your work" (Exodus 20:9). For what purpose is [the phrase] "and do all your work" added [given that the Rabbis assume that nothing is superfluous in the Torah]? It is to include a person who has a courtyard or a field in a state of decay that he should go and busy himself with them. A man only dies through idleness.[33]

Even though the Rabbis lived in what was largely a patriarchal society, they recognized that women must work in order to live an honorable life. Thus they say that even if woman has a hundred servants, she must do some of the housework herself, because "idleness leads to lewdness and to mental instability."[34] A terse assertion of this view of work as the source of human honor is the Rabbis' interpretation of Deuteronomy 30:19, "Therefore choose life," as saying, "that is, a handicraft."[35]

At the same time, the Rabbis recognized that the kinds of work and the conditions in which one works play a major role in determining the dignity of the work and the worker. In some places, the Rabbis depict certain types of work, notably tanning and skinning animals, as inherently undignified, presumably because these trades are notoriously dirty and smelly.[36] Similarly, one should avoid engaging in trades associated with criminality, such as donkey or camel handling.[37] However, in other places, the Rabbis caution against shunning any kind of work. In one Talmudic episode, Rav instructs Rav Kahana, "Skin carcasses in the marketplace and collect your wages, and do not say, 'I am a *kohen* [a priest by lineage] and a great man, and this is below my dignity.'"[38] That is, earning a living, even in a job that is distasteful or degrading for a person in a particular religious group—and, by extension, social or economic group—is better than taking money on the dole, for the latter is even more humiliating.

A type of work may be oppressive also because it does not fit the age or strength of the worker or because it seems to be pointless. In the Haggadah read at the Passover Seder, the Rabbis interpret "And they [the Egyptians] imposed hard labor upon us" (Deut. 26:6) with reference to Exodus 1:14, that the Egyptians imposed hard labor "ruthlessly" (*b'farekh*, or "with rigor"), and elsewhere they interpret that term as follows:

> "Ruthlessly" (Exodus 1:14). Rabbi Samuel bar Nahmani said in the name of Rabbi Yohanon: They would assign the work of men to women and the work of women to men.[39]

> They would impose a difficult task upon the weak and an easy task upon the strong, a light burden upon the young and a heavy burden upon the old. This was work without end and futile, for the Egyptians wanted not only to enslave them [the Israelites] but also to break their spirit.[40]

In our own era, the Nazis were expert in forcing Jews and others to transfer one pile of dirt or rocks to a given place, only to be required to transfer it back to the original place, a good example of the endless and futile work intended to break the spirit of someone whose work should be of some benefit and therefore mean something.

Finally, dignity in work and in life in general is a function of how others regard you, especially if they make their negative feelings known. Rabbi Jill Jacobs has demonstrated this in a rabbinic ruling on contemporary work conditions at the lowest level of skill and salary (custodians, people who make beds in hotels, etc.). She points out that often what really bothers such people, as evidenced especially in contract negotiations, is that "they don't respect us," as evidenced by the crushing demands and few breaks (even to go to the bathroom) that some employers impose on their staff and the general attitude they express in words and deeds to their low-ranking employees.[41]

The same point applies, though, to all of our human interactions. One telling example of this in rabbinic literature concerns the duty the Torah imposes on children to honor their parents.[42] As we will discuss in somewhat greater detail below, the Rabbis interpreted that duty to apply to middle-aged children of elderly parents, requiring them, among other things, to feed their parents when they cannot feed themselves.[43] On this the Rabbis note the importance of not only carrying out the duty, but of doing it with an attitude of respect:

> A man may feed his father on fattened chickens and inherit Hell [as his reward], and another may put his father to work in a mill and inherit Paradise.
>
> How is it possible that a man might feed his father fattened chickens and inherit Hell? It once happened that a man used to feed his father fattened chickens. One time his father said to him: "My son, where did you get these?" He answered: "Old man, old man, eat and be silent, just as dogs eat and are silent." In such an instance, he feeds his father fattened chickens, but he inherits Hell.
>
> How is it possible that a man might put his father to work in a mill and inherit Paradise? It once happened that a man was working in a mill. The king decreed that his aged father should be brought to work for him. The son said to his father: "Father, go and work in the mill in place of me [and I will go to work for the king]. For it may be [that the workers for the king will be] ill-treated, in which case let me be ill-treated instead of you. And it may be [that the workers for the king will be] beaten, in which case let me be beaten instead of you." In such an instance, he puts his father to work in a mill, but he inherits Paradise.[44]

MEDIEVAL AND MODERN JEWISH SOURCES

The classical rabbinic texts discussed above demonstrate that concern for human dignity supersedes both positive and negative commandments, generates both exemptions and obligations, and is activated by challenges to the physical and the social needs of an individual, which brings up issues related to the conditions for shame. Perhaps this principle had a glorious but short-lived run, disappearing from the stage of Jewish legal discourse in later centuries?

No, in fact, it has retained its power, though it is not cited as sweepingly in later sources as in classical rabbinic literature.[45]

In the section of his code of Jewish law entitled "Laws of Repentance" (4:4), Maimonides lists five sins from which it is difficult to desist because they are treated casually by most people. Among them is dignifying oneself through the humiliation (even passive) of another. Because most people are indifferent to the humiliation of others or fail to defend someone being shamed because they are worried that then they themselves will be demeaned, there is little social motivation for the offender to repent and restore respect to his neighbor.

Rabbi Moses Isserles permits a couple whose dowry arrangements were delayed to marry on Friday night, despite the prohibition of marrying on the Sabbath (which lasts from a little before sunset Friday to about an hour after sunset on Saturday), because "it would shame the bride and groom if they were not married" (O. H. 339:4).[46] This, granted, is an extraordinary circumstance that should be avoided when possible by arranging for the dowry and wedding on weekdays. Human dignity, however, is cited eighty-one times in the *Shulhan Arukh*, the authoritative sixteenth-century code of Jewish law, and in its primary commentaries to permit otherwise forbidden actions.

In his essay "Congregational Dignity and Human Dignity: Women and Public Torah Reading," Bar Ilan University professor Daniel Sperber assembles a diverse assortment of ways in which human dignity has been cited in recent centuries.[47] Sperber says that the Talmudic principle about human dignity superseding established laws "has been given wide application" in various halakhic contexts. In the responsa literature, Sperber finds numerous references to human dignity superseding a rabbinic law. For example, despite the fact that the Mishnah says that if a man cannot have children with his wife within ten years of marriage, he must divorce her and marry another woman in order to fulfill the commandment "Be fruitful and multiply,"[48] a sixteenth-century legal ruling of Rabbi Joseph bar Lev not only permitted the man to stay married to his first wife when marrying a second woman to procreate, but insisted that he do so, citing the principle of human dignity.[49] Rabbi Abraham Yitzhak HaKohen Kook waived the disqualification of women from participating in producing a Torah scroll, allowing them to sew together its panels, by reference to human dignity.[50]

Rabbi Eliezer Waldenberg, a twentieth-century Israeli Orthodox rabbi who specialized in bioethics, cites human dignity to allow a hearing-impaired person to wear (and carry) a hearing aid on the Sabbath, despite the prohibition of carrying in the public domain on that day.[51] First he considers whether the use of a hearing aid can be justified under the rubric of protecting health or avoiding danger, for which other laws, including those of the Sabbath, are superseded. Having rejected this rationale, he turns to the dignity of a hearing-impaired individual, and uses the Talmud's reasoning with great force and sensitivity:

> We have learned from that said [in the Talmud and codes] that the prohibited act of carrying *muktzeh*[52] [on the Sabbath] was permitted in deference to human dignity, lest the person be humiliated, whether in his own eyes or in the eyes of others, due to being unable to carry [e.g., smooth rocks for wiping] in any way. And if so, it seems that there is no greater matter of human dignity than preventing embarrassment and humiliation of the hearing-impaired person due to inability to hear those who speak to him. One cannot describe the great humiliation, shame, and discomfort caused to him when he walks among people and in synagogue and is isolated, unable to hear what is happening, unable to reply to that said to him, for this is more a matter of dignity than the subjects mentioned [in the Talmud]. Moreover, great anguish is mixed together with humiliation at his inability to participate in public prayer, and to hear the Torah chanted, and to respond [in the prayer service along with the rest of the congregation] "*Amen, yehei shemei rabbah*" and *kedushah*, and similarly, his inability to fulfill the package of commandments, small and great. Thus, it is certainly proper to permit him to carry *muktzeh* because of such a great instance of human dignity, and to allow the hearing-impaired person to carry a hearing aid on Shabbat.

Rabbi Waldenberg writes compassionately about two levels of human dignity at risk: the humiliation of being socially excluded from the life of one's community and the anguish at being unable to fulfill the commandments. In the beginning of his ruling, Rabbi Waldenberg stipulates that his permission applies only to cases in which the hearing-impaired person agrees not to turn the device on and off on the Sabbath, which, in Orthodox interpretations, would violate the Torah's ban on lighting or extinguishing a fire on the Sabbath (Exod. 35:3), a capital offense (Exod. 31:12–15). From his perspective, this act, which is done quite casually at other times, would violate a primary category of labor prohibited on the Sabbath. Moreover, there is a concern for misleading appearance: other Jews might see him using the hearing aid and assume that they may operate electrical appliances on the Sabbath. Even though these are reasonable concerns that could lead to capital offenses, Rabbi Waldenberg sets them aside in favor of the need for the hearing-impaired person to have a dignified part in Jewish society.

This example demonstrates that human dignity as a legal consideration is not limited to *temporary* dispensations but can also be summoned for a *permanent* accommodation. It shows that even when there is a danger that the limited permission of a rabbinically prohibited act could arguably lead to the violation of a biblically prohibited act, we are allowed to be lenient for the sake of human dignity. Rabbi Waldenberg notes both the social and the religious elements of exclusion, and he makes human dignity a legitimate and powerful consideration of the law.

In light of this long, well-established, and broad application of the value of human dignity, Sperber cites the human dignity of women to justify their permission to read the Torah in public, even if some people still consider this to violate the dignity of the men in the congregation. Human dignity is a central value of Jewish theology and law. Similarly, in making her case for the expansion of women's ritual participation within Orthodoxy, Tamar Ross describes the role of values such as human dignity within Jewish legal discourse in clarifying the *telos* or ideal vision of Jewish law.[53]

Rabbi Aaron Lichtenstein, former head of Yeshivat Har Etzion, published an article on the role of human dignity in halakhah in the Israel Defense Force's (IDF) journal, *Mahanayim*.[54] He observes that many rabbinic authorities have been reluctant to cite human dignity explicitly in their rulings, but that this value is frequently the background motivation for a rabbi's decision. Rabbi Lichtenstein understands this reluctance, and indeed fears that the liberal citation of human dignity could undermine the authority of rabbinic norms in general. Nevertheless, he argues that this hesitation to cite human dignity explicitly results in the weakening of a significant Jewish legal and theological principle. If Jewish law is reduced to the mechanical application of precedent without concern for its moral motivations, its religious significance is greatly diminished.

Since 1950, the State of Israel has passed eight "Basic Laws," largely related to the functioning of the government and army. Israel, like Great Britain, which ruled that area of the world from the end of World War I to 1948, does not have a written constitution, but Israel is creating a constitution over time from the ground up by adopting Basic Laws that are intended to be part of the ultimate constitution. In 1992, the Israeli parliament, the Knesset, passed

"Basic Law: Human Dignity and Freedom." In four of its twelve clauses[55] it establishes a broad entitlement to dignity in Israel.[56]

> Basic human rights in Israel are grounded in the recognition of human worth, in the sanctity of human life and freedom, and these are honored in the spirit of the principles included in the declaration establishing the State of Israel.
>
> 1. This basic law is intended to protect human dignity and freedom in order to secure in basic law the values of the State of Israel as a Jewish and democratic state.
> 2. It is forbidden to harm the life, body, or dignity of a person in that he is human.
>
> . . .
>
> 4. Every person is entitled to protection of his life, body and dignity.

This Basic Law has been cited in a broad array of appeals to the Israeli Supreme Court in cases considering the rights of Arab citizens, those of Jewish settlers expelled from Gaza, and the complaint of Alice Miller, a female Israel Air Force pilot.[57] Same-sex relationships have been granted legal recognition by Israel's Supreme Court on the grounds of human dignity in cases awarding social security and inheritance benefits to a male partner of a male military officer and in the registration of two women as the mothers of an adopted child.[58] Our purpose in citing this Basic Law and its application in protecting the rights of gay and lesbian Israelis is to demonstrate the centrality of human dignity, not only within the discourse of traditional Jewish legal sources but also in the modern State of Israel.[59]

WAR

With this grounding in the depth of thought about human dignity in Jewish sources and its broad application to many areas of life, we turn now to three areas of life where human dignity is especially threatened because of the violence involved—namely, war, family violence, and abortion—and then to some new areas of research where concerns of human dignity are important, particularly sexual orientation and genetic engineering. We begin with war, where the sole intention is to inflict harm on one's enemies, either in defense or in aggression, and where human dignity would seem to be undermined by the act inherent in the very meaning of war, namely, killing other people.

The Bible describes many wars, from the war of the four kings against five, in which Abram participated (Gen. 14), to the Exodus from Egypt, to the wars against Amalek and the seven Canaanite nations, repeated often in different eras, as described in the Torah itself and then in Joshua, Judges, 1 and 2 Samuel, and 1 and 2 Kings. Some of those wars are defensive, but many are to carry out the command of God to conquer the Canaanite lands (e.g., Deut. 7:1–5, 22–26; 9:1–5). Some of the actions during the biblical wars are downright gruesome, as, for instance, Yael's pounding a tent pin into the head of the sleeping enemy general, Sisera (Judg. 4:21). Some are even genocidal, as in God's command to kill all the inhabitants of the seven Canaanite nations (Deut. 20:16–18) and the command of God to Saul to kill not only the soldiers of Amalek but also its women, children, and animals (1 Sam. 15:2–3).

In the midst of these stories of war, however, the Torah establishes some rules to diminish war's severity and its threats to human dignity. Specifically, Deuteronomy 20 demands that Israelite forces allow enemy forces to surrender peacefully before attacking them, thus diminishing the carnage even though humiliating the enemy by forcing complete surrender on them. Deuteronomy 21:10–14, however, has a provision that has the effect of preserving the dignity of at least some of the people involved in war—namely, the enemy's women taken as wives. Specifically, it provides that such women be given a month's time to mourn their father and mother, whose household they are leaving through this marriage, and that if later the man wants to divorce her, he may do so, but as a free woman and not as a slave sold to someone else.

Later Jewish sources go in two different directions regarding war. The Hanukkah story, as told in the book of Maccabees of the Apocrypha, celebrates the military victory of the Maccabees over the Syrian Greeks in the name of religious freedom, and that is part of the story Jews repeat in song and story every Hanukkah.[60] The Talmud, however, says nothing about such a military victory and instead defines Hanukkah as the celebration of the miracle of the oil (left over in the Temple to rededicate it after the Syrian Greeks sullied it) that was supposed to last only one day and instead lasted eight.[61] The focus of the holiday thus shifts from celebrating a human military victory, albeit in the name of religious freedom, to a miracle wrought by God. This undoubtedly reflects the Rabbis' frustration with wars after the Romans destroyed the Second Temple in 70 CE and with it the Second Jewish Commonwealth, and after the Romans again quashed a Jewish revolt against them in 132–35 CE. In line with this reticence to glorify war, the liturgy for Hanukkah praises *God* for standing up against the Greeks and does not even mention the human fighters involved, the Maccabees.

The Talmud itself, however, is ambivalent on this issue. Although it reacts as described above to the Hanukkah story, shifting the emphasis from human military action to God's miracles, it also says that the Torah commands, "If anyone comes to kill you, kill him first,"[62] based on their interpretation of Exodus 22:1–2 that, in their understanding of those verses, establishes the duty of self-defense. This then leads to the Rabbis' classifications of various forms of war, including these three: the war of conquering the Canaanites to establish the nation of Israel there, as explicitly commanded by God; obligatory wars of self-defense; and optional wars to expand the Land of Israel's territory. They then describe the varying requirements for waging such wars and the rules of engagement.[63]

For two millennia, from the end of the Maccabean state circa 63 BCE to the establishment of the State of Israel in 1948, Jews did not have their own armies, and so Jewish discussions about war during that long period were both rare and theoretical. Jews often fought in their nation's armies, but they could not decide as Jews which wars to wage and how to wage them. Modern Israelis, however, have frequently fought wars, both to establish the State of Israel and to defend it. In the process, they have developed a Code of Ethics that governs the IDF's conduct of war. In that code, human dignity is listed as one of its three "basic values," and it is defined as follows: "Human Dignity—The IDF and its soldiers are obligated to protect human dignity. Every human being is of value regardless of his or her origin, religion, nationality, gender, status or position."[64] Even before that official document on this subject, David Ben Gurion, the first prime minister of the State of Israel, created the doctrine of "purity of arms," which is asserted as a value for the IDF and is described in the Code of Ethics as follows:

> Purity of Arms—The IDF servicemen and women will use their weapons and force only for the purpose of their mission, only to the necessary extent and will maintain their humanity even during combat. IDF soldiers will not use their weapons and force to harm human beings who are not combatants or prisoners of war, and will do all in their power to avoid causing harm to their lives, bodies, dignity and property.[65]

In practice, this ideal has often come into conflict with another value articulated in the Code, namely, to risk one's own life and the lives of one's fellow soldiers as little as possible, and therefore the training of Israeli soldiers, sailors, and airmen includes a series of concrete cases in which these values conflict so that military personnel know how to balance these values when they come into conflict.

The IDF, like all military forces, has been criticized for falling short of these ideals in practice.[66] Armed conflict is inherently undignified, especially when it involves civilian populations whose involvement is ambiguous. Checkpoints, home inspections, and other intrusions into the privacy of individuals, some of whom are not engaged in threatening conduct, are humiliating, even if they are deemed by military commanders to be necessary for the protection of life. The U.S. military has likewise struggled to ensure that its ideals of dignity are observed in practice by soldiers who are themselves frightened or even bored (as in the 2003 outrages at the Iraqi prison of Abu Ghraib).[67] The demands of dignity are difficult to observe in theaters of conflict, but it is there that they may be most important, not only for individual soldiers and civilians, but also for the success of restoring peace and justice to a society convulsed by war.

In an article that Elliot Dorff wrote for a symposium on Judaism and war that was later published in the journal *Philosophia*, he articulated another set of implications of human dignity for conduct in war that are very much part of the ethical norms and expected practice of the IDF:

> War does not justify rape or other forms of torture, humiliation, or injury of the enemy not required to defend oneself and one's community. This stems directly from the respect that we must have for all human beings as creatures of God, created in the Divine Image. This leaves open the rare possibility recognized by the Israeli Supreme Court of some forms of physical pressure to reveal the whereabouts of terrorists about to kill many people (the "ticking bomb" case), but only if such procedures can be demonstrated to prevent such terrorism.[68]

According to the UN, 200,000 women and children have been raped during the Congo's long conflict,[69] and that is just the most egregious of many recent examples to demonstrate that bans on rape and other forms of humiliation during wartime are not taken for granted in much of the world. The Jewish tradition's insistence on human dignity, however, puts such conduct off limits, even during wartime, when many of the usual rules of civil society, including the ban on killing others, are suspended.

Thus, human dignity is very much a contemporary concern in the unfortunate arena of war, where it is perhaps most starkly called into question. Even in that inherently inhumane context, however, traditional and contemporary Jewish sources have attempted to insert considerations of human dignity in both the deliberations of when to wage war (*jus ad bellum*), how to wage it (*jus in bello*), and how to treat one's former enemies after the war is over (*jus post bellum*), when the justification of self-defense to harm one's enemies ceases and a nation must reinstate its normal duty to treat others, including one's former enemies, with respect. In Israel today, with recurrent *intifadas* and continuing official states of hostility on the part of some Arab nations toward Israel and official peace with others, deciding exactly what context one is in—outright war, semiwar, or peace—is itself a challenge, and so how to balance considerations of human dignity with the equally crucial commitment to self-defense on both personal and national levels is an ever-present matter of debate and changing public policy in Israel as it strives to put both of these values into practice.

Israel, of course, is not perfect in accomplishing this, any more than any other nation is. Furthermore, because of conflicting Jewish and Arab narratives about Israel and many other factors, it is impossible to discuss the Arab–Israeli conflict in purely objective and philosophical terms. The continued conflict between Israel and several of her immediate neighbors, the many forms of terrorist attacks, and the Israeli occupation of the Palestinian population of the West Bank since 1967 with its accompanying demeaning checkpoints and home invasions have made dignity an exceptionally difficult value to implement. Nevertheless, the naming of dignity as a Basic Law of the State of Israel and as a cornerstone of the IDF Code of Ethics allows for the identification of abuses and the possibility of their remediation.

ASSAULT

With the exception of the circumstances of self-defense and participation in a justified war, Jewish law prohibits assault on anyone, and it recognizes that in addition to the physical harm involved, victims of assault may also suffer from psychological harms, including humiliation. The Mishnah therefore stipulates that the perpetrator must pay five different remedies to the victim—for the injury itself, for medical costs to heal the injury, for time lost from work, for the pain suffered, and for the shame or embarrassment involved in being vulnerable in this way.[70] One who attacks others has in the process undermined their dignity, which minimally includes their safety and with it their bodily and psychological integrity and honor.

If this is true in general, it is true even more in family configurations. As individuals and as a society, we would hope that families are loving, supportive, and, especially, safe environments. Thankfully, for many of us this is true. Those fortunate enough to grow up or currently live in such a home, however, then mistakenly think that everyone had such a home while growing up and has one now.

The statistics tell a very different story. Spousal abuse, child beating, and hitting elderly parents are all much too common to ignore.[71] Being assaulted in any of those family configurations undermines one's sense of dignity even more than when one is assaulted by a stranger, for one expects that of all the people in the world, one's family will be least likely to harm you. This fact may also add a sense of shame that one has failed to build a "happy family" and guilt that one may have brought it upon herself or himself. So the humiliation is psychologically scarring in addition to being physically dangerous.

People expect, in fact, just the opposite—that one's family will be the most important source of one's sense that one is not only respected but loved. When that does not happen and when, on the contrary, one is abused by family members, it is downright devastating to one's sense of self-respect. Spousal and parental abuse is inexcusable and deeply harmful; child abuse in many cases is even worse, akin to murder in its effects on the child's sense of self-respect and his or her capacity for love and being loved. Both authors of this chapter have written detailed articles on family violence and its psychologically destructive effects on the people involved.[72]

Finally, attacking disabled people constitutes another special case of the indignity entailed in assault. Abusing those with atypically functioning bodies and minds completely violates Jewish norms. As indicated earlier, precisely because many people, upon seeing someone who is disabled either physically or mentally, might say to themselves, "Thank God that is not me," or might respond with a negative aesthetic reaction, the Jewish tradition requires typically abled people, on seeing a disabled person, to bless God for making people different from one another.[73] The prayer educates all of us emotionally and religiously, for it is saying that everyone must recognize that disabled people are created in the image of God just as much as typically abled people are and deserve to be treated as such. The Torah demands, "You shall not insult [or curse] the deaf, or place a stumbling block before the blind. You shall fear your God: I am the Lord" (Lev. 19:14), a verse that the Rabbis interpret to apply not only to cursing the deaf but to cursing any unfortunate person, and not only to placing stumbling blocks before the physically blind, but also to giving people incorrect information and to tempting people who are especially vulnerable to violate the law.[74] So abusing disabled people violates not only the general laws prohibiting assault but also these special laws and theological convictions applying to the disabled, who share the same dignity that abled people have by virtue of being created in the image of God and who, in any case, are, as the disabled community rightly says, "the temporarily abled." In the end, Judaism bids all of us to create an inclusive community in which all people are invited and empowered to participate fully.

ABORTION

The Torah, in its original Hebrew version, provides that if men who are fighting hit a pregnant woman and that causes her miscarriage, the penalty for the lost fetus is money, the amount of which depends on how far along she was in the pregnancy, while the penalty for injuries to the woman is "life for life, eye for eye," etc. (Exod. 21:22–25). The Rabbis later interpreted these verses to make the penalty for personal injuries monetary also, but they understand the Torah to be making a clear distinction between the life of the mother, who is a full human being, and that of the fetus, who is not. They therefore rule in a Mishnah (ca. 200 CE)—in a time long before safe Caesarian sections—that if the mother is having difficulty in childbirth such that her life is at stake, those attending to her must go into her womb and dismember the fetus because even at the end of the ninth month "her life takes precedence over its life"—that is, the fetus does not have the same legal status as the mother does as a full human being.[75]

Undoubtedly grounded in what the Rabbis witnessed in miscarriages, they maintained that for the first forty days of pregnancy, the fetus was "simply liquid,"[76] and from that point on it was "like the thigh of its mother."[77] Based on this analysis of the status of the fetus, abortions in Jewish law come in three categories: (1) where the mother's life or physical or mental health is at stake (the latter interpreted narrowly to mean that she would go insane if she did not abort), then an abortion *must* be done, in line with the Mishnah cited above; (2) where there is an increased risk to the mother's physical or mental life or health beyond that of normal pregnancy (e.g., the mother has diabetes) or, according to many modern rabbis, including the Conservative Movement's Committee on Jewish Law and Standards, when the fetus has a lethal or devastating genetic disease, such as Tay–Sachs or Fragile X, then an abortion *may* be done;[78] but (3) normally abortions are not allowed.

Because the fetus is not viewed as a full human being, for the Jewish tradition feticide is not homicide, and so the usual ban on abortions is not a function of the ban on murder; it is rather the ban on self-injury. No man or woman has the right, according to Jewish law, to injure his or her body, for God owns our bodies, and we have the fiduciary duty to take care of them. Thus the dignity of the mother outweighs the dignity of the fetus when her life or health is at risk, but the fetus—and even sperm and ova—have the dignity of being the creative components of human life and therefore need to be treated with respect. What that respect requires varies with the circumstances, but it does require, for example, that abortions be justified for the reasons mentioned above.

In this way, the Jewish tradition takes a stance on abortion different from that of the Roman Catholic Church, on one end of the spectrum, and secular law, on the other, the two positions that most people living in Western countries know and see continually at odds with each other in politics and in the press. *Donum vitae* (*Instruction for Human Life in Its Origin and on the Dignity of Procreation*) was issued by the Vatican's Congregation for the Doctrine of the Faith on February 22, 1987. It reaffirms the position of the Roman Catholic Church since the first century that abortion under almost any circumstances is prohibited, and the very title of that document relates the ban on abortion to human dignity. Canon 1398 of the Code of Canon Law, in fact, requires immediate excommunication for any woman who has an abortion. But Canon 1324, paragraph 3, makes an exception if the woman's life is at stake, and papal statements offer absolution for those who repent for having had an abortion. The ban on abortion is based on the Catholic view that life begins at conception, and so abortion is homicide. Recent statements of the United States Conference of Catholic Bishops extend that position even to a zygote in a petri dish, where the pre-embryo has no chance of developing into a human being unless implanted into a woman's uterus, and consequently they prohibit embryonic stem cell research that kills the embryo in the process of removing its inner cell mass for research purposes. They also ban in vitro fertilization because that process usually leads to destroying any unused embryos.[79]

On the opposite end of the spectrum is secular law in most Western countries, except some that are heavily Roman Catholic. To take U.S. law as one example of this view, in 1973 the U.S. Supreme Court in *Roe v. Wade* defined the fetus in a woman's womb as part of her body and therefore completely subject to her will as to whether to maintain the pregnancy or abort it before it reaches viability (that is, the ability of the fetus to survive outside of the uterus after birth). At that point—which *Roe* defined as the third trimester (starting at 28 weeks) but which neonatology has subsequently advanced in at least some cases to twenty-three or twenty-four weeks of gestation—states may impose restrictions on abortions, but not, according to the Supreme Court *Casey v. Planned Parenthood* (1992) decision, to the extent that such restrictions effectively make it impossible for a woman to procure an abortion.

The Jewish tradition's concern with, and interpretation of, human dignity leads it to take a position on abortion intermediate between those of the Roman Catholic Church and U.S. law. Thus, on one hand, unlike the Catholic position, it recognizes the difference between what is potentially a human being and what is actually so. In fact, we have very good hormonal evidence that approximately 75 percent of fertilized ova in a woman's womb will miscarry,[80] most in the early months of pregnancy and some even before a woman knows that she is pregnant, so a fertilized egg is not a person; it is something that has a one-in-four chance of becoming a person. The woman, in the meantime, is definitely a human being, and so Jewish law treats a pregnant woman as an actor with inherent worth, not just a container for the fetus.

On the other hand, Jewish law recognizes that all of us begin as fertilized egg cells, and so justifications are required to terminate a pregnancy; it is not just a matter of the mother's will alone. Not wanting another child is a very good reason to use birth control; to terminate a pregnancy for that reason is, in most cases, not a sufficient warrant. Human dignity requires us to respect even sperm and ova, let alone zygotes and then embryos and fetuses, for we all began that way. Sometimes the woman's dignity overrides that of the fetus, for she is a full human being and the fetus is not, even, as the Mishnah says, in the last month of pregnancy if her life requires an abortion at that point. But the developing human being within her does require justifications for abortion, and they need to be stronger to abort in later stages of pregnancy than in earlier ones.

This discussion about abortion should not blind the reader to the larger context of how Judaism understands sexual activity. As Elliot Dorff has written in his *Rabbinic Letter on Human Intimacy*, Judaism sees sexual activities not as dirty or demeaning but rather as actually commanded between husband and wife for both their mutual pleasure and for procreation, and his letter addresses the values that should inform sex outside of marriage. Now that the United States and much of the Jewish community have extended the institution of marriage to same-sex couples, these same values pertain in any marriage. One of those is the dignity of one's sexual partner, and so sexual activity must be consensual for both married and unmarried couples. This positive attitude toward sex within Judaism is complemented by its understanding that sexual activities, though a great gift that God has given us, should be done in private, and that one's dress and speech should demonstrate the modesty that human dignity requires in public.[81]

SEXUAL ORIENTATION AND GENDER IDENTITY

The past half century has been dominated in many cultures by various rights movements, all of which have asserted more or less explicitly that human dignity requires equal treatment—regardless of race, gender, sexual orientation, gender identity, or physical and mental ability. Similar arguments had been advanced by Jews in Western societies for centuries (recall Shylock's soliloquy "Hath not a Jew eyes?"), and in recent decades the Jewish community has generally, although not consistently, supported the rights agenda.[82] Classical Jewish texts such as those cited above about humans being created in the divine image and the obligation to love one's neighbor as oneself (Lev. 19:18) have been cited to support these newly vocalized expressions of human dignity. And yet it is also the case that many classical Jewish norms have been experienced as obstacles, not resources, for the expansion of the realm of human dignity.

After all, Jewish classical texts are patriarchal, told from a male perspective, with females related to as "other" and frequently as subject to male demands. The Sages recognized that some people occupied intersex categories, and yet their normative world was deeply binary, with men and women each assigned distinct social, legal, and ritual roles. Rabbinic texts do not classify people by sexual orientation, but they do prohibit and even criminalize sexual intimacy between members of the same sex. Great sensitivity is expressed in biblical and rabbinic texts for the dignity of the elderly, the infirm, and those who are disabled. Yet there remains a hierarchy of Jewish obligation and thus of dignity in classical Jewish sources such that a healthy free Jewish male occupies the upper echelon of Jewish community.[83]

The authors of this chapter have dedicated much of their Jewish legal writings to addressing these tensions and to expanding the application of human dignity to people who have been excluded or even oppressed by our tradition. Together with Rabbi Avram Reisner, we wrote a 2006 responsum entitled "Homosexuality, Human Dignity and Halakhah," (see note for link) from which we have quoted above. Our core argument was that human dignity is such a powerful value of Jewish tradition that it has the capacity to supersede all but the most explicit biblical norms found to undermine the dignity of gay and lesbian people.[84] Separately, we have each written on the subjects of disability and old age,[85] and through our association with Conservative Judaism's Committee on Jewish Law and Standards, we have participated in addressing discrimination against deaf people, women, and transgender people.[86]

Tension between traditional norms and contemporary perceptions of social experience is not surprising, nor need it incapacitate responsible leaders. Our method includes both respect for and generous criticism of former generations of Jewish scholars together with curiosity and sympathy for the experiences of our contemporaries, leading us to interpretations of Jewish law that respect the wisdom of the ages and the dignity claims being expressed in our day.

GENETIC ENGINEERING

A final concern that demands mention is the expanding range of challenges and opportunities for human dignity posed by the revolution in genetic engineering. Elliot Dorff has presented an expansive view of the issues involved in stem cell research, genetic identity, genetic testing, and genetic interventions in *Jews and Genes: The Genetic Future in Contemporary Jewish Thought*, coedited with Laurie Zoloth.[87] Daniel Nevins has studied the many issues involved and came to halakhic conclusions in his responsum, "Halakhic Perspectives on Genetically Modified Organisms."[88] He concludes that modifications of the human genome intended to promote human health may be permitted, but genetic interventions intended merely to enhance human appearance or performance violate Jewish teachings about the sanctity of life.

Genetic engineering has the potential to expand the realm of human dignity by treating diseases such as cancer and by restoring physical strength and even mental acuity. Allowing humans to live healthier, fuller, and longer lives is certainly a boon to the cause of human dignity. Yet there are also ethical challenges posed by this rapidly evolving field. Through gene editing tools such as CRISPR-Cas9, permanent changes to the human genome can be made, giving scientists far more control in determining the structure of human life. The ability not only to treat disease but also to enhance human abilities may paradoxically undermine human dignity. Wealthy parents with access to the latest technology will increasingly be able to design offspring with certain physical and intellectual capacities and with disease resistance and other biological benefits that may make class distinctions permanent. As income inequality continues to increase, we have already arrived at a stage in which lifespan differs dramatically based on wealth.[89] Will wealthier humans soon use gene editing essentially to create a new species of humanity? What then will become of the core concept that all humans are created equally in the divine image? As Jews and as humans, we are committed to finding the proper balance, with the goal of expanding the realm of human dignity and supporting social solidarity based on the essential equality of all people.

EPILOGUE

It is fitting that we end with a statement of human dignity from the Hebrew Bible, the first authoritative document of Judaism. It is this view of the human being that underlies everything we have discussed above on the Jewish tradition's view of human dignity:

> What are humans, that You have been mindful of them, mortals, that You have taken note of them, that You have made them little less than divine, and adorned them with glory and majesty; You have made them master over Your handiwork, laying the world at their feet, sheep and oxen, all of them, and wild beasts too; the birds of the heavens, the fish of the sea, whatever travels the paths of the seas. O Lord, our Lord, how majestic is Your name throughout the earth! (Psalm 8:5–10)[90]

NOTES

Abbreviations in the following notes:

M. = Mishnah, edited ca. 200 CE
Y. = Jerusalem (Palestinian) Talmud, edited ca. 400 CE
B. = Babylonian Talmud, edited ca. 500 CE
M.T. = Maimonides's *Mishneh Torah*, completed in 1177 CE
S.A. = Joseph Karo's *Shulhan Arukh*, completed in 1563 CE, with glosses later added by Moses Isserles to indicate where northern European Jewish practice differed from the Mediterranean practices that Karo recorded

1. B. *Berakhot* 19b; B. *Shabbat* 81b, 94b; B. *Eruvin* 41b; B. *Megillah* 3b; B. *Bava Kamma* 79b; B. *Menahot* 37b, 38a; Y. *Berakhot* 3:1; Y. *Kilayim* 9:1; Y. *Nazir* 7:1, et al.

2. Genesis 1:27; see also Genesis 5:1.

3. For an extended analysis of the various meanings attributed to this phrase in classical rabbinic literature (but not after that), see Yair Lorberbaum, *In God's Image: Myth, Theology, and Law in Classical Judaism* (New York: Cambridge University Press, 2015; originally published in Hebrew in 2004). For another treatment of the various meanings of this phrase, extending into medieval Jewish philosophy and mystical writings, see David Mevorach Seidenberg, *Kabbalah and Ecology: God's Image in the More-Than-Human World* (New York: Cambridge University Press, 2015), 43–232.

4. See Genesis 1:26–27; 3:1–7, 22–24.

5. See Genesis 2:18–24; Numbers 12:1–16; Deuteronomy 22:13–19. Note also that *ha-middaber*, "the speaker," is a synonym for the human being (in comparison to animals) in medieval Jewish philosophy.

6. Maimonides, *Guide of the Perplexed*, trans. Shlomo Pines (Chicago: University of Chicago Press, 1963), pt. 1, chap. 1.

7. See Deuteronomy 6:5; Leviticus 19:18, 33–34, and note that the traditional prayer book juxtaposes the paragraph just before the Shema, which speaks of God's love for us, with the first paragraph of the Shema, which commands us to love God.

8. Consider the prayer in the traditional, early morning weekday service, *Elohai neshamah she-natata bi*, "My God, the soul (or life-breath) that you have imparted to me is pure. You created it, You formed it, You breathed it into me; You guard it within me"; Jules Harlow, ed., *Siddur Sim Shalom* (New York: Rabbinical Assembly, 1985), 8–11. Similarly, the Rabbis describe the human being as part divine and part animal, the latter consisting of the material aspects of the human being and the former consisting of that which we share with God; see *Sifre Deuteronomy*, para. 306; 132a. Or consider this rabbinic statement in *Genesis Rabbah* 8:11: "In four respects man resembles the creatures above, and in four respects the creatures below. Like the animals he eats and drinks, propagates his species, relieves himself, and dies. Like the ministering angels he stands erect, speaks, possesses intellect, and sees [in front of him and not on the side like an animal]."

9. *Genesis Rabbah* 24:7.

10. Deuteronomy 21:23.

11. B. *Sanhedrin* 46b.

12. See *The Cambridge Companion to the Talmud and Rabbinic Literature*, ed. Charlotte Elisheva Fonrobert and Martin S. Jaffee (New York: Cambridge University Press, 2007), for a survey of recent scholarship on the rabbinic canon.

13. M. *Avot* (*Ethics of the Fathers*) 2:10.

14. M. *Avot* 3:14.

15. Rabbi Akiva's statement reminds us that Jewish texts discuss the dignity not merely of humans, but of *creations*. The Hebrew term *briyyot*, "creations," indicates that human dignity is a derivative of divine dignity. As a consequence, the Jewish value of human dignity applies broadly to all humans, and not only to Jews.

A second consequence is that human dignity is secondary to divine dignity. This prioritization is expressed in the Talmud by citing Proverbs 21:30: "There is no wisdom, nor comprehension nor counsel against the Lord." That is, even those qualities of wisdom that most highly exalt humanity in rabbinic eyes pale in comparison to God's glory. Moreover, if the wise oppose God, they forfeit their own claims to dignity. On the other hand, the degradation of another human is seen as a degradation of the divine image, and the Sages therefore took extraordinary measures to protect human dignity.

Nachum Rakover studies the concept of human dignity in Rakover, *Gadol Kvod Habriot—kvod ha-adam k'erekh-al* ("Great Is Human Dignity": Human Dignity as an Overriding Value) (Jerusalem: Ministry of Justice, Mishpat Ivri Library, 1998 [Hebrew]); published in English as *Human Dignity in Jewish Law*. He observes that although *kevod habriot* (honor due to God's creatures) is a significant concern of the Tannaim (Rabbis of the first two centuries CE) in extending God's dignity to God's creatures, it is in Amoraic sources from the third to the sixth centuries CE that it develops into a legal principle with jurisgenerative power.

16. M. *Sanhedrin* 4:5. Some manuscripts are less universalistic. They read: "Anyone who destroys one *Israelite* soul is described in Scripture as if he destroyed an entire world, and anyone who sustains one *Israelite* soul is described in Scripture as if he sustained an entire world." A Hasidic *bon mot* (from Martin Buber, *Tales of the Hasidim* [New York: Schocken, 1961], 2:249–50) reminds us that we must balance this recognition of our divine worth with a proper dose of humility. Rabbi Bunam said: A person should always have two pieces of paper, one in each pocket. On one should be written, "For me the world was created." On the other should be written, "I am but dust and ashes" (Gen. 18:27).

17. For a thorough discussion of this blessing and concept in the Jewish tradition, see Carl Astor, *Who Has Made People Different: Jewish Perspectives on the Disabled* (New York: United Synagogue of America, 1985).

18. M. *Avot* 4:20.

19. Other sources add nuance to this ruling, discussing whether the stature of the Sage is to be considered, whether it matters if the violation is intentional or not, whether stripping would be necessary if he had no undergarments, and whether another person

who noticed the mixture of linen and wool on his neighbor should wait until they reach a private place before informing him. It is possible that *only* a Sage is required to humiliate himself in this fashion.

20. This may refer to ossuaries, which typically left enough space between the bones and the lid to intercept ritual impurity.

21. Miguel Perez Fernandez, *An Introductory Grammar of Rabbinic Hebrew*, trans. John Elwolde (Leiden: Brill, 1997), sec. 16.13a (108–9). See also Moshe Z. Segal, *Dikduk Leshon HaMishnah* (Tel Aviv: Devir, 5696 [year on the Jewish calendar]), sec. 230 (and also sec. 232), 130. He describes this construction as yielding "an activity that is constant and continuous."

22. The fuller reference is Psalm 8:5–6: "What is man that You have been mindful of him, mortal man that You have taken note of him. That You have made him little less than divine, and adorned him with glory and majesty" (New Jewish Publication Society trans.). We thank Benjamin Sommer for this association and for the grammatical sources in note 21.

23. See *Tosfot*, s.v. לעשות נחת רוח לנשים, and the parallel sources in *Rosh HaShanah* 33a, etc.

24. This survey has in fact been limited to those passages that cite our entire phrase, "Great is human dignity, for it supersedes a law of the Torah." However, *kevod habriot*, the Hebrew for "human dignity," appears explicitly or implicitly in many other contexts, such as B. *Hagigah* 16b, which is described by Sperber (see below in the text).

25. See discussion by Eliezer Berkowitz, *Not in Heaven: The Nature and Function of Halakha* (New York: Ktav, 1983), 23.

26. See Rashi to B. *Sukkah* 36b, s.v. *mutar l'hakhnis*; B. *Beitzah* 32b, s.v. *v'haha*; B. *Menahot* 38a, s.v. *b'lav d'lo.*

27. Some primary sources on shaming another include M. *Bava Kama* 8:1, 6; B. *Bava Kamma* 86a–b, *M.T.* "Laws of Injury and Damage," 1:1; Tur/*S.A.* H.M. 120:3; B. *Mo'ed Katan* 27b.

28. B. *Mo'ed Katan* 27b.

29. Shame is one of the five components of an assault that requires compensation even if the other four components (physical injury, pain, medical treatment, time lost from work, as according to M. *Bava Kamma* 8:1) do not apply: B. *Bava Kamma* 85a–86a. The Talmud's discussion of shame being measured not only by the victim's feelings but also by the family or community recognizing that the victim has been shamed: B. *Bava Kamma* 86b.

30. B. *Nedarim* 49b.

31. Genesis 2:15; Exodus 23:12.

32. M. *Avot* 1:10.

33. *Avot D'Rabbi Natan* 11.

34. M. *Ketubbot* 5:5.

35. Y. *Pe'ah* 15c. Along these lines, Atul Gawande discusses the positive health outcomes that follow when people in residential care are dignified with responsibilities, such as caring for pets and plants; Gewande, *Being Mortal* (New York: Henry Holt and Company, 2014), chap. 5.

36. B. *Kiddushin* 82b.

37. B. *Kiddushin* 82a.

38. B. *Pesahim* 113a.

39. B. *Sotah* 11b; *Exodus Rabbah* 1:11 (on Exodus 1:14).

40. *Midrash Hagadol*, on Exodus 1:14.

41. Rabbi Jill Jacobs, "Work, Workers, and the Jewish Owner," http://www.rabbinicalassembly.org/sites/default/files/assets/public/halakhah/teshuvot/20052010/jacobs-living-wage.pdf.

42. Exodus 20:12; Deuteronomy 5:16.

43. B. *Kiddushin* 31b. See note 80, below.

44. Y. *Pe'ah* 1:1 (15c); cf. B. *Kiddushin* 31a–b; *S.A. Yoreh De'ah* 240:4. The text in the Jerusalem Talmud does not make it completely clear that the king specifically demanded that the father come to work for him, but that is the only way that the story works, as the commentators say there and as Rashi says with reference to the abbreviated version of the story in the Babylonian Talmud.

45. A search on the Bar Ilan Responsa Project (version 12+) yields 440 citations, 248 of them from responsa.

46. See discussion in Rabbi Joseph Telushkin, *A Code of Jewish Ethics* (New York: Bell Tower, 2006), 1:279.

47. *The Edah Journal*, 3:2, 2002 (Elul 5763), http://www.edah.org.

48. M. *Yevamot* 6:6.

49. Responsa of Maharibal, pt. 1, sec. 40.

50. Responsa of *Da'at Kohen*, sec. 169.

51. Responsa of *Tzitz Eliezer*, vol. 6, sec. 6, para. 3.

52. *Muktzeh* means touching an object, such as a match, which is used primarily for a purpose prohibited on the Sabbath. Striking the match would violate the biblical prohibition of burning, but even touching the match violates the rabbinic fence around the law of *muktzeh*, designed to protect the person from mistakenly violating the biblical prohibition and thus being at least theoretically subject to the death penalty.

53. Tamar Ross, *Expanding the Palace of Torah: Orthodoxy and Feminism* (Waltham, MA: Brandeis University Press, 2004), esp. chap. 4, "The Meta-Halakhic Solutions of Modern Orthodoxy," 65.

54. *Mahanayim*, no. 5 (new series) Iyyar 5753. We thank Rabbi David Rosen for providing us with his translation of this article. A somewhat longer version, delivered as a lecture by Rabbi Lichtenstein, under the title "*Kevod Ha-beriyot:* Human Dignity in Halakha," is available in a transcript and translation prepared by Aviad Hacohen and David Silverberg at the Yeshivat Har Etzion Israel Koschitzky Virtual Beit Midrash.

55. The full text of "Basic Law: Human Dignity and Liberty" is available at http://www.knesset.gov.il/laws/special/eng/basic3_eng.htm. Here is the official translation:

1. *Purpose.* The purpose of this Basic Law is to protect human dignity and liberty, in order to establish in a Basic Law the values of the State of Israel as a Jewish and democratic state.

2. *Preservation of life, body and dignity.* There shall be no violation of the life, body or dignity of any person as such.
3. *Protection of property.* There shall be no violation of the property of a person.
4. *Protection of life, body and dignity.* All persons are entitled to protection of their life, body and dignity.
5. *Personal liberty.* There shall be no deprivation or restriction of the liberty of a person by imprisonment, arrest, extradition or otherwise.
6. *Leaving and entering Israel.* (a) All persons are free to leave Israel. (b) Every Israel national has the right of entry into Israel from abroad.
7. *Privacy.* (a) All persons have the right to privacy and to intimacy. (b) There shall be no entry into the private premises of a person who has not consented thereto. (c) No search shall be conducted on the private premises of a person, nor in the body or personal effects. (d) There shall be no violation of the confidentiality of conversation, or of the writings or records of a person.
8. *Violation of rights.* There shall be no violation of rights under this Basic Law except by a law befitting the values of the State of Israel, enacted for a proper purpose, and to an extent no greater than is required.
9. *Reservation regarding security forces.* There shall be no restriction of rights under this Basic Law held by persons serving in the Israel Defense Forces, the Israel Police, the Prisons Service and other security organizations of the State, nor shall such rights be subject to conditions, except by virtue of a law, or by regulation enacted by virtue of a law, and to an extent no greater than is required by the nature and character of the service.
10. *Validity of laws.* This Basic Law shall not affect the validity of any law (*din*) in force prior to the commencement of the Basic Law.
11. *Application.* All governmental authorities are bound to respect the rights under this Basic Law.
12. *Stability.* This Basic Law cannot be varied, suspended or made subject to conditions by emergency regulations; notwithstanding, when a state of emergency exists, by virtue of a declaration under section 9 of the Law and Administration Ordinance, 5708-1948, emergency regulations may be enacted by virtue of said section to deny or restrict rights under this Basic Law, provided the denial or restriction shall be for a proper purpose and for a period and extent no greater than is required.

56. See discussion of this Basic Law in Rakover, *Gadol Kvod Habriot*, 14–17, and the full Hebrew text on 193, appendix IV.

57. Israeli Supreme Court decisions may be searched at http://www.court.gov.il/heb/index.htm and at http://www.nevo.co.il.

58. Although the primary consideration in the latter case, which was decided in favor of the two mothers on January 10, 2005, was for the good of the child, the court also found that to exclude the plaintiffs from consideration as a family based on their being the same gender would violate their dignity as established in the 1992 Basic Law.

59. We thank Ronen Hausirer for his assistance in accessing these cases. See also Orit Kamir, שאלה של כבוד: ישראליות וכבוד האדם (Israeli Honor and Dignity: Social Norms, Gender Politics and the Law) [Hebrew] (Jerusalem: Carmel, 2005).

60. See Seth Schwartz, *The Ancient Jews from Alexander to Muhammad* (Cambridge: Cambridge University Press, 2014), 45.

61. B. *Shabbat* 21b.

62. B. *Berakhot* 58a, 62b; B. *Yoma* 85b.

63. M. Sotah 8:7 (44b). See also B. *Eruvin* 45a, and compare that to M. *Eruvin* 4:3; T. *Eruvin* 3:6; Y. *Eruvin* 4:3 (21d); and Saul Lieberman, *Tosefta Kif'shuta* (New York: Jewish Theological Seminary of America, 1962), 342–44. For a summary and discussion of the Jewish laws of war, see Elliot N. Dorff, *To Do the Right and the Good: A Jewish Approach to Modern Social Ethics* (Philadelphia: Jewish Publication Society, 2002), chap. 7.

64. https://www.idfblog.com/about-the-idf/idf-code-of-ethics/.

65. Ibid.

66. See Breaking the Silence, *Our Harsh Logic: Israeli Soldiers' Testimonies from the Occupied Territories, 2000–2010* (New York: Henry Holt and Company, 2012).

67. For an overview of the Abu Ghraib story and the broader context of torture and degradation as U.S. tools of war during these years, see https://en.wikipedia.org/wiki/Abu_Ghraib_torture_and_prisoner_abuse.

68. Elliot N. Dorff, "War and Peace: A Methodology to Formulate a Contemporary Jewish Approach," *Philosophia* 40, no. 4 (2012): 661.

69. Aryn Baker, "War and Rape," *Time*, April 18, 2016, 38.

70. M. *Bava Kamma* 8:1.

71. For some of the statistics on family violence, see Elliot N. Dorff, "Family Violence," in *Love Your Neighbor and Yourself: A Jewish Approach to Modern Personal Ethics* (Philadelphia: Jewish Publication Society, 2003), 158 and its endnotes; and his rabbinic ruling, "Family Violence" (775–76n8), for the Conservative Movement's Committee on Jewish Law and Standards on which that chapter is based, http://www.rabbinicalassembly.org/sites/default/files/assets/public/halakhah/teshuvot/19912000/dorff_violence.pdf.

72. For Dorff's essays on this, see the previous note. See also Daniel S. Nevins, "Between Parents and Children," in *The Observant Life: The Wisdom of Conservative Judaism for Contemporary Jews*, ed. Martin S. Cohen (New York: Rabbinical Assembly, 2012), 673–92.

73. B. *Berakhot* 58b. For a detailed description of Jewish responses to disability, see Carl Astor, *Who Has Made People Different.*

74. Applied not only to the deaf but to cursing all unfortunate people: B. *Sanhedrin* 86a. Applied not only to putting a stumbling block before the blind but to giving false advice: *Sifra* on Leviticus 19:14. Applied to tempting people to violate the law: B. *Pesahim* 22b; B. *Mo'ed Katan* 17a; B. *Bava Metzi'a* 75b.

75. M. *Ohalot* 7:6.

76. B. *Yevamot* 69b.

77. B. Yevamot 78a; B. *Sanhedrin* 80b; B. *Hullin* 58a.

78. Rabbis Ben Zion Bokser and Kassel Abelson, "A Statement on the Permissibility of Abortion" (1983), http://www.rabbinicalassembly.org/sites/default/files/public/halakhah/teshuvot/20012004/07.pdf. For a related set of considerations in the different setting of preimplantation genetic diagnosis (PGD), see Rabbi Mark Papovsky, "Choosing Our Children's Genes: The Use of Preimplantation Genetic Diagnosis" (2008), http://www.rabbinicalassembly.org/sites/default/files/public/halakhah/teshuvot/20052010/Popovsky_FINAL_preimplantation.pdf, in which he permits PGD only when the disease being tested for is either lethal or severely debilitating and there is no cure.

79. United States Conference of Catholic Bishops [USCCB], *United States Catechism for Adults* (Washington, DC: USCCB, 2008), 392–93.

80. Allen J. Wilcox et al., "Incidence of Early Loss Pregnancy," *New England Journal of Medicine* 319 (1988): 189–94. See also http://miscarriage.about.com/od/riskfactors/a/miscarriage-statistics.htm?utm_term=miscarriage%20statistics&utm_content=p1-main-1-title&utm_medium=sem&utm_source=msn_s&utm_campaign=adid-ca20ee5f-efb9-49dd-ae8d-de9f47737e3c-0-ab_msb_ocode-28795&ad=semD&an=msn_s&am=broad&q=miscarriage%20statistics&o=28795&qsrc=999&l=sem&askid=ca20ee5f-efb9-49dd-ae8d-de9f47737e3c-0-ab_msb.

81. For a description of Judaism's approach to sex, see Dorff, *Love Your Neighbor and Yourself*, chap. 3 ("'This Is My Beloved, This Is My Friend': Sex and the Family"), originally published as a pamphlet that is now out of print: Dorff, "This Is My Beloved, This Is My Friend": A Rabbinic Letter on Human Intimacy (New York: Rabbinical Assembly, 1996).

82. Shakespeare, *Merchant of Venice*, 3.1.51–59: Shylock says, "I am a Jew. Hath not a Jew eyes? Hath not a Jew hands, organs, dimensions, senses, affections, passions; fed with the same food, hurt with the same weapons, subject to the same diseases, heal'd by the same means, warm'd and cool'd by the same winter and summer, as a Christian is? If you prick us, do we not bleed? If you tickle us, do we not laugh? If you poison us, do we not die? And if you wrong us, do we not revenge? If we are like you in the rest, we will resemble you in that."

83. This is quite literally the case in the Talmud's discussion of *arakhin* or the "market value" of humans in the slave market, which was used to determine the value of a pledge to the Temple, occupying a full tractate of the Mishnah, following the lead of Leviticus 27. This patriarchal view is even more prominently displayed, if only because it is part of the daily liturgy and therefore more well known, in the blessings in the early morning liturgy that thank God for "not making me a Gentile . . . for not making me a slave . . . and for not making me a woman," for Gentiles are, according to Jewish law, obligated for only the seven laws that God gave, according to the Talmud, to non-Jews; Jewish slaves are exempted from the 248 positive commandments because their status as slaves presumably means that they cannot perform them; and women are exempted from about 20 of the 613 commandments, but free males are subject to all of them. To change the ethnocentrism and sexism involved in these blessings, especially as most people would understand them absent this rubric of increasing obligation to God's command-

ments, Conservative Jewish liturgy since 1946 has transformed them to thanking God for "making me in God's image . . . for making me a Jew . . . and for making me free"; see *Sabbath and Festival Prayerbook* (New York: Rabbinical Assembly of America and United Synagogue of America, 1946), x and 45.

84. Dorff, Nevins, and Reisner, "Homosexuality, Human Dignity and Halakhah," https://www.rabbinicalassembly.org/sites/default/files/assets/public/halakhah/teshuvot/20052010/dorff_nevins_reisner_dignity.pdf (2006). See also the appendix to this rabbinic ruling, approved in 2012, "Rituals and Documents of Marriage and Divorce for Same-Sex Couples," https://www.rabbinicalassembly.org/sites/default/files/assets/public/halakhah/teshuvot/2011-2020/same-sex-marriage-and-divorce-appendix.pdf.

85. So, for example, Elliot N. Dorff, *Matters of Life and Death: A Jewish Approach to Modern Medical Ethics* (Philadelphia: Jewish Publication Society, 1998), chaps. 7–9, on end-of-life medical issues; Elliot N. Dorff and Laura Geller, "When Alzheimer's Turns a Spouse into a Stranger: Jewish Perspectives on Loving and Letting Go," in *The Sacred Encounter: Jewish Perspectives on Sexuality*, ed. Lisa J. Grushcow (New York: CCAR Press, 2014), 549–64; Daniel Nevins, "The Participation of Jews Who Are Blind in the Torah Service," in *Jewish Perspectives on Theology and the Human Experience of Disability*, ed. William Gaventa and Judith Abrams (Binghamton, NY: Haworth Pastoral Press, 2006); Daniel Nevins, "Between Parents and Children," in Cohen, ed., *The Observant Life*, 673–92.

86. Dorff and Nevins have contributed input, approving votes, and, in the first two examples, concurring opinions to each of the following rabbinic rulings approved by the Conservative Movement's Committee on Jewish Law and Standards: Pamela Barmash, "The Status of the Heresh [Deaf Person] and Sign Language," https://www.rabbinicalassembly.org/sites/default/files/assets/public/halakhah/teshuvot/2011-2020/Status%20of%20the%20Heresh6.2011.pdf; Barmash, "Women and Mitzvot," https://www.rabbinicalassembly.org/sites/default/files/assets/public/halakhah/teshuvot/2011-2020/womenandhiyyuvfinal.pdf; and Leonard Sharzer, "Transgender Jews and Halakhah," https://www.rabbinicalassembly.org/sites/default/files/public/halakhah/teshuvot/2011-2020/transgender-halakhah.pdf.

87. Elliot N. Dorff and Laurie Zoloth, eds., *Jews and Genes: The Genetic Future in Contemporary Jewish Thought* (Philadelphia: Jewish Publication Society, 2015).

88. Daniel Nevins, "Halakhic Perspectives on Genetically Modified Organisms," http://www.rabbinicalassembly.org/sites/default/files/public/halakhah/teshuvot/2011-2020/nevins-gmos.pdf.

89. See Beth C. Truesdale and Christopher Jencks, "The Health Effects of Income Inequality: Averages and Disparities," *Annual Review of Public Health* 37 (March 2016): 413–30.

90. We have adapted this translation from the *JPS Tanakh* (1985), shifting from the singular "man" to the plural and gender-neutral "humans" and such since that is clearly the verse's intention.

five

DIGNITY

A Hindu Perspective

Christopher Key Chapple

The topic of dignity in Hindu traditions will be considered from a variety of perspectives in this chapter, beginning with theological and sociological analysis from classical texts. On the one hand, dignity within Hinduism derives from a sense of intimacy with the transcendent self, referred to in the sacred literature as the *ātman*. In the Upaniṣads, this self is identical with the Brahman, as indicated in the phrases *So'ham* (I am that) and *Tat Tvam Asi* (Thou art that).[1] On the other hand, external markers indicate clearly actions that will earn one a status in society that commands dignity and respect. The term for this defining social code is *dharma*, a sense of how, why, and when to perform actions in order to maintain the world order.[2] A sense of this innate sense of propriety will be conveyed through two early narratives: the story of a young man in search of his true identity, and the fable of an adopted daughter whose devoted parents ensure her well-being. Both these stories emphasize discovering one's place within a complex world.

Next I will explore the inversion of hierarchies for the sake of the greater good from a Gandhian perspective. Gandhi, an original anticolonialist and among the first postcolonialists in Asia, challenged the notion that European culture and civilization improved the lot of the masses. He came to reject many aspects of what we today call "development" as inherently oppressive to the human spirit. He suggested that greater meaning and dignity can be found in not acquiescing to the notion that fast transportation, the manufacture and distribution of medicines, and abstract learning enhance the human condition. In his theory of village economy, the less complicated one's life, the greater the degree of happiness.

Then I will explore ways in which dignity may be defined in contemporary, post-Gandhian India. Vinoba Bhave (1895–1982) implemented a land-distribution program known as *Bhū Dān* (gift of land) that broke apart big estates and gave millions of people the means to be self-supporting. India played an important role in drafting the UN's Universal Declaration on Human Rights (UDHR), particularly through the advocacy of Hansa Mehta on behalf of women. Drawing from the tradition of yoga psychology and ethics, tools for the uplift of the self will be explored in the context of postcolonial India. The work of several contemporary activists, writers, and scholars will be explored, including B. R. Ambedkar, who helped craft the Constitution of India to guarantee human rights for all people, especially the former untouchables; Swami Agnivesh, who continues to engage grassroots activism for the marginalized; Anutosh Varshney, who has documented effective avoidance of violence; Pramila Jayapal, whose account of village life in India shows growing vitality within the burgeoning middle class; and Suketu Mehta, whose real-life accounts of life in Mumbai demonstrate human tenacity and resilience despite all odds.

I end the chapter with some reflections on how human dignity in India derives from an inner core wherein the certainty of one's identity and place within the world leads to a higher sense of connectivity with one's immediate group and the larger social order.

HUMAN PERSON AS A DIVINE AND SOCIAL BEING

The Hindu view of the human person stands in marked contrast to that found in the Judeo-Christian and Islamic traditions. The early Upaniṣads (ca. 800 BCE) teach that the inner self (*ātman*) connects with universal presence, or Brahman, that pervades all reality. Men and women, through their participation in "offerings and sacrifices, become the world of the gods."[3] Human reality finds intimacy with the divine.

Hindu social traditions, as articulated in Sanskrit legal literature dating from 600 BCE, posit four essential goals to be achieved in order for the human being to abide in a state of dignity: material sufficiency (*artha*), pleasure (*kāma*), community participation (*dharma*), and a sense of spiritual purpose and accomplishment (*mokṣa*). These four were to be achieved according to one's social location. The Vedas (ca. 1500 BCE) describe a social order homologous to the human body. Farmers and laborers (*Śūdras*) work the soil and are the foundational feet of social order. Those who transport and buy and sell the food and other goods produced by the Śūdras make up the merchant class (*Vaiśyas*), correlated to the legs. Protection through government falls to the warriors (*Kṣatriyas*), the strong arms of landowners and kings. At the top of the social structure one finds the priests, physicians, and lawyers, the Brahmins who have mastered, through extensive oral training, the Sanskrit texts that empower them to perform ritual and also dispense medicine and justice. Paramount to this system is the notion of dharma, the idea that a life purpose has been allotted to each individual and that each group can find meaning through the accomplishment of that dharma. Dharma, in a sense, provides dignity within work, and work helps to protect and restore the vulnerable.

The hierarchical nature of Hindu social structures cannot be denied. Georges Dumézil, the French cultural historian, has noted that similar stratification can be found throughout the Indo-European world, which includes speakers of Slavic, Romance, and Germanic languages.[4] Shared root words and early cultural practices can be found throughout northern India and Persia, Russia, Eastern and Western Europe, and the British Isles. Sanskrit and Avesthan, older cousins of classical Greek and Latin, through their speculative literatures, offer hierarchical templates for defining the human person that continue to inform social organization in the modern era. By examining the Hindu definitions, attitudes, and approaches to human dignity one can explore archaic structures that undergird much of what may be identified as the "Western world," in contrast to the very different articulations found in Chinese and other cultural spheres. Taoism and Confucian traditions, for instance, place great emphasis on the cultivation of harmony, and traditional African philosophical traditions value Ubuntu, defined as interpersonal respect.

In considering the four goals of human life, the Dharmaśāstra literature assigned specific roles to the four groups described above. Although early texts such as the *Chāndogya Upaniṣad* (ca. 800 BCE) suggest social mobility was possible within this system (see particularly the story of Satyakama, below), eventually the *varṇa/jāti* system arose, emphasizing endogamy to ensure clear delineations of responsibility and expectations arising from birth. The word *varṇa* applies to the broad categories of workers, merchants, landowners, and literati, while *jāti* describes the hundreds of clans and subclans that proliferated over the course of more than two millennia. For instance, before entering the sanctum sanctorum of any Hindu temple, a Brahmin must identify his *Gotra*, the name of the Vedic sage said to be the original progenitor of his lineage.

During the colonial era of European expansion and imperialism, the Portuguese were the first to describe this complex social system, employing the term *casta*, which in French and English was simplified to the word "caste." Early chroniclers and missionaries during the colonial period described social practices that kept each group separate and distinct, including refusal to share food or to even touch a person of another group. Marriage would be arranged within one's own group. Two stories describe the complexity of this emergent system of social organization. The story of Satyakama Jabala underscores the continuity of the human with the forces of nature and subverts the standard caste narrative. The story of the Ṛṣi and the mouse similarly shows human embeddedness in nature yet also reinforces the endogamous narrative. Both extend one's sense of dignity beyond the exclusively human realm to include animals as important agents.

THE EDUCATION OF SATYAKAMA JABALA

During the early period when India was lightly settled, cowherds were sent out into the forests and meadows to tend to flocks in distant quarters.[5] One story of a young drover named Satyakama reveals that a time of aloneness for him in the wild became a time of great discovery. This young man learns about his personhood in relationship to his birth origin and hence caste identity and about the operations of the self in relationship with the world. He learns these lessons only partially from a human teacher. Profound truths are communicated by the elements of nature and by animals. The story of Satyakama Jabala appears in the fourth book of the *Chāndogya*, one of the two oldest Upaniṣads, dating perhaps from 2,800 years ago. This story also indicates a journey to self-discovery and lays out the insights to be gained for Satyakama Jabala to become a renowned guru or spiritual teacher.

The story begins with a narrative about caste identity. Society clearly expects an individual to know his or her social location. In this case, the youth later known as Satyakama did not know the identity of his father, and so he asks his mother. She responds that she does not know which man caused her pregnancy, stating that she kept company with many different men, clearly placing herself outside parameters of caste respectability. Because of his guilelessness and sincerity, she gives him the first name Satyakama (desirous of truth) and advises him to use her name, Jabala, as his surname, staking a claim for her and his inherent dignity. He then sets out to find a teacher, prompted to quest more deeply for his identity. The famous teacher Haridrumata Gautama, when approached by Satyakama, asks him his lineage. When Satyakama repeats the story told by his mother, he praises his honesty and agrees to teach him the nature of the self. First, however, Satyakama must render service. Haridrumata Gautama charges the young man with tending a herd of 400 cattle. Rising to the task, Satyakama vows not to return until the herd grows to a thousand heads. He retreats into the landscape for a period of years where he encounters four magical experiences that transform him into a sage, a man of wisdom.

The first encounter begins when a bull from the herd notifies Satyakama, "We have reached a thousand."[6] Then the bull himself proceeds to tell Satyakama the first of four teachings about the nature of Brahman. He alerts Satyakama to the four directions: east, west, south, and north, resulting in an experience of the shining (*prakāśa*). The bull indicates that further teachings would come from the fire. That night, the fire instructs Satyakama about the worlds to be found in the earth, the atmosphere, the sky, and the ocean. After another day of driving the cattle back toward the home of Haridrumata Gautama, a swan comes in the evening and tells him of the fourfold nature of the luminous: fire itself, the sun, the moon, and lightning. A diving bird gives Satyakama the final teaching, a fourfold analysis of that which supports experience: the breath, the eye, the ear, and the mind.

Through these four encounters, Satyakama learns the importance of locating oneself within the four directions. He grasps the vast expanse of the earth below, the surrounding air, the largeness of space, and the unfathomable ocean. He moves on to understand the many manifestations of fire and light and then discovers the inner working of the human being, living in a body through the senses and the mind. When he returns to his teacher, Haridrumata Gautama proclaims to Satyakama, "You shine like a knower of Brahman!"[7] Satyakama became himself a great teacher, sharing wisdom based on his experience in a living universe. Rising from lowly status, he distinguishes himself through his process of inquiry, through his obedience to his teacher, his willingness to listen to the lessons of the natural world, and his learned sense of emplacement within the world. To hold oneself with dignity, in this case, requires intimacy with the outer world of the four directions and the four great zones of earthly being: earth, atmosphere, sky, and ocean. Dignity then requires mastery of fire in its various forms, and of one's own proprioceptive and perceptual faculties, respiratory, sensory, and mental capacities. By fully understanding the outer world and the inner world, freedom can be found, inspiring respect from others.

THE ṚṢI FINDS A SUITOR FOR HIS DAUGHTER

A story from the Hitopadeśa (ca. 600 BCE) conveys a similar sense of search that might be interpreted as "knowing one's place."[8] In a positive sense, the story below lauds finding home within one's own community. In a negative light, it might be seen as a cautionary tale to not outreach one's social expectations. Whereas Satyakama seemingly transcended his birth-given ontological status and gained esteem and fame, in this story the message seems a bit more cautious.

The story of the Ṛṣi and his daughter deals with a different phase of life, that of the dutiful impulse of parenthood. One day a Ṛṣi, a composer of Vedic hymns, is performing his ablutions as usual at the nearby river. A falcon flies overhead. It releases from its talons some freshly caught prey, a mouse that falls into the river, unharmed. The Ṛṣi cups the mouse in his hands and places it safely onto a leaf on the shore and then, having finished his morning bath, begins walking home. Midway he is struck with a feeling of immense responsibility toward the mouse. It dawns on the Ṛṣi that this encounter was somehow auspicious and that his task is not yet complete. He returns to find the mouse still drying off in the sun. He invokes a special mantra and transforms the mouse into an infant girl. The Ṛṣi places her in swaddling and then brings her home to his wife. The couple had been childless; now they devote their doting attention to rearing this little girl.

In traditional India, the task of the parent includes arranging for the marriage of one's children. The Ṛṣi, who clearly had developed a deep love for his daughter, takes this responsibility very seriously, and seeks out the most appropriate match for this miracle given from the heavens. Because of her propitious origins, the Ṛṣi aims very high, choosing as her first suitor Sūrya, the Sun himself. He approaches Sūrya and explains that his daughter came from the sky itself and therefore is his equal. Sūrya demurs and remarks, "Yes, I am powerful, but there is one more powerful than I. The cloud, which seems so soft and gentle, nonetheless occludes my rays and mutes my power. Ṛṣi, approach the cloud; it will make a better match for your girl." The Ṛṣi then approaches a billowy cloud, made of water vapor. The cloud also demurs: "Yes, I can be billowy, light or dark, thin or thick and yes I can overpower the Sun.

But there is one better than I. The wind slices me into pieces, forces me to give up my form into countless drops of rain, destroying my magnificence. Ṛṣi, approach the wind." The Ṛṣi calls out to the wind: "Come here, O great Vāyu. . . . You will meet your match in this daughter of mine, arisen from the sky and the river, beautiful, and ready for marriage." Vāyu, like the others, explains his own limits: "O Ṛṣi, it is true that I can travel the face of the earth and that my power courses through the veins of all that lives. But I also have limits. Whether in the heat of the day or the darkness of night, one great force stops my wanderings: the mountain. The mountain, with its great majesty, is the most powerful and the most worthy suitor for your beloved daughter. Approach the mountain and offer to him the hand of your daughter in marriage." The Ṛṣi travels along the base of the mountain and looks up at its immense grandeur, covered with forests, seeming to boasting with its spectacular granite boulders. Certainly, nothing could be more grand. However, the mountain too speaks from a place of humility. He grumbles, "You flatter me and, yes it would be nice to think that I am above all other beings. But look closely and you will see that one being always gets the best of me, tunneling into hillocks, lacing passages underneath the roots of my forests and around the boulders that adorn me like massive jewels. The smallest of beings can also be the most powerful. Behold the greatest being of all: the mouse!"

The Ṛṣi approaches a hole in the face of the mountain. He calls out to the mice and asks them to send him the best of mice to step up and meet his future spouse. The best of the mice steps forward and proclaims, "Indeed, your daughter is lovely. However, she is too large for my lair. How can she fit inside when it is time to sleep?" With that, the Ṛṣi reverses his original spell. His daughter, for whom he had cared for a period of twelve years, returns to her original form and then joins the best of mice as his wife and queen.

This story evokes dignity and vulnerability in multiple ways. The Ṛṣi and his wife, once childless, find full dignity within their home by rearing their beautiful daughter. He had rescued this most vulnerable being from the clutches of the falcon, extending her protection and love. He sought to find for her the most suitable, dignified spouse, yet sun, clouds, wind, rain, and even the mountain itself reveals its own vulnerability. The mouse, humble yet tenacious, manifests great dignity when it states the obvious to the Ṛṣi. And the Ṛṣi himself becomes humble by acquiescing to the mouse's request that the beloved daughter be reinstated to her original form. This story highlights the emotions of parenthood, wherein one seeks to find dignity for one's children, a process that requires care, attention, and eventually dispassionate love and surrender.

Interestingly, the story focuses almost exclusively on the emotions of the father. Neither wife nor daughter exerts agency. Nonetheless, the deep feelings of the Ṛṣi speak to the supreme values of responsibility and care that well up from within the heart of an individual and go far beyond external mandates. This might also be seen as a call to compassion for all orphans, for all vulnerable beings, heaven-sent or human.

In both these stories, the main characters achieve a state of dignity despite difficult circumstances. Jabala's son rises to a position of great prominence and respect, despite his obscure birth. This in turn elevates his mother. The once-childless Ṛṣi finds completion through his dedication to a vulnerable mouse. At the end of the tale, daughter is happy and parents are happy, having learned their respective places in the world. This opens to the question of dharma: What is one's duty, one's place, one's responsibility in the world? The *Bhagavad Gītā* states: "Better to do one's own dharma even incorrectly than to usurp the dharma of another" (XVIII:47).[9] Henry David Thoreau interpreted this passage to signal "to thine own self be true." In the dignity of work, one finds meaning. We now turn to a strong advocate for human dignity from a Hindu perspective, Mahatma Gandhi (1869–1948).

GANDHI, DIGNITY, AND VULNERABILITY

Gandhi regarded dharma as the key to a reciprocal society.[10] He advocated for dignity through labor and himself cleaned latrines and required all members of his intentional communities (ashrams) in South Africa and India to do the same. From a modern Western sensibility this might seem like a harmless enough task, partly because of the ubiquity of flush toilets and sewerage systems, cleansers, and brushes. However, moving human waste from the collection pit to the field to be used as fertilizer in South Africa or India would only be performed by specialists spurned socially by others. Gandhi, by taking on this fetid task, outraged his contemporaries and even his wife. However, in order to build a just society, he insisted that those with privilege participate in all aspects of human labor.

For Gandhi, education was not a necessary prerequisite for dignity. In his core manifesto, *Hind Swaraj*, or Indian Self-rule, he proclaimed that book learning was not necessary for all people. Gandhi's idea prevailed for many decades; not until the 2000s was universal access to education for children mandated. Nonetheless, India made tremendous progress in the realm of education.

Before independence from British rule in 1947, literacy stood at 25 to 30 percent. By the 1980s it had risen to more than 70 percent. The noted economist and Nobel Prize winner Amartya Sen has proclaimed universal education to be key for ending poverty in India,[11] in direct contradiction to Gandhi's original manifesto. For Gandhi, education would allow one to serve and control the senses. Gandhi stated that it would not be necessary to make education compulsory and that building strong character traits takes priority over book learning. He stated that "we must not make of it a fetish."[12] Gandhi emphasized life skills. It would seem that this practical approach to education would be irrelevant in today's global economy. However, his standards for a good education entailed the cultivation of service and self-control, which are not necessarily included in today's curriculum, though they certainly have their merits. By suggesting that character counts more than the accumulation of facts, Gandhi is looking for a quality of life that defies quantification. Gandhi resists what today is called the neoliberal drive toward consumer economies, preferring to emphasize that human happiness can be found in the building of strong character, not in the accumulation of possessions.

This brings us back to the question of human dignity and a revisiting of the Gandhian project. According to Gandhi, self-respect is of utmost importance. It accords one a sense of dignity and self-worth. He claimed that self-respect can be best achieved through labor. In protest of British manufacturing policy that saw the export of cotton to be milled in English factories, woven into cloth, and then sold on the vast Indian market, enriching the British Empire but pauperizing India, he began a campaign to spin and weave. Casting off the shackles of consumer complicity with style, his homespun garments, known as *khadi*, even today signal rebellion against the forces of market hegemony. For decades, he spent hours each day with his spinning wheel and started an all-India resistance movement that contributed to the downfall of British colonial rule.

Key premises of Indian thought that informed Gandhi's worldview can be summarized as follows. Origins are obscure. We cannot be certain from where we came or at what point of time things began. The Vedas articulate an unformed foundation, a realm of nonexistence (*asat*), a mist from which arise distinct worlds, depending on human desire. Through desire, humans craft their world, creating boundaries and distinctions, separating heaven from earth, light from darkness. In this constructed world, sustained by sacrifice, meditation, and prayer, individuals gather into community, moving from the unformed to the formed. Intention and desire direct communities and individuals to select various options, symbolized by various deities, all seen as provisional tools for attaining a goal, whether worldly or sublime. Dharma sustains those who choose to uphold the world. Followers of dharma aspire to fit into the cosmic flow of life (*ṛta*). Renouncers, particularly the practitioners of yoga in its various forms, strive for an elevated sense of cosmic connection, known as *samādhi*. For both the worldly and the spiritually inclined, precepts set forth ideals for behavior that respect the need for acknowledging the ongoing flux or flow between the unspeakable realm of origin, the *asat*, and the realm of manifest activity. These precepts, observed by Vaiṣṇavas, Śaivas, Jainas, Buddhists, and Sikhs in India, include respect for all forms of life, a mandate to be truthful and honest, and cautions against the dangers of greed and lust. These precepts shape both personal and social ethics. Gandhi championed these central percepts. In his life work, he constantly reminded his followers of the importance of *satyāgraha* (holding to truth), *ahiṃsā* (nonviolence), and *aparigraha* (nonpossession).

Gandhi's core text arguing for independence from the British Empire, *Hind Swaraj*, was published in 1910. In this text he critiques the basic policies of the colonial occupation and calls for a reexamination of some fundamental assumptions regarding the good life. His ideas diverge radically from the development model of recent decades. This model, popular in India since the 1990s, places great value on expanding economies, growing transportation networks, reducing of illiteracy, and reducing morbidity. Though Gandhi's ideas on these topics would most likely have changed given new information, his cautions about their apparent benefits contain some wisdom and an opportunity for introspection and reflection.

For Gandhi, dignity can only be experienced or earned from a place of direct encounter of a transcendent reality, of the sort described in the Vedic term *ṛta* and the yoga meditation term *samādhi*. For Gandhi, the obstacles to human dignity in India were to be found not only with the British but also with any form of injustice toward the downtrodden, whether impoverished low-caste Hindus, women of all faiths, or disadvantaged Muslims.

Gandhi advocated a village economy. This involves the consumption of local foods, and the wearing of clothes spun and woven by each individual. He also encouraged small-scale technologies, which, for instance, involve solar cook stoves, locally generated electricity, and self-transport using bicycles. In the words of Lloyd and Susanne Rudolph, we might now need to heed "Gandhi's postmodern emphasis on human capital, decentralized production, and appropriate technology."[13] The human must be valued for his or her dignity, not as a potential customer or consumer.

Pathways to Dignity in Gandhi's *Hind Swaraj*

Examining *Hind Swaraj*, Gandhi's seminal work, we see that three ideas promote human dignity. The first has to do with its general philosophy of self-effort, indicated in the title "Self-rule" and attested to by the reading list that influenced the Mahatma. The title refers not only to Hind/India as a country but also to the people of India themselves. Gandhi proclaimed that by mastering themselves individually and collectively, Indians would find the will to govern themselves and cast off their colonial oppressors, which in fact transpired thirty-seven years after the publication of *Hind Swaraj*. The second idea entails Gandhi's abiding critique of transportation, and his related call for maintaining a slow-paced life. The third topic is Gandhi's critique of physicians and his general approach to health care.

*Self-Rule (*Swaraj*).* The following passage from the *Yogavāsiṣṭha* explains the importance of self-determination in Gandhian thought:

> There are some who, due to their desire,
> have incapacitated themselves to such an extent
> that they cannot squeeze their fingers together
> sufficiently enough to hold water
> without scattering several drops.
> On the other hand, there are some who,
> by efficacious actions, take on the responsibility
> of seas, mountains, cities, and islands,
> as well as families, for whom even the earth itself
> would not be too much.[14]

The *Yogavāsiṣṭha* was recommended to Gandhi by his Jaina teacher, Raichandbhai, also known as Rajchandra Ravjibhai Mehta (1868–1901).[15] It advocates the cultivation of human will and effort in order to effect change in the world. Gandhi struggled to find strength within India and within the Indian psyche. In the *Yogavāsiṣṭha* he found a philosophy that urges one to take action and that rejects any form of submissiveness. This strength must be directed inward, however, and not against an external enemy. From Rajchandra and his own mother, Gandhi learned and lived an undying commitment to nonviolence. Nonetheless, he advocated inner warfare, heeding the advice of the second chapter of the *Bhagavad Gītā*. According to his personal secretary, Narayan Desai, Gandhi recited the last eighteen verses of the Yoga of Understanding daily, adhering to the ideas encapsulated in verse 64: "With the elimination of desire and hatred, even though moving among the objects of the senses, the one who is controlled by the self through self-restraint attains tranquility."[16] Combining strength, adherence to nonviolence, and self-control, Gandhi set himself and others on a path that changed the course of world history.

Gandhians today continue to espouse the ideals and realities of self-control, moving toward self-sufficiency, dignity, and self-respect. Gandhian ideals prompt one to ask the following questions in regard to human dignity: How much is enough? How much food? How much entertainment? How large a car? How large a house? From a Gandhian perspective, true happiness comes with ingenuity and restraint, not through unbridled consumption. By gaining control of our senses the human community can attain dignity through *swa-raj*, self-rule.

Transportation, Industrialization, and Technology

Thousands of new cars pour onto the roads of India each week, the new mark of middle-class status. The rapidity of change in the developing world staggers the imagination, with innovations in many instances following some basic Gandhian precepts, at least at first glance. For instance, India has engineered and put into production the world's least expensive car, at one-tenth the price of an average American sedan. Cell phone technology has put mobile communication within the reach of nearly all India's population without the need to construct a network of costly telephone lines. The Internet and inexpensive public access to computers has allowed India to leap into a position of leadership in the area of information technology. Perhaps Gandhi would have embraced these changes. However, in 1910, Gandhi warned of the shortfalls and pitfalls of even the railroad. Gandhi suggested that a better use of public funds would have been to improve irrigation systems, allowing local areas to flourish. He suggested that railways facilitate the spread of disease and that "good travels at a snail's pace—it can have little to do with the railways."[17] In his critique of railroads, Gandhi calls into question the very premises of progress and speed. He writes: "Honest physicians will tell you that, where means of artificial locomotion have increased, the health of the people has suffered. . . . I cannot recall a single good point in connection with machinery."[18] Although we hesitate to think in categories of either/or and recognize that both irrigation and transportation result in positive outcomes, daily life through improved access to water would have been a good use of imperial resources. Today, alongside the railways, both air travel and automotive transport have increased exponentially, resulting in a faster pace of life, and, to an extent, an increase in disease. The AIDS problem has been exacerbated in India by truckers, patrons of sex workers, bringing the disease home to remote villages.

Gandhi states, "Machinery is like a snake-hole which may contain from one to a hundred snakes . . . where means of artificial locomotion have increased, the health of the people has suffered. . . . Nature has not provided any way whereby we may reach a desired goal all of a sudden."[19] He advocates the slow-paced life of the village, wherein all needed goods and services are provided locally. The simplicity advocated by Gandhi would entail little or no need for transportation of goods or persons. By adhering to a village economy, and by remaining content within one's community, basic human needs could be fulfilled.

Today, great virtue is seen in scaling back our modes of transportation. Emphasis is being placed on mass transit options and ride sharing. In quiet ways, Gandhian principles are being reasserted by individuals who compost, grow their own vegetables, and minimize their own transport and oil consumption needs by living close to work, who drive rather than fly when possible, purchase low-emission vehicles, and preferably walk or cycle frequently. Though Gandhi could not have anticipated the massive looming problem of global warming, he certainly saw the ills that accompany complexity. His call for simplicity and abstinence from reliance on machinery remains relevant.

As the planetary population continues to urbanize, a host of difficulties arise that result in a loss of human dignity: reliance on agribusiness, alienation from the rhythms of nature, and a loss of a sense of community. In the developing world, which now provides the bulk of manufactured goods, we see the increase of what Gandhi lamented in Europe a century ago, when he wrote, "Machinery has begun to desolate Europe. Ruination is now knocking at the English gates. Machinery is the chief symbol of modern civilization: it represents great sin."[20] With great prescience, Gandhi wrote, "And those who have amassed great wealth out of factories are not likely to be better than other rich men. It would be folly to assume that an Indian Rockefeller would be better than the American Rockefeller."[21] Gandhi lamented, "The workers in the mills of Bombay have become slaves."[22]

Health Care and Human Dignity

For Gandhi, growing up in an era before antibiotics and in the proximity of the Jaina community, death was not a mystery nor were extraordinary measures employed to avoid death. In fact, the Jaina tradition of fasting unto death (*sallekhanā/santhara*), a practice still enacted by monastic and lay Jainas worldwide today, undoubtedly informed his worldview. Hence, death with dignity would be an essential part of a Gandhian approach. He considered the manner of death far more important than the avoidance of death, advocating a spiritual approach. He considered medicine to be a "parasitical profession"[23] and wrote that "doctors have nearly unhinged us."[24] His attitude toward medicine was one of high suspicion, and he regarded reliance on physicians as feeding human weakness:

> How do these diseases arise? Surely by our negligence and indulgence. I over-eat. I have indigestion, I go to a doctor, he gives me medicine, I am cured, I over-eat again, and I take his pills again. Had I not taken the pills in the first instance, I would have suffered the punishment deserved by me, and I would not have over-eaten again. The doctor intervened and helped me to indulge myself. My body thereby certainly felt more at ease, but my mind became weakened. A continuance of a course of medicine must, therefore, result in loss of control over the mind. . . . Had the doctor not intervened, nature would have done its work, and I would have acquired mastery over myself, would have been freed from vice, and would have become happy.[25]

Though this approach seems to arrogate all illness to the mind without taking into account truly debilitating conditions beyond human control, Gandhi nonetheless offers insight and wisdom. The rise of diabetes worldwide has been caused in part by the increase of caloric intake. Many diseases, including those related to alcoholism and smoking, arise because of human behavior.

Gandhi, as a vegetarian, considered the life of animals to be sacred and advocated for the protection of animals. He was a vocal antivivisectionist. He wrote:

> European doctors are the worst of all. For the sake of a mistaken care of the human body, they kill annually thousands of animals. They practise vivisection. No religion sanctifies this. All say that it is not necessary to take so many lives for the sake of our bodies. These doctors violate our religious

> instinct. Most of their medical preparations contain either animal fat or spirituous liquors; both of these are tabooed by Hindus and Mahomedans. . . . The fact remains that the doctors induce us to indulge, and the result is that we have become deprived of self-control and have become effeminate. . . . To study European medicine is to deepen our slavery.[26]

Anticipating the rapaciousness of pharmaceutical companies, he also observed, "Doctors make a show of their knowledge, and charge exorbitant fees. Their preparations, which are intrinsically worth a few pennies, cost shillings. The populace in its credulity and in the hope of ridding itself of some disease, allows itself to be cheated."[27] As one reflects on the disproportionate compensation given to physicians, particularly in the United States, and the extreme expense of both medicine and insurance, Gandhi's homespun remarks continue to be poignant.

In his nineteen-point call for action, he proclaimed that a doctor, in order to exert the strength needed for Swaraj, "will give up medicine, and understand that, rather than mending bodies, he should mend souls."[28] He called all physicians to abjure vivisection:

> It is better that bodies remain diseased rather than that they are cured through the instrumentality of the diabolical vivisection that is practised in European schools of medicine. In a radical acceptance of the inevitable, he considered it more noble for a patient to succumb rather than subject himself or herself to drugs: if any patients come to him, [the doctor] will tell them the cause of their diseases, and will advise them to remove the cause rather than pamper them by giving useless drugs; he will understand that, if by not taking drugs, perchance the patient dies, the world will not come to grief, and that he will have been really merciful to him.[29]

Although this advice would often be imprudent today given the advances of modern medicine, the adoption of a more noninterventionist approach would help reduce the modern doctor's propensity for ordering expensive tests and prescribing too many medications. This of course would need to be complemented by a less litigious attitude in the health-care field.

Mahatma Gandhi offered a blueprint for ending colonial rule both politically and psychically. He offered a scathing critique of Western definitions of personhood and dignity, challenging the wisdom of the Euro-American traditions of law, medicine, and education.

Gandhi advocated simple living. He held deep suspicions about the benefits of European civilization, including its insistence on mechanized transport and its fetish for medicines of dubious efficacy. The wisdom he shared regarding self-reliance remains relevant for the contemporary postmodern world, with modifications. Our economy has become globalized and knowledge-based. It is no longer manipulated only by governments, but now also by corporations. If Gandhi were alive today, he no doubt would stand in awe of cell phones, the Internet, and so many other accoutrements of daily life. He would be relieved at the number of nations that have cast off the shackles of colonialism, but he would remain concerned about the host of social justice issues that are still unresolved, not only in India, but in China, the nations of Africa, and elsewhere. He would, however, still bear witness, as do modern Gandhians, against the power of corporations, the unbridled greed of business, and the frivolous embrace of materialist consumerism that now pervades the globe.

POSTCOLONIAL GANDHIANS

The legacy of postcolonial Gandhians has been mixed. All Gandhians strive to enhance human dignity. Gandhi worked tirelessly to overcome the stigma associated with being born in a "low" Jati. The drafter of the Constitution of India, B. R. Ambedkar (1891–1956), was the first low-caste person from India to receive a PhD in the United States, from Columbia University. The Constitution of India includes numerous provisions to overcome discrimination against Scheduled Tribes and Scheduled Castes. In order to ensure social mobility, university admission and government employment have been guaranteed for disadvantaged groups. In urban areas in particular, one's family of origin plays a lesser role in one's social standing, though pressure to marry "in-group" remains and many rural areas still practice caste discrimination. This practice is not restricted to Hindu communities but can also be found among Muslims and Christians.

Following Gandhi, Vinoba Bhave (1895–1982) implemented a land-distribution program known as *Bhū Dān* (gift of land) that broke apart big estates. He and his followers walked the length and breadth of India, educating landowners that if they relinquished one-sixth of their holdings, every Indian family could take title to enough to become financially self-sufficient. They met with great success. Most farms in India are little more than an acre. Nearly half of India's population today works the land. Eventually, a constitutional amendment was passed mandating that no single person may own more than sixteen acres. This renders U.S.-style agribusiness untenable, yet many challenges remain, such as the marketing to farmers of seed, chemical fertilizers, herbicides, and pesticides by multinational companies, a practice severely criticized by Vandana Shiva and others.

Since the time of Gandhi, India has experienced many changes and evolutions. Prime Minister Jawaharlal Nehru (1889–1964) instituted a form of Soviet-friendly socialism that favored industrialization within India and withdrawal from the world economy that under the British had been so disadvantageous. No international company was allowed majority ownership in India and, despite the gains in education mentioned above, and the successful food security measures implemented by Prime Minister Indira Gandhi (1917–84), India remained impoverished. As recently as the 1980s, the trunk highways between major cities could not accommodate two lanes of traffic. When Rajiv Gandhi (1944–91), Nehru's grandson, became prime minister, a liberalization of policies took place that modernized the economy. Foreign investment was allowed, infrastructure projects began, and India entered the world economy. This shift to a market consumerist model resulted in migrations to cities and ownership of private automobiles and housing units. On the one hand, this change brought about a sense of autonomy that could bolster a sense of individual dignity. On the other hand, it has contributed to the sense of the primacy of individual needs and desires, diminishing reliance on family and clan identity. Studies of the emerging middle class in India have revealed an increase in materialism—and in stress.[30]

DIGNITY AND HUMAN RIGHTS ON THE WORLD STAGE

The UDHR, adopted in 1948, endures as a global document of conscience. It advanced a process of decolonization that began with Gandhi and continued with the liberation of numerous countries from their colonial rulers in the subsequent decades. The UDHR provided an idealistic, optimistic tone for the rebuilding of the world order following World War II. It crafted a language for assessing the human person that emphasized rights and responsibilities that accord to men and women based on their innate dignity.

The drafters of the UDHR were quite thorough in their attempt to be inclusive of the world's philosophical perspectives. Additionally, discussions of gender played an important role in the drafting of the document, both in terms of the ideas contained in the document and the leadership of the commission. Eleanor Roosevelt (1886–1962) served as the chair of the Human Rights Commission of the UN from its inception in 1947 until 1951. Though he had passed away, Franklin Roosevelt cast a long shadow on the proceedings, particularly as his wife reminded the group from time to time of his advocacy of "four freedoms": freedom of speech, of belief, freedom from fear, and from want.[31] The UDHR created a benchmark for public policy in the latter half of the twentieth century, and, it can be argued, helped prevent greater strife through the difficult period of the Cold War.

Work on the UDHR began within months of the end of World War II. Two Asian members of the committee are of particular note for the discussion of dignity and assertion of the rights of women. P. C. Chang insisted on including the Chinese Confucian *Ren*, which he translated as "two-man mindedness." The sense of this delicate concept was eventually rendered as the word "dignity,"[32] and from the nuanced language of the document, a sense of the original intent can be gleaned from its emphasis on humane, person-to-person thinking. Hansa Mehta, an independence activist and legislator from newly created free India, served on the drafting committee and played a significant role in ensuring a special place for women in the document. Mehta was particularly effective in broadening the language of the document so as to steer away from male universals. At her insistence, and over the objections of Eleanor Roosevelt, the preamble reads "inherent dignity . . . of all members of the human family" rather than "mankind," and the first article states that "all human beings are born free and equal in dignity and rights."[33] As Mary Ann Glendon has noted, Mehta "made sure the Declaration spoke with power and clarity about equal rights for women well before they were recognized in most legal systems."[34] Mehta had been imprisoned by the British during the anticolonial struggle and was "battling back home against purdah, child marriage, polygamy, unequal inheritance law, and bans against marriages among different castes."[35] She warned that the language of "all men" would explicitly ban women, while Roosevelt insisted that the term would include women. Eventually, Roosevelt yielded.

The UDHR, in a sense, created a global context for women's leadership, particularly in Asia. Hansa Mehta, sensitive to the suffering caused by misogyny in the world, emphatically insisted that gender be put on the table as a global issue to be recognized, confronted, and negotiated. Recognition of the dignity of women in South Asia saw the rise of the world's first female prime ministers, in India, Sri Lanka, Pakistan, and Bangladesh.

The first statement of the preamble to the UDHR emphasizes the importance of dignity: "Whereas recognition of the inherent dignity and of the equal and inalienable rights of all members of the human family is the foundation of freedom, justice and peace in the world."[36] It then continues in the first five articles to emphasize the specific ways in which dignity must be valued:

> Article 1. All human beings are born free and equal in dignity and rights. They are endowed with reason and conscience and should act towards one another in a spirit of brotherhood.
>
> Article 2. Everyone is entitled to all the rights and freedoms set forth in this Declaration, without distinction of any kind, such as race, colour, sex, language, religion, political or other opinion, national or social origin, property, birth or other status. Furthermore, no distinction shall be made on the basis of the political, jurisdictional or international status of the country or territory to which a person belongs, whether it be independent, trust, non-self-governing or under any other limitation of sovereignty.
>
> Article 3. Everyone has the right to life, liberty and security of person.
>
> Article 4. No one shall be held in slavery or servitude; slavery and the slave trade shall be prohibited in all their forms.
>
> Article 5. No one shall be subjected to torture or to cruel, inhuman or degrading treatment or punishment.[37]

The discourse of dignity provided a foundation for emphasizing humane actions in the postwar, Cold War era. However, with the rise of neoliberalism and the triumph of consumer capitalism worldwide, dignity has become somewhat eclipsed by a crass materialism that came into vogue in the 1980s and 1990s. Globalization of the world economy has brought a new set of challenges that may best be met with renewed conversations about meaning, justice, and recovery of human dignity.

PSYCHIC OBSTACLES TO DIGNITY IN VOW-BASED TRADITIONS OF ASIA

Returning to our discussion of Hindu traditions, an analysis of the human person as found in the Upaniṣads and complexified in later philosophies might provide some methods for a new engagement of human dignity. The assessment of the human condition in the traditions of India revolves around the philosophy of *karma*. Karma comes in two large categorical groupings: *puṇya* and *pāpa*. *Puṇya* means "auspicious," "pure," or "good." *Pāpa* means the reverse: "inauspicious," "impure," or "evil." For Hinduism and the related traditions of Buddhism, Jainism, and Sikhism, a key term specifies the cause of *pāpa* karma: *kleśa*, or "affliction," a negative quality arising from inauspicious acts that shapes a person's disposition.

It is important to note the underlying worldview and presuppositions of Hindu traditions: the microcosm reflects the macrocosm, and the macrocosm can be found in the microcosm. The Vedic hymn in praise of the primal person (*puruṣa*) makes this correlation clear: the lower realms of the body are associated with heavier elements of earth and water, encapsulated in the word *Bhū*; the middle realms of the body are associated with heat and air (*Bhuva*); the uppermost region of the body extends into and reflects space (*Sva*). From the *Yoga Sūtra*'s third chapter, and from various Upaniṣads, we also find the supposition that by understanding the inner workings of the body, one comes to understand the world at large. Therefore, inner processes become inseparable from outer manifestations. The latent results in the patent, the mark in the marker and the marked. The subtle body (*sūkṣma śarīra*) determines the gross body (*sthūla śarīra*). Past actions known variously as impressions (*saṃskāras*) and habit patterns (*vāsana*) determine the nature of the world through the prism of each individual experience. What one finds within expresses itself throughout. The governing engine in the world-creating process, according to the Indian traditions of Yoga, Sāṃkhya, and the *Bhagavad Gītā*, is the *Buddhi*, the repository for all past impressions. These latencies, according to Patañjali, can be categorized into five afflicted modalities, the *kleśas* that vitiate action and block goodness and human dignity.

The first *kleśa*, *avidyā* (lack of wisdom), is said to be the origin point of the other four. Patañjali explains this flaw as follows: thinking that evanescent things last forever, mistaking the impure to be the pure, expecting happiness in domains that eventually deliver pain, and assuming that one can find the true self in the realm of definition, attribution, and appropriation. One example of a resulting loss of dignity might be found in compulsive overeating or overconsumption of any resource. One might blunder into thinking that because this food tastes good, more of it must be better, or, because this car is fast and large, it must be a better car. Ignorance of this sort can lead to obesity and to overreliance on fossil fuels. The most delicious of desserts, in the long run, can be deadly, and the most impressive of cars can also be the most destructive. Likewise, the acquisition of an elaborate wardrobe or the collection of multiple degrees might serve as a mask or persona for the self, but all such identifications eventually fall short of providing lasting or significant meaning or otherwise contributing to human dignity.

The second *kleśa* is *asmitā* (egotism). By making oneself the measure of all things, one runs the great risk of a harmful narcissism. This can operate on both the personal level and in the greater society. If one is only concerned about one's own creature comforts, then others may be neglected or ignored. A parent who disregards the needs of a child creates a world of grief. The society that thinks itself the best and the most important ruptures connections with other peoples, other nations. A society stuck in utter self-concern and isolationism would be blind to human dignity. By enabling rampant pollution for the sake of ego-driven creature comfort, corporations and governments surrender any interest in the common good in favor of profits.

The third *kleśa* is *rāga* (overwhelming, insatiable attraction and attachment). The allurement of owning things, and thereby gaining identity and recognition and even respect, has long been an essential aspect of the human condition. Marco Polo, reporting on the many luxuries to be found in Asia, created a market for Indian spices and Chinese silks. These and other comforts have driven the world economy for centuries. Since the seafaring times of the age of exploration, newer, faster, and increasingly more polluting transport modalities have been invented to speed the pace of trade. First, steam engines on boats, then on trains, then the internal combustion engine in automobiles and eventually airplanes have all allowed the desire for goods to escalate, to the point where most of the people of the developed world have taken up patterns of compulsive appropriation of goods, many of which go unused and which ultimately tend to detract from rather than enhance human dignity. The hording of material goods to achieve and display status does not result in happiness.

The fourth fettering category of karma is *dveṣa* (the state of overwhelming aversion and negativity). One continually acquires (through attraction) in order to find happiness, but in *dveṣa*, one finds fault with all things. Rather than attempting to be part of a solution, aversion prevents one from taking any action at all or, what is even worse, becoming an impediment to any possible solution. Politicians are famous for fanning the flags of animosity, as seen in the standoff between opposing parties whose sole purpose seems to be the ability to tear down the opposition. Some individuals and organizations hate the very idea of regarding others as worthy of respect and dignity and with harsh demagoguery revile groups they consider to be "outsiders." All empathy or caring disappears.

The fifth category of *kleśa* karma, *abhiniveśa* (returning to engage in activity), offers some hope for human dignity. This aspect of karma is said to remain even among wise, spiritually liberated individuals. It speaks to the undying human propensity to keep busy, active, and productive. This particular aspect of karmic residue speaks like an interior voice, urging even the most advanced meditator and sage to reenter the world, but from an enlightened state. Such individuals have conquered both inner and outer negativity and impurity. They spontaneously engage the world in accord with a higher moral purpose, holding their own dignity and upholding the dignity of others. Like the Buddhist Bodhisattva, such a person works toward the alleviation of the suffering of all beings.

Overconsumption, whether of energy sources, food, material goods, and the rest, proceeds from the abiding presence of unresolved desires within the human psyche. According to Indian philosophy, one can overcome these temptations through the application of will and adherence to the vows extolled by Mahatma Gandhi. Freedom and dignity can be found through overcoming *kleśa* karma, undoing the drives that propel the individual to remain enmeshed in negativities.

THE RELATIONAL HUMAN: CONFLICT AND THE COLLECTIVE

The emphasis on individual self-improvement leading to dignity can only be understood in the context of Indian family structures and the overall concern for societal propriety. Traditional Indic values embrace a relational view of the self. The human person does not arrive in this world alone but enters immediately into a web of relationships. The child relies utterly on the parents, and only after a period of years does the child of whatever culture attain a degree of autonomy. People in India, regardless of caste or creed, celebrate and reinforce the interrelationships among family members in a variety of ways. These include special rituals in naming a child and honoring the close friendship bond between brothers and sisters in a bracelet exchange ceremony of protection (*rakhi*). Additionally, the majority of marriages in India even today are arranged by the family, and most families flourish in extended family communal living arrangements. These rituals confirm the family unit as the central source for one's identity in India.

The question of human dignity in light of Hindu principles and practices can prompt multiple and often contradictory analyses. In the 1970s, anthropologists working in India developed a series of terms to account for the theory of the human person in Indian culture. Ronald Inden's study of marriage and rank in Bengal and McKim Marriot's studies of Hindu village life have suggested that the caste system and social relationships in India do not correspond to the idea of class in the West, but they rather are grounded in a type of "monism" wherein all persons share in a common, unifying force, regardless of status. Following Dumont's analysis that the concept of the 'individual' does not apply to traditional South Asian social structures,[38] Marriot and Inden have offered a theory of the person as "dividual": "Persons are 'dividuals' or unique composites of diverse subtle and gross substances derived ultimately from one source; and they are also divisible into separate particles that may be shared or exchanged with others."[39] Thus, in this interpretation, every person has both a universal and subindividual dimension. On the one hand, all persons are derived from "a single, all powerful, perfect, undifferentiated substance or principle,"[40] which is referred to elsewhere by Marriot as indicative of an underlying "monism."[41] On the other hand, persons are continually exchanging "pieces" of themselves with one another, "channeling and transforming heterogeneous ever-flowing, changing substances."[42] The use of the term "monism" indicates the acceptance of a philosophical absolute; the idea of transaction seems to correspond to the mundane or relative level of existence.

In this interpretation, society is maintained by mutual support, each group or unit an integral part of the whole:

> Each caste's inborn code enjoins it to maintain its substance and morality, its particular occupation and its correct exchanges with other castes. Indian thought does not separate "nature" and "morality" or "law," so that castes are, in Western terms, at once "natural" and "moral" units of society. These units make up a single order, one that is profoundly particularized.[43]

> The act of worship was, then, at both the caste and clan level, the act of dharma par excellence, a concise statement or symbol of the ordered unity of the total community. By worshipping a higher more divine genus, by wealth and food in accord with its capacity to give, a genus subordinated its own gain (*artha*) and enjoyment (*kāma*) to the higher goal of nourishing and upholding the embodied Veda, the primary source of community well-being

> and prosperity, and transformed its own embodied rank into the share of well-being, fame, and respect it rightly deserved.[44]

Through ritual, the underlying unity of Hindu social structure is revealed.

In brief, the interpretation of Marriot and Inden is that indigenous Hindu sociology is not one of conflict and domination, but rather a system of mutual support through ritual transaction: all castes arise from a monistic source, and caste rules are symbolic of that archetypal, monistic structure. Through the interplay of "higher" and "lower," society is maintained in a highly structured fashion, based in the concepts of dharma and *svadharma*, one's own dharma. Both personal and societal fulfillment are found in the performance of dharma.

From the perspective of universal dignity, this could be seen as both inspirational and problematic. On the one hand, this scenario gives dignity to manual labor. The workers hold value as support for the upper echelons of society and provide the nourishment and foundation for all human endeavor. On the other hand, as these roles became prescriptive rather than descriptive with the passing of centuries, this poetic description of specialization of labor became a tool for suppression based on one's heredity. The modern Constitution of India, composed by Ambedkar, a member of an untouchable caste and converted to Buddhism at the end of his life, includes provisions that erode the power of caste and work for a more open, equal-opportunity society.[45] Most recently, Amartya Sen has underscored the need for universal education to lift persons from poverty.[46] The winds of change within India have brought a burgeoning middle class that has begun to claim economic rights and build a lifestyle that benefits from development and progress. However, these benefits need to extend to the lower classes of India, many of whom have remained trapped in conditions of bonded labor with no access to education. Swami Agnivesh (b. 1939) has campaigned tirelessly to draw attention to the nearly 200 million people within India who have little or no hope of gaining an education or sharing in the rapidly developing economy of India.[47] These people, for whom the traditional system of caste and family relationships form no safety net, would be the most important beneficiaries of a Western-style human rights campaign in India.

Today India finds itself caught in a tension between traditional values and an emerging, uniquely Indian form of modernity. Upper- and middle-caste Hindus continue to celebrate the traditional forms of dharma, which combine personal responsibility with civic awareness expressed through social mores and law. This population continues to fulfill its birth-given duties and does so with a sense of purpose and dignity. At the same time, India continues to define its own version of the modern secularist worldview, which, for some, needs to undo all forms of discrimination based on caste or religion. Several persons of low-caste birth have risen to positions in parliament and several have held governorships of India's many states. The vision of Gandhi and Ambedkar to erase all caste distinctions has produced many successes and demonstrated that education and equal opportunity can help empower those whose options have been restricted for generations by the caste system.

Traditional Hindu values give priority to family and social roles, not to the individual; modern secular Gandhian values seek to undo the injustices caused by the caste system. These two views are not necessarily contradictory. Hinduism does not place greatest value on wealth and comfort. It lists wealth (*artha*) as the first of four goals, but considers pleasure (*kāma*), social stability (*dharma*), and spiritual liberation (*mokṣa*) to be successively superior. Ironically, the highest goal is to be achieved by the diminishment of wealth. The greatest saints of Indian culture have been among its poorest citizens. Gandhi's greatest subversion of British colonial rule came through his advocacy for people to back away from the economic juggernaut, to renounce consumption of manufactured British goods. His own great campaigns were often punctuated with fasting, and he urged others to follow his example.

Despite the heroic efforts of people of goodwill and the protections accorded Scheduled Castes and Scheduled Tribes and religious minorities in India, from time to time conflict arises. The partition of India in 1947 resulted in horrendous bloodshed and mass migrations: Hindus to India and Muslims to east and west Pakistan. Mahatma Gandhi was killed by an assassin incensed with his liberal policies. Indira Gandhi was assassinated by her Sikh bodyguards in 1984, her son by Tamil separatists in 1991. The Babri Masjid (mosque) in Ayodhaya was torn down in 1992 by Hindu activists, resulting in riots and counterriots.

Ashutosh Varshney, a professor of political economy at the University of Michigan, dedicated ten years to researching the causes of violence in twentieth-century India, focusing on instances of Hindu–Muslim rioting from 1950 to 1995. To conduct the research, he employed a team of twelve investigators who worked with three pairs of cities, three riot-prone, three riot-free. In his survey of Aligarh and Calicut, Hyderabad and Lucknow, and Ahmedabad and Surat, he discerned and documented a clear pattern:

> When organizations such as trade unions, associations of businessmen, traders, teachers, doctors, lawyers, and at least some caste-based political parties (different from the ones that have an interest in communal polarization) are communally integrated, countervailing forces are created. . . . A synergy emerges between the local wings of the state and the local civic organizations, making it easier to police the emerging situations and prevent it from degenerating into riots and killings. Unlike violent cities when numerous rumors and skirmishes, often strategically planned and spread, are quickly transferred into riots, such relationships of synergy in peaceful cities nip numerous, small clashes, and tensions in the land.[48]

People who come into regular contact with other persons who do not share their ethnicity or religion are less likely to demonstrate prejudice or harbor negative emotions about members of other groups.

Varshney relies on field research and historical analysis to affirm the efficacy of intergroup relations for the maintenance of societal harmony, but Arvind Sharma of McGill University suggests that human dignity in India can derive from traditional Hindu categories. He states that the quest for dignitarian human rights aligns with the Hindu quest for material sustenance (*kāma*); legal aspects can be reflected in political and economic structures (*artha*); the moral mandate of protecting human dignity correlates with the pursuit of law or justice (*dharma*); and that the religious impetus behind dignity and human rights shares a common ground with the Hindu quest for liberation (*mokṣa*). Sharma notes that the Hindu view of rights starts with the cosmos, not the individual,[49] and that caste, certainly a historical impediment to human rights, is not the same as racism.[50] Sharma states that, according to Gandhi and others, caste can sometimes help protect human dignity because of its emphasis on the collective and not the individual, a position that would probably not receive universal acclaim in India or elsewhere.

Recent writers have grappled with the paradox of India through thick description without providing an overarching theory to account for or in some way attempt to reconcile the seeming disconnect between outer injustice and inner calm. I began this chapter with a discussion of the definition of the human person as innately transcendent and connected with realms much larger than the localized self. The Upaniṣads extol the microcosmic body as inseparable from the macrocosm, and yoga traditions provide meditative and ethical technologies through which one can feel the experience of higher connection. One such technique is the performance of *pūjā*, a ritual generally performed privately on a daily basis, with large ceremonies keyed to an annual calendar. Constantina Rhodes, in her book *Invoking Lakshmi: The Goddess of Wealth in Song and Ceremony*, describes preparing for the autumn celebration of the goddess, a nine-day festival honoring Sarasvatī (goddess of knowledge), Lakṣmī (goddess of wealth), and Durgā (a heroic goddess). She focuses on the worship of Lakṣmī, examining each of the sixteen aspects of *pūjā*, from the invocation through bathing and clothing the deity image, making vegetative offerings, offering food and money, waving of lights, and a farewell. She participates in an urban *pūjā*, held in an upper-middle-class neighborhood of New Delhi. Rhodes writes:

> Toward the end of the ceremony, Veena lit another lamp, this one with camphor, which sent out an initial blaze of sparks and then settled into a diamond-like, piercingly brilliant white light along with an astringent and pungent fragrance. Very suddenly things got quiet. Of their own accord the children gathered close to the altar, standing still and with an attitude of expectation. I noticed that the street noise had subsided, and the darkening room seemed to spread with light. Within an instant, everything had changed. A deep and peaceful fullness settled over the house. That yogic point of perfect quietude flooded the heart and stilled the mind. I let go of compulsive, dualistic queries. . . . In that moment when the *pūjā* imploded into perfection . . . existence with the world and transcendence beyond the world seemed as one.[51]

The ceremony prompts an inner experience of connection, wherein the distinction between higher and lower, self and other, human and divine, dissolves.

Although seemingly inner-focused, it is important to bear in mind that this ceremony has taken place within the context of a family that has spent many hours preparing the proper foods, conducting the sixteen required components, welcoming relatives and friends, and that others in the neighborhood have been doing the same. The emphasis here is on the collective, not the individual.

This sense of collectivity was also noted by Pramila Jayapal. In her book *Pilgrimage to India: A Woman Revisits Her Homeland*, Jayapal describes returning to her country of birth, which she had left at the age of four for an international upbringing in Southeast Asia and collegiate and graduate studies in the United States. While working for the Institute of Current World Affairs, she traveled through all parts of India, urban and rural, discovering the rhythm of life experienced by her ancestors. She discovered great privation and wealth, and during her two years there encountered "people for whom life still revolved around family, community, spirituality, and land."[52] She discovered that in the village of Kamalsagar near Varanasi, as elsewhere in India, land had been donated to Harijan (formerly regarded untouchable) farmer folk, many of whom prospered through subsistence agriculture. In this particular village, the Brahmins, who previously relied on Harijan labor, themselves were engaged in farming. Jayapal noted that the Brahmin women were generally better educated than the men. Jayapal draws upon her own reflections and emotions to describe how she, a modern development worker employed by an international health organization, grappled with the contrast between her own world of seeming plenty, somewhat bereft of soul, and the culture of India, steeped in connections. She writes: "We in the so-called 'developed' world fool ourselves all too often. . . . We allow ourselves to be surrounded by human-made things and forget that we are here by grace, not by right."[53] She contrasts the now-downcast Brahmins with the industrious and enthusiastic beneficiaries of post-Gandhian governmental policies.

Suketu Mehta similarly returned to the city of his birth after having completed high school, college, and a master's program in the United States. From the dual perspective of insider/outsider he documents lives on the ground in his native Mumbai, including dance hall performers, politicians, slum dwellers, jewel merchants, and religious renouncers. He follows the lives of one family who moves from a one-room lean-to in the slums to a two-room flat in a housing development of dubious quality. He also travels back to their village of origin for a family wedding. In the one-room hovel, the entire family—mother, father, two sons plus a daughter—transformed their day living space into a dormitory at night, mother and father sleeping under the table, brothers on one side, sister on the other. When they moved to the more spacious apartment, Mehta notes, "Having grown up in one room, they don't know what to do with the extra room when at long last they get it."[54] The designated "bedroom" stays vacant; everyone prefers to sleep in the common room until one of the sons brings a wife into the family. Mehta notes:

> In families like the Thakkars, there is no individual, only the organism. Everything—Girish's desire to go abroad and make and send back money, Dharmendra's taking a wife, Raju's staying at home—is for the greater good of the whole. There are circles of fealty and duty within the organism, but the smallest circle is the family. There is no circle around the self.[55]

From the sensibility of Western individualism, this arrangement might seem suffocating. However, despite hesitation about being labeled romantics or naïve orientalists, many observers who travel to India find admirable human dignity in this cultural system that emphasizes and prioritizes family and group identity. Feeling part of a greater unit provides a sense of belonging that many in neoliberal, contemporary, consumer-based societies find woefully lacking.

CONCLUSION

The Hindu vision of human dignity derives from two loci, one internal, the other external, yet linked with an internal sense of connectivity and group belonging. The Upaniṣads and the practices of yoga emphasize that human meaning can be found in moments of stillness wherein the life force of the individual feels part of a great whole. This experience of solitude might be found in a remote, peaceful place, such as an ashram, or it might even be experienced in the midst of other people, as found in a celebratory family *pūjā* or a great festival, such as the Kumbha Mela, a periodic gathering of millions along the banks of India's sacred rivers. The "self" experienced in these moments leaves behind all fettering identities and concerns. All afflicted karmas fall away in this instant of meditative repose. No accomplishments, no possessions, no status can define or contribute to this form of internal dignity.

Somewhat paradoxically, this aspirational definition of human personhood as inseparable from the cosmos contributes to a sense of the collective. Because no "thing" can provide dignity, dignity can be found only by surrendering one's selfishness for the sake of the group. Dignity, or a sense of propriety, can only be gained through the benefit of others. In a conversation with Yajnavalkya, his wife, Maitreyi, learns:

> Not for the love of the husband is a husband dear,
> but for the love of the Soul [*ātman*] is the husband dear;
> Not for the love of the wife is a wife dear,
> but for the love of the Soul [*ātman*] is the wife dear;
> Not for the love of children are the children dear,
> but for the love of the Soul [*ātman*] are the children dear.
> (IV.5.6)[56]

The same is said in regard to cattle, Brahmins, Kṣatriyas, worlds, gods, the Vedas, and all beings. By seeing all phenomena as inseparable from the World Soul, a transcendent reference point is given. In this can be found dignity.

In the *Bhagavad Gītā*, the highest accomplishment of human life requires the transcendence of all categorizations, seeing oneself as inseparable from the selves of others: "The knowledgeable ones view with equal eye an educated Brahmin, a cow, an elephant, a dog, or an outcaste" (V.18).[57] The beloved community excludes no one; dignity must be accorded to every being.

NOTES

1. Robert Ernest Hume, *The Thirteen Principal Upaniṣads* (London: Oxford University Press, 1930), 23–31.

2. See *Bhagavad Gītā* III:20, where Krishna advises Arjuna, "You must act, attending to no less than the holding together of the world"; Antonio T. de Nicolás, *The Bhagavad Gītā: The Ethics of Decision Making* (Berwick, ME: Nicolas-Hayes, 2004), 43.

3. *Bṛhadāraṇyaka Upaniṣad* I.4.7, as translated in Robert Ernest Hume, *The Thirteen Principal Upaniṣads* (London: Oxford University Press, 1930), 85.

4. See Georges Dumézil, *The Destiny of the Warrior*, trans. Alf Hiltebeitel (Chicago: University of Chicago Press, 1970).

5. Retold from various translations, most notably Hume, *The Thirteen Principal Upaniṣads*, 218–22.

6. Ibid., 219.

7. Ibid., 221.

8. The following sources were consulted for the retelling of this story: Patrick W. Olivelle, trans., *Pañcatantra: The Book of India's Folk Wisdom* (New York: Oxford University Press, 1997), McComas Taylor, *The Fall of the Indigo Jackal: The Discourse of Division and Pūṇabhadra's Pañcatantra* (Albany: State University of New York Press, 2007), and Franklin Edgerton, trans., *The Panchatantra Reconstructed*, vol. 2, *Introduction and Translation* (New Haven, CT: American Oriental Society, 1924).

9. Adapted from the translation by Antonio T. de Nicolás, *Avatára: The Humanization of Philosophy through the Bhagavad Gītā* (New York: Nicolas Hays, Ltd., 1976), 158.

10. Important recent works on Mahatma Gandhi include Tara Sethia, *Gandhi: Pioneer of Nonviolent Social Change* (Boston: Pearson, 2012), and Veena Howard, *Gandhi's Ascetic Activism: Renunciation and Social Action* (Albany: State University of New York Press, 2013).

11. See Amartya Sen, *The Argumentative Indian: Writings on Indian Culture, History and Identity* (New York: Penguin, 2005), 112–15, 243–47, 342–44.

12. Mohandas Gandhi, *Hind Swaraj and Other Writings*, ed. Anthony J. Parel (New York: Cambridge University Press, 1997), 102.

13. Lloyd I. Rudolph and Susanne Hoeber Rudolph, *Postmodern Gandhi and Other Essays: Gandhi in the World and at Home* (Chicago: University of Chicago Press, 2006), 27.

14. Christopher Chapple, *Karma and Creativity* (Albany: State University of New York Press, 1986), 105–6.

15. Anthony J. Parel, introduction to *Hind Swaraj and Other Writings*, by Mohandas Gandhi, ed. Anthony J. Parel (New York: Cambridge University Press, 1997), xlix.

16. Adapted from de Nicolás, *Avatára*, 91.

17. Gandhi, *Hind Swaraj and Other Writings*, 47.

18. Ibid., 110.

19. Ibid., 110–11.

20. Ibid., 107.

21. Ibid., 108.

22. Ibid.

23. Ibid., 62.

24. Ibid., 63.

25. Ibid.

26. Ibid., 64.

27. Ibid., 65.

28. Ibid., 117.

29. Ibid.

30. See Joanne Punzo Waghorne, *Diaspora of the Gods: Modern Hindu Temples in an Urban Middle Class World* (New York: Oxford University Press, 2004), and Waghorne, *Place/No-place in Urban Asian Religiosity* (Singapore: Springer, 2016). See also Sara Dickey, *Living Class in Urban India* (New Brunswick, NJ: Rutgers University Press, 2016).

31. Hume, *The Thirteen Principal Upaniṣads*, xviii.

32. Mary Ann Glendon, *A World Made New: Eleanor Roosevelt and the Universal Declaration of Human Rights* (New York: Random House, 2001), 100.

33. The Universal Declaration of Human Rights [UDHR], UN, http://www.un.org/en/universal-declaration-human-rights/index.html.

34. Glendon, *A World Made New*, xx.

35. Ibid., 90.

36. UDHR.

37. Ibid.

38. Louis Dumont, *Homo Hierarchicus: The Caste System and Its Implications*, trans. Mark Sainsbury (Chicago: University of Chicago Press, 1970), 41, 232–33.

39. McKim Marriot and Ronald Inden, "Toward an Ethnosociology of South Asian Caste Systems," in *The New Wind: Changing Identities in South Asia*, ed. Kenneth David (The Hague: Mouton Publishers, 1977), 232.

40. Ibid., 231.

41. McKim Marriott, "Hindu Transactions: Diversity without Dualism," in *Transaction and Meaning: Directions in the Anthropology of Exchange and Symbolic Behavior*, ed. Bruce Kapferer (Philadelphia: Institute for the Study of Human Issues, 1976).

42. Marriott and Inden, "Toward an Ethnosociology of South Asian Caste Systems," 233.

43. McKim Marriott and Ronald B..Inden, "Caste Systems," *Encyclopedia Britannica*, 15th ed. (Chicago: Encyclopaedia Britannica, 1975), 983.

44. Ronald B. Inden, *Marriage and Rank in Bengalis Culture: A History of Caste and Clan in Middle Period Bengal* (Berkeley: University of California Press, 1976), 148–49.

45. See Nicholas B. Dirks, *Castes of Mind: Colonialism and the Making of Modern India* (Princeton, NJ: Princeton University Press, 2001), 255–75; Eleanor Zelliot, *From Untouchable to Dalit: Essays on the Dalit Movement* (New Delhi: Manohar, 1996); Gail Omvedt, *Dalits and the Untouchable Revolution: Dr. Ambedkar and the Dalit Movement in Colonial India* (New Delhi: Sage Publications, 1994).

46. See Amartya Sen, *Development as Freedom* (New York: Knopf, 1999).

47. For articles by Swami Agnivesh, see https://www.swamiagnivesh.com/articles.php.

48. Ashutosh Varshney, *Ethnic Conflict and Civil Life: Hindus and Muslims in India* (New Haven, CT: Yale University Press, 2002), 11.

49. Arvind Sharma, *Hinduism and Human Rights: A Conceptual Approach* (New Delhi: Oxford University Press, 2004), 36.

50. Ibid., 39.

51. Constantina Rhodes, *Invoking Lakshmi: The Goddess of Wealth in Song and Ceremony* (Albany: State University of New York Press, 2010), 2–3.

52. Pramila Jayapal, *Pilgrimage to India: A Woman Revisits Her Homeland* (Seattle: Seal Press, 2001), 6.

53. Ibid., 7.

54. Suketu Mehta, *Maximum City: Bombay Lost and Found* (London: Headline, 2004), 503.

55. Ibid., 516.

56. Adapted from Hume, *The Thirteen Principal Upaniṣads*, 145.

57. Adapted from the translation by de Nicolás, *Avatára*, 105.

six

JEWISH AND HINDU PERSPECTIVES ON DIGNITY

Responses

Christopher Key Chapple and Elliot N. Dorff

RESPONSE BY CHRISTOPHER KEY CHAPPLE

Judaism and Hinduism share many features. Both claim antiquity, with aspects of their narratives and practices dating from at least 4,000 years ago. Both ground their faith in texts, the Torah for Jews, the Vedas for Hindus. Commentaries on these core texts make up an ongoing vital tradition for each. Orthopraxy distinguishes each tradition, most notably in the areas of food laws and the practice of endogamy. Judaism and Hinduism each developed traditions of priesthood and temple sacrifice that require long years of preparation through education and training.

Dorff and Nevins define dignity through rabbinical responses that apply scriptures to real-life dilemmas and circumstances. By virtue of the human capacity to speak and to think with reason, persons merit being treated with respect, even if they have committed a crime (92). Hindus would certainly agree that human dignity can be found in the capacity to think and reason. However, one difference between the traditions might be found in the Hindu attribution of dignity to animals on the grounds that every animal might be someday born as a human and that every human, depending on deeds committed, could be reborn as an animal. Judaism does not tolerate cruelty to animals, but always places priority on the needs of humans.

Dignity, according to Judaism, can be found in work and the right to work, as seen in the rabbinical pronouncements "work is great" and "love work." The

Hindu tradition, as expressed in the *Bhagavad Gītā*, extols work not for the sake of work itself, but advises that all work must be undertaken for the sake of the greater good, without attachment to the fruits of one's labor. Lord Krishna, one of the ten Avataras of Vishnu, the god symbolizing maintenance of the world, proclaims to his student Arjuna: "Work always for the sake of work alone, never for the fruits of action" (BG II:47). The entire fifth chapter of this important text focuses on Karma Yoga, stating that through the performance of work well done, in accord with one's station in life (*svadharma*) and with the intent of upholding all aspects of the world (*lokasaṃgraha*), one can achieve freedom while engaged in daily activities.

Doff and Nevins identify five aspects of dignity of contemporary concern that merit consideration: war, family violence, abortion, sexual orientation, and genetic engineering. As in the Jewish tradition, the Hindu tradition does not have a single authoritative voice on any one of these or other ethical issues. Just as the Jewish faith relies on the opinions of rabbis (or the Rabbis) recorded and remembered over many centuries applied to contemporary circumstances, so also Hinduism has produced many and sometimes conflicting views. Torah, Mishnah, Gemara, Midrash, commentaries, and responsa literature are the Jewish sources for discussing and possibly adjudicating troublesome issues. For Hindus, analogical analyses of the Vedas, the Upaniṣads, the Dharmashastras, the Arthashastra, and the Mahabharata and Ramayana, along with their many commentaries, serve as resources for developing and defending moral views. Each of these will be cited in responding from a Hindu perspective to the five issues related to dignity.

War has flared up many times over the long history of the Indian subcontinent. The Vedas narrate the sometimes violent advance of warriors across the northern reach of India. The Arthashastra gives advice on the waging of war, including best practices for espionage. The Mahabharata tells of grand alliances between kingdoms that line up behind two sets of cousins competing for dominance. The resulting warfare paints a picture in the aggregate of the futility and sadness and inanity of waging war. Gandhi interprets the *Bhagavad Gītā*, a critical portion of the Mahabharata, as warning that one must gain self-mastery, not domination over others. The Upaniṣads emphasize the need for self-understanding, with little reference to conflict, while the Dharmashastras lay out the duties of all the respective *varṇas*, or four major social groups, noting that the "job," or *dharma*, of the warrior (*kshatriya*) requires skilled performance in war. The other social groups are not exempt from participation:

the merchants (*vaiśyas*) help fund warfare, Brahmins give counsel, and farm-workers (*śūdras*) will often be armed and sent into battle.

For most of India's history, as many as 600 kingdoms, known as Rajas, existed, adjacent to one another, separated by forests, mountains, and deserts. Occasionally, amalgamations such as Aśoka's empire 2,300 years ago and the Gupta Empire (320–550) were formed. The Mughal Empire (1526–1857) turned many Hindu kings into vassals, as did the overlapping period of British presence and eventual rule (1858–1947).

In ancient times, every twelve years the king would undertake a roaming ascetic sabbatical, renouncing his comforts to follow a sanctified horse, staking a claim on those areas where the horse ventured. At the end of the year the horse would be slain and the new territory annexed. Standing armies would defend the borders and ensure that taxation would be collected. Brahmin experts in law would advise the king on all matters and disputes. In the Ramayana, Brahmins ask King Dasaratha to send his son to police the forests and rid them of dacoits, who disturb those on spiritual retreat. Eventually, Rama rescues his wife, Sita, who had been abducted by Ravana, the king of Lanka, the island kingdom. Rules are clearly found in the Dharmashastras and the Arthashastra for the waging of war, but in the actual narratives, ambiguity arises regarding the right course of action. For instance, the protagonists in the Mahabharata fight treacherously and against the rules, and, according to some versions of the Ramayana, Rama lacks trust in his own wife, resulting in her self-demise.

This brings us to the second topic, family violence. The Vedas and Upaniṣads include loving narratives of family harmony, with fidelity between husband and wife and deep affection between many named parents and their children. However, the Mahabharata tells the horrific tale of family conflict leading to violence on a massive scale. As in all great tragic literature, the narrative serves to warn about the results of treachery with an eye to avoiding future similar situations. Many in India will not allow the text to be kept in their homes because of its woeful content. In summary, two sets of cousins dispute one another's claims of sovereignty over a wealthy kingdom. The five Pandavas, born of four different divine fathers, are driven out by their hundred male cousins, the Kauravas, born of a blind king. Because of his blindness, this elder king had yielded rule to his younger brother, but then assumed regency when his brother died. As the 105 cousins reach adulthood, no agreement regarding succession can be reached. The five are banished with their families for thirteen years. Hatred simmers in the hearts of the one hundred for this time, and although the five defeat the hundred, only sadness lingers in the aftermath. This dystopic tale serves to remind families to negotiate differences and cultivate harmony whenever possible.

The challenges of joint-family living complicate the need for peace within a family. Up until the liberalization of the 1990s, virtually all Indian families followed the pattern of joint-family living. All brothers lived under the same roof, welcoming in wives who would serve under their common mother-in-law, preparing meals and sharing the responsibilities of rearing children. Each child would be raised in the constant company of aunts and uncles and cousin-sisters and cousin-brothers. The matriarch, who generally survived her husband, would be the arbiter of all disputes. This pattern can still be found in much of India and in many Indian diaspora communities. With the growth of the middle class and the increase in wealth in India, it is now more common to see nuclear households owning their own flats, often in proximity to other family members. It is also increasingly common for women to work outside the home, though in public spaces men generally still outnumber women.

The system of dowry remains an entrenched problem in India. Marriage entails complex negotiations between families, with the expectation that a woman will bring significant resources into the husband's family. One heinous crime, condemned by all faiths in India, remains the immolation of young women who do not meet expectations of the husband's family. This form of family violence has resulted in the advocacy for civil divorce, which had not been permitted in the Dharmashastra texts.

Abortion has been a topic of enduring concern throughout Asia for reasons quite different from those found in Christian countries. The male gender holds greater prestige in the Indian family unit. A girl only resides temporarily within her birth family, but the male child will remain part of the family until his death. A girl takes financial resources away from the family in the form of dowry; the male child earns income that benefits his brothers and parents. Family dignity relies on the success of its sons, not its daughters. Hence, with the advance of genetic testing and visual fetal scans, it has become commonplace for some families to abort female fetuses. This practice has been denounced by most Hindu leaders and declared illegal by the state and federal governments in India, yet it is still practiced, skewing the sex ratio in India overall by as many as ten percentage points depending upon the region. A major campaign in India advocates for the dignity of the female child. Additionally, high-profile rape cases in recent years have energized advocacy for the dignity of women.

Ambiguity in the realm of sexual orientation has been known in India for millennia, with early literature telling of the "third sex" wherein the body of a male manifests desires like that of a female, and the reverse. Even today, bands of Hijras, men who dress as women and sometimes undergo gender-altering surgeries, can be seen in India. Hijras support themselves as entertainers and generally live in their own version of a joint-family compound. In many Hindu devotional communities, men will dress as women in order to participate in women's rituals, singing fervently to the chosen deity as one's lover. In 2013, the Supreme Court of India reinstated sodomy laws, reversing its setting aside of British-era sodomy laws in 2009, letting section 377 inherited from British law in 1860 to remain on the books, though reportedly it is seldom enforced. The LGBT movement has gained momentum in many areas of India, with rallies and Western-style advocacy. Additionally, in some states of India, Hijras have entered politics and gained seats in local governments. Hindu texts acknowledge the presence of alternative forms of sexual identity, most notably with the hero Arjuna going in disguise as a woman dance teacher for a full year before the great Mahabharata war.

Genetic engineering opens many possible ethical conversations from Hindu perspectives. Swasti Bhattacharyya, author of *Magical Progeny, Reproductive Technology: A Hindu Bioethics of Assisted Reproductive Technology*, has outlined a methodology for approaching a wide range of Hindu responses to modern issues. She uses the birth narratives of the five Pandava brothers, one fathered by the god of Dharma, another by Indra (god of war), another by the god of Wind, and twins fathered by the rising and setting sun, to explore attitudes toward technologies, such as in vitro fertilization, gamete transfer, and sperm donation. The Hindu tradition clearly embraces the creation of life by extraordinary means, according to these narratives, and one might extend this logic to an expected embrace of enhancement of human well-being through genetic engineering. However, given the many unforetold consequences of human and divine mixing, including the strife and warfare generated from jealousy over the success, power, and beauty of the Pandavas, discussion might be needed about the advisability of using genetic engineering without safeguards in place.

Dignity has many faces and each tradition has its own definitions and cultural needs. In my chapter on Hindu dignity, I argue that dignity derives from an innate divinity, a sense that the small self of personhood reflects and embodies the larger macrocosm in all its magnificence. My response here asks that more difficult questions be asked: How does the call to dignity translate when applied to issues of war, family violence, abortion, sexual orientation, and genetic engineering? Because of its status as a "disorganized religion,"[1] Hinduism does not have a central board of authorities that might be able to provide a standard answer on any of these or other topics. Nonetheless, the rich textual and narrative traditions of the Hindu faith provide resources for constructive reflection on developing an informed response on how best to foster human dignity even in challenging circumstances.

RESPONSE BY ELLIOT N. DORFF

Although there are some places where the concept and practice of dignity in Judaism very clearly differ from those in Hinduism, in many places in Chris Chapple's chapter I found myself saying, "It depends on which expression of Judaism you are talking about." This is true from his very first paragraph, in which he states, "The Hindu view of the human person stands in marked contrast to that found in the Judeo-Christian and Islamic traditions" because "the early Upaniṣads (ca. 800 BCE) teach that the inner self (*ātman*) connects with universal presence, or Brahman, that pervades all reality" (129). He is certainly right about that distinction if we are talking about the biblical or rabbinic tradition, for in those classical expressions of Judaism each person is an independent and unique creature of God, and one's dignity is at least partly a function of that individuality. The later Jewish mystical tradition (*kabbalah*), however, especially in the books produced between the thirteenth and sixteenth centuries CE, say exactly the same as what the Upaniṣads say, namely, that we need to dissolve our sense of distinctiveness as much as we can to become part of God. The Kabbalah also has a doctrine of transmigration of souls from one life to another, similar to the Hindu tradition.

Similarly, although the goal of life for Judaism is to be holy like God (Lev. 19:2) and ultimately become "a kingdom of priests and a holy nation" (Exod. 19:6), there are certainly elements of the classical Jewish tradition that emphasize the importance of harmony, as do the Taoist and Confucian traditions. So, for example, the following early rabbinic source uses a play on words in the Hebrew to make its point:

> "You are children of the Lord your God. You shall not gash yourselves (*lo titgodedu*) . . ." (Deuteronomy 14:1): that is, do not make of yourselves separate groups (*aggudot*) but rather all of you should be one group (*aggudah*), as it says, "God founded His vault (*aggudato*) [singular] on the earth" (Amos 9:6).[2]

Granted, this is speaking about harmony within the Israelite society rather than harmony between humans and nature, but you get even that expressed in the Torah itself, when it proclaims that the Israelites must not violate the sexual prohibitions in Leviticus 18 lest the land become defiled by such behavior and "spew you out for defiling it" (Lev. 18:28). Similarly, the African emphasis on interpersonal respect is embodied in the rabbinic insistence that we honor all God's creatures (*kevod ha-briyyot*), which, as Rabbi Nevins and I describe in our chapter in this volume, is construed to be so important that it supersedes even some biblical and rabbinic commandments. So although these varying traditions are certainly not the same, I would be careful about drawing clear lines of demarcation among them on their depictions of the nature of humans, the proper goal of human life, or the way in which dignity is understood and put into action.

However, there certainly are some clear differences (and similarities) between the Jewish and Hindu traditions on aspects of human dignity. Here are some points of comparison:

1. *One's own unique identity.* Chapple cites the *Bhagāvad Gītā* as stating, "Better to do one's own dharma even incorrectly than to usurp the dharma of another" (135). Jewish sources do not imagine that anyone could take on the identity of another or act in the exact same way. On the contrary, the Mishnah emphasizes the uniqueness of each one of us by comparing God's creation to human creation. Human beings create a mold for making coins, and each coin comes out the same. God, on the other hand, creates each of us in the image of God (Gen. 1:27, 9:6), and yet each one of us is unique.[3] This is a recognition and appreciation of both God's special powers and the significance of the individuality of each person—all before the discovery of DNA! Furthermore, uniqueness conveys value, much as an original Picasso is much more valuable than any of its reprints or photographs. Thus this same Mishnah goes on to say that because each person is unique, anyone who saves a person saves an entire world (namely, the person and all of his or her descendants), but anyone who kills a person destroys an entire world—a saying that appears four centuries later in the Qu'ran. Many centuries later, this idea appears in an oft-quoted Hasidic bon mot:

> Before his death, Rabbi Zusya said: "In the coming world, they will not ask me: 'Why were you not Moses?' They will ask me: 'Why were you not Zusya?'"[4]

2. *Work.* "In the dignity of work, one finds meaning" (135). This Hindu teaching is also affirmed by Judaism. First, although the Sabbath is probably a Jewish innovation and it gives both humans and animals the dignity of desisting from work so that their value apart from their work is recognized, the Torah balances the importance of stopping work one day in seven with working the other six, which is also one of God's commandments: "Six days shall you do your work, but on the seventh day you shall cease from labor so that your ox and donkey may rest, and your bondman and the stranger may be refreshed" (Exod. 23:12). Later the Rabbis say, "Great is work, for it honors the workmen."[5] Conversely, "A man only dies through idleness."[6] Even Torah study, which the Rabbis valued greatly, must be balanced by work:

> An excellent thing is the study of the Torah combined with some worldly occupation, for the labor demanded by them both makes sin to be forgotten. All study of the Torah without work must in the end be futile and become the cause of sin.[7]

This is very similar to Gandhi's insistence that those with privilege participate in all aspects of human labor. Furthermore, the Rabbis of the Talmud recognized the importance of all sorts of work, as did Gandhi, for although a few of them belonged to wealthy families, the vast majority were engaged in labor themselves. So, for example, Rabbi Joshua was a charcoal-burner;[8] Rabbi Meir was a scribe;[9] Rabbi Yose bar Halaphta worked in leather;[10] Rabbi Yohanan made sandals;[11] Rabbi Judah was a baker;[12] and Rabbi Abba Saul aided a baker as a kneader of dough[13] and had formerly been a gravedigger.[14] Furthermore, even though the Rabbis were engaged in what they saw as the most honorific activity, study of the Torah in its broadest sense, they valued manual labor:

> It was a favorite saying of the Rabbis of Yavneh: I am a creature [of God], and my neighbor is also His creature. My work is in the city, and his is in the field. I rise early to do my work, and he rises early to do his. As he cannot excel in my work, so I cannot excel in his work. But perhaps you say, "I do great things [by studying Torah], and he does small things [by manual labor]." No, we have learned that [it matters not whether] a man does much or little, as long as he directs his heart to Heaven.[15]

3. *Medicine, Education, and Law.* Like Gandhi, the Rabbis did not like physicians; one Mishnah even says, "The best of physicians is destined for

Gehinom (hell)"[16]—probably because patients were frustrated by the fact that doctors at that time could not cure their diseases. But in the last 1,500 years or so there has been a virtual love affair between Jews and medicine, with many rabbis becoming both clinicians and medical researchers and with doctors seen and honored as the partners of God in healing. Also unlike Gandhi, the Jewish tradition very much prizes education, and so parents have the duty to teach their children both Torah and a trade.[17] His opposition to a focus on law is also not shared by Judaism, which sees law as not only an important vehicle for social order, but also as a means to inculcate good moral character and to connect with God.[18]

4. *Character education.* Unlike Gandhi, the Jewish tradition sees learning of the Torah and the later rabbinic tradition as important parts of inculcating good character traits in both children and adults in a variety of ways, which I discuss elsewhere.[19] At the same time, many voices within the tradition recognize that book learning is not sufficient. So, for example, Maimonides, an important twelfth-century rabbi, philosopher, legal codifier, and physician, says this:

> We teach Torah only to a student who is morally fit and pleasant in his ways, or to a student who knows nothing [and therefore may become such a person with learning]. But if the student goes in ways that are not good, we bring him back to the good path and lead him to the right way, and then we check him and [if he has corrected his ways] we bring him in to the school and teach him. The Sages said: Anyone who teaches a student who is not morally fit is as if he is throwing a stone to Mercury [i.e., contributing to idolatry]. . . . Similarly, a teacher who does not live a morally good life, even if he knows a great deal and the entire people need him [to teach what he knows because nobody else can], we do not learn from him until he returns to a morally good way of life.[20]

Later, in the nineteenth century, Rabbi Israel Lipkin Salanter created the Mussar movement with the specific goal of supplementing the text study of rabbinical students with character education techniques that drew on methods of group psychology.[21]

5. *Marriage.* As in the story of Ṛṣi and his wife, in Judaism marriage is an ideal and constitutes a rise in status, for only in marriage can people fulfill

the Torah's commandments to provide for each other's needs for lifetime companionship, sexual fulfillment, procreation, and raising the next generation. Because "it is not good that a person be alone (Genesis 2:18)," the Rabbis assert that "even if a man has many children [by one or more previous marriages], he must not remain without a wife."[22] Furthermore, the Rabbis recognized that being married and having children increases a person's maturity and sensitivity to aspects of life that one would not be expected to know if single. So the Rabbis rule, for example, that only a man who has children is eligible to judge a capital case, for only such a person can truly know the value of life—of both the culprit and the victim.[23]

6. *Endogamy.* The concern for endogamy appears in the very earliest stories of Genesis (e.g., 24, 27:46–28:5),[24] but it was for maintaining the identity of the clan and its religious practices, not the socioeconomic class. But the Rabbis maintain that although any Jew may marry any other, it is *wise*, but not legally required, for a man to marry a woman more or less his own age[25] and to marry a woman of the same or lower socioeconomic status so that her relatives do not look down on him.[26] On the other hand, because Judaism prizes knowledge of the Jewish tradition as much as it does, a man should seek to marry the daughter of a rabbi or scholar so that he can be assured that his own children will be learned, for Torah learning is more respected than wealth in the Jewish tradition.[27]
7. *Infertility.* Like the Ṛṣi and his wife, many of the couples in the Bible suffer from infertility and from the heartache and family jealousies and frictions that it causes.[28] Because American Jews go to college and graduate school in percentages far higher than the general population and thus postpone marriage until after the ages when people are most likely to be able to procreate, infertility is a major problem in the contemporary Jewish community, and so, with some limitations, Jews embrace artificial reproductive techniques to enable them to have children.[29]
8. *Children.* Conversely, children are seen as a major blessing (e.g., Psalms 128) and are, together with the Land of Israel, God's blessings to Abraham and Sarah, Isaac and Rebekah, and Jacob and Rachel.[30] Furthermore, again like the story of Ṛṣi, the plight of orphans is a major concern, and so the Prophets complain of people neglecting or cheating both widows and orphans, and the Talmud asserts that one way to "act justly and do right at all times" (Psalms 106:3) is to raise an orphan in one's house and ultimately marry him or her off.[31]

9. *Groups within the community.* Although there is no formal caste system in Judaism, the Pharisees, whose form of Judaism most influenced what we know as Judaism today, got their name by virtue of the fact that they separated themselves (*perushim*) from the common folk when eating because they did not trust them to adhere properly to Jewish dietary laws.
10. *Changing social status.* Like Satyakama, anyone of any background can rise to high status through inquiry. So, for example, Hillel and Rabbi Akiba, two very important figures in rabbinic Judaism of the first two centuries CE, were both shepherds before they became oft-quoted rabbis. What enabled them to become rabbis, however, was not "obedience to his teacher" (132) but rather the knowledge and skills to ask questions, challenge one's teachers and peers, and apply Judaism in new ways. This is one manifestation of the feisty nature of Judaism, such that the Talmud is one page after another of arguments. That Judaism encourages questions and challenges to authorities and to accepted ways of doing things, albeit within a context and in a tone of mutual respect, may be the most profound distinction between Judaism and Hinduism—and, for that matter, between Judaism and many other religions—a distinction in mode of being in this world rather than in any particular substantive doctrine.
11. *Humans and other animals.* In contrast to the story of Ṛṣi and the mouse, Judaism sees human beings as distinct from other animals by virtue of the image of God embedded within us. Exactly what the image of God is within us humans is a matter of debate in Jewish sources, with some maintaining that it is our spiritual nature, some our ability to reason, and some our ability to distinguish good from bad, which is what the garden of Eden story seems to be saying. The Torah itself and later Jewish law require Jews to minimize the pain of animals in our use of them and in slaughtering them for food, but even in the Kabbalistic tradition there is no sense that the dignity that humans have by virtue of the divine imprint within them is shared by animals.

NOTES

The following abbreviations are used in the notes for this chapter:

M. = Mishnah (edited ca. 200 CE)
T. = Tosefta (ca. 200 CE)

J. = Jerusalem (Palestinian) Talmud (ca. 400 CE)
B. = Babylonian Talmud (ca. 500 CE)
M.T. = Maimonides's code, the *Mishneh Torah* (1177)
S.A. = Joseph Karo's code, the *Shulhan Arukh* (1565), with glosses by Moses Isserles to indicate where the practice of northern European (Ashkenazic) Jews differed from that of Jews living in the countries surrounding the Mediterranean Sea (Sephardic Jews)

1. Statement from Varun Soni, dean of religious life at the University of Southern California.
2. *Sifre* 44:31on Deuteronomy 14:1; B. *Yevamot* 13b, 14a.
3. M. *Sanhedrin* 4:5.
4. Martin Buber, *Tales of the Hasidim: The Early Masters* (New York: Schocken, 1975), 251.
5. B. *Nedarim* 49b.
6. *Avot D'Rabbi Natan* 11.
7. M. *Avot* (*Ethics of the Fathers*) 2:2.
8. B. *Berakhot* 28a.
9. B. Eruvin 13a.
10. B. *Shabbat* 49b.
11. M. *Avot* 4:14.
12. J. *Haggigah* 77b.
13. B. *Pesahim* 34a.
14. B. *Niddah* 24b.
15. B. *Berakhot* 17a.
16. M. *Kiddushin* 4:14.
17. B. *Kiddushin* 29a.
18. For a discussion of the variety of ways in which law accomplishes these goals, see Elliot N. Dorff, *Love Your Neighbor and Yourself: A Jewish Approach to Modern Personal Ethics* (Philadelphia: Jewish Publication Society, 2003), 337–44.
19. Ibid., 323–37.
20. *M.T. Laws of Study* 4:1.
21. For a brief description of this approach, see Ira F. Stone, "Mussar Ethics and Other Nineteenth-Century Jewish Ethical Theories," in *The Oxford Handbook of Jewish Ethics and Morality*, ed. Elliot N. Dorff and Jonathan K. Crane (New York: Oxford University Press, 2013), 127–33. For a more extensive description, see Immanuel Etkes, *Rabbi Israel Salanter and the Mussar Movement* (Philadelphia: Jewish Publication Society, 1993).
22. B. *Yevamot* 61b; *M.T. Laws of Marriage* 15:16; *S.A. Even Ha-ezer* 1:8.
23. T. *Sanhedrin* 7:3; B. *Sanhedrin* 36b.
24. For a discussion of this aspect of Jewish family law and practice, see Elliot N. Dorff and Arthur Rosett, *A Living Tree: The Roots and Growth of Jewish Law* (Albany: State University of New York Press, 1988), 469–70.
25. B. *Yevamot* 101b.

26. B. *Yevamot* 63a.

27. B. *Pesahim* 49a.

28. Sarah: Genesis 15:2–4, 18:1–15. Rebekah: Genesis 25:21. Rachel and Leah: Genesis 30:1–8, 22–24, 35:16–20. Hannah: 1 Samuel 1:1–20.

29. For a discussion of this, see Elliot N. Dorff, *Matters of Life and Death: A Jewish Approach to Modern Medical Ethics* (Philadelphia: Jewish Publication Society, 1998), chaps. 3 and 4.

30. Genesis 15:5, 17:4–21, 18:18, 22:15–18, 26:4–55, 28:13–15, 32:13.

31. B. *Ketubbot* 50a.

seven

DIGNITY

A Protestant Perspective

David P. Gushee

INTRODUCTION

Discussions of the concept of human dignity are now omnipresent in theology, philosophy, ethics, law, and politics, but Protestant theologians and ethicists appear to have made few original contributions to discussions related to the meaning of human dignity, its grounding or justification, and its real-world normative implications. Of course, it is certainly questionable whether airtight boundaries between Protestant, Catholic, and Orthodox approaches to human dignity can be identified. There is extensive borrowing and overlap in this post-denominational age, and the concept of human dignity is an aspect of the broader Christian tradition, shared by the whole Church.

Yet, I have been asked to offer a Protestant perspective, based on my monograph *The Sacredness of Human Life* (*SHL*).[1] I was not intending to offer a distinctively Protestant ethic of human dignity in that book. However, dialogues with other scholars have clarified for me ways in which my own account of human dignity has some particularly Protestant contours, most notably in the warrants that I offer for this concept but also in other ways. Therefore, I accepted this assignment to offer a Protestant take on human dignity. (I prefer to call it *the sacredness of human life*, though I will also use the dignity terminology here once I clear the intellectual brush away.)

The invitation to write this chapter provides a welcome opportunity for me to review, reconsider, and perhaps revise some of the claims made in *SHL*. In this I have been helped considerably by participation in a 2012 Oxford

University conference on human dignity, hosted by the estimable Christopher McCrudden. The volume that emerged from that conference, *Understanding Human Dignity*,[2] now functions as a profoundly helpful aid to reflection for all who work on these issues, and I will engage it extensively here. I am also grateful for three classrooms of sharp Mercer University students, one undergraduate and two graduate, who have worked through these issues with me in recent years.

MEANINGS AND DEFINITIONS

Sacredness and Dignity

To understand what is meant when people say that (human) life is *sacred* or that humans have *dignity* requires some etymological detective work and intellectual history. I undertook some of that work for *SHL* and believe that it has stood up well.

The English adjective *sacred* emerged from a now-obsolete Middle English verb *sacre*, which meant "to consecrate, make holy, or dedicate to a deity."[3] In its original meaning, something or someone could be described as sacred insofar as it could be said that some agent, or Agent, had made or declared it sacred. The same holds true today. Nearly anything can be declared or consecrated as sacred—a dog, a horse, a spot of land, a building, a document, an office, or a person. All it takes is for someone (with the proper authority) to declare or consecrate it as such, and for some relevant community of persons to respect that consecration. Think of *sacred texts* like the Bible, *sacred places* like cathedrals, or *sacred offices* like the papacy. There are "secular" national variants—sacred texts like the U.S. Constitution, sacred places like Gettysburg, or sacred offices like the presidency. In my favorite sport, baseball, there are what can only be described as sacred places, like Boston's Fenway Park, sacred figures like Jackie Robinson (the first black player in the major leagues), and sacred statistical achievements like Ted Williams batting .406 in 1941.

Once an object, place, office, person, or whatever is declared sacred by some authoritative agent, behavioral implications follow. These are often summarized in terms of obligations to feel and think and behave toward these sacred things with something like dignity, respect, reverence, or awe. Because X is sacred, we must treat it with reverence. "Don't shout in the cathedral; it is a sacred place." "Don't disrespect the pope." Sanctions are often threatened against those who "violate" the sacredness of the object or person or place in question, because that sacredness is viewed as *inviolable*—which means "*must* never be violated," not "*can* never be violated." Such violations can be called *desecrations*, and they are a serious offense against the community for whom the object, place, or person has been authoritatively declared and communally accepted as sacred.

Human history and practice reveal that many objects, places, and persons have been declared or consecrated as sacred. This appears to be just something that human beings do—we elevate some objects over others, some places over others, some days over others, some foods over others, some persons over others, some roles over others, some classes over others, some languages over others for special consecration, and require that members of the relevant communities respond by offering due respect and reverence to that which has been consecrated.

To say that *human life, as such, is sacred* is to make the radical claim that humanity as a collective, and each and every human being as an individual, has been authoritatively consecrated and declared to be sacred and must be viewed and treated as such. Not just the king, but every person. Not just my kin, but every family, clan, and tribe.

Today, the term "human dignity" often functions with equivalent meaning to what I have just described as the meaning of the sacredness of human life. But though "sacredness of human life" is mainly used in religious circles, human dignity is used both in religious contexts and in secular ones, the latter including philosophy and domestic and international law. The English term "dignity" comes from the Latin *dignitas*. Dignity means "worthiness, elevation, nobility, honor, and distinction. . . . It originally emerged from the classical world and carried the connotation of rank."[4] The term carries much of its original connotation even in egalitarian-leaning, English-speaking lands. To say that a person "carries himself with dignity" conjures up mental images of fine etiquette, posture, and dress, or perhaps emotional restraint, verbal self-control, and polite decorum. In other words, the term still carries a whiff of the English "noble" classes with which it was originally associated centuries ago.

To say that *human life, as such, has dignity* has by now come to mean that humanity as a collective, and each and every human being individually, not just those of high human rank and noble birth, has been declared to be dignified, or bears intrinsic dignity, and must be viewed and treated as such. Everyone,

one might say, is a noble, even the "lowest" "commoner." It is easier to miss the religious connotation of sacredness when one instead uses the term "dignity." This is because sacredness more clearly demands some answer to the question of agency: *Who exactly declared or consecrated every human being as sacred?* Dignity can more easily simply posit a worth or value, often declared to be "intrinsic," to human beings as such, and not worry over who exactly decided that human beings should be viewed in this way. In common parlance, the terms have at least sometimes become interchangeable. I personally prefer, however, to deploy the term "dignity" as a consequence-term following from the central claim that human life is sacred:

> Human life is sacred: this means that each and every human being has been set apart for designation as a being of elevated status and dignity. Each human being must therefore be viewed with reverence and treated with due respect and care, with special attention to preventing any desecration or violation of a human being.[5]

Notice that this basic definition covers all of the bases suggested above: it applies to each and every human being, it elevates their rank "as if" all are nobility, and it requires appropriate corresponding action from others, notably, to view and to treat all others with reverence, respect, and care, and to prevent particularly egregious kinds of harm to others.

Agency and Justification

Whether we speak of each and every human being as sacred, or of human dignity, we still face the monumental problems of agency and justification. If framed in terms of agency, the question is, "Who exactly has declared/consecrated human dignity/sacredness?" If framed in terms of justification, the question is, "What are the rational warrants for making and/or accepting the claim that human beings as such are sacred/have dignity? How do we *know* that human beings have dignity?"

One of the features of *SHL* that seems to make it a distinctively Protestant work is my argument that "the only agent (Agent) who could imagine designating all human beings as sacred, and who could have the authority to do so, is God."[6] More pointedly, I declare that "the conviction that each and every human being is sacred comes to humanity from beyond humanity. It is an aspect of divine revelation and could only have come to us that way."[7]

To be more precise, my claims related to the justification for the conviction that each and every human life is sacred look something like this:

- Descriptively, it can be observed that human beings often declare and act as if certain objects, places, or persons are sacred or of exalted dignity.
- Descriptively, it can be observed that human beings often declare and act as if certain objects, places, or persons are insignificant or even profane, of low or no worth, and therefore of no moral value.
- Descriptively, at least for "Western cultures," that is, those shaped by the nexus of "Athens" and "Jerusalem," the idea that each and every human being should be viewed as sacred seems to have been birthed not in classical Greco-Roman culture but in the nexus of the biblical faiths of Judaism and Christianity, and is frequently suggested or articulated in their religious traditions in succeeding centuries.
- Descriptively, it can be observed that both Jews and Christians, as recorded in the pages of their sacred scriptures and in their long histories as peoples, have sometimes succeeded and sometimes failed to act in accord with the idea that each and every human being has dignity or sacred worth; but the concept has never disappeared, and moral leaders have often returned to it.
- Critics of various types have raised compelling challenges to the credibility of every nontheological justification for human dignity or sacredness of life.
- I justify or ground my conviction that each and every human life has dignity or sacred worth by claiming that it is an aspect of divine revelation, recorded in the biblical canon and then developed over centuries as an aspect of Jewish and Christian theology and ethics. (Lacking the relevant expertise, I will not attempt to make or to dispute similar claims about Islam or other religions.)

Alternative Warrants for Human Dignity

My approach is distinguishable from most secular and many Catholic efforts to ground human dignity. Many such thinkers offer some account of what it means to be human, often by naming distinctively or normatively human characteristics, powers, potentialities, needs, interests, or vulnerabilities. This account is then used to ground claims to human dignity, both its content and its normative implications. In *Understanding Human Dignity*, a wide array of such inductive moves from (purported) human nature and experience are described or attempted. I will name just a few of them here.

For Catholic ethicist Margaret Farley, as quoted by fellow Catholic David Hollenbach, the "obligating features of personhood" are autonomy and relationality.[8] Hollenbach renames autonomy as "freedom" and adds "basic needs," such as for food or health care.[9] Thus he claims to reason inductively, from observation about human freedom(s), relationships, and basic needs, to the claim that "human dignity" is the term given to refer to these three ramifying characteristics of personhood that demand concrete respect from other human beings and in human community.[10] Hollenbach goes on to quote the Vatican II document *Gaudium et spes* to name three other "secular warrants for human dignity": the transcendence of the mind; the sacredness of conscience; and the excellence of liberty.[11] He argues that these warrants are rationally knowable to anyone and thus are not dependent on Church doctrine or teaching, though they are reflected in Church doctrine and teaching.

Sifting through other essays in *Understanding Human Dignity*, one finds an array of similar efforts to ground dignity in aspects of the human. These aspects include rationality, personality, freedom, conscience, relationality, love, subjectivity, mutuality, uniqueness, unfathomability, and transcendence. Even though there might be a dimension of "mystery" here,[12] there is just something about being human that demands respect, summarizable in a norm that can be called *human dignity*. The concrete particular obligations that follow from such a respect for dignity are the subject of ongoing exploration, argument, and development, but the dignity standard is both warranted and widely recognized.

I am not convinced. Here's why: many individuals, communities, and societies over millennia have observed the same great capacities, profound depths, and grave needs of their fellow human beings and have not chosen to respond by believing in or practicing a norm of respect for the dignity of any, some, or all of their neighbors. Often, quite the contrary.

There's a second alternative warrant for human dignity. Some legal scholars at the 2012 Oxford Conference simply accepted the idea that human dignity is "a human concept . . . a social and political construct."[13] Constitutions or statutes enshrine this human concept in law. Judges interpret and therefore, in effect, "mak[e] dignity"[14] through their evolving rulings. This, then, is essentially a warrant for human dignity claims based on the existing fact that many human communities have chosen to create such a concept and enshrine it in law, and it appears to offer some value for creating decent human communities.

This social constructionist account of human dignity makes its own kind of sense. But it is not satisfying. Here's why: shifting legal concepts based on the current will of political communities seem to be a flimsy basis for belief in a concept as central as human dignity/sacredness of human life. What a community enshrines into law it can also strip from law. Consider 1933 Germany.

A third major alternative way to ground claims to human dignity is presented by the UN Universal Declaration of Human Rights (UDHR) (1948).[15] All italics are added by me for further comment:

> Whereas recognition of the inherent dignity and of the equal and inalienable rights of all members of the human family *is the foundation of freedom, justice and peace* in the world,
>
> Whereas disregard and contempt for human rights *have resulted in barbarous acts* which have outraged the conscience of mankind, and *the advent of a world* in which human beings shall enjoy freedom of speech and belief and freedom from fear and want has been proclaimed as the highest aspiration of the common people,
>
> Whereas it is essential, if man is not to be compelled to have recourse, as a last resort, to rebellion against tyranny and oppression, that human rights should be protected by the rule of law,
>
> Whereas *it is essential to promote the development of friendly relations between nations,*
>
> Whereas the peoples of the United Nations have in the Charter *reaffirmed their faith in fundamental human rights,* in the dignity and worth of the human person and in the equal rights of men and women and have determined to promote social progress and better standards of life in larger freedom,
>
> Whereas Member States *have pledged themselves to achieve,* in co-operation with the United Nations, the promotion of universal respect for and observance of human rights and fundamental freedoms, and
>
> Whereas a common understanding of these rights and freedoms is *of the greatest importance for the full realization of this pledge,*
>
> Now, Therefore THE GENERAL ASSEMBLY proclaims THIS UNIVERSAL DECLARATION OF HUMAN RIGHTS as *a common standard of achievement* for all peoples and all nations.

This cardinal text for modern human dignity and human rights offers soaring and memorable language but no real warrant for its claims other than *aspiration*, *faith*, and *consequentialism*. Having just lived through every evil that was done during World War II, the UN, among others, said that humanity could never go back there again. We have to long for,[16] aspire to, believe in, and together create the kind of world in which people respect human dignity, otherwise . . . the abyss. But if we do believe in and seek to create such a world, we can achieve freedom, justice, and peace at last.

This also is unsatisfying as a warrant for human dignity. Here's why: it is easy to see why skeptics could consider such a claim akin to believing in unicorns. Michael Rosen claims that "dignity is humbug,"[17] and, if this is its best warrant, I would have to agree with him. It is certainly true that human existence apart from belief in and respect for human dignity has proven to be a very scary prospect, but that is not much of a justification for a belief. For several years in my childhood the idea of living in a world without the existence of Santa Claus was a frightening prospect, but this did not create the real existence of a jolly red-suited man who crosses all the world's time zones to deliver presents to worthy children on Christmas Eve. A need to believe does not warrant a belief.

A THEOCENTRIC-VOLUNTARIST WARRANT

My own approach to warranting belief in the sacredness of life/human dignity is quite distinct from any of the foregoing. I am not attempting any form of natural law or inductive reasoning. I am not adopting a social constructionist approach or simply accepting the current existence of a moral or legal norm. Nor do I believe in human dignity because I fear the consequences of not doing so or just want to live in a world like that.

Instead, I am offering a *theocentric warrant* for human dignity. Here's one basic way I have said it:

> To speak in religious terms of the sacredness of each and every human life . . . is basically to claim that all human beings are something like cathedrals that have been consecrated by God and must not be violated. God has consecrated the human being, each human being, who is now sacred, and must be treated accordingly.[18]

Why has God consecrated human beings as sacred? Because the God who created human beings has the authority to do so, has decided to do so, and has done so. All it takes is the divine will to do so, though a very plausible case from sacred scripture can be made that God's primary motivation is love for his creation and its creatures, the same love that motivated the creation in the first place.

My overall approach here might be described as a *voluntarist* or *decisionist* paradigm (challenged by John Tasioulas for "de-centering" humanity[19]). I emphasize divine freedom rather than anything intrinsic in humanity that might demand or evoke a designation of human sacred worth from God or anyone else. I am further claiming that we "know" that God has declared human life sacred through the traces left in divine revelation, notably in the sacred canonical scriptures and in Jesus Christ. All efforts to find in the Bible some other or deeper reason for God's decision to declare human life sacred should be viewed as speculative. We do not need to know why. We need to hear God's word about sacred human worth, and God's consequent and related commands, and act accordingly.

A Formal Definition of Sacredness/Dignity with Biblical Warrants

All of the foregoing offers background to the formal Christian (if you will, Protestant) definition of the sacredness of human life that I offer in *SHL*:

> Human life is sacred: this means that God has consecrated each and every human being—without exception and in all circumstances—as a unique, incalculably precious being of elevated status and dignity. Through God's revelation in Scripture and incarnation in Jesus Christ, God has declared and demonstrated the sacred worth of human beings and will hold us accountable for responding appropriately. Such a response begins by adopting a posture of reverence and by accepting responsibility for the sacred gift that is a human life. It includes offering due respect and care to each human being that we encounter. It extends to an obligation to protect human life from wanton destruction, desecration, or the violation of human rights. A full embrace of the sacredness of human life leads to a full-hearted commitment to foster human flourishing.[20]

Notice certain key decisions embedded in this formal definition:

1. A clear emphasis on divine decision and agency in consecrating human life.
2. Reinforcement of the claim that sacredness/dignity applies to each and every human being without exception and in all circumstances.

3. This means that no action of a human being can cause divinely ascribed sacredness/dignity to be forfeited.
4. Individual human uniqueness and preciousness are noted.
5. Human worth is beyond calculation, so it cannot be quantified, commodified, or traded.
6. Every life, not just some lives, have elevated status and dignity by divine decision, regardless of human perceptions or preferences.
7. The entirety of biblical revelation speaks to this divine decision, and all of that revelation must be plumbed for traces and direction, as *SHL* goes on to do in chapter-length explorations of creation themes, legal texts, prophetic exhortations and promises, Gospel narratives and teachings, and early Church narratives and instructions.
8. The incarnate Christ is the pinnacle of God's self-revelation, and this includes God's revelation of divine will related to how human beings should be viewed and treated.
9. Many behavioral obligations follow, including reverence, responsibility for others, respect and care, life and dignity protection, a commitment to universal human rights, and finally the ongoing task of fostering human flourishing.

SUMMARIZING AND EXTENDING MY NORMATIVE ACCOUNT

Let me now summarize my claims in terms that connect this chapter to others included in this book. All authors were asked to reflect on certain key questions, and this will provide a path to summarization, a bit of extension, and a connection with other authors. We will also note these connections as appropriate.

Human dignity/sacredness is the ascribed worth belonging to each and every human being by virtue of the decision of God, our Creator. It is an ascribed status, neither earned nor intrinsic. It is not inherent in being human as such, or intrinsic to any characteristics of the human, or subject to the growth or diminution of particular human capacities or attributes.

Human dignity cannot be quantified. No one has more sacred worth, or less, than anyone else. It is a universally and equally distributed divine gift. Human dignity is not contingent on the existence, survival, or flourishing of any particular human capacities, such as spirituality, rationality, morality, decision-making, or relationality. Therefore, a person can neither gain nor lose, either by his or her own choices or by that of others, nor by physical developments or decay, their dignity. This is a way to say that human dignity is *inalienable*.[21]

This does not mean that it is impossible to offend the dignity or violate the sacredness of another human being. All kinds of acts violate human dignity, many of which are named in sacred scripture, such as violations of human bodily integrity, including assault and murder. The obligation to prevent such indignities and violations is central to the moral norm I am describing here. Such violations offend God and God's decision to declare each human being sacred; they harm the persons who are attacked; they are experienced as humiliations, indignities, or desecrations by the victims and those who most love them. But nothing can take away the divinely ascribed sacred worth of a human being. Slaves or the tortured are infinitely precious and sacred to God even when they are being treated as worthless by other people.

This is a reminder that the exquisite divine gift to human beings of dignity creates tasks, moral obligations. The human being who discovers the divine decision and declaration that each human being is sacred discovers extensive obligations to herself and to others. The communities of faith that seek to live in obedience to God's word constantly are called to reflect upon and to seek to practice the obligations that come with this divine word. The divine decision to declare human life sacred has been communicated to human beings by God in divine revelation, notably sacred scripture and Jesus Christ. This revelation is extensive, though complex, and subject to varying particular interpretations and applications. It is by no means reducible to (implications of, or speculations about) the *imago Dei* theme, but extends through the entire canon.

This divine declaration has been received and heard by the Jewish and Christian communities, as has been evidenced by the development of theological and ethical doctrines and practices over time that reflect it. The communities primarily responsible for hearing, obeying, and communicating this divine revelation to others are those to whom this revelation was originally directed: Jews and Christians. But these communities have the obligation to bear witness to this revelation in word and deed.

Human beings who have not heard or responded favorably to this or any other aspect of divine revelation can sometimes intuit aspects of it. But it cannot be said that the sacredness of each and every human life is a belief that can simply be intuited or arrived at naturally, certainly not in humanity's fallen state apart from relationship with God. Various philosophical theories or approaches point to aspects of human existence or experience that arouse respect for human abilities and potentialities or evoke compassion for human immiseration and suffering—these are pointers in the direction of human dignity/sacredness, but are not sufficient guides or grounding.

The post–World War II emergence of a global human dignity ethic and human rights ethic and jurisprudence should be understood as in part a response to the enormous desecrations of human dignity from 1914 to 1945, and in part an extension of previous developments in politics and moral theory. Now, after seventy years of intellectual and legal development of human dignity ethics and law, it can seem like "everyone knows" that human dignity is fundamental, equal, and universal and/or that human life is sacred. But (1) there are still plenty of dissenters, in theory and in practice, and (2) there is no agreed warrant for this belief in human dignity, other than (3) the recognition after 1945 that human survival is imperiled if we cannot learn to treat one another with a modicum of dignity. Still, this new global human dignity ethic and legal norm has numerous points of connection with ancient Jewish and Christian moral tradition and provides an opportunity for shared reflection, advocacy, and moral practice.

Dignity and Conflict: Torture

This is a book about dignity and conflict. Other contributors will offer full-length treatments of particular issues related to human conflict or to conflicting readings of the implications of human dignity for particular moral issues. Because these other authors are examining a range of issues at length, I do not need to attempt to do the same in this chapter. However, it seems to me that my own account of human dignity/sacredness needs fleshing out with application to particular issues. I do this in *SHL* at some length. Here I would like to offer brief treatments of the issues of torture and LGBTQ equality, neither of which is discussed in *SHL*. I believe that this discussion will reveal both the potential and certain of the limits, not only of my approach to human dignity, but also to human dignity/sacredness as a moral norm.

Let us here follow international legal norms and define torture as follows:

> For the purpose of this Convention, the term "torture" means any act by which severe pain or suffering, whether physical or mental, is intentionally inflicted on a person for such purposes as obtaining from him, or a third person, information or a confession, punishing him for an act he or a third per-

> son has committed or is suspected of having committed, or intimidating or coercing him or a third person, or for any reason based on discrimination of any kind, when such pain or suffering is inflicted by or at the instigation of or with the consent or acquiescence of a public official or other person acting in an official capacity. It does not include pain or suffering arising only from, inherent in, or incidental to, lawful sanctions.

This text from the UN Convention against Torture[22] excludes torture on the part of lone individuals or even criminal gangs, or torture motivated merely by sadism or malice. It intends to cover torture understood as state action, usually motivated by security considerations, and often incidental to interrogation of detained civil or foreign enemies. Torture, thus defined, is banned by international law, by several international conventions, by the laws of war, and by the laws of multiple nations, including the United States, where it is a felony punishable by a lengthy prison term. Torture is often treated in moral philosophy as banned without exception and in all circumstances, a rare "unexceptionable" moral norm.

Often, though not always, one warrant given for these moral and legal bans on torture is "human dignity." In my published work on torture, I have always grounded my own absolute moral opposition to torture in the sacredness of human life. So I have every interest in strengthening rather than weakening moral and legal opposition to torture.

But now consider again my fullest, most formal definition of the sacredness of life:

> Human life is sacred: this means that God has consecrated each and every human being—without exception and in all circumstances—as a unique, incalculably precious being of elevated status and dignity. Through God's revelation in Scripture and incarnation in Jesus Christ, God has declared and demonstrated the sacred worth of human beings and will hold us accountable for responding appropriately. Such a response begins by adopting a posture of reverence and by accepting responsibility for the sacred gift that is a human life. It includes offering due respect and care to each human being that we encounter. It extends to an obligation to protect human life from wanton destruction, desecration, or the violation of human rights. A full embrace of the sacredness of human life leads to a full-hearted commitment to foster human flourishing.[23]

Is a ban on torture clearly derivable from this definition of the sacredness of human life? I have suggested as much in the past. But further experience has left me less certain of this than in the days, a decade ago, when I was a leading antitorture activist. A more precise way to say it is that I remain deeply and existentially convinced of the wrongness of torture, but I am less sure than I was a decade ago that this position can be unassailably grounded simply in the moral conviction that human life is sacred, or in human dignity. If I think that I know that torture is wrong because human life is sacred, and you also believe that human life is sacred but do not believe that torture is in every case wrong, we have at least an epistemological problem, if not a conceptual one.

Certainly there are resources for opposing torture embedded in this definition. It is hard to see how one can view a human being with reverence, or accept responsibility for the unique gift that is a single human life, and proceed to torture that person. It is hard to square torture with the obligation to show due respect and care for a person. It is hard to make torture align with preventing the desecration of another human being or preventing the violation of his or her rights. It is certainly clear that being tortured does not contribute to any human being's flourishing. All of this is true, or at least defensible. But it is still reasonable to ask whether more is needed to derive an absolute ban on torture. Perhaps, for example, torture could be seen as prima facie immoral, but this immorality could be overridden in cases of emergency.[24] That is how many other moral norms are understood to work. Unexceptionable moral norms are quite rare in most contemporary accounts of ethics.

Or, perhaps my account based on divine revelation needs more concrete, rule-like ethical guidance from sacred scripture itself. Maybe we need to be able to show not just a presumption against torture based on the broad conviction that human life is sacred, but also posit specific moral commands banning torture, or at least moral commands prescribing concrete norms related to, for example, how prisoners of war should be treated. One might have imagined that the Bible would offer such concrete moral principles or even moral rules, but, alas, it does not. There are a range of relevant narratives and principles, including the story of the tortured Jesus, or the concept of the sacredness of human life itself. But that does not amount to a clear ban on torture in the Bible.

Moving the discussion back out to human dignity/sacredness of human life also begs the question of whose lives are being valued as sacred. A national security rationale for torture that is even remotely defensible always involves some kind of balancing claim, in which the suffering inflicted on these particular prisoners is justified by the likely greater quantity of suffering prevented on the part of innocents who are at risk in war or terrorism. We torture two people here tonight in order to get the information that prevents their compadres from tomorrow murdering 200 and maiming another 2,000. My analysis earlier claimed that human dignity/sacredness is not quantifiable, tradeable, or comparable in this way, but this was exactly the justification for "enhanced interrogation techniques" offered by policymakers in the George W. Bush administration and elsewhere.

Finally, it is certainly the case that just to claim "sacredness of human life" as moral norm does not resolve the technical questions of what precise actions constitute torture, or the just slightly less severe category of "cruel, inhuman, and degrading treatment" that is not quite torture. Certainly in the Bush administration, lawyers for the White House argued not for torture but for a definition of torture narrow enough to allow for a wide range of techniques that previously had been banned. This involved much parsing of what exactly constituted "severe" physical and mental pain—parsing that was ultimately repudiated by later White House officials but that actually was used in interrogation policy for several crucial years.

All of this at least raises the question of what kind of moral norm sacredness of human life actually is, and whether it does the work its advocates, including this writer, have claimed for it. Here it seems better at providing a foundation for more concrete moral rules banning torture than it does at banning torture on its own.[25] An even more skeptical rendering would be that it simply is too vague and abstract to offer significant action-guides and thus fails to be a helpful moral norm at all.[26]

Dignity and Conflict: LGBTQ Inclusion

The issue of full social and religious equality for lesbian, gay, bisexual, transgender, queer, intersex, and other persons whose gender identity and sexual orientation deviate from the norm may raise even more interesting questions for the sacredness of human life/human dignity ethic. It is certainly the case that the long history of stigmatization, social contempt, criminalization, and violence toward LGBTQ persons in Western cultures cannot be described as conforming to a sacredness of life/human dignity ethic. One of the signal achievements of the LGBTQ activist community has been to delegitimize such attacks on gender and sexual minorities among vast majorities in the Western world.

But what of other questions, which now have become more pressing: Does sacredness/dignity require abandonment of belief in a God-given design for human sexuality and gender expression that would reject same-sex activity or ban transitioning from a male to a female via surgery? Does sacredness/dignity require the full inclusion of LGBTQ persons in Christian community on the exact same terms as all other persons, with full and equal access to all the same rights and responsibilities as everyone else? Does sacredness require churches to bless same-sex marriages, ordain gay ministers, and support congregants transitioning genders?

One of the most (painfully) memorable aspects of the 2012 Oxford conference on dignity was the exchange about gay marriage between traditionalist presenters Christopher Tollefsen and Robert George, on the one hand, and inclusivist presenter Edwin Cameron, on the other.[27] Their positions were fundamentally incompatible and irreconcilable, yet both used the language of human dignity as their grounding. Tollefsen, backed by George, spoke of the "dignity of marriage." Cameron, a gay South African jurist, spoke of the dignity of the gay individual who should not be denied access to marriage.

I now think that this division goes back to a primal split about the concept of human rights that has roots in late medieval Europe and has worsened dramatically in modernity and postmodernity. A good way to get at this split is to juxtapose a traditionalist "right order" approach against a "subjective rights" vision.[28] Right-order advocates believe that there is an observable moral/natural/divinely ordained order to the world in which humans live, and human dignity is only rightly understood and advanced if human beings choose to conform their individual lives, their relationships, and their social institutions to this order. If people can be said to have "individual rights," these are limited to choices that can be made within the parameters of this order.

Thus, on this view, a male has what might be described as a natural or individual right to marry the female of his choice, and vice versa, but neither has the "right" to marry a person of the same sex, because this is not actually "marriage" and is not in keeping with right order. A person has the right to have one or more children but does not have the right to kill any of them. A person can choose from among any number of professions, but one of them cannot be, say, prostitution. Right-order advocates reject a number of popular contemporary rights claims, such as the "right" to an abortion or the "right" to assistance in suicide.[29] Just because a person in her freedom wants something, this does not make it a right. What she wants must conform to right order and be within the zone of licit freedom.

A subjective-rights approach is far less confident in making or accepting claims about right order, whether natural or divinely given. At least, these thinkers believe that such claims do not belong in the public sphere or public law. This view has been deeply affected by growing social pluralism but, more broadly, is characteristic of modern liberal democracy going back to its origins. In liberal democracy, on this account, law exists primarily to protect human autonomy up to the boundary of harm to others. Any just law treats all citizens equally. The state offers no substantive account of right order or the human good, allowing individuals to define the good for themselves and to exercise their autonomy to pursue that good as they see it—again, up to the limit of harm to others. Freedom and equality are, then, the two cardinal norms for modern liberal democracy.

The consequences follow for how gay marriage is viewed. Right-order advocates, most often though not always religious, very often oppose gay marriage based on a conviction that it violates moral order. They reject any claim that sacredness/dignity warrants overturning what they understand to be this moral order, discernible from reason, nature, or revelation. They sometimes argue that gay marriage violates the dignity of marriage in the name of a misunderstood dignity for individuals. This in turn leads a secular philosopher such as Michael Rosen to conclude that (traditionalist religious) renderings of "dignity" actually undercut core modern commitments to autonomy and equality. Those who are really committed to the latter norms are best served by abandoning dignity language and staying away from its religious advocates, who are always apt to resurface with right-order claims that violate autonomy and equality.[30]

Subjective-rights advocates, on the other hand, generally support gay marriage as the latest step in humanity's long march toward respecting every person's autonomy and granting full social equality to not just some but all persons. They believe that denial to gay persons of access to social benefits and responsibilities available to the sexual majority is a clear violation of both equality and freedom and therefore also a violation of their human dignity. As readers well know, these matters are contested daily in our homes, churches, legislatures, courtrooms, and political campaigns.

As with torture, it is hard to see how the sacredness/human dignity norm can cash out in a way that resolves this issue. It does not appear capable of definitively adjudicating the conflict between right-order and subjective-rights approaches. Instead, all that really seems to happen is that moral views become more deeply entrenched as all sides claim the ultimate warrant of dignity/sacredness for their most deeply held convictions. Legal scholars often also express concern that dignity offers no "justiciable" value and offers no solid or precise substantive norms for legal decision-making,[31] which would include legal decision-making related to gay marriage. This raises acute questions as to the actual value of dignity/sacredness, either as a moral or legal norm.

WHAT DO WE LEARN? WHAT KIND OF NORM IS THIS?

In an ethics introduction,[32] Glen Stassen and I describe four levels of moral norms, from the most abstract to the most concrete: (1) basic convictions, (2) principles, (3) rules, and (4) particular judgments. If envisioned as a pyramid, basic convictions are the base, then up a level is principles, up another level is rules, and at the top are particular judgments. The higher up the pyramid one goes, the more specific and concrete are the moral norms, or action-guides. Each level down is somewhat more abstract and less concrete. Basic convictions are the most foundational moral norms, having to do with broad beliefs about reality, God, humanity, and moral responsibility, but they are also the most abstract and the least concrete.

Consider this example:

> Particular judgment: I will give $10 to the next homeless person who asks for my help.
>
> Moral rule: Give alms to the poor (a clear and concrete biblical command/practice).
>
> Moral principles: Generosity, mercy, love.
>
> Basic Conviction: God is generous, merciful, and loving, and calls me to be the same.
>
> So I give $10 to the homeless person today as an expression of my obedience to the moral rule in scripture to give alms to the poor. This rule is itself a concretization of the moral principles widely articulated in scripture of generosity, mercy, and love, especially for those in greatest need. Those principles are derived not just from specific biblical teachings but from the overall biblical picture of the character of God and God's will.

If you grant the cogency of this four-level depiction of moral norms, consider this: What level of moral norm is sacredness/dignity? It's certainly not a particular judgment, nor is it a moral rule. It might be viewable as a broad moral principle, like justice or love. But it is better seen as a basic conviction, from which more concrete moral principles and even more concrete moral rules might be derivable.

I do not believe this means that sacredness/dignity has no value as a moral concept or conviction. It is clearer to me now than when I wrote *SHL*, however, that its value lies at the basic conviction level, informing and helping to shape correlated moral principles, rules, and particular judgments. But no one can claim unassailable "proof" of the rightness, or wrongness, of the principles, rules, and judgments one might derive by making appeal to one's dignity ethic. This is a sobering judgment, but a fair one, I think.

CONCLUDING REFLECTIONS

Thinking back on the entire discussion thus far, I acknowledge other theoretical complexities with the sacredness of human life, even if it functions as a basic conviction rather than as a more concrete moral principle or rule. Many of these complexities are addressed in *SHL*, to which I refer the reader. But they include the following:

1. To speak of the sacredness of human life has sometimes meant denigrating other species by comparison. This need not be the case, but an account must be offered for the divinely declared and revealed worth of other creatures.[33]
2. To speak of the sacredness of human life does not resolve questions of exactly when life begins to count as human or ceases to count as human. Nor does it resolve the related question of whether a human being can cease to be a person while remaining a human. These issues must be addressed by arguments and cannot simply be handled by definitions.
3. My account of the ascribed rather than achieved sacredness/dignity of human life has made no effort to reflect on human efforts to maximize our (God-given) potential across so many different dimensions. Does this not matter at all? It does, I say, not for the concept of sacredness of life as discussed here, but for other dimensions of human flourishing.
4. The moral obligations that follow from viewing all life as sacred are expansive and demand much of human beings in relation to their neighbors. But I am not suggesting that all of us are responsible in the exact

same way for the protection of particular persons' human dignity and flourishing. These responsibilities are diffused to different persons, relationships, and agencies of society.

5. My revelational account of dignity/sacredness can be critiqued for not adequately accounting for the human capacity to grasp concepts of dignity apart from biblical revelation or faith. I think this is especially the case when one considers the very broad demand of oppressed persons for dignified treatment. No divine revelation appears to be needed to trigger such a demand. Perhaps a provisional conclusion relates to the idea of the epistemological privilege of the oppressed. That is, those on the receiving end of violations of their sacred worth "know" what dignity means, or should mean, far more readily than those who are doing the victimizing.
6. I have not emphasized here as much as in *SHL* the complexity of reading the sacredness/dignity norm in, through, and sometimes despite canonical texts that do not all fully reflect that norm. This requires a reverent but not uncritical theology of scripture, which I offer in *SHL* but have not developed here.

I still believe that the idea that each and every human life is sacred is one of the grandest legacies of biblical faith to the world. I still believe that it helps to protect the moral fabric of human civilization and actually contributes to saving human lives. I share the idea that we need a concept like this even if we cannot agree on how to ground it in our pluralistic world. I have spent too much time studying the horrors of the twentieth century to think anything else. And yet even the most robust concept of human dignity/sacredness of life is only the beginning of moral inquiry and action, not the end of it.

NOTES

1. David Gushee, *The Sacredness of Human Life* (Grand Rapids, MI: Eerdmans, 2013).
2. Christopher McCrudden, ed., *Understanding Human Dignity* (Oxford: Oxford University Press, 2014).
3. Gushee, *The Sacredness of Human Life*, 18.
4. Ibid., 19 (italics omitted).
5. Ibid., 24 (italics omitted).
6. Ibid., 25.
7. Ibid. (italics omitted).

8. David Hollenbach, "Human Dignity: Experience and History, Practical Reason and Faith," in *Understanding Human Dignity*, 129.

9. Ibid., 131.

10. Ibid.

11. Ibid., 135.

12. James Hanvey, "Dignity, Person, and the *Imago Trinitatis*," in *Understanding Human Dignity*, 226, and Janet Soskice, "Human Dignity and the Image of God," in ibid., 241.

13. Catherine Dupré, "Constructing the Meaning of Human Dignity: Four Questions," in *Understanding Human Dignity*, 116.

14. Ibid.

15. See http://www.un.org/en/universal-declaration-human-rights/index.html.

16. Bernhard Schlink, "The Concept of Human Dignity: Current Usages, Future Discourses," in *Understanding Human Dignity*, 633.

17. Michael Rosen, "Dignity: The Case Against," in *Understanding Human Dignity*, 143.

18. Gushee, *The Sacredness of Human Life*, 25.

19. John Tasioulas, "Human Dignity and the Foundations of Human Rights," in *Understanding Human Dignity*, 294.

20. Gushee, *The Sacredness of Human Life*, 33 (italics omitted).

21. Christoph Goos, "Würde des Menschen: Restoring Human Dignity in Post-Nazi Germany," in *Understanding Human Dignity*, 89.

22. See https://treaties.un.org/doc/Publication/UNTS/Volume%201465/volume-1465-I-24841-English.pdf.

23. Gushee, *The Sacredness of Human Life*, 33 (italics omitted).

24. Goos, "Würde des Menschen," 89.

25. Christopher McCrudden, "In Pursuit of Human Dignity: An Introduction to Current Debates," in *Understanding Human Dignity*, 15.

26. Rosen, "Dignity," 146.

27. See Edwin Cameron, "Dignity and Disgrace: Moral Citizenship and Constitutional Protection," in *Understanding Human Dignity*, 467–82; Christopher Tollefsen, "The Dignity of Marriage," in ibid., 483–500; and Robert P. George, "Response to Tollefsen and Cameron," in ibid., 501–8.

28. Discussed briefly in Gushee, *The Sacredness of Human Life*, chap. 7; also see John Milbank, "Dignity Rather Than Rights," in *Understanding Human Dignity*, 189–205.

29. Dupré, "Constructing the Meaning of Human Dignity," 120.

30. Rosen, "Dignity," 147–52.

31. Conor Gearty, "Socio-Economic Rights, Basic Needs, and Human Dignity: A Perspective from Law's Front Line," in *Understanding Human Dignity*, 161, and Christoph Möllers, "The Triple Dilemma of Human Dignity: A Case Study," in ibid., 186.

32. David Gushee and Glen Stassen, *Kingdom Ethics*, 2nd ed. (Grand Rapids, MI: Eerdmans, 2016).

33. Gushee, *The Sacredness of Human Life*, chap. 11.

eight

DIGNITY

An Orthodox Perspective

Aristotle Papanikolaou

DIGNITY IN THE HUMAN RIGHTS DOCUMENT OF THE RUSSIAN ORTHODOX CHURCH

One of the most recent Orthodox theological reflections on the concept of dignity has been given in an official document on human rights issued by the Russian Orthodox Church (ROC).[1] In this chapter, I will analyze the way in which the ROC develops a particular "Orthodox" understanding of human rights based on a theological interpretation of "dignity" that is itself grounded in the classical Christian distinction between the image of God and the likeness of God. I will then trace the meaning ascribed to the image/likeness distinction within the Orthodox tradition, culminating in the contemporary Orthodox theology of personhood. I end by arguing against the ROC's "Orthodox" notion of human rights, which rests not on a mistake in theological anthropology, but in the elision between the ecclesial and the political.

The Russian Orthodox Church's Basic Teaching on Human Dignity, Freedom and Rights (*DFR*), approved by the Bishops' Council of the Moscow Patriarchate in 2008, was the culmination and crystallization of rhetoric discernible in Russia since the collapse of the Soviet Union, but especially at the start of the new millennium.[2] This document can be interpreted as a correction to the Declaration on Human Rights and Dignity by the Tenth World Russian People's Council, which is not an official organization of the ROC, even if the president is the patriarch of Moscow and its seat is at the Danilov Monastery on the premises of the Moscow Patriarchate.[3] In the 2006 Declaration on Human Rights and Dignity, the World Russian People's Council offered an interpretation of human rights based on the link between human "dignity" and human rights through the concept of morality. In other words, although one's "worth" was a given, one's dignity is not a given but a quality acquired by enacting moral principles. The World Russian People's Council was attempting to express an understanding of human rights counter to that of Western liberalism: human rights are not inherently based on the inherent equal worth of all human beings, and thus cannot be used as a basis for the freedom to commit immoral acts. Predictably, and corresponding to the anti-Western positioning of this document, such immoral acts include especially the freedom of sexual expression, which entails but is not limited to gay marriage.

In the 2008 *DFR*, there is no mention of human "worth," but the ROC did manage to maintain the link between dignity and morality. Rather than distinguishing between an inherent worth and a dignity that is earned, the ROC distinguishes between a God-given ontological dignity (I.4) that is "inherent" to human nature even after the Fall (I.1) and a dignified life (I.2). It is in relation to the notion of a "dignified life" that the ROC retains the link between morality and dignity that was evident in the 2006 declaration. What the ROC is attempting to convey is that by virtue of creation, all human beings are given by God an inherent dignity, but, as a result of the Fall and of sin, this dignity has become distorted (I.1), darkened to the point of indiscernibility (I.4), resulting in human "indignity" (I.5), and in the "derogation" and "humiliation" of one's own dignity and that of others (III.1). Up to this point, one would not find much that is controversial in the ROC statement about dignity. It recognizes an irreducible worth of all human beings, which sin obfuscates. The challenge is somehow to confront sin so as to embody, make manifest, and reveal a dignity that already exists. Such an interpretation of dignity is a fairly standard adaptation of the image and likeness distinction (I.2) to a concept—dignity—that actually has had no history in the Orthodox tradition until fairly recently.

What is original in the *DFR* is that the ROC offers an interpretation of human rights based on the distinction between inherent dignity and a dignified life. The ROC argues that because dignity is distorted as a result of sin, obedience to moral principles is the way to restore the dignity inherent to all humans:

> According to the Orthodox tradition, a human being preserves his God-given dignity and grows in it only if he lives in accordance with moral norms

> because these norms express the primordial and therefore authentic human nature not darkened by sin. Thus there is a direct link between human dignity and morality. Moreover, the acknowledgement of personal dignity implies the assertion of personal responsibility. (*DFR*, I.5)

> The development and implementation of the human rights concept should be harmonized with the norms of morality, with the ethical principle laid down by God in human nature and discernable in the voice of conscience. (*DFR*, III.2)

The need for morality for a dignified life means that humans cannot have the "right" to freely exercise their will in whatever way they choose. The basic point is that whatever is defined as a right cannot sanction immorality. What is unique about the ROC's logic is not so much the use of an anthropological distinction between image and likeness so as to justify a particular regime of governance, but that such a distinction is now translated into the modern language of dignity and human rights. By making such a move, the ROC is attempting to simultaneously affirm and deny a so-called clash of civilizations.[4] It denies a clash of civilizations by demonstrating that it is not against modern liberal *notions* of human rights and dignity; it affirms a clash of civilizations by rejecting the dominant Western liberal *understandings* of these concepts. Rights, according to the ROC, should be defined so as not to contradict human beings' duty or responsibility to live a dignified life, or, at the very least, so as not to encourage human indignity caused by sin.

It comes as no surprise, then, that the ROC would seek to not only deny rights claimed on the basis of "legislative and public support given to various vices, such as sexual lechery and perversions," but also deny those based on "the worship of profit and violence . . . abortion, euthanasia, use of human embryos in medicine, experiments changing a person's nature and the like" (*DFR*, III.3). A little more unusual is the ROC's claim that "human rights should not contradict love for one's homeland and neighbours" (III.4), which the ROC justifies by claiming that the "Orthodox tradition traces *patriotism*[5] back to the words of Christ the Savior Himself: 'Greater love has no one than this, that he lay down his life for his friends' (John 15:13)." The ROC amplifies: "One's human rights cannot be set against the values and interests of one's homeland, community and family. The exercise of human rights should not be used to justify any encroachment on religious holy symbols things [*sic*], cultural values and the identity of a nation" (IV.1). Such rights are excluded because, for the

ROC, "in Orthodoxy, there is an immutable conviction that in ordering its life a society should take into account not only human interests and wishes but also the divine truth, the eternal moral law given by the Lord and working in the world no matter whether the will of particular people or people's communities agree with it or not" (III.2).

The ROC is, ironically, appropriating the modern concepts of human rights and dignity to promote a political configuration against which human rights and dignity language was meant to protect.[6] It does so by positioning its interpretation of human rights and dignity against "secularized standards of human rights" (*DFR*, III.2). Although the freedom of conscience is designated as a right (IV.3), it is relegated to the private sphere, because the ROC promotes a public political space infused with the moral principles of Orthodox Christianity (as interpreted by the ROC) and enforced legislatively by the state. The language of rights and dignity is still used, but within this specific religiously inflected moral horizon. What has formed the basis for a plurality of moralities in the West is being used to define a morally homogeneous space as an identity marker against the West. According to the ROC, laws against "gay propaganda" and arrests for "blasphemous" expressions do not violate rights, and thus dignity, since they only violate the morality that facilitates a "dignified life." Also significant is that this rhetoric by the ROC has geopolitical significance, insofar as it is being used by Vladimir Putin to carve out a new ideological divide based on the opposition between traditional and liberal values.[7] According to Putin's rhetoric, he is not against democracy, but he is globalizing the American culture wars for the sake of demarcating a stable Russian identity based on the fusion of nationalism and religion.

The ROC's notion of acquired dignity might sound odd and lead one to the impression that the ROC does not affirm an inherent value to human life, in a way that is strikingly similar to positions held by Peter Singer and Ronald Dworkin.[8] The ROC's position, however, is not claiming that a human has no worth, and, thus, no entitlement to rights until a certain point of development. The distinction between inherent dignity and dignified life is much closer to the argument advanced by Timothy Jackson, who distinguishes claims to rights based on sanctity and those based on dignity.[9] For Jackson, dignity is acquired, and it serves as the basis for interest-based rights that are meant to realize just relations within public political space. As examples of such earned dignity-based rights, Jackson mentions the right to vote or the right to operate a motor vehicle. Jackson even reserves the word "person" for those who have acquired such dignity. His intent, however, is not to support the views of Singer or Dworkin, but to counter them. He does so by arguing that there can be no acquired dignity if not for the affirmation of need-based rights that are based in the inviolable sanctity of the human being, which rights ultimately ground our duties to love those who have not or cannot acquire the dignity of personhood. For Jackson, the affirmation of the sanctity of all human beings allows for the realization of acquired dignity; as a result of this sanctity, the human being is owed certain rights so as to develop toward personhood, and, if that is not possible, then these need-based rights are still valid and the only way to protect from depersonalization. It is only because of God-given sanctity, for example, that someone suffering from Alzheimer's can be affirmed as unique and inviolable, even if their capacities render them a "nonperson."

Even though the position of the ROC resonates with that of Jackson's, there are fundamental differences beyond the conclusions each draws for the right to gay marriage. The ROC is arguing that although there is inherent dignity, the duty of the human is to grow toward holiness, which allows for the restriction of certain rights that make a claim to sinful action; Jackson argues that the human is given sanctity that grounds need-based rights that allow for protection of inviolability and development of capacities toward dignity. There is a clear gospel-law framework informing Jackson's understanding of image and likeness, while the ROC is drawing from the Orthodox tradition's understanding of deification, or *theosis.* I would argue, however, that although the Orthodox understanding of deification does lend itself to a certain inherent worth-development model of dignity, a more careful analysis of the dynamics of *theosis*, or what I call divine–human communion, leads to an understanding of dignity and its implications for human rights much closer to Jackson's position.

DIGNITY AS IMAGE AND LIKENESS

In working toward a foundational understanding of "dignity" within the Orthodox tradition, one has first to begin by admitting that there is no such concept within the Greek patristic tradition, whose texts are authoritative for Orthodox theology. There is no equivalent in Greek for *dignitas*, and, in terms of what the original Latin was attempting to convey as an acquired status, the closest Greek word might be *taxis*, "order," "office," "rank," which was often based on a person's *charisma* (gift, skill). Theologically, the meaning of this term was often seen through the lens of deification, as divine–human communion was an event of hierarchically arranged relations between various symbolic offices based on particular gifts. "Hierarchy" in this sense was not understood as a top-down form of communication, but an acknowledgment that certain symbols, human offices, and otherwise were more symbolically charged than others in the relational event of divine–human communion.[10]

When it comes to the modern notion of dignity as inherent, immeasurable, and of equal worth, not surprisingly our attention must be toward the distinction between image and likeness. Early in the Christian tradition, theological anthropology was shaped by the notion that the human was made according to the image and likeness of God.[11] The distinction itself is based on Genesis 1:26, "Then God said, 'Let us make man in our image, after our likeness.'" References to this distinction are ubiquitous throughout the patristic tradition, and it is meant to affirm that in the creation of the human, God's being is communicated to the human being as God "breathed in something of his own breath" (Gen. 2:7). How exactly to conceptualize human participation in God such that the human images God is one of the fundamental questions that has driven the Christian intellectual tradition.

Throughout the patristic texts, the basic point is that image refers to a "primordial gift," while likeness refers to a "calling to be realized."[12] This primordial gift was eventually defined in terms of godlike characteristics, such as rationality, free choice, and perception, which are wired into the human and reflect something of God. These capacities are static in that they are indelible qualities of the human, but also dynamic in the sense that they form the basis of moving toward the likeness, which is the realization of divine–human communion through the actualization of virtue.[13] What prevents movement toward the likeness is sin, which causes human capacities to function wrongly, but can never erase the fact that the human has capacities reflective of God's being.

Irenaeus of Lyons was one of the first early Christians writers to build a theological anthropology around the image and likeness distinction.[14] Irenaeus provided the basic architecture that was to shape Greek patristic thinking on the human person, including the position that at creation the human was made in both the image and the likeness of God, and what was lost at the Fall was the likeness.[15] The human by virtue of her being created always presences the divine, but since the Fall, she reflects this divine presence to a greater and lesser degree. The restoration to the likeness, however, is not to become again like

Adam, but to become like Christ, the Son of the Father, who makes possible this restoration. To participate in divine–human communion, which is to iconize God's very being, is to image Christ, who is the image of the Father. This manifestation of the likeness after the Fall is available to all humans without any discrimination, since "there is no longer Jew or Greek, there is no longer slave or free, there is no longer male or female; for all of you are one in Christ" (Gal. 3:28).

In terms of understanding the inherent, indelible worth of the human being as equal to all human beings without discrimination, the distinction between image and likeness of God establishes this "human dignity" on three levels: (1) at creation, where all humans are created in the image and likeness of God; (2) at the Fall, where all humans are affected by the effects of sin; (3) and at salvation, which is available to all humans in equal measure and whose possibility sin cannot preclude. In the end, however, priority is given to the salvific pole because the equality affirmed at the level of creation and sin is ultimately interpreted in light of the communion with God, for which the human was created. This divine–human communion is what has been restored in Christ, and it is the realization of all that the human was created to be *in* God. Vladimir Lossky succinctly states, "It is in the context of the Incarnation (say rather: it is by the fact, by the event of the Incarnation) that the creation of man in the image of God receives all its theological value, which remained unperceived (or somewhat impoverished) in the letter of the sacerdotal narrative of the creation as seen by critical exegesis."[16] It would be wrong, however, to interpret this theological anthropology as saying that the human only has worth to the degree that the human acquires holiness, but, it is not simply by virtue of creation that all humans have equal worth, because humans were created *for* communion with God. It is, thus, by virtue of the human potential to be in communion with God, to iconize God's being, to love as God loves, which is possible for all humans regardless of their capacities and by virtue of their creation, that humans have equal worth. Another way to put this is that it is in this communion with God that is finally revealed the equal worth of all humans that has always been reflected on the side of God.

DIGNITY AS IRREDUCIBLE UNIQUENESS

In contemporary Orthodox theology, the distinction between image and likeness would continue to shape theological anthropology, but it would now be interpreted within the framework of one of the most important developments in twentieth-century Orthodoxy—the theology of personhood. Still, even in those theologians most responsible for an Orthodox theology of personhood, one would be hard-pressed to find references to "dignity." This does not mean, however, that this theology of personhood does not affirm human dignity understood as equal and inherent worth.

The development of contemporary Orthodox theology of personhood is a much-debated and complicated story. Most contemporary Orthodox theologians have argued that this theology of personhood was first developed during the theological debates of the fourth century, and there are those, of course, who dispute this claim.[17] It is clear, however, that certain features of the contemporary Orthodox understanding of personhood are a result of the modern context. For example, the Orthodox theology of personhood rests on a distinction between nature and person, in which nature is identified with necessity and person/hypostasis is identified with freedom. Vladimir Lossky was the first to popularize this way of understanding "personhood":

> "person" signifies the irreducibility of man to his nature—"irreducibility" and not "something irreducible" or "something which makes man irreducible to his nature" precisely because it cannot be a question here of "something" distinct from "another nature" but of *someone* who is distinct from his own nature, of someone who goes beyond his nature while still containing it, who makes it exist as human nature by this overstepping and yet does not exist in himself beyond the nature which he "enhypostasizes" and which he constantly exceeds.[18]

Elsewhere he elaborates that "the idea of person implies freedom vis-à-vis the nature. The person is free from its nature, is not determined by it."[19]

The antinomy, however, between nature-as-necessity and hypostasis-as-freedom is evident in Sergius Bulgakov, even if Bulgakov never developed a "theology of personhood." This antinomy between necessity and freedom in human subjectivity is also discernible in German idealist philosophy.[20] Although one can identify the distinction between *hypostasis/prosopon* and *ousia* in the Trinitarian and Christological controversies of the fourth century, the mapping of the freedom/necessity distinction onto the *hypostasis/ousia* distinction resulted from Bulgakov's engagement with German idealist philosophy. As he states, "In the creaturely spirit, nature is givenness or unfreedom. It is necessity that is realized in the freedom of the person."[21] Bulgakov, however, does not see such a development as an unauthorized invasion of philosophy into theology, since he sees the German idealist appropriation as indebted to early Christian debates and, in this sense, somewhat continuous with this patristic tradition.[22]

Lossky was the one who appropriated[23] the mapping of the necessity/freedom distinction onto the Trinitarian/Christological nature/person distinction in such a way as to unhinge it from traces of German idealism and situate it squarely within the Trinitarian theology. Lossky effectively would make use of Bulgakov's understanding of the person/nature distinction in terms of necessity and freedom and patristicize it against Bulgakov, making it appear as if the mapping of one distinction onto the other emerged solely within the patristic tradition.[24]

Lossky interpreted the image/likeness distinction through the lens of the distinction between nature = necessity and person = freedom in way that would influence later Orthodox theology, but this does not, ironically, clearly resonate with patristic formulations of this image and likeness. The major difference is that for Lossky, the two dimensions of human existence—nature and *hypostasis* (person)—image the Trinitarian life of God. The categories of nature and person in Trinitarian theology express the antinomic unity-in-diversity of God's Trinitarian life. In an analogous way, humans are meant to relate to one another so as to possess the nature that is in common but in such a way that manifests the irreducible uniqueness of each person. Lossky states, "The ineffable distinction of the Three Persons and the One Nature in God, should find the same mysterious distinction in beings created in God's image. *It is only on this basis that a correct formulation of the teaching on the Church and the world can be found.*"[25] The category of person is meant to indicate the uniqueness of the human being that is irreducible to nature, or to specific characteristics of nature. It is this notion of personhood as irreducible uniqueness that resonates with the modern notion of dignity.

To clarify, the human being, according to Lossky, "is not merely an individual of a particular nature, included in the generic relationship of human nature to god the Creator of the whole cosmos, but he is also—he is chiefly—a person, not reducible to the common (or even individualized) attributes of the nature which he shares with other human individuals."[26] Since the human person is irreducible to nature, Lossky disagrees with the identification of the "image of God" with the "higher faculties" of the human being, such as the human intellect, even if such an identification can be found in someone such as St. Gregory of Nyssa.[27] Lossky almost anticipates postmodern antiessentialism in resisting any understanding of the human being as a "something," as an object reducible to essentialist categories.

The person as person is called to be free from the "necessity" and the "domination of nature," and it is in this freedom that one sees the image of God in the human person.[28] By freedom from the necessity and domination of nature, Lossky means free from the limitations inherent in created nature, from being defined and thus reduced to a specific trait or characteristic of nature, and from the effects of sin that have divided the common human nature into individuals with each defining herself over and against other individuals, rather than in the personal existence of unity-in-diversity. In the fallen world, "human beings tend to exist by excluding each other. Each himself by contrasting himself with others, i.e. in dividing—in parceling out—the unity of nature, each owning a portion of human nature for himself, so that 'my' will contrasts 'myself' with all that is 'not I.' In this light, what we call a person is not that, but an individual."[29] In one of the few references to dignity in the entire Eastern Christian intellectual tradition, Lossky declares that "the truth of man is beyond all conditioning; and his dignity consists in being able to liberate himself from his nature, not by consuming it or abandoning it to itself . . . but by transfiguring it in God."[30]

It would be a mistake to interpret this transfiguration of nature as a negation. The nature/person distinction is meant to express the unity-in-diversity of created existence, even if it is obfuscated by sin. Lossky affirms that "as a natural creature, man is part of this integral, created world." The human being, however, is more than simply being a part of the whole: "As a self-aware created person, each man is a single being, absolutely unique, which cannot be reduced to anything else, which is distinct from everything, undefinable and rationally unknowable."[31] To *be* a human person is simultaneously "transcending the nature which it 'enhypostasizes,'" and this transfiguration/transcending results "by virtue of a singular and unique relation to God who created him 'in His image.'"[32] Personhood is, in the end, a gift of unique relationship with the living God, which renders each human being unique. In the sense that humans are never not in relation to this God, humans are always "in the image," but in the sense that we were created for divine–human communion, *theosis*, which was made difficult because of sin, this irreducibly unique relationship is a manifestation (not achievement) through participation in the divine energies of God. Insofar as the human being is never not in unique relation with God, who never reduces the human being to the common nature, then this human is always "in the image"; insofar as deification manifests this uniqueness such that the human reflects the life of God, then the human person is "according to the likeness," "manifesting God in the extent to which his nature allows itself to be penetrated by deifying grace. Thus the image—which is inalienable—can become similar or dissimilar, to the extreme limits: that of union with God, when deified man shows in himself by grace what God is by nature, according to the expression of St. Maximus; or, indeed that of the extremity of falling away which Plotinus called 'the place of dissimilarity' . . . placing it in the gloomy abyss of Hades."[33]

John Zizioulas developed Lossky's theology of personhood, but he made more explicit what is implicit in Lossky—personhood as irreducible uniqueness is realized in the event of communion. He would further define Lossky's understanding of personhood as freedom from the necessity as an *ecstatic* dimension of personhood, while irreducible uniqueness that *is* personhood indicates the *hypostatic* dimension.[34] Zizioulas also affirmed Lossky's understanding of the image of God in the human as imaging the Trinitarian life, but he amplified by stating that the human images God's Trinitarian life, but in such a way as "to mirror the communion and otherness that exists in the triune God."[35] Zizioulas, however, links the theology of personhood to a Eucharistic ecclesiology in such a way that is not evident in Lossky and that infuses his understanding of all aspects of theology. His argument is, in short, that personhood as an ecstatic event of freedom from the necessity of nature and for the Other is a relational event that simultaneously constitutes the human being as hypostatic, or as irreducibly unique. Such an event is that of the body of Christ, where the human being relates to God the Father as and in the Son and by the Holy Spirit and, in so doing, relates to all Others, human or otherwise, in love and freedom.

What is also distinctive about Zizioulas's theology of personhood is that he argues that the image of God that is wired into the human being is indicated by a drive toward personal uniqueness. This drive is implicit in the phenomenology of the question, "Who am I?"

> The human being, by asking the question, "Who am I?" expects to raise the particular to the level of ontological primacy. This is built into this question of his being, as we have already seen. In so doing, man wishes to be God, for the conditions that we have set out for this ontology of personhood exist only in God. Is that the *imago Dei* in man? I believe it is. But the realization of this drive of man toward personal ontology cannot be provided by created being.[36]

Zizioulas also points to the human creation of art[37] and to the procreative act[38] in order to illustrate for us the human longing for uniqueness and freedom. In the end, however, this longing for uniqueness is tragic in the sense that it is impossible within the limits of created existence. Death thwarts such longing, reducing all to sameness. Such a longing is fulfilled only if there exists an eternal relationship in which the human being, together with all of creation, is constituted as free and irreducibly unique. It is for this reason that the Eucharist is the event par excellence of personhood, because it is the event of being constituted as the body of Christ and, as such, as children of God.

Again, it may seem as if Zizioulas is saying that humans have worth only if they realize a particular relationship with God, but such an interpretation is a misreading. First, it is important to indicate that although the idea that personhood as irreducible uniqueness is a relational event may sound jarring, it is remarkable how much it resonates with human experience. Zizioulas is not saying that one is a human person only if certain capacities are developed—he explicitly, as with Lossky, disavows such an interpretation. He is saying, however, that our being as irreducibly unique is constituted in particular relations. Such an understanding of personal uniqueness rings true especially if one considers how Nazi concentration camps and the Soviet Gulags are clear examples of structures of relationships that depersonalize the human being, constituting him or her as nonunique and unfree while subjecting him or her to extreme forms of oppression. In such situations, the human being can claim to be unique and free from the oppressor, but the reality is such that this cry for recognition is ignored. As liberation theologians have rightly argued, the relational matrix of the concentration camp or the Gulag or of extreme poverty renders such human being as "nonpersons." The only basis for justifying this claim to uniqueness and freedom in the midst of oppression is an eternal relationship with God, who is eternally relating to each human being in such a way as to always be constituting the human being as unique and free, even if fallen conditions do not allow for the realization of such an experience of personhood. The relational understanding of personhood in terms of freedom and uniqueness is also clearly manifested in those who suffer from Alzheimer's disease, which is a disease that seeks to destroy one's uniqueness and freedom. For those who suffer from Alzheimer's, their capacity to remember the details of their own unique story or the people who are a part of that story disintegrates and they are trapped in a world of confused thoughts and fleeting images. In such a state, the only hope for affirming the uniqueness of the Alzheimer's patient is through their loved ones, who have always related to the Alzheimer's patient as "Helen," "Maria," "George," or "Seraphim," even as the Alzheimer's patient cannot remember his or her own unique name. It is also becoming clear that the experience of violence leaves a trace on the body, subjecting the human being to a certain kind of necessity that damages one's capacity for relationality and one's sense of self-worth. In the experience of violence, the victim attempts to transcend this necessity to restore the capacity for relationality and is enabled by certain kinds of relationship.[39]

In developing this contemporary theology of personhood, Lossky and Zizioulas affirm the antinomic dimension of being "in the image" as inalienable and yet-to-be-realized. Furthermore, they further define the notion of dignity as equal worth in terms of irreducible uniqueness. What Zizioulas, however, emphasizes is that irreducible uniqueness is not an essential quality inherent to the human but an event of relationship. The human being is never not irreducibly unique, because the human is always in relationship to the eternal God who loves each uniquely. God does not stop loving us because of sin; sin only makes it difficult for the human to experience the love of God that is always being offered. To say, also, that humans are constituted as irreducibly unique in particular relations does not mean that we are unique *because* God loves us; we do not possess inherent worth *because* God has created us. It is, of course, by virtue of this creation that the human being exists, but once created our inherent worth simply *is* by virtue of who we are. God does not love us *because* . . . ; God simply loves us, and it is in this love that we discover we are unique and, hence, are constituted as irreducibly unique, as dignified.

BACK TO THE RUSSIANS

We see in contemporary Orthodox theology a broad consensus that, based on the theological distinction between image and likeness, each human being is affirmed as having a worth that is equal to all other human beings. There is also agreement that all are affected by sin, but that each human being has the capacity through grace to be in a divine–human communion. The human being was created in relation to God for the sake of deepening this divine–human communion. The incarnation of Christ provided new hope for what sin made difficult. There is, thus, an affirmation that spiritual progress in *theosis* is possible for all and to each according to their histories and capacities, and this spiritual movement only manifests the irreducible uniqueness that one *is* in relationship to the living God. To understand the full range of the equivalency of "dignity" within the Orthodox tradition, one must see the various dimensions of being human. It is not as simple as saying that just by virtue of being created by God that each human being has equal worth, even though this is affirmed in the tradition, both past and present, as I have indicated.

What cannot be ignored is that the modern notion of "dignity" emerged in relation to thinking about the public political space, and it is difficult today to hear the word without thinking of the political. It is also interesting that the most sustained Orthodox theological analysis on specifically the word "dignity" comes from the ROC's document on human rights. It would therefore be important to assess whether, in fact, the ROC's conclusions are the inevitable result of Orthodox understandings of the human person in terms of equal worth and irreducible particularity, even when considering and accepting the call to divine–human communion.[40]

First, it must be recognized that the language of human rights has a political purpose and is meant to structure relations within a public political space. In light of this, the ROC document does convey the sense of the Orthodox tradition that, insofar as human rights language allows humans to make justifiable demands on each other, then humans were created for the kinds of relations that are simply more than what can be achieved through the assertion of rights. Put differently, rights language simply does not indicate all that is possible for humans. Nor could one agree with Nicholas Wolterstorff's claim that God has the right "to be worshipped" and "to our obedience to such commands as God may issue."[41] God creates the not-God out of love for love; to say that God has a right to our love has the force of obligation, which is not loving God for God's sake. In this sense, rights language cannot make sense of the event of divine–human communion for which the human was created, whether that be on the side of God or the human.

Human rights language thus has something to do with structuring relations in the public political space, which is not the ecclesial/sacramental space. The political space cannot assume that all who occupy this space share the same beliefs. For the Christian, it means that it is the space where the stranger and even the enemy is encountered most intensely. The public political space has a purpose analogous to, but not identical with, the ecclesial/sacramental space.

The ROC's mistake is not so much understanding "dignity" in antinomic terms of both inalienability and process; the ROC's mistake is in eliding the ecclesial and the political and seeing the latter as that whose purpose is to facilitate divine–human communion.[42] The ROC's theological error is not in terms of theological anthropology, but in terms of the relation between theological anthropology and ecclesiology (and, one could add here, Trinitarian theology). What is missing from the ROC document is the affirmation within the tradition, clearly evident in both Lossky and Zizioulas but in different ways, that divine–human communion is an event given within the Church. What the ROC calls "dignified life" is an ecclesial reality and, as such, can form the basis of structuring the public political space in a form analogous to the ecclesial/sacramental space. Put another way, the goal of the public political space is not *theosis*, but something like *theosis* in the attempt to structure relations among those who do not share common beliefs about what is ultimate. If, in fact, the human worth, or dignity, is an event of irreducible uniqueness constituted through particular forms of relationships, then the public political space must be structured in such a way as to maximize the conditions for the possibility for irreducible uniqueness, or, in other words, for not being rendered a "nonperson." Dignity as irreducible uniqueness in the political space is analogous to dignity as an ecclesial and sacramental reality; as such, in the political space it must account for the structuring of relations based on fear and sin.

In light of the distinction between the ecclesial/sacramental and the public political space, the language of human rights is meant to provide the normative structures of human relations whereby the human person is treated as a unique and irreducible human being. A public political space structured in this way the Orthodox can judge as mirroring sacramental communities in which humans are constituted as unique and irreplaceable. Zizioulas himself states, "Pursuant to the idea of personhood as something relational . . . people all have the same value and the same rights because they themselves represent unique and unrepeatable identities for those with whom they are in a personal relationship. Therefore, *the law is obligated to respect and protect everyone, regardless of one's characteristics, because every man bears a relational identity, and with that, is a unique and unrepeatable person.*"[43]

If the ecclesial and public political spaces are not to be elided, then it makes no theological sense to exclude rights that would contradict love for "homeland" or "patriotism" or allow for "blasphemy" or "gay marriage." In excluding such rights, the ROC extends the ecclesial/sacramental space into the public political space univocally as a way of justifying a soteriological application of human rights language. Such a move is theologically unwarranted on the basis of the ROC's own affirmation that the human was created for divine–human communion, since to use the power of the state to enforce the morality that is meant to structure a life toward divine–human communion would be to apply the language of human rights to what is possible only within the ecclesial/sacramental space, and would be to elide the political and the ecclesial/sacramental space. Put another way, if one affirms that the human was created for *theosis*, then there is no theological justification for the Christian to assert historical or cultural privileges within a public political space. The Christian is called to work toward political structures that maximize the conditions for the possibility of realizing irreducible uniqueness, which would involve affirming human rights language that allows what would be unthinkable within an ecclesial/sacramental space. As an example, if God has created the human with the ability to freely reject God, then the Church cannot use the power of the state to outlaw public expressions of this rejection, which may even manifest themselves as blasphemous.

What the ROC also forgets is that the so-called dignified life to which it gives witness is an ascetical struggle to love as God loves, which means to love the stranger and the enemy. In seeing the political as an arena demanding the *askesis* of love, we are reminded of Jackson's project of arguing for the relevancy of love for politics. If the goal of the public political space is justice, then such justice cannot be achieved without obligations to love based on the affirmation of the sanctity of the human being. This love-based justice would require of the Christian to affirm laws and rights that would structure just relations among human beings who do not share the same beliefs. In a similar fashion, if the ascetical journey for divine–human communion is a learning how to love that results in a relational event of irreducible uniqueness, the political is one of the many deserts in which that struggles occurs. In the public political space, the ascetical struggle occurs in the face of others who are often determined to destroy all that we cherish. In the face of the political other as either friend or foe, this love-driven *askesis* works for a justice that would structure relations that facilitate the realization of personhood as irreducible uniqueness—dignity. The temptation, however, is to exercise one's "right" to violence and force against those to whom we relate as Other. Such violence and force are especially evident in laws against so-called gay propaganda in Russia. It is in the enforcement of such laws where we see, ironically, the negation of dignity, most especially by those who seem to support it.

NOTES

1. See https://mospat.ru/en/documents/dignity-freedom-rights/.

2. For an excellent overview of the role of the Russian Orthodox Church in Russian politics, see Irina Papkova, *The Russian Orthodox Church and Russian Politics* (Oxford: Oxford University Press, 2011). Papkova concludes that the ROC's influence within Russian politics was insignificant, even if media coverage made it appear to be more pervasive. Since 2011, however, it is clear that Vladimir Putin has used Russia's religious past to carve out a new East/West ideological divide not demarcated by capitalism versus communism, but by godless, Western liberal values versus traditional religious values. Putin has effectively globalized the American culture wars and linked them to Russian nationalism.

3. For an excellent analysis and comparison of the two documents, together with a historical overview of the ROC rhetoric on human rights and dignity since the collapse of the Soviet Union, see Kristina Stoeckl, *The Russian Orthodox Church and Human Rights* (New York: Routledge, 2014). See also Stoeckl, "Moral Argument in the Human Rights Debate of the Russian Orthodox Church," in *Christianity, Democracy and the Shadow of Constantine*, ed. George Demacopoulos and Aristotle Papanikolaou (New York: Fordham University Press, 2017). My analysis of the 2006 Human Rights Declaration of the World Russian People's Council is based on Stoeckl's analysis. I have also benefited greatly from the research of the Postsecular Conflicts Project, funded by the European Research Council, whose principal investigator is Kristina Stoeckl, and for which I serve on the Advisory Board.

4. On this, see Stoeckl, *The Russian Orthodox Church and Human Rights.*

5. Emphasis mine. I know of absolutely no precedent in Orthodox hermeneutics that uses this passage to justify "patriotism."

6. For such appropriation, see the recent construction of http://orthodoxrights.org/.

7. Anyone who doubts that Putin is using Russia's Orthodox history and theology as a way of carving out a Russian identity against Western liberalism will, I hope, be convinced by the picture of Putin at the church of Protaton Karyes, standing in a throne that once was occupied by the Byzantine emperor but is now traditionally occupied either by a bishop or the abbot of a monastery; see http://www.sandiegouniontribune.com/news/2016/may/28/putin-visits-orthodox-monastic-community-at-mount/.

8. Peter Singer, *Practical Ethics* (Cambridge: Cambridge University Press, 1993); Ronald Dworkin, *Life's Dominion: An Argument about Abortion, Euthanasia and Individual Freedom* (New York: Knopf, 1993).

9. Timothy P. Jackson, *Political Agape: Christian Love and Liberal Democracy* (Grand Rapids, MI: William B. Eerdmans, 2015).

10. Ashley Purpura, *God, Hierarchy and Power: Orthodox Theologies of Authority from Byzantium* (New York: Fordham University Press, 2017). I thank Ashley for conversations and insights around this theme.

11. For an excellent summary of the basic idea of the Orthodox understanding of the distinction between image and likeness, see Verna Harrison, "The Human Person as Image and Likeness of God," in *The Cambridge Companion to Orthodox Christian Theology*, ed. Mary B. Cunningham and Elizabeth Theokritoff (Cambridge: Cambridge University Press, 2008), 78–92.

12. Peter Bouteneff, *Beginnings: Ancient Christian Readings of the Biblical Creation Narratives* (Grand Rapids, MI: Baker Academic, 2008), 80.

13. Harrison, "The Human Person as Image and Likeness of God," 78.

14. Bouteneff, *Beginnings*, 80.

15. Ibid.

16. Vladimir Lossky, "The Theology of the Image," in *In the Image and Likeness of God*, ed. John H. Erickson and Thomas E. Bird (Crestwood, NY: St. Vladimir's Seminary Press, 1974), 136.

17. Most notably, John Behr, *The Nicene Faith*, vol. 2, *The Formation of Christian Theology* (Crestwood, NY: St. Vladimir's Seminary Press, 2004); and Lewis Ayres, *Nicaea and Its Legacy: An Approach to Fourth-Century Trinitarian Theology* (Oxford: Oxford University Press, 2004).

18. Vladimir Lossky, "The Theological Notion of the Human Person," in Erickson and Bird, eds., *In the Image and Likeness of God*, 120. See Lossky, *Orthodox Theology: An Introduction*, trans. Ian Kesarcodi-Watson and Ihita Kesarcodi-Watson (Crestwood, NY: St. Vladimir's Seminary Press, 1989), 72: "The Person . . . is then man's freedom with regard to his nature, 'the fact of being freed from necessity and not being subject to the domination of nature, but able to determine oneself freely' (St. Gregory of Nyssa)." No reference is given for the quote from Nyssa.

19. Vladimir Lossky, *The Mystical Theology of the Eastern Church* (Crestwood, NY: St. Vladimir's Seminary Press, 1976), 122.

20. On this point and its influence on Bulgakov, see Brandon Gallaher, *Freedom and Necessity in Modern Trinitarian Theology* (Oxford: Oxford University Press, 2016).

21. Sergius Bulgakov, *The Bride of the Lamb*, trans. Boris Jakim (Grand Rapids, MI: William B. Eerdmans, 2002), 128. This is but one of numerous citations in Bulgakov's work mapping the freedom/necessity distinction onto the person/nature distinction.

22. For an excellent analysis of "dignity" in Bulgakov's thought, and in light of the ROC's recent statements on dignity and human rights, see Regula Zwahlen, "Sergej Bulgakov's Concept of Human Dignity," in *Orthodox Christianity and Human Rights*, ed. Alfons Brüning and Evert van der Zweerde (Leuven: Peeters, 2012), 169–86.

23. Together with many other categories of Bulgakov, such as kenosis of the Son and kenosis of the Holy Spirit, antinomy, individual versus person, and reference to the Incarnation as "fact" that serves as foundation for all theology. On this point, see Aristotle Papanikolaou, "Eastern Orthodox Theology," in *The Routledge Companion to Modern Christian Thought*, ed. Chad Meister and James Beilby (London: Routledge, 2013), 538–48.

24. This move by Lossky never really took into account the fact that Bulgakov was the first in the history of Eastern Christian thought to provide a history of ideas that

would show the development of patristic thought, both in terms of continuity and discontinuity. What differentiates the two theologians is that Bulgakov saw recent developments in German idealist philosophy as indebted to the Christian tradition, but in need of correction. He was not shy, however, in this correction to indicate what was right about German idealist thought. Lossky saw the relation between philosophy and theology more in terms of an absolute break.

25. Vladimir Lossky, "Personality and Thought of His Holiness Patriarch Sergiy," trans. A. Chulyukina, *Journal of the Moscow Patriarchate* 40, no. 12 (1984): 69 (emphasis mine).

26. Lossky, "The Theology of the Image," 137.

27. Ibid., 138. See also Lossky, *Orthodox Theology*, 103.

28. Lossky, *The Mystical Theology*, 119.

29. Vladimir Lossky, "Redemption and Deification," in Erickson and Bird, eds., *In the Image and Likeness of God*, 106–7.

30. Lossky, *Orthodox Theology*, 72.

31. Lossky, "The Personality and Thought of His Holiness Patriarch Sergiy," 268.

32. Lossky, "The Theology of the Image," 137.

33. Ibid., 139.

34. See John Zizioulas, *Being as Communion* (Crestwood, NY: St. Vladimir's Seminary Press, 1985).

35. John Zizioulas, *Communion and Otherness: Further Studies in Personhood and the Church*, ed. Paul McPartlan (London: T&T Clark, 2006), 4–5 and 249.

36. Ibid., 108.

37. Ibid., 206–49.

38. John Zizioulas, *Being as Communion*, 50–53.

39. On the effects of violence and trauma on the body's capacity for relationships of trust and intimacy, see, especially, Bessel van der Kolk, *The Body Keeps the Score: Brain, Mind, and Body in the Healing of Trauma* (New York: Penguin, 2014). See also Judith Herman, *Trauma and Recovery* (New York: Basic Books, 1992). See also Aristotle Papanikolaou, "Person, Kenosis and Abuse," *Modern Theology* 19, no. 1 (2003): 41–66; Papanikolaou, "Liberating Eros: Confession and Desire," *Journal of the Society of Christian Ethics* 26, no. 1 (2006): 115–36; and Papanikolaou, "The Undoing and Redoing of Virtue," in *Orthodox Perspectives on War*, ed. Perry T. Hamalis and Valerie Karras (Notre Dame, IN: University of Notre Dame Press, 2017).

40. For a more substantive account of what follows, see Aristotle Papanikolaou, *The Mystical as Political: Democracy and Non-Radical Orthodoxy* (Notre Dame, IN: University of Notre Dame Press, 2012), esp. chap. 3. See also Pantelis Kalaitzidis, "Individual versus Collective Rights: The Theological Foundation of Human Rights. An Eastern Orthodox View," in *Orthodox Christianity and Human Rights in Europe: A Dialogue between Theological Paradigms and Socio-Legal Pragmatics*, ed. Elisa Diamantopoulou and Louis-Léon Christians (Brussels: Peter Lang, 2018).

41. Nicholas Wolterstorff, *Justice, Rights and Wrongs* (Princeton, NJ: Princeton University Press, 2008), 248 and 281.

42. According to Zwahlen, Bulgakov makes a similar distinction, though expressed in terms of law and morality. See Zwahlen, "Sergej Bulgakov's Concept of Human Dignity," 173.

43. John Zizioulas, "Law and Personhood in Orthodox Theology," in *The One and the Many: Studies on God, Man, the Church and the Word Today* (Alhambra, CA: Sebastian Press, 2010), 408 (emphasis original).

nine

PROTESTANT AND ORTHODOX PERSPECTIVES ON DIGNITY

A Response

Matthew R. Petrusek

Reading the Protestant and Orthodox conceptions of dignity in tandem provides an illuminating reminder of how much the two forms of Christianity share—and how much they do not. Indeed, dignity offers an excellent heuristic for identifying and analyzing the traditions' underlying theological similarities and differences while also demonstrating, more broadly, how much theology makes a difference for ethics.

In this response, I will compare David Gushee's and Aristotle Papanikolaou's respective conceptions of the *imago Dei* and how they relate to dignity. On the surface, it may appear that, despite the foundational role the *imago* plays in both Protestantism and Orthodoxy, there may be more differences than similarities with respect to the particular function of the *imago* in justifying the existence and nature of dignity. For example, Gushee recognizes that humans are made in the image and likeness of God, but he maintains that dignity comes from God *declaring* that humans are sacred in and through Jesus Christ rather than from any ontological feature of humanity. Papanikolaou, in contrast, draws on the Orthodox distinction between "image" and "likeness" to argue that humans retain an intrinsic goodness after the Fall that endows them with universal worth. In other words, Gushee appears to embrace a "relational" conception of dignity; Papanikolaou advances an "inherent" one.

Yet a closer reading demonstrates that the two are not as far apart as they may appear. Papanikolaou upholds an inherent dimension to dignity, but he also describes it as "irreducible uniqueness," which, he argues, is not primarily the consequence of God having created human beings but rather because of God's choice *to love* humans in an "event of relationship." This "event" points to a surprising affinity between Protestantism and Orthodoxy: both conceive of human worth primarily through the lens of relationality rather than ontology, which means, despite their different interpretations of the effect of sin, that both traditions locate dignity in God's active will rather than God's one-time act of creation.

It is just past this point, however, that the two traditions diverge, for what seems to be the beginning and end of the story for Gushee is just the beginning for Papanikolaou. Orthodox theology recognizes a *process* (or, in Papanikolaou's language, a "manifesting") of becoming more fully human by conforming oneself to Christ—what Orthodoxy calls "theosis" and what Papanikolaou translates as "divine–human communion." There does not appear to be anything substantively analogous to this qualitative moral and spiritual growth in Gushee. In this sense, then, Gushee's conception of dignity is "static"; Papanikolaou's is "dynamic."

The role of sanctification in distinguishing Protestant theology from Orthodox (and Catholic) theology is well-established.[1] However, I will argue that it takes on distinctive ethical significance in this context: tying dignity to a form of moral and spiritual growth—that is, seeing dignity not only as fixed but also teleological—provides the grounds for claiming that dignity is vulnerable to human action. It is this very vulnerability, I will argue, that provides a coherent explanation for why dignity is in need of protection, which, in turn, helps establish a coherent grounding for the necessity of "rights." Papanikolaou's theology can explain how dignity is vulnerable in this way; however, it is not clear that Gushee's formulation of dignity as a divine "ascription" can do the same. Thus, notwithstanding the foundational similarities between the Protestant and Orthodox accounts of dignity, I will argue not only that the dissimilar underlying theologies render different conceptions of dignity's vulnerability to human action, but also that this difference has profound ethical implications.

RELATIONAL DIGNITY IN GUSHEE'S THOUGHT

Gushee's chapter begins by distinguishing his conception of dignity from secular and Catholic ones. Catholic and secular accounts disagree on the *ultimate* source of dignity, but both, Gushee believes, locate dignity in the human person, primarily in the form of the existence and exercise of constitutive human capacities, including rationality, freedom, relationality, love, subjectivity, mutuality, unfathomability, and transcendence (178). Gushee's argument against grounding dignity in these kinds of capacities is in part a historical one. He writes, "Many individuals, communities, and societies over millennia have observed the same great capacities . . . and have not chosen to respond by believing in or practicing a norm of respect for the dignity of any, some, or all of their neighbors" (178). Gushee also rejects formulations of dignity that make positivist legal appeals (e.g., "dignity exists because it is written in a constitution") or appeals based on sheer affirmation, which he sees in the Universal Declaration of Human Rights. He notes, "It is easy to see why skeptics could consider such a claim akin to believing in unicorns" (180).

Gushee's alternative justification of dignity—or, as he prefers to call it, "the sacredness of human life"—takes the form of a "theocentric-voluntarist warrant." As he explains, "My overall approach here might be described as a *voluntarist* or *decisionist* paradigm. . . . I emphasize divine freedom rather than anything intrinsic in humanity that might demand or evoke a designation of human sacred worth from God or anyone else" (181; Gushee's emphasis). Another key passage fills out Gushee's view:

> Human dignity/sacredness is the ascribed worth belonging to each and every human being by virtue of the decision of God, our Creator. It is an ascribed status, neither earned nor intrinsic. It is not inherent in being human as such, or intrinsic to any characteristics of the human, or subject to the growth or diminution of particular human capacities or attributes. (182)

Gushee emphasizes, moreover, that this view of dignity is not reducible to the *imago Dei*; it is, rather, extracted from the entire Christian canon, with special emphasis on the revelation of Christ's redemptive love for humanity in the New Testament. He writes, "The divine decision to declare human life sacred has been communicated to human beings by God in divine revelation, notably sacred scripture and Jesus Christ. This revelation is extensive, though complex. . . . It is by no means reducible to (implications of, or speculations about) the *imago Dei*" (183). Furthermore, the *reason* God has chosen to declare humans as sacred, Gushee maintains, is located within the mystery of the divine will itself: "Why has God consecrated human beings as sacred? Because the God who created human beings has the authority to do so, has decided to do so, and has done so" (180). In short, humans have dignity because God wills that humans have dignity, and we can know this—indeed, the implication is that we can *only* know this—based on the one place where God, for Gushee, reveals God's will: the Bible.

There is much to learn from Gushee's theoretical derivation of dignity's existence and nature and the compelling way in which he applies it to the problem of torture and LGBTQ inclusion. For the purposes of comparison, however, I want to highlight that his conception of dignity appears to be entirely *relational* in nature. By "relational" in this context, I mean, as Gushee explicitly recognizes, that dignity is decidedly *not* ontological or intrinsic: human beings have dignity *only* because God has established (and presumably continues to maintain) a value-conferring *relationship* with humans after creation and after the Fall. This is what I take Gushee to mean by claiming that dignity is an "ascribed" status; "to ascribe" is to give something to someone that otherwise does not constitutively belong to them. Humans may "enjoy" dignity in the form of being granted the benefits of being deemed as dignified. But it is not "in" us ontologically; it is not, in other words, "natural" to us. The proper focus of human dignity is thus not ultimately the human. It is God and, more specifically, Jesus Christ.

In framing dignity this way, Gushee's standpoint represents a foundational theological-anthropological position in the Protestant tradition: one cannot speak about the human person without speaking about God; and one cannot speak about God from any other standpoint than what has been revealed in scripture.[2] Identifying human value in an ontological sense from this perspective (e.g., claiming that humans have value because of something inherent in humanity) would not only be putting carts before horses; it would be claiming that carts can propel themselves! This is the kind of idolization of the human in "human dignity" that Gushee's account of dignity wants to reject categorically: to claim that human life is sacred is to claim that God, the only source of the sacred, *deems* it so by choosing to enter into relationship with human beings. The *imago Dei* thus explains who humans are, but it does not, primarily, explain why we have value. Gushee affirms, "The only agent (Agent) who could imagine designating all human beings as sacred, and who could have the authority to do so, is God. . . . [T]he conviction that each and every human being is sacred comes to humanity from beyond humanity" (176).

DISTINGUISHING "IMAGE" AND "LIKENESS" IN PAPANIKOLAOU'S ACCOUNT OF DIGNITY

Papanikolaou seems to take a different approach to establishing the existence and nature of human worth. He notes that the language of dignity has only recently emerged in Orthodox thought, and, in particular, in the Russian Orthodox tradition, which much of his chapter focuses on. The recognition that humans have value by virtue of being made in the divine image and likeness, however, has a long history in Orthodoxy, and it is here, particularly in the distinction between "image" and "likeness" in the *imago Dei*, that Papanikolaou locates his distinctive understanding of dignity.

Unlike Gushee, Papanikolaou recognizes dignity as having roots in something *inherent* in humanity, which he identifies as the "image" of God in all human beings. Drawing on the document *The Russian Orthodox Church's Basic Teaching on Human Dignity, Freedom and Rights*, Papanikolaou upholds the view that, though sin obscures the original created goodness in human beings, it does not totally eclipse it. The goal for humanity thus becomes recognizing the value that *is already present in humans*, despite the obfuscating influence of sin. As he writes, "[There is] an irreducible worth to all human beings. . . . The challenge is somehow to confront sin so as to embody, make manifest, and reveal a dignity that already exists" (195). Papanikolaou affirms that this dignity is "inherent" (195) and "inviolable" (198) in the sense that nothing can extirpate or otherwise diminish it. It is a constitutive feature of human beings qua human beings, and a defining characteristic of what it means to be made in God's "image."

Drawing on the *imago Dei* in this way appears to mark a substantial difference with Gushee. Gushee rejects the claim that dignity is inherent; Papanikolaou seems to embrace it. And where Gushee downplays the centrality of the *imago Dei* in justifying the existence and nature of dignity, Papanikolaou locates the *imago* at the heart of the Orthodox conception. This discrepancy, in turn, points to broader theological differences related to the severity of sin: whereas Gushee appears to affirm that sin has stripped humanity of its original created goodness (at least goodness that can generate dignity), Papanikolaou, in line with Orthodox theology more generally, appears to interpret sin as having distorted humanity's goodness but not destroyed it. This differing emphasis also helps explain why Gushee locates dignity in the *redemptive Christ*, while Papanikolaou locates it (at least as it pertains to the "image" of God in human beings) more in the *God of creation.*

These differences certainly hold in the comparison between the Protestant and Orthodox conceptions of dignity. However, it is important to note that Papanikolaou's own interpretation of "inherent" as it applies to dignity does not necessarily mean "ontological," at least in the sense of some "thing" that is constitutively located exclusively within human beings. Drawing on classical and contemporary Orthodox theologians, Papanikolaou complicates the definition of the *imago* by developing dignity through the prism of what he calls the "irreducible uniqueness of personhood" (205). To be a unique person, he argues, is to be an individual whom God has chosen to love as a gift of God's grace—not because of anything intrinsic in the person. Papanikolaou writes, "God does not love us *because* . . . ; God simply loves us, and it is in this love that we discover we are unique and, hence, are constituted as irreducibly unique, as dignified" (206; emphasis original).

This love, Papanikolaou specifies, takes the form of an encounter made possible by God alone, which he defines as an "event of relationship" (206). As he explains, "Personhood is, in the end, a gift of unique relationship with the living God, which renders each human being unique" (203). To say that dignity is inherent from this perspective, therefore, is not to claim that humans somehow possess ontological value that God chooses to love; rather, it is God's love itself that generates that value "within" human beings *because* God is in relation with them. Papanikolaou thus frames dignity as a consequence of God's ongoing and active will, a result of God *choosing* to be in relation, rather than the result of a "one-time" creative act.

Given this interpretation of "inherent," it would therefore be misleading to claim that there is a clean, dichotomous distinction between the Protestant and Orthodox formulations of dignity, with Gushee representing a "relational" view and Papanikolaou representing an "ontological" or "inherent" view. Papanikolaou's theological construal of dignity as an "event of relation" profoundly complicates such a simple categorization. Both he and Gushee ultimately conceive of dignity—"the sacredness of human life" for Gushee and the "irreducible uniqueness of personhood" for Papanikolaou—in relational terms. Human dignity is not *in* human beings for either; rather, it is *in* the relationship that God establishes with human beings. And the implication, for both, is that God must continuously *will* this relationship for dignity to "exist." In short, there may be much more substantive agreement between the Protestant and Orthodox accounts of dignity than first appears.

Dignity as a Gift *and* Goal

However, foundational theological differences between the two accounts remain, especially in light of Papanikolaou's claim that we must understand dignity not only in terms of the "image" of God but also of the "likeness." Drawing again on *The Russian Orthodox Church's Basic Teaching on Human Dignity, Freedom and Rights*, Papanikolaou reemphasizes that the "image" of God identifies who humans are in the form of a potentiality to be realized or manifested. The "likeness" of God, in contrast, defines who humans are *called to become* by overcoming sin, that is, to become like Christ. Although God's grace plays an indispensable role in transforming the human being from the image of God, which is disfigured by sin, into Christlikeness, which is liberated from sin, human action, in the form of freely choosing to live according to God's will, is equally indispensable. In other words, for Papanikolaou humans can choose to contribute to the realization of their full humanity by living morally virtuous lives—or not.

Papanikolaou recognizes this process of sanctification as "theosis," though he prefers to say "divine–human communion" in order to capture the full relational aspect of the *imago Dei*: God bestows value on humanity by choosing to enter into loving "event relationships" with human beings, and yet these relationships *call* humans to enter into deeper communion by being conformed, and conforming themselves, to Christ. Drawing on Vladimir Lossky, he explains,

> Insofar as the human being is never not in unique relation with God . . . then this human is always "in the image"; insofar as deification [divine–human communion] manifests this uniqueness such that the human reflects the life of God, then the human person is "according to the likeness," "manifesting God in the extent to which his nature allows itself to be penetrated by deifying grace. Thus the image—which is inalienable—can become similar or dissimilar, to the extreme limits: that of union with God, when deified man shows in himself by grace what God is by nature . . . or, indeed that of the extremity of falling away which [the ancient Greek philosopher] Plotinus called 'the place of dissimilarity' . . . placing it in the gloomy abyss of Hades." (203)

In other words, God calls all human beings to communion, and the way that human beings move towards the fulfillment of this communion is to cooperate with God's grace by living a moral life and seeking to be conformed to the perfection of Christ. In this way, Papanikolaou adds a teleological dimension to his relational view of dignity. Dignity is not a static gift of the divine; it becomes *more* or *less* depending on how the individual responds to the divinely initiated and sustained relationship that generates it in the first place.

On this point, Papanikolaou's view differs substantially from Gushee's, who claims that dignity is *not* "subject to the growth or diminution of particular human capacities or attributes" (182). Although Papanikolaou carefully qualifies that failing to grow in holiness does not make an individual "less human," he agrees with the Russian Orthodox Church document in affirming that individuals who choose not to participate with God's grace morally *lose* something in the form of an unfulfilled potential. As he writes, "There is . . . an affirmation that spiritual progress in *theosis* is possible for all and to each according to their histories and capacities, and this spiritual movement only manifests the irreducible uniqueness that one *is* in relationship to the living God" (206–7). As this passage implies, to move against the current of this "spiritual movement" is to become something less than fully in relationship with God, less than what one is called to become, and, consequently, less than fully dignified.

Moreover, Papanikolaou underscores the moral implications of this spiritual progress by recognizing that those who ultimately fail to make it, either by their own fault or the fault of others, are in danger of what he identifies as being rendered a "nonperson" (198). Dignity is thus not only a gift of divine relationship. It is a goal that every human is called to pursue by letting herself or himself "be penetrated by deifying grace"—or choosing to reject that grace.

Dynamic Dignity and the Moral Importance of Vulnerability

This additional dimension of Papanikolaou's account of dignity is one that Gushee may find theologically foreign. Notwithstanding the shared "relational" structure both authors attribute to dignity, Gushee does not add any teleological characteristic to the *imago Dei* or human worth, and the reason appears to be theological: to wit, because he does not conceive of the normative human relationship with God in terms of a "process" of moral and spiritual growth, there are no theological grounds for speaking of the *imago Dei* and dignity in dynamic terms. Scripture, for Gushee, reveals that God has chosen to declare that human beings are sacred. He frames this declaration as an affirmation of a true state of affairs—"humans are sacred because God wills them to be sacred"—and *not* as a potential to be realized. There is not, in this sense, any more work to do beyond recognizing what God has done and what God, presumably, continues to do. Indeed, given that Gushee locates dignity exclusively in God's will in this way, it appears that *nothing* can diminish, enhance, or otherwise alter it.

This difference with Papanikolaou is instructive because, again, it points to underlying theological differences. It is not surprising that Papanikolaou attributes a teleological dimension to dignity given Orthodoxy's conception of *theosis* (or "divine–human communion"), just as it is not surprising that Gushee's Protestant formulation of dignity does *not* emphasize moral or spiritual growth, especially growth that the individual could claim credit for (e.g., "allowing" oneself to be penetrated by God's grace to become more Godlike, as we see in Papanikolaou's account) given Protestantism's general emphasis on God doing *all* of the salvific work. Dignity helps reveal some unexpected similarities between Protestantism and Orthodoxy in this context, but it also, perhaps entirely expectedly, confirms underlying theological differences.

Ethical Implications of Theological Differences

I want to examine the *ethical implications* of these theological differences. Gushee's formulation of dignity as a divine declaration of sacredness opens up an interesting question about whether and how dignity, as he conceives of it, is vulnerable to moral harm. It is important to highlight that Gushee believes it is; indeed, he says so explicitly, observing, for example, "All kinds of acts violate human dignity, many of which are named in sacred scripture, such as violations of human bodily integrity, including assault and murder. The obligation to prevent such indignities and violations is central to the moral norm I am describing [in the chapter]" (183). Gushee also notes elsewhere in his chapter that saying that dignity is inviolable means saying that it *must* not be violated, not that it *cannot* be violated (180). In other words, Gushee may not define dignity as teleological, but he does believe that dignity is vulnerable to harm, which grounds, for him, the moral obligation to refrain from doing such harm.

However, the issue remains whether dignity defined only as a divine "ascription" of value can sustain the claim that it is vulnerable to harm in the ways that Gushee claims. For if dignity is located in *only* the divine and a result of the divine will alone, how, and in what way, could human beings possibly threaten it? What action could "undo" or "diminish" God's declaration that every human life is sacred? What, besides another act of God's will, could possibly affect the integrity of that sacredness which, ontologically speaking, belongs *only* to God?

These kinds of queries point to even more foundational questions about the relationship between the divine and human beings (or the Creator and the created). For example, if we take one of God's attributes to be noncontingency, meaning that whatever else defines God, God is, at least, the only being that does not depend on any other being for its existence—which is an attribute, I presume, that Gushee would agree with—then how can we claim that that which is *contingent* could in any way "violate," in the sense of harm or diminish, that which is *noncontingent*? To be sure, we could, within Gushee's framework, claim that certain actions violate God's will in the sense of "act contrary to." But violating God's will by not following what God has commanded with respect to human dignity does not *harm* or *diminish* God or, presumably, any value-conferring relationship that God chooses to establish with human beings. God and God's will remain the same no matter what humans do or do not do, which would imply that, so long as we define dignity *solely* according to God's will and locate dignity *only* within God, we are defining human dignity in a way that is, by definition, invulnerable to human action.

This observation points to a much broader discussion that requires wading into even more complex (and long-standing) theological debates, but it is important to pose two questions in this context: (1) Can a theological voluntarist position, such as Gushee's, generate a conception of dignity that is vulnerable to moral harm? And (2) if not, what are the moral implications of defining dignity as *invulnerable* in this way? How, for example, would we define "rights" in relation to dignity, if we take one of the fundamental functions of rights to be to protect dignity? How could rights protect something that, by definition, could not be protected? How, also, could we provide reasons to *respect* dignity if the integrity of dignity remains untouched no matter whether it is respected or not? Moreover, what *urgency*, if any, is there to act in dignity's name if its integrity is and always will be intact because of the invulnerability of the divine decree?

However we may be able to address these questions from Gushee's perspective, Papanikolaou's formulation of dignity can, I believe, clearly account for vulnerability to moral harm. Notwithstanding the shared way in which he and Gushee both define dignity in relational terms, Papanikolaou's recognition of the teleological character of dignity provides the conceptual grounds for being able to claim that human action *can* harm dignity. Although the inherent dignity that finds its ground in the "image" of God may be invulnerable to human action given that, like Gushee's account, it is located entirely in God and God's will, Papanikolaou makes it clear that dignity as it relates to the "likeness" of God *is* vulnerable to human action, for better or worse: although no human can fully become Godlike without God's grace, we can, for Papanikolaou, either freely choose to cooperate with that grace (to allow it to "permeate" oneself) or to reject it. What humans choose to do, or not to do, in other words, can and does have a direct influence on whether and how humans fully realize the potential to "manifest" the full nature of God within themselves and enter fully into "divine–human community." It is for this reason, in the end, that Papanikolaou can coherently speak of the danger of violations of dignity rendering human beings "nonpersons."

Such a claim, however, would not make sense from Gushee's perspective; if one's moral personhood is located in one's dignity, and one's dignity is located in God's will, and God's will is invulnerable to human action, then *no action* could possibly strip an individual of her or his personhood, rendering her or him a "nonperson." However, by adding the recognition that dignity is not only a gift of the divine will but also a goal that human beings are called to fulfill by cooperating with God's grace (or not) to become like God, Papanikolaou provides the grounds for identifying conditions under which one might *fail* to become more Godlike and, hence, not realize the full potential of her or his personhood. This vulnerability, in turn, provides the grounds for identifying actions that (1) *enhance* individuals' dignity by helping them realize the potential embedded in their dignity, and that (2) *harm* human dignity by serving as obstacles to the realization of the potential embedded in their dignity.

From this perspective, for example, we might be able to provide a justification of "rights" on the grounds that they specify the actions that humans ought and ought not to do in order to fulfill their God-given potential. Respecting these rights would not only be acting in accordance with God's will; it would also be *protecting* another human being's vulnerable humanity. Gushee, in contrast, certainly supports the idea of a "commitment to universal human rights" (182), but it is not clear what, specifically, those rights would be protecting within his framework; for again, if dignity is located exclusively in the divine will, and the divine will is immune to human action, then rights, it seems, would be rendered moot, at least specifically with regards to the protection of human dignity.

CONCLUSION

Certainly, much more needs to be said about the relationship between dignity's vulnerability and invulnerability; about the definition of God primarily in voluntarist terms (as opposed, for example, to defining God as "eternal law," as in the thought of St. Thomas Aquinas); about questions of dignity's universality and equality if, epistemologically, *knowing* that dignity is universal and equal depends on *particular* revelation; about what specific rights might be necessary in order to protect dignity defined as a goal (among many other important questions); but the comparison between the rich accounts of dignity in Gushee and Papanikolaou ultimately leads to two instructive conclusions: (1) comparing different theological traditions on specific ethical questions, such as the existence and nature of human dignity, can yield surprising theological similarities, as we see, for example, in Protestantism and Orthodoxy both rejecting an ontological definition of dignity in favor of a relational one; and (2) such comparisons can also point to long-standing theological differences, as we see in the conflicting interpretation of the possibility of spiritual and moral growth in relation to dignity.

Whichever conception one may ultimately point to as the "right" or "better" one, the comparison itself helps us remember that theology makes a difference for ethics. Different descriptions of God in relation to humanity produce different conceptions of human dignity; and different conceptions of human dignity, in turn, not only give us different answers to the question about what it means, normatively, to be human, but also about whether and how the integrity of that humanity might, or might not, be in danger.

NOTES

1. I do not mean to claim that there is no conception of "sanctification" within some forms of Protestantism or that "sanctification" means the same thing within Catholicism, Protestantism, or Orthodoxy. Indeed, one of the ongoing matters of debate between Catholicism and Eastern Orthodoxy in particular is how, precisely, to define sanctification; as this response notes, the Eastern Orthodox account of "becoming Godlike" usually prefers to use the language of deification, or *theosis*, rather than "sanctification" (Papanikolaou prefers "divine–human communion"). I thus do not wish to claim that sanctification is the same in Orthodoxy and Catholicism or that there is no conception of sanctification in the Protestant traditions (indeed there are, for example, in the thought of John Calvin or John Wesley). Rather, what I wish to highlight for this response is that (1) the Protestant account of dignity by Gushee does not substantively appeal to *any* conception of becoming Godlike in order to justify and explain its particular formulation of dignity; and that (2) the Orthodox account of dignity by Papanikolaou *does* make such an appeal. This difference, I believe, is important to highlight.

2. Several classic texts come to mind. Think, for example, of the opening lines of John Calvin's great *Institutes of the Christian Religion* in which he recognizes that one cannot know oneself without knowing God: "Our wisdom, in so far as it ought to be deemed true and solid wisdom, consists almost entirely of two parts: the knowledge of God and of ourselves. But as these are connected together by many ties, it is not easy to determine which of the two precedes and gives birth to the other" (Calvin, *Institutes of the Christian Religion*, I.1, http://www.ccel.org/ccel/calvin/institutes.iii.ii.html). Martin Luther also famously claims in his *Heidelberg Disputation*, "The love of God does not find, but creates, that which is pleasing to it" (Thesis 38, LW 31, 41), stressing the position that worth is *not* in human beings but *only* in God. Or think of the great Reformed theologian Karl Barth, writing in *The Humanity of God*, "In his divinely free volition and election, in this sovereign decision . . . God is *human*. His free affirmation of man, His free concern for him, His free substitute for him—this is God's humanity"; Barth, "The Humanity of God," in *The Humanity of God*, trans. John Newton Tomans and Thomas Wieser (Louisville, KY: Westminster John Knox Press, 1960), 51; here again, we see that speaking about humanity requires us to first speak about God since *only* God can and does represent what it fully means to be human in the person of Jesus Christ. The Lutheran theologian Helmut Thielicke has also written extensively about what he describes as "alien" human dignity—"alien" because, though imputed to humans, dignity only properly belongs to God. As he writes, "[The] character of the *imago Dei* as . . . something alien is supremely brought out by the fact that . . . as true ontic possession . . . it is ascribed solely and exclusively to Jesus Christ . . . in the absolute sense, Jesus Christ is the only man"; Thielicke, *Theological Ethics*, vol. 1, *Foundations*, ed. William H. Lazareth (London: Adam & Charles Black, 1966), 171. Although these authors represent richly diverse accounts of "Protestant" understandings of human worth, there is in all of them the recognition that the starting and ending point of speaking about "human" dignity is God rather than anything intrinsic to the human being. Gushee's formulation of dignity, I believe, falls within this broad distinctively Protestant understanding.

ten

DIGNITY

An Islamic Perspective

Zeki Saritoprak

INTRODUCTION

Islamic conceptions of dignity are rooted in a theocentric vision and anthropological claim that all humans possess the *imago Dei* and a dignifying status as children of Adam. In fleshing out these conceptions, I draw primarily on passages from the Qur'an and classical, medieval, and modern commentaries. I undertake a comprehensive theological and linguistic analysis of the Qur'anic terms *al-ins*, *al-nas*, and *al-insan*, used to describe humanity. As the art of the Most-Beloved and Most-Merciful and the vice-regent (*khalifa* [*pl. khulafa'*]) of God on earth, humanity possesses inherent physical and spiritual dignity that enjoins legal commands and moral duties. I also explore, however, the ways in which certain passages of the Qur'an depict human beings as weak and vulnerable to deception and desire. I argue that, at its essence, dignity in the Islamic tradition reflects an awareness of human frailty and human reliance on God.

In explicating Islamic perspectives on dignity canvassed in the Qur'an, I engage Muslim scholars and mystics from differing historical contexts, including al-Tabari (d. 923), Abu Mansur al-Maturidi (d. 944), Abd al-Karim al-Jili (d. 1306), Ibn Kathir (d. 1373), Muhammad Hamdi Yazir (d. 1942), and Bediüzzaman Said Nursi (d. 1960). Through their commentaries on the sayings of the Prophet, we can gain insights into the ways in which Islamic thought disabuses notions of superiority, emphasizes effort and duty over lineage, and affirms that the path of justice involves respect for others and supplication before God.

In Islam, all creation is important because everything was created by God. Within the realm of creation, though, human beings have a special place and are the most important creatures in the universe. If the universe is a tree, human beings are the fruit. This is arguably an axiom of the Islamic tradition, and the importance of human dignity is outlined in the major sources of Islam, in particular the Qur'an. Before exploring what the theological sources say about human dignity, some etymological information is useful. The term that is used for the dignity of human beings is a derivative of the root k-r-m, *karam*. As a noun, the word that is defining human dignity is *al-karama*. In contemporary literature, because of the Islamic source's use of this term, human dignity has been terminologically spoken of as *karamat al-insan*, literally "the dignity of human beings." Basically, *al-karama* is the term that all related references use to refer to the dignity of human beings. A second word from the same k-r-m root is used to call someone or something noble, has connotations of honoring someone, and is used to indicate the dignity of human beings. The Qur'an uses this second, transitive form when it speaks of the dignity of human beings: "Surely We have dignified [*karramna*] the Children of Adam and carried them in land and sea, and We have given them good things as sustenance. And We have made them superior to many other creatures that We created" (17:70).[1] This dignity is generally understood as the superiority of human beings over other creatures. That God has dignified human beings means God has made human beings superior in comparison to other creatures. The opposite of the word *al-karama* is *al-ihana*, which connotes humiliation. The technical word *al-karama* should also not be confused with the Sufi understanding of the term, which describes extraordinary events performed by mystics.

As an adjective, the k-r-m root becomes *al-karim*, which means "honorable" or "the one who is dignified and honored." To indicate the honorable position of someone, the Prophet would often use the word *al-karim*. For instance, when describing the prophet Joseph, after whom chapter 12 of the Qur'an is named, the Prophet of Islam said: "He is *al-karim*, the son of *al-karim*, the son of *al-karim*, the son of *al-karim*. Joseph [is] the son of Jacob the son of Isaac the son of Abraham." This indicates that Joseph and his ancestors were all honorable and dignified by God because they have the honor of prophethood, knowledge, beauty, chastity, and character.[2] Also *al-Karim* is one of the 99 Names of God. God is the Most-Honorable and the Most-Generous. In other words, God gives bounties extensively to human beings so His honor and generosity are unlimited. Human beings are also called *al-karim*, but their *karama* is by definition limited.[3] Therefore the term that is used to define human dignity has several connotations, and, in fact, all of them are taken into account when we speak of the dignity of human beings. These connotations are honor, dignity, majesty, exaltedness, chastity, generosity, and kindness. These are all considered the qualities that contribute to the dignity of human beings. Furthermore, human beings are honorable just because they are human beings. With this regard, all human beings share the same honor regardless of their skin color, religious affiliation, and other characteristics. This is because the Qur'an speaks of the dignifying of the children of Adam and is part of what separates human beings from other creatures.

There are several specific reasons why human beings are dignified in Islam. One is that God made human beings with His own hands (see Q 38:75). This means that God gives paramount importance to human beings, and, as such, they are the most special art of God. Similarly, there are verses which state that God put into human beings a part of His spirit (Q 32:7–9) and that human beings are dignified because they have been made in the most beautiful way, that is, they were made in the image of the Divine name al-Rahman, the Most-Merciful (Q 64:3). It can be argued that among Muslim theologians there is a consensus on the dignity of human beings to the extent that, even during times of war, it is not permissible to mutilate the body of an enemy. This is a legal command that requires Muslims to dignify human beings qua human beings, enemy or friend.

With this in mind, we should now turn to what the classical Islamic sources, especially commentaries of the Qur'an, have to say on the subject. They are scholars of their time, but some elements of what they have to say are useful to us today, others not. Thus, my approach is not simply to repeat them, but instead to build upon them and use them to frame my own interpretation. The obvious need for modern interpretation and analysis aside, it is refreshing to see how even early commentators were very progressive, and the modern world can benefit from their understandings. It is important to note that many Western philosophers and humanists have developed a specialized literature on human dignity. For example, August Comte and those who followed him approached humanity in a very independent way that disconnects humanity's relationship with the Divine. This approach has led some people to erect a statue to humanity, as literally happened in 1983 in Brazil. The Islamic approach to humanity is considerably different. Humanity is the art of God, but it should not be considered an object of worship. Therefore, since Islam is a theocentric tradition, any idea that suggests worshipping human beings and making human beings the standard for moral rule and worship will be at odds with the core teachings of the religion on the nature of humanity and be rejected by Muslims. In other words, humanity is to be loved and to be honored because it is the art of the Most-Beloved and the Most-Beautiful. Human beings are expected, as the thinkers of the Book of the Universe, to contemplate how they were created as a Divine art (Q 41:53). And further, the Qur'an commands human beings to contemplate within themselves (Q 30:8). More importantly, human beings are expected to serve each other, and this service again has a Divine connection because serving one another leads to the pleasing of God. The Prophet of Islam said: "The best of human beings are those who are the most beneficial to human beings."[4] With this in mind, let me turn to the understanding of humanity in the Qur'an and Hadith.

In the Qur'an, the nature of humanity is spiritual. In fact, every human being can become so high in dignity and honor that he or she can reach a certain level of perfection. Because spirituality is so essential in human life, I will first briefly examine how mystics have understood human dignity, then I'll examine more closely what the Qur'an and the sayings of the Prophet, the two major sources of Islam, say about humanity. Because thoroughly examining the mystical dimension of human dignity is beyond the scope of this chapter, two examples—one from the classical and one from the modern period—should suffice. One of the most well-known and significant works on human dignity is by Abd al-Karim al-Jili (d. 1306). Al-Jili's famous book is generally known simply as *Al-Insan al-Kamil* (*The Perfect[ed] Human*). The same title is also given as an honorific to the Prophet of Islam, and al-Jili describes the Prophet of Islam as a model for human dignity and a perfect human being. In the entirety of the creation of human beings, if one makes a pyramid of perfection, the pinnacle contains the prophets of God. Among the prophets of God, the five elite prophets—Noah, Abraham, Moses, Jesus, and Muhammad—are the most perfect examples for humanity. In fact, the Qur'an speaks of the Prophet of Islam as "a beautiful example" (33:21). Also, Abraham and "those with him"[5] are presented as models for human beings (60:4–6). One section of *Al-Insan al-Kamil* directly speaks of the perfect human being. Here, al-Jili describes the Prophet of Islam. This section is the foundation of the book, and the entire book is an explanation of the dimensions of this perfect human being.[6] As the culmination of perfection, al-Jili describes the journey of human beings toward the eternal life.

In the Islamic pyramid of creation, technically speaking, angels are higher than human beings, but because human beings have free will and can improve themselves, they may become higher than angels. However, if they use their capabilities in the wrong direction, these dignified and precious human beings will become lower than animals. If human beings make the effort to improve themselves, they will join the group of human beings on whom God has bestowed His favors and bounties (Q 1:7). As al-Jili describes, they will reach their eternal abode and become eternal. Thus it is interesting also to see that some Muslim theologians use the name *Dar al-Karama* for Paradise. Literally, this means "the Abode of Dignity" or, descriptively, "the Abode where the Divine bounties are plentiful." Furthermore, the significance of being honored by God is that human beings can supplicate to God as they wish. They can ask God for what they want and when they want it. Because of this honorable position, even if they make mistakes, their repentance is acceptable. This is true even if they break their promise and repent again. Al-Qushayri (d. 1074), the prominent mystic and commentator of the Qur'an, cites a hadith qudsi: "I gave you before you asked Me. I forgave you before you asked for forgiveness."[7]

A modern example of literature on human dignity is found in the work of Bediüzzaman Said Nursi (d. 1960), a prominent scholar-mystic from Turkey. This is Nursi's commentary of the Qur'anic verse: "Surely We have created human beings in the best form. Then We returned them to the lowest of the low, except those who believe and do good deeds" (95:4–6). This work has been translated into various languages, with one of the translations in Arabic being *al-Insan wa al-Iman*, or *Human Beings and Faith*. In his magnum opus, called the *Treatises of Light*, Nursi elaborates on the importance of human beings extensively, but in this treatise, he specifically focuses on humanity and faith and how human beings can have spiritual elevation through faith and connection with the Divine.[8]

THE QUR'AN AND HUMANITY

In Islam, the most important source of theological and religious knowledge is the Qur'an, the Holy Book of Islam. Therefore to understand human dignity in Islam, one should start by understanding what the Qur'an says about human beings. The three most important words in the Qur'an for human beings or people are *al-ins*, *al-nas*, and *al-insan*. All of these terms derive from the same root, a-n-s, which means "sociable, nice, or friendly," and, importantly, these three words also connote a level of civilization. The first word to mention is *al-ins*, which is usually translated as "human beings" or "humankind."[9] The most commonly used variant in the Qur'an is *al-nas*, which means "the people" or "humanity." However, the third term, *al-insan*, is perhaps the most well-known word for human beings found in the Qur'an. This term is used as a shorthand for *banu Adam*, which means "the children of Adam." The children of Adam are honored by God and are the most eminent creatures in the realm of creation. The Qur'an also uses the word *bashar*, which literally has something to do with skin and corporality, but is used to mean "human" as opposed to deity. In the Qur'an, God instructs the Prophet of Islam to say, "I am only a *bashar*" (18:110). That is to say, I am not a deity: I am a human being.

Since the most well-known term for human beings is *al-insan*, it is appropriate to examine some relevant verses in order to see how it is used in the Qur'an. It should be noted, however, that the concept of *al-insan* in the Qur'an is not monolithic. It is a large idea that in itself would require a major study to examine fully. Human beings are remarkably dignified in the Qur'an, but there are verses that speak of the negative characteristics of humanity. One verse says, "God wants to lighten your burden, and human beings[10] [*al-insan*] are created weak" (4:28). Another verse describes *al-insan* as the ones who deny God's bounties and are excessive wrongdoers (14:34). Another verse notes their psychological weakness: "Human beings pray for evil as they pray for good, and human beings are ever hasty" (17:11). The Qur'an further says: "And human beings are more than anything prone to dispute" (18:54). Another Qur'anic verse speaks of humanity's relationship with the Divine: "Surely We have created human beings, and We know what their souls whisper to them, and We are closer to them than their jugular veins" (50:16). Yet another verse challenges human beings because of their irresponsible actions: "Do human beings assume they will be left without aim?" (75:36).

In connection with *al-insan*, one must also make mention of Satan. According to the Qur'an, Satan is the enemy of human beings and always wants to benefit from human weaknesses. He is an extraordinary enemy who can ruin the future for human beings if they are not strong enough to resist. Also, the Qur'an speaks of another enemy of human beings that is within themselves. This is *al-nafs al-ammara*, or "the evil-commanding soul." The evil-commanding soul is described by many Muslim mystics as the outpost of Satan in human beings. This is not to say that human beings are evil, but to underline the fact that if human beings do not work hard to achieve perfection, they can easily become victims of these negative forces. The Qur'an gives the story of Adam and how he and his wife were deceived by Satan; therefore one can see a constant warning in the Qur'an to human beings about the possibility of being deceived. In almost all Qur'anic verses where Satan is mentioned, he is described as the enemy of human beings and must be taken seriously.[11]

The Qur'an presents human beings as the vice-regents of God on earth. The following two verses are probably the most quoted Qur'anic verses on the dignity and importance of human beings. The first verse is related to the importance of human beings and their superiority over other creatures. The verse says, "Surely We have honored the Children of Adam and carried them in land and sea, and We have given them good things as sustenance. And We have made them far superior to many other creatures that We created" (17:70). Scholars of Islam and Qur'an commentators have given many explanations of this verse that reflect the value of human beings. Some commentators refer to the human capacity of reasoning. Others refer to the capacity of speech or to the beauty of the human face. One of the earliest commentators of the Qur'an, Abdullah bin Abbas, who was also one of the companions of the Prophet, comments on the above verse by saying, "Eating with their hands, while other creatures eat with their mouths, made human beings superior over other creatures."[12] In fact, another Qur'anic verse speaks of the fingers of human beings as a Divine gift. Indicating that God could have made human hands and feet like the hooves of camels and donkeys, the Qur'an says: "Yes, indeed we are able to make whole his [their] very finger tips" (75:4). The commentator al-Tabari (d. 923) would say being supervisors over other creatures is what makes human beings superior.[13] Scholars generally take the Qur'anic language to be inclusive, that is, to include both believers and unbelievers as honored because both are the creation of God and have received the bounties of God. This honor is related to the ability to reason and distinguish between what is right and wrong and consequently to make choices, that is, to have free will.

From a theological perspective, all human dignity is derived from God, the Creator. God through His gifts to human beings has endowed them with a noble place in the cosmos. That place is as *khalifa*, or God's representative on earth. In Islamic theology, creation can be considered a pyramid. Human beings, on the whole, are somewhere near the top of that pyramid. Generally speaking for contemporary Islamic theology, human beings, because of their quality and encompassing knowledge, are considered above rocks, microbes, plants, animals, and even angels, though some have accepted archangels as being higher than human beings. Theologically speaking, human beings are supervisors over all creatures. Human superiority is a theological truth laid out in several Qur'anic verses that speak of the bowing down of angels before Adam and Adam's knowledge of "the names." These verses are the foundation of this belief in the superiority of human beings over other creatures. However, there are also verses that speak of human beings' accountability and their responsibility to God, to fellow human beings, and to the environment. In other words, human beings are superior over other creatures, but are not permitted to do whatever they please. Human beings' actions among themselves and toward other creatures have to be in accordance with Divine command. They can do anything that is allowed, but must avoid anything prohibited.

The most notable verses that discuss humans' superiority use the word *khalifa*. *Khalifa* is the Arabic word for "successor," which was also used for the successors of the Prophet. Among the places where *khalifa* is used, the most important for a discussion of human dignity is in 2:30–37. This long section is part of the conversation God had with the angels related to Adam, the first human being and the first prophet. The Qur'an says:

> And remember when your Lord said to the angels: "Surely I am placing a *khalifa* on the earth." They said: "Will You place on it one who will cause corruption and will shed blood, while we are exalting You with Your praise and sanctifying You?" He said: "Surely I know what you do not know." And He taught Adam the names of all [things that have a name], then presented them [i.e., the things He had taught Adam the names of] to the angels, saying: "Tell Me the names of these things, if you are truthful." They said: "Exalted are You! We have no knowledge except that which You have taught us. Surely You, only You, are the Most-Knowledgeable, the Most-Wise." He said: "O Adam! Inform them of their names," and when he [Adam] informed them of the names of things, He [God] said: "Did I not tell you that I know the secret of the heavens and the earth? And I know what you display and what you hide." And remember when We said to the angels, "Prostrate to Adam," they all prostrated except Iblis. He arrogantly avoided [doing so] and became one of the disbelievers. And We said, "O Adam, you and your wife stay in the Garden and you both eat freely as you desire, and do not go near this tree or you both will be among the wrongdoers." But Satan caused them both to slip up and took them both away from what they had been in [of the

> bounties]. And We said, "Go down all of you. Some of you are enemies to others of you. And for you on earth there is a place of dwelling and enjoyment for a time." And then Adam received from his Lord some words [of revelation] and He [God] accepted his [Adam's] repentance. Surely He alone is the One who accepts repentance and the Most-Merciful. (2:30–37)

Theologians' commentaries on these verses generally state that God wanted to show the importance of consultation because God did not need the angels' opinion. God tells the angels that He will create on earth a *khalifa*. Yet, the angels appealed to their superiority as innocent, peaceful creatures who spend their existence praising God, whereas this *khalifa* would shed blood and cause destruction on the earth. The angels' concern is that human beings will love bloodshed on earth, but the Divine response is clear. It indicates that even if some of them will commit evil actions, the good will outweigh the bad. Even if those who do good are low in number, they will be higher in value. God tells the angels several times in these verses that He knows things the angels do not, and, in order to show the superiority of these *khulafa'*, God teaches all names to the first of them, whom we know to be Adam.[14] This shows that these *khulafa'* are knowledgeable and therefore honorable and the angels are asked to recognize them. God then tests Adam and the angels, asking them for the names. Adam's knowledge is superior because he is capable of learning and developing and possesses free will, but angels are static and do not possess these abilities.

HUMANITY'S VICE-REGENCY

We have established that human beings are God's *khulafa'* on earth. But, what does it mean to be a *khalifa*? Commenting on verse 2:30, al-Tabari says, "Khalifa is when you say: Someone succeeded someone on this matter. When he [or she] takes the place after that person, the person becomes his [or her] *khalifa*. . . . That is why for the Sultan, the title Khalifa is given because he succeeds the previous ruler and takes his place."[15] Muslim theologians and commentators of the Qur'an have elaborated on this concept. Surely it is an honorable positon given to human beings by God to the extent that angels were asked to show their respect for this new creature by bowing before him. Some recent theologians, such as Said Nursi, go further by saying that the Qur'an equates the earth with the heavens in many verses because of the honorable position of the earth as the home of these *khulafa'*. Being on earth, humanity adds to the value of the earth in comparison to the heavens. It should be remembered that according to Muslim theologians, the highest of these *khulafa'* are the messengers of God, particularly the five elite prophets, and therefore their having lived on earth, makes the earth equal in comparison to the much larger heavens. A recent Turkish commentator, Muhammad Hamdi Yazir (d. 1942), interprets these verses as if God is saying to the angels about human beings the following: "I will give these *successors* certain authority from my own power and free will. They will be able to exercise their authority over creatures as my representative. In my name they will apply some of my rules and carry them out. They are not the originator of these rules and will not carry them out for themselves. On the contrary, they will be representing Me and they will be My apprentices and be commanded to use their free will to apply My will, My commands, and My laws. And they will practice this generation after generation."[16]

It is evident, therefore, that these verses indicate the importance of human beings as the *khulafa'* of God on earth. This dimension of human beings is frequently emphasized. For example, al-Qushayri, in commenting on these verses, says that it is God who has created all of Paradise and what is in it, and the Throne with what it encompasses of design and beauty. But He never consulted with angels saying He is creating Paradise or the Throne or angels. Instead, to show the honor and privilege given to human beings in the personality of Adam, God speaks to the angels and tells them He will create a *khalifa* on earth.[17]

In general, commentators on the Qur'an speak of *khalifa* as the representative of God on earth, but there are commentators who understand the word in a different way. Since the word *khalifa* itself has the connotation of succession and representation, a minority of commentators understand the word to describe the succession of one generation of human beings to the next. Most prominently, Ibn Kathir (d. 1373) takes this approach. Despite not being well known in the Islamic tradition, this way of approaching *khalifa* is interesting for a study of the idea of human dignity. For Ibn Kathir, the word *khalifa* means "a nation succeeds one to another, century after century and generation after generation."[18] He then proceeds to list a long lineage of these successors, which includes the great figures. This idea is not at odds with the majority opinion and, in my view, enhances it by showing how humanity is part of a living chain that stretches from Adam to us today.

The prophets of God are the highest human beings in the realm of humanity, and therefore they deserve this title of *khalifa* more than other human beings. Theologically speaking, the prophets were exceptional human beings and are often called perfect human beings. Further, they directly represented God on earth and spoke on behalf of God. In the Qur'an, we have the stories of many of these great human beings. As an example, let us examine the story of David. The Qur'an speaks very positively of David as someone who received God's bounties to the extent that even mountains were commanded to be co-worshipers of God with him (34:10). He is known as the one who constantly returned to God, *al-awwab* (38:17), and David is directly addressed by God as *khalifa*: "David! Surely We have made you *khalifa* on the earth; therefore judge with truth [and justice] between people, and do not follow [your] desire such that it will deviate you from the way of God. Surely those who deviate from the way of God have an awful punishment, for they have forgotten the Day of Reckoning" (38:26). This verse clearly states the importance of David as the representative of God on earth, but it also indicates two important qualities that should be followed by all the offspring of Adam. The Qur'an, by addressing David, indirectly addresses all *khulafa'*, asking them to have two essential qualities.

The first of these is to act justly and to serve justice. Justice is the foundation of human society. In fact, one of the names of God is the Most-Just. If human beings do not follow the way of justice, they cannot be representatives of God on earth. Justice is emphasized because human beings have great capacity for justice and injustice toward their fellow human beings, other creatures, the environment, and so on, and the evil-commanding soul can easily lead them to transgressions. Following the path of justice is a challenge, but human dignity requires it. Justice is so significant that chapter 55 of the Qur'an, on four occasions, emphatically asks human beings to establish justice: "And He raised the heaven and He established the balance so that you not transgress the balance. And establish the measurement with justice and do not come up short of the balance" (55:7–9). The second quality is self-awareness of human weaknesses. Human weaknesses can deviate humanity from the path of justice to the path of desires. Therefore, God addresses David, and through David addresses all human beings, saying that they should not follow the path of desire. This will deviate them from the path of justice. Human beings are not to follow desires that can cause them to do injustice and to transgress on the rights of others. It can be argued that these qualities of justice and self-awareness are, at least in part, what distinguish the human community from animal communities.

One of the most quoted verses of the Qur'an dealing with the dignity of human beings says, "Surely We have created human beings in the most beautiful form" (95:4). The verse indicates human physical and spiritual dignity. It also indicates that such a creature of the Divine deserves to be the vicegerent of God on earth. Human beings, as God's most sophisticated creatures, are given this position. According to the Islamic theology, human beings are pure by nature. Yet, despite the natural goodness of human beings, they are capable of committing evil. Indeed, as can be seen from verses 2:30–37, above, even Adam committed sin. However, unlike in the Christian tradition, there is no concept of "original sin"; there is no transmission of the sin of Adam and Eve to their offspring. It is strongly emphasized in Islam that no one is to bear another's burdens (6:164, 17:15, 35:18, 39:7, and 53:38). That is to say, children are not responsible for the crimes of their parents. Everyone is responsible only for his or her own actions. Furthermore, in Islam, all children until the age of puberty are considered innocent and pure, and it is only when a human being reaches puberty that he or she becomes responsible and accountable.

It is for this reason that in the realm of creation, human beings are the ones whose level of quality is nonstatic. Individual human beings can be lower than animals or higher than angels. Perhaps the best examples of this in the Qur'an are Pharaoh and Moses, and many other examples can be given from human history. Theologically, this is related to the dualistic nature of human beings. In describing human arrogance Nursi gives the following description of human beings:

> O human beings! There are two aspects in you. One is of creativity, existence, goodness, positivity, and action. The other is destruction, nothingness, evil, negativity, and passivity. In regard to the first aspect, you are lower than a bee and a sparrow and weaker than a spider and a fly. In regard to your second aspect, you exceed the mountains, the earth, and the heavens. You have taken upon your shoulder the burden that they were afraid to take so you assume a circle larger than they do. The reason for this is that when you do good deeds and when you do something creatively, you do it according to your capacity and to the extent of your hands and according to your own power so you can do positive, creative things accordingly. But when you do bad things and are destructive, then your evilness transmits and your destruction spreads.[19]

A basic understanding of human beings' positive and negative characteristics is fairly self-evident, but in the Islamic tradition part of what makes one's angelic qualities manifest and leads to a fuller recognition of human dignity is not simply doing good deeds and refraining from evil ones. It is also in understanding the frailty and impotence of human capacities and human beings' reliance on God for all human advances. Nursi continues:

> This means that human beings' domination and human advances and the attainments of civilization, which are to be observed, have been made subject to them not through their attracting them or conquering them or through combat, but due to weakness. They have been assisted because of their impotence. They have been bestowed on them due to their indigence. They have been inspired with them due to their ignorance. They have been given them due to their need. And the reason for their domination is not strength and the power of knowledge, but the compassion and clemency of the Sustainer and Divine mercy and wisdom. They [Divine mercy and wisdom] have subjugated things to them [human beings]. Yes, what dresses human beings, who are defeated by vermin like eyeless scorpions and legless snakes, in silk from a tiny worm and feeds them honey from a poisonous insect is not their own power, but the subjugation of the Sustainer and the bestowal of the Most-Merciful, which are the fruits of their weakness.[20]

Perhaps paradoxically then, it is human beings' own weakness before God that is the source of human achievement. As the famous Muslim mystic Uwais al-Qarani in his supplication says, "You are the Great and I am the meek. You are the Powerful and I am the weak. You are the Giver and I am the beggar. . . . You are the Healer and I am the sick."[21] Human beings are dignified not because they are great and powerful creatures. Human dignity comes from their supplication to and relationship with the Divine and the status of human beings as the addressees of God. Human beings are imputed this dignity at birth, and that dignity qua being human cannot be taken away. For instance, a thief still has a certain level of dignity because he or she is still a human being. That person's humanity might be extensively affected by his or her actions, which can cause it to fall down a few rungs in the ladder of humanity, but still that person's position can be reclaimed through repentance. It is like a candle that can burn brightly but also be covered or even put out and still be relit. Whether the candle is out or burning brightly, for the candle to burn to its fullest, there must be constant positive actions and intentions. This takes us to the concept of contemplation in the creation of human beings through which the relationship with the Divine is strengthened.

CONTEMPLATIVE HUMANITY

The Qur'an emphatically states that the main purpose of the creation of human beings is to worship God. It says, "I have not created human beings and jinn [invisible creatures parallel to human beings] except that they worship Me" (51:56). The concept of worship has a large connotation. Praying five times a day is an act of worship, but so is clearing the path for others so that they can easily walk and are not harmed. In fact, the Prophet emphasized that to be beneficial to others is a form of worship. Similarly, many solitary spiritual acts are also acts of worship. Indeed, within the tradition of Islamic spirituality there is a well-developed literature on such personal acts of worship. For present purposes, I will concentrate on one, contemplation, for its direct connection to human dignity.[22]

There are many Qur'anic verses that invite human beings to contemplate the signs of God in nature. For instance, the Qur'an says, "And on the earth are signs [e.g., mountains, seas, trees, fruit, etc.] for those who are sure in faith. And in yourselves [there are signs], will you not see [them]?" (51:20–21); "We will show them Our signs in the horizons and in themselves until it becomes clear that it [the Qur'an] is true. Is it not enough that your Lord is the Witness over everything?" (41:53). Other verses invite human beings to contemplate their own existence: "It is God the One who created the earth for you as a sheltered place and the sky as a ceiling and formed you and beautified your images and provided you with good sustenance. That is God your Lord. And Exalted is God, the Lord of the worlds" (40:64). There is also an emphasis on the importance of the creation of human beings. A Qur'anic verse says, "Then We made the drop [of semen] into a clot [of blood]. And then We made the clot into a lump [of flesh]. And then from the lump We made bones and We clothed the bones with flesh. Then We made it another creature. Exalted is God. He is the Most-Beautiful of creators" (23:14). In his commentary on this verse, al-Razi (d. 925) says, "If you want, just contemplate only one organ among the organs of the human being, and that is the eye. He [God] created the black pupil of the eye, and then circled it with the whiteness of the eye. He then covered it with the blackness of the eyelash. God then framed that blackness of the eyelash with the whiteness of the eyelid, then created the blackness of the eyebrow. He then created above that the whiteness of the forehead. God then created the blackness of hair. Let this just be as an example of the Divine creation in human bodies."[23] From here, al-Razi goes further and compares this world to a city: "This world is similar to an urbanized village, or a well-prepared guest house. All of its benefits are directed to human beings. The human in this world is similar to a president who is served, or to a ruler who is obeyed, all other animals compared to him are like slaves. All this shows that human beings, in the sight of God, through His dignifying of them, have a very special place."[24] Indicating the importance of human status in the universe, Umar, the second caliph, while defending the rights and dignity of a Coptic Egyptian, admonished his governor in Egypt by saying, "How can you enslave people while they are born from their mothers as free?"[25] This indicates the free nature of every human being and shows that slavery is anathema to the dignity of humanity as strongly advocated by the Islamic tradition.

God has given human beings a special status in the realm of creation and subjugated all other creatures to them, and one of humanity's duties is therefore to be thankful, but not all human beings are grateful for this Divine gift. In fact, the Qur'an says, "It is God who has made the night for you to rest in it and the day for you to see. Surely God has bestowed bounties upon human beings, but most human beings are not thankful" (40:61).[26] People are either grateful or ungrateful (76:3). Those who develop their angelic qualities and are aware of the Divine bounties are seen as grateful, while those who develop their satanic qualities are seen as ungrateful. Similar to other traditions, this dualism in the Qur'an takes the form of right being good and left being bad. This is most notable in 56:27–44. The Qur'an here speaks of the beauties of paradise, which "the people of the right [hand]" (56:27) will receive, and the torments of hell for "the people of the left [hand]" (56:41). Further, chapter 56 goes on to note that it is these people who "persisted in the great sin" (56:46). But it should be emphasized that it is only those who fail to correct their behavior who are doomed.[27] Nevertheless, whether individual human beings are good or bad, humanity as a whole is still the reflection of the Qur'anic verse: "Surely We have honored the Children of Adam" (17:70). Thus, since the Qur'anic language on the dignity of human beings is comprehensive, regardless of one's faith or beliefs, all human beings are considered dignified by God simply on account of their being human beings.

In Islam, there are two distinct ways in which an individual praises God. One is the conscious praising of God, and the other is unconscious. The former is the praise of the believers, and the latter is the praise of the body's organs, tissues, and such. In other words, the human body itself, including all of the living cells of the body, regardless of the consciousness of the individual human being, praises God continuously. It does so through what is called its "tongues of exposition." Therefore, a person who does not believe in God may not consciously praise God, but the cells of the body of such a person still praise God. Perhaps for this reason, on the Day of Judgment the limbs or organs of a human being may testify against that person (see Q 36:65). This is why human beings, just because they are human beings, deserve respect and dignity.[28] Jabir bin Abdillah narrates that on one occasion he was with the Prophet and a funeral procession passed by them. The Prophet stood up for it, and his companions stood up with him. And they said, "O Messenger of God, the deceased person is Jewish." The Prophet responded, "When you see a funeral procession, stand up for it."[29] By this he indicated his respect for the dignity of every human being, regardless of that person's religion and ethnicity. Hence, in Islam there should be no animosity toward others, even to someone with whom you may have a disagreement.

IMAGO DEI

Perhaps because of the prominent place of human beings vis-à-vis the Divine names, the Prophet said, "When you fight your brother, avoid striking the face because God created the Children of Adam in His own image";[30] on another occasion, the Prophet said: "God created human beings in the image of al-Rahman."[31] This does not mean that there is anthropomorphism in Islam, as if to say, God is like human beings, but it is to indicate that human beings are the reflection of the Divine names or attributes. Indeed, Islamic theologians have often said that whatever comes to the mind of human beings, God is different from that. Theologians have used such sayings of the Prophet to demonstrate that human beings, among all creatures of God, are the most important mirrors of the Divine names. Because of this encompassing aspect of human beings, every human being is a universe. In other words, a universe is folded into every human being. The Qur'an equates the killing of one human being to the killing of all human beings and the saving the life of a human being to saving the lives of all human beings (5:32). Among the Divine names for which human beings are mirrors are *al-Basir*, the One who sees everything; *al-Sami'*, the One who hears everything; *al-Khabir*, the One who is aware of everything; and *al-Mutakallim*, the One who speaks and has the power of all languages. Not only are humans' outer senses reflections of Divine names, but our inner senses, of which there are thousands, are too reflections of the Divine names. For example, our sense of compassion reflects the Divine name *al-Rahman*, the Most-Compassionate. Our sense of mercy reflects the Divine name *al-Rahim*, the Most-Merciful. Our sense of love mirrors the Divine name *al-Wadud*, the Beloved or the One who loves. Our inner ability of patience indicates the Divine name *al-Sabur*, the Most-Patient. Our sense of peace and tranquility indicates the Divine name *al-Salam*, the Peace. Thus, just as mirrors, glasses, and even bubbles show the reflection of the light of the sun, human beings reflect attributes and names of God.

Muslim theologians have spoken in detail on these human capacities and how they are reflections of the Divine names. Indeed, the vast majority if not all Muslim theologians are in agreement on this fact. Some would say that human beings have thousands of inner and outer senses, each of which reflects one or more Divine names. As an indication of the importance of human beings, a line in one of the poems attributed to Ali, the fourth caliph, says, "O human beings, do not think you are a small creature. A great world is folded in you."[32] That is because human beings received *al-Amana*, or the Divine Trust. They are elevated and have become the addressees of God. In the realm of creation, it is only human beings that are carrying *al-Amana* according to the Holy book of Islam: "We offered al-Amana to the heavens, and to the earth, and to the mountains, but they shrank from the burden and they were afraid of it. And human beings accepted this offer. But surely some are extremely unjust and ignorant" (Q 33:72). This is an extraordinarily precious duty, but at the same time it gives a remarkable accountability. God has given human beings free will. People are free to exercise it as they wish because in Islamic teachings, this life is a test. Some members of the human family will do much wrong and will be ignorant, while others will be wholesome and knowledgeable.

HUMAN BEINGS' POTENTIAL

The Qur'an encourages human beings to be aware of their potential and capacities. Yet at the same time, the Qur'an complains that human beings are reckless: "O human beings, what has deceived you about your Generous Lord, the One who created you and shaped you and made you symmetrical? In whatever form He desired, He composed you" (82:6–8). These verses remind human beings of their relationship to the Divine: they are created, not the Creator, and they are created in the most beautiful form. As we have seen, on the one hand, human beings have the capacity of being greater than angels to the extent that angels are proud to serve them, and, on the other, human beings have the capacity to be lower than animals. Some Islamic scholars, considering this aspect of human nature, use the "Analogy of the Seeds." If you put some seeds into the ground and give them enough water, sunlight, and, if necessary, fertilizer, they will grow and be fruitful trees and in turn will result in thousands of new seeds. But if you neglect the seeds, neither planting them nor giving them nourishment, the seeds despite their innate capacities will rot and never bear fruit and will become forgotten. Human beings with their inner and outer capacities can be likened to these seeds. If they are given appropriate spiritual nourishment, human beings will develop and become a tree with thousands of fruits in the realm of eternity. If human beings fail to develop these capacities, they ultimately will become like the rotten seed, without fruit and spiritually barren.[33] In other words, if human beings follow the way of their egoistic desires, rather than pursue spiritual developments, they will lose their almost limitless capacity, and their life will be only this short, temporary, physical life. But if they follow their angelic qualities, consider the body given to them as a house of God for their spirit, and use their skills and senses for the betterment of society and to help others in ways that will further their mirroring of the Divine names, human beings will be the most important trees that will result in thousands of seeds and fruits and will enjoy the realm of eternity.

Muslim mystics considering this capacity of human beings have developed a concept to idealize such a state of humanity. This state is *al-insan al-kamil*, "the perfected human being" or "the person who has reached perfection." Through spiritual training, and a strong relationship with the Divine, human beings are encouraged to reach the state of perfection. As we briefly mentioned above, such a level of perfection is found in the messengers of God who worked for the betterment of human beings in this life and in the afterlife; in the messengers who invited their fellow human beings to righteousness. A society made up of people striving to live the life of perfection would be considered a society of bliss. Indeed, Muslim theologians have called the era of the Prophet, "The Era of Bliss." Mystics have developed codes of behaviors to keep human beings on the right path in the way of perfection. This idea is most famously described by al-Jili. The reason that al-Jili used the "Perfect Human Being" for the Prophet is because of the encompassing message of the Prophet. Spiritual development is not something to be achieved and finished. It is a constant struggle until the end of life for an individual and until the end of time for humanity in general. Because God has not put limitations on human capacities, vast fields of spiritual development are open to human beings, but there are tests that must be passed to reach them.

I have examined the idea of human dignity vis-à-vis the Qur'anic understanding of what distinguishes human beings as magnanimous creatures of God, but we must also discuss how human beings are to interact with one another. For this, it is best to look carefully at one of the most important verses from the Qur'an on the subject. The verse says, "O human beings! Surely We have created you from male and female, and have made you nations and tribes that you may know one another. Surely the noblest of you, in the sight of God, is the best in conduct. Surely God is All-Knowing, All-Aware" (49:13).

Human beings are social creatures. The Qur'an gives paramount importance to the development of positive relationships among human beings. In fact, in the language of the Qur'an all of humanity is one family from one father and one mother. In addition to the verses we have looked at, there are many other verses that encourage good manners and positive relationships between human beings. The Qur'an describes a group of God-fearing people as those who give charity in their good and difficult times and those who swallow their anger, forgiving people. "Surely God loves those who do what is beautiful" (3:134; see also 2:195, 3:148, 5:13, and 5:93). Similarly, another verse says, "Good deeds and bad deeds are not the same. Repel [the bad] with what is most beautiful and then between you and whom there is enmity it shall become as if he were a close friend" (41:34).[34] In other words, just as Jesus said to love one's enemy, the Qur'an says to be kind and do good to one's enemy. The Qur'an encourages people to follow certain moral principles. Therefore forgiveness is a wholesome quality of a human being, and responding to evil with good is also an important element of Qur'anic morality. As al-Tabari says in his commentary, "Respond with your kindness to their ignorance against you; with your forgiveness to their wrongdoing to you; with your patience to the difficulties that they impose upon you."[35] A similar verse says, "And the servants of God are those who walk on earth humbly and when some ignorant [people] speak against them, they just say peace" (25:63). The Qur'an makes it clear that human beings have been put on this planet to live together and carry out their social lives with respect and kindness, not with arrogance, cruelty, or claims of ethnic superiority.

In 49:13, this aspect is emphasized clearly, and perhaps this verse is the most repeated when human relationships are being considered. This particular verse covers at least five critical points. First, the addressee is all human beings, unlike some other verses directed specifically at believers. Second, the human family is one since all humans share the same father and the same mother. Third, division into nations and tribes is a Divine plan, and all are part of the extended human family. Fourth, the reason for such diversity is to "know one another" and not to fight one another. Fifth, there is no superiority of a color of skin or ethnic background over others; white is not greater than black, and black is not greater than white. The same holds true for nations. The best of people are simply the best in conduct. The verse is considered a foundation for Islamic understandings of human relationships. If humanity reaches this level of understanding, perhaps social problems will be much easier to solve. In order to reach this level of understanding, the preceding verse is more specific and in fact prepares human minds for the next step.

Whereas 49:13 addresses all human beings, the verse just before it addresses believers. The goal is to develop good relations between believers specifically, which eventually will contribute to the general betterment of humanity: "O believers! Avoid many suspicions as some of them are sinful. Do not spy on one another. Do not gossip. Does one of you love to eat the flesh of his dead brother? You will abhor it. Then be God-fearing. Surely God is the Acceptor of repentance and God is the Most-Merciful" (49:12). This verse puts in place a specific foundation for the betterment of society. For instance, showing the abhorrence of gossip and comparing it to eating the flesh of one's brother is a very powerful way of alleviating such a social problem. Once the Prophet of Islam was asked what gossiping is, and the Prophet said, "to mention your brother [or sister] with something he [or she] dislikes. If what you say is true it is gossiping. If what you say is false, it is gossiping and calumny."[36] Additionally, the Prophet admonished even those who were listening to gossip that this was akin to gossiping themselves. A society that avoids these social diseases will be able to cooperate and promote harmonious interpersonal relationships.

It is worth mentioning the occasion of the revelation of 49:12 and 13. There are several different stories regarding the revelation, and perhaps they all are relevant. When the Prophet asked Bilal, an Ethiopian who converted to Islam and was purchased out of slavery, to call for prayer, Bilal went up onto the Ka'ba and called for prayer. At this point some pagans in Mecca became upset. Harith bin Hishan said, "Does not Muhammad have someone other than this black crow?" Itab bin Sayyid, who was among the most eloquent of the pagans, said, "My father was lucky because he did not see this day [in which a black person is inviting people to prayer]." Based on these conversations, it is believed that this verse was revealed to indicate that all humans are equal and there is no superiority of one racial or ethnic group over another. Therefore, the Qur'an prohibits claiming the superiority of one ethnicity over another because the origin of all human beings is the same, and thus there is no basis for such claims of superiority. The Prophet of Islam practiced this Qur'anic principle throughout his life. His appointment of Bilal is but one example of this. A second story that some consider the occasion of the revelation concerns Abu Hind, a young freed slave. The Prophet asked the tribe of Benu Bayadah to marry one of their women to Abu Hind. They said, "How can we marry our daughters to our slaves?"[37] There is another story on the occasion of this verse's revelation in which the Prophet passed by a black slave in the market of Medina, who was shouting, "Anyone who buys me, my condition is that he will not prevent me from praying five times a day behind the Prophet." A man bought this slave and allowed him to have his prayer behind the Prophet. The Prophet would see him in every prayer. One day, he could not see him. The Prophet learned that he was sick and went to visit him and wish him well. After a few days, the man's sickness worsened. The Prophet again visited him. When the man passed away, the Prophet himself prepared his funeral prayer.[38] The commentators suggest that the end of the verse in question, which says that God is Knowing and Aware, alludes to this story that God knew what was in the heart of this individual: kindness and faith. Even though he appeared black, for the Messenger of God he was a great person of faith. Also, this incident was difficult for the Prophet's companions to understand, which could be another reason for the revelation of the verse.

Commenting on 49:13, Abu Mansur al-Maturidi (d. 944), one of the great scholars of Islam in the Middle Ages, gives two meanings to the verse. According to the first meaning, God says, "We have created all human beings from one source and that is Adam and Eve and therefore all become brothers and sisters. There is no superiority of one brother or sister over others because of their ancestors. Their ancestors are given to them and they did not acquire them. What counts for honor is merit and good conduct."[39] For the second meaning, al-Maturidi understands that God has created all human beings, including kings, subjects, freemen and slaves, men and women, from the liquid of male and female. Since all people are from such liquid drops that are ugly and stinky, human nature finds it detestable. By mentioning this, the Qur'an draws our attention to the meaninglessness of claims of superiority through ancestors or tribes.[40]

Muslim commentators reject the notion that people can claim honor based on who their ancestors were, because this is not something over which an individual has control. One has no right to claim something that is beyond his or her control and for which he or she has not produced effort. The Qur'anic verse clearly states, "And for human beings there is nothing except the result of their own efforts" (53:39). Therefore, fearing God and having good conduct are the criteria for superiority, and not one's lineage; from the Creator's perspective, all people are at root the same.

The Prophet of Islam furthers this idea of superiority of effort and not lineage. There are several sound hadith on the subject, which when taken together straightforwardly show that the spiritual lineage of the prophets is not through their relatives, but through the scholars (*ulama*).[41] Al-Razi narrates a story from his own time, the thirteenth century, that serves to illustrate this:

> There were some people in Khorasan [a historical region in Central Asia that today is split between Iran, Tajikistan, and Afghanistan] closer to Ali, the cousin of the Prophet by blood, but they were impious. There was also a black servant who was accelerated through knowledge and effort. People would come to him for blessings. One day he went out of his home to go to the mosque. A good number of people followed him. The Sharif [the one with closer blood ties to Ali] encountered him [while the Sharif was] drunk and the people were throwing themselves in front of the Sharif to keep him away, but the Sharif managed to get close to the servant and said: "You are the one with black hands and feet, the son of infidels, but I am the son of the Messenger of God. . . ." The black servant responded, "O, honorable Sharif, I whitened my inner [self] and you blackened your inner [self]. People see the whiteness of my heart over the blackness of my face. I took the lifestyle of your father and you took the lifestyle of my father. People are seeing me in the behaviors of your father and seeing you in the behaviors of my father. They think that I am the son of your father and you are the son of my father. They treat you as they treat my father and they treat me as they treat your father."[42]

Some commentators refer to Jesus's and Muhammad's statements when discussing the verses in question. People asked Jesus, "Who are the most honorable of people?" Jesus took two handfuls of soil and said, "Which of these are more honorable?" Then he mixed them and threw them and said, "All people are from soil. The best of them are the best in conduct."[43] Similarly, the Prophet of Islam, while pointing to his chest, said, "God doesn't look at your body and appearance, but he looks at your heart."[44]

CONCLUSION

It is fitting to end with the words from the last sermon of the Prophet.[45] Here, he again emphasizes this same notion: "O human beings, surely your Lord is One and your father [Adam] is also one. There is no superiority of an Arab over a non-Arab, and there is no superiority of a non-Arab over an Arab. Also there is no superiority of black over white and white over black. The only superiority is through piety." After his sermon, the Prophet repeatedly asked, "Lo! Did I convey the message?" And his companions said yes, "We are witnesses that you conveyed the message." Then the Prophet said, "Let those who are present convey the message to those who are absent."

NOTES

1. I have consulted available translations as a guide, but all translations from the Qur'an should be considered my own.

2. Muhammad bin Muhammad al-Zabidi, *Taj al-Arus* (Dar al-Hidayah, n.d.), 33:350. For the hadith reference, see al-Bukhari, *Al-Sahih*, hadith no. 3390.

3. Muhammad bin Makram bin Ali al-Ifriqi, *Lisan al-Arab* (Beirut: Dar Sadir, 1414H [=1993/4 Gregorian]), 12:511.

4. Abdullah Muhammad al-Quda'i, *Musnad al-Shihab* (Beirut: Muassasat al-Risale, 1988), 2:223.

5. This is the language used by the Qur'an. It is generally taken to mean the early prophets, who are considered his offspring, including Isaac, Ishmael, Joseph, and Jacob.

6. Abd al-Karim al-Jili, *Al-Insan al-Kamil fi Marifat al-Awakhir wa al-Awai'l* (Cairo: al-Matba'at al-Azhariyya, 1316H [= 1898/9 Gregorian]), 2:44–49.

7. 'Abd al-Karim al-Qushayri, *Lataif al-Isharat*, ed. Ibrahim al-Basyuni (Cairo: Al-Ha'at al-Misriyya al-Amma li al-Kitab, n.d.), 2:360.

8. Bediüzzaman Said Nursi, *Sozler*, in *Rislae-i Nur Kulliyati* (Istanbul: Nesil Yayinlari, 1996), 132–42. For an English translation, see Bediüzzaman Said Nursi, *The Words*, trans. Sukran Vahide (Istanbul: Sozler Nesriyat, 1992), 319–40.

9. In the past, *al-ins* was often translated as "man" or "mankind." However, this should not be taken to mean that only male human beings are being referred to. In many instances, this being just one example, gender-neutral language in the Qur'an has been rendered this way in English, occluding the real Qur'anic meaning.

10. Formally in Arabic, *al-insan* is singular, but making it plural in English translation is more in keeping with my understanding of the meaning of the word in the Qur'an.

11. A partial list of such verses is 2:168, 6:142, 7:22, 12:5, 17:53, and 36:77.

12. Abu Muhammad bin Mas'ud al-Baghawi, *Tafsir al-Baghawi*, ed. Abd al-Razzaq al-Mahdi (Beirut: Dar Ihya' al-Turath al-Arabi, 1420H [= 1999/2000 Gregorian]), 3:145.

13. Muhammad bin Jarir al-Tabari, *Jami' al-Bayan fi Ta'wil al-Qur'an*, ed. Ahmad Muhammad Shakir (Beirut: Mu'assasat al-Risala, 2000), 17:501. For other similar commentaries, see Abu Hayyan Muhammad bin Yusuf al-Andalusi, *Al-Bahr al-Muhit*, ed. Sidqi Muhammad Jamil (Beirut: Dar al-Fikr, 1420H [= 1999/2000 Gregorian]), 7:84–86.

14. The commentaries on this verse are not in agreement as to what the "names" refers. Some say that it is to the names of creatures, but others argue that it refers to the Divine names. Answering this question, though, does not affect the larger point of this discussion.

15. al-Tabari, *Jami' al-Bayan fi Ta'wil al-Qur'an*, 1:449.

16. Muhammad Hamdi Yazir, *Hak Dini Quran Dili* (Istanbul: Matbaa-i Abüzziya, 1979), 1:300.

17. al-Qushayri, *Lataif al-Isharat*, 1:75.

18. Ismail bin Kathir, *Tafsir al-Qur'an al-Azim* (Beirut: Dar al-Andalus, 1966), 1:216.

19. Nursi, *Sozler*, 136.

20. Ibid., 141.

21. Quoted in Zeki Saritoprak, *Islamic Spirituality: Theology and Practice for the Modern World* (New York: Bloomsbury Academic, 2017), 223.

22. I discuss a number of these in Saritoprak, *Islamic Spirituality*.

23. Fakhr al-Din al-Razi *Mafatih al-Ghayb* (Beirut: Dar Ihya al-Turath al-Arabi, 1420H [= 1999/2000 Gregorian]), 21:373.

24. Ibid., 274.

25. Yusuf bin Hasan al-Hanbali *Mahd al-Sawab fi Fadai'l Amir al-Mu'minin Umar bin al-Khattab*, ed. Abd al-Aziz bin Muhammad (al-Madina: Imada al-Bahth al-Ilmi, 2000), 2:473.

26. An almost identical verse is 27:73. Other similar verses are 2:243, 10:60, 12:38, and 34:13.

27. To elaborate further on this point would lead to a discussion of sin in Islam. Suffice it to say that the concept of sin in Islam is similar, with notable differences, to that found in the Christian tradition. For example, sin can be forgiven, but it is only God who can forgive sins. For more on sin in Islam, see Saritoprak, *Islamic Spirituality*, 67–71, 80–81, and 104–5.

28. The subject at hand is human beings, but the same idea holds for all living and even nonliving things. Though the process for human beings may be on a higher level be-

cause of their place as the supervisors of all creation, the bodies of all created things praise God and deserve dignity and respect. It is this idea that forms an important basis of Islamic environmentalism.

29. al-Bukhari, *Al-Sahih*, hadith no: 1311. A version of this hadith is also found in Muslim bin al-Hajjaj, *Al-Sahih*, hadith nos: 960 and 961.

30. Muslim, *Al-Sahih*, hadith no: 2612.

31. Shihab al-Din al-Alusi, *Ruh al-Ma'ani*, ed. Ali Abd al-Bari Atiyya (Beirut: Dar al-Kutub al-Ilmiyya, 1450H [= 1994/5 Gregorian), 8:49.

32. Shihab al-Din Ahmad bin Muhammad al-Khafaji, *Inayat al-Qadi wa Kifayat al-Radi ala Tafsir al-Baydawi* (Beirut: Dar Sadir, n.d.), 7:112.

33. For Nursi's version of this analogy, see Nursi, *Sozler*, 136–37.

34. In about forty places, categories of people that God loves and ones that God does not love are cited in the Qur'an. The Qur'an says God loves those who repent and clean themselves (2:222), the God-fearing ones (3:76, 9:4, 9:7), those who are patient (3:146), those who trust in Him (3:159), the just ones (5:42, 49:9, 60:8), those who are clean (9:108), and so on. God does not love the transgressors (2:190, 5:87, 7:55), those who cause corruption (2:205), the arrogant (4:36, 31:18, 57:23), wrongdoers (3:57, 3:140, 42:40), those who openly say bad words (4:148), those who are corrupt (5:64, 28:77), those who are wasteful (6:141, 7:31), those who are dishonest (8:58), and so on.

35. al-Tabari, *Jami' al-Bayan fi Ta'wil al-Qur'an*, 21:421.

36. Muslim, *Al-Sahih*, hadith no: 2589.

37. Scholars of al-Azhar Islamic Research Center, *Al-Tafsir al-Wasi li al-Qur'an al-Karimt* (Cairo: al-Hay'at al-Amma li Shuun Matabi al-'Amiriyya, 1988), 3:1049.

38. Ismail Haqqi, *Ruh al-Bayan* (Beirut: Dar al-Fikr, n.d.), 9:91.

39. al-Maturidi, *Ta'wilat Ahl al-Sunnah*, ed. Majdi Baslum (Beirut: Dar al-Kutub al-Ilmiyya, 2005), 14:76.

40. Ibid.

41. See al-Bukhari, *Al-Sahih*, hadith no: 67; and Ahmad bin Hanbal, *All-Musnad*, hadith no: 9972

42. al-Razi, *Mafatih al-Ghayb*, 28:114.

43. Ismail Haqqi, *Ruh al-Bayan*, 9:91.

44. Muslim, *Al-Sahih*, hadith no: 2564.

45. For the full version of the Prophet's last sermon, see Scholars of al-Azhar Islamic Research Center, *al-Tafsir al-Wasit li al-Qur'an al-Karimt*, 3:1049.

eleven

DIGNITY

A Humanist Perspective

William Schweiker

The idea of human dignity is a hotly debated topic in Western and, increasingly, global moral and political thought. Appeals to human dignity are found and contested within human rights discourse, the claims of indigenous peoples, plans for economic development and distributive justice, and classic and emerging forms of democratic governance. This is the case, in part, because ideas of human dignity have always been located within the networks of practices, values, ideals, and norms that structure religions, cultures, and societies. For instance, there are profound differences between the meaning of what we now call "dignity" within a warrior culture, such as ancient Greece, and the various appeals in the biblical religions to the idea of human beings created in the image of God. In a heroic culture, "dignity" can be won or lost, increased or decreased, insofar as it designates height, glory, and strength and also the honor accorded these forms of human excellence and social status. Conversely, if human dignity is an image of the divine within human beings, then the respect owed a person, including self-respect, is seemingly impervious to the agent's or the community's actions, rank, or excellence. Rather than a concept of "status," dignity in this created sense is "constitutive" of the meaning of being human.[1] There seems to be a great divide between constitutive and status conceptions of dignity, and between those who hold that any conception of human dignity requires divine or religious sanction and those who deny the need for religious or theistic claims.[2]

In the light of these examples, one must admit that the meaning of human dignity is context-dependent, even if some religious and philosophical positions claim the universalizability and stability of the idea of human dignity. Important for this chapter is that, however conceived, dignity is bound to and interwoven with a humanistic outlook on life, broadly understood. Dignity and humanism are naturally bound together within the legacies of Western and, nowadays, non-Western thinking, say, in Africa and China.[3] The purpose of this chapter is, accordingly, to situate the idea of human dignity both within the networks of thought and life broadly called "humanistic" and within the forms of religious and secular humanisms, and also in relation to some "anti-humanist" critics.[4]

At the outset of this inquiry, one crucial point and two caveats must be noted. First, it is crucial to note that there is no "orthodox" conception of "humanism." In fact, the idea is so variously used and so variously understood that some might wonder if it is not a vacuous concept, one unable to provide clear orientation for careful reflection on the human condition. Humanists disagree on what defines humanism. Tzvetan Todorov, a prominent nonreligious "neo-humanist," isolates three features of humanism: "the *autonomy of the I*, the *finality of the you*, and the *universality of the they*."[5] That is, humanists (1) value the freedom to conduct and shape their own lives, (2) are dedicated to the equality and respect of persons, and (3) are committed to a universal community of justice. Jacques Maritain, a renowned Catholic thinker, proposed a more robust definition of humanism. Humanism, Maritain wrote, "tends essentially to render man more truly human, and to manifest his original greatness by having him participate in all that which can enrich him in nature and in history . . . ; it at once demands that man develop the virtualities within him, his creative forces and the life of reason, and work to make the forces of the physical world instruments of his freedom."[6] Given the diversity of accounts of humanism, what follows is obviously one thinker's rendering of humanism in relation to human dignity. I make no pretense to being comprehensive or exhaustive in my treatment of humanism. However, Alasdair MacIntyre is surely right to describe a tradition as an extended argument.[7] What is at issue, then, is some account of the subject matter in question, the point of central dispute, around which the argument driving a tradition is to be identified. I agree with much of what Todorov and Maritain hold about humanism, but for the sake of this chapter I begin with a broader definition in order to specify the point of dispute in what we might call the "humanist tradition."

On my account, a humanist is someone who holds that human beings have a special—if not unique—importance and worth within the myriad forms of life on Earth that is shared by all human beings as such. The idea of "dignity" is thereby a natural way to articulate, define, and advance that importance and worth and to designate its universal scope. The point of central dispute is about the source of human dignity, and if it does or does not link human beings to some transcendent or sacred reality. This focus on dignity does not mean that all people are or should be alike. Human diversity, distinctiveness, and otherness are great humanistic values. All it means is that to be human—in whatever way of life one adopts—is to be accorded a special importance and worth qua being human.[8] At dispute, ultimately, is what it means to be a human being. It is my hope that the basic convictions of humanism and the various types of humanism I describe will find widespread agreement. But that intention remains, when all is said and done, a hope.

The first caveat to the argument to follow is that the forms of "humanism" to be charted are found in Western religious and philosophical thought, even though parallels can be found in other cultures. I am not attempting to write a global account of humanism. The second caveat is that "antihumanists" are not antihuman, but, rather, thinkers, and patterns of thought, that contest the network of beliefs and values set forth by humanists. In this respect, antihumanism serves as a foil in the following inquiry rather that its focus.

My argument here moves along three lines of inquiry. First, I isolate some generally shared convictions held among humanists. These convictions have been adduced from ancient and contemporary humanistic writings, but they represent in outline my understanding of a humanistic outlook on human life and our world. Second, I will briefly map a typology of humanistic positions with respect to whether dignity is a term of "status" or is instead "constitutive" of the human being and, conjointly, whether it is conceived in religious or nonreligious terms.[9] It might seem that religious traditions back "constitutive" conceptions of dignity and nonreligious outlooks forward ideas about dignity as "status," but matters are more complex. Finally, based on that analytical and typological work, I sketch two challenges to the future of human dignity and then briefly note a humanist response to them. This conclusion will draw on deep humanistic ideas about human dignity and the worth of life itself.

The point of the argument is that a humanistic conception of "dignity" is not found in the distinction and relation between status and constitution, as I called them, nor even in religious or nonreligious sanction for dignity. A humanist idea of dignity is to be found in how the set of convictions to be analyzed below provide a framework within which dignity and its features are understood and what that means for the orientation of life worthy of one's humanity. In this respect, what is distinctive about a humanist conception of dignity is the framework of convictions that motivate a life dedicated to respecting and enhancing the dignity of human lives.

With a sense of the direction of the chapter's argument in hand, it must be stated, finally, that the orienting reason for undertaking this inquiry is the sense that we find ourselves in a global situation where different ideas about dignity can too easily fund destructive relations among people. In this situation there is the grave need to forge a future worthy of our humanity around new ways of thinking about human dignity.[10]

SHARED CONVICTIONS

Throughout the ages, humanists have shared some interconnected ideas about the meaning, value, and purpose of being human. These convictions provide the framework within which human dignity is conceived. Generally eschewing an overly "systematic" or architectonic picture of human "nature," certain convictions are endemic to a humanistic outlook on life. We can briefly isolate four basic convictions, and note a fifth religious conviction not shared by all humanists.

An Ontological Conviction

The most counterintuitive conviction shared by humanists was forcefully put in the fifteenth century by Pico della Mirandola in his famous *Oration on the Dignity of Man*.[11] Pico's claim, recall, is that human beings have no set or determined "nature" but may rise to moral heights or fall into brutishness through their own will and action. Human beings are incomplete projects and so have the task to fashion and define their individual characters and communal lives. Obviously closely related to the idea of dignity as status, the deeper claim is that human beings are complex, tensive, "mixed" beings, neither reducible to sheer matter and biological processes nor souls trapped in bodies. Rather, human beings must navigate the various and sometime conflicting desires, thoughts, and values that permeate experience in order to constitute their lives with some measure of wholeness or integrity.

Given this ontological conviction, humanists see freedom as a fundamental value. It is the capacity of humans to negotiate conflicts and thereby to rise to new heights of joy, pleasure, friendship, and responsibility or to sink into conflicts in self that too easily shred human life into pieces. Freedom is neither the capacity to leap out of one's given context in a radical act of choice to constitute the self, as some existentialists have argued, nor is freedom epiphenomenal, to be explained in terms of some deeper, underlying determined causality, whether biochemical, physical, or metaphysical. Freedom is real and valued, but limited; it is precious, but vulnerable to the forces of the world, others, and even oneself. Put otherwise, human beings are multidimensional creatures that cannot be known or valued from merely one perspective, such as our bodiliness or rationality. This fact denotes not only the vulnerability of being human, but also, as Pico argued, something about human dignity. Dignity is thus a matter of human making, a status, but it is rooted in the constitutive nature of being human as a free moral agent.

An Epistemological Conviction

Intimately related to the conviction about being human is a conviction about the character of human knowing. Thomas Aquinas noted, "Things are known according to the mode of the knower."[12] That principle means two things with respect to human knowledge. First, as "mixed" beings, human beings always know through a combination of sensation, ideation, imagination, and—most fundamentally—language. Human knowledge is not just a matter of pure sensory experience, as ardent empiricists seem to hold, nor is knowledge about pure ideas, such as in high idealism. The human imagination tracks between sense and idea with its own creative power, even as human beings use language to grasp the meaning of their worlds and their lives, to communicate with others, and to open new domains of meaning. Little wonder that the study of languages and literature has been central among humanists.

Second, the epistemic principle of humanism carries with it a challenge to which the work of interpretation is the answer. Insofar as human beings are mixed creatures and freely shape the character and direction of their lives, then human beings will, come what may, understand things differently according to the tenor of their lives. The saint and the sinner no less than the wise and the foolish or the rich and the poor "see" and "know" different worlds. Human beings inhabit different, if overlapping, worlds of meaning. Two things thereby follow. One thing is that humanists are not surprised by profound human disagreements and are acknowledged skeptics, to greater and lesser degrees. That is, insofar as "things are known according to the mode of the knower" and no one is perfectly wise, morally pure, or without foibles, then one can and should reserve judgment about the ultimate veracity and clarity of one's beliefs. Humility is a virtue for humanists insofar as it enacts a basic fact of human knowing. It is no wonder that humanists have been advocates for tolerance rooted in humility about the capacity of human beings to grasp truth with utter clarity.

Another consequence of the fact that human beings inhabit different emotional, linguistic, moral, political, cultural, gendered, and racial "worlds" is that the work of human knowing and understanding is through the labor of interpretation. What we interpret are the practices, myths, symbols, concepts, and narratives human beings "make" in order to orient their lives.[13] There is, put technically, an essential hermeneutical dynamic to human knowing. And although the "objects" of interpretation are actions, myths, symbols, and such that articulate domains of meaning, the purpose of interpretation is to understand the meaning of our lives and our worlds and to provide orientation for personal and social life. Humanists have thereby advocated the study of both hermeneutics (the art of interpretation) and the art of persuasion (rhetoric) even while they hold a healthy mistrust of the certainty of their beliefs.

An Existential Conviction

Humanists revel in the wild diversity of ways of being human and the diversity of human characters as the subject of joy, scorn, satire, and praise. (Think, for instance, of Erasmus's *Praise of Folly*, John Kennedy Toole's *The Confederacy of Dunces*, or Miguel de Cervantes's *Don Quixote*). Yet such delight and criticism express more basic convictions. Humanists hold, first, that human beings are "progressive beings."[14] That is to say, it is possible for human beings to improve their lot in life, to seek more noble or refined character, and to fashion more relatively just and humane communities. The "progressive character" of human existence is of a piece with the ontological conviction, yet it becomes an existential conviction when an individual or community actually seeks to advance and improve their character and way of life. This conviction underscores the importance of virtue and the centrality of the whole of the moral life for humanistic thinking. In religious terms, the drive for progress finds expression in ideas about saints, human deification, or transformed heavenly bodies. This drive for improvement is not only found in humanistic thinkers, of course. Consider some transhumanists, who want to improve the "human" form of life through technological, medical, or genetic means in an ongoing war against death. The idea of humans as progressive beings can take humanistic and nonhumanist expressions. A humanist seeks to perfect but not to overcome our all-too-human mode of being in the world with others.

The distinctively humanistic conception of human beings as progressive creatures includes a strong emphasis on education. The Latin idea of *humanitas*, from which we get the "humanities," combined the Greek ideas of *philanthrôpia* (loving what is human) and *paideia* (education) and was bound to the areas of study basic to civic life (e.g., language, grammar, philosophy, law).[15] Often enough today, one is considered a "humanist" simply if one is a student and/or scholar of the "humanities." The emphasis on education in the robust sense of cultivating character and a whole way of life, individual and social, is found both in religious humanists, such as Erasmus or Melanchthon, and in "secular" humanists, such as John Dewey or the American Humanist Association.[16] Importantly, for humanists, knowledge is not an end in itself. Insofar as human beings are progressive creatures, then education ought to serve to respect and enhance the integrity of human life. Many of the great humanistic universities of the nineteenth and twentieth centuries take as their mottos these ideas: the Humboldt University of Berlin (*Universitas litterarum*, "University of Letters"); Johns Hopkins University (*Veritas vos liberabit*, "The truth will set you free"); and the University of Chicago (*Crescat scientia; vita excolatur*, "Let knowledge grow from more to more; and so let life be enriched). Human beings are "progressive beings," which means for the humanist that we are learning creatures.

Here too one sees the importance of hermeneutics and rhetoric for humanists. To learn means to come to understand others, oneself, and one's world through the interpretation of whatever makes a claim to meaning, especially the whole realm of human culture. Further, social life, if it is to endure and not tumble into the fires of hatred and conflict, must supplant force with persuasion. The philosopher Alfred North Whitehead made the point in words any humanist would endorse: "Civilization is the victory of persuasion over force."[17] In these terms, humanism is a commitment to "civilization" as a possible state of human beings as learning creatures.

An Axiological Conviction

Fourth is the axiological conviction, that is, a conviction about what has value and worth. For a humanist, a human being has unconditional worth, or dignity. As Immanuel Kant famously put it, human beings are ends in themselves, not to be valued as means to other ends.[18] Human beings have worth (*Würde*) and not just a price or value. For religious thinkers, especially theists, human dignity is found in relation to the divine, the highest or supreme good, that bestows constitutive dignity on human beings and grants the capacity to seek the perfection of their natures. For nonreligious humanists, dignity is a status to be attained—to be virtuous or to build a community of justice—or it is simply constitutive of being human qua human. As George Kateb has recently put this: "In the idea of human dignity to recognize oneself as sharing in a common humanity with every human being is the primordial component of individual identity. Its positive center, however, is belief in one's uniqueness together with the uniqueness of every human being."[19] Human beings are part of the community of life on this planet, but no other living species is of equal worth with human beings. Yet it is also the case that the community of life does not exist or derive its value from its utility for human beings. Humanism, despite its critics, is not necessarily anthropocentric in its axiology, even if human beings have a distinctive worth or dignity.[20] This dignity, we can further say, is found in human responsibility for itself and for the other forms of life on Earth.

Human freedom and its progressive learning capacities are intertwined for the humanist with the moral claim of responsibility on human beings. For some humanists in the West, especially classical and Renaissance humanists, the idea is that perfection, or attaining the right to be happy, as Kant later put it, is the purpose of life. For many contemporary humanists, often called "neohumanists," the claim of responsibility is found in the obligation towards others, their protection and well-being, rather than just the perfection and happiness of the self. Neohumanists such as Tzvetan Todorov and Martha Nussbaum often worry that striving for personal perfection can lead to a neglect or even denial of the quotidian needs and goods of finite life.[21] That is especially the case, they hold, among religious outlooks supposedly aimed at otherworldly perfection. In order to avoid that possibility, neohumanists speak of "lateral transcendence," that is, the capacity of human beings to go beyond themselves in respect and care for others, rather than religious or "vertical" transcendence. We return to this issue below, but now it is enough to note that a humanist conception of "dignity" or intrinsic worth is interwoven with the other basic convictions found among humanists. It is also bound to a form of self-transcendence insofar as self-respect and responsibility for others exceed and transform one's actual life into a condition of life that manifests and/or achieves the dignity of being human.

A Religious Conviction

It is not possible in one chapter to explore all the possible forms of religious humanism. Yet this type of humanism does seem to share three points that can be illustrated by classic Christian humanism.[22] The first point shared by religious humanists is that God, the divine, or the sacred must be known and experienced with respect to the humanist framework of our other four convictions. That is to say, the human–divine relation or encounter does not destroy or negate the distinctly human mode of life. This is why Christian humanists often focus their theological reflection on Jesus as the Christ since in Christ the divine is incarnate in human form.[23] As St. Athanasius put it in his treatise on the Incarnation, "God became Man so that we might become God."[24] Yet Christian ideas about *theosis* or divinization are not, despite what neohumanist critics might claim, against human existence. The point is that the divine does not despise the human condition, but in fact dwelt among us as a fully human being.

The first shared point among religious humanists is that they remain staunchly humanistic rather than denying the distinctly human mode of being. This is evident in the way that Christian humanists have been committed to education, and to the arts of interpretation and rhetoric. This first point is also related to a second one—religious humanists hold that the reach, depth, and scope of our humanity is greater than their nonreligious colleagues believe. Indeed, humanity, they hold, reaches to and participates in the sacred. No wonder that Christian humanists have held that the core of the religious and moral life is the love of God and the love of neighbor as oneself. Human love is both a form of lateral and vertical transcendence, to use the terminology of neohumanists. Sometimes, as in the thought of St. Paul and some others, the point is pressed to the extent that the two forms of love are unified.[25] "For the whole law is summed up in a single commandment: 'You shall love your neighbor as yourself'" (Gal. 5:14; cf. Lev. 19:18; Matt. 7:12, 19:19; John 13:34). This reading of the double-love command in terms of the "Golden Rule" shows the profoundly humanistic understanding of transcendence in Christian thought, which parallels other religious traditions.

The conception of transcendence in terms of love of God and neighbor among Christian humanists along with their insistence on a humanistic framework of thought and life relates to the final third point shared among kinds of religious humanists. St. Irenaeus put it well for Christians: "The glory of God is man alive" (*Gloria Dei est vivens homo*). For a Christian humanist this aliveness is found in Christ and not simply in the self, and, further, the divine glory is not a matter of the divine self-relations, say, among the persons of the Trinity, or even in God's self-glorification, but in vivifying human and nonhuman life. It is in this light that Christian humanists understand human perfection: that "perfection" is to be fully alive in love and this, rather than an otherworldly reality, is, in truth, the glory of God.

Obviously, not all humanists are religious believers. Yet it is the case that, as seen with respect to Christian humanists, some forms of religious conviction and practice are fully consistent with a humanistic framework of convictions. In our current global situation perhaps the most pressing task facing religious people is to humanize their religious commitments and practices.[26]

DIGNITY: STATUS AND/OR CONSTITUTION

Having analyzed some convictions that are basic to a broadly humanistic outlook and a conception of "dignity," it is now possible to isolate some "types" of humanism on the question of human dignity. This typology is developed around two lines of inquiry: (1) whether dignity is understood primarily in terms of "status" and "constitution," as I have called them, and, (2) whether or not a conception of dignity is necessarily related to an idea or belief in a transcendent supramundane reality, conceived in terms of God, gods, or nontheistic reality. Obviously, any typology cannot capture or examine in detail all possible positions on the subject matter in question, in this case, humanistic conceptions of "dignity." What is sought is a map of options within which specific positions can be roughly located. For the sake of brevity, I refer to religious and nonreligious forms of humanism, realizing that these can take many shapes.

Dignity as Constitutive of Being Human

For many religious and nonreligious humanists (again broadly conceived), dignity, or intrinsic worth (*Würde*), is simply written into our humanity. This dignity might be predicated of "reason" as the specific difference between human and nonhuman creatures, or it might be designated as the "image of God" stamped on the human soul by God in creation. Still others, such as Kant, argue that dignity is found in the human capacity to legislate laws for one's own free action. Without further detail, the point of these positions is that human dignity is a constitutive part of humanity and therefore must be ascribed to each and every human being; it is universal in scope. The question then becomes, as the sad histories of racism and sexism attest, not who among humans has dignity, but rather who is or is not truly human. Once acknowledged as genuinely human, individuals or communities have irreducible worth, are ends in themselves. This means that dignity is intrinsic to humanity, but vulnerable because one's humanity can be denied.

It must be admitted that in the history of Western thought this conception of dignity as a vulnerable but intrinsic fact of being human has been a two-edged sword. Specific conceptions of being human—say, the human is a rational, social animal or a member of a specific community, polis, or race—have been used to exclude people from the recognition of their dignity. Sadly, too often peoples have identified being human exclusively with their own group or race and thus elided the universal scope of human dignity. Indeed, many criticisms of "humanism," religious and nonreligious, focus on the failure of those who speak of human dignity to acknowledge it in those people outside their cultural, racial, or ethnic identities. Certainly, this criticism is warranted for the famous "Enlightenment" figures who championed the "rights of man" while owning slaves (Thomas Jefferson), doubting the rational capacities of nonwhite races (Kant), and, of course, insisting on the inferiority of women (Jean-Jacques Rousseau).[27] Ironically, too often humanists who insist on the constitutive dignity of "man" have denied the full scope of "human" dignity. No wonder that some contemporary antihumanists have proclaimed the end of "man," meaning by this the end of the Enlightenment's illusory universalism regarding "human" dignity.[28]

However, a constitutive idea of human dignity is also two-sided. The same thinkers who failed to live by the full measure of their commitments in fact provided concepts needed for the full participation of everyone in democratic procedures (Jefferson), the backing for human rights (Kant), and the critique of social systems that enslave human beings, including women (Rousseau). That is to say, the idea of universal, intrinsic dignity, whether endowed by God or simply a feature of being human, has exerted pressure on societies and political institutions to extend human social, political, ethnic, racial, and sexual rights to all people.[29] Indeed, the many and various movements for civil rights around the world, from India to the United States, and from South Africa to China, are unimaginable without a humanistic conception of intrinsic or constitutive human dignity.[30] The ancient Romans called a slave a "speaking tool" (*instru-*

mentum vocale), but the progress of global civilization has been an arduous struggle to extend the recognition of human dignity to all people. A commitment to the constitutive character of human dignity, even if culpably incomplete in its early expressions, determines a social, political, and economic task to be undertaken: the achievement of dignity as recognized status. Insisting on the constitutive nature of human dignity sets an agenda, a task, to be undertaken so that the dignity of people will be recognized simply by virtue of their humanity.

Dignity as the Status of a Human Being

No doubt the most ancient conception of dignity was linked to the status an individual could attain in relation to the moral, religious, and cultural values of some specific community. In the Greek world, for instance, virtue or excellence was originally predicated of anything—a ship, a shield—that fulfilled its "function" in the highest degree. Among the ancient Stoics and even later idealists such as F. H. Bradley, "virtue" was excellence in the role of one's social station.[31] In this context, "dignity" was not a given-yet-vulnerable constitutive feature of being human, but, rather, an excellence, height, or supremacy achieved by an individual or community. It was a specific status of that person or community. Dignity could be won or lost and was not an attribute of the human qua human. This seemed to be the force of Pico's claim that human beings lack a nature and are free to rise or fall under their own will and lights. Jean-Paul Sartre made a similar argument in his famous essay "Existentialism as Humanism."

The implication of conceiving of dignity as a status to be achieved is that not everyone can or will achieve it. Aristotle, for instance, insisted that not everyone would attain well-being or happiness (*eudaimonia*), either because the winds of fate might destroy one's life and goals or because those endowed with lesser mental and moral capacities could not achieve human excellence, virtue. The Stoics, too, thought that in principle everyone could attain wisdom, but in fact very few would actually become sages. For existentialists, people can deny the radical choice to define one's identity. Sartre, for example, was open in principle to the free choice of anyone to live authentically, but he held that too many people were mired in inauthentic, slavish, and conformist ways of life.

The idea of dignity as status captures a dearly held humanistic conviction: human beings are progressive creatures. It also expresses the profoundly social nature of human life and dignity insofar as a dignified status is always defined by the values of some community and recognized—or not—within that community. Indeed, for thinkers in the ancient world, such as Aristotle, the standard or model of virtue was the individual deemed as such by a community according to its beliefs about human excellence. Given this "Great Man" criterion, someone might be recognized for his or her dignity in one culture, but not in another. Indeed, the shift from ancient heroic culture to the virtues and values of later cultures indicates just this kind of development. It was only when the question was asked by Aristotle, Plato, and others whether there was a human function as such (that is, a specific excellence of distinctly human capacities) that the criterion for dignity as status was given deeper philosophical and religious sanction. Because of this progression, dignity as status became linked to ideas about the constitutive dignity of a defining function of being human.

Many of the same criticisms that have been levied at the constitutive conception of human dignity have also dogged claims about dignity as status. After all, if the criterion for recognizing dignity is community-based and a community does not esteem the virtues of some people (say, women) or denies others the capacity to attain dignity (say, slaves) or contends that one is born into a specific caste that lacks dignity (say, *Dalits*, or untouchables, in traditional India), then dignity cannot be a universal attribute of being human. Furthermore, if dignity resides in the excellence of some capacity or function constitutive of humans as such, then those deemed nonhuman or subhuman simply lack dignity. Yet in the same way, a conception of dignity grounded in capacity or function also opens a path to dignity for those previously excluded when and where an individual does in fact excel in action and achieve an excellence, say, in the arts, athletics, the military, and so on. In this respect, dignity as status has also been a two-edged sword in the social history of the West. It has been used both to deny and to grant dignity to individuals and groups of people.

The Paradoxes of Dignity

Yet it is not surprising that humanism itself, given its intimate connection to the discourse of dignity, has come under criticism. Some have argued (on religious and nonreligious grounds) that humanism is anthropocentric, either denying the sovereignty and supreme good of the deity, as James M. Gustafson has argued, or denying the worth of nonhuman animals through an invidious speciesism, as Peter Singer has called it. Other critics advocate a form of antihumanism insofar as they seek a completely different semantic and conceptual framework for understanding being human and the dignity and vocation of human beings. Martin Heidegger, in his famous "Letter on Humanism," rejected existentialist positions like Sartre's, arguing that humanism presupposed a forgetfulness of Being and embodied a basic framework, a *Gestell*, that reduces Being to standing reserve for human technological use. Against the humanist outlook as he understood it, Heidegger claimed man is the shepherd of Being whose task is to tend to Being and its meaning. Likewise, current strands of thought called "transhumanism" seek to transcend through technological and biochemical means the form of human existence and its bondage to death. All of these movements and thinkers challenge a humanistic framework for understanding the status and vulnerability of human dignity.[32]

Rather than considering further the various critics of humanistic ideas about dignity, I think it more apt to note two paradoxes of dignity so conceived, a conceptual and a social paradox. The conceptual paradox has been helpfully identified and analyzed by Matthew Petrusek.[33] It is this: if dignity is constitutive of being human, then it would seem that there is no reason to defend it, since, per definition, it is simply given with human existence and in that respect invulnerable to human action. Conversely, if dignity is vulnerable this might undercut any notion of equality and universality to the concept while also posing practical challenges to its defense. Yet, at least within a humanist framework, the two basic forms of dignity (status and constitution) can become interrelated because each is explicated in the other one. If dignity as status relies on some conception of a constitutive function of being human, then the two ideas are related. Likewise, dignity as constitutive laid out the task, and so the status, of recognizing all people as having equal dignity. If not in theory, then at least in practice, the two forms of dignity within a humanist outlook imply each other and thereby elide what I have called the conceptual paradox.

Matters are more complex with respect to the social paradox, as I am calling it. By this I mean that each of the forms of dignity explored above depends, in different ways, on processes of recognition, that is, the ways in which human dignity, however conceived and sanctioned, is acknowledged as such. This fact is, importantly, consistent with the humanist conviction about the profoundly social nature of human life and also the arts of interpretation and persuasion for the orientation and conduct of individual and social life.

What then is the paradox? In order to make any appeal to dignity, however conceived, there must be someone who can recognize and respond to that dignity. The responses might be one of neglect, denial, abuse, esteem, or respect, but someone must recognize the call of dignity. The paradox here is that whether conceived as constitutive dignity, dignity as status, or some interrelation of these forms of dignity, each is interdependent with a response to recognition. Lacking recognition, the claim of dignity persists, but it lacks moral, political, and religious salience. Little wonder, then, that humanists worry about the knowledge of and response to the claim of the dignity of another and oneself. This knowledge is of a piece with humanist epistemological commitments, and so admittedly subject to doubt and error and also the need for interpretation and learning. Indeed, a basic humanist concern is how best to hone or tutor one's perceptions so as to recognize and respond to the claim of other people's dignity. Humanists of various stripes have advanced three related, but different, accounts of moral perception: a religious one; a social account; and a broadly phenomenological one. Just a few words about each account will have to suffice for the purposes of this chapter.

First, religious accounts of dignity often require the cultivation of religio-moral perception through various spiritual practices (e.g., prayer, contemplation and meditation, worship) aimed at the perception and experience of the divine or sacred in relation to the mundane realities of human life. These practices are meant to enlighten, awaken, redeem, or restore persons to a purified state in order to know and perceive their spiritual condition and with it the claim of others' dignity on oneself. In fact, in some traditions (e.g., Buddhism) there are moral practices required in order to advance spiritually.[34] In theistic traditions there is another layer of reflection: insofar as the divine knows people in the depths of their hearts, human recognition of dignity is related to and sanctioned by divine recognition. Accordingly, the tutoring of perception is the work of coming to see, know, and respond to the claim of dignity as God sees, knows, and responds. For instance, among Christian theologians, the claim is that through the grace of Christ and the discipline of loving, one is to come to know and love the neighbor and oneself in God. As St. Augustine argued in *De doctrina christiana*, the proper recognition of the other in God sanctions the equal and universal recognition of the dignity of all people. This is to fulfill the so-called double-love command, that is, to love God and to love the neighbor as oneself. For Christian humanism, this training in love is also the pedagogy of freedom, insofar as one's moral agency is integral to the life of faith.[35] However, it is crucial to note that any human practice and human striving for perfection in love is utterly reliant on divine grace. For the Christian humanist, the human being in sin—though not utterly devoid of created goods or capacities—cannot redeem, restore, and transform itself. Perfection in love is a work of grace and of human striving.

Second, social accounts of recognition explore the social processes of giving and withdrawing respect for dignity. Examples include various social institutions or spheres (family, market, politics, civic organizations, educational institutions, etc.), patterns of mutual recognition, and free reason-giving with respect to shared norms germane to the sphere structure social life. In this respect, there is, in principle, the recognition of status and excellence internal to these various social practices even as social inclusion, at least in advanced democratic societies, rests on some notion of dignity not reducible to social processes. For instance, the constitutions of most modern nation-states include the recognition of basic rights not dependent on the state itself in order to warrant the inclusion of every citizen within the scope of those rights. This means, of course, that a social account of dignity is usually dependent on a constitutive idea of dignity. Yet the point here is not about the origin or grounds of dignity, but, rather, its recognition. The argument is that social life itself relies on and enacts patterns of mutual recognition, and this is important for the acknowledgment of human dignity.[36] The various struggles for civil rights around the world—racial, religious, economic, sexual, ethnic—can be seen as struggles for social recognition when social processes restrict or exclude people from the domain of rights consistent with full participation in the social order.

Finally, some humanists offer "phenomenological" accounts, in the broad sense, of recognition. Two have been basic in the contemporary debate about humanism. First, Kant, as the champion of human dignity and worth, was the first to put respect for persons, including oneself, at the core of morality. For Kant, "respect" is an odd phenomenon since it is, on his terms, a "moral feeling" produced solely by reason and applies only to persons and not things. In fact, this "feeling" is respect for the moral law, and thus, Kant insists, morality itself is regarded as an incentive for action.[37] Kant's position, and those like his, argues that the human capacity for free, rational action evokes the feeling of respect and so the acknowledgment of the dignity of oneself and others. Some, such as Jürgen Habermas, link this process to the logic of intersubjective communication, or, in a somewhat different way, to capacities needed for people to exercise their freedom and attain some measure of well-being (as Amartya Sen and Martha Nussbaum have argued). Whatever the case, this broadly Kantian account of the recognition of and respect for human dignity is about the constitution of free moral agency.[38]

Emmanuel Levinas develops another phenomenology of recognition in his "humanism of the other."[39] Levinas worries that most Western thought has been developed from the perspective of the knowing and acting "I" or self and that this approach reduces the otherness of others to the same, to the self. In order to escape the grip of such thinking, what he calls "ontology," one must begin with the "face" of the other and the command it enunciates: "Do not murder me!" It is this command issued by the other that constitutes the self in a relation of infinite responsibility. One does not, on this account, assume responsibility for others; one is constituted as a self by the claim of responsibility uttered by the other in her or his complete vulnerability. The philosophical task, accordingly, is to unfold the phenomenology of this claim to responsibility and what it means for the whole scope of human life and conduct.

With these three responses to the paradoxes of dignity, we have, I think, a fair account of the types of humanism, religious and nonreligious, on the question of the grounds and acknowledgment of human dignity. The only question remaining concerns humanism and the future of dignity. We turn now to consider that question.

THE FUTURE OF DIGNITY ON EARTH

There are, it would appear, two major challenges to human dignity now defining the future of human and nonhuman life. One challenge to the idea of human nature is the claim that we should, as transhumanists argue, seek to transcend or overcome the human lot through technological or biochemical means in a war against the reality of death. For example, transhumanists ask, "Why not download memories and experiences into a computer so that one's personal life is freed from the vulnerability and morality of the human body?" Because they seek to transcend the human frame, one might see these and other transhumanist ideas as the final apotheosis of Pico's oration on human dignity. If humanity has no set nature, why not seek to overcome our current mortal condition?

At stake here is the question of the degree to which human dignity is bound to the created and/or evolved constitution of our species and whether our finite condition can and ought to be affirmed as intrinsically good, even in the face of suffering and death. In response to that challenge, the humanist must, I contend, insist on the constitutive goodness of our finite condition and on the meaning and dignity of human existence as unfolding within the ways in which that condition sustains and yet also limits human freedom. Stated otherwise, human freedom on this humanist account is found within the labor of human responsibility, that is, to respect and enhance the integrity of life, rather than in seeking a nonhuman or suprahuman form of existence. Hans

Jonas, a Jewish philosopher, put the point well. He argued that it is imperative in our situation to ensure that responsibility remains on Earth, and therefore we must be dedicated to the "Idea of Man" since it is human beings who are the bearers and agents of responsibility.[40] Yet this affirmation of "Man" must entail, on my account, respect for and the enhancement of the constitutive integrity of the species-nature of human beings. In this respect, the future of dignity is a future in which human finitude is respected and treasured as the necessary condition for any enhancement of life.

The second challenge to human dignity concerns the connections between human life—granting, from a humanist perspective, its axiological distinctiveness—and other forms of life on Earth. There is little doubt about the massive challenges that now face life on this planet from climate change and other forms of human action on the environment. These environmental challenges are intrinsically linked to the future of human well-being, and to the possibility and demand for justice among peoples and within human communities. Given this essential connectedness among forms of life on this planet and the fact that human distinctiveness, most basically, is found in the responsibility human beings bear for the integrity of finite life, the dignity or intrinsic value of nonhuman life now demands recognition.

In order for the dignity of nonhuman life to incite action aimed at addressing the manifold ecological challenges we now face, our moral perception of the goodness of the community of life must be tutored and refined.[41] Here, too, the humanist concern for education and moral perception becomes important, and in three ways.

First is so that we can perceive the worth (*Würde*) and not just the price or utility of nonhuman life. Without the sense of the claim of this worth upon our responsibility, it is hard to imagine any viable response to environment challenges. But this means, of course, massive political, civic, and international effort, both to educate people and to respond to those challenges. Sadly, it is not at all clear that there is sufficient political will to coordinate such massive efforts. In this situation, humanists must direct their energies to the work of education and also civic engagement in order to awaken the public will, while also remaining utterly realistic about the seemingly intractable nature of the problem.[42]

The second reason why humanist concerns for moral perception and education are important in the face of global environmental challenges is the tragic nature of a lack of response to those challenges. The tragedy of any failure of nations and peoples to respond to environmental challenges is obvious. A lack of response means either the demise or the severe limitation of the dignity of future human and nonhuman life. In the worst case, the tragedy here is that it would mean the end of human free choices. Environmental and survival necessity would rule decisions, thereby dooming the future for free human agents. Without some measure of freedom of choice, there can be no conflicts that demand choices and so no meaningful human agency. All "choices" would be necessitated by environmental facts and therefore not really choices. Ironically, in order to ensure the future of human agency, some measure of vulnerability and risk must be accepted and even affirmed. Yet no such choices are possible when environmental destruction necessitates a course of action impervious to human need, intention, or deliberation.

The third reason a concern for perception and moral education is crucial in our situation is that, granting—at least for the moment—that some element of choice remains, then individuals and communities must develop the means to reason through complex problems about respect for and the sustainability of future life. The demands of our day seem to outpace conventional forms of ethics. They at least demand revisions in them and thus reflection on and the development of patterns of moral reasoning. Now is not the time or place to enter into current debates about practical reasoning and environmental questions, but it is clear that a humanist has much at stake in those debates. They are also a constant reminder of the fallibility and limitation of human judgment. Yet in the face of these threats to the future of dignity on Earth, those human limitations cannot and must not forestall decisions about how to respect and enhance the integrity of life.

FROM HUMAN DIGNITY TO THE INTEGRITY OF LIFE

The dignity of human nature and the worth of nonhuman life form the horizon of this inquiry into humanism and dignity: they open up once again inquiry into the most basic tenants of humanism, namely, that one can and must speak of the intrinsic worth of being human and that human beings are in some measure distinctive in worth in relation to other forms of life on Earth. How should we formulate the dignity of human beings once the scope of worth is seen to exceed human existence, even as human beings now have a distinctive responsibility for the future of forms of life?

The movement from classical humanism to neohumanism, I suggested, is found in the shift from the development and perfection of the self to responsibility for the other, the finality of the you, as Todorov put it. The task now,

I suggest, is to advance a form of humanism that interrelates human dignity with the worth of nonhuman life. The centerpiece of that kind of humanism, I further contend, is the integrity of life, seeing human dignity as found in the responsibility to respect and enhance the integrity of living things.[43] That shift in axiology must be matched, I believe, with a new engagement between humanism's religious convictions and the myriad forms of hypertheism. I call that outlook on life "theological humanism," the moral and religious focus of which is responsibility for the integrity of life.[44] However named, this chapter has demonstrated how and under what terms humanism remains an indispensable voice in the global debate about human dignity.

NOTES

1. Various thinkers, including Matthew Petrusek (one of the editors of this book), make something like this distinction between status and constitution. For another recent example, see George Kateb, *Human Dignity* (Cambridge, MA: Belknap Press of Harvard University Press, 2001), and his distinction between status and stature. For my purposes, what is important is the interaction among these conceptions rather than their differences.

2. Many other examples of the diverse meanings of dignity could be considered. For religious traditions, such as Buddhism, that lack a constitutive conception of an enduring or substantial "self" and see the root human problem as the desire for possession and status, conceptions of dignity as status and as constitutive are simply unnecessary. Insofar as that is the case, some other means must be found to make sense of the idea of human dignity. It is not possible in this chapter to consider the details of nontheistic traditions in terms of their conceptions of the ultimate or unconditioned.

3. See, for example, J. De Gruchy, ed., *The Humanism Imperative in South Africa* (Stellenbosch: Sun Press, 2011), and Tu Wei-ming, "Confucianism," in *Our Religions*, ed. Arvind Sharma (New York: HarperCollins, 1993), 139–228.

4. It should be noted that this terminology of religious and nonreligious forms of humanism and the idea of "antihumanism" are clearly contemporary designations. Virtually every classical humanist in the West, ranging from Cicero to medieval Scholastics, was a religious thinker in some respect. Even with the rise of the difference between Northern and Southern forms of humanism during the Renaissance, wherein "Northerners," such as Thomas More and Erasmus, were obviously more orthodox Christians than were Southern, Italian humanists, a religious dimension to human life was never denied. Secular humanism is an invention of the nineteenth and twentieth centuries. Likewise the idea of "antihumanism" owes its legacy to various twentieth-century philosophical critiques of classical humanism.

5. Tzvetan Todorov, *Imperfect Garden: The Legacy of Humanism* (Princeton, NJ: Princeton University Press, 2014), 30 (original emphasis).

6. Jacques Maritain, *Integral Humanism* (Notre Dame, IN: University of Notre Dame Press, 1996), 153. I thank John Buchman for calling this citation to my attention.

7. Alasdair MacIntyre, *Three Rival Versions of Moral Enquiry: Encyclopedia, Genealogy, Tradition* (Notre Dame, IN: University of Notre Dame Press, 1990).

8. For the importance of this point in religious ethics, see Richard B. Miller, *Friends and Other Strangers: Studies in Religion, Ethics, and Culture* (New York: Columbia University Press, 2016).

9. The usual provisos about "typologies" are at play in this chapter. A typology is an abstraction from the welter of positions about a specific topic, in this case, human dignity, with respect to some shared discourse ("humanism") in order to isolate the relative insights and oversights of logical options. A typology makes no claim to provide an exhaustive account of any one position since its purpose is not analytic depth, but, rather, to survey conceptual and axiological options on the given topic.

10. Without meaning to sound alarmist, it can be hardly doubted that there are many political, social, and even intellectual movements that rage against the idea of universal human dignity in the name of ethnic and political communities, religious fundamentalism, distinctive racial, gendered and class identities, and also some ecological ideas. In our time, to champion a humanistic conception of dignity is as difficult as it is important, or so I hold.

11. Giovanni Pico della Mirandola, *Oration on the Dignity of Man*, trans. A. Robert Gaponigri (Washington, DC: Gateway Editions, 1996). It is interesting to note that when Thomas de Vio (Cajetan), theologian and later cardinal, debated Pico at Ferrara in 1494, he was proclaimed the victor and triumphantly celebrated by his students. Already, the question of the human relation to the divine was at dispute among avowed humanists. For an account of humanistic theology and the struggle for justice, see Santiago Piñón, *The Ivory Tower and the Sword: Francisco Vitoria Confronts the Emperor* (Eugene, OR: Pickwick, 2016).

12. Thomas Aquinas, *Summa theologiae* I, 14, 1.

13. Edward W. Said, *Humanism and Democratic Criticism* (New York: Columbia University Press, 2004), and William Schweiker, *Mimetic Reflections: A Study in Hermeneutics, Theology and Ethics* (New York: Fordham University Press, 1990).

14. J. S. Mill, *On Liberty*, in *John Stuart Mill: On Liberty and Other Essays* (Oxford: Oxford University Press, 1991), 5–130.

15. See Werner Jaeger, *Paideia: The Ideals of Greek Culture*, 3 vols. (Oxford: Oxford University Press, 1954).

16. John Dewey, *Reconstruction in Philosophy* (New York: H. Holt & Co., 1920).

17. Alfred North Whitehead, *Adventures of Ideas* (New York: Simon and Schuster, 1967), 83. Whitehead attributes the quote to Plato: "The creation of the world—said Plato—is the victory of persuasion over force." Mark Skousen, referencing Whitehead, says, "The triumph of persuasion over force is the sign of a civilized society"; see Skousen, "Persuasion vs. Force," in *Everything Voluntary: From Politics to Parenting*, ed. Skyler J. Collins (Salt Lake City: Skyler J. Collins, 2012), 26.

18. Immanuel Kant, *Critique of Practical Reason*, 2nd ed., trans. Mary Gregor (Cambridge: Cambridge University Press, 2015).

19. Kateb, *Human Dignity*, 17.

20. For examples of these criticisms of humanism, see James M. Gustafson, *Ethics from a Theocentric Perspective*, 2 vols. (Chicago: University of Chicago Press, 1984); Peter Singer, *Unsanctifying Human Life* (Oxford: Blackwell, 2002); and Dana Haraway, "A Cyborg Manifesto: Science, Technology, and Socialist-Feminism in the Late Twentieth Century," in *Simians, Cyborgs and Women: The Reinvention of Nature* (New York: Routledge, 1991).

21. Martha Nussbaum, *Upheavals of Thought* (Cambridge: Cambridge University Press, 2001); Tzvetan Todorov, *Facing the Extreme* (New York: Henry Holt, 1996).

22. For a brief recent account, see R. William Franklin and Joseph M. Shaw, *The Case for Christian Humanism* (Grand Rapids, MI: William B. Eerdmans, 1991). For a very different position, see Karl Barth, *The Humanity of God* (Louisville, KY: Westminster/John Knox Press, 1996).

23. See William Schweiker, "Flesh and Folly: The Christ of Christian Humanism," in *Who Is Jesus Christ for Us Today?* Festschrift for Michael Welker, ed. A. Schuele and Günter Thomas (Louisville, KY: Westminster/John Knox Press, 2009), 85–102.

24. Athanasius, *De Incarnacione*, trans. T. Herbert Bindley (London: Religious Tract Society, 1903), 142.

25. See William Schweiker, "And a Second Is Like It: Christian Faith and the Claim of the Other" *Quarterly Review* 20, no. 3 (2000): 233–47.

26. See William Schweiker, "Humanizing Religion," *The Journal of Religion* 89, no. 2 (2009): 214–35.

27. See William Cohen, "Thomas Jefferson and the Problem of Slavery," *Journal of American History* 56, no. 3 (1969): 503–26; Immanuel Kant, "Of the Different Human Races," in *Kant and the Concept of Race*, ed. and trans, John Mikkelsen (Albany: SUNY Press, 2013), 55–73; Jean-Jacques Rousseau, *A Discourse on Inequality*, trans. Maurice Cranston (London: Penguin, 1984).

28. Michael Foucault, *The Order of Things: An Archeology of the Human Sciences* (New York: Random House, 1970); see also, for example, Judith Butler, *Gender Trouble: Feminism and the Subversion of Identity* (London: Routledge, 1990); and Susan Kehman, *The Feminine Subject* (Cambridge: Polity, 2014).

29. Lynn Hunt, *Inventing Human Rights: A History* (New York: Norton Books, 2007).

30. On this, see Barbra Bennett and Elizabeth Bucar, *Does Human Rights Need God?* (Grand Rapid, MI: William B. Eerdmans, 2005).

31. F. H. Bradley, *Ethical Studies* (Oxford: Oxford University Press, 1876); Epictetus, *Discourses, Fragments, Handbook*, trans. Robin Hard (Oxford: Oxford University Press, 2014), see, esp., 90–92, on "How may the actions that are appropriate to a person be discovered from the names applied to him?"

32. Gustafson, *Ethics from a Theocentric Perspective*, 1:73; Singer, *Unsanctifying Human Life*, 1–25; Martin Heidegger, "Letter on Humanism," in *Martin Heidegger: Path-*

marks, ed. William McNeill (Cambridge: Cambridge University Press, 1998), 239–77; Max More and Natasha Vita-More, *The Transhumanist Reader* (Chichister: Wiley and Sons, 2013).

33. See, for instance, Matthew Petrusek, "Human Capacities and the Problem of Universal Human Dignity: Two Philosophical Test Cases and a Theistic Response," *Journal of Moral Theology* 5, no. 1 (2016): 37–64.

34. See David Clairmont, *Moral Struggle and Religious Ethics* (Chichister: Wiley and Sons, 2011); Iris Murdoch, *The Sovereignty of the Good* (New York: Routledge, 1970).

35. This is part of the force of Erasmus's argument against Martin Luther's claim about the "bondage of the will." See E. Gordon Rupp and Philip S. Watson, eds., *Luther and Erasmus: Free Will and Salvation* (Philadelphia: Westminster Press, 1969).

36. See Jürgen Habermas, *Moral Consciousness and Communicative Action*, trans. Christian Lenhardt and Shierry Weber Nicholsen (Cambridge, MA: MIT Press, 1999); Axel Honneth, *The Struggle for Recognition* (Cambridge: Polity, 1995); Paul Ricoeur, *The Course of Recognition*, trans. David Pellauer (Cambridge, MA: Harvard University Press, 2005); Michael Sohn, *The Good of Recognition: Phenomenology, Ethics, and Religion in the Thought of Levinas and Ricoeur* (Waco, TX: Baylor University Press, 2014); Charles Taylor, *Ethics of Authenticity* (Cambridge, MA: Harvard University Press, 1991).

37. Immanuel Kant, *Critique of Practical Reason*, trans. L. W. Beck (Indianapolis, IN: Bobbs-Merrill, 1956).

38. Habermas, *Moral Consciousness and Communicative Action*; Amartya Sen, *Development as Freedom* (New York: Random House, 1999); Martha Nussbaum, *Women and Human Development: The Capabilities Approach* (Cambridge: Cambridge University Press, 2000).

39. Emmanuel Levinas, *Humanism of the Other*, trans. Nidra Poller (Urbana: University of Illinois Press, 2006).

40. Hans Jonas, *The Imperative of Responsibility: In Search for an Ethics of the Technological Age* (Chicago: University of Chicago Press, 1984). Also see William Schweiker, *Responsibility and Christian Ethics* (Cambridge: Cambridge University Press, 1995).

41. This is one point where my argument departs radically from Jonas's and others like him. In order to incite action, Jonas argues, one must rely on a "heuristics of fear." My claim, more in line with humanist convictions, is that it is the perception of goodness and the aim of the good that incites action.

42. Some scholars have adopted an idea developed within public policy discussion to characterize the environmental challenge, namely, the idea of "wicked problems." Wicked problems are those social problems of such complexity that no simple answer is possible, and, further, any answer adopted will increase the problem even while addressing part of it. In popular terms, wicked problems involve a catch-22: no matter what is done, the problem is rendered all the more complex and seemingly intractable.

43. See William Schweiker, *Dust That Breathes: Christian Faith and the New Humanisms* (Oxford: Willey-Blackwell, 2010).

44. See David E. Klemm and William Schweiker, *Religion and the Human Future: An Essay on Theological Humanism* (Oxford: Wiley-Blackwell, 2008).

twelve

ISLAMIC AND HUMANIST PERSPECTIVES ON DIGNITY

A Response

Jonathan Rothchild

Dignity is under attack across the globe, and the preceding chapters have asserted that religious traditions view dignity as a foundational principle for reflection on divine–human relations and practical deliberation about the meanings of moral goods. A conversation between humanism and Islam is needed in our contemporary context for at least two important reasons: first, it can help mediate current disagreements between Islamic thinkers and Western, liberal thinkers on the nature and status of human rights; second, it can challenge longstanding, Eurocentric biases embedded in Western humanistic accounts of dignity. Addressing these two concerns represents the wider aim of my response. My primary purpose is to perform a comparative analysis of the chapters from William Schweiker and Zeki Saritoprak, focusing on the anthropological assumptions underpinning their accounts of dignity and drawing out the ethical implications of these assumptions. I argue that they share two central claims: dignity is intrinsic, but also vulnerable; and upholding dignity requires attention to personal aspects (seeking moral goods) and interpersonal aspects (granting respect and undertaking responsibility). Dignity, in my judgment, necessarily requires a kind of coinherence between vulnerability and responsibility.

I first compare and contrast their anthropological assumptions, highlighting dignity, vulnerability, and responsibility. Next, I consider the ethical implications of these assumptions in light of questions raised by disability. I also engage thinkers from Protestantism—my own tradition—in order to expand the comparative analysis of dignity. Third, I briefly explore aspects of Islamic humanism, including Eurocentric interpretations, and I make modest constructive proposals regarding contemporary debates about human rights.

Before moving to these substantive matters, I want to note a few methodological points. It is inevitably reductive to compare two traditions given their own internal debates and disagreements, even if both Schweiker and Saritoprak acknowledge that their accounts represent respective *interpretations* of the humanist and Islamic traditions. Second, a short response does not provide adequate space for one to marshal the resources of a fully comparative religious ethic. I am simply employing dignity as a bridge concept to place humanism and Islam in conversation and to reflect constructively on current discussions about disability and human rights.[1]

ANTHROPOLOGICAL ASSUMPTIONS AND DIGNITY

Saritoprak provides a rich portrait of the layered anthropology in the Islamic tradition, which has resonance with Schweiker's humanistic conceptions. Modeled on the exemplars of the five elite prophets (Noah, Abraham, Moses, Jesus, and Muhammad), human beings are created as *khulafa'*, or God's representatives on Earth, God's vicegerents, and successors of the Prophet, and therefore enjoy superiority over other creatures and seek friendship and relationality (*al-ins*) with one another. As we noted in the introduction to this book, Islam pursues a notion of dignity that is ontological and inherent. Saritoprak writes that "all human dignity is derived from God, the Creator" (233), where "human dignity comes from their supplication to and relationship with the Divine and the status of human beings as the addressees of God" (239). Though Schweiker identifies a variety of foundations for the intrinsic worth (*Würde*) of humans, including the *imago Dei*, he locates a claim similar to Islam that emerges in theological humanism: "Insofar as the divine knows people in the depths of their hearts, human recognition of dignity is related to and sanctioned by divine recognition" (266). In Islam, this divine–human encounter underlies dignity and inspires the pursuit of perfection (*al-insan al-kamil* as the perfected human being mirroring the perfection of God *al-Kamil al-Mutlaq*, or the Unlimited Perfect). This perfection, according to Saritoprak's reading of the Qur'an, materializes in terms of the acquisition of knowledge and good conduct. Acquisition of knowledge is a key theme in the Qur'an and a distinguishing feature of being human even vis-à-vis angels: "Adam's knowledge is superior because he is capable of learning and developing and possesses free will, but angels are static and do not possess these abilities" (235). Capability or a dynamic capacity for knowledge, where "the Qur'an encourages human beings to be aware of their potential and capacities," resonates with Pico della Mirandola's sense of humans as "incomplete projects" (255) and what Schweiker identifies as dignity as status and "a dearly held humanistic conviction: that human beings are progressive creatures" (263).

If humans have intrinsic worth and are continuously developing their capacities, what are the challenges and obligations that accompany being human? Both authors view vulnerability and responsibility as two fundamentally interrelated modes of being related to dignity, which indicates that aspects of dignity can be diminished or enhanced through individual and interpersonal actions. From an Islamic perspective, vulnerability is expressed as the "frailty and impotence of human capabilities and human beings' reliance on God for all human advances" (239). As Saritoprak explains, this frailty is intensified by the presence of Satan. Though Islam does not have a Christian conception of original sin ("there is no transmission of the sin of Adam and Eve to their offspring"; 238), human beings have a dualistic nature—they are both angelic and satanic (241). The extent to which human beings maintain the full enjoyment of their dignity depends in part on their cultivation of virtue and good action. Saritoprak declares that "if human beings follow the way of their egoistic desires, rather than pursue spiritual developments, they will lose their almost limitless capacity, and their life will be only this short, temporary physical life" (244).[2]

Schweiker's conception of vulnerability within human dignity is also connected to human frailty. Although not preoccupied with the condition of sin, Schweiker maintains that sin affects pursuit of perfection and necessitates that human striving is supported by grace. Sin does not completely obviate dignity, which maintains its intrinsic character. Nonetheless, Schweiker contends that dignity still remains vulnerable because "in order to make any appeal to dignity, however conceived, there must be someone who can recognize and respond to that dignity" (265). He characterizes this recognition aspect as the social paradox where "each of the forms of dignity . . . depends, in different ways, on processes of recognition, that is, the ways in which human dignity, however conceived and sanctioned, is acknowledged as such" (265). Acknowledgment affirms the inherently relational dimensions of dignity that reflect a relational anthropology and a deep sense of interconnectedness that animates and concretizes human dignity.

Both Saritoprak and Schweiker also discuss responsibility as a key feature of dignity. Saritoprak views responsibility as grounded in the status of humans as *khalifa*, where "everyone is responsible only for his or her own actions" (238) even as other Qur'anic verses "speak of human beings' accountability and their responsibility to God, to fellow human beings, and to the environment" (234). This responsibility for others unfolds as respect for persons independent of their status. Saritoprak points to the story about the Prophet, who, upon learning that a funeral procession was for a deceased Jewish person, insists that "respect [is owed] for the dignity of every human being, regardless of that person's religion and ethnicity" (242). Schweiker similarly maintains that responsibility emerges out of one's own dignity and in response to the dignity of the other: "Human freedom on this humanist account is found within the labor of human responsibility, that is, to respect and enhance the integrity of life, rather than in seeking a nonhuman or suprahuman form of existence" (268).

ETHICAL IMPLICATIONS: THE CASE STUDY OF DISABILITY

In the same way that Islamic and humanist traditions are not uniform in terms of their beliefs and practices, Protestant—my own tradition's—perspectives are not monolithic (and have not been in Reformation, post-Reformation, and contemporary contexts). We can identify general Protestant sensibilities, namely, an emphasis on the individual (say, in terms of individual salvation and one's individual experience of God *pro nobis*) and on the needs of the neighbor (expressed, for example, in Martin Luther's idea about becoming a Christ for the neighbor or Paul Ramsey's understanding of biblical justice as measured by the real need of the neighbor).[3] These ideas have been criticized by Protestant and non-Protestant theologians in terms of their deleterious effects on the environment and economic priorities,[4] retributive punishment,[5] and mutual sexual pleasure.[6] My task here is not to engage in a critical conversation regarding these critiques, but rather to use these ideas as constructive lenses for engaging ideas about dignity in Saritoprak and Schweiker.

I have noted several anthropological features, namely, dignity, vulnerability, and responsibility, similarly discussed by Saritoprak and Schweiker. In drawing out some of the ethical implications of their perspectives, I turn to issues concerning dignity and disability. In his analysis of dignity, Saritoprak quotes the Qur'anic description of the physical and spiritual dignity unfolded in creation: "Surely We have created the human being in the most beautiful form" (238).

What might disabled, deformed, or broken bodies offer as potential counter-models to this "beautiful form"? To be sure, theologians in many traditions have struggled with this question and unfortunately collapsed ideas about disease, disability, sin, and healing. Eliding disability and theological accounts of healing reinscribes marginalization and disempowerment. Jewish theologian Julia Watts Belser writes: "But the *imperative* to be healed—the assumption that disabled bodies and minds all desire and require healing—functions as a form of violence and a kind of imperialism."[7] Does Saritoprak's account of dignity sufficiently account for disability and related issues of violence and imperialism? He views humans as possessing intrinsic dignity and striving towards perfection, and he defends the claim that humans should respect persons regardless of their race, religion, or gender. Is disability included in this list? Does it represent a difference that warrants respect or subjugation (and remolding into the beautiful form)? Some scholars argue that the concept of disability is not found in the Qur'an,[8] whereas others point to the unique challenges faced by disabled women in Islamic cultures.[9]

My reading of Saritoprak is that his conception of dignity in terms of vulnerability and responsibility can coinhere in ways to empower respect for persons with disabilities. Saritoprak explains that there is no concept of original sin in Islam (which is, to varying degrees, markedly different than what most Protestant thinkers would claim), but he upholds that all persons are vulnerable as they negotiate their dual natures and try to progress in knowledge. Martin Luther analogously contended that a shared feature of existence—sin—equalizes everyone, because abled and disabled alike cling to the mercy of Christ.[10] Saritoprak similarly insists that Islamic tradition not only demands respect for difference but also "draws our attention to the meaninglessness of claims of superiority [that emerge out of that difference such as] through ancestors or tribes" (248). In this regard, the Islamic tradition appears compatible with the distinction Lutheran theologian Gilbert Meilaender makes between two interrelated forms of discourse about human dignity: "We need the language of human dignity to talk about matters that involve the integrity and flourishing of the human species, and we need the language of personal dignity to express respect for persons regarded as equal and non-interchangeable individuals."[11]

Though he does not directly address disability, Schweiker is cognizant of the distorted visions of certain humanists "who insist on the constitutive dignity of 'man' [and thereby] have denied the full scope of 'human' dignity" (262). In affirming the full scope of human dignity, Schweiker submits that dignity "cannot be known or valued from merely one perspective, such as our bodiliness or rationality" (256). This nonreductionist sense of dignity, according to Schweiker, lays the groundwork for a capacious axiological commitment "found in human responsibility for itself and for the other forms of life on Earth" (259). In thinking with Schweiker and the humanist traditions vis-à-vis dignity, disability, and responsibility, I want to push two points. First, do humanistic traditions sufficiently account for relationality as the mode in which dignity is experienced and enhanced? Pentecostal theologian Amos Yong notes, "There is the fact that the more severely or profoundly disabled express and manifest their self-identity precisely in and through the relationships of interdependence with others."[12] Interdependence, which elicits and sustains a dignity-based care in a relationship between disabled and abled persons, coalesces constitutive and status understandings of dignity. These relationships of interdependence seem to cut through the paradoxical relationship between constitutive and status understandings of dignity—as Schweiker envisions them—and affirm them in ways that coinhere (as I have also suggested above with respect to Saritoprak's account).

Second, do secular and theological forms of humanism account for another aspect of relationally based dignity, namely, sacrifice? Take, for example, the case of caregivers for significantly disabled persons. To what extent is there—even within the context of interdependence described above—a sacrifice of one's own dignity understood as privileging one's agency, knowledge, and well-being?[13] In *The Cost of Discipleship*, Lutheran theologian Dietrich Bonhoeffer portrays the disciples as ones who relinquish their dignity to take on the sufferings of others: "These men without possessions or power, these strangers on earth, these sinners, these followers of Jesus, have in their life with him *renounced their own dignity*, for they are merciful. As if their own needs and their own distress were not enough, they take upon themselves the distress and humiliation and sin of others."[14] The cost of discipleship may surpass "reasonable" expectations for responsibility for the dignity of others, but it—like the experiences of abled and disabled in interdependent relationships—nevertheless challenges humanistic accounts to reimagine the scope and depths of responsibility beyond awareness, tolerance, and respect.

ISLAMIC HUMANISM: PAST AND PRESENT

I turn now to another feature of a discussion between Islamic and humanist traditions, Islamic humanism. Sadly, the devastating bombings in the city of

Aleppo, Syria, are but one recent example of the human costs of conflict. It is, however, a particularly visceral representation of the ways in which human dignity—including the lives of women and children—can be callously denied and indiscriminately decimated. It is estimated that more than 16,000 civilians died in bombings in 2016.[15] The story of Aleppo certainly includes tragedy and suffering, but it also offers a message of hope. Aleppo is also an ancient city that witnessed Islamic–Christian dialogue and the proliferation of Islamic humanism. Abdulrazzak Patel describes the efforts of Jirmānūs Farhāt (1670–1732) and others, who "produced numerous works that they appropriated and adapted from the Muslim humanist tradition and made available to their Christian audience."[16] Reclaiming this kind of dialogue and potential collaboration can help provide a constructive pathway for promoting dignity. In this concluding section, I briefly discuss historical forms of Islamic humanism and constructively explore current debates regarding human rights, which represent the formal legal and political mechanisms for acknowledging and protecting human dignity. After briefly describing some figures within the Islamic humanist tradition, I explore issues of Eurocentrism and the prospects for Muslim–Christian dialogue.

Islamic humanists historically developed dialogical frameworks for theological, philosophical, and jurisprudential interpretations. Examples of Islamic humanists include the tenth-century philosopher and jurist Al-Fārābī (d. 950) and fourteenth-century historian Ibn Khaldun (1332–1406). Lenn Goodman describes Fārābī as one who studied Greek science, logic, and philosophy and found "Islam itself as something both alien and intimately familiar."[17] Goodman suggests that Fārābī could receive the tradition more critically in virtue of being open to multiple perspectives and recognizing "that there are limits in all human articulations of values, no matter how universal the underlying ideas."[18] Self-reflexive awareness of these limits opens space for dialogue and the dignity of the other. More recent examples of Islamic humanists include Muhammad Iqbal (1877–1938). Similar to Fārābī, Iqbal engaged sources of human knowledge outside of the tradition as a method of reconstructing Muslim philosophical and legal traditions and finding compatibility with contemporary secular human rights discourse.[19] Ebrahim Moosa demonstrates that thinkers such as Iqbal were influenced by classical and medieval hermeneutical approaches to jurisprudence; Moosa contends that "the claim that Islamic law is immutable denies the historical evolution of the legal system over centuries."[20] David Ingram similarly identifies the sustained influence of "the eighth-century Hanafi School, whose interpretation of *shari'a* emphasizes the role of analogical reasoning and rational deliberation about the common good."[21] These hermeneutically informed interpretative strategies constitute a central strand within humanistic traditions and are important for current discussions about human rights.

To appreciate the ways in which Islamic humanism can continue to contribute to global conversations about dignity and human rights, we must recognize Eurocentric perspectives that have blunted the contributions of Islamic humanism. Abdulrazzak Patel succinctly states that Western humanists have played a significant role in perpetuating Eurocentric biases against Islamic humanism: "In fact, nowhere is Eurocentrism more historically perverse than in Western humanists' neglect of the medieval Islamic world, where the idea of humanism originated; and nowhere are the effects of its narratives more profound than in the neglect of humanism as it was practiced from the end of Islam's 'golden age' in the thirteenth century to the Arab renaissance (*nahdah*) in the nineteenth."[22] Though Schweiker is aware of diverse forms of humanism across the globe (e.g., "Dignity and humanism are naturally bound together within the legacies of Western and, nowadays, non-Western thinking, say, in Africa and China") (253), and Saritoprak appeals to commentators of primarily "classical Islamic sources" (229), both authors could augment their accounts of dignity through appeal to Islamic humanism. An additional factor contributing to the Eurocentric bias against Islamic humanism pertains to the colonial contexts of many Muslim communities that have suffered oppression.[23]

Islamic humanistic approaches offer insight into contemporary social issues and moral problems. Islamic humanists critically interrogate traditional assumptions and practices and dialogically engage a range of experiences, sources, and perspectives; such deliberative practices can help confront challenging issues such as gendered violence.[24] This critical interpretation resonates with Schweiker's conception of hermeneutical interpretation and Saritoprak's sense of nonprivileged discourse about one's own narrative. Emphasizing these aspects in concepts within the Islamic tradition (e.g., Qur'an as reading; *ijtihad* as jurisprudential hermeneutics; *ta'wil* as interpretation), Edward Said posits that the task of the humanist is "to be both insider and outsider to the circulating ideas and values that are at issue in our society or someone else's society or the society of the other."[25] Inhabiting this hermeneutical space, what Lutheran theologian Paul Tillich described as the "boundary," enables the humanist to be part of a (religious) tradition while also conversant with diverse perspectives within a pluralistic context. Standing within two worlds enables one to gain insight and knowledge of self, other, and the world, and to affirm one's own dignity and the dignity of others. It also works to deconstruct binaries between the religious and the secular and between Islam and the West.[26]

The drive for knowledge, which we noted as an anthropological feature of both Saritoprak's and Schweiker's accounts, can further enhance protections for dignity. Khaled Abou El Fadl observes connections between knowledge, happiness (*sa'ada*), and justice: "The more a believer knows about himself, about other people and cultures, and about the world, the more such a believer will be capable of understanding the balance (*mizan*) that is necessary in striving for justice with the self and others (*qist*)."[27] Knowledge of self and other militates against *jahiliyya*, or "ingratitude," "selfishness," "arrogance," "lack of awareness," or "moral ignorance,"[28] all of which create the conditions for intolerance, social fragmentation, and attenuated respect for human dignity. El Fadl affirms that knowledge of the other is a condition for peace, and it should not be limited merely to tolerance, as Schweiker advocates in his call for responsibility for the other, and as Catholic thinkers such as David Hollenbach have also encouraged.[29] El Fadl states that the "grace of *ihsan*, which calls on people to approach one another not just with mercy and sympathy, but with empathy and compassion"[30] grounds authentic knowledge of the other and contrasts with "puritanical movements [that] tend to be unsympathetic to narratives of social suffering."[31]

Human rights offer a critically important way to recognize and promote dignity and to respond to the "narratives of social suffering." Scholars such as Abadir M. Ibrahim see convergences between early Islamic conceptions of rights based on human dignity and contemporary expressions of human rights: "Imam Abū Hanīfah and his followers [around 750] developed an intricate theory of the rights of humanity (*al-'ismah bi al-âdamiyyah* [inviolability is due for all human beings for being human]) that has an abiding resemblance to the understanding in contemporary human rights."[32] Despite this convergence (and others involving thinkers such as Muhammad Iqbal, noted above), why have Muslim scholars and countries been marginalized within contemporary discussions about and formalizations of human rights? Abdulaziz Sachedina attributes this marginalization to several factors, including perspectives that the UN Universal Declaration of Human Rights is "insensitive to particular Muslim cultural values" and has "implied hostility to divergent philosophical or religious ideas."[33] These obstacles—and the Eurocentric biases we noted above—need to be taken seriously as human rights discussions unfold between nations, regions, cultures, and religion. Real protections for dignity are at stake in these discussions.

I turn finally to the prospects for hope in Islamic–Christian dialogue on dignity and human rights. Resonating with the insights developed in the chapters by Saritoprak and Schweiker, "A Common Word between Us and You" (a 2007 open letter from Muslim leaders and scholars to Christian leaders and scholars) appeals to the Great Commandment—Love of God and Love of the Neighbor—as a shared basis for Muslims and Christians. Repudiating this basis as "simply a matter of political ecumenical dialogue," the letter advocates that Muslims and Christians "respect each other, be fair, just and kind to one another and live in sincere peace, harmony, and mutual good will."[34] The prospects for achieving a vision requires serious engagement with Muslim and Christian traditions, humanistic strands within these traditions, and contemporary human rights discourse.[35] Differences may continue to constrain dialogue, but placing dignity at the forefront—including a profound sense of our shared vulnerability and responsibility—will inspire our imaginations, our theological and moral convictions, and our commitment to solidarity and the common good.

NOTES

1. See Robin Lovin, "Islamic and Christian Political Thought as Comparative Religious Ethics," *The Muslim World* 106 (2016): 226–33. For an insightful overview of current, "third wave" methods in comparative religious ethics, see Elizabeth M. Bucar and Aaron Stalnaker, eds., *Religious Ethics in a Time of Globalism: Shaping a Third Wave of Comparative Analysis* (New York: Palgrave Macmillan, 2012).

2. I see resonance here with Christian theologians such as Augustine, who holds that humans risk losing their very being when they fail to love God as their highest good; see Augustine, "On the Morals of the Catholic Church," in *Basic Writings of Saint Augustine*, ed. Whitney J. Oates (New York: Random House, 1948), 319–57.

3. See Martin Luther, "Freedom of a Christian," in *Martin Luther: Selections from His Writings*, ed. and with an introduction by John Dillenberger (New York: Anchor Books, 1962), 42–85; and Paul Ramsey, *Basic Christian Ethics* (New York: Scribner, 1950).

4. See, for example, Sallie McFague, *Life Abundant: Rethinking Theology and Economy for a Planet in Peril* (Minneapolis: Fortress, 2001).

5. See, for example, T. Richard Snyder, *The Protestant Ethic and the Spirit of Punishment* (Grand Rapids, MI: Wm. B. Eerdmans, 2000).

6. See, for example, Christine Gudorf, *Body, Sex, and Pleasure: Reconstructing Christian Ethics* (Cleveland: Pilgrim Press, 1995).

7. Julia Watts Belser, "Violence, Disability, and the Politics of Healing: The Inaugural Nancy Eisland Endowment Lecture," *Journal of Disability and Religion* 19, no. 3 (2015): 178 (original emphasis).

8. Maysaa S. Bazna and Tarek A. Hatab, "Disability in the Qur'an," *Journal of Religion, Disability, and Health* 9, no. 1 (2005): 5–27.

9. Majid Turmusani, "Disabled Women in Islam," *Journal of Religion, Disability, and Health* 5, no. 2–3 (2001): 73–85.

10. See Stefan Heuser, "The Human Condition as Seen from the Cross: Luther and Disability," in *Disability in the Christian Tradition*, eds. Brian Brock and John Swinton (Grand Rapids, MI: William B. Eerdmans, 2012), 184–215.

11. Gilbert Meilaender, *Neither Beast Nor God: The Dignity of the Human Person* (New York: New Atlantis Books, 2009), 87.

12. Amos Yong, *Theology and Down Syndrome: Reimagining Disability in Late Modernity* (Waco, TX: Baylor University Press, 2007), 185.

13. I want to note an important caveat about my example. I am in no way suggesting that disabled–caregiver relationships are one-sided, including experiences of sacrifice and relinquishing one's agency. My earlier emphasis on interdependence as the mode of these relationships remains operative here. Disabled–caregiver relationships often can be mutually beneficial in terms of increased self-awareness, mutuality, and compassion (even in cases where the caregiver is a paid medical professional).

14. Dietrich Bonhoeffer, *The Cost of Discipleship*, rev. and unabridged ed. (London: SCM Press, 1959), 100 (original emphasis).

15. See information provided by the organization I am Syria, http://www.iamsyria.org/death-tolls.html.

16. Abdulrazzak Patel, "AHR Roundtable: The Trajectory of Arab Islamic Humanism: The Dehumanization of a Tradition," *American Historical Review* 120, no. 4 (2015): 1347.

17. Lenn Goodman, *Islamic Humanism* (Oxford: Oxford University Press, 2003), 4.

18. Ibid., 16.

19. See Ebrahim Moosa, "The Dilemma of Islamic Rights Schemes," *Journal of Law and Religion* 15, no. 1/2 (2000–2001): 185–215.

20. Ibid., 194.

21. David Ingram, "How Secular Should Democracy Be? A Cross-Disciplinary Study of Catholicism and Islam on Promoting Public Reason," *Politics, Religion, & Ideology* 15, no. 3 (2014): 386.

22. Patel, "AHR Roundtable: The Trajectory of Arab Islamic Humanism," 1344.

23. See Abdullah al-Ahsan, "Law, Religion, and Human Dignity in the Muslim World Today: An Examination of OIC's Cairo Declaration of Human Rights," *Journal of Law and Religion* 24, no. 2 (2008–2009): 569–97.

24. Shannon Dunn, "State of the Field Essay: Gender, Violence, and Social Justice in Islam: Muslim Feminist Scholars in the Public Eye," *Journal of Law and Religion* 31, no. 3 (2016): 293–305.

25. Edward Said, *Humanism and Democratic Criticism* (New York: Columbia University Press, 2004), 76.

26. See, for example, Onir Muftugil, "Human Dignity in Muslim Perspective: Building Bridges," *Journal of Global Ethics* 13, no. 2 (2017): 157–67.

27. Khaled Abou El Fadl, "When Happiness Fails: An Islamic Perspective," *Journal of Law and Religion* 29, no. 1 (2014): 110.

28. Ibid.

29. See David Hollenbach, *Christian Ethics and the Common Good* (Cambridge: Cambridge University Press, 2002).

30. Fadl, "When Happiness Fails," 118.

31. Ibid., 120.

32. Abadir M. Ibrahim, "A Not-So-Radical Approach to Human Rights in Islam," *Journal of Religion* 96, no. 3 (2016): 348.

33. Abdulaziz Sachedina, *Islam and the Challenge of Human Rights* (Oxford: Oxford University Press, 2009), 5, 6.

34. "A Common Word between Us and You," http://www.acommonword.com/the-acw-document/. For further analysis, see Anas Malik, "Reconciliation between Muslims and Christians: Collective Action, Norm Entrepreneurship, and 'A Common Word between Us,'" *Journal of Religious Ethics* 41, no. 3 (2013): 457–73.

35. For an excellent analysis, see Irene Oh, *The Rights of God: Islam, Human Rights, and Comparative Ethics* (Washington, DC: Georgetown University Press, 2007).

Part II

CASE STUDIES

INTRODUCTION TO PART II

The contributors in part II discuss urgent case studies in which various forms of violent conflict implicate and threaten human dignity. Authors draw upon a range of sources and engage theological, philosophical, and critical theory perspectives. They describe the theological, legal, cultural, and political causes and contexts of the conflicts, and they propose constructive ways for confronting conflict and promoting and protecting human dignity.

In chapter 13, "Dignity and Conflict: Gendered Violence," Hille Haker defines dignity in terms of what she calls "vulnerable agency." Agency, she specifies, is vulnerable to two different kinds of harm: ontological harm (or injury) and moral harm (or violence). However, Haker also emphasizes that vulnerability need not only be conceived of as a source of danger; in the individual's openness to the other, vulnerability also allows for new and often unexpected opportunities for moral growth and flourishing. Haker applies this reconceptualization of dignity and autonomy to the moral problems of reproductive rights and sexual violence, particularly in relation to women.

In chapter 14, "Dignity and Conflict: Religious Violence," Nicholas Denysenko addresses the current conflict between Ukraine and Russia. The conflict includes the Orthodox Moscow Patriarchate's questioning of the Christian identity of the Ukrainian Greco-Catholic Church (UGCC) and Orthodox Kyivan Patriarchate (KP) and its depiction of them as heretics, which has implications for human dignity. To confront these critiques, Denysenko defines foundational sacramental identity established at baptism and chrismation in the Byzantine liturgical tradition and explores the polemical exchanges about this tradition in the Ukraine–Russia conflict. He develops a constructive proposal for recovering the "anthropological maximalism" of sacramental identity rooted in the notion of each Christian as a servant of God within a context of Christian plurality. Denysenko hopes that this recovery can help facilitate reconciliation between Ukraine and Russia.

In chapter 15, "Dignity and Conflict: Racial Violence," Terrence Johnson begins with the 1963 bombing of the 16th Street Baptist Church in Birmingham, Alabama, that killed four young girls. Exploring the roots of normalized, racialized violence created and perpetuated in conceptual schemes, moral imaginations, and religious sources tethered to national interests, Johnson addresses the objectification of black bodies, racially motivated killings, and unhealed racial wounds. He engages the Black Lives Matter movement's conception of dignity as a distinct political, aesthetic, and moral category independent from—though resonating with—deeply religious or Afro-Christian motifs and metaphors. Johnson constructively develops an African American moral humanism framed by the tension between black bodies and liberal political ideas. Drawing on Delores Williams's category of the wilderness and Victor Anderson's reformulation of the grotesque as markers informing his politico-aesthetic conception of human dignity, Johnson seeks to imagine alternative moral and political frameworks for expanding our views of human dignity.

In chapter 16, "Dignity and Conflict: Criminal Justice," William O'Neill defends the dignity and worth of the human person—innocent and guilty. He first undertakes an expansive genealogy of modern appeals to dignity and rights, and then offers an alternative account of both dignity and rights. He locates major foci in a neo-Kantian morality of liberal rights and an appeal of neo-Hegelian ethics to the common good of the state; these approaches fund theories of punishment within individualistic, social contracts that do not favor restorative concerns, such as reintegration of the offender into the community. In responding to these approaches, O'Neill turns to a dignitarian interpretation of rights (exemplified in the Truth and Reconciliation Commission in South Africa), which supports relationships of mutual dependency while rejecting collectivism. He develops a threefold hermeneutic of rights—deconstructive (critical), constructive, and reconstructive—to confront empirical data on criminal justice, including racial, ethnic, class, and gender disparities. O'Neill articulates a restorative critique that brings into relief the systemic antinomies of the prevailing retributive regime.

In chapter 17, "Dignity and Conflict: Immigration," Victor Carmona employs the perspective of Catholic human rights theory to analyze the externalization of border enforcement and the ongoing refugee crisis. He develops a Catholic critique of the border enforcement policy of the United States, Mexico, Turkey, and the European Union, and he constructively defends—on the grounds of human dignity—proposals for protecting and promoting a right to permanent residence or resettlement. After discussing migrant deaths, readmission agreements, distributive justice, and the rights of immigrants and refugees, Carmona draws on modern Catholic social teaching and its conception of dignity as a transcendent and concrete fundamental norm connected to a broad range of human rights. He appropriates David Hollenbach's framework of personal, social, and instrumental rights to undertake a sustained analysis of John XXIII's encyclical *Pacem in terris* in order to engage constructively the intersections between and among peace, natural moral order, political and socioeconomic rights (including rights of movement), the common good, and the international political system and roles of states.

In chapter 18, "Dignity and Conflict: Ecology," Dawn Nothwehr draws on diverse theologians and philosophers to develop an understanding of dignity that informs, and is informed by, what she calls "integral ecology." Nothwehr argues that human dignity defined as both an inherent feature of all human beings and a goal that humans should seek to attain calls us to recognize that the value of human beings cannot and should not be separated from the value of all life itself. Highlighting the perils materialism and instrumental forms of reasoning pose to our planet, she stands with Pope Francis in calling for a renewed recognition of the inextricable connection between the good of humanity and the good of our planet.

In chapter 19, "Dignity and Conflict: Religious Peacebuilding," Ellen Ott Marshall probes dignity as a cause for conflict and a criterion for the means of conflict. She argues that the *imago Dei* grounds individual rights and maintains relationships, and she constructively proposes that the *imago Dei* inspires and sustains nonviolent resistance to physical and structural violence by holding together rights and responsibilities and justice and reconciliation. Analyzing the meanings of conflicts and peacebuilding and the ways in which religion affects them, Marshall contends that resistance becomes the basis for promoting dignity, justice, and reconciliation. She considers recent examples such as the Black Lives Matter movement and engages the writings of thinkers such as Palestinian Quaker Jean Zaru to explore the prospects for religious peacebuilding. She concludes with a discussion of moral injury—experienced, for example, by soldiers who violate their core moral beliefs—to illustrate ways in which the image of God is diminished and restored over time.

thirteen

DIGNITY AND CONFLICT

Gendered Violence

Hille Haker

I remember well what happened that day, almost thirty-five years ago. It was a rather trivial experience, and yet I will never forget it. I was a student in my first year at the university and had sustained an injury to my knee—torn knee ligaments during a volleyball match. Knee surgery was still considered risky in those days, and so the doctors elected to wait for the swelling to go down before making a decision. Eventually they said that I needed a cast, from my thigh to ankle. I was sent to Dr. B. I was more annoyed than anxious, upset only about the inconvenience it would mean for me to even get from my dorm to the classrooms over the next few weeks.

I was a patient, and certainly vulnerable. I was in pain and could not help myself overcome it. But *as* a patient, I did not feel very vulnerable, because, after all, my pain was very identifiable, it was caused by an injury, and it concerned my leg only: I did not, for example, need to undress before multiple people, no boundaries were to be crossed that would increase my dependency, and although I was indeed in terrible pain, I was relieved that the doctors were trying to take care of my body, and to take care of me. The location of my pain eased the anxiety that I had always felt around doctors, an anxiety that one needs to overcome as a patient.

The incident only lasted one minute. I had to sit down in front of Dr. B. in my underwear, and he began to measure my leg. When he came to my upper thigh, he paused and asked me to lie down. He silently took out a pen, measured again, and then slowly, very slowly (or, in other words, far too slowly) drew a line on my upper thigh. He knew that I knew what was happening, what he was doing, not merely as a doctor any longer but as a male. By crossing a boundary of professionalism, crossing the boundary of my body, taking it into possession as an object of sexual arousal, he transformed himself and transformed me in a blink of an eye. It was a game with and of power, played on the field of sexuality, and Dr. B., I sensed, enjoyed every second of it. He did not say a word. I froze. And yet, the moment passed—quickly, I should say, in "objective" time, but dragged on endlessly in my "subjective" experienced time. Dr. B. did not say a word. And I, too, was silent, still frozen, dispossessed but at the same time bound in a spell of violence, as if struck by an external force I could not escape.

After the incident, he left the room, and, slowly, the spell vanished. For the next couple of minutes, I tried to comprehend what had happened, asking myself whether what I had just experienced had been "real" and what to do next. I felt sick; my body's pain was transformed into another pain, the pain of shame. My body was tense. It remembered, remembered so well. It connected this incident with past incidents, adding yet another element to the history, my history, of moral injury through sexual violence. It did not matter how trivial it might look for the world around me—I had been broken, again, and I understood, then, that it would never end.

Because his assistants dealt with the next steps of preparing the cast, I never saw the doctor again. I wanted to file a complaint, but in the end I did not because I was too ashamed. Furthermore, I slowly internalized the view from the outside, and I had to admit that nothing had happened. Or rather nothing that I could have explained or proven. The doctor could always claim that marking the line for the cast was part of the procedure and that I had just reacted to his attention in a hypersensitive fashion. He would claim that I had misinterpreted the situation. I knew that I had no words to defend my version of the story, no proof except for what both of us knew, which he would deny. Hence, there seemed to be no public language, no public category that sufficiently described my experience, and so I fell silent, just telling as many friends as possible never ever to go to this doctor—a minor act of resistance.

My body can actualize this experience of moral transgression at any moment. It is stored in my conscious memory. It belongs to a family of experiences of the same kind, all of which my body remembers, which is to say: I embody these memories.

"THE DIGNITY OF MAN [HUMANS] IS UNTOUCHABLE. TO RESPECT AND PROTECT IT IS THE DUTY OF ALL STATE AUTHORITY."[1]

Article 1 of the German constitution, the *Grundgesetz*, starts with these words, establishing "human dignity" as the cornerstone of the rule of law; it is immediately followed by the commitment to inviolable and inalienable human rights. It seems to me that all three semantic connotations of the terms: "dignity" is not to be "*touched*"; "human rights," insofar as they are *inviolable* and *inalienable*, are the basis of any human community, peace, and justice in the world. They are binding on the nation's legislative, executive, and judicial branches.

The dignity clause in this constitution, which is also expressed in international law and has been adapted, for example, also in the South African post-apartheid constitution, has often been critiqued—if not ridiculed—for its vagueness and/or Western bias. Over the last decade, the critique has become louder, particularly in the field of bioethics. Ruth Macklin, one of the most prominent American bioethicists, has called the concept of dignity "useless" because it does not add anything to the concept of autonomy;[2] Steven Pinker, self-announced leader of the ethics of biomedical progress, calls it "a squishy, subjective notion, hardly up to the heavyweight moral demands assigned to it," though even he concedes that it might play a relative role when it is "precisely specified" and not a "contentious moral conundrum" or religious, Judeo-Christian bulwark against biomedical inventions.[3]

In this chapter, I will defend the concept of dignity and interpret it through an analysis of vulnerable agency. This understanding accounts for the inter-subjective dimension of agency and humans' vulnerability in its different dimensions. Dignity is a paradoxical concept: on the one hand, it rests upon the faculty of self-reflective agency; on the other, however, this capacity not only comes in degrees, because it can also only be actualized in inter-actions with others. The concept of agency must be understood in its active and passive senses: we are active, as agents, but at the same time patients, who are acted upon by other agents; our agency is, moreover, actualized in the response to others—self-reflective agency is response-ability. Dignity, understood this way, is paradoxical because what functions normatively as unconditional status is still conditional, dependent on the actualization in inter-action.

I will start from the perspective of vulnerability. This move should not be interpreted as an argument that weakens human agency; rather, I will reveal what is concealed in the agency-as-autonomy concept, namely, the complexity of intersubjective agency that is entangled with vulnerability. I will proceed in two steps: first, I will develop the concept of vulnerability in its ontological, moral, and structural dimensions; second, I will turn to two contexts that concern women's agency, namely, the move towards so-called social egg freezing within the broader context of reproductive technologies and sexual violence against women. Although my conceptual argument will apply to both "man's" and "woman's" dignity, my contextual focus will be on the vulnerable agency of women. As we will see, my experience of many years ago is part of the overall social reality that renders women in all cultures especially vulnerable to moral harms.

THE CONCEPT OF VULNERABILITY

When Alasdair MacIntyre published *Dependent Rational Animals*, he had clearly sensed a shift in ethics brought about mainly by frustration over liberal ethics approaches that said much about autonomy and little about dependence and relationality.[4] MacIntyre argued for the integration of an anthropological concept of interdependency, but he also fully embraced the feminist "care ethics," which had become prominent during the 1980s and 1990s.[5] Although the ethics of care and interdependency are not identical with the ethics of vulnerability, both approaches share a critique of the sovereign, atomistic agent, and both embrace "relational" agency as the basis of any ethical theory. Vulnerability differs from dependency, however, because it considers relations exactly as one site in which vulnerability is played out: relations are not necessarily the "solution" to human vulnerability; they are also, as I will argue below, the site where vulnerability is negotiated or played out. Vulnerability encompasses the radical ambiguity of human relations. We do not "naturally" develop into agents; rather, we are addressed and shaped by others *as* (potential, actual, or former) agents, in order to see ourselves as agents, beings who are able to act on one's own account. Vulnerability refers as much to the social constitution of the self as to the general affectability of human beings. For my purpose here, it suffices to outline a conceptual framework of vulnerability and hence distinguish its three dimensions: ontological, moral, and structural vulnerability. This framework will help to gain a deeper understanding of what is at stake in the concept of human dignity.

Ontological Vulnerability as Affectability

Ontological vulnerability refers to humans' affectability as the "openness to the world" as part of the human condition. Vulnerability stresses the risk that the affectability and openness entails. The Latin verb *vulnerare* means "to wound"; its passive form is "to be wounded." Human beings are susceptible to suffering because they are first and foremost living organisms, and as such are in need of some basic provisions; when they lack these, they cannot survive. Furthermore, just like their nonhuman counterparts, humans are susceptible to wounding themselves and/or being wounded without any intention by others: one may, as I did, step on the foot of a teammate during a volleyball match and tear knee ligaments—all of this without having to blame oneself or others for the pain. We may be, at a certain moment, at the wrong place at the wrong time and get hit by a falling tree branch; or we may be born on an island that is going to be flooded because of some natural disaster.[6] Our vulnerability is an element or dimension of living life as an organism: just as rodents will flee from the sources of danger, we too are reacting to the contingencies of our lives. For those beings who are dependent on others to survive, cultures and communities are ways of reducing the risks of the environment (spatial vulnerability), and the threats of particular times, as, for example, the different seasons of the year or different life stages (temporal vulnerability).[7] I call this vulnerability "ontological" because it does not matter whether we "feel" vulnerable or invulnerable: human beings *are*, by their nature, vulnerable, that is, susceptible to incidents and/or conditions beyond their control. Vulnerability in this sense renders us weak, powerless, incapable, and passive, unable to control the "external" (environmental) or "internal" (body-related) forces.

Ontological vulnerability, however, also is the condition for a most basic openness to the world. In her book *The Ethics of Vulnerability: A Feminist Analysis of Social Life and Practice*, Erinn Gilson critiques the one-sidedness of recent conceptualizations of vulnerability, which often stress only the weakness and lack (or loss) of control linked to harm while not attending to the positive side of vulnerability that is better articulated as "openness" to the world. Ontological vulnerability in its most general form is "an unavoidable receptivity, openness, and the ability to affect and be affected," and therefore also entails the susceptibility to be affected positively: "Understanding oneself as vulnerable therefore involves an understanding of the self as being shaped through its relationships to others, its world, and environs."[8] In order to be affected by others in this positive sense, one must actively open up to others, taking the risk to embrace one's lack of control, which in turn holds the promise to be transformed by new experiences.[9] In a culture that emphasizes autonomy as control over one's body, it is difficult to interpret this sense of vulnerability, especially the positive dimension of the openness to be affected by another person or being, exactly because "vulnerability" is such an ambiguous term. It is therefore not trivial to point out that an ethics of vulnerable agency responds to the ontological vulnerability in both its negative and positive implications.

Moral Vulnerability as Susceptibility to Harm

Moral vulnerability is the crux of the ethics of vulnerable agency, because it must acknowledge the necessary moral risk to affect the other in and through one's actions while critiquing and opposing, at the same time, any intentional (i.e., moral) harm that is being inflicted—in short: the ethics of vulnerable agency walks the thin line of dignity as concept of agency and dignity as limiting concept for actions.

The body—especially the skin and the passages between the exterior and interior body (mouth, nose, anus, vagina, breast, penis, etc.)—that we have and who we are as "embodied rational beings" renders human beings "receptive" to benefits (good) and harms (evil) done by other human beings. Similar to the ontological dimension of vulnerability, moral vulnerability is not exclusively tied to the negative interpretation. I agree with Erinn Gilson and others in critiquing Judith Butler, who over the last years has developed one of the most important concepts of moral vulnerability, because she sometimes overemphasizes the violence that is involved in the constitution of the self or subject. In her earlier ethical works, Butler tends to reduce the theory of self-constitution to the necessary condition of "subjection" to the framing and/or norms of intelligibility, which we must internalize in order to become subjects in the first place.[10] In her more recent works, however, Butler articulates more clearly the ways in which self-constitution rests upon "affectability," including the positive addresses by others.[11] The following insights of self-constitution that I discern from Butler's broader view are crucial for my concept of moral vulnerability, because they explain the ontogenetic evolution of agency through self-constitution as social identity formation:

1. We are affected by the touch, the voice, and the gaze of someone else, usually the primary caretakers, before we touch others, speak, and return the gaze—in other words: senses are prior to any reflective self-consciousness, and they perform our sense of self.[12]
2. In order to become a self/subject, it is necessary to internalize the frames and norms of intelligibility that precede the self, rendering others as the "first authorities" and the self necessarily not the "inventor" or "creator" of values but first the recipient of and then the respondent to the judgments and addresses of others. Butler stops her deliberation at this point, but wondering whether it is ever possible to "give an account" of oneself, I hold that self-constitution is, at the same time, the constitution of the moral self as moral agent, who in a continuous learning process of evaluations and self-evaluations emerges as a "response-able self."[13]
3. The experience of unity and conformity with others (the "sameness" or identifiability), as well as difference and dissonance (the selfness or individual uniqueness) is necessary for the constitution of the self, but, at the same time, this dialectic is also a source of breaks and ruptures, and potentially a source of moral injuries. The moral self, this means, is necessarily a vulnerable agent, other to others and other to themselves.

Moral vulnerability, I maintain, applies to a living being who can only become a self (a subject, or an agent) on the condition that it is addressed in encounters that acknowledge its particular status as a unique member of the community of moral agents. This is the paradox of any concept of dignity: normatively speaking, dignity cannot be "lost" because it refers to the capability of agency, but in its dependence on being actualized in encounters with others, dignity is in fact subject to social encounters of recognition. Self-constitution is moral self-constitution—being recognized as this being, a unique, yet identifiable person, belonging to others in one's singular, individual identity, enables us to understand ourselves as responsoric, response-able agents. Furthermore, because there is no self without identity, and no identity without relations, the self is positioned in the complex semantic field of relations: every agent is, for example, a child of particular parents, at a particular place and time, the kinship and social position identifiable or signified by the boundary of one's bodily existence. The vulnerable agent is the agent who belongs to a community of others while being other to all others, and other to themselves.[14]

Self-constitution, this means, is not only a process of learning to take the perspective of others, as G. H. Mead famously held, but it is in part also a process of internalizing the evaluative recognition by others—"to belong" means to be recognized as being of the "same kind" as the "others," yet as being a "unique" individual.[15] As a result of this process of (moral) individuation, a person will learn to trust the evaluations of others and see herself as someone with a particular moral status for others and herself. If successful, it will enable her to keep the tension between the conformity (sameness) with others and the difference to them (individuality) in balance. Hence, the sense of dignity rests upon the interplay or "dialectic" between the social and individual identity.[16] As I will show below, moral injury is so damaging because it questions this balance between belonging to the "world" of others as moral agent and at the same time being a unique other—the balance between the *idem* and the *ipse*, as Paul Ricœur coined it.[17] The denial of this status of being the "same" and "unique" matters because individuals are receptive to others, and because they are essentially social beings. If one's dignity must be actualized in *every* interaction with another person, the denial of one's sameness and/or uniqueness not only misrecognizes, but it also puts at risk the very foundation of the socially mediated self, to be oneself as one agent among other agents.

To be susceptible to moral harm differs from susceptibility to pain and injury inherent to ontological vulnerability, though of course moral vulnerability arises out of one's ontological state of vulnerability. As ontological vulnerability is first and foremost the susceptibility to any pain and suffering, moral vulnerability is first and foremost the susceptibility to someone else's wrongdoing. Thus moral vulnerability coincides with and yet differs from its ontological kin insofar because it not only entails the passive experience of being injured or wounded. It also entails the interpretation that another person deliberately harmed or continues to harm oneself.

In his thorough study on torture and rape, Jay Bernstein has argued that torture and rape are extreme cases that not only violate the dignity of a person, but may irreversibly harm the person. Following Jean Amery, Bernstein points to the possibility that victims of torture lose their sense of a moral status and belonging. But we need to be careful here: experientially speaking, one's experiences of recognition, together with one's sense of having survived misrecognition, disrespect, and the violation of one's dignity, may become the resource of resistance; it is exactly why many victims of sexual assaults call themselves survivors rather than victims.[18] Dignity does not entirely rest upon one's social identity, as it does not entirely rest upon one's individual identity; it rests upon the dialectic of the same and the self.[19] In contrast to Amery's painful account of his torture, the seemingly more "harmless" practices—practices that go unnoticed by a society or social group—are often not perceived, not interpreted, and therefore not acknowledged as moral harms.

With the term "moral vulnerability," I not only refer to the harm done but also to the injured person's moral sense of being (morally) humiliated and not just—coincidently—injured. Without sensing and interpreting the other's intention, we cannot distinguish a nonintentional injury from wrongdoing. But this means, too, that we cannot just take an act itself (or the result of an act) as the criterion for our moral judgment. We need to inquire into the others' intentions.[20] As long as we are only called to examine our own motives—and this is what Kant and most moral theorists are interested in—we are mostly faced with the problem of conscious or unconscious self-deception, or *akrasia* (the weakness of will, or the blending of motives). But when we depend on our moral sense and on interpretation to judge another person's acts, it is much more difficult to distinguish between an accidental injury and a morally inflicted harm.[21] It is very unlikely, on the one hand, that my volleyball teammate intentionally got in my way so that I would step on her foot; if I had interpreted it this way, however, I would be correct in my sense and subsequent judgment that I was not merely injured but indeed harmed by her action. When, on the other hand, I sensed that the doctor approached me in a sexual way, transforming me into an object that evoked sexual pleasure for him, I was right in interpreting this as humiliating, even though I may have had no way to prove it as long as he would not confirm my interpretation.[22]

Because social and moral norms are so intertwined, the gap between the (moral) self and the other, and between the self and society, matters in these "negotiations" or interpretations; for if self-identity consists of the dialectic of conformity and dissonance with others, the individual's experience of humiliation may not conform with the social norms or interpretations of shame. In other words, if there is no public or social perception of wrongdoing (and, hence, no language and no frame for the intelligibility of an evaluation), no harm is acknowledged.[23] And if there are no provisions, for example, sanctions or laws that are enforced, there is little else to rely upon than the word of the perpetrator, who must admit his transgression. Independent of what the individual may have sensed, her experience is socially rendered unspeakable, inaudible, and invisible.[24]

Does this mean that we do not know that our dignity is violated when there is no linguistic, social, or legal framework that allows the experience to be interpreted as such? And still more troubling: Are we perhaps, in these cases, hurt and injured but not morally harmed? Would this then mean that I was not morally harmed because I had no language for what I can only now, decades later, interpret and narrate as an everyday sexual assault? Let me try to give a tentative answer to this serious problem entailed in the paradox of dignity—a moral concept dependent on social interpretations—to which I referred in my introduction: like pain, moral harm isolates the one who experiences it. And yet, we do have a language of pain and suffering. The same holds true for shame. We may repress it. We may think we are wrong, that our feeling is wrong. But as a general rule, I would hold, experiences are indeed articulated and expressed, even though the words may be vague and the sensations blurry—in most cases, the question is not whether there are words for shame or pain—the question is *whether* our sometimes diffuse interpretations are heard and how they are heard. I therefore believe that ethics would be better served by exploring and examining the sites of interpretation or negotiation, or, put differently, the social sites where the dialectic of social and individual identity is being played out.

Let me explain my plea for a hermeneutical ethics as complement to a normative ethics of dignity in view of an example that has become famous in (feminist) ethical debates, even though I am aware that it requires a thorough contextual analysis to do justice to the very context I am speaking about. Western ethicists often argue for the universal (normative) concept of human dignity and human rights. One of the hardest cases these ethicists have been confronted with over the last decades is the case of female genital cutting. In several traditions, this practice is considered an initiation rite that introduces girls to the social world of adulthood and female identity, and it is not only practiced in faraway countries, such as in African countries, but also in immigrant cultural groups in Western societies. In the 1990s, human rights scholars who were horrified by this practice began to fight for its abolition. Often, however, they found themselves confronted with criticism from cultural theorists who defended the practice in the name of an "ethics of difference" or cultural diversity, claiming that what Western liberals may see as a human rights violation is not interpreted as such by those who practice female genital cutting. Up to today, the ethical conflict divides the "universalists" and the "particularists," especially in feminist ethics.

Does the ethics of vulnerable agency offer anything new? Or is it merely one other theory of ethics that imposes the normative concept of dignity upon those who do not even *feel*, nor *agree*, that their dignity has been violated? Does one have to sense moral shame to be violated in one's dignity? Whose story is heard? And whose story is unspoken?

If one considers the practice as a site of interpretation and negotiation of social and individual identity, female genital cutting can be discerned as a practice that endows women with a moral status—honor or recognition—in their given culture. Social recognition always comes with a price, a kind of "subjection," as we have seen in Butler's analysis. Many women pay it because the alternative in their given societal context would be social exclusion; in extreme cases this might lead to their social death, the loss of acknowledgment and sense of belonging. Would women who undergo the practice of genital cutting say that they are morally harmed by it? Maybe they would acknowledge the pain associated with it, but this harm seems to become justified as a means to a greater end, namely, to be recognized in one's social identity. If we try to understand this judgment, genital cutting suddenly becomes comparable to other bodily interventions, including "Western" practices that are, too, justified as means to greater ends—we only need to think of the trend towards vaginal cosmetic surgery in the United States. It all depends on whom and what we see, or whom and what we want to see. Ethically, this attention to plural ways of understanding and the necessity of interpretation means that transformations of understandings may be the result of a conversation but not the object of it, and certainly not the entry point of intercultural interpretations. Ethical analyses of "female genital mutilation," however, strangely enough often put the blame on the agents—the women who subject the girls to a seemingly painful practice, rendering the girls as the passive victims of a human rights violation. This focus on the individual actions shames the practice of mutilation and blames those who practice it, concealing the fact of the negotiation of individual and social identity that is an important element, if not the central motive, of the practice in the first place.

But this is what has happened since the 1990s, requiring what I take to be a hermeneutical ethics that scrutinizes and critiques the models of interpretation. In the Western popular media, the abolition campaign created the "victimized female" in African countries and cultures, with decontextualized images of sexualized violence. In constructing the conflict as a violation of dignity and rights, the individual act of harming was highlighted, while the social normative order that motivates and legitimizes the practice was faded out. Yet, in an attempt to give women a voice—a move that the ethics of vulnerable agency considers, too, as constitutive—human rights activists and ethnographers alike lifted up the experiential narratives in order to find out what women themselves thought and how they understood the practice. However critical we must be of just using narratives to make an argument, women did speak up, and their voices have indeed changed the perception of female genital cutting considerably. Depending on the narratives, they supported or corrected the readers' own perceptions. In their accounts, many women have addressed the physical harm of the procedure and the social risks for women who opt out. Some no longer see the practice as "cutting" but indeed as "mutilation," thereby rendering it an unjustified means to the end of social inclusion. The different words that are used therefore carry the weight of a massive cultural and social value transformation.

Analyzing the experiential narratives of vulnerability to harm, ethicists must attend to the conflict of priorities the women are facing. They must, first, take a position as listeners, addressed by the interpreted experiences; only then are they, second, able to respond responsibly to the women and their narratives. Because they are response-able, in their response they will point to the moral dilemma the women face: women are socially recognized *sub conditione*, they are subjected to a painful, often irreversible surgery that has no physical benefit for themselves, and they are caught in a violent circle of "voluntary coercion." Hence, the ethical response will indeed emphasize the normative dimension of dignity, namely, the right not to be harmed, yet it will spell it out concretely as the right to social inclusion that must not come with the price of sacrificing one's bodily integrity; in solidarity with the minority group of women, ethics will strive to imagine other ways of women's social identity, reinterpret (or, to maintain my terminology, renegotiate) the terms of women's social identity and social agency.

Finally, however, the ethical conversation must entail the acknowledgment that anybody's social identity requires negotiations for social inclusion, even though the sites of negotiation may differ. As we will see below, there is rarely a clear cultural "we" and "them." If we looked, only for one moment, at the sexualized violence in all societies as a site of negotiated social identity, would we not be able to see the commonality of being silenced about the moral harm that is the price of social recognition? There are, after all, multiple ways to create social identities *sub conditione*, and to regard the harm in other cultures may well prevent one from regarding the everyday harms in one's own cultural and social contexts. Hence, to conclude my question of how we know that we are harmed when there is no social language or public and legal recognition of it, the problem of interpretation is, at the same time, also the solution to how we may sense an experience as moral harm, because it is rarely the case that cultures are completely unaffected by alternative, often subversive interpretations of the dominant normative narratives. What we perceive as moral harm is, in part, a question of attending to the stories of those affected by its pain.

We are so used to associating vulnerability with the susceptibility to suffering that it is easy to overlook that there is also moral vulnerability as a risk of morally affecting the other and being affected by them in a positive way. I call this the risk to transform the other and be transformed ourselves in the inter-action. Hence, the concept of moral vulnerability must also be developed as the ambiguity in affecting each other, in the address-and-response between agents in any interaction. Any action that affects another person risks harming the other as much as being harmed in return. That is the risk of moral agency that acknowledges the vulnerability entailed in any interaction. Moral vulnerability, as its ontological kin, is present in any personal and social encounter, and, therefore, it is a concern for the actor as much as for those affected by the action. How to encounter, and not to encounter, another person with respect and recognition is exactly the issue at stake in an ethics of vulnerable agency.

My example above has alluded already to the method this ethics entails: it requires the attentiveness of active listening to the other and the hermeneutic endeavor to understand the other before responding. Furthermore, however, it requires a normative ethics that upholds the response-ability that renders us accountable for our actions; seen from the positon of the vulnerable agent, this ethical approach starts with the question of what we must do to the other—because we can do it, because we are response-able, it is an ethics of human obligations. Seen from the perspective of the vulnerable agent as patient, however, it is an ethics of human rights, guaranteeing that certain claims on others are justified. These are the negative and positive human rights as they are spelled out as civil and political rights, but also as the social, economic, and cultural rights declaration, which is more open to interpretation in its scope. For the ethics of vulnerable agency, justification of obligations and rights must be correlated with contextual interpretations. To accept obligations when they can be justified and to claim those rights that can be justified is only possible when we strive to understand each other in our differences and commonalities, and in the different positions in our relationships. And because our relationships are necessarily mediated by social practices and structures that entail social norms and values, the ethics of vulnerable agency is incomplete unless it attends explicitly to structural vulnerability. Ultimately, the ethics of vulnerable agency—and any ethics of dignity—is a normative ethics that should be correlated with a critical hermeneutics of social practices, social structures, and institutions.

Structural Vulnerability as States of Suffering and Threatened Trust in the World and Others

Structural vulnerability refers to particular states of vulnerability. Age, illness, disability, or similar factors that increase the risk of suffering may elevate what I have called the ontological dimension of vulnerability. If one happens to be born in a region of environmental risks, such as from earthquakes or flooding, one may easily live in a constant state of insecurity. But states of vulnerability also entail the more specific socially inflicted risks incurred by one's socioeconomic status, ethnicity, sex, or religion. States of moral vulnerabilities are often described in terms of structural injustice against particular social groups, such as discrimination or marginalization. Such states of vulnerability, which Butler contrasts with precariousness, "precarity," reduce the social agency of persons and deprive them of the same security, safety, and opportunities to social freedom in the public space that other groups possess.[25] Many studies demonstrate that in each of the above-mentioned "states of vulnerability" women are affected more than men, rendering them at greater risk to structural vulnerabilities in both the ontological and the moral sense.

Over the last decades, feminist theory has reinterpreted the theory of justice and focused on participatory justice and the personal, social, and political empowerment of women.[26] Feminist scholars, especially, reacted to both the denial of women's autonomy and social agency, predominantly in the field of reproduction and sociopolitical participation, and to the language of "victimization" in political discourses. But when we look at structural vulnerability from the perspective of vulnerable agency, it becomes clearer that much more than autonomy and empowerment is at stake. Structural vulnerability is a big obstacle to developing a positive sense of one's moral agency, or that dimension of vulnerable agency that entails openness to the "world" or to the "other."[27] Structural vulnerability diminishes the excluded or marginalized groups' trust that their increased risks will be acknowledged and the burden be shared, but also that others will not constantly harm and/or shame them, especially in the public sphere.

What is needed in all areas of vulnerability, we have seen, is the acknowledgment that vulnerable agency is still moral agency, understood as moral response-ability. Regarding structural vulnerability, however, moral agency must be spelled out in agents' different scope and degrees of response-ability: in light of unequally distributed (ontological and moral) vulnerabilities, all parties must be enabled and willing to take responsibility for their actions, but all agents must acknowledge that the scope of action may differ according to their different social power.

Excluded or marginalized groups, the ethics of vulnerable agency claims, are not only passive victims of injustice (that their voices are not heard does not mean that they do not have voices or agency), but they also are silenced by a code of honor that is embedded in social norms. Individuals or groups may be socially speech-less and socially invisible, but every struggle for recognition rests upon the experience of being rendered inaudible and invisible. Again, developing a public language of respect and recognition is crucial: it must rest upon the understanding of ontological and moral vulnerability, and, furthermore, of the structural vulnerability as different states of increased risk to misrecognition and injustice. The shared experiences, narratives, and public grievances are necessary steps to a social transformation that embraces exactly all dimensions of vulnerable agency.

I will next turn to two distinct contexts in which this concept of vulnerable agency serves as a lens of interpretation. The first context, human reproduction, helps us to understand how the concept of agency-as-autonomy pushes the ontological, moral, and social vulnerability to the background, rendering an ethics of vulnerability as an alternative rather than a superfluous interpretation to the concept of dignity-as-autonomy; the second context, sexual violence, demonstrates how moral vulnerability is indeed the result of a social "honor code" that, in addition to the physical and psychical harm, not only silences but profoundly damages a woman's dignity. Both contexts address especially the vulnerable agency of women located in the United States.

AUTONOMOUS VERSUS VULNERABLE AGENCY

Much of the history of modernity can be regarded as a particular reaction to the condition of ontological vulnerability as I have described it above; modernity, one might say, begins with the birth of the idealized sovereignty of the human subject.[28] In their famous work "The Dialectic of Enlightenment," Max Horkheimer and Theodor W. Adorno, the "founding fathers" of the Frankfurt School and of Critical Theory, reflect on the central concept of nature, which the modern conception of rationality strives to overcome by instrumental reason. Multiple feminist studies have addressed the nature/culture divide as a highly gendered dualism, and I do not wish to repeat this debate here. Rather, I want to exemplify in one particular area the effect of instrumental reason's victory over any other kind of reason and interpret it in light of the above analysis of vulnerability. My purpose is to demonstrate how natural processes are transformed into constraints, rendering them deficient modes of human existence that must be fought against, controlled, or altogether replaced by technologies. I will show that the myth of invulnerability promises an agency that is based on the notion of increased autonomy. It comes, however, with the price of losing the openness to the receptivity that I have claimed is the positive side of vulnerability, because it is the "motor" of intersubjective, responsoric agency.

The beginning and end of life are passages "into" and "out of" life associated with an increased level of vulnerability. In an age that emphasizes autonomy, control, and sovereignty more than anything else, any lack (or loss) of control is perceived as a threat. But how can we control "life itself"? How can we control death? Over the last century, more and more effort has been undertaken to understand better what "life" is, what its origins are, and what makes us human. The medical sciences of the nineteenth and most parts of the twentieth centuries aimed mainly at understanding nature and repairing the human body, but today's life sciences are in fact turning into "constructive" sciences, concerned with making or constructing life. Those elements of human nature that were always considered beyond human control are no longer a normative limit of human intervention; life itself has turned into the mere material that scientists take as the starting point for potentially infinite modifications and interventions.[29] "We have got to the point in human history where we simply do not have to accept what nature has given us,"[30] states researcher Jay Keasling, one of the prominent researchers in synthetic biology. The life sciences necessarily incorporate an instrumental use of the human body, creating ever-new ways to gain control over its processes. In an instrumental sense, our whole body, including the brain, is the material that can be used for whatever purpose we like as long as we ask for the consent of the "owner"; in the intersection of science, technology, and market economy, this "utilization" is evidently linked to new opportunities of commodification and self-commodification.[31] It is justified as a means to a greater end: autonomy, understood as the control over our own bodily nature.

Kant, in contrast, argued against such an application of instrumental reason to human beings, and claimed that human beings have dignity: as agents they are subjects and must therefore not be acted upon as mere means to other agents' ends. In a phenomenological sense, however, the utilitarian understanding is considered reductionist; but Kant, too, only emphasizes the dimension of self-reflective agency, ignoring the fact of embodiment that ultimately renders an objective view of one's body impossible: we not only have a body that we can use as we use any other material in the world that we encounter—we are at the same time our body, entangled in it as embodied selves.[32] But even this is too narrow and must be broadened to the phenomenology of social agency. The normative analysis of structural vulnerability should make us pause before becoming too optimistic about procedural rules and the exclusive reliance on consent to legitimize the current broadening of commodification.[33]

Considered against this broader backdrop, it is no coincidence that the beginning and end of life are at the center of twentieth- and twenty-first-century life sciences, aimed at reducing the contingency of birth and death, or, in other words, aimed at gaining as much control over their associated risks as possible.

AUTONOMY AND THE CONTROL OF THE BODY IN REPRODUCTIVE TECHNOLOGIES

In the second half of the twentieth century, at the beginning of the era of assisted reproductive medicine, researchers regularly justified their pursuit of developing the technology of in vitro fertilization by claiming they were just "giving nature a helping hand."[34] Today, reproductive technologies, in concert with the other sciences, aim at overcoming nature rather than "helping" it to function "naturally"; at least one can say that the social imagery has transformed into the goal of "designing" or "engineering" human embryos. Women have long been particularly targeted as those who will profit most from the scientific progress in this area.

The latest step in the direction of "full control" over a woman's body that I will take as an example here concerns "social egg freezing." The envisioned autonomy concerns not only women but also men, companies, and even states.

By freezing women's egg cells at an early age, it is argued, women will profit by being able to plan how to combine work and family; men will profit because they may not be pushed into active family planning because of their female partner's age; companies will profit because some companies will expand their business plans while others gain more security for their investment and personnel planning. Since the balancing of professional life and family life is thereby highly privatized, states will also profit because they no longer need to engage in the regulation of the labor market to ensure more gender justice. Some companies, such as the market leader EggBanxx, encourage women to freeze a good number of their egg cells as an "insurance" against the "ticking clock" of their nature, their aging body, and the loss of their reproductive capabilities.[35] Apple and Facebook announced in 2015 that they would at least partly share with their female employees the costs for storage (Apple invests up to $20,000 per woman), and companies that market the storage have begun to target young (affluent) women who will invest in this biomedical insurance. At present, the costs are estimated for the United States with $40,000 per individual woman over a period of twenty years.

A certain group of women—the affluent—may well embrace this offer as an empowerment of their agency, understood as autonomy. After all, it is in line with the promise of modernity, operating with exactly the same model of mastery over nature that underlies the overall (cultural) concept of autonomy, choice, and individualized pursuit of happiness that is depicted as the idealized good life. But as seducing as this effort to reduce the susceptibility to (future) suffering may be, the fight against the "natural" processes of the body comes with a price, both socially and individually. On a social level, we are less and less able to uphold any other rationality than the instrumental, utilitarian concept of life, of living together, and of social cooperation. Instead of investing in how best to master the *relation* between nature and culture, we almost exclusively invest in the mastering of nature *by* culture. On an individual level, the darker sides of assisted reproductive technologies are rarely told: the costs for the procedure and the storage can only be paid by those who are affluent in the first place; women hand over some power over their body (or body parts) to companies; those who "opt out" may risk to be sidelined in a company's career and personnel planning; men may decide even later than today to commit to a family. And even though only a few women may think that they will indeed use these eggs in the future, it is not clear what effect the egg freezing will have on their reproductive choices. If the same women will count on the advances of assisted reproduction, they will then be faced with all the risks of assisted reproduction.

More strikingly, however, than these immediate effects is that this exemplary new service contributes to a much broader transformation of the social practice of reproduction and its accompanying values, a transformation that began with the introduction of assisted reproductive technologies in the 1980s. The effort to overcome the aging process (of egg cells) and to expand the time span of reproduction by biomedical technologies is one more step to "normalize" assisted reproduction as a means of procreation. Furthermore, the technological "fix" of the female aging body with respect to reproduction (and, one should add, the health of the offspring) is slowly considered as a rational, if not even a responsible, choice for young women who fear that their body will "fail" them in the future. Social egg freezing is promoted and conceived as buying time and furthermore justified as technological empowerment and contribution to women's social equality, yet without ever naming the underlying causes of their inequality and without attending to the diversity of how women are affected by social injustice, depending on their socioeconomic status or their ethnicity.

Ontological, or natural, vulnerability, we can now see, is conceived merely as a biological obstacle to women's freedom, equality, and good life, but there is no attention to the moral and structural vulnerability that may exacerbate the underlying ontological vulnerability. When women's egg cells can be safely extracted, stored, thawed, and used in the future, at the right time and with the right person, the story goes, women's autonomy will indeed be increased. Most importantly, however, social egg freezing is a market service offered only to those who can afford it or who work for a company that has set up its own scheme of cost-sharing. Socially, it means that the "normal" aging of the female body (or body parts) together with sexual reproduction is transformed into the new "un-normal."[36] Ironically, the technological "assistance" is sold as a necessary part of women's sovereign and autonomous agency.

Even though vulnerability has become a prominent concept in bioethics over the last years, it is rarely reflected in view of these social ethical implications. The problem with many of the new technologies is not that they expand autonomy and control. They may well do so. Rather, it concerns the unquestioned premise that this autonomy and control over nature will result in a better life. As Horkheimer and Adorno, however, argued, instrumental, technical rationality will ultimately dominate our understanding of what it means to be human; even though (potentially) "liberated" from the contingencies of nature, we may well lose what I have called the positive dimension of vulnerability, namely, the openness to be affected in surprising, unforeseen, and uncontrollable ways. If this receptivity or "affectability" by an other, the openness to something unexpected, including a new life to which one may give birth, is considered a problem that needs to be contained or controlled, we may gain instrumental agency, but at the price of the responsoric agency, which necessarily includes the receptivity and thereby the risk of being transformed by the other.

One may argue, therefore, that we misunderstand ourselves in striving towards an ever-greater autonomy. But this is not the only point. The notion of autonomy as sovereignty ignores the interplay or dialectic between one's sameness and uniqueness I explored earlier, which is necessarily socially mediated. One's active role of recognizing an other as other is as important as the passivity of being recognized. The autonomy model, I would now hold, has a place for the other, but it does not have a place for this alterity; it transforms the "other" into a means for one's own well-being—limited only by the moral prohibition of harm—a prohibition that already seems extrinsic or even alien to one's own striving. In contrast, the ethics of vulnerable agency argues that the "other" must indeed never be merely a means; rather, the other—and it matters that this otherness cannot be defined from the outset—may be an occasion for an *encounter* that has the potential to transform one's own self-understanding. This insight into the necessity of alterity, an insight that nobody stressed more than Emmanuel Levinas, is one more reason why the ethics of vulnerable agency requires a hermeneutics in addition to the normative analysis of rights and obligations: the latter defines, ultimately, the justified claims the other can make; the former, however, keeps the question who the other is, and who the other is in relation to the agent, open. It is the experience of the event, the encounter, or the *Widerfahrnis*, that calls for an interpretation in order to understand and respond, rather than the judgment on the other's worth for me. The ethics of vulnerability embraces autonomy, but it understands it and reinterprets it as the capability to open up to the other, the capability to respond to the other, instead of looking for ever-more ways how to expand one's power and control.

Instrumental rationality, however, may not only impoverish the responsoric agency, which I have now redefined as agency, but it also displaces rather than overcomes the contingency of the human condition, because the customer, client, or patient is not necessarily as "sovereign" as it may appear in the imagery of control. In the example of egg freezing, a woman's body is more and more controlled by other people. Ultimately, the new technologies establish a new regime of what Foucault called "biopower," subjecting the self to its inherent rationality. Moreover, other people, rather than nature, define the parameters of one's pursuit of happiness, or one's life—the people who have the power over the costs, over the quality control, over the modification of those cells defined as "not fit enough to be used for fertilization," or the power over the property rights of body parts. In short, the idealized sovereignty of agency is transformed into an ideology of social control.

Although human reproduction concerns men and women, reproductive technologies, together with the social discourse and bioethics, construct it as a highly gendered issue. First and foremost, reproduction is about women's negative freedom (their wish not to reproduce) and women's positive freedom (their wish to reproduce with the help of medicine or technologies).[37] Feminist ethics, however, should critique reproductive technologies when they become an ideology of invulnerability, concealing the moral and structural causes of the vulnerability that technologies strive to overcome—arguably women would be much more empowered if they gained more social control, for example, over the conditions of the workplace and reproduction. There are certainly multiple reasons for a "gendered" approach to human reproduction; one reason is the particular lack (and loss) of control over one's life by pregnancy. But although pregnancy is mostly seen as a time of increased women's vulnerability, one may claim with the same right that it increases women's agency. In this case, however, agency is not exclusively defined in line of control but entails the experience of receptivity and openness to transformations by new experiences. Similarly, one could argue that pregnancies also render men more vulnerable in their interactions with their female partners, because they also must learn new ways of interaction.[38] If vulnerability concerns both the susceptibility to harm and the openness, the *risk* of being transformed in the receptivity to an other, social practices should create the spaces for human reproduction as a site of such receptivity and openness to the unexpected, uncontrollable, and new. The concept of vulnerable agency therefore enables us to reinterpret moral agency without either sacrificing autonomy or denying the particular vulnerability of certain life phases. Vulnerable agency means exactly this: to cultivate and create the spaces in one's life for "something new" to transform one's self-understanding. Receptivity is not the opposite of agency—it is an essential dimension of it.

Hence, the alternative narrative to the technological mastery of human reproduction would need to give a voice to the experiences of women who see reproduction not merely as an "obstacle" or "threat" to their autonomy but as a time of vulnerable agency. Opening up to one's own receptivity and to being affected by another being whose very life one cannot control is not an argument against autonomy—and not even against any of the new reproductive technologies—as long as they maintain the potential for the agents to be transformed, and thereby enriched, rather than hindered in their vulnerable agency. The world of instrumental reason has no language for such a narrative, because it conceptualizes the objects of knowledge differently. Nothing is wrong with applying instrumental reason as long as it is embedded in the broader practical rationality. Practical rationality, in its necessary link to morality, defines social practices differently, returning the body to where it belongs: to the individuals who are not just living machines but embodied moral agents.

VULNERABLE AGENCY AND SEXUAL VIOLENCE AGAINST WOMEN

Reproductive technologies operate with a reductionist understanding of autonomy and agency, undermining the openness to the "other" as part of women's agency, but I will now explain why sexual violence exploits and violates exactly this openness towards the other in acts of moral violations of women's dignity, harming, damaging, and potentially destroying their socially mediated self-identities. As I have claimed above, self-constitution and moral agency rest on the ability to balance the tension between one's social identity (one's sense of belonging to the shared social world) and one's individual identity (one's sense of oneself as unique)—or, in other words, to uphold the dialectic of the *idem* and *ipse* dimension of the self. Because of this dialectic, moral harm not only harms physically or psychically, but it also "gets under the skin" because it is an attack on a person's moral integrity, understood exactly as this balance between *idem* and *ipse* that constitutes self-identity as a sense of belonging by way of social mediation.[39] We have seen already that moral vulnerability is tightly linked to the act of shaming and the experience of shame. Shaming and shame are socially mediated concepts, marking the fine line between "decent" and "indecent" behavior. Moreover, since shame, in its "family relationship" with sexuality, refers back to the vulnerability of the human body, specific acts of shaming are often connected to speech acts concerning sexuality, and moral injuries are most traumatic when they concern the "nakedness" of our embodied selves.[40]

In his literary works, the South African author John Coetzee often engages with this embodied vulnerability. In his short story "The Problem of Evil," for example, the protagonist Elizabeth Costello argues that writers should not depict human vulnerability, because it is a source of shame. Especially the expressions of physical vulnerability are shameful and obscene, Elizabeth argues, and they should be left where they belong: out of or off the scene. In embedding this argumentation about narrative ethics in a narrative that does exactly the opposite, namely, dragging multiple obscenities into the scenes of the story, Coetzee demonstrates his extraordinary skill of dialectic judgment as the core of his poetics. In the story, Elisabeth Costello herself is haunted by memories of a sexual assault, which are so "obscene" that she can only endure them "off-scene," in the restroom of the conference venue where she has made her argument of keeping experiences of shame in the shadows of the public. In the meltdown of the otherwise sovereign writer's agency, namely, in the narrated rupture of place, time, and rationality that suddenly is habituated by the "devil" whose existence Elizabeth would have vehemently denied only minutes before, Coetzee demonstrates that vulnerability is inescapable. It is therefore no coincidence that Elizabeth is depicted as an aging woman, lonely, doubtful, and insecure, but in the self-consciously created masked or staged social identity, she is a sovereign, self-confident, famous, seemingly undamaged and hence (almost) invulnerable celebrated author.[41]

As a response to the necessary crossing of bodily boundaries, medical ethics, for example, has developed particular protocols that must be followed, most prominently the patient's consent to any medical intervention—not only a "no" but a "yes" to medical interventions—in order to maintain a patient's autonomy and respect of her dignity and human rights. Consent is considered key to the respect of a person's autonomy, and by now, mirroring medical ethics guidelines, it has become the cornerstone, too, in the ethical discussion on how to best respond ethically to potential and actual sexual assaults. But as consent alone is insufficient to protect patients from moral harms in the context of medicine, it is also insufficient to protect individuals from sexual assaults.[42] In my experience of many years ago, the very act of marking my thigh with a pen could be seen as part of a medical procedure that I had consented to. But this *same* act of marking my thigh with a pen transformed into a sexual assault. In order to see it that way, someone must interpret the doctor's act as I sensed and experienced it—or find some evidence of wrongdoing in order to give my narrative a shared or public meaning. Almost all cases of sexual assault, rarely witnessed by third parties, depend in the same way on interpretation, and it is not only the perpetrators' denial of crossing any boundaries but also the underlying social values and norms that often prevent the assaulted persons' experiences from becoming "publicly" acknowledged narratives—they are concealed by a well-functioning code of silence. The social norms, namely, those that shame the victims and leave them, rather than the perpetrators of violence, ashamed, have indeed a dramatic silencing effect.[43]

Sexual assault is radically underreported, but, according to the 2011 FBI report that Muhs quotes, in the United States, a forcible rape occurs every 6.3 minutes. Moreover, correcting the FBI outdated definition and adding the (conservatively) calculated nonreported cases, it is estimated that the number would rise to *one rape in almost every minute*, reaching the staggering number of almost 470,000 women raped in 2011 alone. Women, studies show, do not report sexual assaults because they do not trust that the police or the whole system of law enforcement will help them. They are, in fact, structurally vulnerable.[44] And the statistics demonstrate that their mistrust is not unjustified: the Rape, Abuse & Incest National Network reports that 97 of every 100 rapists receive no punishment.[45] Victims of rape are frequently confronted with assumptions such as "no does not mean no"; "victims must have sent misleading messages"; or "rapists are strangers." Hence, women (as any victim of sexual violence) are questioned implicitly or explicitly as to whether they have "provoked" the assault. In rape trials, Diehl observes, victims may be questioned about their behavior preceding and also during the assault—whether they have objected (enough), showed signs of disapproval, or signs of resistance.[46] As Finch and Munro show, the role of alcohol, associated with many rapes in which both parties know each other, is unjustly used to blame the victims.[47] To transform the culture of an assumed implicit consent to sexual advances, the reversal of the slogan "No is No" to "only a Yes is a Yes" is a good starting point to better understand the underlying cultural and moral patterns of sexual assaults as patterns of misrecognition. Diehl states:

> "Yes." It is a simple enough word, but one that is often presumed from silence, drunkenness, or even sleeping. According to a new law in California, "yes" as it applies to consensual sex, is something that is "affirmative, conscious, and voluntary." Lack of protest or resistance does not mean yes. Silence does not mean yes. Intoxication, relationship history, incapacitation, or sleeping cannot be used to assume consent.[48]

The California law is from 2014. Diehl argues, correctly in my view, that the focus on consent would shift from "blaming the victim" to the responsibility of the assaulter to procure consent. Yet, it is still mostly interpreted as the explicit consent to be given by *women*. The concept of vulnerable agency, in contrast, requires one instead to interpret sexual acts as one site among others of personal, socially mediated, and morally challenging interactions between agents, requiring the respect and recognition of each party at any given moment.

Victims of sexual violence are easily trapped in the binary of being regarded either as agents (able to consent, for example) or purely passive victims. The concept of vulnerable agency transcends this binary. Obviously, reclaiming women's agency in the context of sexual violence does not mean to shift accountability away from the perpetrators. That is the reason why it is so important to understand exactly what are the moral injury and harm that victims suffer. Sexual assaults not only harm women physically and psychically, but women are morally harmed because they are denied the socially mediated conformity and sameness as an agent among other agents, and/or denied their uniqueness (selfness) as an embodied individual who is necessarily different from any other being. Rendering her "just another body" who can be used for sexual pleasure morally shames and misrecognizes a person in her dignity. Jay Bernstein rightly emphasizes this in his study on torture and dignity, which includes rape as of the same kind as torture—it is the betrayal of the existential and moral trust that another person will not return one's openness (vulnerability) with humiliation. The moral injury and damage of the self, he rightly claims, rest on the always possible reversal of self-constitution in an act of violence. What is damaged in rape? It is one's responsoric agency, upon which the whole concept of dignity relies. The phrase "the dignity of a woman is untouchable," we can now see, is a purely normative phrase, a warning, so to say, that a person is severely damaged in her moral identity if her dignity is touched.

This interpretation is certainly in line with the historical context. After the end of World War II and the Nazi genocide, the authors of the German constitution were all too aware of the fact that human dignity had been, and could be again, violated. A norm such as article 1 in the German constitution does not articulate this history; it abstracts necessarily from the (historical) experience it responds to. But this means that the other side of normativity, namely, historical experiences, is missing. The principle or norm of dignity, therefore, must be reinterpreted in what Walzer calls a "reiterative universalism."[49] Vulnerable agency is my attempt to interpret the paradoxical nature of the norm of dignity that grounds any concept of moral agency in situating it in actualizations, in the concrete contexts of historical experiences.

For a more radical shift of morality concerning sexual violence to happen, it is crucial to understand that sexual assaults happen in the context of and against the backdrop of social norms (or myths), which also define what is "decent" and "indecent" behavior. Appiah has shown that social and moral transformations are successful when the "honor code," that is, the norms of shame and shaming, shift.[50] In the case of sexual assaults, it is the apparent code of silence that renders victims invisible and inaudible and contributes to the fact that the social honor code of sexual assault as a "normal" pattern of sexual interactions is maintained. As dire as the overall pandemic of sexual violence against women is, there may, however, be hope at least in one area: a moral transformation may well be under way concerning the "rape culture" in U.S. colleges after many victims have begun to speak up. After all, one condition for the reversal of the reversal, for the reconstitution of self-constitution in the sense we described in the first part of the chapter, together with the necessary trust that is a constitutive element of any socially mediated identity, is the moral (and this means public) recognition of the victims/survivors.[51] The most important moral lesson in this context that we can learn from the concept of vulnerable agency that I have proposed here is this: yes, a woman's trust in the world is severely damaged by the violation of her dignity. But the other side is also true: she also embodies all other experiences in the memories of her life story. As long as these include experiences and encounters in which the trust in others was not betrayed, these, too, make up her identity. Such memories and experiences of recognition may well pave the way to the reconstitution of the moral self and a new balancing of the conformity with others and the uniqueness of oneself. Communities of solidarity among survivors and relations that entail recognition are important factors in both creating a public language and a renewed sense of belonging.

Both major Western ethics traditions that are predominant in the United States, liberalism and utilitarianism, link freedom to justice; a reinterpretation of the concept of dignity as vulnerable agency is strikingly different from both traditions insofar as it highlights the respect of, the responsibility by any, and the responsibility for vulnerable agents to ensure that the susceptibilities to suffering and harms do not destroy their freedom as openness to the world and others in the different contexts and the plural ways of interactions. In a society that does in fact value justice as much as freedom, the principle of autonomy is a necessary but not sufficient condition to ensure that political priorities are set to fight injustices. Yet, in a culture that is so predominantly shaped by an individualistic understanding of autonomy and freedom, it is very tempting to define freedom and justice along the lines of sovereignty, forgetting that moral agency is indeed relational, socially mediated, and entangled in the dialectic of sameness and belonging, on the one hand, and selfhood and uniqueness, on the other. Although the moral theory of dignity sets the standard of respect and recognition on the basis of historical experiences of disrespect and misrecognition, it is the interpretation of moral agency—entailing the three dimensions of ontological, moral, and structural vulnerability—that enables us to spell out the necessary steps towards a social transformation of injustices. The necessary condition for this transformation is the acknowledgment of our shared, yet unique and different vulnerable agency—so that justice will be done to all those whose dignity is, and continues to be, violated.

NOTES

1. Art. 1: (1) "Die Würde des Menschen ist unantastbar. Sie zu schützen, ist Verpflichtung aller staatlichen Gewalt. (2) Das Deutsche Volk bekennt sich darum zu unverletzlichen und unveräußerlichen Menschenrechten als Grundlage jeder menschlichen Gemeinschaft, des Friedens und der Gerechtigkeit in der Welt. (3) Die nachfolgenden Grundrechte binden Gesetzgebung, vollziehende Gewalt und Rechtsprechung als unmittelbar geltendes Recht." I have changed the sentence in order to show that potentially the perception of the phrase "human dignity" changes depending on the social contexts of equality and inequality before the law. Ultimately, however, "human dignity" is correct because it does not determine the scope of dignity further.

2. Ruth Macklin, "Dignity Is a Useless Concept," *British Medical Journal* 327 (2003): 1419.

3. Reviewing the President's Council on Bioethics's *Human Dignity and Bioethics*, Pinker polemically asks how the United States reached "a point at which it grapples with the ethical challenges of twenty-first-century biomedicine using Bible stories, Catholic doctrine, and woolly rabbinical allegory?" (Steven Pinker, "The Stupidity of Dignity," *New Republic*, May 28, 2008, https://newrepublic.com/article/64674/the-stupidity-dignity).

4. Alasdair MacIntyre, *Dependent Rational Animals: Why Human Beings Need the Virtues* (Chicago: Open Court, 1999).

5. See, among others, Virginia Held, *The Ethics of Care: Personal, Political, and Global* (Oxford: Oxford University Press, 2006); Held, *Liberalism and the Ethics of Care* (Toronto: University of Toronto, Faculty of Law, 1997); Eva Feder Kittay, *Love's Labor: Essays on Women, Equality, and Dependency* (New York: Routledge, 1999); Fiona Robinson,

Globalizing Care: Ethics, Feminist Theory, and International Relations (Boulder, CO: Westview, 1999); Joan C. Tronto, *Moral Boundaries: A Political Argument for an Ethic of Care* (New York: Routledge, 2009). For a discussion in view of an ethics of vulnerability, see Erinn C. Gilson, *The Ethics of Vulnerability: A Feminist Analysis of Social Life and Practice* (New York: Routledge, 2014).

6. If the flood is caused by human action, it becomes a different question, because our suffering is then caused, or at least partly caused, by an act (or omission) of others that makes us not only *ontologically* vulnerable to injuries but *morally* vulnerable to harm. The latter is the subject of the next section.

7. Not everyone goes as far as Frans de Waal in correlating human and nonhuman behavior, including morality, but current research shows the ongoing interest in comparing modern concepts of morality with nonhuman behavior, with ramifications for the concept of dignity that go beyond my treatment here. See Frans de Waal, *The Bonobo and the Atheist: In Search of Humanism among the Primates* (New York : W. W. Norton, 2014); Frans de Waal and Pier Francesco Ferrari, *The Primate Mind: Built to Connect with Other Minds* (Cambridge, MA: Harvard University Press, 2012); Christine Korsgaard, *Self-Constitution: Agency, Identity, and Integrity* (Oxford: Oxford University Press, 2009).

8. Erinn C. Gilson, *The Ethics of Vulnerability: A Feminist Analysis of Social Life and Practice* (New York: Routledge, 2014), 86.

9. Ibid., 37. Gilson distinguishes between ontological and situational vulnerability, the latter referring to the particular forms of experiences and states of vulnerability. I follow her in the description of ontological vulnerability, but I will describe the "situational" vulnerability more precisely as moral vulnerability in the next section. See also Hille Haker, "Verletzlichkeit als Kategorie der Ethik," in *Zwischen Parteilichkeit und Ethik: Schnittstellen von Klinikseelsorge und Medizinethik*, ed. Monika Bobbert (Berlin: Lit Verlag, 2015), 195–225. In that work, I have called the "ontological" vulnerability "anthropological" to stress its connection to the *conditio humana*; in order to create a more common language, I now take up Gilson's term.

10. See, for example, Judith Butler, *The Psychic Life of Power: Theories in Subjection* (Stanford, CA: Stanford University Press, 1997); Annika Thiem, *Unbecoming Subjects: Judith Butler, Moral Philosophy, and Critical Responsibility* (New York: Fordham, 2008). Thiem provides a good analysis of Butler's work up to the point at which she becomes more explicitly ethical. Butler's earlier theory of subjectivation conflates vulnerability and violence, and it has therefore no criterion to distinguish between the ontological and the moral dimension of vulnerability. Even in Butler, *Precarious Life: The Powers of Mourning and Violence* (New York: Verso, 2004), and Butler, *Frames of War: When Is Life Grievable?* (London: Verso, 2010), it is not clear why the acknowledgment of another person should almost exclusively be tied to her grievability or the potential loss. In Butler's work, the relation between self-constitution and the constitution of the moral self is still ambiguous. The clarification and distinction of the relation between ontological and moral vulnerability, and injury and violence, is therefore also intended to provide a better understanding

of the relationship between self-concepts and moral identity. See Hille Haker, "The Fragility of the Moral Self," *Harvard Theological Review* 97, no. 4 (2005): 359–82.

11. See, especially, Judith Butler, *Giving an Account of Oneself: A Critique of Ethical Violence* (Oxford: Oxford University Press, 2005); Butler, *Precarious Life*; Butler, *Frames of War*; Butler, *Senses of the Subject* (New York: Fordham, 2015).

12. Butler puts this nicely: "No one acts without first being formed as one with the capacity to act" (*Senses of the Subject*, 8).

13. Waldenfels calls human beings "responsoric beings," rendering inter-action pivotal for any theory of philosophical anthropology; see Bernhard Waldenfels, *Antwortregister* (Frankfurt am Main: Suhrkamp, 1994), and Waldenfels, *The Question of the Other* (Albany: State University of New York Press; Hong Kong: Chinese University Press, 2007). For a thorough analysis of the moral self-constitution and the development of self-worth from an ethical rather than psychological perspective, without, however, explicitly developing a concept of responsibility, see J. M. Bernstein, *Torture and Dignity: An Essay on Moral Injury* (Chicago: University of Chicago Press, 2015).

14. Is there a "teleological" implication in the intersubjective concept of agency? Yes. But teleology is tied to a person's life history, articulated in the changing and shifting narratives of one's life that is, on every level, entangled with other stories and histories. For a thorough analysis, see Hille Haker, *Moralische Identität: Literarische Lebensgeschichten als Medium ethischer Reflexion* (Tübingen: Francke, 1991).

15. It is important to interpret the psychic self-constitution as simultaneously moral self-constitution. Butler, as so many others, overlooks the fact that "morality" does not only concern the internalization of norms but the conscious recognition and subsequent return of the "gaze of the other" as a process of recognition; this "gaze" is not necessarily hostile and, therefore, the "norm" of the "other" may well be the norm of love and acknowledgment. It is thanks to the work of Axel Honneth that we are in a much better place to develop the moral language for this process, even though his initial attempts needed to be revised considerably; see Honneth, *The Struggle for Recognition: The Moral Grammar of Social Conflicts* (Cambridge, MA: Polity, 1995). For a revised examination, see Axel Honneth, with Judith Butler, Raymond Geuss, Jonathan Lear, and edited by Martin Jay, *Reification: A New Look at an Old Idea* (Oxford: Oxford University Press, 2007), and Axel Honneth, *Freedom's Right: The Social Foundations of Democratic Life* (New York: Columbia University Press, 2014).

16. Charles Taylor linked in a similar way the theory of recognition with the concept of dignity in Taylor, *Multiculturalism and the Politics of Recognition: An Essay* (Princeton, NJ: Princeton University Press, 1992).

17. Paul Ricoeur's work is indispensable for any analysis of the relation between "conformity" and "dissonance," or the self as another; see Ricoeur, *Oneself as Another* (Chicago: University of Chicago Press, 1992). In his last book, Ricoeur spelled out further the relation between the social mediation and the cognitive dimension of recognition. I will leave the analysis of this important work on recognition aside; see Ricoeur, *The Course of Recognition* (Cambridge, MA: Harvard University Press, 2005).

18. Bernstein, in my view, goes too far in his analysis of torture and rape in claiming the destruction of the self, which throughout his book he calls the "devastation" of oneself together with one's social and moral "standing." But many survivors of torture and rape would object to this radical claim of being entirely destroyed; quite to the contrary, especially survivors of torture claim that their abusers could not take their selfhood away. And even Jean Amery, whom Bernstein quotes as a survivor of torture and who famously claimed that survivors of torture will lose their sense of belonging in the world, still *wrote* about his experiences, contradicting the thesis at least at that point in his life, most likely deliberately so.

19. In his anthropological study, Hans Blumenberg refers to the human capacity to be comforted by others. It is most likely that survivors need the comfort of others in order to relearn trust in others; see Blumenberg, *Beschreibung des Menschen* (Frankfurt: Suhrkamp, 2006); Hille Haker, "Verletzlichkeit als Kategorie der Ethik."

20. In his moral philosophy, Kant knew this and therefore had to turn away from any consequentialist notion of moral "goodness" or "rightness. See, for example, Immanuel Kant, *Groundwork of the Metaphysics of Morals* (Cambridge: Cambridge University Press, 1998).

21. This is the point of Judith Shklar's book on injustice, opposed to "luck"; see Shklar, *The Faces of Injustice* (New Haven, CT: Yale University Press, 1990).

22. Moral philosophy has been suspicious of the moral senses, because they are indeed prone to error; nothing, however, shows that the mere reliance on "rational" judgments is even possible or a better method of moral judgment—*both* depend on interpretation. See Martha C. Nussbaum, *Upheavals of Thought: The Intelligence of Emotions* (Cambridge: Cambridge University Press, 2001).

23. Below, I will call this the honor code that functions, at the same time, as a code of silence—or, rather, a code of silencing.

24. In *Frames of War*, Butler addresses the ungrievability of certain lives who are excluded from the public perception; she hence underscores the connection between the public perception, public recognition, and moral practices, such as the mourning over the loss of lives; see, among many others, the seminal article by Patricia Williams regarding racism: "On Being the Object of Property," in Patricia Williams, *The Alchemy of Race and Rights* (Cambridge, MA: Harvard University Press, 1991), 216–38. See also Gayatri Chakravorty Spivak, "Can the Subaltern Speak?," in *Can the Subaltern Speak?*, ed. Cary Nelson (Urbana: University of Illinois Press, 1988), 271–313.

25. For the elaboration of the concept of social freedom, see Axel Honneth, *Freedom's Right: The Social Foundations of Democratic Life* (New York: Columbia University Press, 2014).

26. For a more thorough analysis of the development of feminist thought in the context of human dignity, see Annika Thiem, "Human Dignity and Gender Inequalities," in *Human Dignity and Gender Inequalities*, ed. Marcus Duewell, Jens Braarvig, Roger Brownsword, and Dietmar Mieth (Cambridge: Cambridge University Press, 2014), 498–504. This is especially important in the context of the Catholic Church:

evoking the notion of women's dignity while at the same time denying women the equal status in the Church is a particularly disgraceful show of disrespect and misrecognition. See, for an analysis of this aspect, Hille Haker, "'So rühmen sie sich stolz, eine Befreiung der Frau vollzogen zu haben' Feministische Theologie und Ethik—Skizze eines Profils," *Theologie und Glauben* 2 (2012): 261–74.

27. This does not exclude that one may become far too open and permeable to others. Rather, it demonstrates how the "positive" openness rests entirely on the trust not to be misrecognized, or stronger, to be acknowledged in one's social and individual identity.

28. Among the many philosophical accounts of the implications of modernity, see Theodor Adorno and Max Horkheimer, *Dialectic of Enlightenment* (New York: Verso, 2016). For the emergence of the modern self, see the seminal study by Charles Taylor, *Sources of the Self: The Making of the Modern Identity* (Cambridge, MA: Harvard University Press, 1989).

29. Nikolas S. Rose, *The Politics of Life Itself: Biomedicine, Power, and Subjectivity in the Twenty-First Century* (Princeton, NJ: Princeton University Press, 2007). By now, life sciences, for example, are driven by the technical understanding of life: genetic interventions aim to modify the human genome; lines between an "automaton" that is still a machine and the "living machine" that transcends exactly this dichotomy of artifacts and biological organisms are blurred; moreover, synthetic biology has begun to construct organisms that would have never emerged in the natural world.

30. Michael Specter, "A Life of Its Own: Where Will Synthetic Biology Lead Us?," *New Yorker*, September 21, 2009, http://www.newyorker.com/reporting/2009/09/28/090928fa_fact_specter.

31. For a thorough analysis, see Donna Dickenson, *Body Shopping: The Economy Fuelled by Flesh and Blood* (London: Oneworld, 2009).

32. Cf. Maurice Merleau-Ponty, *Phenomenology of Perception* (New York: Humanities Press 1962).

33. We can, of course, brush over this fine line and dismiss it as caught in irrational or nonsecular thinking. Pinker's statement from the beginning must be seen in this context: he is appalled by a "conservatism" or "irrationalism" that he sees lurking behind every critique of the paradigm of human progress through the new technologies. As I hope to have argued in the previous section, this critique is as much based on a misunderstanding of the concept of dignity as it is an uncritical affirmation of the underlying epistemology of the life sciences and medicine. Dignity matters not because technologies as such are to be viewed with suspicion, but because the new technologies operate with the reductionist (and therefore wrong) Cartesian conception of the human. The concept of dignity, however, maintains the noninstrumental self-relation of the "embodied self," as does, by the way, international law and human rights conventions prohibiting, for example, organ trafficking. The line between payment and donation, of course, may be blurred when the "compensation" for donation is indistinguishable from payment.

34. Sarah Franklin, *Embodied Progress: A Cultural Account of Assisted Conception* (New York: Routledge 1997).

35. Social egg freezing is to be distinguished from its counterpart, namely, egg freezing because of a medical condition, such as cancer. For a critical analysis of the new phenomenon of "social egg freezing" as another step of women's liberation, see Caitlin E. C. Myers, "Colonizing the (Reproductive) Future: The Discursive Construction of Arts as Technologies of Self," *Frontiers: A Journal of Women Studies* 35, no. 1 (2014): 73–103; Christine Rosen, "The Ethics of Egg Freezing," *Wall Street Journal*, May 3, 2013, C2; D. Stoop, E. Maes, N. P. Polyzos, G. Verheyen, H. Tournaye, and J. Nekkebroeck, "Does Oocyte Banking for Anticipated Gamete Exhaustion Influence Future Relational and Reproductive Choices? A Follow-up of Bankers and Non-bankers," *Human Reproduction* 30, no. 2 (2015): 338; Hille Haker, "Kryokonservierung von Eizellen—neue Optionen der Familienplanung? Eine ethische Bewertung," *Zeitschrift für medizinische Ethik* 62, no. 2 (2016): 121–32.

36. Almost all new reproductive technologies have first been introduced as medical applications for exceptional cases, as is also true for egg freezing. The global market value of assisted reproduction technology (ART) is estimated to be $29 billion by the year 2022. See Grand View Research, *Assisted Reproductive Technology (ART) Market Analysis by Procedures (Frozen Non-donor, Frozen Donor, Fresh Donor, Fresh Non-donor, Embryo/Egg Banking) and Segment Forecasts to 2022* (summary) 2015, http://www.grandviewresearch.com/industry-analysis/assisted-reproductive-technology-market.

37. Hille Haker, "Reproductive Rights and Reproductive Technologies," in *The Routledge Handbook of Global Ethics*, ed. Heather Widdows and Darrel Moellendorf (London: Routledge, 2014), 340–53.

38. The same holds true, of course, for any significant partner, e.g., in nonheterosexual relations: pregnancy changes the way we encounter each other in a particular way, as any radical change in a person's identity transforms their interactions with others.

39. This, of course, is at the core of recognition theory.

40. In Greek terminology, *ᾳἶδώς*, literally, "reservation," or a sense of shame, honor, or respect, is etymologically connected to the term for the sexual organs, *ᾳἶδόίά*. *ᾳἶδώς* is the precursor of *ἁρέτή* (virtue), which becomes the central term of the morally right disposition to act. Interestingly, *δίκη* (justice) is depicted as a daughter of *ᾳἶδώς*, which means that the virtue of justice has its origin in the "reservation" and respect for another person and the "honor" within the public moral order. In contrast, *ἀίσχύνή* (shame) refers to the experience of shame and to the act of shaming as a moral judgment of an act or person. In modern philosophy, shame and the moral sense of the self (or oneself) are inseparable. See, for example, Bernard Williams, *Shame and Necessity* (Berkeley: University of California Press, 1993); J. Ruhnau, "Scham," in *Historisches Wörterbuch der Philosophie*, ed. Joachim Ritter, Karlfried Gründer, and Gottfried Gabriel (Darmstadt: Wissenschaftliche Buchgesellschaft, 2007), 1208–15. See Bernstein for an ethical account of sexual assaults, especially rape, along the same lines as I argue here, with a comprehensive analysis of the literature; Bernstein, *Torture and Dignity*.

41. Cf. John M. Coetzee, *Elizabeth Costello* (London: Secker and Warburg, 2003), "The Problem of Evil," 156–82. For my interpretation of the story, see Hille Haker,

"'Ban graven images': Literatur als Medium ethischer Reflexion," in *Literatur ohne Moral: Literaturwissenschaften und Ethik im Gespräch*, ed. Christof Mandry (Berlin: Lit Verlag, 2003), 67–88.

42. In the following, I will only speak of female victims of sexual assault, but this does not mean that it does not affect any kind of assault and any other gender, on both sides.

43. The following facts are taken from Bradley A. Muhs, who collected official criminal record data up to 2011. It also includes expansive literature on underlying prejudicial assumptions in law enforcement and rape trials; see Muhs, "Fighting the Unfair Fight: Post-traumatic Stress Disorder and the Need for Neuroimaging Evidence in Rape Trials," *Women's Rights Law Reporter* 35, no. 2 (2014): 215–42.

44. It is no coincidence that, for example, the World Health Organization can call sexual violence against women a pandemic—with almost no public reaction.

45. RAINN (Rape, Abuse & Incest National Network) used statistics from the U.S. Justice Department to calculate this number, https://www.rainn.org/news/97-every-100-rapists-receive-no-punishment-rainn-analysis-shows. For more on how RAINN determines their statistics, see https://www.rainn.org/about-rainns-statistics.

46. Beatrice Diehl, "Affirmative Consent in Sexual Assault: Prosecutors' Duty," *Georgetown Journal of Legal Ethics* 28, no. 3 (2015): 503–19.

47. Emily Finch and Vanessa E. Munro, "The Demon Drink and the Demonized Woman: Socio-Sexual Stereotypes and Responsibility Attribution in Rape Trials Involving Intoxicants," *Social & Legal Studies* 16, no. 4 (2007): 591–614.

48. Diehl, "Affirmative Consent in Sexual Assault," 503–19.

49. Michael Walzer, *Thinking Politically: Essays in Political Theory* (New Haven, CT: Yale University Press, 2007).

50. Kwame Anthony Appiah, *The Honor Code: How Moral Revolutions Happen* (New York: Norton, 2010).

51. Bernstein, *Torture and Dignity*.

fourteen

DIGNITY AND CONFLICT

Religious Violence

Nicholas Denysenko

The twentieth century witnessed unprecedented developments in the area of theological anthropology. Beginning at the end of the nineteenth century, Roman Catholic theology began to reflect on the question of human dignity, especially with reference to the challenges posed to laborers.[1] Pastoral concern for the legal rights of workers, access to employment, equal distribution of resources and wealth, and humane living conditions intersected with the restoration of theological reflection on human dignity and the innate goodness of the human person, established by the presence of God's divine image in each person.[2] Orthodox theologians also reflected on theological anthropology, drawing from scripture and patristic sources to renew a vision of humanity as bearing the image of God and called to return to eternal communion. Some of the most poignant literature on the dignity of the human person comes from figures of the "Paris school of theology," a diverse cohort of postrevolutionary Russian theologians whose prodigious output occurred in the aftermath of the revolution and through the tumult of World War II and the Cold War.[3] These theologians and their families had witnessed the brutal violence wrought by the Soviet and Nazi regimes, acts of repression and eradication that were fundamental violations of human dignity. The theologians who wrote about anthropology have their own unique contributions, and writers such as Paul Evdokimov, Nicholas Afanasiev, Alexander Schmemann, and Boris Bobrinskoy drew from the sacramental repository of the Byzantine heritage to connect baptism, chrismation, and Eucharist as activating the Christic offices of priest, prophet, and king in each lay person.[4]

Mother Maria Skobtsova stands out for her appeal to honor the divine image in each human person, including those whom one might traditionally view as dangerous, scandalous, or adversarial.[5] Mother Maria called for the Orthodox Church to reshape its Eucharistic theology so that the daily toil of rehearsing love for all others would amount to participation in the sacrament of the brother or sister. For Mother Maria, loving all others, especially those whom one would prefer to avoid, constituted a renewal of authentic Orthodox spirituality and was the proper path to achieving union with God.[6] Given the complicated circumstances of her own life and vocational trajectory, Mother Maria's innovative teaching was likely inspired by the abject horrors of violence and war of her epoch: she was a witness of the brutal violence that mocked human dignity in its attempt to repress and coerce peoples.[7] Her witness was not limited to the written word, but was also demonstrated by her action, as she herself was a casualty of the genocide committed by the Third Reich against Jews.[8]

For the purposes of this chapter, God's creation of the human being in the divine image establishes the basis for human dignity. For Orthodox and Greek Catholic Christians of the Byzantine rite, the descent of the Spirit in baptism and at the anointing of chrism results in the creation of a Christ, or anointed one. The sacramental rite actualizes the re-creation of the human person who now bears the fullness of human dignity, as baptism washes away all distortions of the image and the continued reception of the Holy Spirit in the Eucharist provides the nourishment needed to sustain the dignity dependent upon the divine image.[9] Although global Orthodoxy has enjoyed a modest renaissance in retrieving the high regard for all of humankind attributed to patristic tradition and grounded by Byzantine sacramental theology—conveniently summarized by Schmemann as "anthropological maximalism," the rehabilitation of human dignity has not resulted in the cessation of polemical fights when traditionally Orthodox nations have come into conflict with neighboring countries and other Christian traditions.[10] The most recent and glaring of these examples is the current conflict between Ukraine and Russia. The violence and war afflicting eastern Ukraine, especially the Donbas region, is a prolonged human catastrophe. Readers should note that the causes of the war are multidimensional and irreducible to a single event, especially since the Euromaidan revolution of Kyiv in November 2013, protesting corruption, was the result of a painful adjustment to national and economic sovereignty in the immediate post-Soviet period.[11] During the process of adjustment, as particular populations within Ukraine longed for more instantaneous economic prosperity, people turned to figures whose ideologies promised a more secure future and present. Some of the Ukrainian populations turned to hopes for economic association with Europe and the West as the path to a more secure future. Other populations, especially those in Ukraine's Donbas region currently afflicted by conflict, tended to favor closer relations with Russia as the best move. Both populations also favored Ukraine's orientation either westward or eastward as natural, cultural, and religious realignments. For those favoring a move to the West, Ukraine was always a nation of multiple religions and Christian denominations, predominantly Orthodox, but open to the West. For easterners, Ukraine was a close sibling of Russia, Belarus, and Moldova in Orthodox faith and culture, sharing common values alien to the West.

As Ukraine struggled to find its footing in the twenty-first century, the conflicting ideologies drew on a long history of religious polemics that drew from the Byzantine legacy of sacramental theology to depict an opposing ideological group as antagonistic and adversarial. The sacramental vocabulary of this legacy is not the only thing implicated in igniting tensions resulting in violent war and its distortion of human dignity, but it has been an important component in composing and communicating narratives that essentially fail to honor the human dignity of the other. In the case of the Ukraine–Russia conflict, the Orthodox Moscow Patriarchate has implicated the Ukrainian Greco-Catholic Church (UGCC) and Orthodox Kyivan Patriarchate (KP) as the aggressors by questioning the legitimacy of their Christian identity and depicting them as heretics and schismatics who actively oppress canonical and faithful Orthodox in Ukraine. The authors of these narratives stretch the employment of words from sacramental vocabulary to align certain religious groups outside of the legitimate Orthodox communion with chauvinists and nationalists who seek the eradication of Orthodoxy from Ukraine to create a fascist state.

I will here define the foundational sacramental identity established at baptism and chrismation in the Byzantine liturgical tradition. I will then survey the history of polemical exchanges that draw from the Byzantine sacramental legacy in the Ukraine–Russia conflict to show how the consistent depiction of the other is designed to delegitimize its standing in the global religious and political communities, while also demeaning its human dignity. The disparagement of human dignity occurs in two tangible ways: first, the aggressors use technical terms to exercise power over the other within ecclesial structures and damage the reputation of the ones described as "schismatics," "radicals," and so on. Second, the aggressors who misuse such terms distort their own capacity to recognize the human dignity of their opponents, which in turn contributes to a vicious cycle of vituperative religious polemics. As a suggestion for remedying this crisis, I will conclude by sketching a proposal for recovering the "anthropological maximalism" of sacramental identity rooted primarily in the notion of each Christian as a "servant of God." This essential and core servant identity is a crucial ingredient for reconciliation between Ukraine and Russia and amelioration of the vicious pattern of violence resulting in the mocking of human dignity in the war in eastern Ukraine.

INTRODUCTION TO BYZANTINE SACRAMENTAL IDENTITY

In the churches of the Byzantine rite, a variety of words convey sacramental identity. Liturgical prayers name God as Father, Son, and Holy Spirit, but also appeal to God with a variety of titles referring to God's relationship with humanity. Such titles for God include "Master," "Lord," "Physician," and "Lover of Humankind" (Philanthropos). The Byzantine Church also uses terms for secondary figures who have contributed to the economy of salvation, particularly Mary, the Mother of God, whom they call "Protectress," "Ladder," and "Victorious Leader," among others. The use of such terms alongside the names of the Holy Trinity, Mary, and the saints poetically shapes the Church's understanding of the figure's role in the ongoing work of salvation freely given by God to humanity. The titles for God, Mary, and the saints are thus theological and ecclesiological.

Just as there are titles for God that denote the divine role in the economy of salvation, the Church employs a variety of liturgical titles for the laity that signify the people's role in exercising the offices of priest, prophet, and king in service to the Church and the world. From the very beginning of one's becoming Christian, identity is formed through the power of words. One of the best examples of a detailed and sophisticated explanation of identity is in the fourth-century preaching attributed to Cyril of Jerusalem.[12] In his procatechesis, which was the final lecture given to prospective Christians on the eve of their baptism, Cyril addresses them, from the very beginning, as φωτιζόμενοι, "those who were about to be illumined": they were on the threshold of joining God's household, a process described as illumination, or being filled with light.[13] By participating in the sacraments of baptism, they will become "the sons and daughters of one mother."[14] Cyril's lecture on the eve of baptism communicates a process of growth, of becoming one who is illumined, one who is joining a royal household and receiving adoption as sons and daughters.

Cyril builds on this prebaptismal vocabulary in the five lectures he delivers on each of the five weekdays following baptism on Pascha. These lectures essentially explain what happened to the person who received baptism. Cyril depicts the baptismal bath as an experience of death and resurrection in imitation of Christ; the participant does not bodily die, but the participant experiences a real death by being a communicant of Christ (ἵνα τῇ μιμήσει τῶν παθῶν αὐτοῦ κοινωνήσαντες ἀληθείᾳ τὴν σωτηρίαν κερδήσωμεν).[15] A feature of sacramental identity is reference to communion: the individual's identity is shaped by the communion. Cyril's instruction here accentuates the primary figure of holy communion: Jesus Christ. Belonging to the holy community of Christ makes the participant a communicant (κοινωνοὶ) of Christ's sufferings and death.[16] The individual person is no longer on a self-governed journey: his or her journey occurs together with Christ's, and it is a journey that begins with death and results in new life. I have referred to Cyril's notion of becoming a communicant of Christ in baptism because this is the cornerstone of Christian identity, the notion of belonging to a holy community.

Note that Cyril adds additional words denoting identity in his series of lectures. In his third lecture, on the anointing with chrism, he seems to elaborate identity by calling the recently baptized "Christs." In fact, one is able to call the Christian a "Christ" because of their participation in Christ (μέτοχοι οὖν τοῦ Χριστοῦ γενόμενοι χριστοὶ εἰκότως καλεῖσθε).[17] In the same lecture, Cyril reminds them that they are communicants (κοινωνοὶ) and fellows (μέτοχοι) of Christ. The fellowship permits them to bear the name of Christ and also to be called "Christians."[18]

The Eucharist ritualizes participation by communing—this time, the term employed by Cyril is μεταλαμβάνομεν, which is the same word used in the contemporary rites of Holy Communion.[19] In other words, the ritual participation of eating, drinking, and anointing is the anthropological way of living in a community; in this case, the community is that of Christ, with his Father and the Holy Spirit. Ritual participation in the Eucharist makes the Christian a Christ-bearer (χριστοφόροι).[20] The ones who are anointed have obtained this privilege because they were given the gift of sharing in the holy community of God. One can be certain in saying that God is the one who gives this gift, but some kind of voluntary action is required on the part of the participant. Participants must agree at some level of their consciousness to partake of this ritual, and this is true even of small children and infants.[21]

THE CONSECRATION OF CHRISM: PRIEST, PROPHET, KING

The Byzantine prayer for the consecration of chrism complements Cyril's sacramental identity program. Byzantine theology views the anointing with chrism as shaping the newly baptized into priests, prophets, and kings, a feature shared with Roman Catholic sacramental theology (as I have written elsewhere).[22] In the Byzantine tradition, the Church consecrates the chrism for anointing new Christians on Holy Thursday (this is not an annual rite, but occurs only as needed). The prayer for the consecration of chrism uses words defining the identity of those who will be anointed:

> Yes, Master, God Almighty, show it, by the descent of your adorable and Holy Spirit, to be a vesture of incorruption and a seal of perfection, imprinting upon those who have received divine baptism your holy name and of your only-begotten son and of your Holy Spirit, that they would become knowledgeable in your view as your citizens, your children and servants, sanctified in soul and in body, free from every evil and redeemed from sin, by the vesture of your incorruptible glory, and that they would be known by this holy sign by the holy angels and archangels and by all the heavenly powers, and that they would be strong against evil and impure spirits, so that they would become for you a chosen people, a royal priesthood, a holy people, sealed through this your pure myron, and having your Christ in their hearts for your dwelling, God and Father in the Holy Spirit: For You are holy, our God, and unto You we send up glory.[23]

The prayer identifies the anointed as "citizens," "children," and "servants" of God; they are chosen and a royal priesthood. One can find this kind of sacramental identity language in the Roman consecration of chrism of the Gelasian sacramentary and in the patristic writings of fathers such as Aphraat and John Chrysostom.[24] The ecumenical movement of the twentieth century retrieved the notion of baptism making Christians into priests, prophets, and kings; the revision of Roman Catholic baptism added a brief formulary accompanying the postbaptismal chrismation of infants and children indicating that they are now priests, prophets, and kings.

SACRAMENTAL IDENTITY IN JOHN CHRYSOSTOM

In his baptismal homilies, preached in Antioch, John Chrysostom engages a vast vocabulary to form identity in the neophytes. A close examination of Chrysostom's homilies indicates that this vocabulary is fluid. In his third baptismal homily from the Stavronikita collection edited by Wenger, Chrysostom uses several titles to form identity in the catechumens:

> Blessed is God, let us say again, who alone has done wonders, who makes and renews all things. Those who were held captive yesterday are now free people and citizens of the Church. Those who yesterday were tarnished by sins are now in boldness and righteousness. For they are not only free, but are holy; they are not only holy, but righteous; they are not only righteous, but are sons; they are not only sons, but are inheritors; they are not only inheritors, but are brothers of Christ; they are not only brothers of Christ, but are also coinheritors; they are not only coinheritors, but are also members, not only members, but also temples, not only temples, but also instruments of the Spirit.[25]

The titles he employs illustrate the process of formation the catechumens are experiencing: they will become citizens of the Church who are free, righteous, and holy. They will also become sons, inheritors, brothers of Christ, coinheritors, members, temples, and instruments of the Spirit.

The testimony of Cyril of Jerusalem, Chrysostom, and the early Byzantine liturgical tradition demonstrates the sacramental identity communicated by ritual participation. A Christian becomes a son and daughter of God, a priest, prophet, king, and citizen, a brother of Christ, and a temple of the Spirit. Perhaps most significant is the notion of the Christian being a communicant, partaker, and fellow of Christ, which is the covenantal basis for both belonging and identity. The basis of this sacramental identity is in the Christian's belonging to the holy community of Christ with his Father and the Holy Spirit. This sacramental identity is profoundly positive, exhibiting the inexhaustible generosity of God, who grants Christians citizenship and privilege in the divine realm. It is essential to remember the significance of ritual participation: the recipient's act of receiving the gift and of participating in Christ's death unveils the divine invitation for the Christian to respond in his or her own activity. Perhaps it is this vision of divine–human symbiosis rooted in Christ and granted to Christians that Alexander Schmemann had in mind when he referred to chrismation as a sacrament manifesting anthropological maximalism.

SACRAMENTAL IDENTITY IN THE RECEIVED LITURGICAL TRADITION: SERVANT OF GOD

The contemporary rites of baptism, chrismation, and Eucharist have retained the sacramental identity I briefly surveyed above. These sacramental rites privilege one final term for the Christian, a word that threads through all of the offices: *servant of God.* Throughout the entirety of a practicing Christian's life, he or she is God's servant. Even after death, the Christian remains God's servant as expressed by the liturgical texts for the offices of the dead.[26] The connotations of "servant" as an identity marker are broad, and the word "servant" is repeated over and over again in the liturgical rites. A participant in the Byzantine liturgy becomes accustomed to the word "servant," possibly to the point where it loses some of its power to shape the identity of the Christian on a daily basis.

The Byzantine liturgy presents a plethora of alternative identities a Christian may or may not assume. Byzantine sacramental theology establishes Christians as priests, prophets, kings, and servants, but it also communicates a vision of the world where God's opponents also have identities and identity markers. The rite of baptism itself offers one snapshot into the depiction of this worldview: at the very beginning, the first exorcism rebukes the devil, casting him and his servants out of the "newly enlisted soldier of Christ our God."[27] The rite depicts the removal of evil from the life of the Christian, who wages a battle against the evil angels and is assured of victory because of the participant's voluntary communion with Christ.

In baptism, the devil is the antagonist who seeks to retain covenant with the Christian.[28] The Church views the devil as offering another community, as an alternative to the one kept with Christ. Since the baptismal bath is the space for entering communion with Christ and dying to covenant with the devil, the exorcism is performed to cast out those who would seek to replace communion with Christ with their own communion. The use of the word "soldier" as an identifying marker in this context suggests a kind of enlistment, loyalty, and the fulfillment of carrying out the orders of the community's leader—Christ.

In the rite of baptism, the exorcisms are preparatory. The three exorcisms conclude with a powerful ritual, where the presider breathes on the mouth, forehead, and breast of the candidate three times, saying each time "drive out of him/her every unclean spirit hiding and lurking in his/her heart."[29] The exorcisms precede the next step in breaking covenant with the devil, where the candidate renounces company with the devil for eternity, punctuated by the candidate's breathing and spitting on the devil.[30] This section of the rite concludes with the creation of the covenant with Christ, with the candidate bowing before Christ and worshipping him, continuing the process of entering into his communion, which will continue with the baptismal bath, anointing with chrism, and participation in Eucharistic communion.[31] We should note the ritual repetition with the casting out of Satan from the Christian's life: the exorcisms and renunciation are not enough. The candidate must be anointed with oil prior to entering the bath to protect him or her from the clutches of Satan, and the blessing of baptismal waters also contains a casting out of demons when the presider breathes on the water in the sign of the cross three times, saying, "Let all adverse powers be crushed beneath the sign of the image of your Cross."[32] The repetitive casting out of demons at each stage of ritual progression has one clear implication: the covenant forged with Christ at baptism is eternal and irrevocable, which means that there is no returning to the communion of the evil one.

The legacy of sacramental vocabulary is a mixed bag in terms of the words used to depict others. The Christian is simultaneously servant and soldier, commissioned to bear Christ's presence to the world, while also eradicating evil and thwarting enemies. The Christian's ability to distinguish a time for witness (servant) from a time for renunciation of evil (soldier) can become complicated. The rites and words employed for the contemporary reception of converts into the Orthodox Church via chrismation elucidate potential problems in the way the ritual texts depict the churches converts are voluntarily leaving, and provides an appropriate example for the way ritual texts can be used to depict non-Orthodox others. We noted above that the Church renounces and casts out the devil from the new covenant the candidates have entered at baptism. In the history of receiving converts through chrismation, the Byzantine Church has introduced new renunciations on the part of candidates, which would demonstrate their fidelity to confessing the Orthodox faith. In late antiquity, former Nestorians and Monophysites were required to furnish a libellus renouncing the heresies of their communities for reception into the Church.[33] The contemporary rituals of reception also call upon candidates to renounce more recent heresies. The rite for receiving converts with a valid Christian baptism begins with an initial renunciation of heresy in an interrogation exercised by the celebrant.[34] After an initial prayer requesting the removal of the candidate's former errors, the candidate faces west and renounces all heresies in an expanded interrogation. The heresies are not explicated in this section, but generalized, and are exemplified by the following excerpt: "Do you renounce all ancient and modern apostasies, heresies, and founders of heresies, and cast them off because they are contrary to God?" "I cast off all ancient and modern apostasies, heresies, and founders of heresies because they are contrary to God." The celebrant then asks the candidate to renounce specific teachings belonging to his or her original faith tradition. For example, the question posed to "non-Chalcedonians" asks: "Do you renounce the false opinion that in our Lord Jesus Christ there are not two natures, divine and human, but one only, the human nature being swallowed up by the divine?"[35]

The second question for converts of "Roman-Latin" origin reads: "Do you renounce the erroneous supposition that the holy Apostles did not receive from our Lord Jesus Christ equal spiritual power, but that the holy Apostle Peter was their prince; and that the Bishop of Rome alone is his successor and that the Bishops of Jerusalem, Antioch, Alexandria and the others are not, equally with the Bishop of Rome, successors of the Apostles?"[36] The second question posed to candidates who were Lutheran is also illustrative: "Do you renounce the erroneous opinion that in the Eucharistic mystery the bread is not transformed into the Body of Christ, yet does not become the Body of Christ, and that the wine is not transformed into the Blood of Christ, yet does not become the Blood of Christ?"[37] The response to each question is "I renounce it/them," or "I forsake it/them." The distinction between general and particular renunciations is relevant to the experience of the candidate and illustrates the magnitude of the change the Church expects her to embrace. The language of the renunciation texts is ecumenically problematic and poses a formidable challenge to the candidate, who will have to navigate potentially painful personal contexts and relationships, assuming the candidate truly interiorizes the renunciations.

RITUAL RENUNCIATION AND THE OTHER AS ADVERSARY

The primary area of pastoral concern emerging from these renunciations is the inherent tension between voluntarily and joyfully entering the Orthodox communion and confronting one's ecclesial past. For converts, their past church experience has been formative, both cognitively and personally. The renunciations call upon the candidate to reject the heresies of their native communities, but I would argue that this approach carries some risk because it is not feasible to view ecclesial teaching and the people who constitute a faith community as mutually exclusive entities. The renunciation of erroneous teachings cannot be both a rejection of false theology and acceptance of the people who continue to belong to that community; a renunciation is essentially a rejection of the whole community, a ritual act with the capacity to shape one's view of the other pejoratively. I would add that this principle of rejecting the other through renunciation is limited to neither converts nor their rite of reception into the Church. The definition of Orthodoxy as the sole true faith, rooted in an ecclesiology of the Orthodox Church as equivalent with the one, holy, catholic, and apostolic Church, reveals a view of the other as outside of that communion. The ritual acts of renunciation are preceded by explanations of how the other faith community is erroneous and thus outside of the Church, and such discourse and depiction of the other as erroneous and extraneous to the Church circulates within Orthodox communities. The renunciation of so-called heresies (e.g., Arians and Nestorians) and schismatics (e.g., Roman Catholics) is formative: it shapes a view of the other as false and erroneous, and outside of the holy community of Christ. When the ritual renunciation becomes an evolving and ongoing narrative that consistently depicts the other as not only erroneous and extraneous, but also adversarial, treacherous, invasive, and evil, the view of the other—in this case, non-Orthodox Christians—becomes distorted. A faulty assumption of the soldier identity enhances the view of the other as adversary, as the Orthodox soldier views others outside of the sacred space of the holy community as warranting renunciation.

I have presented the ritual renunciation of heresies and errors in the reception of converts into the Church as an illustration of a living tradition within the Orthodox Church. Pastorally, many people who become Orthodox suffer from conflicted emotions about and relations with their native faith communities. It is becoming increasingly common for Orthodox converts to view their native communities of faith in adversarial terms: people who are outside of the holy community and thus false. These views exchange in a type of circular cross-pollination with other existing views on people of other faith traditions, which vary and are not always negative or adversarial, but occasionally are pejorative and even hostile. It is no secret that many Orthodox in the world are afflicted with anti-Semitism and hostility towards Islam, attitudes occasionally shaped by extra-ecclesial conflicts. Other Orthodox despise Roman Catholics on account of the Latin sacking of Constantinople in 1204 or the mission to convert Russia. Many Orthodox in the world bear open hostility towards Greek Catholics, a view of the other which is now well known to the global public on account of the tragic Russian aggression in eastern Ukraine.

THE ADVERSARIAL OTHER IN CONTEMPORARY UKRAINE–RUSSIA RELIGIOUS POLEMICS

Much of my recent scholarship has reflected on the problem of narratives and counternarratives, which draws terms from the repository of Byzantine sacramental identity in an attempt to increase the weight of the argument and persuade the world that Greek Catholics and Orthodox Ukrainians are responsible for the war and for the persecution of those who are legitimate members of the holy community, namely, the canonical Orthodox. In the history of Ukraine–Russia religious polemics, the practice of casting the other as a malevolent adversary with a malicious agenda has deep roots. Before summarizing the state of polemical exchange in its contemporary manifestation, a brief overview of the historical events leading up to this point can help us understand how the various parties arrived at this state of affairs. Ultimately, our review will demonstrate that the pejorative view of the other is the result of a complex process of political, economic, and cultural subjugation, and the role of the Churches in Ukraine's political aspirations.

Ecclesial Separation, Part 1: The Union of Brest, 1596

Orthodoxy came to Kyiv (Kiev) in the tenth century, becoming a permanent fixture when Prince Volodymyr baptized the people of Kyiv into the Church of Constantinople in 988.[38] It is important to note that Kyiv was one of a few city-states in the region of Rus', consisting of a mixed people of Scandinavian and Slavic provenance.[39] The city-state of Kyiv enjoyed a particular prominence among the other city-states (namely, Novgorod and Vladimir-Suzdal), and in the eleventh century, the city's interior intellectual life cultivated by Prince Yaroslav obtained enough international prestige that the patriarch of Constantinople permitted it to have its own native presiding bishop.[40] Kyiv's prestige and its status as the ecclesiastical center of the local city-states did not remain unchallenged. In 1169, Prince Andrei Bogoliubskii of Vladimir-Suzdal ransacked and plundered Kyiv in an attempt to elevate the prestige of his own city-state.[41] This event is one example of diversity among the city-states: Kyiv's status as the center and capital did not remain unchallenged. Eventually Kyiv fell, first to the Mongolian Golden Horde in 1240, and then it came under the Kingdom of Poland and the Grand Duchy of Lithuania in the fourteenth century.[42] During this period, Moscow attained ecclesiastical preeminence and the various city-states existed within distinct cultural and political orbits. Kyiv's legacy remained significant in part because it was the first inheritor of the Byzantine political, cultural, and intellectual repository. But by the fourteenth century, Kyiv and its inhabitants were vassals of Western, Roman Catholic realms.

Kyiv's existence in the Polish kingdom significantly shaped the religious orientation of its leaders in the late sixteenth century. In 1596, the entire hierarchy of the Kyivan Church entered into communion with the See of Rome at the Union of Brest.[43] Church historians disagree on the motivation for this union. Most historians attribute the union to the political conditions of the time: communion with Rome and assuming a Catholic identity without relinquishing the Byzantine rite would grant the Ukrainian aristocrats greater political clout, wealth, and access to education for their children.[44] Other historians rationalize the union on ecclesiological grounds: Brest completed what was started by the Council of Florence–Ferrara in 1438–39, and the See of Kyiv had always valued its relations with the Churches of East and West.[45] However one assesses the objectives of the union, the outcome was a permanent division: the hierarchy embraced it, but the majority of the laity rejected the union and remained Orthodox. In 1620, Jerusalem patriarch Theophanes consecrated a new hierarchy for the Orthodox Metropolia of Kyiv, and the Kyivan Orthodox Church entered into what some have called a golden age under the leadership of the Moldovan-born metropolitan Peter Mohyla, who negotiated the tensions between East and West by emphasizing excellent education of the clergy and their knowledge of both their native traditions and the Western Christianity they encountered on a daily basis.[46]

The Orthodox refutation of the Union of Brest became a historical error in the Orthodox version of the historical narrative. The majority of the Greek Catholics were under the rule of the Polish kingdom and the Austro-Hungarian Empire up until the twentieth century, but the cohorts of Greek Catholics who came into contact with imperial Russia were permanently struck by the memory of Tsar Nicholas I's attempt to coerce Greek Catholics in imperial Russia to convert to Orthodoxy.[47] In the early twentieth century, tensions between Greek Catholics in Poland and Orthodox in western Ukrainian regions ruled by imperial Russia were thick, the result of complicated political-religious confrontations that had taken place throughout the eighteenth and nineteenth centuries.[48] The memoirs of Metropolitan Evlogy (Grigorievskii), who was bishop of Kholm and later archbishop of Volyn, attest to the local Orthodox memory as one of bitter conflict resisting Uniate proselytism.[49] In summary, both sides experienced some kind of disparagement that damaged their sense of human dignity when they encountered one another.

Two succeeding events of the twentieth century occurred in which these adversarial views of the other boiled over into conflict. The first event was in 1946, when the Russian Orthodox Church presided over an orchestrated council in L'viv.[50] The UGCC had experienced a particularly tumultuous period during the consistently shifting grounds of political rulers. From the beginning of the twentieth century, the Greek Catholics in western Ukraine found themselves under Austro-Hungarian, Polish, western Ukrainian, Ukrainian, German, and Soviet rule. Furthermore, the battles for Ukrainian sovereignty raged longest in western Ukraine, and many Greek Catholics had invested their hopes in the Ukrainian Insurgent Army.[51] When western Ukraine was granted to the Soviet Union as part of the fateful Yalta agreement in 1945, Joseph Stalin consolidated his control over Christians in the Soviet Union by forcibly coercing the Greek Catholics to hold a phony council celebrating their return to the Orthodox Church. The Greek Catholic Church was also illegal in Ukraine at this time. From the perspective of the Greek Catholics, this pseudocouncil was a deliberate act of religious persecution and contributed to their view of the Russian Orthodox Church as the adversarial other and close collaborator with the merciless Soviet regime. To make matters worse, the Orthodox Church publicly celebrated the victorious return of the Greek Catholics to Orthodoxy for several decades afterwards, even publishing articles in vernacular Ukrainian on the joy of their return to the true Church in the official organ of the Orthodox Church in Ukraine.[52]

These tensions simmered among Greek Catholics in the West, and the situation came to a head again at the end of the Soviet era during Gorbachev's rule, when the Soviet government authorized the legalization of the Greek Catholic Church in 1989. Millions of Greek Catholics who had been coerced into conversion to Orthodoxy returned to their Church, and violence erupted as conflicts emerged on parish property ownership.[53] As the end of the Soviet era loomed, western Ukraine was a center of Ukrainian patriotism and nationalism, and the legalization of the openly patriotic UGCC, along with the unexpected return of the equally patriotic Ukrainian Autocephalous Orthodox Church (UAOC), posed unexpected challenges to the hegemony of the Moscow Patriarchate, which was the only Church from the Byzantine tradition tolerated in Ukraine during the Soviet period.

The end of Soviet rule and the emergence of an independent Ukrainian republic put an end to the favored status of the Moscow Patriarchate in Ukraine.

From the time of independence onwards, the UGCC and Orthodox bodies independent of Moscow have challenged the role and especially the public positions of the Moscow Patriarchate in Ukraine. Despite the emergence of Christian competition in Ukraine, the Moscow Patriarchate retained the most adherents of the Churches following the Orthodox tradition. More importantly, the two Churches encountered one another with much greater frequency than they had in the periods when each found itself under the rule of a neighboring realm. As they encountered one another, the historical memories of wrongs committed by the other contributed to their public positions on the other. For the Orthodox under Moscow, Greek Catholics had betrayed Orthodoxy and were thus schismatic. Furthermore, they did not belong to the critical mass of people who drove the Nazi aggressors from Soviet territory during the Great Patriotic War. By definition, they were thus schismatics (ecclesially) and chauvinists (politically), an assignment of identity possible only by a uniform inscription of political association upon all Greek Catholics. The recent memory of the Greek Catholics' voluntary decision to return to communion with Rome and seize parish property served to enflame these perceptions. For Greek Catholics, the Orthodox were religious persecutors who voluntarily collaborated with the Soviet regime and participated in an attempt to eradicate a legitimate religious group for a malevolent political purpose.

Ecclesial Separation, Part 2: The Creation of an Independent Orthodox Church in Ukraine (1921)

In the aftermath of the reconstitution of the Orthodox Kyivan Metropolia in 1620, the Ukrainians enjoyed a brief victory over their Polish rulers during the great uprising in 1648. In 1654, the leaders of the uprising signed an agreement with the Russian Crown at the Treaty of Pereiaslav, and Kyiv fell under a predominantly Russian orbit until the Revolution of 1917. From 1654 to 1685, the Orthodox See of Kyiv remained under the jurisdiction of Constantinople, but in 1686, Constantinople permitted the patriarch of Moscow to ordain the Metropolitan of Kyiv.[54] Moscow interpreted this act as a transfer of jurisdiction. As with the Union of Brest, historians disagree on the significance of this change in jurisdiction. Some argue that the reunification of Kyiv with Moscow was a reconstitution of the principalities of Rus', this time under Muscovite leadership instead of Kyivan. Others argue that Kyiv resisted this change and refer to 1686 as an annexation, referring to the two-plus centuries afterwards as a period of Russians systematically eradicating Ukrainian identity from Church life.[55]

As the collapse of imperial Russia approached, Ukrainian ideologues began to dream of an autonomous Ukraine, and with a sovereign republic, an independent Church.[56] Ukraine had two opportunities to claim an independent Church: the first came in 1918, when Patriarch Tikhon of Moscow authorized the convocation of an all-Ukrainian council for the Ukrainians to determine their own ecclesial course.[57] Conciliar work was interrupted several times because of civil war, and it embarked on the path of remaining a part of the Moscow Patriarchate. Yet the council itself is considered by some to be dubious since Russian monarchist bishops forcibly removed pro-Ukrainian delegates from the voting assembly.[58]

As control of Ukraine changed no fewer than five times from 1917 to 1920, a group of Ukrainian Orthodox intellectuals continued their work in attempting to liberate the Church from Muscovite control. A series of negotiations with bishops from Moscow failed during this period, and in 1921, the Ukrainian group declared independence from Moscow, established its own episcopate, and named itself the first-ever Ukrainian Autocephalous Orthodox Church (UAOC).[59] The ecclesiological basis of the first UAOC was innovative: they modified the rite of consecration of bishops and significantly revised both traditional Church canons and the rules concerning marital prohibitions for candidates for the episcopal and presbyteral offices of the Church. The 1921 UAOC was a minority voice within Ukraine, but it was popular among intellectuals and grew rapidly until the Soviet authorities liquidated it between 1927 and 1930. A second version of the UAOC emerged in 1941 in Polish cities with predominantly Ukrainian populations, and it differed from its predecessor by retaining all traditional canonical and liturgical norms of the Church, but it still came into conflict with the Church of Moscow.

The majority of the leaders of the World War II–era Church emigrated to Western Europe and North America where diaspora Ukrainians were quite outspoken about the political agendas of the Moscow Patriarchate, often rallying together with diaspora leaders of the Greek Catholic Church. In 1989, the UAOC appeared on the scene for the third time in Ukraine, and declared itself an Orthodox patriarchate in 1990. By 1992, this group separated into two, the UAOC and the newly formed KP, with the KP the larger and more influential of the two. As the KP slowly grew in Ukraine, it came into conflict with the Ukrainian Church under Moscow, especially during the recent crisis of the

Maidan revolution, annexation of Crimea, and war in eastern Ukraine. On December 15, 2018, the KP, UAOC, and two bishops of the Moscow Patriarchate united into the Orthodox Church of Ukraine (OCU), and received canonical autocephaly from the Patriarchate of Constantinople on January 6, 2019. Despite this attempt to resolve the issue, the polemical infighting between the Moscow Patriarchate and the OCU continues to rage.

When the 1921 UAOC adopted the innovative path to independence, they obtained a stigma of ecclesial illegitimacy. Immediately, bishops of the Moscow Patriarchate referred to them as "self-consecrated, without grace, and uncanonical" in correspondence. For their part, the Ukrainians presented their own depiction of the Church under Moscow: it was the "old" Church, composed of servants of the tsar, not of Christ, and worst of all, it persecuted the Church in Ukraine through the political medium of the Russian Empire. For this reason, the leader of the 1921 UAOC, Metropolitan Vasyl Lypkivsky, unashamedly defined himself as a Church revolutionary who sought to destroy the chains used by the institutional Russian Church to enslave the Ukrainian people.

This kind of polemical exchange was passed on from one generation to the next in intra-Church discourse in Ukraine, despite the fact that each of the Churches in question had experienced a series of transformative developments, both positive and negative. An excellent example of the longevity of the terms used to identify the other during this period comes from the letter of Moscow patriarch Pimen to Patriarch Athenagoras in 1972. Athenagoras's friendly meeting with the leader of the American diaspora Ukrainian Church, Metropolitan Mstyslav Skrypnyk, precipitated Pimen's letter. Pimen wrote to Athenagoras to chastise the latter for engaging an uncanonical and illegitimate group in dialogue. The following excerpt from Pimen's letter discloses the identity of the other inscribed by the Moscow patriarch on the independent Church of Ukraine:

> In the beginning of the 1920's a group of native Ukrainian chauvinists, consisting of a small portion of parish clergy and faithful of the eparchies of our Church in Ukraine, decided to separate from the Mother Church on account of phyletistic motives. These anti-ecclesial acts found no support in our episcopate, and the clerical leaders of the Russian Orthodox Church placed the proper canonical prohibitions on the schismatics. Then, ignoring this warning and without the blessing of the primate of the Russian Orthodox

> Church, his holiness, Patriarch of Moscow and all Rus' Tikhon, the separatists convoked a council in October 1921 called "the all-Ukrainian Council of clergy and laity." . . . This pseudo-council proclaimed the existence of the Ukrainian Autocephalous Orthodox Church. The leader of the separatists, archpriest Vasyl Lypkivsky (deposed at the time), was elected as "bishop" of the new "church" by the delegates of the "council" . . . the ordination itself was performed by deposed presbyters and laity by the placing of the relics (hands) of the hieromartyr Macarius, Metropolitan of Kiev, on Lypkivsky. This blasphemous act was repeated for the next "ordination" to "bishop" on archpriest Nestor Sharaivsky (also deposed). The character of these "ordinations" provided the basis for the assignment of the name "self-consecrated" to the schismatics among the faithful.[60]

Noteworthy in Pimen's letter is the amalgamation of terms: the 1921 UAOC was chauvinistic, illegal, a false council, blasphemous, and unrecognized by the legitimate Orthodox. One might summarize these terms as "illegitimate." The remainder of Pimen's letter attributes the same illegitimacy to the second UAOC that emerged in World War II, along with new pejorative notions of ecclesial illegitimacy corrupting the Church's status in global Orthodoxy.

Pimen's letter exemplifies the kind of language used to define another Church (Orthodox in this case) in a dispute over jurisdiction. Let us summarize how this abbreviated review of development in the history of the Orthodox Church of Kyiv has resulted in the vituperative religious polemics of this day. The most obvious problem is the use of insulting and offensive terms to define the identity of the other. Some of these terms come from the sacramental and ecclesiological Byzantine legacies: heretics and schismatics. Russian bishops referred to Greek Catholics and dissident Ukrainian Orthodox as heretics and schismatics, and also invented new terms we might view as belonging to the larger tree of "schismatic," such as "self-consecrated," "without grace," and "uncanonical." The Moscow Church also affixed political labels on these groups, conveniently adding new layers of *dubia* to the ecclesial ones already present: "chauvinistic," "nationalists," and "collaborators with fascist aggressors." The addition of the new identity terms to the established ecclesial ones punctuates the complete illegitimacy of the Church in question: they are altogether evil and malevolent. Pimen's letter represents the faulty "soldier" identity of Orthodoxy: the letter proposes to defend Orthodoxy by renouncing illegitimate and evil adversaries outside of the holy community.

Our review of the history of this development discloses the political and cultural complexities contributing to separation, rivalry, disagreement, and anger. The ultimate outcome on the part of the ones on the receiving end of these messages is a complete diminishment of human dignity. According to their enemies, they are demonic, not human, and are certainly not priests, prophets, kings, Christ-bearers, and servants of God. The sending of one insult results in an offensive response, creating a vicious cycle of ecclesial infighting, and, tragically, contributing to the history of human catastrophe in twentieth- to early twenty-first-century Ukraine. The preceding review establishes a lens through which we can understand the dynamics and effects of the contemporary intra-Christian polemics in Ukraine.

CONTEMPORARY INTRA-CHRISTIAN POLEMICS IN UKRAINE

Since November 2013, there have been numerous examples of intra-Christian polemical exchanges illustrating the inscription of adversarial identity on the other. I will cite a recent example illustrating this view of the other from Moscow patriarch Kirill's statement at the recent meeting of the heads of the Orthodox Churches in Chambesy:

> Over thirty churches of the Ukrainian Orthodox Church have now been taken over and at least ten are under the threat of attack by schismatics and nationalists, who are trying to prevent what is happening as voluntary transition of believers to the so-called Kyiv patriarchate. In actual fact, it was a real bandit, raiding takeover: they hold a meeting of people who are unrelated to the community, then they fake the charter documents with the authorities' assistance, take over the church using nationalist militants, and they throw the church community and the priest out in the street . . . schismatics and their semi-bandit military groups ignore court rulings.[61]

Note the strategic construction of this statement: the schismatics are also bandits, raiders, and unlawful. Patriarch Kirill's recent statement is consistent with other documents he has issued, including his letter to Ecumenical Patriarch Bartholomew on August 20, 2014, when he blamed "Greek Catholics and schismatics" for promoting hostility in Ukraine and requested Patriarch Bartholomew's assistance. Kirill's assignment of blame in his February report is consistent with other documents he has issued. These two brief references to Kirill's statements elucidate the beginnings of a pattern of assigning blame to schismatics and Greek Catholics while appealing to other Orthodox bishops for assistance. Metropolitan Hilarion Alfeyev's statements made to the participants of the Fourth European Orthodox–Catholic Forum (Minsk, June 2–6, 2014) fit this pattern:

> Sadly, the Greek Catholics have played a very destructive role in allowing this situation to develop. The words of their leading archbishop, hierarchs and clergy and an extremely politicized position have brought about the polarization of society and a worsening of the conflict which has already led to numerous victims. Unlike the canonical Ukrainian Orthodox Church, which has been able during these difficult months to unite people of various political persuasions, including those who have found themselves on both sides of the barricades, the Uniates have ostentatiously associated themselves with only one of the belligerent forces. The aggressive words of the Uniates, actions directed at undermining the canonical Orthodox Church, active contacts with schismatics and the striving to divide a single multinational Russian Orthodox Church have caused great damage not only to the Ukraine and her citizens, but also to the Orthodox-Catholic dialogue. All of this has put us back a great distance, reminding us of the times when the Orthodox and Catholics viewed each other not as friends but as rivals.
>
> Allow me to use this platform to appeal to all our partners in the Orthodox-Catholic dialogue to do all that is possible to cool down the "hotheads" among the Uniates, to halt the actions of the Greek Catholics in making the crisis in the Ukraine worse.[62]

The statements of the two high-ranking Russian bishops demonstrate how one can integrate a select vocabulary from the Byzantine sacramental heritage into public discourse on assigning blame for the war in eastern Ukraine.

However one views the political situation in Ukraine, this construct is simply too convenient of a fusion of a view of the other shaped by the language of sacramental identity. For the purposes of this construct, let us assume that "Uniates" are schismatics at best or heretics at worst from the perspective of the Russian bishops. The adherents of the KP fall under the grouping of schismatic, though they too have been accused of heresy on account of the allegation of ethnophyletism. The point is that the perspectives on the other introduced above fit this paradigm because upon becoming Orthodox, a convert would presumably have to renounce a native faith community that was either schismatic or heretical, or both. One can apply this paradigm to the Moscow Patriarchate's attitude towards these two Churches because the patriarchate views both groups as completely outside the holy community of Christ. Essentially, the current statements of the Moscow Patriarchate exemplify the preference for the soldier identity, as they renounce external threats to the Holy Communion. The soldier metaphor also identifies the Moscow Patriarchate as a protector or defender of those who are alleged to have caused the violent conflict resulting in death. In other words, the Moscow Patriarchate establishes the canonical Church as both the victim of the conflict and the only legitimate body equipped to defend the dignity of those persecuted by "Uniates" and "schismatics."

Regardless of one's views on the legitimacy of the Moscow Patriarchate's allegations, the attitude portrayed towards the KP and the UGCC here has two fundamental problems. The first problem is the linear construct of legitimacy: the fact that the Kyivan Patriarchate and Greek Catholic churches are outside of the holy community renders them unlawful by definition. The juxtaposition of "canonical" with "unlawful," "dissenting," and "destructive" is too convenient and suggests that the existence of the two Churches outside of the Holy Communion is both the cause and source of unlawful actions that have resulted in violent war, which has resulted in the distortion of human dignity.[63] The fundamental flaw of this perspective is not in the convenient linear pattern of legitimacy producing lawful behavior, but in the unfortunate consequence of rejection and renunciation of those outside of the Holy Communion, which is legitimized by sacramental practice and reinforced in internal ecclesial discourse. The second flaw of this approach, which is much graver, is the absolute absence of any interior examination of conscience on the part of those who claim they belong to the holy community. The assumption of legitimacy is absolute and leaves no space for the possibility of moral failure, which makes it impossible to discuss the situation objectively and perhaps even assume some responsibility for the problem. Thus, the assumption of canonical legitimacy with its yield of lawful activity is absolute: the proponents of such positions are incapable of introspective reflection on whether or not they may have contributed to the human catastrophe in Ukraine because of their absolute trust in the steadfastness of canonical legitimacy guaranteed by citizenship in Christ's holy community. Finally, anyone even vaguely familiar with the history of post-

Soviet Ukraine knows that relations among the Orthodox and between Greek Catholics and Orthodox have been strained on account of the adjustment to the ever-changing political conditions of the country. The increase in the vitriol between the groups is certainly not the only cause of civil strife, but it has contributed to enflamed tensions between groups of divergent political persuasions.

The ultimate outcome of the voluntary creation of narratives that construct a malevolent caricature of the other on the foundation of sacramental vocabulary goes beyond angry clergy and faithful in the Churches. Receiving such communication in an already emotionally charged environment of despondency, punctuated by poverty and economic struggle, is a diminishment of the basic human dignity of the other. As a sad result, the use and abuse of Byzantine sacramental vocabulary has contributed to violent conflict and bloodshed, where the violation of dignity devolves into human catastrophe.

CONCLUSION

I will conclude by proposing an approach to using the language of Byzantine sacramental theology in a way that honors the human dignity of all. I apply this approach to both the global Orthodox Church and to the conflicts and divisions within Ukraine and between Ukraine and Russia. The first matter concerns the incompatibility of the fundamental cornerstone of Byzantine sacramental identity established at baptism with the tendency to depict the other as adversarial. The language describing one's Christian identity is potent and has the capacity to become transformative, but, in contemporary discourse, it seems either to be relegated to a utopian ideal promulgated from the pulpit, at best, or it is used to distinguish an ecclesial elite within the holy community from inferior people outside of it, at worst. This results in what should be a potent sacramental character becoming thoroughly impotent. The problem does not lie in the sacramental vocabulary of baptism itself: it continues to retain the divine grace needed to transform humans into the priests, prophets, kings, and servants God has called them to become.

In postmodern religious and political discourse, a new hermeneutic for the use of such sacramental vocabulary must be developed so it can become potent on the global scale. Orthodox Christianity has simply become too familiar with the method of juxtaposition and differentiation in the era of the religious marketplace and pluralism. The contemporary identifying marker of *servant of God* needs to acquire more power and replace the faulty soldier motif so the ritual action shapes the activity of daily life. I would like to suggest that the cornerstone of sacramental identity, the Holy Communion founded on Christ, is the key to understanding the implications of being God's servants. Christians who have received the gift of belonging to the realm of God and the privilege of bearing the titles of son and daughter have a moral obligation to perform these offices in their daily lives, to transfer the voluntary ritual participation of receiving God's gift to the voluntary carrying out of God's will in the world. The global Orthodox community can restore the potency of sacramental identity by prioritizing it in liturgical formation and by privileging the positive aspects of self-identity over the temptation to identify one's self in comparison with the other. Disparaging the other in an attempt to illuminate one's own sanctity and legitimacy not only violates human dignity, but it also contradicts the Orthodox liturgical and ascetical tradition, which calls upon faithful to remember their enemies in love. To be blunt, the Christian should compare oneself with Christ so that one is ever becoming priestly and prophetic without recourse to celebrating superiority over the other in an inflated elitism.

The second approach is to adopt the inherent sacramental asceticism of the Eucharistic liturgy that demands that the Eucharistic participant remember all others of the cosmos. As I have written elsewhere, the liturgy of St. Basil depicts the holy community as describing itself as unworthy of the privilege of belonging.[64] Christians participate in the communion on the basis of God's grace; there is absolutely nothing they have done to earn or merit this privilege. The Church, praying the anaphora, says that "we have done nothing good upon the earth." One should not view this statement as self-deprecatory, but a healthy comparison of the human's modest contributions with those of God, who grants the privilege of partaking of divine life. This self-understanding of constantly striving to become good enables the community to appraise the other as one to be welcomed and embraced, and not as an adversary seeking to snatch the kingdom from the spiritual elite. The anaphora of St. Basil invites the Church to adopt a positive view of the other by remembering all possible others. Even enemies are remembered ("those who hate us" are included in the commemorations). I propose that this Eucharistic spirituality epitomized by the anaphora of St. Basil nourishes and sustains the sacramental identity established at baptism. By constantly striving to be priestly people and understanding that one can never merit the privileges of the holy community, one is able to see the other as a person worthy of remembrance in God's bosom, whether or not that other is a real adversary. In this vein, the Eucharistic spirituality of the anaphora of St. Basil is an organic completion of the sacramental identity established at baptism and has the capacity to restore the proper place of sacramental identity as the catalyst of moral action.

It might seem utopian and even unrealistic to ask pastors to adopt a paradigm shift in liturgical formation. I have here attempted to disclose the potency of baptismal sacramental identity to heal division and foment reconciliation within the world by elevating the human dignity established by the sacraments. I am convinced that hierarchical commitment to restoring the primacy of the Christian as God's servant whose work is to reconcile the world to God can awaken the senses needed to inspire Churches to perform their moral responsibility in the time of war. That moral responsibility begins with adopting a view of the other as a person created in God's image who is worthy of remembrance, as opposed to an adversary and competitor. The conversion of the Christian who honors the image of God in a former adversary can inspire the beginning of the end of the violence and war that mocks human dignity and results in catastrophe throughout much of this world. As the twenty-first century progresses, may we become joyful witnesses to a period of Christian rapprochement that becomes a model for honoring human dignity through the reception of the gift of belonging to Christ's holy community.

NOTES

1. See, for example, Leo XIII's encyclical *Rerum novarum*, http://w2.vatican.va/content/leo-xiii/en/encyclicals/documents/hf_l-xiii_enc_15051891_rerum-novarum.html.

2. Regis Duffy and Angelus Gambatese, eds., *Made in God's Image: The Catholic Vision of Human Dignity* (New York: Paulist, 1999).

3. See Antoine Arjakovsky, *The Way: Religious Thinkers of the Russian Emigration in Paris and Their Journal, 1925–1940*, trans. Jerry Ryan, ed. John Jillions and Michael Plekon, foreword by Rowan Williams (Notre Dame, IN: University of Notre Dame Press, 2013); Aidan Nichols, *Theology in the Russian Diaspora: Church, Fathers, Eucharist in Nikolai Afanasiev, 1893–1966* (Cambridge: Cambridge University Press, 1989); Antoine Kartachoff, "Orthodox Theology and the Ecumenical Movement," *The Ecumenical Review* 8, no. 1 (1955): 30–35; John A. Jillions, "Ecumenism and the Paris School of Orthodox Theology," *Theoforum* 39, no. 2 (2008): 141–74.

4. Nicholas Denysenko, *Chrismation: A Primer for Catholics* (Collegeville, MN: Liturgical Press, 2014), 96–114.

5. Michael Plekon, *Living Icons: Persons of Faith in the Eastern Church*, foreword by Lawrence Cunningham (Notre Dame, IN: University of Notre Dame Press, 2002), 59–80. For additional scholarship on St. Maria, see Plekon, "The 'Sacrament of the Brother/Sister': The Lives and Thought of Mother Maria Skobtsova and Paul Evdokimov," *St. Vladimir's Theological Quarterly* 49 (2005): 313–34; Sergei Hackel, *Pearl of Great Price: The Life of Mother Maria Skobtsova, 1891–1945* (London: Darton, Longman & Todd, 1982); Katerina Bauerova, "Emigration as Taking Roots and Giving Wings: Sergei Bulgakov, Nikolai Berdyaev and Mother Maria Skobtsova," *Communio viatorum* 4 (2012): 184–202; Natalia Ermolaev, "Modernism, Motherhood and Mariology: The Poetry and Theology of Elizaveta Skobtsova (Mother Maria)" (PhD diss., Columbia University, 2010).

6. See Nicholas Denysenko, "Retrieving a Theology of Belonging: Eucharist and Church in Postmodernity, Part 2," *Worship* 89 (2015): 22–26.

7. See "Insight in Wartime," in *Mother Maria Skobtsova: Essential Writings*, trans. Richard Pevear and Larissa Volokhonsky, intro. Jim Forest (Maryknoll, NY: Orbis, 2003), 126–39.

8. Mother Maria died after taking the place of a Jew on a train bound for the gas chamber. Her colleague Fr. Dimitry Klepinin also suffered violence for protecting Jews from Nazi persecution. See https://incommunion.org/2004/10/18/father-dimitry-klepinin/.

9. For a comprehensive treatment of the Byzantine notion that Christ re-creates the divine image and sustains it in baptism, chrismation, and Eucharist, see Denysenko, *Chrismation*.

10. Alexander Schmemann, *Of Water and the Spirit* (Crestwood, NY: St. Vladimir's Seminary Press, 1974), 82.

11. The chapter surveying the post-Soviet period of Ukrainian independence in Serhii Plokhy, *The Gates of Europe: A History of Ukraine* (New York: Basic Books, 2015), 323–36, establishes the background to the 2013 revolution.

12. Auguste Piedagnel, ed., *Cyrille de Jérusalem: Catéchèses mystagogiques*, trans. Pierre Paris, Sources chrétiennes 126 (Paris: Cerf, 1966). I cite from Piedagnel's critical edition for the texts of the mystagogical catecheses; I cite from F. L. Cross, ed., *St. Cyril of Jerusalem's Lectures on the Christian Sacraments* (Crestwood, NY: St. Vladimir's Seminary Press, 1995), for the sole citation from the Greek text of the procatechesis.

13. In Cross, ed., *St. Cyril of Jerusalem's Lectures*, 2.

14. Ibid.

15. In Piedagnel, ed., *Cyrille de Jérusalem: Catéchèses mystagogiques*, 114.

16. Ibid., 116.

17. Ibid., 120.

18. Ibid., 128.

19. Ibid., 136.

20. Ibid.

21. When Holy Communion is distributed in the Byzantine rite, there are always some children who refuse participation for some reason.

22. Denysenko, *Chrismation*, 118–39.

23. *L'Eucologio Barberini gr. 336*, 2nd ed., ed. Stefano Parenti and E. Velkovska, Bibliotheca Ephemerides liturgicae, subsidia 80, ed. A. M. Triacca and A. Pistoia (Rome: Edizioni liturgiche, 2000), number 141, 143 (my translation). Also see Denysenko, *Chrismation*, 6–7.

24. For the translation of the prayer for the consecration of chrism in the Gelasian sacramentary, see E. C. Whitaker, *Documents of the Baptismal Liturgy*, ed. Maxwell Johnson (Collegeville, MN: Liturgical Press, 2003), 212–43. See Paul Meyendorff's citation of Aphraat's *Demonstrations* in Meyendorff, *The Anointing of the Sick* (Crestwood, NY: St. Vladimir's Seminary Press, 2009), 39.

25. John Chrysostom, "Baptismal Homily no. 3:5," in *Huit catéchèses baptismales inédites*, ed. and trans. A. Wenger, Sources chrétiennes 50 (Paris: Cerf, 1957), 153.

26. See the English text for the funeral of the dead at https://web.archive.org/web/20160304025913/http://www.anastasis.org.uk/funeral.htm.

27. The office of baptism at https://web.archive.org/web/20160305185715/http://anastasis.org.uk/baptism.htm.

28. See the exorcisms performed during the first portion of the office of baptism in ibid.

29. Ibid.

30. Ibid.

31. The covenant with Christ is forged following the utter rejection of Satan; the candidate turns around, professes unity with Christ three times, and bows down before Christ.

32. The text asks that the waters be freed of evil presence: "We pray you, Lord, let all airy and invisible spectres withdraw from us, and do not let a demon of darkness hide itself in this water, and do not let an evil spirit, bringing darkening of thoughts and disturbance of mind, go down into it with the one who is being baptized" (office of baptism).

33. Miguel Arranz, "Évolution des rites d'incorporation et de réadmission dans l'Église selon l'Euchologe byzantine," in *Gestes et paroles dans les diverses familles liturgiques: Conferences Saint-Serge XXIVe semaine d'etudes liturgiques, 1977*, ed. A. Postoia and A. Triacca, Bibliotheca Ephemerides Liturgicae Subsidia 14 (Rome: Centro Liturgico Vincenziano, 1978), 75.

34. *The Great Book of Needs*, expanded and supplemented, vol. 1, *The Holy Mysteries*, trans. St. Tikhon's Monastery (South Canaan, PA: St. Tikhon's Seminary Press, 1998), 62–64.

35. Ibid., 73.

36. Ibid., 75.

37. Ibid., 76.

38. Plokhy, *The Gates of Europe*, 32–37.

39. Ibid., 23–35.

40. Ibid., 37.

41. Ibid., 44–48.

42. Ibid., 63.

43. Ibid., 86–90.

44. Ibid., 86–87.

45. For the background on this matter, see the historical study of Ihor Mončak, *Florentine Ecumenism in the Kyivan Church: The Theology of Ecumenism Applied to the Individual Church of Kyiv* (Rome: Ukrainian Catholic University in the name of Pope Clement, 1987).

46. See Frank E. Sysyn, "The Formation of Modern Ukrainian Religious Culture: The Sixteenth and Seventeenth Centuries," in *Religion and Nation in Modern Ukraine*, ed. Serhii Plokhy and Frank E. Sysyn (Edmonton and Toronto: Canadian Institute of Ukrainian Studies Press, 2003), 13–16. Also see Plokhy, *The Gates of Europe*, 91–92.

47. Orest Subtelny, *Ukraine: A History*, 4th ed. (Toronto: University of Toronto, 2009), 211.

48. See the comprehensive treatment by Barbara Skinner, *The Western Front of the Eastern Church: Uniate and Orthodox Conflict in 18th-Century Poland, Ukraine, Belarus, and Russia* (DeKalb: Northern Illinois University Press, 2009).

49. Metropolitan Evlogy, *My Life's Journey: The Memoirs of Metropolitan Evlogy*, part 1, trans. Alexander Lisenko, intro. Thomas Hopko (Crestwood, NY: St. Vladimir's Seminary Press, 2014), 109–17.

50. Bohdan Bociurkiw, *The Ukrainian Greek Catholic Church and the Soviet State (1939–1950)* (Edmonton and Toronto: Canadian Institute of Ukrainian Studies, 1996).

51. Plokhy, *The Gates of Europe*, 280–96.

52. Based on an archival paper of Bohdan Bociurkiw titled "The Russian Orthodox Church in Ukraine, 1961–79," from the Bohdan Bociurkiw Memorial Library, University of Alberta, in Edmonton.

53. Subtelny, *Ukraine: A History*, 578–79.

54. See Victor Zhivov, "The Question of Ecclesiastical Jurisdiction in Russian-Ukrainian Relations (Seventeenth and Early Eighteenth Centuries)," in *Culture, Nation, and Identity: The Ukrainian-Russian Encounter, 1600–1945*, ed. Andreas Kappeler, Zenon E. Kohut, Frank E. Sysyn, and Mark von Hagen (Edmonton and Toronto: Canadian Institute of Ukrainian Studies, 2003), 1–18. Also see James Cunningham, *A Vanquished Hope: The Movement for Church Renewal in Russia, 1905–1906* (Crestwood, NY: St. Vladimir's Seminary Press, 1981), 23–30, and Zenon Kohut, *Making Ukraine: Studies on Political Culture, Historical Narrative, and Identity*, foreword by Frank Sysyn (Edmonton: Canadian Institute of Ukrainian Studies, 2011), 135–50.

55. The dispute over 1686 erupted into a crisis when the Patriarchate of Constantinople annulled the right of Moscow to ordain the metropolitan of Kyiv. On October 11, 2018, Constantinople restored its jurisdiction over the Church in Ukraine. Moscow severed communion with Constantinople soon afterwards. Constantinople granted autocephaly (independence) to the Orthodox Church of Ukraine on January 6, 2019.

56. See Arseny Zinchenko, *Визволитися вірою: життя і діяння Митрополита Василя Липківського* (*Liberation through Faith: The Life and Activities of Metropolitan Vasyl Lypkivsky*) (Kyiv: Dnipro, 1997), 83–100.

57. Hyacinthe Destivelle, *The Moscow Council (1917–1918): The Creation of the Conciliar Institutions of the Russian Orthodox Church*, ed. Michael Plekon and Vitaly Permiakov, trans. Jerry Ryan, foreword by Metropolitan Hilarion (Alfeyev) (Notre Dame, IN: University of Notre Dame Press, 2015), 44.

58. See Ivan Wlasowsky, *Нарис Історії Української Церкви*, vol. 4, XX ст., 2nd ed. (New York: UAOC, 1990), 43–44. Also see Metropolitan Feodosij (Protsiuk), *Обособленческие движение в Православной Церкви на Украине* (Moscow: Krutyskyj Podvoria, 2004), 119.

59. This period witnesses to numerous instances of correspondence between the Ukrainian group and the bishops under Moscow. Readers should note that both sides frequently attempted to reconcile with the other in good will, but were unable to reach agreement on the fundamental issue at stake: the absolute independence of the Ukrainian Church from Moscow. Note that this was the first of three UAOCs to emerge in Ukraine through the course of the twentieth century.

60. Osyp Zinkewich and Oleksander Voronyn, eds., *Мартирологія Українських Церков*, vol. 1, *Українська Православна Церква* (Baltimore: Smoloskyp Publishers, 1987), 662–66.

61. "Orthodox Churches under Threat in Ukraine," Religious Information Service of Ukraine, http://risu.org.ua/en/index/all_news/orthodox/orthodox_world/62270/.

62. "Metropolitan Hilarion Alfeyev: Actions of the Uniates Have Caused Great Damage Not Only to Ukraine and Her Citizens, but Also to the Orthodox-Catholic Dialogue," Russian Orthodox Church Department for External Church Relations, https://mospat.ru/en/2014/06/03/news103524/.

63. My examples draw from the Moscow Patriarchate; the counternarratives of the KP and UGCC occasionally employ the same polemical strategy using different words.

64. Denysenko, "Retrieving a Theology of Belonging . . . Part 2," 27–37.

fifteen

DIGNITY AND CONFLICT

Racial Violence

Terrence L. Johnson

Human dignity has always been a guiding principle in African American social justice movements. Racial uplift ideology and the Talented Tenth are two fine examples of African American political traditions that recognized human dignity as distinct from the achievement of liberty or voting rights. In this chapter I attempt to make explicit human dignity's distinct political-aesthetic role in shaping African American politics and political thought, namely, through the idea of an African American moral humanism.

One of the most explicit examples of African American moral humanism can be found within the Black Lives Matter movement (BLM). Although BLM founders Opal Tometi, Patrisse Cullors, and Alicia Garza do not explicitly turn to African American religious rhetoric or moral tropes, their writings and statements on "dignity," "restorative justice," and affirmation of the human worth of "Black queer and trans folk" characterize what Womanist ethicist Katie Cannon calls the "moral wisdom" of African American women who appeal to a set of sociocultural norms that emerge from and sit in tension with Afro-Christianity and the non-Christian traditions, such as hoodoo, conjure, and divination. "The moral wisdom that exists in the Black community is extremely useful in defying oppressive rules or standards of 'law and order' that unjustly degrade Blacks in the society. It helps Blacks purge themselves of self-hate, thus asserting their own validity."[1] BLM's meetings and public protests often integrate African American spirituals and religious-oriented ceremonies, according to researcher Hebah Farrag, within debates on justice and state violence to remind the community of the need to incorporate multidimensional responses to antiblack racism. Weaving together "religious" and political responses to oppression is a reminder of black religion's role in shaping black political movements in the United States. To be sure, contemporary debates over black religion's influence on BLM demonstrate the political viability, however weak, of African American religions in social justice movements, such as BLM. As I shall demonstrate, BLM reflects the values and principles of a long-standing tradition I call "African American moral humanism."

This chapter is organized as follows. First, I analyze white violence against African Americans, from 16th Street Baptist Church bombing in Birmingham, Alabama, in 1963 to current examples of racial violence and the emergence of the BLM. Second, I examine the characterizations of human dignity in the writings of Anna Julia Cooper, an exemplary social critic whose writings provide a historical context for understanding human dignity within African American religion and religious cultural criticism. Third, I sketch out the political uses of human dignity within two fundamentally distinct, but overlapping traditions: Womanist thought and African American religious cultural criticism. Specifically, I will focus on Delores Williams's category of the wilderness and Victor Anderson's reformulation of the grotesque as markers that fundamentally inform my development of African American moral humanism in general and the politico-aesthetic dimension of human dignity in particular. Fourth, I discuss the politico-aesthetic dimension of human dignity. Lastly, I explain how African American moral humanism informs contemporary African American political thought.

An analysis of human dignity will illuminate the deeply interwoven role of moral humanism within African American religion and political thought. What I call African American moral humanism reflects the constant but shifting moral perspectives that inform black religious subjectivity and influence political imaginations within black life. The moral humanism characterized here corresponds to the description developed by Cornel West in *Prophesy Deliverance!* As he describes it, the humanist perspective within black religion "acknowledges the complex interplay between practicality and ideology, electoral politics and structural social change."[2] The moral humanism I am developing is framed by the tension between black bodies and political liberalism. This tension exposes the degree to which ideal liberalism brackets, ignores, and isolates the comprehensive commitments that our *color-blind* liberal philosophy appeals to in its efforts to adjudicate social problems fairly. In other words, political liberalism promotes color-blind policies to reduce discriminatory behavior and practices. The move, however, leads to unintended political consequences:

ignoring the ways public culture and moral beliefs construct blacks and their bodies as lacking innocence and humanity and therefore in need of subjugation, imprisonment, and death.

Many will disagree with my argument. For I imagine Womanist thought and African American cultural religious criticism as moral and political traditions that play a major role in developing an African American humanist project that sits alongside the humanisms outlined by William R. Jones, Cornel West, Anthony Pinn, and Melanie Harris.[3] This hermeneutical shift points to non-Christian traditions within black life that establish the epistemic groundwork for the emergence of BLM. Indeed, according to Harris, humanism within Womanist thought privileges "the theo-ethical perspectives, communal and social actions of black women and black women foremothers" in an effort to understand more deeply the epistemic shifts black women have employed in African American religion, ethics, and political discourses.[4] The moral framework established by Harris and others sets the stage for exploring more deeply African American moral humanism within black politics and political thought.

I will not spend much time examining whether the retrieval of human dignity is successful in developing new approaches for dismantling structural racism. Instead, I will turn inward, and from within the veil of blackness examine the meaning and implications of this shift on the moral and religious dimensions of black politics and political thought. This is not a form of navel-gazing, or an attempt to imagine an unobstructed black definition of human dignity. It is a strategy of sorts—a reconfiguration and recentering of African American intellectual thought in an effort to disrupt, dismantle, and deconstruct how *we*, in the broadest sense of the term, conceptualize and construct blackness in public life. This strategy is without a particular goal, other than to imagine alternative moral and political paradigms, however limited they might be, for expanding our competing and overlapping views of human dignity.

FROM BIRMINGHAM TO BLACK LIVES MATTER: RACIAL VIOLENCE AND THREATS TO DIGNITY

Less than a month after the Rev. Dr. Martin Luther King Jr.'s riveting "I Have a Dream" speech at the March on Washington in 1963, the dreamer's vision of social justice and racial harmony was subdued by white violence against blacks in Birmingham, Alabama. The 16th Street Baptist Church was nearly split in half Sunday, September 15, 1963, by a bomb left near the side entrance of the church. Amidst the rubble, shattered stain-glass windows, and a decapitated crucifix were four slain black girls, all wearing white dresses: Denise McNair, Carole Robertson, Addie Mae Collins, and Cynthia Wesley.[5]

In his eulogy at the funeral of three of the four girls, Reverend King called the bombing one of the most "vicious and tragic crimes ever perpetrated against humanity."[6] Though the girls died nobly, King proclaimed, the bombing symbolized the tragic sense of black life. The girls, like so many other blacks in slavery and during segregation, King suggested, had been robbed of their innocence, not because of haste, poor judgment, or accident but because of a shifting but sustained belief in the innate inferiority of black people.[7] Within this cultural narrative, whites could justify the unconscionable slaughter of African Americans without fear of public or divine retribution.

King made every effort in his eulogy to reassemble the broken limbs of the dead, conjuring from the carnage an innocence denied to them in life. He reminded the grieving audience of the beauty, "dignity," and human "worth" of the slaughtered girls. "These children—unoffending, innocent, and beautiful—[are] . . . martyred heroines of a holy crusade for freedom and human dignity."[8] The dreamer lifted the lingering veil of affliction, anger, and anguish from among the parishioners, if only momentarily, to bear witness to Afro-Christianity's belief in divine justice, even as violence engulfed a nation already simmering in a racial war over segregation and the expansion of political rights. The outcry over the church bombing was a sign of the increasing momentum of the civil rights movement. These girls, Denise, Carole, Addie Mae, and Cynthia, King reminded the audience, did not die in vain. "The [spilled] blood of these innocent girls may cause the whole citizenry of Birmingham to transform the negative extremes of a dark past into the positive extremes of a bright future. Indeed, this tragic event may cause the white South to come to terms with its conscience."[9] Echoing the faith of the Negro spirituals and Afro-Christianity's belief in God's promise to stand with the oppressed, King implored his audience to embrace black innocence, beauty, and human dignity as the tools needed to transform the "conscience" of white southerners and the nation. This affirmation of human dignity stood in direct opposition to the nation's moral doctrine of black inferiority.

The 16th Street Baptist Church bombing was a grim reminder of the random and ongoing violence against blacks in an antiblack society. Though many liberal white Christians and Jews joined in solidarity with blacks to denounce the church bombing, many national and local leaders characterized the attack as an isolated incident committed by lone thugs and brutes. James Baldwin took a different position. He described the bombing as reflecting the will of the "people who rule the State."[10] The bombers, as did the Ku Klux Klan, stood in union with the moral and political conscience of far too many legislators, government officials, and businessmen. This was another reminder of the nation's racial code, the codification of black subjugation within the ethos and ethics of American democracy. It was, indeed, an indication of how law, public culture, and moral beliefs coalesced to fuel antiblack racism and condone violence against innocent black bodies. Baldwin said:

> A mob cannot afford to doubt: that the Jews killed Christ or that niggers want to rape their sisters or that anyone who fails to make it in the land of the free and the home of the brave deserves to be wretched. But these ideas do not come from the mob. The idea of black persons as property, for example, does not come from the mob. It is not a spontaneous idea. It does not come from the people, who knew better, who thought nothing of intermarriage until they were penalized for it: this idea comes from the architects of the American State. These architects decided that the concept of Property was more important—more real—than the possibilities of the human being.[11]

Baldwin contextualizes white violence against African Americans in three important ways: first, he links racial violence to the nation's long history of anti-Semitism; second, he points to the calculated efforts to reinforce in public culture the racist trope of the hypersexualized black man who longs to rape white women as an attempt to strike fear among whites; lastly, he illustrates how the Protestant work ethic is retrieved to hold African Americans blameworthy for their own economic and political subjugation. Baldwin's argument is striking: beliefs in black inferiority were created and reproduced through conceptual schemes, moral imaginations, and religious doctrines that aligned with the nation's normative political and economic principles. Such principles, in far too many instances, cultivated and reinforced in public life and culture views of blacks as disposable and malignant. Within this context, racial violence was normalized and deemed acceptable by those who believed sincerely in black inferiority and white (male) superiority.

The ongoing racial violence against blacks in the United States is akin to what Anthony Pinn calls in *Terror and Triumph* a "ritual of reference," a "repeated, systematic activity conducted in carefully selected locations that is intended to reinforce the enslaved's status as object."[12] The objectification of black bodies, I might add, is symbolic and material as it intentionally and without design severs, dismantles, mutilates, and often murders blacks in an effort to maintain white domination. Hortense Spillers characterizes the ritualization of violence against black bodies rather poignantly. The black body, she argues, is seized "by externally imposed meanings and uses: (1) the captive body becomes the source of an irresistible, destructive sensuality; (2) at the same time—in stunning contradiction—the captive body reduces to a thing, becoming *being for* the captor."[13] The bodies of the slain girls are tied to a bigger social conundrum. On the one hand, the bodies are a reminder of the absence of humanity within black women's bodies; on the other hand, they represent what Spillers calls "a common historical ground" on which the New World emerges: the subjugation and exploitation of black bodies for political, economic, and moral reasons. To return to this history, especially within King's eulogy, is to begin the messy work of confronting the nation's senseless history of murdering African Americans without cause or reason. Once again, we are reminded, as Toni Morrison writes in *Beloved*, that the past is never dead—only erased from our visibility but always lingering in our discourses, signs, symbols, and narratives. King's eulogy, like Morrison's novel, exposes the nameless faces and narratives we too often choose to ignore or bury.

More than half a century following the 16th Street Baptist Church bombing, white violence against African Americans continues to plague a nation whose racist history many believed was exonerated by the election of its first African American president in 2008. From the deaths of Trayvon Martin (2012) and Jordan Davis (2012) to the Charleston, South Carolina, massacre at Mother Emmanuel AME Church (2015) to the police shootings and deaths of Michael Brown (2014), Eric Garner (2014), Tamir Rice (2014), and Sandra Bland (2015), the nation is once again witnessing an unprecedented number of racially motivated killings of African Americans. The resurgence of violence against African Americans, most notably by police officers, is a glaring reminder that we live in what acclaimed law professor Michelle Alexander calls the "new Jim Crow." This is a political and economic system framed by a language of liberty, equality, and equal opportunity that relies on a "new racial caste system" to justify legal discrimination against mostly black and brown men and women. This racial caste is evident in the criminal justice system and the disproportionate number of African Americans and Latinx incarcerated in the

United States.[14] Christian ethicist Barbara Mitchell believes a fundamental moral dimension in politics—and implicitly within the racial caste—remains unaddressed: the "unhealed" racial wounds from the trauma of white supremacist beliefs and practices. "Full civil and political rights and economic opportunities are crucial for the advancement of African Americans. However, these material assets do not, in the final analysis, heal the wound that remains such a painful part of the story of the black presence in America."[15] Psychic wounds are as potent as political and economic hardships, especially when subjugation and violence are deemed appropriate by moral beliefs that correspond to national interests. To this end, racism is a moral *and* political problem. Mitchell reinvokes human dignity as a necessary moral and political category that deserves sustained attention in twenty-first-century debates on race and justice as white violence against blacks reemerges.

This brings me to one of my central points in my analysis of an African American moral humanism: unlike the political vocabulary framing the civil rights movement, which employed human dignity as an extension of political rights, BLM defines human dignity not as a continuation of political rights but as a distinct political, aesthetic, and moral category that must be explored and embraced more explicitly and wholeheartedly in politics and political theory. Mitchell anticipates this argument in *Black Abolitionism*, arguing that "the failure to acknowledge the full humanity of blacks has fostered an undercurrent of dissatisfaction that manifests itself not only in the perpetually disaffected underclass of blacks but even in the corporate halls and the academy."[16] Prolonged attention to human dignity provides an opportunity for new scholarly direction in the study of African American politics and political thought as it expands the boundaries of the political and creates the conceptual space to examine the moral and religious dimensions of political thought.

BLM shifts the meaning and use of human dignity in three critical ways: first, it detangles human dignity from the private sphere of individual morality; second, the movement reclaims the category without draping it in deeply religious or Afro-Christian motifs and metaphors that locate human dignity as an extension of *imago Dei*; third, human dignity is reconfigured into a politico-aesthetic category.

What we are witnessing within BLM's political vocabulary is as significant as the late stages within the civil rights movement when young organizers created the Student Nonviolent Coordinating Committee, which, many believe, fundamentally overhauled African American politics in the late 1960s. Similarly, BLM is changing the tone and content of political debates by forcing mainline African American political leaders, clergy, and scholars to tackle issues often left off the table in traditional debates on voting rights and urban renewal: the criminal justice system, sexuality, gender, queer, transgender, and disability concerns. In fact, BLM advocates four major guiding principles: "diversity," "restorative justice," "globalism," and "collectivism." Keeanga-Yamahtta Taylor writes in *From #BLACKLIVESMATTER to Black Liberation*, "Not only do the 'new guard's' politics stand in sharp contrast to those of the 'old guard' but so does their approach to organizing. Beyond being led by women, the new guard is decentralized and is largely organizing the movement through social media."[17] The structures in and through which BLM organizes social protest and the attention to black bodies and their criminal and social-sexual dysfunctions establish within BLM's platform an organic interest in and understanding of the political value of human dignity and worth. How does this resonate with African American religious cultural criticism?

MAPPING RIGHTS AND HUMAN DIGNITY IN AFRICAN AMERICAN RELIGIOUS CULTURAL CRITICISMS

Religious cultural criticism dates back to the literature and oral traditions of African slaves in the South. Public intellectuals and social critics ranging from Anna Julia Cooper and Frederick Douglass to Martin Luther King Jr. and Angela Davis have employed religion and moral tropes to denounce slavery and its legacy in America. As Pinn asserts:

> Slavery's power lies in the eradication of Africans as subjects and the manner in which the enslaved African is re-created in the context of the New World as an object, depersonalized, a nonbeing. As such, enslaved Africans occupied a strange space in that they existed outside the recognized boundaries of human community while also being a necessary part of the same community—as a workforce and as the reality against which whiteness was defined.[18]

In postslavery America, the white/black binary deepened during Jim Crow as the social and cultural norms reinscribed black inferiority and white superiority and renewed efforts to cement legalized segregation. In fact, Pinn asserts, institutional efforts to marginalize blacks reflected a deep preoccupation with the black body as representing "something," though clearly not human or humanity.

Anna Julia Cooper is an exemplary model for exploring black bodies in public life because she employed human dignity and worth as tropes to guide her political thinking and moral imaginations. Though deeply rooted in a moral vocabulary dripping in Victorian sensibilities and the politics of respectability, she nonetheless challenged the parochial constructions of race and gender by speaking boldly of the intersectionality of gender, class, and race. Not only did she expose in her writings the commodification of black women's bodies, but Cooper also grappled with moral doctrines of black inferiority that were inscribed in what she called the "Negro question." This question served as a heuristic tool for examining the "ethics" of the codes, symbols, and habits that simultaneously converged to dehumanize and to liberate blacks.

In her most widely read and discussed work, *A Voice from the South*, Cooper weaved together an insightful autobiographical and cultural analysis of the political and social challenges facing African American women and families at the turn of the twentieth century. Vivian May describes Cooper's prose as "transgressive" in its ability to employ modes of writing that "are normatively opposed—one perceived to be the mark of narrow and definitively biased reflection, the other the sign of neutral, objective, and universal knowing. Not only does Cooper reject a false divide between head and heart and self and other, but she repeatedly demonstrates how the supposed impartiality of the third person is often used as a mask to hide both the bias and the locatedness of the powerful, who employ the third person to present themselves, erroneously, as neutral observers of reality untainted by identity, emotions, or social location."[19] Cooper's prose sheds some light on the content of her analysis insofar as she examined race and gender dialectically, exposing their ontological social characterizations in an effort to undermine their political and ethical potency.

By inserting competing modes of writing and thinking, Cooper revealed the limits of exploring social content without examining the social contexts from which it emerged. For instance, in her reflections on the human dignity and the worth of women, Cooper asserted an unusually compelling argument in light of the epistemic terrain she operates in: moral agents are encumbered by the traditions, habits, and customs of their ancestors. Indeed, we are born into histories we did not create, and any political, economic, or social assessment of an individual or group requires some heavy lifting beyond the scrutiny of the immediate social context. "In order to reform a man, you must begin with his great grandmother," Cooper wrote.[20] Contemporary cultural critics could too easily dismiss Cooper's argument if they were unaware of her creative prose and the historical circumstances shaping her. Cooper was writing during a time when philanthropic foundations were studying "Negro problems" and trying to use data to understand the social, political, and economic issues facing blacks. W. E. B. Du Bois's *The Philadelphia Negro*, published in 1899, nearly seven years after the publication of *A Voice from the South*, inaugurates what would become a privately funded sociological study to "understand" Negro problems. I agree with May's argument that Cooper's writings were intended to disrupt the use of the objective science that was invoked to support beliefs in black criminality, inferiority, and inhumanity. Cooper echoed this point in her work: "Weaknesses and malformations, which today are attributable to a vicious schoolmaster and a pernicious system, will a century hence be rightly regarded as proofs of innate corruptness and radical incurability."[21] Cooper asserted an argument many have credited to Du Bois: the idea that social circumstances do not reflect the cultural, moral, or philosophical values of a people. In far too many instances, Cooper suggested, society assumed that impoverishment and impoverished economic circumstances were tied to a group's humanity and individual's self-worth.

In *A Voice from the South*, for instance, Cooper explicitly identified moral "heroism" and "moral heroes of humanity" as fundamental models needed to promote the intrinsic value and worth within every human being. Indeed, Cooper wrote, "He must *believe* in the infinite possibilities of devoted self-sacrifice and in the eternal grandeur of a human idea heroically espoused."[22] Cooper reclaimed moral heroism as a way to characterize the intrinsic value and "infinite possibilities of an individual soul," of every moral agent's ability, I suggest, to transgress social boundaries.[23] Cooper's analysis underscored the political usefulness of human worth and dignity without relying on God-talk to justify the inherent value of blacks and black bodies. These are the fundamental components of African American moral humanism and are also retrieved, in varying degrees, in Womanism and African American religious cultural criticism.

WOMANISM AND WILDERNESS EXPERIENCE

Cooper sets the groundwork for introducing Womanism into the conversation on African American moral humanism and the politico-ethical dimension of human dignity. Womanist thought develops the major themes employed by black women to imagine, describe, and portray their understanding of and responses to the social context under consideration. According to ethicist Melanie Harris, Womanism privileges the "theological voices and theo-ethical reflections of black women" in an attempt to provide a richer account of theological and moral inquiry in black life.[24] To this end, Womanism interrogates the religious subjectivity of black women's political imagination and activism. Without this narrative, we too easily dismiss the religious influence in black politics.

Delores Williams's characterization of Womanism is a case in point. She frames human dignity as a political category and underscores the degree to which political resistance against state violence may not necessarily lead to immediate liberation. Instead, freedom manifests itself in the struggle to obtain human dignity. Womanism, unlike its predecessor, black theology of liberation, implicitly distinguishes rights from freedom. Both are necessary and wanted, but Womanism recognizes the importance of securing human dignity within a social context of black subjugation and exploitation. Indeed, Womanism, which emerged from the margins of scholarly studies within African American religious thought, anticipated the hermeneutical shift and development we are currently witnessing in BLM.

Womanist examinations of theology and literature opened the way for a multidimensional exploration into the academic study of black women in the United States and African diaspora. Williams inaugurates the discipline of Womanist thought in her groundbreaking work *Sisters in the Wilderness.* As Harry Singleton describes it, Williams "calls for a reconceptualization of the meaning of the Exodus narrative not only in socio-political terms but also in moral terms, i.e., God sanctioning Hebrew violence as a vehicle for liberation."[25] Part of Williams's reconceptualization involves expanding the epistemic terrain on which we examine black religion. Dianne Stewart calls this shift an effort to create an analysis of "wholeness" within the academic study of black women in particular and African American religions in general: "Womanist theological method involves a multidimensional analysis of oppression, a religiocultural analysis, a sociopolitical analysis of wholeness, and bifocal analysis."[26] An example of Williams's attempt to incorporate an analysis of wholeness is within the conceptual model of the wilderness.

From the onset of slavery and into the antebellum period, black women found within the wilderness narrative, for instance, a source of strength and a reflection of their own human dignity and worth. As Williams writes in her groundbreaking work, the wilderness narrative tells the story of an Egyptian named Hagar, a pregnant runaway slave in search of refuge from an abusive slaveowner. In the wilderness, a "risk-taking faith" emerged within Hagar, and, according to Williams, it manifested itself when Hagar, without doctrinal or ecclesiastical permission, named the God she met in the isolated space: "Thus we can speak of Hagar and many African American women as sisters in the wilderness struggling for life, and by the help of their God coming to terms with situations that have destructive potential."[27] The wilderness, unlike accounts in colonial America that depicted it as hostile and in need of domination, represented for slaves a place of spiritual meaning and promise.

The wilderness narrative provides two important resources for Afro-Christianity: first, it represented a place where religion was pursued and embraced as a source for establishing a relationship with Jesus. If persistent, women and men in the wilderness would meet Jesus and receive from him the spiritual and physical strength to battle the racist social world standing outside the wilderness. Second, the wilderness experience was transformative as it created the context for reflection and established a relationship between "Jesus and slave" that in turn fostered the necessary "healing" and subsequent "conversion of the slave's more secular bent to a thoroughly religious bent."[28] This interior religious revival provided the courage and strength to return *home*, to the slave community, and to fight against injustice.

The wilderness experience, according to Williams, is where "destruction," "impeding death," and "God" all stand with outstretched hands awaiting those courageous enough to persevere and remain hopeful when it is far easier to sit in nihilistic pessimism than to imagine freedom. As Williams notes, the wilderness signifies "a near-destruction situation in which God gives personal direction to the believer and thereby helps her make a way out of what she thought was no way."[29] The wilderness narrative, long overlooked by black theologians, resonates with Williams because it gives an account of how women and men, in particular Hagar and her son Ishmael, can find meaning, dignity, and worth while in bondage or in dire social circumstances. Williams's account of the wilderness is by no means an attempt to justify suffering, or even to call it redemptive. Rather, the wilderness narrative focuses on survival and the techniques developed to promote individual and group well-being and assure a people that, according to Williams, destruction and death cannot materialize in isolation from God. This does not mean God condones or employs dread and suffering to entice her followers; instead, I believe, the wilderness is a reminder of the agency we possess even in dire situations. God or an angel appearing in the wilderness, to be sure, is a symbol of the strength within every human being to face the circumstances at hand with courage. Indeed, within the wilderness model, one may never experience liberty or political equality, but one is always capable of embodying and exerting freedom.

Williams's reconfiguration of the wilderness narrative is rather generative for reflecting on the legacy of slave religion and its religious strivings. Alongside Cooper's insistence on framing justice in the context of ethics and ethical duties, the wilderness serves as a model for imagining African American moral wisdom as a dialogical exchange between text and author/subject. Like the wilderness account, African American moral wisdom is not concerned with discovering the right answers; rather, it is designed to cultivate a meaningful, creative, and disruptive exchange in an effort to uncover what was hidden. As one can see, there is a direct link between Womanism and BLM. Indeed, Womanism underscores the fundamental politico-aesthetic dimensions of BLM's platform. For instance BLM privileges queer and trans folk, the disabled, and undocumented workers in an effort to reimagine and transgress "the narrow nationalism that can be prevalent within Black communities, which merely call on Black people to love Black, live Black and buy Black, keeping straight [cisgender] Black men in the front of the movement while our sisters, queer and trans and disabled folk take up roles in the background or not at all."[30] BLM's platform also calls for renewed efforts to "nurture the beloved community" and "practice empathy" as individuals "acknowledge" and "affirm" difference among those in the struggle to achieve freedom and human dignity.

GROTESQUE AND RACIAL APOLOGETICS

Victor Anderson's *Beyond Ontological Blackness* is one of the most profound and compelling reflections on black theology of liberation published in recent decades. Among his many concerns is the degree to which African American religious criticisms remain preoccupied with creating a "counterdiscourse" to what he calls categorical racism. As Anderson describes it: "Categorical racism and white racial ideology justified the racial consciousness of the modern age by providing rhetorical conditions for positively differentiating the European cultural genius from others."[31] This racial consciousness is established by a white/black binary, which seems to create for Anderson an unpromising account of race and racial categories.

As he sees it, the preoccupation with validating black humanity and intellectual traditions compelled many African American theologians and historians to turn to archives, slave narratives, writings, and social protest in an effort to establish a coherent and compelling account of African American intellectual traditions. This move served two primary purposes: first, to create an epistemic platform from which to establish black thought; and second, to ignite a cultural and intellectual movement based on validating black aesthetics and human dignity. This doubleness within African American religion is unusual in the context of Western modernity, because Europeans were more often than not given the luxury of exploring the realm of ideas without the cultural imperative to justify European existence and humanity. Though noble, Anderson asserts, this counterdiscourse within African American religion in general and black liberation theology in particular is counterproductive because it has limited the epistemic framework for imagining black life to a narrow black/white binary, which envisioned blacks as always struggling to overcome white racism and hegemony.

In far too many instances, Anderson argues, African American religious scholarship at the turn of the twentieth century was shaped and informed by "racial apologetics." According to Anderson, "it is an apologetic that sought to ameliorate blacks' alienation from the progressive democratic movements of Western culture, politics, aesthetics, philosophy, and morals."[32] Racial apologetics created the conditions for the emergence of a "black heroic genius," a figure reclaimed to explain the historical significance of black thought in the Western world. But it had unintentional consequences. Instead of reflecting the breadth of intellectual thought among the formerly enslaved, it reinscribed parochial models of black masculinity and made universal masculinist ideas of culture, religion, and identity.

Following in the tradition of Du Bois's tragic soul-life and Cornel West's tragic-comic sensibility, Anderson turns to the black literary tradition for resources that might eclipse black/white models of racialization.[33] Anderson wants to displace the political, upset its stronghold on black life, and bury the heroic in an effort to offer a new rendering of blackness in ways that "resist eclipsing individuality under collectivity." He's right. But this, too, is the problem: whether or not blacks can emerge, ever, as individuals distinct from or at least in tension with the collective black is possibly unlikely in the current moment. The issue Anderson wants to avoid—conceptualizing blacks as a problem people—sits at the very heart of the new Jim Crow era: blacks are condemned to a violent death by virtue of their blackness.

Anderson's criticism leaves African American religions facing a number of concerns. On the one hand, Anderson imagines blackness as a category in need of critical and robust interrogation. He does not assume the "black" possesses inherent intellectual "second-sight" to think in tension with the overly generalized categories of race, gender, and sexuality. This is his major point of contention with traditions such as Womanist thought: "Because black life is fundamentally determined by black suffering and resistance to whiteness (the power of nonbeing), black existence is without the possibility of transcendence from the blackness that whiteness created."[34] Without the employment of a radical hermeneutics of suspicion, Womanist's categories such as the wilderness may reinforce the kind of racial rigidity Anderson rejects. On the other hand, Womanist thought challenges the appropriateness of liberation theology in light of the continued suffering of black women. Instead, it focuses on the competing and overlapping ways black women survive within the wilderness.

Racial apologetics and the subsequent rise of the black heroic genius undermine, Anderson argues, African American intellectual traditions. "It subjugates the creative, expressive activities of blacks (whether in performance arts or literature) under the symbolism of black heroic genius . . . It makes race identity a totality that subordinates and orders internal differences among blacks, so that gender, social standing, and sexual orientations are secondary to racial identity."[35] Anderson understands why previous generations of theological and religious intellectuals, writers, and artists developed ways to justify black existence and humanity. But this move privileges a racial identity that reflects a dualism and objectification unhelpful for exploring the nuances of black life. The result: ontological blackness.

Ontological blackness is far too static and does not reflect the richness of black life. He turns to the grotesque as a way to lay claim to the richness and complexity of black life. Anderson reformulates Nietzsche's notion of the grotesque as a way to introduce a more complicated understanding of black traditions and religious philosophies and to disrupt the degree to which religious critics define culture as "ultimate or total." He defines the grotesque as "a controlling unit idea or benchmark" that is "open to the creative interplay of an undifferentiated unity of experience that comes into focus only by the activity of squeezing the eye."[36]

The grotesque employs four important frameworks for expanding philosophical reflections in general and developing African American moral humanism in particular. First, the grotesque does not attempt to resolve racial pain or suffering. Instead, it exposes the conversations about those issues as ways to expand the debate on race. Anderson says the grotesque "recovers and leaves unresolved prior and basic sensibilities such as attraction/repulsion and pleasure/pain differentials."[37] To this end, Anderson's project does not seek a resolution. Instead, second, the grotesque is comfortable with "nonresolution," ambiguity, and possibly even confusion as blacks try to make sense of the liminal nature of race, gender, and identity. Third, ambiguity creates the conditions, Anderson asserts, "for creative ways of taking an object or subject."[38] Fourth, the grotesque seeks to undermine efforts to systematize or synthesize antiblack racism, for instance, into one thing. The "grotesque disrupts the penchant for cognitive synthesis by highlighting the absurd and sincere, the comical and tragic, the estranged and familiar."[39] This appears to be Anderson's attempt to acknowledge how discourse and systems reproduce themselves through ordinary habits and practices that are not always coherent or evident.

THE POLITICO-AESTHETIC DIMENSION OF HUMAN DIGNITY

The politico-aesthetic addresses some of the concerns of racial essentialism raised by Anderson. Indeed, the politico-aesthetic is aimed at exposing, for instance, the reinvention of the white/black binary, the assumed superiority of whites and inferiority of blacks. The white/black binary, once operative in the form of legalized segregation and Jim Crow, emerges in the postmodern social context as a set of discourses, social symbols, and cultural practices aimed at privileging a seamless racial ideal of white over black. According to Evelyn Brooks Higginbotham "racial categories . . . are strategically necessary for the functioning of power in countless institutional and ideological forms, both explicit and subtle."[40] The politico-aesthetic dimension of human dignity tries to repair and cultivate within black politics and political thought what modernity, the Atlantic slave trade, and Jim Crow nearly eviscerated: human dignity. Human dignity is not static, intrinsic, or necessarily inherited but a dimension of human life that one pursues and struggles to embody. Lewis R. Gordon best describes the argument I am building: "The Black, as a function of the modern world, has lost something. For many blacks, this has been the historic dignity of their humanity. But the effort to reclaim their humanness raises the question of whose standards are its exemplars."[41] For Gordon, the effort to reclaim their humanity and human dignity happened simultaneously in art forms such as jazz and poetry and during social protest. Sometimes they failed as they struggled to embrace human dignity, and other times they achieved their goals. The politico-aesthetic reclaims the black body as a starting point for defining human worth and dignity. This recentering of black bodies from political margins, according to Hortense Spillers, is a chilling reminder of the pressing need among blacks to focus on freedom in the robust sense, instead of clinging to a discourse of equality in isolation of the comprehensive goals needed to obtain freedom:

> Even though the captive flesh/body has been "liberated," and no one need pretend that even the quotation marks do not *matter*, dominant symbolic activity, the ruling episteme that releases the dynamics of naming and valuation, remains grounded in the originating metaphors of captivity and mutilation so that it is as if neither time nor history, nor historiography and its topics, shows movement, as the human subject is "murdered" over and over again by the passions of a bloodless and anonymous archaism, showing itself in endless disguise.[42]

Here, Spillers is challenging the viability of political struggles that focus on the dominant liberal narrative, the acquisition of rights, at the expense of building a unique political vocabulary that addresses the moral and political justification of black dehumanization and exploitation. This black feminist critique raises serious challenges to mainline African American liberal approaches to ameliorating antiblack racism by securing voting rights.

As we observed in the first section, Reverend King during the heyday of the civil rights movement adhered to a liberal rights-based agenda established in a belief that constitutional rights would serve as a guarantor of human dignity and worth. Michael Eric Dyson notes in *I May Not Get There with You: The True Martin Luther King, Jr.*, that for the young King, prior to "1965, the imagery of a buoyant American democracy filled King's speeches and sermons."[43] But King grew weary as white hostility to full equal rights for blacks deepened and materialized into violent attacks against blacks. "King came to the conclusion that black oppression has generated a 'terrible ambivalence in the soul of white America' . . . This is a far cry from the King who assured whites of their basic humanity, who was convinced that we must separate white sinners from the sin of white supremacy."[44] The early King retrieved a moral vocabulary that included human dignity as a legitimate conceptual scheme, but the category was subordinate to his more vigorous appeal to the acquisition of political rights. I wonder if segregation, in a strange and convoluted way, created the space in which human dignity was never questioned. Indeed, maybe segregation created the cultural, social, and moral conditions for producing counterpublics where blacks, and King in particular, took for granted human dignity when the right to vote and equal access were pressing concerns. Possibly, human dignity was assumed in those counterpublics because the politics of respectability was a cornerstone of black politics and a guiding theological doctrine in black sacred spaces, such as the church and mosque. In other words, human dignity was a fundamental concept within intraracial political discourse, religious imagination, and civil society.

CONCLUSION: FINDING HUMAN DIGNITY

Having examined various historical, theological, cultural, and political dimensions of dignity and racial violence, I want to bring these strands together in my constructive reflections on African American moral humanism in black political thought. Building on Anthony Pinn's important work in humanist thought, I depict here a moral humanism that is fundamentally an ongoing "quest for complex subjectivity."[45] Humanism, as Pinn describes it, "frames a quest for life full and healthy, the making of meaning in such a way as to capture perspective on and attention to the looming questions of our very complex and layered existence."[46] My work attempts to extend Pinn's humanism to include a more robust account of black politics and aesthetics.

African American moral humanism is designed to frame the multidimensional approaches to discuss ethics, politics, spirituality, beauty, and morality without turning to religious claims or theological evidence to justify African American freedom. Womanist thought takes seriously the encounters between God and black women within the wilderness, but it also privileges black women's experience in literature, art, and music as legitimate sources for religious inquiry. The meeting with God does not necessarily weigh more than religious subjectivity expressed in black women's literature. This is an example of theo-ethical commitments within Womanist theology. To this end, the moral humanism I am piecing together takes seriously the performative dimensions of blackness and black identities in our many publics and moves away from theo-ethical commitments; that is, African American moral humanism acknowledges that subjects produce and reconfigure their subjectivities without any coherency or allegiance to a codified religious or cultural method.

The shift away from theism to politico-aesthetics underscores the range of philosophical approaches created by blacks to probe human dignity. We see signs of this in Williams's category of the wilderness. To be fair, she defines it as a place where women meet God, but the God she imagines is a symbol of the strength the women must muster up from their resilience and dogged faith to fight against all odds. The moral humanism I am advancing is also evident in Anderson's reconfigured category of the grotesque. Anderson's heuristic paradigm is designed to help us sit with the tensions of categorical racism, for instance, as we look for ways to find meaning in social categories that often limit rather than fuel human imagination and will. Anderson states, "The grotesque ought not to be thought of as an opposition between two diametrically opposed sensibilities such as would occur in binary dialectics. Yet the grotesque does have to do with the sensibilities that are oppositional, such as attraction and repulsion, and pleasure and pain differentials."[47] The grotesque serves as a helpful epistemic tool for challenging racial essentialism and Anderson's cult of the heroic genius. By heroic genius he means the modes of framing African American experiences that in many stances foreclose grappling with the complex subjectivities of raced and gendered bodies. In his effort to build an epistemic terrain sturdy enough to hold our creative tensions, Anderson's heuristic model, I believe, is threatened by what I call the moral problem of blackness.[48] How does one embrace the complexity of human subjectivity in a social context where the ritual of black dehumanization is performed routinely in our basic public institutions and reinscribed in cultural habits and practices?

A case in point is BLM: its characterization of human dignity and racial dehumanization weaves together aesthetics and politics to establish a political rhetoric and philosophy that challenge social injustice from a multidimensional viewpoint. But the debate is focused on *black lives*—the specific ways law, politics, and culture treat blacks and black bodies as inherently criminal, abject, and immoral. The central aim of the movement is noteworthy, justifiable, and necessary. Yet I wonder, thinking alongside Anderson, if the effort to inscribe human dignity and worth onto blackness is a doomed project. Following Anderson's criticism of racial representation and the black heroic genius, public intellectuals, artists, and activists must remain skeptical, or at least cautious, of efforts to create a counterdiscourse, as such a move might in fact objectify blackness in ways that deepen our reliance on categorizing humans.

Still, BLM advances, according to Taylor in *From #BLACKLIVESMATTER to Black Liberation*, and has "created a feeling of pride and combativeness among a generation that this country has tried to kill, imprison, and simply disappear."[49] Taylor's provocative descriptive account of BLM underscores the political paradigm shift away from mainline racial liberalism based on integration and political rights to substantive criminal justice policy reform. What is underplayed in her work is the degree to which BLM's focus on human dignity also reflects an effort to overhaul black politics. The move is aimed at an internal reform along with a critical transformation of social structures. Of particular interest for my chapter is the movement's effort to include marginal groups within black life based on the argument for human dignity.

BLM is calling for an end to "narrow nationalism" that focuses on black power in relationship to economics and political solidarity. Instead, it calls for an affirmation of "Black queer and trans folks, disabled folks, black-undocumented folks, folks with records, women and all Black lives along the gender spectrum."[50] By making gender central to its political model, BLM has transformed the narrative of black politics and political thought to punctuate four important points: restorative justice, robust diversity, globalism, and family-friendly public spaces. What is strikingly clear is the centrality of gender and spaces historically designated as women's spaces. This hermeneutical turn is in line with Womanist's ethical vision and liberation ethic. Cannon writes, "An inclusive liberation ethic must focus on the particular questions of women in order to reveal the subtle and deep effects of male bias" in religion and politics.[51]

How, then, do blacks recover from racial trauma without relying on a racial apologetics? The answer is at least twofold: (1) critical self/communal reflection; (2) resistance and opposition to oppressive structural systems. Let's first consider self/communal reflection. Baldwin offers an intriguing analysis of how African Americans might heal themselves from the onslaught of psychic and political trauma: "To do our first works over."[52] What does he mean by this? "To do your first works over means to reexamine everything. Go back to where you started, or as far back as you can, examine all of it, travel your road again and tell the truth about it. Sing or shout or testify or keep it to yourself: but *know whence you came*."[53] Here, Baldwin focuses on memory as a site of return where one pursues, investigates, and imagines the "past" not as a particular place or historical moment but as an active journey to nowhere. Baldwin's approach is generative in three important ways. First, it develops an ethical imperative to awaken and encourage moral subjects to rethink the ordinary, the dull, and mundane. Second, the move creates a framework for articulating the tensions and contradictions of one's understanding of identity and politics. Third, the ethical imperative destabilizes one's assuredness in truth and objectivity, race, and identity.

How do we confront the challenge of restorative justice raised in BLM? Are the founders referring to a restoration between blacks and whites or an internal reconfiguration of intraracial relationships? The answer is unclear. What is obvious is the need to strengthen black self-image and consciousness. The founders write on their website: "When we say Black Lives Matter, we are talking about the ways in which Black people are deprived of our basic human rights and dignity . . . Black queer and trans folk bearing a unique burden in a hetero-patriarchal society that disposes of us like garbage and simultaneously fetishizes us and profits off of us is state violence."[54] BLM is more than a rhetorical trope articulated to convince whites and public officials of the intrinsic value of black life. It is a call to embrace the diversity and richness of black sexuality and gender. The link between the criminal justice system and black queer and trans folk is remarkable. It is recovered to further delineate the comprehensive nature of our political life. Black queer and trans folk are undervalued. Interestingly enough, the discussion of systematic racism is employed in tension with the need to "value" black life. The value here and throughout the BLM website corresponds to human dignity, the sense of wanting to affirm and see epistemic value in blacks and their bodies.

In far too many instances, however, black political rhetoric leans heavily on beliefs that assume the infrastructures and political doctrines of modernity, slavery, and segregation will bend to political rhetoric and social unrest. Indeed, the notion of overcoming antiblack racism presumes there is a chance that one person or a collective group can unravel discourses, institutions, cultural beliefs, and socioeconomic systems by mere subversion, assimilation, moral suasion, or rugged will. Such beliefs reflect bad faith—this idea of choosing to believe in a lie, at its most remarkable level. African American moral humanism, leaning on Baldwin, Williams, Pinn, and Anderson, shifts the conversation away from overcoming hegemony to imagining cultural contexts in which human dignity and worth are expressed in the lives of African Americans, reflected in the justice they frame with their hands, and executed in their actions. This does not mean moral agents should accept injustice, or, for that matter, abandon radical civil disobedience to fight against oppression; instead, it means accepting freedom, and believing in a radical disposition that one is born free and one's choices and actions extend and sustain individual and group freedom. Beliefs in a radical freedom are not only necessary for achieving human dignity and worth, but are prerequisites both for surviving in the wilderness and developing creative encounters between diametrically opposed ideas.

In King's eulogy of the Birmingham bombing victims, he said that Denise, Carole, Addie Mae, and Cynthia had something to say to the world.

> They have something to say to every minister of the gospel who has remained silent behind the safe security of stained-glass windows . . . They have something to say to every Negro who passively accepts the evil system of segregation, and stands on the sidelines in the midst of a mighty struggle for justice . . . They say to us that we must be concerned not merely about *WHO* murdered them, but about the system, the way of life and the philosophy which *PRODUCED* the murderers.[55]

Their deaths reflect the evil of antiblack racism and the tragic price of blackness. No one is shielded from this history and the dripping blood from the millions who have been slaughtered. But we are all condemned to confront this tragic history and its lingering legacy both in moral reflection and political agency. This is the price we must pay to pursue human dignity in order to one day gain the *right* to call ourselves human.

NOTES

1. Katie G. Cannon, "Moral Wisdom in the Black Women's Literary Tradition," in *Presenting Women Philosophers*, ed. Cecile T. Tougas and Sara Ebenrek (Philadelphia: Temple University Press, 2000), 61.

2. Cornel West, *Prophesy Deliverance! An Afro-American Revolutionary Christianity* (Philadelphia: The Westminster Press, 1982), 90.

3. See Anthony Pinn, *Why Lord? Suffering and Evil in Black Theology* (New York: Continuum, 1995), and Melanie Harris, "Womanist Humanism: A Deeper Look," *Cross Currents* 57 (Fall 2007): 471–72.

4. Harris, "Womanist Humanism," 392.

5. Frank Sikora, *Until Justice Rolls Down: The Birmingham Church Bombing Case* (Tuscaloosa: University of Alabama Press, 2005), ix.

6. Martin Luther King Jr., "Eulogy for the Martyred Children," in *I Have a Dream: Writings and Speeches That Changed the World*, ed. James M. Washington (New York: Harper, 1992), 116.

7. By innocence I do not mean what James Baldwin referred to in *The Fire Next Time* as a lack of awareness, or denial of the tragic. I mean innocence as fragile, blissful, earnest, and curious. Such characteristics reflect the humanity rarely attributed to blacks.

8. King, "Eulogy for the Martyred Children," 16.

9. Ibid.

10. James Baldwin, *The Price of the Ticket: Collection Nonfiction, 1948–1985* (New York: St. Martin's Press, 1985), xviii.

11. Ibid., xix.

12. Anthony Pinn, *Terror and Triumph: The Nature of Black Religion* (Minneapolis: Fortress Press, 2003), 49.

13. Hortense Spillers, "Mama's Baby, Papa's Maybe: An American Grammar Book," *Diacritics* 17, no. 2 (1987): 67 (original emphasis).

14. Michelle Alexander, *The New Jim Crow: Mass Incarceration in the Age of Colorblindness* (New York: New Press, 2011), 11–14.

15. Barbara Mitchell, *Black Abolitionism: A Quest for Human Dignity* (Maryknoll, NY: Orbis Press, 2005), 153.

16. Ibid.

17. Keeanga-Yamahtta Taylor, *From #BLACKLIVESMATTER to Black Liberation* (Chicago: Haymarket Books, 2016), 168.

18. Pinn, *Terror and Triumph*, 16.

19. Vivian May, "Writing the Self into Being: Anna Julia Cooper's Textual Politics," *African American Review* 43 (Spring 2009): 18.

20. Anna Julia Cooper, *A Voice from the South* (New York: Oxford University Press, 1988), 235.

21. Ibid., 28.

22. Ibid., 297 (original emphasis).

23. Ibid., 298.

24. Harris, "Womanist Humanism," 393.

25. Harry Singleton, "In God (And Sarah) We Trust: An Analysis of Delores S. Williams' Critique of Black Theology," *Journal of Intercultural Disciplines* 8 (2010): 3.

26. Dianne M. Stewart, "Womanist Theology in the Caribbean Context: Critiquing Culture, Rethinking Doctrine, and Expanding Boundaries," *Journal of Feminist Studies in Religion* 20 (Spring 2004): 67.

27. Delores Williams, *Sisters in the Wilderness: The Challenge of Womanist God-Talk* (Maryknoll, NY: Orbis, 2004), 109.

28. Ibid., 113.

29. Ibid., 108.

30. Black Lives Matter, "About the Black Lives Matter Network," http://blacklivesmatter.com.

31. Victor Anderson, *Beyond Ontological Blackness: An Essay on African American Religious and Cultural Criticism* (New York: Continuum, 1995), 61.

32. Ibid., 78.

33. For more information on tragic soul-life, see Terrence L. Johnson, *Tragic Soul-Life: W.E.B. Du Bois and the Moral Crisis Facing American Democracy* (Oxford: Oxford University Press, 2012).

34. Ibid., 92.

35. Ibid., 85.

36. Victor Anderson, *Creative Exchange: A Constructive Theology of African American Religious Experience* (Minneapolis: Fortress Press, 2008), 10–11.

37. Ibid., 11.

38. Ibid.

39. Ibid.

40. Evelyn Brooks Higginbotham, "African-American Women's History and the Metalanguage of Race," *Signs* 17, no. 2 (1992): 253–54.

41. Lewis R. Gordon, "When I Was There, It Was Not: On Secretions Once Lost in the Night," *Performance Research* 12, no. 3 (2010): 11.

42. Spillers, "Mama's Baby, Papa's Maybe," 68 (original emphasis).

43. Michael Eric Dyson, *I May Not Get There with You: The True Martin Luther King, Jr.* (New York: Touchstone Book, 2001), 38.

44. Ibid., 39.

45. Anthony Pinn, "Humanism as a Guide to Life Meaning," in *What Is Humanism and Why Does It Matter?*, ed. Anthony Pinn (Bristol, CT: Acumen Publishing, 2013), 33.

46. Ibid., 34.

47. Anderson, *Beyond Ontological Blackness*, 127.

48. See Johnson, *Tragic Soul-Life*.

49. Taylor, *From #BLACKLIVESMATTER to Black Liberation*, 190.

50. See http://blacklivesmatter.com/about/.

51. Cannon, "Moral Wisdom in the Black Women's Literary Tradition," 127.

52. Baldwin, *The Price of the Ticket*, xix.

53. Ibid. (original emphasis).

54. See http://blacklivesmatter.com/herstory/.

55. King, "Eulogy for the Martyred Children," 16 (original emphasis).

sixteen

DIGNITY AND CONFLICT

Criminal Justice

William O'Neill

> Imagine that you yourself are building the edifice of human destiny with the object of making people happy in the finale, of giving them peace and rest at last, but for that you must inevitably and unavoidably torture just one tiny creature, that same child who was beating her chest with her little fist, and raise your edifice on the foundation of her unrequited tears—would you agree to be the architect on such conditions? Tell me the truth.
>
> —Ivan's question to Aloysha in *The Brothers Karamazov*[1]

Time and again, the architects of mass atrocity have answered Ivan's question. Walter Benjamin's *Angelus Novus*, the "angel of history," still presides over "the suffering and passion of the world."[2] Yet unrequited tears, too, find their voice, for example, in the UN Universal Declaration of Human Rights's (UDHR) *cri d'coeur* against "crimes which have outraged the conscience of humanity."[3]

In this chapter, I will explore the ethical implications of what the UN Charter calls our "faith in fundamental human rights, in the dignity and worth of the human person," not only for the innocent, but for the guilty.[4] In the first section, I will briefly consider the genealogy of our modern appeal to dignity and rights in complex, pluralist polities. For just how dignity grounds rights and which rights remain contested questions. In the second section, I will turn to the place (rhetorical *locus*) of human rights in criminal justice, looking not only to Western uses of rights, but to rights' rhetoric in the Truth and Reconciliation Commission (TRC) in South Africa. Differing interpretations of rights, I will argue, underwrite a continuum, ranging from retributive to restorative justice.[5] In the final section, I will argue further that the dignitarian tradition of rights favors a more robust restorative approach to criminal justice, looking, in particular, at mass incarceration in the United States.

OUR COMMON FAITH

Whether we see the "tiny creature's . . . unrequited tears" as morally tragic or merely an unimportant failure of global politics is never given *tout court.* "Pity" says Cynthia Ozick, "is not 'felt,' as if by instinct or reflex. Pity is taught." And for Ozick, the source of pity is the divine admonition against idolatry, against Moloch "demanding human flesh to feed on." In the "absence of the Second Commandment, the hunt for victims begins."[6] The suppression of pity is a desecration of the *imago Dei*, an effacing of dignity. In Martha Minow's words, "A most appalling goal of the genocides, the massacres, systematic rapes, and tortures has been the destruction of the remembrance of individuals as well as of their lives and dignity."[7] Our faith in dignity and human rights, conversely, is a stay against atrocity, against forgetting. And yet, as we shall see, there is no simple logic binding dignity and rights. Indeed, what Mary Ann Glendon calls the "dignitarian" strand of rights in the UDHR is but one of several interpretations woven into our controversies regarding criminal justice.[8]

A Brief Genealogy

We begin with a biblical gloss. The priestly creation narrative, writes John Donahue, "reaches its summit in Genesis 1:26: 'Let us make humankind in our image, according to our likeness.'" In its original context, the image of God (*imago Dei*) signifies that we are "God's representatives," and hence worthy of honor. Other exegetes say we are "created to be God's counterparts, creatures analogous to God with whom God can speak and who will hear God's word." In either interpretation, concludes Donahue, "all men and women prior to identification by race, social status, religion, or sex are worthy of respect and reverence."[9]

Later Christian tradition provides a metaphysical basis for such worthiness in identifying the *imago Dei* with the godlike (analogical) properties of intelligence and freedom.[10] For it is by our "intellectual nature," says Aquinas, that we are proper subjects of natural law, participating, albeit imperfectly, in the divine, eternal law.[11] Yet, circumscribed within an intricate, hierarchical teleology, Aquinas's affirmation of dignity did not perspicuously yield a doctrine of equal "subjective rights." For the origins of *jus subjectivum*, we must rather look to a tributary of natural law or right in late twelfth-century canonical jurisprudence. For it is here, *in nuce*, that the "dignitarian" strain of human rights emerges in "the religiously oriented systems of the medieval era."[12] Multiple variations are worked upon the theme as Renaissance poets such as Pico della Mirandola extol our godlike freedom, and Reformation controversies bequeath us a right to religious liberty.

Giving pride of place to such individual rights, the modern natural lawyers of the seventeenth and eighteenth centuries look less to the natural finality of the common good than to the natural convergence of rational (prudential) wills.[13] Indeed, with the eclipse of the divinely inspired *bonum commune*, natural law itself succumbs to the "secularized doctrines of the Enlightenment."[14] The disenchantment of modern natural law theory, adumbrated in Grotius, emerges clearly in the writings of Hobbes and Pufendorf.[15] In a nominalist vein, Hobbes opposes liberty as the "Right of Nature" (*jus naturale*), "to use [one's] power, as he will himself, for the preservation of his own nature," to the "Law of Nature (*lex naturalis*)," which "determineth, and bindeth."[16] For stripped of Grotius's "natural sociability," it is "the foresight of their own preservation" that leads "men, (who naturally love liberty, and dominion over others,)" to submit to "that restraint upon themselves, (in which we see them live in commonwealths)."[17] Society is itself a grand artifice, "an artificial man" created by our mundane *fiat*—a *fiat* in its natural state unbridled by faith in human dignity. And in such a state of natural enmity, natural "justice and injustice have there no place."[18] Rather, justice emerges with Leviathan, so that crime, no less a voluntaristic construction, becomes an offense against the sovereign's rights.

In the Lockean strand of liberal rights theory, by contrast, our natural state remains a peaceable kingdom. Deferring to the "judicious Hooker," Locke grounds the civility of mores in our natural equality, from which springs "the obligation to mutual love." And yet the "law of nature" regulating our natural "state of liberty" turns less on Aquinas's (or Hooker's) *bonum commune* than the domain of individual, prepolitical rights.[19] Indeed, private property becomes the regnant metaphor of rights, the preservation and protection of which underwrites the social contract. Locke's doctrine of natural rights thus betrays its Whiggish inspiration; for the contract is effected by propertied males to remedy the "inconveniences" besetting their defense of property rights in the state of nature. And in remedying such inconveniences, citizens cede their natural right of punishment to the state.

Rousseau, too, appeals to the doctrine of a social contract. Yet where Hobbes's *pactum subjectionis* resolves the will of all into the will of one, Rousseau depicts the social bond (*lien social*) as the will's self-limitation; indeed it is only "with civil society" that we acquire "moral freedom, which alone makes man the master of himself." *Pace* Hobbes, freedom is found, not in slavery to the appetites, but in "obedience to a law one prescribes to oneself."[20] Sovereignty arises through a "reciprocal commitment," so that in contracting, "as it were, with himself" each person "finds himself doubly committed, first as a member of the sovereign body in relation to individuals [*souverain*], and secondly as a member of the state [*état*] in relation to the sovereign."[21] So it is that the "extravagant shepherd" of the *Confessions* justifies the sovereignty of the general will (*volonté général*), at once harking back to the natural rights championed by Locke, yet anticipating the Romantic historicization of law as the "general will" of the *Volk*.[22]

Purifying Rousseau's doctrine of the general will, Kant regards the formal generality, or "universal voice," of will as entirely *sui generis*: the will's transcendental freedom is itself the "*ratio essendi*" of the moral law. Freedom of the will (*die Willkür*) is internally limited by practical reason itself, in the autonomous "self-legislation" of *der Wille*.[23] Expressed in synthetic *Naturrecht*, the categorical imperative (in its various formulae, including that of respect for persons as "ends in themselves") abstracts entirely from the realm of prudential experience, formulable in hypothetical imperatives. The original contract, whereby "all (*omnes et singuli*) the people give up their external freedom in order to take it back again immediately as members of a commonwealth, that is, the people regarded as the state (*universi*)," is "a mere idea of reason."[24]

Civic virtue, for Kant, is thus no longer the natural fruition of prudence (Aristotelian *phronesis*), but rather a rein upon it as the "subjective principle of self-love."[25] The boundaries between morality, for example, "subjective rights, and [prudential] self-love" have become "distinct and sharp."[26] Yet in so severing us from the realm of ethical (*sittliche*) experience, Kant leaves us a dubious heritage.[27] For nature has ceased to tell a moral tale: the "good will" alone is good, final, and "without qualification."[28] Divested of natural finality, freedom, say Kant's critics, is perforce confined to the private realm or "the inward domain of consciousness."[29]

Now, such "moral self-consciousness . . . inwardly related to itself alone" falls prey to Hegel's censure, for "it has identity without content." Morality (*Moralität*), arising from the "pure unconditioned self-determination of the will," says Hegel, is finally reduced to "an empty formalism" from which "no immanent doctrine of duties" may be derived.[30] Concrete social bonds, once derived from the ethical ideal of the common good (the positive determination of freedom, or *libertas*, for Augustine and Aquinas), must now be constructed, in a nominalist vein, through the exercise of individual or collective will.[31] So too for Kant, adjudication of guilt and punishment is perforce retributive; it restores, not the thicker bonds of traditional communitarian membership, but the formal (procedural) rule of abstract right. Punishment is just deserts for violating the social contract. Roger Sullivan observes, "Justice may be mitigated by benevolence, but the criminal still owes *society* a strict debt to restore the reciprocal contractual relationship between obedience to the law and benefits received form living under the law."[32]

Kant's Romantic critics such as Herder thus bid us return to the concrete ethical life.[33] For only in the "concretely personal," the historic *mythos* of the *Volk* or state, could Kant's "organic" conception of a kingdom of ends be redeemed.[34] Yet Hegel's sublation of *Moralität* into the realm of ethics (*Sittlichkeit*) was to prove no less ephemeral. No longer anchored in the dialectical unfolding of Objective Spirit, ethics becomes "something relatively 'local and ethnocentric.'"[35] Ethical substance, that is, is fragmented in our myriad traditions, and (social) nature, in Weber's words, is thoroughly "disenchanted."[36] And so, in brief, the genealogy of our modern (or postmodern) rhetorical rivalries: variations wrung upon the neo-Kantian morality (*Moralität*) of liberal *rights* rhetoric, and the appeal of neo-Hegelian (or Aristotelian) ethics (*Sittlichkeit*) to the common good of *Volk* or state.

CRIMINAL JUSTICE: RETRIBUTIVE AND RESTORATIVE REGIMES

Our all-too-brief traversal of the origins of modern rights rhetoric underscores the complex relationship of faith in dignity and natural or human rights. As Brian Tierney notes in his magisterial treatise, the origins of "subjective rights" (*jus subjectivum*) in late medieval canonical jurisprudence betray little of the social atomism, abstract formalism, or disenchantment marking modern liberal uses.[37] The "idea of natural rights in its earlier formulations," says Tierney, was consistent with "the communitarian values of traditional societies." Traces of the earlier, communitarian ideal persist in the dignitarian strain of human rights where, in Glendon's words, "individual and community are bound together in reciprocity."[38] The communitarian motif is likewise sounded in Pope John XXIII's incorporation of human rights within the civic common good and in regional charters such as the African Charter on Human and Peoples' Rights.[39] Still, for many critics and partisans alike, "bourgeois civil rights" now fill up the space (rhetorical *locus*) of rights as "the standard maximalist morality of the West."[40]

Further variations, of course, are worked upon such rights in differing liberal theories, and even more in the practices they rationalize, such as in criminal justice. And yet characteristic motifs emerge, permitting us to speak of a liberal strain of "rights talk." As we saw above, with the eclipse of the religious ideal of the common good in early modernity, rights are envisioned as powers or properties of sovereign selves—subjects emancipated from "all tutelage" of traditional mores.[41] What John Rawls terms the "fact of pluralism" in (post)modernity dispels any political appeal to a comprehensive conception of the good.[42] Bonds of "civic friendship" are frayed and "natural" solidarities fragmented. Indeed, the very irreconcilability of our local and ethnocentric conceptions of the good leads us to cherish the "liberties of the moderns" as our foremost rights. "The only freedom which deserves the name," writes J. S. Mill in a justly memorable phrase, "is that of pursuing our own good in our own way." Our liberty, in turn, is parsed as our several immunities or negative rights, limited principally by (negative) duties of forbearance. For we must, says Mill, respect others' liberty, neither depriving them of their own good nor impeding "their efforts to obtain it."[43]

Dignity, of course, plays a role in such rhetoric, but, deprived of divine sanction, as Eliot might say, it is "politic, cautious, and meticulous"—respecting Mill's "negative" liberty, but divested of formal and final causality. Civic bonds, once derived from the medievals' *bonum commune*, must now be constructed through exercise of Locke's fiduciary contract, if not Hobbes's imperious Leviathan. Positive legal obligations, accordingly, extend primarily to fellow citizens privy to the social contract underlying the moral legitimacy of the state. The state, in turn, will protect citizens against the "inconveniences" of the state of nature and, in social democracies, provide a modicum of welfare, but the fictive, legal contract remains "disinterested." Citizenship does not entail civic friendship (the bonds of Aristotelian *philia*), much less Ozick's pity or empathy for victims.

Retributive Justice

Criminal justice follows suit. In liberal regimes, powers to enforce or punish, no longer diffused through intermediate associations of the medieval *civitas*, are ceded to the state. And just as punishment emerges as the state's prerogative, so crime appears as an offense against the general will underwriting our reciprocal social contract. For Kant, we saw, the criminal must repay the strict moral debt incurred to society; justice is entirely retributive. Other strands of liberalism look rather to a consequential calculus, favoring rehabilitation, incapacitation, or deterrence.[44] In either case, however, adversarial adjudication of guilt and punishment restores the formal (procedural) rule of abstract right or law, that is, the coercive prerogatives of the bureaucratic state, but not the thicker bonds of traditional communitarian membership. Under the rubrics of an individualistic social contract, repaying the offender's "debt to society" favors neither reparations for victims (recognizing victims' positive rights) nor reintegration of the offender into the community.

Restorative Justice

The contrasting motifs of restorative justice emerge against this backdrop. For, to its partisans, what must be restored is less the abstract right of the status quo ante than the bonds of moral relationship—not only between victim and offender, but within the moral community itself. One of its leading theorists, the Mennonite theologian Howard Zehr, describes restorative justice as "a process to involve, to the extent possible, those who have a stake in a specific offense and to collectively identify and address harms, needs, and obligations, in order to heal and put things as right as possible."[45] For proponents of restorative justice, victim–offender reconciliation programs (VORPS), sentencing circles, or family group conferences (FGCs) represent an effective alternative to prevailing regimes of retributive justice.[46] For Zehr, these restorative gambits are not merely different, more efficient moves in the prevailing penal system; rather, "restorative justice provides an alternative framework for thinking about wrongdoing," encompassing a variety of practices. And yet, as Zehr concedes, neither retributive nor restorative justice is a rigidly limited conception.[47]

Some interpretations of retributive justice include restorative elements, while restorative practices need not exclude retributive sanctions. Indeed, proponents of restorative justice differ as to their proper balance, for example, whether restorative practices should replace, complement, or be integrated within criminal justice systems. Still, a family resemblance emerges: Where in retributive regimes, "crime is a violation of the law and state," restorative justice views "crime as a violation of people and relationships." And where "justice requires the state to determine blame (guilt) and impose pain (punishment)," restorative justice "involves victims, offenders, and community members in an effort to put things right." Finally, in retributive systems, offenders "get what they deserve," while restorative justice looks rather to redressing "victim needs and offender responsibility for repairing harm."[48]

Critics of restorative justice, for their part, object that such informal, broadly participatory practices threaten due process and the impartiality of justice–blind law. And so too, rival liberal and communitarian politics differ in interpretations of just what is to be restored. Sentencing circles emerged from First Nation communities in Canada and FGCs from traditional conciliation practices in New Zealand and Australia. Yet for restorative critics, the ideal of repristinating a communitarian ethos for modern, pluralist polities is illusory if not inimical to individual rights. Indeed, redressing victim needs and offender responsibility may mitigate justice with benevolence, but, Kant reminds us, criminals still owe society a strict moral debt to restore the contractual relationship.

A Rapprochement?

Must we then choose between modern liberal rights rhetoric—what Michael Sandel calls the "politics of rights" in retributive regimes—and the rival, communitarian "politics of the [particular] common good" in restorative justice?[49] The complex genealogy of dignity and rights touched on above belies a simple opposition. For not only are retributive and restorative threads sometimes interwoven; restorative practices themselves, I will argue, turn on a richer, dignitarian interpretation of rights—a rhetorical *via media* supporting relationships of mutual dependency while rejecting collectivism. Here, the proceedings of the Truth and Reconciliation Commission (TRC) in South Africa are especially illuminating, for they not only display the rhetorical force (*locus*) of human rights in practice, but do so in an explicitly restorative vein.

Forged of political necessity, the South African TRC was charged by the "Promotion of National Unity and Reconciliation Act of 1995" to promote "unity and reconciliation by providing for the investigation and full disclosure of gross violations of human rights committed in the past."[50] Of the three Committees of the Commission, the first to begin hearings was, fittingly, the Human Rights Violations Committee, which focused primarily on the victims of apartheid. Through two years of the public testimony, the Committee sought to establish victims' identity and ultimate fate, and find those responsible for the atrocities.

For some, provision of conditional amnesty (contingent upon full disclosure of politically motivated crimes) represented an abdication of strict, retributive justice. For Archbishop Desmond Tutu, chair of the TRC, however, rights-based justice was not exhausted by retribution:

> Retributive justice—in which an impersonal state hands down punishment with little consideration for victims and hardly any for the perpetrator—is not the only form of justice. I contend that there is another kind of justice, restorative justice. . . . The central concern is not retribution or punishment but, in the spirit of *ubuntu*, the healing of breaches, the redressing of imbalances, the restoration of broken relationships. This kind of justice seeks to rehabilitate both the victim and the perpetrator, who should be given the opportunity to be reintegrated into the community he or she has injured by his or her offence.[51]

Rights let us name atrocity; let victims speak. In the TRC, "our nation," writes Tutu, "sought to rehabilitate and affirm the dignity and humanity of those who were cruelly silenced for so long, turned into anonymous, marginalised victims."[52] Here, testimony evokes what was systemically effaced. "Now through the Truth and Reconciliation Commission," writes Tutu, victims "would be empowered to tell their stories, allowed to remember and in this public recounting their individuality and inalienable humanity would be acknowledged."[53] Lukas Baba Sikwepere, blinded in a brutal attack by police in Cape Town and later tortured, testifies: "I feel what—what has brought my sight back, my eyesight back is to come back here and tell the story. But I feel what has been making me sick all the time is the fact that I couldn't tell my story. But now I—it feels like I got my sight back by coming here and telling you the story."[54] Telling the story is, at once, part of Baba Sikwepere's story, what is woven into collective memory.[55] And so too the converse; in Jean Baudrillard's words, "forgetting the extermination is part of the extermination itself."[56]

The telling of stories is, to be sure, no panacea; many stories remained untold in the TRC, nor is the "disclosedness" of truth tantamount to reconciliation.[57] Still, when TRC submitted its five-volume report on October 29, 1998, the years of anguished testimony had forged a remarkable narrative linking the stories of more than 23,000 victims such as Lukas Baba Sikwepere into what Charles Villa-Vicencio describes as "the greater story that unites."[58] In victims' testimony, the TRC revealed the distortions and evasions of apartheid. But the disclosure of atrocity is also a clearing for new stories to be told, both personal and collective. The TRC set the stage for creating a new national narrative that would seek to redeem the *cri d'coeur* "never again."

Now the naming or disclosure and systemic redress of atrocity in the TRC culminated in the specific redress of victims, enacted within practical limits by the Reparations and Rehabilitation Committee of the TRC. For depriving victims of their basic human rights generates a secondary or ancillary set of special rights (and correlative duties) of reparation, restitution, and/or retribution: to victims, fitting reparation was owed—though not always provided—perpetrators must fully disclose their complicity, and those failing to do so were subject to retributive sanction.

The sway of restorative justice, aiming at "the healing of breaches,"[59] is necessarily limited. As Primo Levi writes, even legal punishment cannot exact a just "'price' for pain."[60] Yet, as we have seen, the invocation of rights, in the spirit of *Ubuntu*, permitted not only the disclosure of crime or atrocity, but also the systemic redress of implementing a rights regime, and the interpersonal redress of victims in reparation. Here, in the TRC's pursuit of restorative justice, the "politics of rights" emerged as the sine qua non of the "politics of the common good"—a rapprochement underwritten by the dignitarian tradition of human rights.

A Schema of Rights

In the preceding section, I argued that the restorative practice of the TRC belied any simple opposition of the politics of rights and the common good. Tutu's appeal to *Ubuntu*, we saw, "thickened" the regnant, liberal doctrine, recalling the origins of *jus subjectivum* in "the communitarian values of traditional societies." Yet such a restorative inflection of rights raises several questions. In what respects does dignity ground rights, and which rights? Just how can the dignitarian tradition contribute to the healing of breaches, the restoration of broken relationships? And can the restorative use of rights be effectively reconciled with liberal insistence upon due process, impartiality, the satisfaction of moral debt? Let me, then, briefly parse our dignitarian interpretation—admittedly but one of several possible reconstructions of our "common faith." We begin with dignity.

(1) Dignity, we may say, is a normative or evaluative property, supervenient upon describing persons as (potential) practically rational agents. Many qualifications are required here, but suffice for the moment to say that we are worthy of respect or reverence precisely as "prospective purposive agents," capable of forming, revising, and rationally pursuing a conception of the good.[61] Though dignity (we shall see) serves as the proximate ground of human rights, dignity may itself be ultimately grounded in differing sacred or secular systems of belief, for example, the biblical "*imago Dei*," African traditional religion's *Ubuntu*, or Kant's transcendental epistemology. What marks the dignitarian tradition is not a knock-down, foundationalist justification, but rather an overlapping consensus—a family resemblance of use.[62]

(2) Such a consensus, exhibited in the UDHR, provides that persons may never be treated merely as means to another's ends. Persons, that is, have equal worth, not price, so that, in Gene Outka's words, the absolute value accorded each person is "incommensurable with the value of contingent desires satisfied or profits secured."[63] As such, dignity is inalienable, imprescriptible, and permanent; in no circumstances can dignity be exchanged, forfeited, or overridden. The notion of dignity or worth thus differs "from every kind of merit, including . . . moral merit, in respect to which there are vast inequalities among persons."[64] Persons, as Baba Sikwepere eloquently reminds us, never cease to matter.

(3) Human rights, in turn, exhibit our respect for persons' dignity, while basic human rights preserve the conditions or capabilities of exercising such practically rational (discursive) agency. In ascribing worth, rather than mere price, to persons as agents, we implicitly valorize the prerequisites of their exercising agency, that is, not only our negative, civil liberties, but entitlements to basic security and subsistence claims—claims rightly enjoyed, asserted, or enforced. Such basic rights—including, a fortiori, liberties of effective participation—are morally (and legally) exigent, serving, in Ronald Dworkin's felicitous words, as "trumps" against collective aims or other, less basic rights (e.g., property rights).[65] It was thus that the Human Rights Committee of the TRC supplied the rubrics under which victims such as Baba Sikwepere testified.

(4) Precisely as warranted claims, basic rights imply correlative duties. Such duties include not merely (a) forbearance or noninterference in the enjoyment of civil liberties, basic security, and welfare, but (b) protection against "standard threats" to their enjoyment (e.g., legal discrimination) and (c) provision, for example, of child nutrition or basic health care where necessary. Negative duties let us name crime or atrocity—the critical or deconstructive hermeneutical use; while positive duties, in turn, generate structural imperatives for the legal instantiation of a rights regime—the constructive use. In Brian Orend's words, "The contemporary human rights movement has, as probably its main goal, the effective translation of the moral values inherent in human rights theory into meaningful and concrete legal rights."[66]

(5) The legal instantiation (or schematization) of rights, we may say, thus emerges as a regulative ideal in both international and domestic jurisprudence, for example, in the TRC. And implementing such a regime, as Amartya Sen reminds us, is "consequentially sensitive."[67] A teleological note is thus sounded—instantiating a comprehensive rights regime as a discursive common good, incrementally realized in the "greater story that unites." Just so, rights appear, not as discrete properties or powers of sovereign selves abstracted from the ensemble of social relations, but rather as "grammatical rules" (in Wittgenstein's terms, a "deep grammar") configuring our legal rhetoric.[68] And like grammar, rights hang together. We do not, after all, speak grammar, but grammatically.

(6) We may say, then, that a grammatically sound or well-formed legal system will preserve and protect the basic rights of all affected. Law, as Aquinas understood, is promulgated for the common good, construed now, not in perfectionist, teleological terms, but as the "morality of the depths," the structural guarantee of equal basic rights.[69] But to assert the suasive force of equal basic rights is to recognize relative vulnerability; for in no regime are equal basic rights equally threatened. Indeed, precisely our moral/legal entitlement to equal respect or consideration justifies preferential treatment for those whose basic rights are most imperiled[70]—in Camus's phrase, our taking "the victim's side."[71] And, as we have seen, such a discriminate response finds expression in the graduated legal/moral urgency of differing human rights, that is, the lexical priority of agents' basic rights over other, less exigent claims, for example, property rights; and in the differing correlative duties presumed for realizing the same human rights.[72] In short, a well-formed legal regime will fittingly protect those most vulnerable to standard threats or systemic deprivation, for example, religious, racial, or ethnic minorities.

(7) Finally, the *critical* or *deconstructive* use of rights (naming atrocity) and the *constructive* use in systemic redress (instantiating legal guarantees against deprivation) combine in what we might call the *reconstructive* use: interpersonal redress in recognizing victims' rights to fitting reparation and the corresponding moral debt incurred by perpetrators. The violation of basic human rights generates ancillary rights of reparation, permitting the TRC to adjudicate the victims' rights of victims and perpetrators' responsibilities, without, however, "essentializing" either. In sum, dignity provides the proximate grounds for ascribing basic rights as the "morality of the depths," even if dignity is itself underwritten by an overlapping consensus of differing, even incommensurable, moralities of the heights (comprehensive notions of the good). The regulative ideal of a rights regime, in turn, lets us *critically* name crime or atrocity, *constructively* redress systemic deprivation or distortions (e.g., in instantiating a rights-based legal regime), and *reconstructively* redress broken relationships (e.g., in reparation for victims). Just as the ethical rhetoric of basic rights permits the impartial legal adjudication of individual violations (violations of forbearance), while condemning institutional distortions, for example, of apartheid (systemic violations of protection and provision), so too rights rhetoric recognizes the particular, ancillary rights accrued by victims, for example, to reparation, and duties of perpetrators, for example, to make reparation, if not restitution.

As in the victim-centered hearings of the TRC, crime is not primarily an offense against the bureaucratic prerogatives of the state, but a breach of moral bonds—the civic *philia* born of mutual respect and reverence. So too, the participatory rights of victim, and even offender, remain salient. "This kind of justice," Tutu reminds us, "seeks to rehabilitate both the victim and the perpetrator."[73] On such a continuum of legal justice, retributive sanctions play a subordinate role. Punishing the perpetrator, writes Nigel Biggar, is but one of several "secondary and subordinate" considerations in criminal justice, including reparation, deterrence, rehabilitation.[74] Here too, we might argue, retributive sanctions, for example, in the international criminal courts (Arusha, the Hague, and the ICC), serve restorative ends, that is, the denial of impunity as deterrence—our redeeming the cry of "never again." Finally, impartiality and due process fall under the regulative ideal of instantiating a restorative rights regime; appropriate safeguards must, insofar as possible, be implemented. Yet, as we shall see, we cannot simply identify such procedural safeguards with prevailing institutional practices in retributive regimes.

A CASE IN POINT: MASS INCARCERATION IN THE UNITED STATES

What might a dignitarian interpretation of rights say to our prevailing retributive regime in the United States? Several caveats are in order: practices, especially those as complex as "meting and doling out" justice, seldom fall unproblematically under theories, even those ostensibly backing them. Indeed, I will argue that several liberal-philosophical motifs, such as attenuated social bonds and the bureaucratic prerogatives of the state in criminal justice, are so exacerbated in our prevailing carceral regime as to threaten other central values, such as impartiality and due process. Yet remedy lies in the critique.

For, as I argued in the preceding section, the dignitarian strain of human rights underwrites a comprehensive assessment of both retributive and restorative regimes in our threefold hermeneutic of rights: deconstructive (critical), constructive, and reconstructive hermeneutical (or rhetorical) uses. Rights are at play (1) in a *critical* assessment of prevailing regimes bearing on questions of "legitimacy, legislative justice, jurisdiction and controversy, as well as deference and enforcement."[75] Where rights, especially of the most vulnerable, are imperiled, we speak of systemic redress, namely, (2) the *constructive* role of rights. What set of causal factors contribute to systemic deprivation? And which legal policies, practices, and institutions will best instantiate a basic rights regime, all things considered? And finally, critical and constructive uses combine (3) *reconstructively* in interpersonal redress: How are ancillary rights and duties, for example, victims' rights to reparation, effectively redeemed?

Let me first set the stage. According to recently published figures from the U.S. Bureau of Justice statistics, the rate of incarceration in the United States nearly quadrupled between 1980 and 2009. Inmates incarcerated in prison or jail number 2.2 million. This is the highest official rate of incarceration in the world (at 731 per 100,000 population). Including those in probation or on parole, the total number of citizens under the aegis of corrections departments now reaches 7.1 million, an increase of almost 300 percent since 1980. Today, 1 out of every 137 Americans is incarcerated.[76]

Disaggregating for race and ethnicity, black men "are six times as likely to be incarcerated as white men and Hispanic men are 2.7 times as likely. For black men in their thirties, about 1 in every 12 is in prison or jail on any given day. More than 60% of the people in prison today are people of color." 1 of 3 black males will be imprisoned; 1 of 6 Latino men. 1 of 18 black women will suffer a similar fate compared to 1 in 111 white women.[77] Felony disenfranchisement deprives "1 of every 13 African Americans" of the right to vote.[78] Such systemic inequities, writes Michelle Alexander, perpetuate the "New Jim Crow" of "racial caste" and "racialized social control."[79] In Adam Gopnik's words, "Mass incarceration on a scale almost unexampled in human history is a fundamental fact of our country today . . . as slavery was the fundamental fact of 1850. In truth, there are more black men in the grip of the criminal-justice system . . . than were in slavery then."[80] The dramatic increase in prison populations over the past half century stands "in sharp contrast to that of the preceding fifty years, during which time there was a gradual increase in the use of incarceration commensurate with the growth in the general population."[81] So too, our current incarceration practices differ markedly from those of other Western democracies with comparable crime rates. Amnesty International reports that the "USA stands virtually alone in the world in incarcerating thousands of prisoners in longer-term or indefinite solitary confinement."[82] So too, racial and ethnic minorities disproportionately suffer the ultimate sanction, capital punishment, where "poor and marginalized groups have less access to the legal resources needed to defend themselves." Since the reinstitution of capital punishment in 1973, "150 US prisoners sent to death row have later been exonerated. Others have been executed despite serious doubts about their guilt."[83] Punitive attitudes prevail in what William Stuntz calls the "harshest" judicial system "in the history of democratic government,"[84] despite evidence of other mitigating factors underlying decreases in violent crime.

A similar punitive stance favors summary apprehension, detention, and deportation of around 10.5 million undocumented migrants—"illegal aliens"—in the United States.[85] According to the Office of Immigration Statistics of the Department of Homeland Security, "Immigration enforcement agents and officers initiated new enforcement actions against 805,071 inadmissible or deportable aliens in FY 2016. These actions included 274,821 inadmissibility determinations by the Office of Field Operations, 415,816 Border Patrol apprehensions, and 114,434 ICE arrests. ICE placed 352,882 aliens in civil detention facilities; and ICE and CBP together removed or returned 450,954 aliens."[86] Despite promises of reform, the overwhelming majority of "those detained are held in jails or jail-like facilities . . . at a cost of over $2 billion."[87] In fiscal year 2018, more than 45,000 parents and children seeking asylum were held in family detention facilities, often in appalling conditions.[88] In my ministry at the Federal Women's Prison in Dublin, California, the majority of the women I serve are poor migrants, some of whom will be summarily deported after completing their sentence. Many of the women are forcibly separated from their children for five to fifteen years, their punishment exacerbated terribly by the punishment thus inflicted on their children. It is not surprising to hear a woman pray for her child who is now also incarcerated. Yet, the crimes for which the women stand convicted are typically nonviolent drug offenses.

A Restorative Critique

Consider then our threefold, restorative hermeneutic of rights. Marked racial, ethnic, and class disparities recall Tennyson's Ulysses, who "mete[s] and dole[s] unequal laws."[89] The critical hermeneutic of rights (1), we saw, becomes, a "pedagogy of seeing," of naming rights violations. Crime appears primarily as a violation of dignity, of the respect and reverence due moral persons as such; only in a secondary vein does it appear as an offense against the state.[90] Just so, such a pedagogy of seeing extends beyond legal adjudication to systemic assessment, that is, racial, ethnic, class, and gender disparities. That more than 60 percent of those incarcerated in prison "are now racial and ethnic minorities" is unconscionable, belying the very rule of law, as is the damaging effect of such mass incarceration for minority communities and families. And the neglect of gender in sentencing, as we have seen, poses equally grave questions, not only for women convicted of nonviolent offenses but also for their families and dependents—children forcibly separated from their mothers by an impersonal state are no less "victims." Gender, race, and ethnicity render women of color particularly vulnerable.[91]

Systemic redress (2), we noted above, bids us consider the constellation of factors generating such disparities—the complex causal nexus of "racial caste" and "racialized social control." In our punitive regime, the economy of exclusion signified by the social contract (distinguishing citizens and aliens) proceeds apace as "criminals" or "illegal aliens" are denied the very "right to have rights." What Hannah Arendt says of forced migrants pertains no less to all those suffering the "loss of home and political status," for example, through mass incarceration and felony disenfranchisement. Such loss, says Arendt, is tantamount to "expulsion from humanity altogether." The "alien" is not the exemplar of humanity in general (the generalized other), but, like the criminal, "a frightening symbol of difference as such."[92] The symbolization of difference, whether of "illegal aliens" or "criminals," likewise blurs the lines between retribution and vengeance or scapegoating (the sublimation of vengeance) in our punitive regime. The will to punish, independent of consequential considerations such as deterrence, remains a potent force in polities where social bonds are already frayed and violence naturalized. Vengeance, especially against "frightening symbols of difference," seems to have its own cathartic rationale even where less punitive measures suffice for deterrence or reparation.

At play here is a perverse dialectic where our punitive regime constructs its own object: the alien becomes "illegal," the young black man the "criminalblackman."[93] As crime is voluntaristically constructed through the state's bureaucratic fiat, so bodies become illegal, criminal. Difference is feared and punished, reproducing (essentializing) the very differences we fear and, consequently, punish. As Alexander argues, our ostensibly impartial, "colorblind" criminal justice system thus rationalizes, and effectively erases, its racial and ethnic partiality or bias.[94]

Our restorative critique thus brings into relief the paradoxes or, perhaps better, systemic antinomies of our prevailing retributive regime. For our economy of exclusion betrays the very impartiality and due process that would render retribution just. So too, the endemic plea-bargaining of mass incarceration undermines any equitable apportioning crime to moral desert. Federally mandated minimum sentences, affecting so many of the women to whom I minister, effectively deny judicial discretion and equity in the rule of law. And recidivism undermines consequentialist legitimation of rehabilitation and deterrence: the Justice Department itself acknowledges the failure of reintegration. Half of all former state convicts will be incarcerated again within three years of their release: "Sixty-two percent of . . . confined youth . . . have previously been in custody. Among those, 40% have been confined 5 or more times."[95] Indeed, as John Tierney observes, "Some social scientists argue that the incarceration rate is now so high that the net effect is 'crimogenic': creating more crime over the long term by harming the social fabric in communities and permanently damaging the economic prospects of prisoners as well as their families. Nationally, about one in 40 children have a parent in prison. Among black children, one in 15 have a parent in prison."[96]

Surely, redressing the systemic racial, ethnic, class, and gender disparities in punishment is exigent, as is reform of sentencing procedures, felony disenfranchisement, and the juvenile waiver system. So too, the systemic aims of rehabilitation, incapacitation, and deterrence are necessarily qualified by the ethical exigencies of (3) interpersonal redress, such as victims' rights and offenders' duties. Moral desert thus rests less in rectifying a contractual relationship than in restoring relationships of mutual respect—Ozick's pity. In many instances, informal, restorative processes (VORPS, FGCs, etc.) may thus better provide for victims' reparation and the offender's rehabilitation and reintegration into community. The basic rights of offenders, even if legitimately curtailed, retain their moral force: cruelty is *never* permissible, nor is vengeance ever justified.

Assessments of deterrence, moreover, must thus themselves be rights-based, integrating both forward- and backward-looking considerations. Where less coercive, restorative measures than protracted incarceration serve the purposes of deterrence and reparation, they would necessarily be preferred in sentencing. To be sure, neither interpersonal nor systemic redress dictates a univocal practice. Informal victim–offender programs may, for instance, be unsuitable for crimes of sexual or spousal abuse. Neither, as we saw in my ministry at Federal Women's Prison, can we always assume a simple demarcation of "victim" and "offender." Systemic and interpersonal redress must be taken together, in a dynamic and fluid judicial praxis.

CONCLUSIONS

It would take us well beyond the scope of this chapter, and my own competence, to say more. My aim has been modest. In the first main section we explored the complex genealogy of dignity and rights, distinguishing the regnant liberal rhetoric of rights from a more communitarian strain at play in traditional and non-Western uses. In the second section, we argued that such a dignitarian interpretation offered a rhetorical *via media* between the retributive politics of rights and restorative politics of the common good. Our reconstructive assessment of the South African TRC in the third section let us apply the fruits of our restorative schema to the punitive regime of mass incarceration in the United States—this "harshest" of modern judicial systems.

We, too, must answer Ivan's question. For the "hunt for victims" began long ago—in the economies of exclusion begetting slavery, Jim Crow, and the scapegoating of migrants. In these pages, I have argued that restorative justice offers the rudiments of an answer: a pedagogy of seeing, and of redress, systemic and interpersonal. Still tears are unavenged. Still there is a place for pity.

NOTES

1. Fyodor Dostoevsky, *The Brothers Karamazov*, trans. Richard Pevear and Larissa Volokhonsky (New York: Vintage Books, 1990), 245.

2. Walter Benjamin, "Theses on the Philosophy of History," in *Illuminations*, ed. Hannah Arendt and trans. Harry Zohn (New York: Schocken, 1968).

3. Universal Declaration of Human Rights (UDHR), Preamble, http://www.un.org/chinese/center/chbus/events/hurights/english.htm.

4. Charter of the United Nations, Preamble, http://www.un.org/en/sections/un-charter/preamble/index.html.

5. Systems of retributive criminal justice may be rationalized on utilitarian or positivist grounds; my concern here is merely with the retributive and/or restorative implications of a rights regime.

6. Cynthia Ozick, "Notes toward a Meditation on 'Forgiveness,'" in Simon Wiesenthal, *The Sunflower: On the Possibilities and Limits of Forgiveness*, rev. ed. (New York: Schocken, 1997), 214.

7. Martha Minow, *Between Vengeance and Forgiveness* (Boston: Beacon, 1998), 1.

8. Cf. Mary Ann Glendon, *A World Made New: Eleanor Roosevelt and the Universal Declaration of Human Rights* (New York: Random House, 2001), 227.

9. John R. Donahue, "The Bible and Catholic Social Teaching: Will This Engagement Lead to Marriage?," in *Modern Catholic Social Teaching: Commentaries and Interpretations*, ed. Kenneth R. Himes (Washington, DC: Georgetown University Press, 2004), 16.

10. For differing interpretations of dignity as pertaining to status, intrinsic value, or behavior, see Michael Rosen, *Dignity: Its History and Meaning* (Cambridge, MA: Harvard University Press, 2012), 1–62.

11. Thomas Aquinas, *Summa theologiae* I, q. 93.

12. Brian Tierney, *The Idea of Natural Rights: Studies on Natural Rights, Natural Law, and Church Law, 1150–1625*, Emory University Studies in Law and Religion (Atlanta: Scholars Press, 1997), 347. The idea of subjective right, says Tierney, was not "dependent on any particular version of Western philosophy. . . . The one necessary basis for a theory of human rights is a belief in the value and dignity of human life" (ibid.).

13. See Richard Tuck, "The Modern Theory of Natural Law," in *The Languages of Political Theory in Early-Modern Europe*, ed. Anthony Pagden (Cambridge: Cambridge University Press, 1987), 117.

14. Tierney, *The Idea of Natural Rights*, 347.

15. Cf. A. P. d'Entreves's assertion that the doctrine of natural law as "set forth in the great treatises of the seventeenth and eighteenth centuries," from Pufendorf's *De Jure Naturae et Gentium* (1672) to Burlamaqui's *Principes du Droit Naturel* (1747) and Vattel's *Droit des Gens ou Principes de la Loi Naturelle* (1758), "has nothing to do with theology. . . . The self-evidence of natural law has made the existence of God perfectly superfluous"; A. P. d'Entreves, *Natural Law: An Introduction to Legal Philosophy* (London: Hutchison, 1970), 55.

16. Thomas Hobbes, *Leviathan*, chap. 14, in *British Moralists, 1650–1800*, ed. D. D. Raphael (Oxford: Clarendon, 1969), 1:38–39. Hobbes thereby separates what Suárez merely distinguishes. See Tierney, *The Idea of Natural Rights*, 301–15.

17. Hobbes, *Leviathan*, chap. 17, 1:52.

18. Ibid., chap. 13, 1:38.

19. John Locke, *The Second Treatise of Government*, ed. Thomas P. Peardon (Indianapolis: Bobbs-Merrill, 1952), 4–6.

20. Jean-Jacques Rousseau, *The Social Contract*, trans. Maurice Cranston (New York: Penguin Books, 1968), bk. 1, chap. 8, 65.

21. Ibid., bk. 1, chap. 7, 62.

22. Ernest Barker, introduction to *Social Contract: Essays by Locke, Hume, Rousseau* (Oxford: Oxford University Press, 1947), xxx. Ultimately, writes Barker, "I must reflect that if I am the thousandth part of a tyrant, I am also the whole of a slave. Leviathan is still Leviathan, even when he is corporate" (xxxv).

23. Rousseau, *Social Contract*, bk. 2, chap. 7, 84. Immanuel Kant, *Critique of Practical Reason*, trans. Lewis White Beck (Indianapolis: Bobbs-Merrill, 1956), 5.

24. Immanuel Kant, *The Metaphysical Elements of Justice: Part I of the Metaphysics of Morals*, trans. John Ladd (Indianapolis: Bobbs-Merrill, 1965), 315–16

25. Immanuel Kant, *Religion within the Limits of Reason Alone*, trans. Theodore M. Greene and Hoyt H. Hudson (New York: Harper and Row, 1960), 31.

26. Kant, *Critique of Practical Reason*, 36.

27. Louis Dupré, *A Dubious Heritage: Studies in the Philosophy of Religion after Kant* (New York: Paulist Press, 1977), 1–17.

28. Immanuel Kant, *Groundwork of the Metaphysic of Morals*, trans. H. J. Paton (New York: Harper and Row, 1964), 393 (1).

29. John Stuart Mill, *On Liberty*, ed. Gertrude Himmelfarb (New York: Penguin Books, 1974), 71. Cf. Dupré, *Passage to Modernity*, 131; Hannah Arendt, "What Is Freedom," in *Between Past and Future: Eight Exercises in Political Thought* (New York: Viking Press, 1968), 143–71.

30. G. W. F. Hegel, *Hegel's Philosophy of Right*, trans. T. M. Knox (Oxford: Oxford University Press, 1952), para. 135.

31. See Jürgen Habermas, "Private and Public Autonomy, Human Rights and Popular Sovereignty," in *Between Facts and Norms*, trans. William Rehg (Cambridge, MA: MIT Press, 1996), 107–8.

32. Roger Sullivan, *Immanuel Kant's Moral Theory* (Cambridge: Cambridge University Press, 1989), 243 (original emphasis). See Kant, *Critique of Practical Reason*, 37; Kant, *The Metaphysics of Morals*, 321–460.

33. Hegel, *Hegel's Philosophy of Right*, para. 137.

34. Cf. Lewis White Beck, *A Commentary on Kant's "Critique of Practical Reason"* (Chicago: University of Chicago Press, 1960), 125.

35. Richard Rorty, "The Priority of Democracy to Philosophy," in *The Virginia Statute of Religious Freedom: Two Hundred Years After*, ed. Robert Vaughan (Madison: University of Wisconsin Press, 1988), 259.

36. Max Weber, "Science as a Vocation," in *From Max Weber: Essays in Sociology*, ed. H. H. Gerth and C. W. Mills (New York: Oxford University Press, 1946), 148.

37. See Brian Tierney, *The Idea of Natural Rights*, 8, cf. 13–89; cf., Annabel S. Brett, *Liberty, Right and Nature: Individual Rights in Later Scholastic Thought* (Cambridge: Cambridge University Press, 1997).

38. Glendon, *A World Made New*, 227. Glendon cites David Kommers, "German Constitutionalism: A Prolegomenon," *Law Journal* 867 (1991): 1838–73. For Glendon, the "rights bearers" of the UDHR "tend to be envisioned within families and communities; rights are formulated so as to make clear their limits and their relation to one another as well as to the responsibilities that belong to citizens and the state" (227).

39. Though a constant motif in modern Catholic social teaching, dignity becomes a ground of *equal* human rights only in postwar doctrine, most notably with John XXIII's encyclical *Pacem in terris*, and in the conciliar texts *Gaudium et spes* and *Dignitatis humanae*. See Michael Rosen, *Dignity: Its History and Meaning* (Cambridge, MA: Harvard University Press, 2012).

40. Michael Walzer, *Thick and Thin: Moral Argument at Home and Abroad* (Notre Dame, IN: University of Notre Dame Press, 1994), 46. Habermas speaks of the "positivation" (*Positivierung*) of classical natural law in modernity, characterized by natural rights or liberties of rational self-interest; Jürgen Habermas, *Theory and Practice*, trans. J. Viertel (Boston: Beacon Press, 1974), 84; cf. Habermas, *Between Facts and Norms* (Cambridge, MA: MIT Press, 1998), 42–45, 56–57, 100–105.

41. Hannah Arendt, "The Perplexities of the Rights of Man," in *The Origins of Totalitarianism* (New York: Harcourt, Brace, & World, 1966), 290.

42. Rawls's "Kantian constructivism" and Habermas's discourse ethics both offer intersubjective interpretations of Kant's formal, canonical formulation of the categorical imperative. Rawls and Habermas thus look less to Kant's ideal of a "kingdom of ends" than to the purely formal, procedural requirements of universalization.

43. J. S. Mill, *On Liberty*, ed. Gertrude Himmelfarb (New York: Penguin Books, 1974), 72.

44. In utilitarian interpretations, collective aims typically "trump" individual rights. In liberal theory, by contrast, deterrence would be justified only if punishment corresponds to guilt. In practice, criminal justice systems may incorporate liberal, positivist, and utilitarian loci.

45. Howard Zehr, *The Little Book of Restorative Justice* (Intercourse, PA: Good Books, 2002), 37.

46. Cf. Gerry Johnstone and Daniel W. Van Ness, eds., *Handbook of Restorative Justice* (Portland, OR: Willan Publishing, 2007); Andrew von Hirsch et al., eds., *Restorative Justice and Criminal Justice: Competing or Reconcilable Paradigms?* (Oxford: Hart Publishing, 2003); Gerry Johnstone, ed., *A Restorative Justice Reader*, 2nd ed. (London: Taylor and Francis: 2013); Daniel W. Van Ness and Karen Heetderks Strong, *Restoring Justice*, 2nd. ed. (Cincinnati: Anderson Publishing, 2002); Howard Zehr, *Changing Lenses: Restorative Justice for Our Times* (Harrisonburg, VA: Herald Press, 2015).

47. For differing rationales, processes, and programs, see Gerry Johnstone, *Restorative Justice: Ideas, Values, Debates* (Portland, OR: Willan Publishing, 2002), 10–35, 161–71.

48. Zehr, *The Little Book of Restorative Justice*, 21.

49. Michael Sandel, introduction to *Liberalism and Its Critics*, ed. Michael Sandel (New York: New York University Press, 1984), 4, 6, 10.

50. Cf. section 3(1)(a), Promotion of National Unity and Reconciliation Act, no. 34, 1995.

51. Desmond Tutu, *No Future without Forgiveness* (London: Rider, 1999), 51. "Ubuntu," says Tutu, "speaks of the very essence of being human." It "means my humanity is caught up, is inextricably bound up" in that of others. "We say, 'a person is a person through other people.' It is not 'I think therefore I am.' It says rather: 'I am human because I belong.' I participate, I share" (34–35).

52. Tutu, *No Future without Forgiveness*, 32–33.

53. Ibid.

54. Testimony of Lukas Baba Sikwepere, at Human Rights' Commission hearing in Heideveld, Cape Town; as reported in Antjie Krog, *Country of My Skull* (Johannesburg: Random House, 1998), 31; cf. Truth and Reconciliation Commission, *TRC Final Report*, vol. 5, chap. 9, para. 9.

55. See Charles Villa-Vicencio, "Telling One Another Stories," in *The Reconciliation of Peoples: Challenge to the Churches*, ed. Gregory Baum and Harold Wells (Maryknoll, NY: Orbis Books, 1997), 37–38.

56. Jean Baudrillard quoted in James E. Young, *The Texture of Memory: Holocaust Memorials and Meaning* (New Haven, CT: Yale University Press, 1993), 1; cf. Minow, *Between Vengeance and Forgiveness*, 118.

57. See Hans-Georg Gadamer, *Truth and Method*, 2nd ed., trans. E. Joel Weinsheimer and Donald G. Marshall (New York: Crossroad, 1991), 482–85.

58. Villa-Vicencio, "Telling One Another Stories," 34.

59. Tutu, *No Future without Forgiveness*, 51–52.

60. Primo Levi, "The Symposium on Simon Wiesenthal," in *The Sunflower: On the Possibilities and Limits of Forgiveness*, rev. ed. (New York: Schocken Books, 1998), 191.

61. See Alan Gewirth, *The Community of Rights* (Chicago: University of Chicago Press, 1996), 16.

62. See Jack Donnelly, *Universal Human Rights in Theory and Practice*, 3rd ed. (Ithaca, NY: Cornell University Press, 2013), 57–60.

63. Gene Outka, "Respect for Persons," in *The Westminster Dictionary of Christian Ethics*, ed. James F. Childress and John Macquarrie (Philadelphia: Westminster Press, 1986), 542.

64. Joel Feinberg, *Social Philosophy* (Englewood Cliffs, NJ: Prentice-Hall, 1973), 88.

65. Ronald Dworkin, *Taking Rights Seriously* (Cambridge, MA: Harvard University, 1978), xi.

66. Brian Orend, *Human Rights: Concept and Context* (Peterborough, ON: Broadview Press, 2002), 26–27.

67. See Amartya Sen, *On Ethics and Economics* (Oxford: Basil Blackwell, 1987), 73, cf. 47–51, 70–78.

68. Ludwig Wittgenstein, *Philosophical Investigations*, 3rd ed., trans. G. E. M. Anscombe (New York: Macmillan, 1958), pt. 1, paras. 497, 664.

69. Henry Shue, *Basic Rights: Subsistence, Affluence, and U.S. Foreign Policy*, 2nd ed. (Princeton, NJ: Princeton University Press, 1996), 18.

70. See Gene Outka, *Agape* (New Haven, CT: Yale University, 1972), 20. Cf. Ronald Dworkin, *Taking Rights Seriously* (Cambridge, MA: Harvard University Press, 1978), 227.

71. Albert Camus, *The Plague* (New York: Alfred A. Knopf, 1960), 230.

72. Cf. John Paul II, *Sollicitudo rei socialis*, nos. 42–43; Cf. the Medellín and Puebla Conference documents of the Latin American Episcopal Conference, in *Liberation Theology: The Documentary History*, ed. Alfred T. Hennelly (Maryknoll, N. Y.: Orbis Books, 1989); Jean Drèze and Amartya Sen, *Hunger and Public Action* (Oxford: Clarendon, 1989), 37–42.

73. Tutu, *No Future without Forgiveness*, 51.

74. Cf. Nigel Biggar, "Making Peace or Doing Justice: Must We Choose?" in *Burying the Past: Making Peace and Doing Justice after Civil Conflict*, ed. Nigel Biggar (Washington, D.C.: Georgetown University Press, 2003), 12.

75. Dworkin, *Taking Rights Seriously*, viii–ix.

76. The Sentencing Project, "Criminal Justice Facts," https://www.sentencingproject.org/criminal-justice-facts/.

77. The Sentencing Project, "Trends in U.S. Corrections," https://www.sentencingproject.org/wp-content/uploads/2016/01/Trends-in-US-Corrections.pdf.

78. The Sentencing Project, "Felony Disenfranchisement," https://www.sentencingproject.org/issues/felony-disenfranchisement/. The Sentencing Project reports that felony disenfranchisement policies "have a disproportionate impact on communities of color. Black Americans of voting age are more than four times more likely to lose their voting rights than the rest of the adult population" (https://www.sentencingproject.org/publications/felony-disenfranchisement-a-primer/).

79. Michelle Alexander, *The New Jim Crow: Mass Incarceration in the Age of Colorblindness*, rev. ed. (New York: The New Press, 2012), 258. See Laurie M. Cassidy and Alex Mikulich, eds., *Interrupting White Privilege* (Maryknoll, NY: Orbis Books, 2007).

80. Adam Gopnik, "The Caging of America," *The New Yorker*, January 30, 2012, 73. Gopnik notes that in the last two decades, "the money that states spend on prisons has risen at six times the rate of spending on higher education" (ibid.).

81. Ryan S. King, Marc Mauer, and Malcolm C. Young, "Incarceration and Crime; A Complex Relationship," "The Sentencing Project," http://www.sentencingproject.org.

82. Amnesty International, *Solitary Confinement in the USA* (London: Amnesty International Publications, 2013), 1.

83. Amnesty International, "Death Penalty," http://www.amnesty.org/en/what-we-do/death-penalty.

84. William J. Stuntz, *The Collapse of American Criminal Justice* (Cambridge, MA: Harvard University Press, 2011), 3.

85. Jeffrey S. Passel, "Measuring Illegal Immigration: How Pew Research Center Counts Unauthorized Immigrants in the U.S." Pew Research Center, https://www.pewresearch.org/fact-tank/2019/07/12/how-pew-research-center-counts-unauthorized-immigrants-in-us/.

86. DHS Immigration Enforcement, 2016, Office of Immigration Statistics, Annual Flow Report, December 2016, http://www.dhs.gov/sites/default/files/publications/DHS%20Immigration%20Enforcement%202016.pdf.

87. Human Rights First, *Jails and Jumpsuits: Transforming the U.S. Immigration Detention System—A Two-Year Review* (New York: Human Rights First, 2011), i, https://www.humanrightsfirst.org/wp-content/uploads/pdf/HRF-Jails-and-Jumpsuits-report.pdf.

88. Human Rights First, "Family Incarceration Continues to Endanger Children, Impede Access to Legal Information & Waste Government Resources," https://www.humanrightsfirst.org/resource/family-incarceration-continues-endanger-children-impede-access-legal-information-waste.

89. Alfred, Lord Tennyson, "Ulysses."

90. Jean-Marc Éla, "Christianity and Liberation in Africa," in *Paths of African Theology*, ed. Rosino Gibellini (Maryknoll, NY: Orbis Books, 1994), 143.

91. Meda Chesney-Lind notes that "nearly half the women in the nation's prisons are women of color: notably 27 percent are African American and 17 percent are Hispanic. The number of Latinas incarcerated increased by 65 percent in the first decade of this century, a figure that reflects a general population increase, but also the increasing involvement of the criminal justice system in the criminalization of immigration, as well as policies and practices relating to the war on drugs"; Chesney-Lind, "'Remember the Ladies': The Problem with Gender-Neutral Reform," in *To Build a Better Criminal Justice System: 25 Experts Envision the Next 25 Years of Reform*, ed. Marc Mauer and Kate Epstein (Washington, DC: The Sentencing Project, 2012), 42.

92. Hannah Arendt, "The Perplexities of the Rights of Man," 297, 299, 301.

93. Kathryn Russell, *The Color of Crime* (New York: New York University, 1988), cited in Alexander, *The New Jim Crow*, 107. M. Shawn Copeland, *Enfleshing Freedom: Body, Race, and Being* (Minneapolis: Fortress Press, 2010), writes from a Womanist perspective: "A white, racially bias-induced horizon defines, censors, controls and segregates different, other, non-white bodies" (15).

94. Alexander, *The New Jim Crow*, 236–44. Cf. the analogous *mujerista* critique of Ada Maria Isasi-Diaz, *En la Lucha (In the Struggle): A Hispanic Women's Liberation Theology* (Minneapolis: Fortress Press, 1993).

95. See Stephen J. Pope, "From Condemnation to Conversion: Seeking Restorative Justice in the Prison System," *America*, November 21, 2001, 13.

96. John Tierney, "For Lesser Crimes, Rethinking Life Behind Bars," *New York Times*, December 11, 2012, A24.

seventeen

DIGNITY AND CONFLICT

Immigration

Victor Carmona

Over the last two decades, the governments of the United States and the European Union have expanded their efforts to externalize their border enforcement. Most recently, their focus has turned to stopping Central American and Syrian immigrants and refugees at the Mexican and Turkish borders, thus externalizing their border enforcement into those countries. U.S. and European attempts have received increasing attention from migration scholars and human rights advocates because they are placing immigrants and refugees at risk. This chapter engages their work from a Catholic human rights theory perspective.

Unprecedented numbers of men, women, and children are attempting to escape the violence roiling Central America and Syria. According to the UN High Commissioner for Refugees (UNHCR), Guatemala, Honduras, and El Salvador "have recently experienced some of the highest homicide rates ever recorded. While a rate above 10 intentional homicides per 100,000 people per year is classified as 'epidemic,' in Guatemala, homicide rates have reached 30–40 in recent years. In Honduras the homicide rate peaked at over 90 in 2011–2012, and reached 103 in El Salvador in 2015."[1] Those are higher homicide rates than the ones they experienced during their civil wars (which took place between the 1960s and the early 1990s).[2] As for Syria, the situation is dire. More than 2,733,000 refugees have made their way to Turkey, where they are hoping to escape one of the most violent civil wars in the Middle East in recent memory.[3]

This chapter takes up the externalization of border enforcement to analyze how and why it threatens the human dignity of immigrants and refugees. To do so, it focuses on the conflict between a person's right to seek safety in a country other than his or her own and a state's right to enforce its border.

Therefore, I focus on the border enforcement policies of the United States and Mexico, and the EU and Turkey, not on the actions of immigrants or refugees or those of their governments. The chapter has four sections. After surveying the border enforcement policies of the governments in question, I turn to an analysis of the Catholic human rights tradition to suggest that its insights on conflicting human rights claims are valuable. David Hollenbach developed those insights during the Cold War, but they address an ideological intractability that still affects immigration issues in general and our understanding of the conflict at hand in particular. In the third section, I argue that the moral order calls for protecting and promoting the right to residence—to permanent residence or resettlement in some other way—if our governments are to protect and promote the human dignity of foreigner and citizen alike. In the fourth section, I conclude that it is precisely that right that the externalization of border enforcement most places at risk.

THE EXTERNALIZATION OF BORDER ENFORCEMENT: HOW DOES IT WORK AND WHAT IS AT STAKE?

The United States and the EU pursue the externalization of their border enforcement in similar ways. In the case of the EU, François Crépeau, the UN special rapporteur on the human rights of migrants, explains that the externalization "of border control . . . involves shifting the responsibility of preventing irregular migration into Europe to countries of departure or transit."[4] According to his report, the EU uses three primary mechanisms to achieve that end.[5] First, it strengthens the capacity of source and transit countries to control their borders. Second, it reaches readmission agreements with transit countries to deport stateless persons and third-country nationals there—including asylum-seekers with failed applications. Finally, in exchange for their cooperation with the previous two mechanisms, the EU signs mobility partnerships with sending and transit countries, offering them a limited number of work visas for their citizens, usually for high-skilled employment. A similar strategy is at work in the case of the United States, where the emphasis is on the first mechanism and, to some degree, the third. Since the United States and Mexico already have a mobility partnership through the North American Free Trade Agreement, the quid pro quo between the countries takes place in other ways.[6] The concern for Crépeau and other human rights advocates is that these mechanisms have weak or absent requirements to protect and promote the human rights of immigrants and refugees.

Ultimately, a security concern appears to be driving those mechanisms. At their testimony before the Inter-American Commission on Human Rights, Jennifer Podkul and Ian Kysel report that "externalization is often framed through a security lens. Control of migration flows is cast as an effort to prevent 'illegal' (or irregular) immigration or to protect migrants from the dangers of the journey."[7] The reason, they suggest, is that the treatment of migration as a political issue has popularized the presumption that immigrants and refugees represent "an inherent security risk."[8] In the United States, for instance, that was the underlying argument behind the attempt by thirty governors to block the resettlement of Syrian refugees in their states in November 2015.[9] The security lens is pervasive because it allows governments to claim that they are pursuing the safety of citizen and foreigner alike.

The externalization of U.S. border enforcement to southern Mexico is evident in both governments' response to a spike in the number of immigrants and refugees that arrived at the Texas-Mexico border in 2014, during the summer months. According to the Migration Policy Institute, in June alone, the U.S. Border Patrol apprehended 10,631 minors and 16,357 mothers with their children.[10] In July of that year, Mexican president Enrique Peña Nieto announced the creation of the Southern Border Plan "to protect and defend the human rights of immigrants that cross into and transit through Mexico; and to arrange border crossings in a manner that increases regional development and security."[11] Among other objectives, the plan seeks to end human smuggling and trafficking between Central America and Mexico. However, multiple reports, including one by the Congressional Research Service, suggest that "the U.S. government has pressured the Mexican government to stave the flow of U.S.-bound illegal migration from Central America," or conversely that "Mexico has been adequately compensated for its efforts through the Mérida Initiative, which provided $79 million in U.S. assistance above the Administration's request for FY2015, partially to support Mexico's southern border efforts."[12] As part of those efforts, the Mexican government modernized twelve ports of entry across Mexico's southern border to increase security. It also established "12 advanced naval bases on the country's rivers and three security cordons that stretch more than 100 miles north of the Mexico-Guatemala and Mexico-Belize borders."[13] Additionally, in 2014, Mexico's Instituto Nacional de Migración (Migration Policy Institute) (the government's immigration enforcement agency) conducted more than 150 raids on *la Bestia*, or "the Beast," a cargo train that carried 500 to 700 persons three times a week on a dangerous journey to Mexico City.[14]

The effects of the externalization of U.S. border enforcement are apparent throughout southern Mexico and the northern triangle of Central America (Guatemala, Honduras, and El Salvador). Mexico now apprehends more adults and children under eighteen from the northern triangle than does the United States. Together, both countries also deport more people there than ever before. The Migration Policy Institute reports that in FY2015, Mexico apprehended 173,000 adults and 29,000 children, whereas the United States apprehended 110,000 adults and 22,000 children.[15] As for deportees, the UNHCR registered 234,561 deportations from both Mexico and the United States to the northern triangle in 2015.[16] Critics of Mexico's southern border plan point out that the country's immigration officers fail to provide adequate humanitarian screening of those they apprehend. As evidence, they point to the Comisión de Ayuda a Refugiados (COMAR, Mexico's refugee agency), which is severely underfunded and understaffed.[17] Those shortcomings adversely affect the human rights of unaccompanied children in particular.

The EU's response to the ongoing Syrian refugee crisis in Greece also reflects the mechanisms of border externalization and the security lens that justifies it. In response to the crisis, in March 2016, officials from the EU and Turkey announced an agreement to "break the business model of the smugglers and to offer migrants an alternative to putting their lives at risk."[18] Their goal is "to end the irregular migration from Turkey to the EU."[19] To that end, the agreement declares Turkey a safe third country for refugees, giving the EU the ability to deport "irregular migrants crossing from Turkey into the Greek islands" back to Turkey while respecting the principle of nonrefoulement. The UN 1951 Refugee Convention lays out that principle: governments may not "expel or return ('refouler') a refugee in any manner whatsoever to the frontiers of territories where his life or freedom would be threatened on account of his race, religion, nationality, membership of a particular social group or political opinion."[20] Additionally, the agreement states that for each Syrian that the EU deports it will resettle another Syrian from a refugee camp in Turkey. Doing so, the officials reason, should "end the human suffering and restore public order."[21] In exchange, the EU is to pay Turkey €6 billion to compensate the government for costs incurred in caring for and managing Syrian refugees and other refugee or immigrant populations there.[22] Additionally, member states will grant visa-free travel to Turkish citizens and restart negotiations around Turkey's admission into the EU.

The potential effects of the EU's border externalization are troubling. On the one hand, it is not clear that the Turkish government has the institutional capacity to process the number of resettlement applications that will result from the agreement. On the other hand, the EU may be unwilling to resettle those refugees. The Migration Policy Institute reports that "more than 350,000 individuals have crossed from Turkey to Greece . . . in the first nine months of 2015."[23] And the situation is worsening. Just in February 2016, more than 57,000 persons did so.[24] Over half of them were Syrian. That same month, the Turkish government had 200,000 refugee applications to process and had so far only processed 38,595 in favor of the applicant.[25] Moreover, the presence of children under eighteen is, as in the Central American case, quite marked. Of the 57,000 persons who crossed into Greece in February 2016, 40 percent were minors, a number that accounts for more than half of all Syrian refugees.[26] As for the EU's ability to resettle Syrian refugees waiting in Turkish camps, its officials have been unable to reach consensus on how to distribute 120,000 refugees among the EU member countries.[27] As a point of comparison, by June 2016, Turkey had received more than 2,733,000 Syrian refugees.[28] At this writing it is not clear how the military coup attempt in Turkey on July 15, 2016, will affect Syrian refugees living there.[29]

Making Migration as Difficult and Dangerous as Possible

The externalization of border enforcement has a long history. Nearly two centuries ago, the United States institutionalized rules and mechanisms to give itself the ability to exercise "remote control" over who may and may not reach its shores. Already in 1819, Congress had set bureaucratic hurdles and shipping rules with the intent of making the transatlantic passage of poor Dutch and Germans nearly impossible. Aristide Zolberg's history of immigration policy in the United States demonstrates that the government has used similar mechanisms towards similar ends ever since.[30] Most recently, in 1993 the U.S. government developed a strategy that it called "prevention through deterrence."[31] According to research by Wayne Cornelius, it hinged on the presumption that *it is* possible to make illegal border crossings so difficult that immigrants and refugees will end up deciding against taking such a risk.[32]

Human rights advocates argue that by strengthening Mexico's capacity to enforce its borders, the United States is driving immigrants and refugees further underground. Both governments are complicit with other actors in placing their lives at greater risk. In Mexico, advocates note that the government's policies have forced Central American immigrants and refugees to rely on routes that "are increasingly falling under the control of organized crime, human traffickers, *maras* or other gangs."[33] They point to three known immigrant massacres—in which 314 victims died, 72 of them were summarily executed—that took place between 2010 and 2012, and also countless disappearances, to illustrate the growing vulnerability of immigrants and refugees who attempt to transit through Mexico on their way to the United States.[34] Their findings also underline the effect that corruption has on the externalization of border enforcement. Los Zetas, a powerful criminal organization, carried out one of those massacres with the alleged support of local government officials and police.[35] Crépeau reaches a similar conclusion with regard to the EU's efforts and their effects on immigrants and refugees. Not only are they reinforcing smuggling rings, but "migrants are made more vulnerable, corruption is made more potent, exploitation more rife, human rights violations are more prevalent and graver, and ultimately lives may be more at risk than before."[36]

Wayne Cornelius and other researchers have found evidence of a causal relationship between border enforcement policies in the southwestern United States and migrant deaths there, but the International Organization for Migration (IOM) cautions that determining "the link between changes in border enforcement policies and *the number* of migrant deaths is not straightforward."[37] Part of the reason is lack of evidence because governments have not prioritized the collection of data on immigrant deaths. As a consequence, the IOM estimates that more than 6,000 persons lost their lives crossing the U.S.-Mexico border since 1998 (mirroring Cornelius's findings), while more than 22,000 have died attempting to reach Europe since 2000.[38] According to the Missing Migrants Project, 3,814 migrants died worldwide during the first six months of 2016, including 2,954 in the Mediterranean, 166 at the U.S.-Mexico border, and 44 along Mexico and Central America.[39] Since many bodies are lost at sea, in mountainous regions, or the desert, estimates may underrepresent the magnitude of the lives lost.[40] Those facts are sufficient to echo Cornelius's own conclusion. They require a debate, he writes, "not just about the efficacy but the morality of a strategy of immigration control that deliberately places people in harm's way."[41] I have met many Catholics (lay, religious, and ordained) who serve at immigrant shelters and parishes across Guatemala, Mexico, and the United States who echo that call because they have seen the suffering of immigrants and refugees firsthand.[42]

Extending the Rights but Not the Duties of Border Enforcement

Readmission agreements allow governments to deport stateless persons and third-country nationals to transit countries. In the case of the EU, once a member state rejects the application of an asylum-seeker, it considers that person an undocumented immigrant who may be deported accordingly. The logic behind the policy is that by resettling a Syrian from a refugee camp in Turkey for each Syrian that officials deport there, people will end attempts to cross illegally into Greece. Yet the EU has not demonstrated the political will to resettle even 120,000 refugees.

Frank McNamara exposes the juridical logic behind the agreements that EU and Turkish officials signed.[43] They allow member states to exercise an indirect control over a foreign international border by enlisting a third state, in this case Turkey, to execute EU immigration policy. Such control is indirect, he explains, "in that the third State is left to implement that policy."[44] The likely purpose of readmission agreements is that indirect control prevents deportees from engaging the extraterritorial jurisdiction of the European Court of Human Rights (ECHR).[45]

The effect is both practical and ethical. As Silvia Morgades argues, readmission agreements operate as a "contention barrier or as an external protection fence" for the EU.[46] Furthermore, they permit a member state to separate its responsibility for securing the human rights of asylum-seekers from its ability to control its borders. McNamara concludes that "the rights available to asylum seekers upon arrival at the traditional external borders of the EU become illusory—real but unattainable. . . . Asylum seekers are thus placed in a position whereby they encounter European migration control and effectively reach a European border within a third State but that Member State will not be responsible for ensuring rights normally assumed at a border."[47] Readmission agreements offer states, then, a way to extend their border enforcement without the responsibilities that such enforcement generally entails.

Imposing a Global Division of Labor between Rich and Emerging Countries

Mobility partnerships show that the management of migration is an essential aspect of international relations. Although some scholars argue convincingly that the externalization of border enforcement speaks to the failure of domestic immigration reforms—this is the case, they believe, in the United States—

it also speaks to its growing use as a tool of statecraft.[48] Crépeau, for instance, notes "that the partnerships appear to be used *as a means for* the European Union to further pursue its agenda of strengthening border controls through preconditioning limited labor opportunities, largely for skilled migrants, and the promise of visa liberalization/facilitation. . . . Viewed this way," he writes, "the mobility partnership can be described as a mechanism for ensuring the externalization of border controls, *in exchange for* tightly controlled and limited migration opportunities."[49] The rights of immigrants and refugees, then, are not simply a juridical or legal matter but tend to be used as bargaining chips in the management of international affairs.

From this perspective, it is necessary to place mobility partnerships—and the externalization of border enforcement as such—within the broader context of the imbalance of power that is inherent to North–South international relations. In a thorough study of EU asylum policy, Alexander Betts and James Milner analyze a series of bilateral treaties that the EU signed with several African countries over the last fifteen years.[50] Their analysis identifies a conventional logic that, I believe, is also at work in its agreement with Turkey. Simply put, "European states have based their approach on the assumption that their role in the global refugee regime should be predominantly financial, based on funding first asylum within the South, where the majority of the current refugees are situated. Primary responsibility for physical protection should then rest with states in the region of origin, which can be compensated or leveraged into playing this role *through either incentives or coercion*."[51] European politicians and civil servants commonly use that reasoning to favor a global division of labor that the EU imposes through the externalization of border enforcement. It is less expensive for governments from the global North to pay those in the global South to halt and take in refugees than resettling them in Europe, for example, so that "a division of responsibility can be made between North and South."[52] A similar logic seems to be at work in the United States, but it tends to be expressed in security terms. That seems to be the case for those who argue "that Mexico has been adequately compensated for its [enforcement] efforts through the Mérida Initiative," which exists to coordinate binational efforts against organized crime.[53] The unresolved question as to whether the United States enlisted Mexico's support in the externalization of its border enforcement through incentive, coercion, or both, reflects the nature of their unequal partnership.

The externalization of border enforcement furthers a global division of labor that weakens the global refugee regime and raises questions of distributive justice. The UN 1951 Refugee Convention creates an institutional framework that rests on two principles: asylum and burden-sharing. Both are necessary to protect refugees from being deported to countries that threaten their life or freedom because of their race, religion, nationality, membership in a particular social group, or political opinion.[54] The challenge, as Alexander Betts explains, is that the "existing regime has a strongly institutionalized norm of asylum that is widely accepted; however, norms related to burden-sharing are weak and largely discretionary."[55] As a consequence, states are technically obligated to grant asylum to refugees that reach their borders but are not required to assist other states in meeting that obligation. Since most refugees seek asylum in neighboring countries, not in faraway ones, that creates an unbalanced system. Worldwide, in 2015 the top three refugee source countries were Syria, Afghanistan, and Somalia (which displaced 4.9, 2.7, and 1.1 million refugees, respectively), while the countries that most hosted refugees were Turkey, Pakistan, and Lebanon (which in turn received 2.5, 1.6, and 1.1 million refugees, respectively).[56] The problem: although the United States and the EU are the top two contributors to UNHCR, those funds are insufficient to sustain refugee camps that provide basic humanitarian assistance across the global South in countries with already stressed political, economic, and social structures.[57]

THE CATHOLIC HUMAN RIGHTS TRADITION

Jesuit Christian ethicist David Hollenbach has consistently engaged the Catholic conception of human dignity and rights developed in modern Catholic social teaching. Consequently, his thought has become an authoritative source for Catholic thinkers.[58] In this section, I take up his insights into how the Catholic human rights tradition addresses the political reality of conflicting rights claims to analyze the conflict in the Central American and Syrian refugee crises. In the midst of the Cold War, the human rights debate focused on the compatibility of political (i.e., civil) and socioeconomic rights.[59] Generally, liberal capitalist countries espoused the former, while Marxist communist countries highlighted the latter. At the time, the consensus among government officials representing each bloc was that one set of human rights or the other could be implemented, but not both—societies and their governments had to choose one. Hollenbach traced the intractability of the human rights debate to "the incoherence of the concept of right" and to ideologically driven attempts to fragment human rights into unrelated sets of political and socioeconomic rights.[60] An integral account of human rights was necessary. The solution, he argued, is to articulate and apply "an understanding of rights which distinguishes and relates the stable and inviolable element of rights vis-à-vis their mutable and instrumental aspect."[61]

Since conflicting rights claims are endemic to immigration debates, Hollenbach's analysis of the Catholic human rights tradition offers two useful insights. First, his critique of the incoherence of the concept of rights suggests the need for more subtle interpretations of the Catholic tradition's understanding of the human right to migrate; we must distinguish which elements of that right are stable and which are mutable. Second, the ongoing immigration debate in the North American context echoes an aspect of Hollenbach's research. The global conflict between liberalism and Marxism vis-à-vis human rights is different from the ongoing conflict between domestic, economic, and cultural interests vis-à-vis immigrants and refugees. Nevertheless, those conflicts share an important characteristic: both are driven by an analogous ideological intractability that harms any society's ability to discern how to protect and promote all human rights (i.e., political, economic, and cultural), including foreigners' rights to immigrate or seek asylum. From such a perspective, the Catholic human rights tradition underlines that all human rights—and the human rights of all—are ultimately related.

Human Dignity in the Catholic Tradition: A Paradoxical Concept

In the Roman Catholic tradition, human dignity is a somewhat paradoxical concept. Understanding why and how so helps clarify how human dignity relates to human rights in general and the human right to migrate in particular. The concept of human dignity has three important aspects. First, as Hollenbach explains in *Claims in Conflict: Retrieving and Renewing the Catholic Human Rights Tradition*, human dignity is a fundamental norm that lies at "the source of all moral principles."[62] Human beings have worth because, as the tradition understands it, we are made in the image and likeness of God. We are sacred and precious.[63] Human worth, in other words, is inherent to our nature. Second, human dignity is transcendent. No person, society, or authority can bestow it. Neither leaders (be they presidents, kings, or popes) nor citizenship, nor political entity (including legislative bodies) is the source of human dignity. Third, though human dignity is a fundamental transcendent norm, it is also a concrete one. In Hollenbach's words: the "primary referent of the term is not conceptual but existential: concrete existing human beings. At the same time the bare notion of human dignity is nearly empty of meaning. This is so because without further specification the notion of human dignity lacks all reference to particular needs, actions and relationships."[64] On the one hand, human dignity is not identical with any one need, action, or relationship because it is inherent to our nature. On the other hand, as a child of God, a person has a rightful claim to the conditions that are necessary for human flourishing. Human dignity transcends material needs, human relationships, and structures but it does not escape them.

The paradoxical understanding of human dignity in the Catholic tradition clarifies its definition of human rights. As Hollenbach defines them, "Rights are the conditions for the realization of human worth in action."[65] Perhaps one of the most pressing concerns for the Catholic human rights tradition, more so in the aftermath of World War II, is the tendency by political, economic, and social leaders to affirm human dignity and human rights either partially (by acknowledging some human rights but not others) or in the abstract. Against this, the Catholic tradition affirms and differentiates multiple kinds of human rights, including the rights of movement.

The Rights of Movement in the Catholic Tradition

The Catholic tradition differentiates and relates human rights using a twofold process. First, it differentiates rights by domains or sectors of human personality—including rights of movement. According to Hollenbach, the tradition "has identified a number of characteristic needs, freedoms and kinds of relationship which must be met or protected in the life of every individual person."[66] Unlike liberal or Marxist accounts of human rights that protect and promote either political freedoms and relationships or socioeconomic needs and relationships, the Catholic account points out that the conditions of human dignity require all of the above. Bodily rights, political rights, associational rights, economic rights, and the rights of movement are all necessary. In figure 17.1, these sectors are evident as arrows that cut from the outer circle towards the inner circle marked "human dignity." More so, to each of these "essential areas of human existence," Hollenbach explains, "corresponds a set of human rights which defend human dignity within that sector."[67] For example, "bodily rights"—which figure 17.1 illustrates at twelve o'clock—are necessary to protect human dignity. Our embodied nature requires not simply that soci-

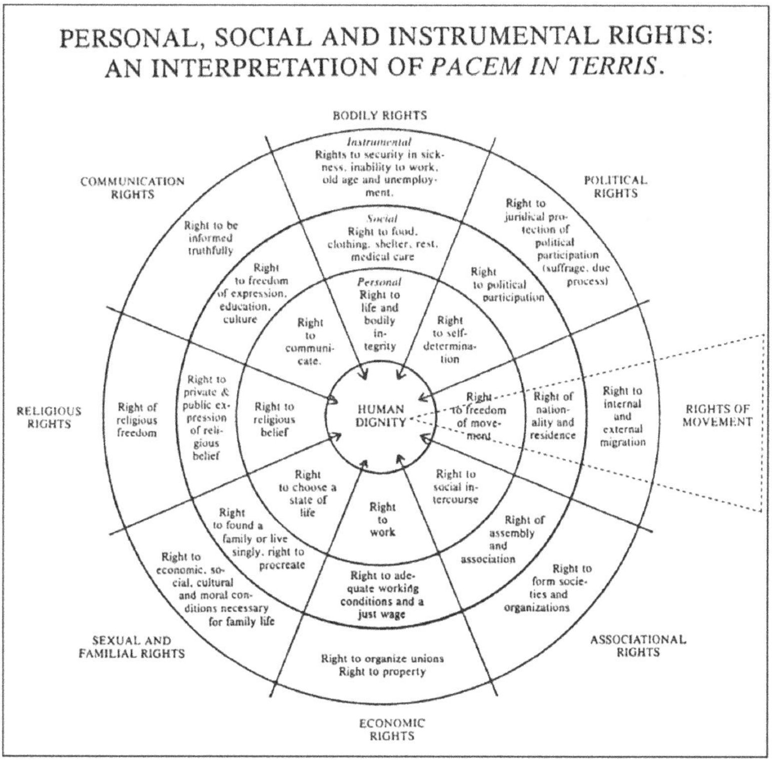

FIGURE 17.1. A Schematic Interpretation of the Rights of Movement. Hollenbach uses this chart to offer "a schematic interpretation" of the relationship between the personal, social, and instrumental human rights in *Pacem in terris*. The inner ring identifies core stable personal human rights. The middle and outer rings identify mutable social and instrumental human rights, respectively. I have added a dashed triangle to highlight the rights of movement, one of eight sectors of human rights (From Hollenbach, *Claims in Conflict*, 98).

eties and their governments affirm the right to life. It also calls on them to secure whatever goods and conditions are necessary to protect that fundamental right for each and every person: food, clothing, medical care, and income assistance to obtain these basic goods in case of incapacity (sickness or old age). As for the "rights of movement"—illustrated at three o'clock—they follow a similar pattern. Societies must secure the right of nationality and/or residence for all persons living in them; likewise, their governments must ensure the right to immigrate and emigrate. Otherwise, freedom of movement, which is essential for human dignity, will suffer.

The Catholic tradition also differentiates and relates three levels of human rights. Since it conceives of persons as "essentially social and institution building beings," as Hollenbach explains, "the *personal rights* which belong to every human being in an unmediated way create duties which bind other persons, society and the state."[68] These three levels of rights—personal, social, and instrumental—are evident as concentric circles that extend out from the inner circle marked "human dignity." Hollenbach goes on to observe that each of these levels is governed by "differing degrees of historical contingency and variability."[69] In general, contingency increases the further the circle extends from its core of human dignity. The tradition differentiates these three levels to underline their historicity, but it also asserts their dynamic unity in service of the protection and promotion of human dignity.

The Catholic tradition affirms that personal rights—including the right to freedom of movement—are stable because they lay claim to goods and conditions that are fundamental to human dignity everywhere and always. Among these, Hollenbach also lists the right to life, self-determination, social intercourse, and work. Social and instrumental rights, however, are mutable (though no less important) because the historical contexts in which societies and institutions must secure those rights are constantly shifting. Generally, that dynamic is more accelerated in industrial and information-age societies, including in the United States and the EU, because the pace of technological, economic, and even social change is greater there than in developing societies.

Social rights—including the right to nationality and residence—are those conditions that must be present in society for the preservation of personal rights and thus of human dignity. The Catholic tradition differs greatly here from the political culture in the United States and some political parties in the EU, which tend to conceive of rights negatively as boundaries that society may not transgress. Instead, the Catholic tradition conceives of rights in a more positive light: they create duties that bind us to other persons and broader society because "human dignity is realized in a positive way through mutuality and social unity."[70] Simply put, human interdependence is real and historically dependent—we rely on one another to live and flourish. *Social rights* depend on and strengthen social bonds. As Hollenbach explains, "Personal dignity is an attribute of the individual, but it is also mediated socially."[71] The implication is that a person may only effectively secure his or her personal and social rights by protecting those of another. Social relationships, therefore, can enhance or hinder the mutual dignity of those who take part in them. Among social rights, Hollenbach also lists the right to food and clothing, to political participation, the right of assembly, and the right to a just wage.

Instrumental rights—including the right to internal and external migration—are those conditions that must be present in macro institutions for the preservation of social and personal rights, and thus of mutual and personal dignity. The Catholic human rights tradition differentiates this set of rights because "social existence," as Hollenbach explains, "is shaped and structured by large-scale institutions such as the state, the law, the economy, the health care system, etc."[72] Institutions have an indirect—though quite significant—effect on human dignity, for example, the UN, the World Bank, national governments, and so on. The implication is that the Catholic tradition acknowledges that institutions and the policies that they pursue do shape social life, even if they do so in unexpected ways. Among instrumental rights, Hollenbach also lists the right to security in sickness, to due process, the right to form organizations, the right to organize unions, and to own private property.

THE MORAL ORDER AND THE RIGHTS OF MOVEMENT IN *PACEM IN TERRIS*

John XXIII wrote *Pacem in terris* soon after a military crisis brought the United States and the Soviet Union to the brink of World War III.[73] In it, he addresses the right to migrate as part of a broader question: How may the world's citizens, their societies, and governments attain world peace, or at the least avert another global war? Peace, the encyclical suggests, hinges on their ability to order properly human and institutional relations according to the natural order itself.[74] In so doing, they may achieve the protection and promotion of political and socioeconomic rights—furthering human dignity in an integral manner—and the legitimate exercise of political authority, which secures these rights—furthering the global common good. Evidently, Pope John's response rests on the principle that "politics, especially political authority, are grounded in the moral order of the universe."[75] The tradition's stance that the moral has primacy over the political is front and center. The closer the whole of the political order comes to reflecting the cosmic order, the nearer to peace the former will be.[76] With this methodological perspective in mind, the encyclical's teaching on the rights of movement becomes apparent.

John XXIII offers his teaching on migration within a broader account of a morally grounded political order that has four distinct spheres: the social sphere, which exists in the order between persons; the national sphere, which orders relations between individuals and public authorities; the international order, which exists between states; and the order subsisting in the global community as a whole. Pope John explicitly addresses the political implications of immigration as an aspect of the moral order that governs two of the four spheres: in the order between persons and in the order between states.

Rights of Movement and the Moral Order between Peoples

In its section on the order between persons, *Pacem in terris* defines the rights of movement and identifies the good they substantiate, namely, human dignity, which the encyclical affirms as membership in the fellowship of humankind. The full text of paragraph 25 states: "Again, every human being has the right to freedom of movement and of residence within the confines of his own State. When there are just reasons in favor of it, he must be permitted to emigrate to other countries and take up residence there. The fact that he is a citizen of a particular State does not deprive him of membership in the human family, nor of citizenship in that universal society, the common, world-wide fellowship of men."[77] A close reading of the text reveals that the realities of the international political system frame the encyclical's analysis. The key concepts at work are the person (i.e., "human being"), his or her homeland (i.e., "his own State"), and the international borders to be crossed to settle elsewhere (i.e., "he must be permitted to emigrate to other countries and take up residence there"). Nonetheless, the text defines the rights of movement in relation to the subject who claims those rights for himself or herself, not in terms of their effects on the rights of either the communities of origin or destination or their political authorities. The state *is not* the subject at hand.

Specifically, paragraph 25 defines three human rights pertaining to people on the move. Using Hollenbach's terminology, those are the personal right to freedom of movement; the social right to residence; and the instrumental right to emigrate and immigrate. Each of those rights substantiates a person's membership in the human family—and thus his or her human dignity—within the bounds of a particular dimension of the political order. Together they secure a person's human dignity in his or her homeland (via the freedom of movement and the right of nationality and residence) and during his or her transition to another land if need be (via the right to emigrate and immigrate).

On this latter point, Catholic rights theory is entirely different from U.S. practice. The history of immigration policy shows that the U.S. Congress fought or negotiated to secure the rights of foreigners to emigrate or exit their homelands (as was the case with the British, German, and Chinese empires, much as *Pacem in terris* affirms).[78] However, the United States does not recognize a foreigner's right to immigrate (neither do most countries) or receive asylum.[79] Even so, Catholic rights theory has a more nuanced stance on the right to immigrate and its implications than what either opponents or advocates of immigrant rights and refugees tend to presume.

Paragraph 25 of *Pacem in terris* affirms the right to residency within the confines of one's homeland, and it also affirms membership in human society, a stance that ultimately grounds, I believe, an immigrant's or refugee's social right to residency in the society in which he or she is seeking safety. Social rights secure the conditions that must be present in any society, including ours, for the preservation of all personal rights and, ultimately, human dignity. Instrumental rights, in turn, secure institutional conditions that are necessary to preserve social rights and, consequently, human dignity. Therefore, it is not possible to affirm that a person has the right to leave his or her homeland and to immigrate to another country without also acknowledging his or her social right to reside in the latter.

Paragraph 25 of *Pacem in terris*, nonetheless, does not require any political community to grant citizenship immediately and automatically to any foreigner who claims his or her instrumental and social rights to immigrate and reside there. On the one hand, Catholic social teaching recognizes a state's right to control its borders to protect the domestic common good. On the other hand, that right is relative, not absolute. (I will explain how so in the next section, which addresses immigration as an aspect of the order between states.) In the U.S. context, the implication is that although the federal government should acknowledge immigration, asylum, and residency as human rights, U.S. society and its government also have the right to determine how a foreigner must integrate if he or she is to become one of their own. Because of an integral understanding of human rights, the tradition affirms that the social rights of all—American and foreigner alike—are at stake. Thus, *Pacem in terris* implies neither that foreigners have a right to citizenship (this would vitiate the social rights of Americans) nor that Americans or Congress have the right to bar them from some form of legal residency, a situation that would eviscerate the social rights of immigrants and refugees (much as is the case of undocumented immigrants living in the United States today). John XXIII, therefore, offers American

Catholics and our fellow citizens a way forward between two morally unacceptable extremes: formal, permanent lack of membership for all foreigners and immediate full social, economic, and political membership for all foreigners.[80]

To summarize, the moral order that exists between persons grounds the freedom of movement as a human right that substantiates the good of human dignity. To that end, societies must protect and promote the social right of foreigners to residency. Governments must facilitate that ability by securing a person's instrumental right not just to leave his or her homeland but also to transit safely across countries to reach the community where he or she intends to settle. From this perspective, the externalization of border enforcement contravenes the moral order and consequently threatens the life of immigrants and refugees precisely because it weakens their human dignity.

To illustrate, as I explained above in the first section, the externalization of border enforcement that the government of the United States and the EU states are pursuing may be increasing the number of migrant deaths along their borders and those of Mexico and Turkey. The strategy of prevention through deterrence is having that effect because it impedes the instrumental right of foreigners to immigrate safely. Additionally, it hinders the capacity of those societies to secure the social right of foreigners to residency—to resettlement. Immigration debates in the United States and Europe may be displaying that limited ability by normalizing dehumanizing rhetoric that serves to advance the view that Muslim refugees or the undocumented represent inherent national security threats that need to be managed accordingly.[81] The externalization of border enforcement and the strategy that underpins it contravene the moral order that exists between persons because they limit the rights of movement that those escaping violence in Syria and Central America are claiming for themselves. In this light, the question for European, Turkish, American, and Mexican peoples is how should these foreigners integrate into their societies, not whether. It is prudent for governments and societies to have security concerns, but this may not be the only lens through which they view immigrants, be they refugees or undocumented.

Border Enforcement Rights and the Moral Order between States

What, then, is John XXIII's teaching on migration in relation to a state's right to control its borders, and what goods does its right substantiate? *Pacem in terris* addresses this question as part of its account of the political order between states, specifically, in its third section, paragraphs 98 and 107. It begins and ends by affirming the human right to emigrate and immigrate. To interpret the text it is necessary to understand how Pope John conceives of sovereignty and international relations.

According to paragraph 98, which sets John XXIII's gloss in motion, truth and justice regulate sovereignty and international order. Peaceful relations between sovereign nations would reflect as much. For this reason, its first sentence counsels that "States must further these relationships by taking positive steps to pool their material and spiritual resources,"[82] that is, they must collaborate. A neo-Thomist presumption that persons in authority use their practical reason to discern the right course of action is at work here. John XXIII expects a country's authorities to discern objectively the international affairs entrusted to them and to act accordingly: in good faith, in truth and justice. From that perspective, the purpose of a country's civil authorities and the border they control are inextricably bound. Both serve the common good and lack any self-referential value. In its last sentence, paragraph 98 explicitly addresses border enforcement in relation to emigration in a manner that underlines Pope John's unconventional understanding of global affairs.[83] It starkly illustrates the need for states to practice solidarity with one another. "We must bear in mind that of its very nature civil authority exists," the pope writes, "not to confine men within the frontiers of their own nations, but primarily to protect the common good of the State, which certainly cannot be divorced from the common good of the entire human family."[84]

Pacem in terris thus conceives of sovereignty and international relations in terms of the common good and solidarity. John XXIII defines the state's right to enforce its borders accordingly. States may enforce their borders because doing so allows them to protect the domestic common good. Yet, civil authorities may so focus on asserting an absolute claim of sovereignty and autonomy that they may hinder solidarity in their exercise of international relations. Simply put, Catholics and other Christians in the United States and Europe may conceive of immigration and refugee policies as they affect their country's sovereignty and the domestic common good. However, the Catholic rights tradition also conceives of those policies as they relate to a nation's solidarity with other peoples. In other words, though we may conceive first and foremost of immigrants and refugees as potential threats to the common good, the Church conceives of migration as a boon to global solidarity and peace.

Thus, *Pacem in terris* envisions borders as demarcating peoples and places within which political authorities pursue the common good, a pursuit to be undertaken in league with other states. John XXIII's reasoning is straightforward: land, capital, and population are unequally distributed across the world. No single state possesses these goods in the correct proportion to autonomously protect and promote its commonweal. Specifically, no state has sufficient arable land, implements, and laborers to secure its needs. Therefore, states need to practice solidarity. "It is imperative, therefore," he argues, "that nations enter into collaboration with each other, and facilitate the circulation of goods, capital and manpower."[85] The implication is that state sovereignty serves to attain the goods mentioned above—and ultimately wealth—in collaboration with others. Since land is difficult to share, the practical solution is to share people and the goods they produce.[86] Pope John's analysis oversimplifies a complex economic reality—especially given globalization today, at its core his is an argument for coordinated resource allocation. Even if the mechanism overemphasizes the government's role, the principle is sound. A more balanced access to the goods necessary for the commonweal of all has a greater probability of leading to peace. The practice of allowing immigrants into our country for the sake of the domestic common good and global solidarity begets peace.

The previous measure of reality has John XXIII advocate "the policy of bringing the work to the workers, wherever possible, rather than bringing workers to the scene of the work."[87] Reflecting pastoral sensitivity and knowledge of the human heart, he argues that this solution is necessary so that "many people . . . be afforded an opportunity of increasing their resources without being exposed to the painful necessity of uprooting themselves from their own homes, settling in a strange environment, and forming new social contacts."[88] States must acknowledge, therefore, that forced migrations are an experience riddled with pain and conflict, both for the sending and receiving nations, and must be avoided.

If states fail to avoid forced migrations for the sake of the common good of their own peoples, then they must act in solidarity to lessen their negative effect by acknowledging the human rights of such immigrants and refugees. In paragraphs 105 and 106, John XXIII writes:

> For this reason, it is not irrelevant to draw the attention of the world to the fact that these refugees are persons and all their rights as persons must be recognized. Refugees cannot lose these rights simply because they are deprived of citizenship in their own states.[89]

> And among man's *personal rights* we must include his right to enter a country in which he hopes to be able to provide more fittingly for himself and his dependents. It is therefore the duty of State officials to accept such immigrants and—so far as the good of their own community, rightly understood, permits—to further the aims of those who may wish to become members of a new society.[90]

The echo of John XXIII's teaching on the rights of movement in the first section of *Pacem in terris* (which addresses the order between peoples) is evident. In paragraphs 105 and 106, he affirms the same personal, social, and instrumental human rights to immigrate, but now does so explicitly in relationship to a state's right to enforce its borders. Here, furthermore, Pope John leaves no doubt as to the duty of government officials to facilitate the instrumental rights of immigrants by granting them entrance into their country. Yet Pope John's intervention with regard to the social right of immigrants remains nuanced. Although he asks government officials to facilitate the integration of immigrants and refugees who desire to join their society by becoming its members (and thus, eventually, its citizens), he leaves the specifics of that question open. The receiving society and/or government may decide against granting them full membership status. Nonetheless, Pope John's instantiation of the personal right to freedom of movement may be startling to Catholics and other Christians in the United States and Europe. In paragraph 106 he seems to fully equate a person's freedom of movement with the instrumental right to immigrate. In my research, I have not found similar papal claims with regard to other personal and instrumental rights that are so closely matched (see figure 17.1). Perhaps, when compared with other sectors, human rights concerning movement are *sui generis* in that respect. If so, it would imply that the right to immigrate is more fundamental to the protection of human dignity than other instrumental rights are.[91]

Interpreters may argue that paragraphs 105 and 106 refer exclusively to the narrow case of political refugees, but its placement in the third section of the encyclical offers sufficient reason to suggest that it includes all those who have been forced from their homeland for economic and social reasons.[92] Nearly thirty years after *Pacem in terris*, the Pontifical Council for the Pastoral Care of Migrants and Itinerant People clarifies this interpretation further in "Refugees: A Challenge to Solidarity."[93] In that document, the pontifical council takes up the definition of refugee that is laid out in the UN 1951 Refugee Convention:

it is a person who leaves his or her homeland "owing to a well-founded fear of being persecuted for reasons of race, religion, nationality, membership of a particular social group or political opinion."[94] Nevertheless, the pontifical council observes that the Refugee Convention's definition fails to include "victims of armed conflicts, erroneous economic policy or natural disasters."[95] These persons are "de facto" refugees, it argues, "given the involuntary nature of their migration."[96]

The normative implication is clear. "In the case of the so-called *economic migrants*," the pontifical council states, "justice and equity demand that appropriate distinctions be made. Those who flee economic conditions that threaten their lives and physical safety must be treated differently from those who emigrate simply to improve their position."[97] The pontifical council's position on this point does not explicitly rest on the position that poverty ultimately means death.[98] Its position, nevertheless, acknowledges the needs of economic refugees who are escaping death. Thus, just border enforcement policies must advance, not hinder, a government's ability to distinguish between political and de facto economic refugees on the one hand, and economic immigrants on the other. From this perspective, though governments may have moral grounds to deport economic immigrants, this is not the case with regard to economic refugees.[99] Neither the pontifical document nor *Pacem in terris* offers specific policy recommendations on how governments may achieve such a distinction. This lies beyond their purview. The perspective offered by both texts, nonetheless, stands in sharp contrast to current practice.

To summarize, the moral order between states grounds their right to control their borders so they may substantiate the domestic common good and global solidarity. It calls for governments to secure some form of residence for foreigners, thus mirroring the pope's stance on the order between peoples. The reasons for this, however, are different in this section of *Pacem in terris*. The moral ground for the state's duty is not—at least directly—the foreigner's human dignity: it is the domestic common good for which all civil authorities are responsible, and it is international solidarity that civil authorities must also pursue through generous immigration and refugee policies. The reason is that states must do so if they are to secure their own commonwealth alongside that of other states. To deny this understanding of the moral order leads to a country's self-destruction and to the weakening of the international system.

To illustrate, the externalization of border enforcement that the United States and the EU are pursuing weakens their governments' ability to distinguish between refugees and economic immigrants. The strategy of prevention through deterrence is a blunt instrument that threatens the same violence—including death—to all persons who are attempting to reach the United States and Europe. It threatens the lives of those who are escaping armed conflicts (as are Syrian and Central American refugees), unsound economic policies, or natural disasters as much as it threatens the lives of those who are pursuing economic opportunity. Furthermore, the externalization of border enforcement is advancing a type of international collaboration that weakens the common good because it is expanding the rights—but not the duties—of the United States and the EU over their borders and those of other states. For instance, these governments are curtailing the extraterritorial jurisdiction of their courts, especially so in the case of the European Court of Human Rights, thus facilitating actions that may further weaken the ability of those societies to administer justice by protecting the human rights of foreigners and citizens alike. Finally, the externalization of border enforcement is also weakening global solidarity. The governments of the United States and the EU have imposed a division of labor between rich and emerging countries to manage the global refugee regime. They advanced this strategy as an alternative to resettling refugees in their societies. Yet, as the Pontifical Council for the Pastoral Care of Migrants and Itinerant Peoples argues, these "camps must remain what they were intended to be: an emergency and therefore temporary solution."[100] Refugee camps have become a permanent solution that is morally untenable because it threatens the social rights of refugees to residence. This strategy does not just present problems of distributive justice. It has shielded U.S. and EU societies from their moral obligation to resettle Central American and Syrian refugees in their midst. This strategy is detrimental not just to refugees, but to the international system itself. In the near future, scholars will likely analyze to what extent fear of immigrants and refugees played a role in the UK's vote to leave the EU and in Donald Trump's election as president of the United States. Both decisions will likely reshape international relations and the management of global population movements for years to come.

The Externalization of Border Enforcement: A Fissure in the Catholic Bishops' Response

Pacem in terris lays the theoretical foundation for a Catholic conception of the human right to freedom of movement and the right of states to control their borders. Nevertheless, it is necessary to acknowledge that the leadership of the Catholic Church is not of one mind when it comes to relying on that tradition to shape its pastoral response in the North American and European contexts. Catholic bishops across the United States and Mexico have taken public stances that reflect an underlying consensus in support of the rights of Central American immigrants and refugees because they are escaping gang violence, but the same is not the case in Europe.[101] The Church's response in Europe suggests a fissure between bishops in Central and Eastern Europe on the one side and bishops in Western Europe on the other.

The fissure is visible in the European bishops' response to concerns over the distinction to be made between refugees and economic immigrants—which gets to a state's right to control its borders—and to the question of integration, which then gets to the freedom of movement. In the early days of September 2015, reflecting what appeared to be a common stance among ecclesial leaders in Hungary, Bishop László Kiss-Rigó suggested that Syrian immigrants are not escaping war but represent, instead, "a kind of intrusion. They aren't refugees," he said, "they are economic immigrants, provocateurs, and who knows what kind of strangers."[102] Hungarian researchers further report that Bishop Gyula Márfi, also of Hungary, believed the main cause of migration to be "*jihad*."[103] At the time, ecclesial leaders in Hungary, the Czech Republic, and Poland appeared to be open to welcoming Christian refugees, but not Muslim ones, in part because of concerns over the latter's (un)willingness or (in)ability to adapt to life in Europe.[104] Ecclesial leaders in Germany, Belgium, and Italy, meanwhile, affirmed that "it is a Christian duty to help the refugees, whatever their origin or religion."[105]

An analysis of the reasons behind the fissure and the explicit or implicit theological-ethical reasoning that led Catholic bishops to reach opposing conclusions are beyond the purpose of this case study. Nonetheless, it is helpful to highlight two differences between the bishops' response in North America and in Europe. First, Catholic bishops in the United States and Mexico are responding to the needs of refugees across societies that, being Protestant and Catholic, mostly acknowledge each other as Christian. The European response needs to account for the challenge of addressing an interreligious dimension, not just an ecumenical one.[106] Second, U.S. and Mexican bishops published a joint pastoral letter on migration in 2003 to identify specific biblical and theological grounds for shared policy principles that inform their joint stance with their respective governments and their immigration policies.[107] And although that pastoral letter is beginning to show its age, it strengthened practices and relationships that continue to inform the stance of the Catholic Church's leaders there, even as the pastoral reality remains in flux. Although in my research I have come across documents that speak to an increasingly active Migration Section at the Caritas in Veritate Commission of the Council of European Bishops' Conferences, there is no evidence of a similar process to the one that the bishops of the United States and Mexico decided to take up nearly twenty years ago.[108] Writing an analogous document in the European context would be a more complicated endeavor, but the process may also strengthen relationships that the Caritas in Veritate Commission appears to be in the process of forging across Eastern, Central, and Western Europe. Such a process may foster greater unity in the bishops' pastoral response to the Syrian refugee crisis.

During early September 2016, representatives from the Catholic bishops' conferences of Central and Eastern Europe met and addressed the ongoing Syrian refugee crisis. Nearly a year after their initial reactions, opposition to lending humanitarian assistance to Muslim refugees seemed to have softened, at least formally. According to a press release, the bishops who were present at that meeting "feel a special duty to help persecuted Christians, but they do not exclude from their hearts any other human person in need of help."[109] Time will tell whether bishops in Hungary, the Czech Republic, and Poland take actions that, in the words of Pope Francis, offer "concrete hope" to Christian *and* Muslim Syrian refugees.[110] The bishops' desire to prioritize the needs of Christians over those of Muslims may require an examination of the internal coherence of the Catholic human rights tradition (in light of the order of charity, for instance) and its usefulness in addressing conflicting right claims in present and future population movements elsewhere in the world.[111]

THE EXTERNALIZATION OF BORDER ENFORCEMENT: A CATHOLIC CRITIQUE

The governments of the United States and the EU are externalizing their border enforcement to Mexico and Syria using three kinds of mechanisms that threaten the human dignity of immigrants and refugees. First, the lack of data makes it difficult to establish direct causality between government actions and the number of migrant deaths beyond those taking place at the U.S.-Mexico border, but the work of scholars and human rights advocates suggests that the strategy of prevention through deterrence developed there has gained global influence. By deliberately placing immigrants and refugees in harm's way, the governments of the United States, Mexico, Syria, and the members of the EU may be complicit in placing the lives of immigrants and refugees at greater risk. That strategy threatens the very lives of those who are escaping military and gang violence by unleashing yet more violence against them. Second, readmission agreements are giving states, especially members of the EU, the ability to shirk their duty to secure the human rights of asylum-seekers who would otherwise be reaching their borders. They allow them to impose that duty on transit countries with governments and societies that have even fewer means to do so. Finally, mobility partnerships further a global division of labor between rich and emerging countries. They highlight the imbalance of power that exists in international relations and its effect on the rights of immigrants and refugees. The United States uses that dynamic to enlist Mexico's support in stopping Central Americans—many of whom are potential asylum-seekers. The EU relies on that imbalance to enlist Turkey's support in stopping Syrians from reaching Greece. In both cases, governments exchanged funds or access to a high-skilled labor market with the effect of weakening the human rights of those who are attempting to escape violence.

Evidently, a noticeable gap exists between a Catholic conception of the rights of movement that protect the human dignity of immigrants and refugees and the mechanisms that governments in the United States and the EU are using to externalize their enforcement to southern Mexico and Turkey. *Pacem in terris* conceives of global migrations as an essential component of global solidarity and peace. That faith-informed perspective stands in stark contrast to the security lens that prevails today, which conceives of immigrants and refugees as inherent threats against that peace.

The Catholic human rights tradition frames immigration as an issue of international relations, that is, as a global phenomenon that plays itself out within the political structure of the nation-state system. As a result, *Pacem in terris* acknowledges the conflict that exists between the foreigner's right to immigrate or seek asylum and the state's right to enforce its borders. In light of the moral order, a Catholic conception of human rights affirms that foreigners have a right to immigrate unless civil authorities objectively conclude that their presence will harm the domestic common good. Therefore, a state's right to enforce its borders is relative to the common good and, I have argued, global solidarity. Border enforcement is not an absolute right. Instead, the tradition gives precedence to the rights of movement because they are necessary to protect and promote the human dignity of immigrants and refugees.

Undoubtedly, that solution may be unrealistic to many Catholics, other Christians, and people of faith in the United States and Europe, and they may well be correct. The tradition's stance may be counterintuitive because it gives greater weight to the goods of human dignity—even in the case of foreigners—than to the domestic common good and to global solidarity than it does to sovereignty as such. The concern, then, tends to be whether a Catholic stance advances open borders. That critique would stand if *Pacem in terris* and the broader tradition *only* affirmed the instrumental right of foreigners to leave their country and enter another. However, the tradition asserts that right (which governments and other institutions may secure through different laws, policies, and mechanisms that objectively protect the domestic common good) because it is necessary to protect and promote a still more important one: the social right to nationality and residence. Thus, John XXIII offers a way forward between two morally unacceptable extremes: denying any form of residency to any and all immigrants or asylum-seekers and offering them full membership or citizenship. The first option would eviscerate the social rights of immigrants and refugees; the second option would vitiate the social rights of the citizens of the United States or the EU.

The mechanisms that the governments of the United States and the EU are using to externalize their borders to Mexico and Turkey—capacity-building in source and transit countries, readmission agreements, and mobility partnerships—threaten the human dignity of immigrants and refugees by weakening not just their instrumental right to cross international borders. They do so to place an essential social right, that of residence, beyond reach. That diminishes the domestic common good of all countries involved and reduces global solidarity. From that perspective, our governments' actions are threatening the very lives of men and women, who are sacred and precious in the eyes of God.

NOTES

1. ACNUR, *Llamado a La Acción: Necesidades De Protección En El Triángulo Norte De Centroamérica, Documento De Discusión (Borrador)* (Geneva/Washington, DC: ACNUR, OEA, 2015), 2. See official English translation.

2. Project Counselling Service–Consejería en Proyectos, *El Contexto Regional Del Desplazamiento Y La Migración Forzada En Centroamérica, México Y Estados Unidos* (México, DF: Project Counselling Service–Consejería en Proyectos, 2016), 9.

3. UNHCR, "Syria Regional Refugee Response," http://data.unhcr.org/syrian refugees/country.php?id=224.

4. François Crépeau, *Regional Study: Management of the External Borders of the European Union and Its Impact on the Human Rights of Migrants* (New York: UN General Assembly Human Rights Council, 2013), 14.

5. Ibid., 14–17.

6. The United States created a special category of NAFTA visas for Mexican citizens, mostly highly skilled employees; see United States Department of State, "Visas for Canadian and Mexican Nafta Professional Workers," https://travel.state.gov/content/travel/en/us-visas/employment/visas-canadian-mexican-nafta-professional-workers.html.

7. Jennifer Podkul and Ian Kysel, *Interdiction, Border Externalization, and the Protection of the Human Rights of Migrants* (Washington, DC: Women's Refugee Commission; Human Rights Institute at Georgetown Law School, 2015), 3.

8. Ibid., 3n5.

9. Arnie Seipel, "30 Governors Call for Halt to U.S. Resettlement of Syrian Refugees," NPR, http://www.npr.org/2015/11/17/456336432/more-governors-oppose-u-s-resettlement-of-syrian-refugees.

10. The term "apprehension" is technically correct, but Central American mothers and children usually turned themselves in; see Muzaffar Chishti and Faye Hipsman, "Increased Central American Migration to the United States May Prove an Enduring Phenomenon," Migration Policy Institute, February 18, 2016, http://www.migrationpolicy.org/article/increased-central-american-migration-united-states-may-prove-enduring-phenomenon.

11. México, Presidencia de la República, "Pone En Marcha El Presidente Enrique Peña Nieto El Programa Frontera Sur," July 7, 2014, search for at http://www.gob.mx/presidencia/prensa/pone-en-marcha-el-presidente-enrique-pena-nieto-el-programa-frontera-sur.

12. Presidents George Bush and Felipe Calderon created the Mérida Initiative in 2007 to fund and coordinate efforts against drug trafficking and organized crime in Mexico; see Clare Ribando Seelke, "Mexico's Recent Immigration Enforcement Efforts," Congressional Research Service, March 9, 2016, 1. See also Clare Ribando Seelke and Kristin Finklea, "U.S.-Mexican Security Cooperation: The Mérida Initiative and Beyond," Congressional Research Service, June 29, 2017.

13. Seelke, "Mexico's Recent Immigration Enforcement Efforts," 1; Seelke and Finklea, "U.S.-Mexican Security Cooperation: The Mérida Initiative and Beyond," 15–16.

14. Seelke, "Mexico's Recent Immigration Enforcement Efforts," 1.

15. Rodrigo Dominguez Villegas and Victoria Rietig, "Migrants Deported from the United States and Mexico to the Northern Triangle," Migration Policy Institute, September 2015, 5, 9.

16. The agency expected at least 234,000 deportations in 2016, an 82 percent increase from 2011, when it registered 128,867; see ACNUR, *Llamado a La Acción*, 6.

17. The report states that there are "only fifteen refugee protection officials to serve the whole country and tend to potential asylum seekers among the one hundred thou-

sand immigrants that Mexico detains each year on average" (my translation); see Project Counselling Service–Consejería en Proyectos, *El Contexto Regional Del Desplazamiento*, 23.

18. Press Office–General Secretariat of the Council, "EU-Turkey Statement, 18 March 2016," news release, http://www.consilium.europa.eu/press.

19. Ibid.

20. United Nations Conference of Plenipotentiaries on the Status of Refugees and Stateless Persons, "Convention Relating to the Status of Refugees," UN OHCHR, http://www.ohchr.org/EN/ProfessionalInterest/Pages/StatusOfRefugees.aspx, art. 33.

21. Press Office, "EU-Turkey Statement, 18 March 2016."

22. Ibid.

23. Natalia Banulescu-Bogdan and Susan Fratzke, "Europe's Migration Crisis in Context: Why Now and What Next?," Migration Policy Institute, September 24, 2015, http://www.migrationpolicy.org/article/europe-migration-crisis-context-why-now-and-what-next.

24. Elizabeth Collett, "The Paradox of the Eu-Turkey Refugee Deal," Migration Policy Institute, March 2016, http://www.migrationpolicy.org/news/paradox-eu-turkey-refugee-deal.

25. "The Asylum Crisis in Europe: Designed Dysfunction," Migration Policy Institute, September 2015, http://www.migrationpolicy.org/news/asylum-crisis-europe-designed-dysfunction.

26. Collett, "The Paradox of the Eu-Turkey Refugee Deal."

27. Banulescu-Bogdan and Fratzke, "Europe's Migration Crisis in Context."

28. UNHCR, "Syria Regional Refugee Response." However, there is a large unregistered refugee population. See Ahmet İçduygu, *Syrian Refugees in Turkey: The Long Road Ahead* (Washington, DC: Migration Policy Institute, 2015), 1.

29. Benjamin Barthe, "Le coup d'Etat, une mauvaise nouvelle pour les réfugiés syriens de Turquie," *Le Monde*, July 16, 2016, http://www.lemonde.fr/europe/article/2016/07/16/le-coup-d-etat-une-mauvaise-nouvelle-pour-les-refugies-syriens-de-turquie_4970423_3214.html.

30. Including, for instance, Chinese "ticketed" labor at the end of the nineteenth and the beginning of the twentieth centuries, and Mexican guest workers between World War I and the middle of the twentieth century; see Aristide R. Zolberg, *A Nation by Design: Immigration Policy in the Fashioning of America* (Cambridge, MA: Harvard University Press, 2006), 110–13.

31. Cornelius references the study by Sandia National Laboratories, a military research facility; see Sandia National Laboratories, *Systematic Analysis of the Southwest Border* (Sandia, NM: Sandia National Laboratories, 1993); Wayne A. Cornelius, "Death at the Border: Efficacy and Unintended Consequences of US Immigration Control Policy," *Population and Development Review* 27, no. 4 (2001): 662.

32. Cornelius, "Death at the Border," 662.

33. Project Counselling Service–Consejería en Proyectos, *El Contexto Regional Del Desplazamiento*, 12.

34. Ibid. See also José Knippen, Clay Boggs, and Maureen Meyer, *An Uncertain Path: Justice for Crimes and Human Rights Violations against Migrants and Refugees in Mexico* (Washington, DC: WOLA, 2015), 20.

35. Knippen, Boggs, and Meyer, "An Uncertain Path," 20–21.

36. Crépeau, "Regional Study," 15, para. 61.

37. Tara Brian and Frank Laczko, eds., *Fatal Journeys: Tracking Lives Lost during Migration* (Geneva: International Organization for Migration, 2014), 12 (emphasis added).

38. Ibid.

39. International Organization for Migration [IOM], "Latest Global Figures: Migrant Fatalities Worldwide," http://missingmigrants.iom.int/latest-global-figures.

40. According to the IOM, "Some experts estimate that for every dead body found on the shores of the developed world there are at least two others that are never recovered"; see Brian and Laczko, *Fatal Journeys*, 15.

41. Cornelius, "Death at the Border," 681.

42. The Mexican and Guatemalan Episcopal Conferences have active pastoral ministries for people on the move, particularly Central American immigrants and refugees. For more information, consult the website of the office for the pastoral care of people on the move of the Guatemalan Conference of Catholic Bishops (in Spanish), http://www.movilidadhumana.com/.

43. Frank McNamara, "Member State Responsibility for Migration Control within Third States—Externalisation Revisited," *European Journal of Migration & Law* 15, no. 3 (2013): 319–35.

44. Ibid., 326–27.

45. Ibid., 327. See *Hiri Jamaa and Others v. Italy* as a counterexample in European Court of Human Rights, "Extra-Territorial Jurisdiction of States Parties to the European Convention on Human Rights," July 2018, 11, http://www.echr.coe.int/Documents/FS_Extra-territorial_jurisdiction_ENG.pdf.

46. Silvia Morgades, "The Externalisation of the Asylum Function in the European Union," in *GRITIM Working Paper Series* (Barcelona, Spain: Universitat Pompeu Fabra, 2010), 12.

47. McNamara, "Member State Responsibility," 334.

48. In their report, Podkul and Kysel speak to the failure of domestic immigration reforms. See Podkul and Kysel, *Interdiction, Border Externalization, and the Protection of the Human Rights of Migrants*, 3–4.

49. Crépeau, "Regional Study," 16, para. 67 (emphasis added).

50. Alexander Betts and James Milner, "The Externalisation of EU Asylum Policy: The Position of African States," in *COMPAS*, ed. Policy and Society Centre on Migration, University of Oxford (Oxford: Oxford University Press, 2006).

51. Ibid., 6 (emphasis added).

52. Ibid.

53. Seelke, "Mexico's Recent Immigration Enforcement Efforts," 1.

54. UN Conference of Plenipotentiaries on the Status of Refugees and Stateless Persons, "Convention Relating to the Status of Refugees," art. 33.

55. Alexander Betts, "The Normative Terrain of the Global Refugee Regime," *Ethics & International Affairs* 29, no. 4 (2015), https://www.ethicsandinternationalaffairs.org/2015/the-normative-terrain-of-the-global-refugee-regime/.

56. UNHCR, *Global Trends: Forced Displacement in 2015* (Geneva: UNHCR, 2016), 3, 13–22.

57. "Contributions to UNHCR for the Budget Year 2016," UNHCR, http://www.unhcr.org/575e74567.html.

58. Hollenbach's research on the Catholic human rights tradition has led to groundbreaking collaborative projects on the theological-ethical study of refugee ethics and the institutionalization of refugee rights; see David Hollenbach, *Refugee Rights: Ethics, Advocacy, and Africa* (Washington, DC: Georgetown University Press, 2008); Hollenbach, *Driven from Home: Protecting the Rights of Forced Migrants* (Washington, DC: Georgetown University Press, 2010).

59. Although the Universal Declaration of Human Rights (1948) affirms both civil and socioeconomic rights, it does not determine which human rights claims governments ought to prioritize; UN Secretariat, "Universal Declaration of Human Rights," http://www.un.org/en/documents/udhr/index.shtml.

60. Yale Task Force on Population Ethics, "Moral Claims, Human Rights, and Population Policies," *Theological Studies* 35, no. 1 (1974): 88.

61. Ibid.

62. David Hollenbach, *Claims in Conflict: Retrieving and Renewing the Catholic Human Rights Tradition*, Woodstock Studies (New York: Paulist Press, 1979), 90.

63. Ibid.

64. Ibid.

65. Ibid., 91.

66. Ibid., 94.

67. Ibid.

68. Ibid., 97 (original emphasis).

69. Ibid.

70. Ibid., 96.

71. Ibid.

72. Ibid.

73. John XXIII wrote the letter soon after the Cuban Missile Crisis of October 1963, when the United States prevented the Soviet Union from delivering its nuclear weapons to Cuba through a naval blockade. They resolved the conflict when the United States agreed to remove its nuclear weapons from Turkey. Their ideological divisions included disagreements over the meaning and purpose of human rights. Leaders in Italy and elsewhere wondered where the Catholic Church stood. Generally, the United States and the Western bloc emphasized political (civil) human rights to further individual freedom, while the Soviet Union and the Eastern bloc highlighted socioeconomic human rights to further material well-being; see Drew Christiansen, "Commentary on *Pacem in Terris* (Peace on Earth)," in *Modern Catholic Social Teaching: Commentaries and Interpretations*, ed. Kenneth R. Himes and Lisa Sowle Cahill (Washington, DC: Georgetown University Press, 2005), 217–43.

74. Ibid.

75. Ibid.

76. Insight from Christiansen. Ibid.

77. John XXIII, *Pacem in terris*, http://w2.vatican.va/content/john-xxiii/en/encyclicals/documents/hf_j-xxiii_enc_11041963_pacem.html.

78. For this history and the actions the U.S. government and its colonial precursors took, please see Zolberg, *A Nation by Design*, chaps. 1–6.

79. "The [Immigration and Nationality Act] expressly notes that the granting of asylum is discretionary, and courts have upheld its denial even when an alien fulfills the requirements of the statutory definition of *refugee*"; see Kate M. Manuel, "Asylum and Gang Violence: Legal Overview," Congressional Research Service, September 5, 2014, 4.

80. This interpretation does not preclude societies from having different practices to convey partial or full membership to a foreigner, nor does it preclude them from creating different juridical structures in that process. It may also sound strange in the abstract, but as a political community the United States already reflects this practice. On one end is the lack of membership (i.e., slavery, undocumented labor), and on the other lies citizenship by birth. In between them lie permanent residency and naturalized citizenship. The former "grants" foreigners the right to due process in most circumstances, for example, and a duty to pay taxes, but not the right to be elected to office or the right to vote. The latter "grants" a new citizen the right to hold elected office and the right to vote, but withholds from them the right to be elected to the highest office in the land or posts deemed sensitive for national security reasons. They have also, unfortunately, not been allowed to do their duty in the past. This happened with naturalized U.S. citizens of Japanese birth during World War II; see Zolberg, *A Nation by Design*, chap. 8.

81. Arnie Seipel, "30 Governors Call for Halt to U.S. Resettlement of Syrian Refugees," https://www.npr.org/2015/11/17/456336432/more-governors-oppose-u-s-resettlement-of-syrian-refugees; Catholic News Agency, "Federal Court Blocks Pence's Ban on Syrian Refugees in Indiana," October 6, 2016, http://www.catholicnewsagency.com/news/federal-court-blocks-pences-ban-on-syrian-refugees-in-indiana-44910/.

82. John XXIII, *Pacem in terris*, 98.

83. This is more striking still when one considers that it was written soon after the Berlin Wall was erected.

84. There is some slippage here in the translations. O'Brien's states: "We must remember that, of its very nature, civil authority exists, not to confine its people within the boundaries of their nation, but rather to protect, above all else, the common good of the entire human family." His translation offers a more direct relationship between the good of a people and the common good of humankind, whereas the Vatican's emphasizes the good of the state. It is also less centered on the state; *Pacem in terris*, 98. See also David J. O'Brien and Thomas A. Shannon, *Catholic Social Thought: The Documentary Heritage* (Maryknoll, NY: Orbis, 2004), 147.

85. Again, O'Brien's translation is clearer in terms of the interpretation for which I am arguing. His text reads: "Consequently, necessity demands a quicker exchange of

goods, or of capital, or the migration of people themselves" (O'Brien and Shannon, *Catholic Social Thought*, 147).

86. Yet there are a few instances in which a country will give up a piece of its territory in favor of another (usually by selling it) so that they may both meet specific needs. For example, the Louisiana Purchase (1803) and the Gadsden Purchase (1854) when the United States bought territory from France and Mexico, respectively. Countries may also unwillingly give up pieces of their territory through war. This was the case with the United States gaining territories in the American Southwest (1848), Puerto Rico (1898–present day), and the Philippines (1898–1946) from Mexico and Spain. In either scenario, the complexity is that whenever a territory transfers hands, questions arise about the membership status of those who were previously foreigners. They may lose their property rights (and other rights) and become foreigners in their own land. The process of forging a new people from two separate ones (conqueror and conquered) is long and arduous; see Oscar J. Martínez, *Border People: Life and Society in the U.S.-Mexico Borderlands* (Tucson: University of Arizona Press, 1994). As a portent of things to come, the island nation of Kiribati is attempting to resettle its population in Fiji, where it is attempting to buy land. The reason: rising sea levels are threatening its population of 850,000 people. The Fijian people are concerned about their potential effect; see Nick Perry, "Island Nation of Kiribati Contemplates Move to Fiji," *Christian Science Monitor*, March 9, 2012, http://www.csmonitor.com/World/Latest-News-Wires/2012/0309/Island-nation-of-Kiribati-contemplates-move-to-Fiji.

87. John XXIII, *Pacem in terris*, 102.

88. Ibid.

89. Ibid., 105.

90. Ibid., 106 (original emphasis).

91. Here I am thinking of Michael Walzer's research on the fundamental importance of membership to access other goods in their particular spheres of justice (as he calls them); see Walzer, *Spheres of Justice: A Defense of Pluralism and Equality* (New York: Basic Books, 1983).

92. Those interpreters may use the subtitles to guide their analysis. However, from a hermeneutical perspective, it is not clear who wrote those subtitles and what criteria they used to place them there. They may agree with me that paragraphs 98 to 100 normatively frame the encyclical's understanding of international relations before it goes on to address specific global problems, including forced migrations, the arms race, and poverty. However, they may guide their analysis using the subtitles to nos. 101 and 102 ("The Proper Balance between Population, Land and Capital"), 103 and 104 ("The Problem of Political Refugees"), 105 and 106 ("The Refugee's Rights"), and 107 and 108 ("Commendable Efforts"). From this perspective the pope's teaching is limited to refugees. Instead, I interpret paragraphs 101 and 102 as addressing forced migrations in the context of the unequal distribution of goods that is at the root of conflict in the international order (forced migrations due to another state's economic stress). Nos. 103 to 105 address the narrower case of political refugees (forced migrations caused by another state's political stress). No. 106,

the text in question, retakes and concludes the broader analysis begun in no. 101. *Pacem in terris* reflects unusual versatility in terms of its consideration that a state's authorities may reach the incorrect conclusion, namely, that when it comes to economic policy, its citizens are expendable. In this sense, those foreigners are not exclusively economic immigrants. They are, in a certain sense, political immigrants. There are, it seems, reasons to blur the line between economic immigrant and political refugee. There may well be such a thing as an economic refugee (an ongoing debate) or a political immigrant.

93. Pontifical Council "Cor Unum" (Pontifical Council for the Pastoral Care of Migrants and Itinerant People), "Refugees: A Challenge to Solidarity," http://www.vatican.va/roman_curia/pontifical_councils/corunum/documents/rc_pc_corunum_doc_25061992_refugees_en.html.

94. UN Conference of Plenipotentiaries on the Status of Refugees and Stateless Persons, "Convention Relating to the Status of Refugees," art. 1.

95. Pontifical Council "Cor Unum," "Refugees: A Challenge to Solidarity," 4.

96. Ibid.

97. Ibid. (original emphasis).

98. Liberation theologians provide this insight, but Fareed Zakaria lays it out well: "Here [in the West] poverty means a bad life. But poverty in the Third World means death. For the 1 billion people who live on less than $1 a day, one bad cold, one unlucky fall, one month of poor rainfall, and they or their children—or both—will likely die. For people who live in these circumstances, moving out from under them is their all-consuming struggle, dwarfing everything else. It would be the same for any of us"; see Zakaria, "How to Change Ugly Regimes," *Newsweek*, June 26, 2005, https://www.newsweek.com/fareed-zakaria-how-change-ugly-regimes-120417.

99. Aside from criminal actions that may warrant their deportation after they have received review through due process.

100. Pontifical Council "Cor Unum," "Refugees: A Challenge to Solidarity, 15.

101. Cáritas Mexicana, "Obispos Del Encuentro De Movilidad Humana Animarán Articulación Entre Instituciones a Favor De Migrantes De Centroamérica Y México," http://caritasmexicana.org/movilidad-humana/obispos-del-encuentro-de-movilidad-humana-animaran-articulacion-entre-instituciones-a-favor-de-migrantes-de-centroamerica-y-mexico. Gustavo Garcia-Siller et al., "Statement of the Bishops of the Border between Texas and Northern Mexico: The Cry of Christ in the Voice of the Migrant Moves Us," Conferencia del Episcopado Mexicano, http://www.cem.org.mx/ing/article/1078-Statement-of-the-bishops-of-the-border-between-Texas-and-Northern-Mexico-The-cry-of-Christ-in-the-voice-of-the-migrant-moves-us.html.

102. Krisztina Barca and András Máté-Tóth, "The Hungarian Religious Leaders' Statements from the Beginning of the Migration," *Occasional Papers on Religion in Eastern Europe* 36, no. 3 (2016): 5.

103. Ibid., 6.

104. *Origins* quotes Bishop Kiss-Rigó of Hungary as saying, "They're not refugees. This is an invasion." The news service also reports that Archbishop Jan Graubner, of the

Czech Republic, "demanded that his country take in only 'Christian refugees.'" As to Poland, it cited reports that Archbishop Henryk Hoser argued that "there's no doubt the integration of Christians will be vastly easier than the integration of Muslims, who may later open ghettos that give birth to violence and terrorism—*let's be realists*"; *Origins: CNS Documentary Service* 45, no. 17 (2015): 282–85 (original emphasis).

105. The bishops in question are Cardinal Reinhard Marx of Germany, Bishop Jean Kockerols of Belgium, and Bishop Gianni Ambrosio of Italy; Commission of the Bishops' Conferences of the European Community, "Refugee Crisis Requires a Common European Solution," in ibid., 282–83.

106. A new book by Christian ethicist Matthew Kaemingk promises to offer a Christian perspective on the specific questions raised by Muslim immigration into the West. Its research may shed light on the historical, political, cultural, and security concerns that Eastern European Christians (including Catholic bishops) are attempting to navigate when discerning their response to the humanitarian needs of Syrian Muslim refugees; see Kaemingk, *Christian Hospitality and Muslim Immigration in an Age of Fear* (Grand Rapids, MI: Eerdmans, 2018).

107. Conferencia del Episcopado Mexicano and United States Conference of Catholic Bishops, *Strangers No Longer: Together on the Journey of Hope* (Washington, DC: USCCB, 2003).

108. Commission Caritas in Veritate, Migration Section, "Challenge of Mercy: Welcoming and Integration of Refugees and Migrants. Dialogue and Charity," paper presented at the Challenge of Mercy: Welcoming and Integration of Refugees and Migrants, Dialogue and Charity, Madrid, Spain, 2016.

109. Martin Kramara, "Meeting of Representatives of Catholic Bishops' Conferences of Central and Eastern Europe," news release by the Bishops Conference of Slovakia, via the Council of Bishops' Conferences of Europe, https://www.ccee.eu/10-09-2016-incontro-delle-conferenze-episcopali-deuropa-centro-orientale/.

110. Pope Francis, "Angelus," September 6, 2015, https://w2.vatican.va/content/francesco/en/angelus/2015/documents/papa-francesco_angelus_20150906.html.

111. One of the strongest theological-ethical arguments that the Catholic bishops of Hungary may be relying on, at least implicitly, for their desire to prioritize the needs of Christian refugees is the order of charity. However, determining whether this is the case (including whether it is an appropriate use of that principle and practice) lies beyond the scope of this case study. For an exploration into how the order of charity intersects with Christian immigration ethics, please see Victor Carmona, "Theologizing Immigration," in *The Wiley-Blackwell Companion to Latino/a Theology*, ed. Orlando Espín (Oxford: Wiley-Blackwell, 2015), 365–86.

eighteen

DIGNITY AND CONFLICT

Ecology

Dawn M. Nothwehr, OSF

In his encyclical *Laudato Si'* (*On Care for Our Common Home*) (*LS*), Pope Francis uses the term "human dignity" five times, adding a human referent an additional sixteen times.[1] He claims:

> Modern anthropocentrism has paradoxically ended up prizing technical thought over reality, since "the technological mind sees nature as an insensate order, as a cold body of facts, as a mere 'given,' as an object of utility, as raw material to be hammered into useful shape; it views the cosmos similarly as a mere 'space' into which objects can be thrown with complete indifference." The *intrinsic dignity* of the world is thus compromised. When human beings fail to find their true place in this world, they misunderstand themselves and end up acting against themselves: "Not only has God given the earth to man, who must use it with respect for the original good purpose for which it was given, but, man too is God's gift to man. He must therefore respect the natural and moral structure with which he has been endowed."[2]

Here, *intrinsic dignity* is clearly directed to an all-encompassing set of subjects, inclusive of but beyond the human subject. Behind these words is Pope Francis's understanding of *integral ecology*, the ontological reality of a common origin of the entire cosmos in the one Creator, the intrinsic value of each element of creation, and the divinely instituted situation of humans in relationship to all of creation.[3] He uses religious and philosophical terms that expose a common truth. He asserts that human dignity and integral ecology hold ethical gravitas flowing from divine intent that condemns violent anthropocentrism that blesses irreparable harm done by humans with absolute disregard for intrinsic dignity—including human dignity.[4]

Pope Francis continues his defense of human dignity, showing threats of past religious errors that justified human raping of the natural world and current dangers of philosophy governing modern technology and scientific experimentation. He says this is the case because

> its [modern technology and scientific experimentation] development was *according to an undifferentiated and one-dimensional paradigm*. This paradigm exalts the concept of a subject who, using logical and rational procedures, progressively approaches and gains control over an external object. This subject makes every effort to establish the scientific and experimental method, which in itself is already a technique of possession, mastery and transformation. It is as if the subject were to find itself in the presence of something formless, completely open to manipulation.[5]

Environmental degradation can be attributed to scientific pursuits using and valuing only empirical data, blinding humanity to other ways, thus alienating people from the natural world. "Our economic exploitation of raw materials and labor-power; the technological imperative to transform the 'raw resources' of nature according to our own wills and fantasies; and the very assumptions about human knowing and desiring that shape the methodology of modern science" manifest this reality.[6] The promise of "power over" nature allures us by promising goodness, yet it makes us impervious to the vital claims nature makes on us. Humans are conflicted and alienated from nature; we are technological and economic tyrants valuing nature quite exclusively for its use to us, while denying its intrinsic value and its many powers that are far superior to our own.

But insights from phenomenology, Christianity, and other great world religions open an alternative to these harmful, reductive ways. Johann Wolfgang von Goethe (1749–1832) was similarly troubled by exclusively empirical epistemological approaches. People were learning to overlook beauty—that is, by appreciating the forms of living beings or apprehending color—beauty that "evokes a kind of wonder and love that is constitutive of our relationship to the things we seek to know."[7] Indeed, Pope Francis also sees that what is at stake "is nothing less than our own dignity."[8]

The new sciences—including ecology, evolutionary biology, astrophysics, and quantum physics—show that everything is interconnected. Integral ecology holds that the entire cosmos is a whole, complete entity, a unity. As theologian Sam Mickey shows, to be fully human is to be integrally linked with the one Earth community that includes all of the planet's habitats, inhabitants, ideas and societies, humans and nonhumans.[9]

I suggest that scientific and religious understanding of integral ecology and of the human person integrally and adequately considered from the viewpoints of phenomenology and Christianity holds promise for uncovering a more robust meaning of human dignity useful for environmental ethics—descriptively and normatively.[10] Resembling Pope Francis, Mickey holds that such humane reflection can "maintain a vision of how science and technology—and markets—can serve the dignity of human life."[11] Religion, with natural and social sciences, reveals the multidimensional complex that defines the human being as a creature existing in an interdependent relationship with the natural world for survival, but also as necessarily making use of humans' unique human capabilities to nurture and care for it. This all-inclusive approach (both/and) leads to a more adequate understanding of the meaning of human dignity.

In this chapter, I use David G. Kirchhoffer's concept to show that human well-being and the sustainability of the Earth are best served when, supported by the natural and social sciences, human dignity is given a multidimensional definition.[12] Kirchhoffer defines human dignity as "the multidimensional existential reality of the human person."[13] He develops this understanding using his "Component Dimensions of Human Dignity" model to define dignity more precisely for contemporary ethics.[14] I also draw on Leonardo Boff's concept of integral ecology to situate the human within the natural world. I suggest that human dignity is more fully actualized when humans heed their status within Earth's integral ecology. Two significant strengths of Kirchhoffer's model and Boff's concept are that (1) they rely on sources that are deemed credible by both secular and religious thinkers, and (2) they are grounded in both empirical and phenomenological data.[15]

This approach fits within a dialogue among world religions, natural sciences, and social sciences toward resolving the global ecological crisis.[16] The worldwide reception of such dialogue is necessary because of the all-encompassing nature of environmental degradation and human conflicts.[17] Here, using Kirchhoffer's multidimensional definition of human dignity, both descriptively and normatively, and grounded in Christian sources—particularly the work of Louis Janssens on *Gaudium et spes* and the "human person integrally and adequately considered"—I also claim that a Catholic ecological ethics evaluation of the human role in environmental degradation denounces and condemns such activity as beyond the bounds of human dignity. Indeed, this moral position stands at the heart of Pope Francis's *LS*.

CHAPTER OUTLINE

This chapter has three major parts. I first examine the sources, content, and components of Kirchhoffer's model, which shows the value of a multidimensional concept of human dignity for contemporary environmental ethics. Kirchhoffer maintains that a precise content for human dignity flounders without an adequate anthropology. Thus, I next expose four time-tested orthodox Christian anthropology sources that give content to Kirchhoffer's understanding of human dignity. Those sources also ground Louis Janssens's classic work interpreting the teaching in *Gaudium et spes* (*The Pastoral Constitution of the Church in the Modern World*) (*GS*) on theological anthropology and human dignity. I focus on Janssens's amplification of "the human person integrally and adequately considered" in *GS* nos. 47–52, which shows the multidimensionality of human existential reality.[18] Last, I address human existential reality as it exists in relation to the destruction of the natural world using Leonardo Boff's four ecologies and his theological notions of "cry of the Earth, cry of the poor" and Sam Mickey's "tactful touch."

I conclude with an analysis of Earth overshoot—an example of a moral event (Joseph Selling)—by engaging human dignity as a descriptive category and normative moral criterion. We will see that an adequate understanding of human dignity and of integral ecology taken together preclude any moral validation of inflicting irreparable damage to the creation—including human persons.

KIRCHHOFFER'S COMPONENT DIMENSIONS OF HUMAN DIGNITY MODEL

Two Understandings of Human Dignity

Human dignity is a good and is conceptualized in two major ways, as (1) *something that all human persons already inherently and inviolably have*, or (2) *something that human persons acquire based on their moral behavior*.[19]

The first conceptualization (inherent dignity) is held on two bases: (a) the ontological status of human persons (e.g., as *imago Dei* or as co-members of the human species); or (b) the capacity of the human person (i.e., the potential inherent in one or more typically human capacities, such as rationality, autonomy, and the capacities to act and to love, among others).

Thinkers supporting the second conceptualization (acquired dignity) include (a) the psychological group that situates human dignity in some subjective sense of self-worth (e.g., a person leading a meaningful life), or (b) the social group that holds that a person acquires dignity to the extent that he or she lives a morally good life in a given social context.

Significant for our purposes is German personalist moralist Klaus Demmer. His position links the conscience with the realization of human dignity, contending that human dignity resides in the given human capacities of reason and free will. He also argues, however, that the realization of this dignity is dependent upon the extent to which the person "responsibly obeys, and hence acts on, the truths known to this conscience: 'Only the awareness of God's judgment can grant ultimate freedom from the judgment of others. The very dignity of the person consists in being judged by God only and living in harmony with her or his own conscience.'"[20] In this way, Demmer bridges and combines the two conceptualizations of human dignity—ontological and acquired.[21]

Reasserting Human Dignity as an Ethics Criterion

Kirchhoffer shows how discounting human dignity as a meaningful ethics criterion is based on unacceptable methodological assumptions.[22] He first proposes an alternative.[23] For him, ethics is a hermeneutical enterprise that seeks to make sense of the meanings inherent in moral behavior.[24] Kirchhoffer uses Janssens's elaboration of *GS* nos. 47–52 concerning "the human person integrally and adequately considered" that exposes the human person as a multidimensional, meaning-seeking, meaning-giving, historical, corporeal subject, who is always intrinsically related to everything that exists.[25] As such, human persons seek to realize a meaningful sense of self-worth in and through their moral interactions with all such relationships, including all elements of creation and the natural environment.[26] In this light, human dignity is a significant ethics criterion.

The Moral Event Defined

The moral event is a multidimensional, time-bound occurrence that includes intentions, physical acts, and circumstances—all of which have a bearing on the moral quality of the episode.[27] All dimensions are open to moral evaluation as good and bad (intentions) and right and wrong (actions). Moral behavior combines the act(s) and the processes of reasoning behind the act(s) and also the circumstances surrounding it.

In this way, Kirchhoffer utilizes a "both/and" paradigm that provides a view of reality that values the complexity and multidimensionality of the moral *Gestalt.* He also emphasizes the historicity of both the human person and the moral event in order to overcome the challenges of moralism and relativism, making us aware of the ever-present possibility that one may be wrong.[28] Relativism is overcome because, despite this possibility, and indeed bearing it in mind, we continue to seek the fullness of the *Truth* in conversation with others.[29] The Truth cannot be reduced to particular interpretations, or indeed to the conversation about it; it is always transcendent. Kirchhoffer expressed this reality utilizing two theological concepts: the Already and the Not Yet, and the Eschatological Proviso.[30] The former acknowledges that although humans already have glimpses of the Truth, we have Not Yet realized the fullness of the Truth. The latter recognizes that no human endeavor can ever fully realize the Truth. We remain perpetual seekers.[31]

Kirchhoffer's Reconstruction of the Criterion of Human Dignity

Using a hermeneutic of generosity, Kirchhoffer argues for the usefulness of human dignity as a criterion for ethics.[32] He develops the Component Dimensions of Human Dignity model, which serves as a descriptive lens through which one can interpret the meanings that particular individuals in particular circumstances ascribe to human dignity, and how these circumstances affect individual moral choices.[33] The same model serves a normative function in that it frames a critique of these particular understandings, for example, where they are reductionist and grounding dignity in an inadequate anthropology.

Human dignity as a descriptive category contains what people believe is significant about their moral lives. Understanding that content is necessary to make any moral judgment. Therefore, Kirchhoffer writes, "The reference to human dignity is not a shortcut allowing to dispense from the handicraft of concrete ethics, but first and most the indication that there are indeed serious ethical questions facing us, questions that challenge us as concrete subjects to bring to bear on them our responsible freedom."[34] We now review Kirchhoffer's model in more detail (see fig. 18.1).

Kirchhoffer asserts that the multidimensional understanding of human dignity is complex. Each of the four major component dimensions of being is

TABLE 18.1. Kirchhoffer's Component Dimensions of the Human Dignity Model

Component Dimension	Complementary Duality: Already	Complementary Duality: Not Yet
Existential	Have (Potential)	Acquire (Fulfilment)
Cognitive-Affective	Inherent Worth	Self-Worth
Behavioural	Moral Good	Morally Good
Social	Others' Dignity	My Dignity

Source: Kirchhoffer, *Human Dignity*, 3 and 208.

fundamental to being human, and they are best understood along an axis of the Already and the Not Yet. Each component dimension is made up by a complementary duality that is mutually revealing and indicative of its realization and potential.[35]

Existential. Kirchhoffer uses Paul Tillich's definition of existential: "An attitude to thinking in which the object of thought is involved rather than detached."[36] At an existential level, all human persons, as such, Already have dignity, but they also possess various capacities, which, when exercised, contribute to the flourishing of human life, but are never fully realized (Not Yet).[37] Also following Tillich, every human person exercises his or her freedom and will, seeking after meaning, significance, and purpose in his or her life. So at the psychological level people are drawn to self-development toward becoming their truest self (Not Yet).[38]

Cognitive-Affective. This component addresses how people experience their existential reality and desire for meaning and self-worth through sensations, perceptions, conceptions, affections, and emotions.[39] Kirchhoffer uses psychologist Gisela Labouvic-Vief's "Cognitive-Affective Development Theory," which holds that as people grow in age and experience, their emotional and cognitive content expands, and their capacity to articulate and comprehend the emotional status of others changes.[40] This enables people to relate more adequately to norms, values, ideologies, and social mores. Thus, self-fulfillment consists in making a fundamental intentional choice (fundamental option).[41] Human dignity is associated with one's fundamental choice or the integral narrative one constructs of one's life, and this is always somewhat subjective and limited.[42]

Behavioral. According to Kirchhoffer, "The human person is a moral being capable of choosing and acting toward a good end in a morally right way."[43] He asserts that behavior is the *actus humanus*: "The use of deliberate reason that aims at a moral purpose to the human provides the key to making an act a genuine *actus humanus* and thus a moral act."[44] Autonomy is thus necessary for moral behavior. Only human actions resulting from deliberation and free choice are open for moral evaluation. One's own and others' evaluations will determine a person's moral character.[45]

Moreover, Kirchhoffer holds that "human dignity is a moral good because it 'represents what has been key to' all other goods that constitute a human person and that as human persons we want to realize."[46] Thus, society should be structured to allow people to develop their capacities, and humans must strive to actualize their own dignity as a sense of self-worth (subjective) and also actively promote the realization of moral good (objective), the inherent dignity of all others. Human dignity is thus normative.[47]

Social. Human persons as corporeal subjects are already situated in historical relationships.[48] A person's context is affected by his or her behavior, and his or her context affects his or her actions. Kirchhoffer argues that context must be accounted for in "how a person conceives of her fundamental choice and the appropriate ways to realize the fullness of the meaning she seeks as a person in the world"; it is "the *conditio sine qua non* of being able to form a fundamental choice in the first place."[49] He continues,

> In making human dignity—both in terms of capacities and in terms of efforts to realize those capacities—a moral good, the necessary gravitas is given to each individual's effort to live out a meaningful existence in their historical circumstances while at the same time holding up an ideal that critiques and corrects all these efforts. This gravitas is what makes the concept of human dignity so important for ethical discourse.[50]

He thus concludes: "My efforts to achieve 'my dignity' must never detract from 'others' dignity."[51]

Because all considerations of morality ultimately also deal with the human subject, without an adequate anthropology, Kirchhoffer maintains, the more precise content of human dignity flounders in ambiguity. It is precisely in pursuit of an adequate anthropology that he turns to the work of Janssens as an interpreter of the Christian anthropology found in *GS*. Thus, I briefly consider several sources that ground such an anthropology.

KEY SOURCES FOR AN ADEQUATE CHRISTIAN ANTHROPOLOGY GROUNDING HUMAN DIGNITY

Current biblical interpretation, ecological theology, theological environmental ethics, and *LS* all raise to high relief the multidimensional, holistic, and personalistic character of an adequate anthropology. Space allows examining only three: key biblical texts; the radically relational creation theology and Christian anthropology of Bonaventure of Bagnoregio (1217–74); and Janssens's treatment of "the human person integrally and adequately considered."[52] These sources expose a multidimensional understanding of human dignity understood as well-being, necessarily grounded in life-giving relationships with the Transcendent, fellow humans, all created beings, and the cosmos itself. To the extent that all of these relationships are life-giving, the honored status of human dignity is possible.

Biblical Literature

Two Samplings from Genesis. Current biblical scholars use exegetical principles mandated in *Dei verbum* (*Dogmatic Constitution on Divine Revelation*), which require a historical critical reading of the texts.[53] These exegetes insist that although there is some honorific character to the human being created in the *imago Dei*, the only divine being is God.[54] The value of creation lies not primarily in its usefulness to humankind (instrumental value) but in its origin as God's work (intrinsic value). In Genesis 2:4b–25, it is clear that God is the main character.

God formed a human being (*adam*) out of the soil (*ha-adam*), and breathed the divine breath of life (*rûah*) into its nostrils, making it a living person (Gen. 2:7).[55] God placed this needy creature in the lush garden of Eden, and directed the person to cultivate and care for it (2:15). God created the animals, and they too received *rûah*. Both humans and other-kind are *nefesh chayah*, "living souls" or "living creatures."[56] Fulfilling God's request, the earth-creature (*adam*) named the animals, seeking a companion among them (2:19). Finding none, God provided Eve (*hawwah*), a living being, equally bearing the *imago*

Dei. These were acts of intimacy, creating an orderly caring bond between the human and other-kind, not giving license for plundering.

When considered in historical context, the *imago Dei* (Gen 1:26–27) is emblematic of God's loving intent to instill a positive self-image and renew the confidence in divine love, care, and presence to an exiled and oppressed people. The royal language recalls ancient Egyptian and Mesopotamian kings, who were considered representatives of their gods and trustees of the gods' possessions.[57] For Jewish exiles, being privileged to represent God and to extend godlike care for creation was an occasion of enhanced self-esteem. Following God's deliberation, the human is created (1:26) and assigned a specific task (1:28). Humans have a distinctive spiritual capacity to relate to God, but they remain creatures among others of God's creation.[58] But there is an interesting break in the pattern of the creation narrative (1:3–25; days 1 to 5) that speaks to an unrealized dimension of Genesis 1.[59] The declaration found after each of the prior creative acts reads, "And it was so." But it is not found after verse 1:26. Human dominion then, remains an unfulfilled divine expectation.

From this sampling, any assertion of human dignity based on the claim to the *imago Dei* was conditioned upon people understanding their rightful status within creation as unique, but not divine. Humans are appointed "keepers and tillers" of "the garden" (Gen. 1:28) to serve and protect creation. Neglecting that task, or, worse, damaging and destroying creation's capacity to renew itself, is to diminish the humans' capacity to bear the *imago Dei* and any claim to the esteemed status (human dignity) it represents. Arguably, today such neglect is manifested in spades across the globe, and the human dignity of both perpetrators and victims has been weakened.

A Sampling from the Gospel according to St. John. John 1:1–18 proclaims the Incarnation.[60] Irenaeus (130–202 CE) and Athanasius (296–373 CE) taught that in the Word made flesh, God became human so that the whole of humanity might be healed, taken up into God, and deified. The Incarnation involves the whole interconnected material world.

Duncan Reid suggests that the Incarnation must be understood in context of John's wider claim that the Word has become flesh (*sarx*).[61] *Sarx* also points to the entire web of life that God sustains and embraces in divine love. Neil Darragh builds on Reid's thought, and specifies, "To say that God became flesh is . . . to say also that God became an Earth creature, . . . a sentient being, . . . a living being (in common with all other living beings), . . . a complex Earth unit of minerals in the carbon and nitrogen cycles."[62] Denis Edwards elaborates, "In Jesus of Nazareth, God becomes a vital part of an ecosystem and a part of the interconnected systems that support life on Earth. . . . Niels Henrik Gregersen calls this the idea of *deep incarnation*."[63] Niels Henrik Gregersen explains: "In Christ, God enters into biological life in a new way and is now with evolving creation in a radically new way."[64] Gregersen elaborates: "In this context, the incarnation of God in Christ can be understood as a radical or 'deep' incarnation, that is, an incarnation into the very tissue of biological existence and system of nature. Understood this way, the death of Christ becomes an icon of God's redemptive co-suffering with all sentient life as well as with the victims of social competition. God bears the cost of evolution, the price involved in the hardship of natural selection."[65]

Here we find a religious and ontological basis for human dignity. Both humans and the created world come from the same source. Through the divine assuming material human form, the world was, in a sense, deified. The divine is engaged in the integral ecology of the entire created world within which humanity lives and thrives. Humans and all of creation live best and thrive "in God" and in an intricately connected web of life. No element of creation thrives in isolation, yet the intrinsic value of each is asserted here, insofar as each is a unique combination of the same "stuff" (*sarx*).[66]

St. Bonaventure of Bagnoregio (1217–74): Creation Theology and Anthropology

St. Bonaventure, a founder of the Franciscan intellectual tradition and spiritual master of the Franciscan Order, provides grounding for the work of Reid, Darragh, Edwards, and Gregersen. Based on the doctrine of the Trinity, Bonaventure presents a highly relational, connected creation theology and multidimensional anthropology.[67] Notably, this creation theology stands in contrast to that of Thomas Aquinas, who stressed an Aristotelian hierarchical view that traditionally dominated Catholic theology and resulted in exalting the value of humans, effectively discounting the value of all other elements.[68]

Creation Theology. For Bonaventure, the Creator, the Triune God, expresses a productive love within the Godhead that is the emanation of the Three Persons. The divine life of the Godhead is thus reflected in the created cosmos (*theophanic*).[69] The sacredness of creation, the intrinsic value of each element, including the dignity of each human, is found in ontological relatedness in God, their common source.[70] All living things are vestiges of God. However, as the *imago Dei* (Gen. 1:26), precisely through God's goodness and grace, they can become a similitude, representing God most closely and distinctively.[71] Divine exemplarity finds culmination in the figure of Christ, the Incarnation of the Divine Word.[72]

God created so that through love creation can be brought into a kind of transforming fullness in union with the divine.[73] Indeed, we could say that the world of creation has its own truth, goodness, and beauty.[74] After the Fall (Gen. 3), the humans' view of God and revelatory creation was obscured, but not lost. Scripture, historical revelation, and, most perfectly, Jesus supplement, clarify, and enable humans to perceive the cosmic revelation as sacramental.[75]

Dignity of the imago Dei *Explained.* Central to Bonaventure's anthropology is the *imago Dei* (Gen. 1:26). God gave humans the ability to know divine goodness through the material world (mediately) and directly (immediately) as do the spiritual beings. The human soul is a body-spirit interconnected (not dualistic) in relationship that reflects the power, wisdom, and goodness of God. The powers of the soul are memory, intellect, and will.[76] The memory includes the capabilities of recalling the past, knowing the present, and anticipating the future; the basic structure of the world; and, insofar as the "image" also characterizes its referent, something about God is also exposed.[77] The human body is connected to the soul and governed by it; the body "is the noblest constitution and organization that exists in nature."[78] Humans are a union of spirit and matter, and thus the human is in the perfect position—the middle—to be the vital link between the two extremes of creation. Like divine beings, humans are spiritual; like the rest of the creation, humans are material. Humans have the capacities to develop and sustain a noble role as mediators between God and creatures. Human dignity is thus understood as both ontologically given and attained.

Human Identity: Image of God and Image of Christ. Humans can receive and participate in life with God by discovering truth and embracing goodness, using their intellect and will.[79] Humans can uncover God's generous, overflowing love and grace, thus finding their true identity and vocation (dignity). Humans are able to realize similarity to the likeness of the Son, who is both human and divine.[80] It is possible for humans to experience profound love that moved God to humble himself and become one like them. Because humans are made like Christ incarnate (exemplarity, Word), human nature is to be like Christ—poor and humble—in relationship to God. Humans are thus deified, and Christlike, though limited.

Human Identity: Mediators. Humans (form and matter, body-spirit beings) are situated in the middle of creation between the simply material beings and the exclusively spiritual beings.[81] The humans' vocation is be mediators between God and creation and guardians of the multiple manifestations of God's self-revelation (Gen. 1:28–30).[82] But humans freely overstepped their role in creation—by breaking their love relationship with the divine, they sinned.[83] Sin's consequences are personal and universal; a false consciousness distorts the image of God and breaks the order and harmony of the world.[84] Christ's passion enabled humans to be reconciled, and God initiates the graced transformation, restoring the similitude of God to each person. Bonaventure's anthropology thus provides both an ontological and a capacity basis for human dignity. When humans sustain mediating God's love and care to creation, they are deified—and retain dignity.

Bonaventure's Influence: Vatican II Theology, Anthropology, and Ethics. At Vatican II (1962–65), the influence of the social and natural sciences concerning human and spiritual development were increasingly recognized. That opened theologians to return to a historically conscious worldview, and to renew views of God and the human person. For example, Karl Rahner's understanding of God as "self-communicating" was strongly influenced by the social sciences, but also by Bonaventure's understanding of the Trinity as a radically related "self-diffusive goodness."[85] Rahner also influenced the theological ethics of Joseph Fuchs and Louis Janssens. Significant about all of this is that a historically conscious worldview enables us to see the interdependence and interrelatedness of all things in God. Such connected relationships originate in the Trinitarian relations that define the "good" toward which all human striving is directed. Indeed it is that (divine) Good that bestows intrinsic dignity on all creation and its capacities to move to perfection.

The Human Integrally and Adequately Considered

Gaudium et spes *and Twentieth-Century Personalism.* A holistic anthropology giving support for the normative status of human dignity as an objective moral criterion emerged in the formulating and interpreting of Vatican II's *GS*. Paragraphs 47–52 of *GS* provide a broad holistic description of the healthy human person. Therein is the grounding for the principle that all human moral activity must be judged as it pertains to the dignity of the human person integrally and adequately considered.[86] This theme was elaborated on by the acclaimed personalist moral theologian Janssens.

Significantly, twentieth-century personalist philosophers also asserted this holistic understanding. Their view of the human person is rooted in a phenomenological and existential analysis of human experience, which is always multidimensional. The person as an acting subject is always embedded in relationships with others, in time, space, and physical and historical reality.[87] Personalists are concerned with all forms of human relations—primary, social, political, economic, and secondary relations brought about by technological and scientific developments. They draw from all forms of knowledge obtainable by reason and faith that clarify the status of the human person.

The human person is a norm and the criterion for morals, but Janssens holds that "this does not mean that the person is raised to the level of supreme value [God]. . . . But in beginning from the viewpoint of the human person and his intentionality, we arrive precisely at the conclusion that the human person is open towards God's [transcendence]."[88] Religious personalists see communion with God as the ultimate fulfillment of the human person. But they also claim that to "begin with the person as norm and criterion, we are better able to demonstrate the place of God in our existence."[89]

Janssens: Eight Essential Dimensions of the Human Person. From *GS*, Janssens elaborates eight fundamental aspects that contribute to the human person integrally and adequately considered, and that must be accounted for in judging any moral act.[90] Space allows only highlighting key features.

(1) "The human person is a subject, not an object as are the things of the world."[91] People are conscious beings with the capacity to knowingly and willingly act. In moral matters, people can act consciously and freely as an expression of their inherent humanity. Each must accept responsibility for one's acts. As self-aware subjects, people can grow in their awareness by learning from their surroundings, and they have the capacity for transcendence, but are limited in their ability to exercise it.[92] People are ontologically free (have free will); each belongs to oneself and can make choices to determine the meaning of one's life and direction toward self-fulfillment—especially to make a fundamental choice, a choice for an ultimate desire that each individual works to realize as the fulfillment of what one's own life means.[93] One's desires mark one's "intentional

wholeness"; how one prioritizes one's desires, defines one's fundamental choice.[94] People have an "intentional wholeness," which makes them conscious that their self-awareness always includes relation to all of creation. Categorical freedom is the option to choose between particular preferences or modes of action.[95] Those cumulatively shape and are integral to one's fundamental choice. One's fundamental choice is realized to the extent that it is lived concretely, in the flesh.[96]

(2) "The person is a subject in corporality."[97] Our physical body affects our subjectivity in a defining way. Our body and soul are one; the body is not accidental, but essential to one's existence.[98] "It is beyond a doubt that air, food, and drink are indispensable goods. Because of the limitation of energies, we need sleep and rest."[99] Clearly, destruction of clean air, water, and arable land violates human dignity.

(3) "Our body forms not only a part of the subject who we are, but also as corporal, a part of the material world. Through this very fact, our being is a being-in-the-world."[100] People are fundamentally related to all that exists. Janssens states: "We form part of the ecosystem and are its only conscious, free and responsible parts; hence personalist morality demands that we aim at the protection of it as preserving our own environment in which clear air, soil, and water are vital goods."[101] He also holds that "the way in which we fulfill our relationships with the reality outside ourselves determines the way in which we fulfill ourselves."[102]

(4) "Human persons are essentially directed toward each other."[103] People are social beings; from childhood they grow and develop their own unique identity through formative interactions with others, for good (life enhancing) or for ill (death dealing). Interactively, people learn values and norms and become moral subjects.[104] Formative interactions can take place with humans, institutions, or the material environment. Destroying the sustainable Earth's environment is alienating and death dealing.

(5) "Human persons are not only essentially social beings because . . . they need to live in social groups and thus in appropriate structures and institutions."[105] Indeed, "cultural realities outside ourselves" constitute the goods of the objective culture.[106] "Every human person needs objective culture in order to fulfill his subjective culture, the unfolding of all his capabilities and possibilities as a human subject."[107] Environmental destruction limits these possibilities.

(6) "Created in the image of God, the human person is called to know and worship Him . . . and to glorify Him in all his attitudes and activities."[108] As Kirchhoffer notes, Janssens's formulation of this dimension is metaphysical.

However, this same point can be expressed in phenomenological terms and be more universally received. Thus, personalist moralist Joseph Selling's restatement: "Any person who seeks the meaning of life is searching for a dimension of being human that is accessible to all while simultaneously transcending each individual. . . . Others will describe the relationship to the transcendent in terms appropriate to their belief system."[109] Environmental destruction militates against transcendent attitudes and is symptomatic of self-centeredness or self-aggrandizement.

(7) "The human person is a historical subject."[110] At various developmental stages, people have different moral capabilities and capacities for finding life's meaning. Spatiality and temporality open opportunities for good or evil. Various influences, norms, and values are present in a society at any moment. Yet, they can change, influenced by current norms and values. Modern fascination with scientific and technological progress brought good, but it also wrought evil, including environmental destruction.

(8) "All human persons are fundamentally equal, but at the same time each is an originality."[111] "Knowing, feeling, desiring and acting we can be caught up in the same values. . . . Fundamental equality explains why moral demands are universalizable, that the same moral obligations apply to all."[112] Simultaneously, each person is unique based on his or her personal givenness. Such diversity is a basis for caring for Earth, our common home.[113]

For Kirchhoffer, these eight criteria provide a framework for an adequate anthropology. Some criteria address dimensions of the particularity of each person, but others stress their commonality or the complex interrelatedness of humans with all of creation. In light of this, the multidimensionality of human dignity and the moral event can be described in terms of ecology.

According to Franciscan liberation ecological theologian Leonardo Boff, the human person is affected by and affects three ecologies—environmental, social, and mental—which in turn shape the reality of integral ecology. Space allows only a summative definition of each.

Integral Ecology: The Relational Context of the Human Integrally and Adequately Considered

Boff holds that environmental ecology concerns relations among various societies, individual humans, and the environment.[114] This approach involves issues of science and technological development. Social ecology explores right relationships that humans encounter as Earth creatures and social beings. Social justice requires "respect for other persons, roles, and institutions and ecological justice requires reverence for the natural world, easy access to its resources, sustainable institutions, and assurance of quality of life."[115] Concerns are "socio-cosmic," including the entire planetary community.[116] Mental ecology arises from the recognition that nature is also within human beings. Here human consciousness conceives and directs healthier processes of subjectivity that relativize socioeconomic well-being by renewing vital natural, cultural, or religious engagements.

Boff's concept of integral ecology includes the three aforementioned ecologies and a holistic visualization of Earth, powerfully symbolized by images of the Earth from space. The Earth and human beings emerge as one. Astrophysics, quantum physics, and molecular biology all show that humans and Earth are evolving with the entire cosmos in processes of cosmogenesis and anthropogenesis.[117] This means that everything is constantly being born and constituting itself, forming an open system, always capable of new acquisitions and new expressions, but also—most significantly—that everything and everyone is related to all else. Put colloquially, "We are all made of stardust!"

Moral Significance of Integral Ecology for Human Development

Ethical significance and consequences for human dignity arise when viewing the human person integrally and adequately considered within the context of numerous relationships (integral ecology). Boff and Mark Hathaway see this exemplified in the Earth Charter, which calls for the emergence of a global society, grounded in a shared vision and principles that embrace democratic political participation, human rights, social and economic equity, nonviolence, ecological integrity, and respect for life.[118] Failure to account for these relationships threatens human dignity as "the multidimensional existential reality of the human person."[119] Simply, to damage anyone or anything is to become an agent of the deprivation of life from another, violating the first principle of all morality—"Do no harm!"—or more.

Boff eloquently illustrates in *Cry of the Earth, Cry of the Poor* how liberation theology and ecology each "seek liberation," responding to the cries of the Earth suffering environmental degradation and to poor people suffering social oppression. The same logic drives dominant populations to plunder the Earth and to oppress the marginalized.[120] Boff's integral ecology and integral liberation make possible the deepest, most thoroughgoing form of human dignity;

both include a personal sense of spiritual fulfillment and a collective sense of social justice. In its cosmological context, the process of integral liberation can be understood as the "conscious participation of humanity" in the cosmogenetic processes of differentiation, subjectivity, and communion.[121]

Human Dignity and the "Tactful Touch"

The etymological study of the word "integral" illuminates a deeper meaning of integral ecology.[122] Becoming integral with the Earth community suggests that humans are of one single, yet multiform community that includes all Earth's habitats, inhabitants, ideas, societies, human- and other-kind.[123] Sam Mickey observes:

> This does not . . . mean that integral ecology calls for humans to stop touching the natural world and let it return to some pristine or original state. . . . The untouched is the limit of touch, where touch makes contact with something else, something different. Integral ecology calls for a touch that attends to its limits, its contacts. It calls for humans to reinvent themselves so that their touch is tactful, so that their practices enhance ecological relations instead of dulling and destroying them. . . . tactful touch means not touching too much, touching lightly and tenderly. An objectifying touch is not tactful. It fails to leave intact the agency or existential value of what is touched. . . . It is stripped of its agency.[124]

Pope Francis teaches in *LS* that integral ecology introduces a new kind of ecological justice, "which respects our unique place in the world, and our relationship to our surroundings."[125] He continues, "When we speak of the 'environment,' what we really mean is a relationship existing between nature and the society which lives in it. Nature cannot be regarded as something separate from ourselves or as a mere setting in which we live. We are part of nature, included in it and thus in constant interaction with it."[126]

THE MORAL EVENT OF LIFE-THREATENING EARTH OVERSHOOT: CONFLICT AND DIGNITY

Kirchhoffer sees the traditional Thomistic Roman Catholic threefold definition of a moral act (act, intention, and circumstances)[127] as insufficient and one that does not account for the complexity of most moral situations, which include "norms, concrete material norms, personal values and disvalues, and so on."[128] Selling's term "moral event" is more adequate because it is "an umbrella term that encompasses all of these sources."[129] The locus for human dignity as the multidimensional existential reality of the human person is within any moral event, itself a multidimensional, time-bound occurrence consisting of intentions, physical acts, and circumstances—all of which have a bearing on the moral quality of the event in which the human subject participates.[130]

Relevant for our purposes is the moral event known as Earth Overshoot Day, the date when humanity's demand for natural resources and services in a given year exceeds what Earth can regenerate in that year.[131] That date has come earlier every year: in 1970 the date was December 23; in 2017 it was August 2; in 2019 it was July 29![132] The following samples illustrate the grave consequences of this reality.

Today, "a fair share" of the planet's livable landmass for each of Earth's 7.5 billion persons is about 4.5 acres.[133] Such an equitable distribution would require that per person, literally everything that sustains human life must come from one's 4.5 acres. But human choices have created vast life-threatening global inequalities. To support an "average lifestyle" in Tanzania takes 2.6 acres versus 22.3 in the United States (plus contextual benefits of infrastructures, food choices, travel options, medical advantages, and conveniences). It would take four to five planets to accomplish a North American lifestyle for all!

The concept of Earth overshoot is defined and supported by a vast amount of data showing the size and the scale of human-caused, morally indictable, planetary, and human devastation. Though access to water and sanitation is a human right, one-fifth of the world's population lives with physical water scarcity, and 500 million more are approaching this situation.[134] The vast majority of the world's hungry people live in developing countries; poor nutrition causes nearly half (45%) of deaths in children under five—3.1 million children each year. Since the 1900s, around 75 percent of crop diversity has been lost from farmers' fields.[135] There is a serious threat to planetary life from the loss of biodiversity. Of the 8,300 animal breeds known, 8 percent are extinct and 22 percent are at risk of extinction.[136]

At best, these data signal the impending demise of the very life of planet Earth and its inhabitants—including humans. At worst, much evidence indicates that conscious human choices have brought us to this point. People have arrogantly forgotten their interdependent creaturely status and their role as the guardians of creation and the representatives of the Creator's care and concern for all. The vulnerable poor have been most egregiously victimized. These behaviors have violated the dignity of both victims and perpetrators, as the following will demonstrate.

An Analysis of Earth Overshoot Using Human Dignity as a Moral Criterion

Human Dignity: A Descriptive Category. Earth overshoot has numerous causes that are thoroughly analyzed elsewhere.[137] Here I simply describe the operative understanding of human dignity that is relevant to the moral event (Earth overshoot) itself, such as mores and other influences, and the operative justification for past moral choices and behavioral strategies.

For centuries, the industrialized Western nations exercised power over the "resources" of the Earth with little regard for its carrying capacity or inhabitants. This activity is known as the "imperial ecology" of Francis Bacon (1561–1626) and René Descartes (1596–1650). Imperial ecology includes economic materialism, and, following the clockmaker god of Deism, asserts human superiority over the rest of creation.[138] Bacon saw humans as lords and masters over nature and Earth elements as merely parts of a machine that could be remade, according to the reason and the imagination of *Homo faber*. He believed that science could restore the world to a paradise, bringing about the biblical "new Jerusalem."[139] Descartes viewed nature as a machine easily understood by analyzing its various parts.[140] To understand nature was to discover the functional relationship between abstractly conceived processes and objects that could be translated into mathematical equations. The key was to bring natural processes into the realm of the conceptual, mathematical understandings—that is, to formulate laws so as to serve human interests. The aim of modern science, Descartes argued, was to "know the power and action of fire, water, air, the stars, the heavens and all the other bodies in our environment . . . and thus make ourselves, as it were, the lords and masters of nature."[141]

Isaac Newton's (1642–1727) genius was reformulating previously known facts and novelties into general laws and principles that could be broadly applied. Newton saw his "mechanical philosophy" as God's omnipotent will, but his theories were simply fulfilling his duty to bear witness of God to others. Newton's work "*Principia Mathematica* convinced Western Europeans that the state of nature was that of martial law. . . . Nature's Eros and ambiguity, its randomness and unpredictability, so familiar to the ancients, are simply ignored or repressed.

Turbulence or frustration became invisible."[142] Eventually Newton student Pierre Simon LaPlace (1749–1827) argued that the universe is completely determined, "so we no longer require the hypothesis of God."[143] Such attitudes and behaviors clash profoundly with the criteria set forth in *GS*, and what Janssens calls the human person integrally and adequately considered—particularly his criteria (3), (4), and (5) above—which make possible the kind of relationships with the Earth and all creatures, that are indicative of human dignity.

Human Dignity: A Normative Criterion. The influences of "imperial ecology" are manifested today in Earth overshoot. This moral event is characterized by disregard for everything I indicated as defining the content of human dignity. "Imperial ecology" and Earth overshoot display an inadequate anthropology and neglect the *imago Dei*, discounting the biblical *nefesh chayah*, ignoring "deep incarnation," and limiting "the human person integrally and adequately considered." The attitudes and behaviors in relation to God, humans, and all of creation dictated by "imperial ecology" and Earth overshoot oppose humans as guardians and mediators in creation. And there is an indifference toward the thoroughgoing cosmic connectedness of integral ecology. Human dignity, as a normative criterion, forcefully condemns Earth overshoot as immoral because it results from human choices that have been made in spite of knowledge that such actions will result in irreparable damage to plants, animals, humans, and life-sustaining planetary systems. Pope Francis summarizes and denounces the conditions creating and sustaining Earth overshoot this way:

> Economic powers continue to justify the current global system where priority tends to be given to speculation and the pursuit of financial gain, which fail to take the context into account, let alone the effects on human dignity and the natural environment. Here we see how environmental deterioration and human and ethical degradation are closely linked. Many people will deny doing anything wrong because distractions constantly dull our consciousness of just how limited and finite our world really is. As a result, "whatever is fragile, like the environment, is defenseless before the interests of a deified market, which become the only rule."[144]

In *LS*, Pope Francis argues for an ecological humanism based on Christian anthropology.[145] He criticizes technology insofar as it serves as a paradigm for technocracy. As such, it models a way of being, shapes our understanding of the world, nature, humans, and animals. Technology is itself a good. However, it has ceased to be an instrument; it has become a power because it destroys and does not support human dignity.[146]

Joël Molinario, theologian and an ecological humanist, defines "technocracy" as "technology supported by discourse that has turned it into the dominant ideology in the world today: reality is completely open to manipulation, domination and transformation. *Every* process of scientific discovery is a good, for there is no longer a single example of restraint."[147] The technocrat is a person who focuses on consumable utility, which turns into domination. Technology becomes the focus of unlimited trust in a better tomorrow with an allure that has made it the dominant cultural paradigm. Economics and politics naturally comply with it, trusting that unlimited technological progress will solve every problem.

Pope Francis holds that though it is never explicitly identified as such, technology controls nearly all sectors of life—markets, finance, biotechnologies, and more. This is problematic because it fails to appreciate the whole of knowledge, yet it has become a global entity, with its many creators scattered abroad and unaware of each other or the full repercussions of their products.[148]

Indeed, psychologist Tim Kasser shows there is a high human price being paid for this materialism, even in its mildest form, where "the good life is accessible through the goods life."[149] Annually, more than $150 billion is spent to embed commercial messages that shape, form, and teach people to organize their lives. Kasser shows that high materialistic aspirations lower personal happiness and life satisfaction, allow fewer daily experiences of pleasant emotions, and trigger higher depression, anxiety, and substance abuse.[150] These realities chip away at human dignity by diminishing human capacities.

Strong materialistic values have a negative effect on social relations and others' well-being. There is a see-saw effect: the higher one's materialistic values, the lower one's pro-social values; thus, people become more or less generous and cooperative. Ironically, the more people focus on material values, the less they care about the Earth that is the source of their material goods! Again there is a see-saw effect between higher or lower materialistic values versus care for the Earth. Human dignity is damaged because such valuing causes humans to harm the common home of fellow humans, other creatures, and Earth systems. People are inhibited from adequately fulfilling life-giving human and planetary relationships. This often results in egregious violations of people and denigration of life-sustaining planetary systems.

Kasser holds that the way forward requires we focus on intrinsic values. Two key causes move people to prioritize materialistic values: feeling insecure or threatened by rejection, economic worries, or fears of death; and high exposure to commercial messages. What promotes intrinsic values is concentration on personal growth, connecting with family and friends, and improving the broader world. That lifestyle is supported by religious values, attention to simple personal lifestyle, or advocating for social policies that promote intrinsic values. These findings align with Kirchhoffer's notion of a proper human dignity that stipulates work for my dignity can never be realized unless I also work for the dignity of all others to whom I am related—the integral ecology of the entire cosmos.

CONCLUSION

Humans are meaning-making and meaning-seeking entities. They live by interacting at multiple levels in numerous relationships, and, within these, they seek purpose and self-worth. Ultimately, they desire a sense of life well-lived. Humans already have dignity, but they can also either acquire it or willfully and utterly forfeit it by choosing acts destructive of self, others, and all of creation. Dignity is both inherent and self-worth. It is a moral good and an end in itself. The dignity of others and one's own dignity are inextricably bound up with each other.

Precisely what constitutes one's idea of dignity depends on numerous influences and one's response to them. The adequacy of a proper understanding of human dignity can be determined in light of the human person integrally and adequately considered (Janssens) and the moral event (Selling). Human existential reality and historicity dictate that a proper normative self-worth (dignity) requires one to always act seeking the dignity of all elements of creation in addition to one's own.

A proper understanding of human dignity is multidimensional, and it provides a framework for understanding and evaluating behavior. As a descriptive category, it helps explore what people do when seeking dignity and why they do it. As a normative criterion, human dignity helps evaluate to what extent a behavior is right or wrong and good or bad and thus assists in making moral decisions. We can evaluate the operative understanding of dignity as a social and moral good, the mores and influences that contribute to that understanding, and behavioral strategies used to achieve human dignity.

Human dignity as a descriptive moral category reveals human flourishing, which requires humans to be guardians and protectors of all creation. When used as a normative criterion, human dignity judges destructive human use of the natural environment negatively because such behavior diminishes, if not destroys, our very humanity. Thus, "human dignity" is a valuable term for grounding principles for environmental responsibility and sustainability in a manner that fits Catholic teaching, exemplified in Pope Francis's *Laudato Si'*. His understanding is distinctively rooted in Catholic social and environmental teachings, but it is indeed catholic (universal). A phenomenological and an inductive both/and approach, his teaching has been understood in both humanistic terms and in those compatible with a variety of religious traditions.[151]

"PROLOGUE: MIDRASH ON NOAH"

A wonderful story from *Midrash Tankhuma*, Parashat Noach, depicts a conversation between God and Noah:

> When Noah came out of the ark, he opened his eyes and saw the whole world completely destroyed. He began crying for the world and said: "God—how could you have done this!?"
>
> God replied, "Oh Noah, how different you are from the way Abraham will be. . . . He will argue with me on behalf of Sodom and Gomorrah, when I tell him that I plan their destruction. . . . But you, Noah, when I told you I would destroy the entire world, I lingered and delayed, so that you would speak on behalf of the world. But when you knew that you would be safe in the ark, that the evil of the world would not touch you. . . . You thought of no one but your family. . . . And—now you complain!?"
>
> Then—Noah knew—he had sinned![152]

Noah's sin was not that he thought of his family. It was that he did not think of everyone else.

Central to protecting the relational structure of creation is to safeguard life itself. If ecosystems are destroyed beyond their capacity to renew themselves or species are allowed to become extinct, they are lost forever. Such is the nature of the moral events of pillaging the environment that result in the ever earlier Earth overshoot date. Such vast losses of biodiversity incriminate humans and eviscerate any claim to dignity by human perpetrators who are agents of such actions. There is virtually no moral justification imaginable for such activity, since (religiously) it endangers the very life of the entirety of God's creation, and (scientifically), as Holmes Rolston III claims, there is need for every creature; there is no "bad" species in the web of life.[153] Ecosystems are living entities that are foundational to life in all its diversity for generating life cycles, keeping selection pressures high, enriching situated fitness, and allowing congruent kinds to evolve in their places with sufficient containment. Ecosystems are integral to the created relational structure.

There can be no human dignity apart from integral ecology, and thus it requires environmental interests be protected through a combination of environmental laws and recognition of environmental human rights. Environmental laws must protect nonhuman species from extinction and provide the basic criteria for making value judgments that determine the role of a nature's part in the entirety. Since planetary systems know no national boundaries, environmental laws need to be international law in order to confront the global ecological crisis. Environmental human rights ought to protect the basic conditions needed by humans to live modestly within the complex relational structure of the cosmos. Minimally, this entails the right and ability of humans to have clean air, water, and food, to live in a healthy environment in harmony with existing ecosystems, and to fulfill their roles as caretakers of creation.

NOTES

1. Pope Francis, *Laudato Si'*, http://w2.vatican.va/content/francesco/en/encyclicals/documents/papa-francesco_20150524_enciclica-laudato-si.html.

2. *LS* no. 115 (emphasis added). He cites in the first quote "Romano Guardini, *Das Ende der Neuzeit*, 63 (*The End of the Modern World*, 55)," and in the second "John Paul II, *Centesimus annus* (1 May 1991), 38: AAA 83 (1991): 841." "Dignity" appears with various grammatical modifiers in *LS* nos. 30, 43, 56, 65, 69, 90, 92, 94, 112, 115, 119, 130, 139, 152, 154, 158, 160, 181, 193, 211.

3. *LS*, chap. 4, "Integral Ecology," nos. 137–62.

4. Especially *LS* nos. 91, 92, 93–95.

5. *LS* nos. 67 and 106.

6. Mark Shiffman, "Between the Knower and the Known—*LS* and the Limits of the Scientific Spirit," *Commonweal Magazine*, March 8, 2016, https://www.commonwealmagazine.org/between-knower-known. David Toolan, *At Home in the Cosmos* (Maryknoll, NY: Orbis, 2001), pts. 1 and 3.

7. Shiffman, "Between the Knower and the Known."

8. *LS* no. 160.

9. Sam Mickey, *On the Verge of a Planetary Civilization: A Philosophy of Integral Ecology* (New York: Rowman & Littlefield, 2014), 17. Mickey discusses work by Thomas Berry and Leonardo Boff. More on Boff below.

10. Descriptive ethics explains what people do when they act morally, why they do what they do; provides valid justifications, reasons, causes, and goals of moral behavior by individuals and societies; provides no evaluation of whether such operations or norms are good, bad, or if the behaviors are right or wrong; and deals with how people believe they ought to behave. Normative ethics addresses how, from an objective perspective, people ought to behave, using arguments and criteria to evaluate human behavior as right/wrong or good/bad. Discussion of both dimensions is necessary for adequate ethical evaluation and practice.

11. Mickey, *On the Verge of a Planetary Civilization*, 17.

12. David G. Kirchhoffer, *Human Dignity in Contemporary Ethics* (Amherst, NY: Teneo Press, 2013).

13. Ibid., 316.

14. Ibid., 2.

15. Ibid., xviii–296.

16. Parliament of World's Religions, Religions and Ecology, https://parliamentofreligions.org/program/climate-action; The Yale Forum on Religion and Ecology, http://fore.yale.edu/religion/; United Nations Environmental Program, *Earth and Faith: A Book of Reflection for Action*, https://www.unenvironment.org/resources/report/earth-and-faith-book-reflection-action.

17. John Haught, *Science and Faith: A New Introduction* (New York: Paulist Press, 2012), 9–20, 120–32.

18. *GS* holds great authority in Roman Catholic magisterial teaching, laying the groundwork for a more adequate understanding of human dignity as a central element of contemporary theological ethics.

19. Kirchhoffer, *Human Dignity*, 76–99. Kirchhoffer provides examples of all categories.

20. Kirchhoffer, *Human Dignity*, 99, cites Klaus Demmer, *Shaping the Moral Life: An Approach to Moral Theology*, trans. Roberto Dell'Oro, ed. James F. Keenan (Washington, DC: Georgetown University, 2000), 16.

21. Kirchhoffer, *Human Dignity*, 99. Kirchhoffer follows Demmer, *Shaping the Moral Life*.

22. Ibid., 125–49.

23. Ibid., 3.

24. Ibid., 165–68. He cites works by Paul van Tongeren and Dietmar Mieth.

25. Ibid., 169–77. More on Janssens follows.

26. Ibid., 14.

27. Ibid., 141–49, 180–83.

28. Ibid., 150–65.

29. Ibid., 158–65.

30. Ibid., 187–89.

31. Ibid., 13.

32. Ibid., 211–13. A *hermeneutic of generosity* appeals to the readers to set aside their own interests or biases, and interpret a text from the perspective of its author. Particularly, such efforts enable readers to encounter their own biases, the role their biases play in interpreting a text, and to better comprehend the author's biases, views, and reasons for writing. See Margaret R. Miles, "Hermeneutics of Generosity and Suspicion: Pluralism and Theological Education," supplement, *Theological Education* 23 (1987): 34–52; Lucretia B. Yaghjian, *Writing Theology Well: A Rhetoric for Theological and Biblical Writers* (New York: Continuum, 2006), 6; and Hans-Georg Gadamer, *Truth and Method*, 2nd rev. ed., trans. Joel Weinsheimer and Donald G. Marshall (London: Continuum, 2004), 269.

33. Kirchhoffer, *Human Dignity*, 129–30, 235–58.

34. Kirchhoffer, *Human Dignity*, 130, cites Jan Jans, "Enjoying and Making Use of a Responsible Freedom: Background and Substantiation of Human Dignity in the Second Vatican Council," in *Sustaining Humanity beyond Humanism* (*Humanität über den Humanismus hinaus erhalten*) (Aarhus: Societas Ethica, 2003), 101–11.

35. Ibid., 18, 223–24, and 250–51nn23–27.

36. Paul Tillich, *Systematic Theology* (Chicago: University of Chicago, 1957), 2:26.

37. Kirchhoffer, *Human Dignity*, 214–16.

38. Ibid., 225–34.

39. Ibid., 217.

40. Ibid., 218.

41. Ibid., 219, 235.

42. Richard M. Gula, *Reason Informed by Faith: Fundamentals of Catholic Morality* (New York: Paulist 1989), 78–81. More on fundamental choice below.

43. Kirchhoffer, *Human Dignity*, 220.

44. Kirchhoffer, *Human Dignity*, 220, cites James T. Bretzke, *Consecrated Phrases: A Latin Theological Dictionary*, 2nd ed. (Collegeville, MN: Liturgical Press, 2003), 5–6.

45. Kirchhoffer, *Human Dignity*, 221.

46. Kirchhoffer, *Human Dignity*, 242, cites John Dewey, *Lectures on Ethics, 1900–1901*, ed. and intro. Donald F. Koch (Carbondale: Southern Illinois University Press, 1991), 54.

47. Kirchhoffer, *Human Dignity*, 243–44.

48. Ibid., 222.

49. Ibid.

50. Ibid., 245.

51. Ibid., 246.

52. See *Schema constitutionis pastoralis de ecclesia in mundo huius temporis: Expensio modorum partis secundae* (Vatican Press, 1965), 37–38: *personam humanam integre et adequate considerandam*. (Hereafter cited as *Expensio modorum*.)

53. *Dei verbum* (*Dogmatic Constitution on Divine Revelation*), November 18, 1965, http://www.vatican.va/archive/hist_councils/ii_vatican_council/documents/vat-ii_const_19651118_dei-verbum_en.html.

54. See Dawn M. Nothwehr, *Ecological Footprints: An Essential Franciscan Guide for Faith and Sustainable Living* (Collegeville, MN: Liturgical Press, 2012), chaps. 1 and 2. Also Dianne Bergant, *The Earth Is the Lord's: The Bible, Ecology, and Worship* (Collegeville, MN: Liturgical Press, 1998); Jeanne Kay, "Concepts of Nature in the Hebrew Bible," in *Franciscan Theology of the Environment: An Introductory Reader*, ed. Dawn M. Nothwehr (Quincy, IL: Franciscan Press, 2002); Susan Power Bratton, "Christian Ecotheology and the Hebrew Scriptures," in Nothwehr, ed., *Franciscan Theology of the Environment*, 51–52; Claus Westermann, *Genesis 1–11: A Commentary*, trans. John J. Scullion (Minneapolis: Augsburg, 1974); Clarence J. Glacken, *Traces on the Rhodian Shore: Nature and Culture in Western Thought from Ancient Times to the End of the Eighteenth Century* (Berkeley: University of California Press, 1967). James Barr, "Man and Nature: The Ecological Controversy and the Old Testament," in *Ecology and Religion in History*, ed. David Spring and Ellen Spring (New York: Harper & Row, 1974); Gerhardt von Rad, *Old Testament Theology*, vol. 1 (New York: Harper & Row, 1962).

55. See Ps. 104:30; Eccl. 3:19, 21; and Gen. 1:24–26.

56. Kay, "Concepts of Nature in the Hebrew Bible," 27.

57. Westermann, *Genesis 1–11: A Commentary*, 153.

58. Bratton, "Christian Ecotheology and the Hebrew Scriptures," 56.

59. Ellen Davis, "Human Dignity—Genesis 1:26–31," in *Humanity: Texts and Contexts—Christian and Muslim Perspectives*, ed. Michael Ipgrave and David Marshall (Washington, DC: Georgetown University Press, 2011), 73–74.

60. See Nothwehr, *Ecological Footprints*, 22–47.

61. Duncan Reid, "Enfleshing the Human," in *Earth Revealing-Earth Healing: Ecology and Christian Theology*, ed. Denis Edwards (Collegeville, MN: Liturgical Press, 2000), 69–83.

62. Neil Darragh, *At Home in the Earth* (Auckland: Accent Publications, 2000), 124. See discussion of "deep incarnation" in Denis Edwards, *Ecology at the Heart of Faith* (Maryknoll, NY: Orbis Books, 2006), 58–60.

63. Edwards, *Ecology at the Heart of Faith*, 59 (original emphasis). See Neils Henrick Gregersen, "The Cross of Christ in an Evolutionary World," *Dialog: A Journal of Theology* 40 (2001): 205.

64. Edwards, *Ecology at the Heart of Faith*, 59.

65. Ibid., 59.

66. Ibid., 10–11, 38, 84–85; Haught, *Science and Faith*, 9–20; Jack Mahoney, *Christianity in Evolution* (Washington, DC: Georgetown University Press, 2011); Elizabeth A. Johnson, *Women, Earth, Creator Spirit* (New York: Paulist, 1993), 39.

67. Zachary Hayes, "Bonaventure: Mystery of the Triune God," in *The History of Franciscan Theology*, ed. Kenan B. Osborne, O. F. M. (St. Bonaventure, NY: The Franciscan Institute, 1994), 53–60. Pope Francis's *LS* is suffused with St. Bonaventure's creation theology; see, esp., *LS* nos. 11, 66, and, esp., 233 and 239.

68. Catherine Mowry LaCugna, *God for Us: The Trinity and the Christian Life* (New York: HarperCollins Paperback, 1993) 158–67.

69. Bonaventure, *Breviloquium* 2.12 (5:230), cited in Zachary Hayes, *Bonaventure: Mystical Writings* (New York: Crossroad, 1999), 90. All citations are Hayes's translations from *Doctoris Seriphici S. Bonaventurae opera omnia*, 10 vols. (Quaracchi: Collegium S. Bonaventurae, 1882–1902). The first two numerals indicate the section of the text; the numerals in parentheses indicate the volume and the page in that volume.

70. Zachary Hayes, "The Cosmos: A Symbol of the Divine," in Nothwehr, ed., *Franciscan Theology of the Environment*, 250–51. See chapter 2 of Bonaventure, *The Journey of the Soul into God.*

71. Phil Hoebing, "St. Bonaventure and Ecology," in Nothwehr, ed., *Franciscan Theology of the Environment*, 276.

72. Bonaventure, *Collations on the Six Days of Creation* 1.13 (5:332), cited in Hayes, "Bonaventure: Mystery," 74.

73. Hayes, "Bonaventure: Mystery," 63–64.

74. Bonaventure, *Collations on the Six Days of Creation* 3.8 (5:344), cited in Hayes, *Bonaventure: Mystical Writings*, 73.

75. Bonaventure, *The Journey of the Soul into God* 1.15 (5:299), cited in Hayes, *Bonaventure: Mystical Writings*, 77. An artistic work reveals something of the artist; thus, creation reveals the Creator—i.e., is sacramental. To destroy creation is, therefore, sacrilegious. See *LS* nos. 138–39.

76. Bonaventure, *Itinerarium Mentis in Deum* 3 (V, 303ff.), cited in Zachary Hayes, "Bonaventure: Mystery," 81.

77. Hayes, "Bonaventure: Mystery," 82.

78. Ilia Delio, *Simply Bonaventure: An Introduction to His Life, Thought, and Writings* (Hyde Park, NY: New City Press, 2001), 69. She cites Bonaventure, *Breviloquium* 2.10 (V, 228). Thomas A. Shannon, "Human Dignity in the Theology of St. Bonaventure," *Spirit and Life* 7 (1997): 67.

79. Alvin Black, "The Doctrine of the Image and Similitude in Saint Bonaventure," *Cord* 12 (1962): 270.

80. Bonaventure, III *Sent.* d. 1, a. 2, q. 3, resp. (III, 29), cited in Delio, *Simply Bonaventure*, 72.

81. Alexander Schaeffer, "The Position and Function of Man in the Created World according to Bonaventure," *Franciscan Studies* 21 (1961): 320.

82. Ewert Cousins, *Christ of the 21st Century* (Rockport, MA: Element, 1992), 152–55.

83. See Bonaventure, II *Sent.* prooem. (II, 1–6), English translation in Timothy Johnson, *Bonaventure: Mystic of God's Word* (Hyde Park, NY: New City Press, 1999) 57, cited in Delio, *Simply Bonaventure*, 75.

84. Delio, *Simply Bonaventure*, 77. Delio cites II *Sent.* d. 33, a.1, q.2 (II, 75); II *Sent.* d. 19, a. 3, q. 1, concl. (II, 470). Also Bonaventure Hinwood, "'Justice' according to St. Bonaventure," *Cord* 31 (1981): 323–35.

85. LaCugna, *God for Us*, 210–11, and 213n6: "Rahner's theology of self-communication appears to have roots in Bonaventure's vision of the self-diffusive God." Rahner

wrote two early articles on Bonaventure's theology: Karl Rahner, "La Doctrine des 'sens spirituels' au Moyen-Âge en particular chez St.-Bonaventure," *Revue d'Ascétique et de Mystique* 14 (1933): 263–99; Rahner, "Der Bergriff der ecstatis bei Bonaventure," *Zeitschrift für Aszese und Mystik* 9 (1934): 1–19.

86. Louis Janssens, "Particular Goods and Personalist Morals," *Ethical Perspectives* 6, no.1 (1999): 55. He cites *Expensio modorum*, no. 104, pp. 37–38. He also cites *Expensio modorum, resp.*, 104b, p. 37.

87. John Polkinghorne, "Anthropology in an Evolutionary Context," in *God and Human Dignity*, ed. R. Kendall Soulen and Linda Woodhead (Grand Rapids, MI: William B. Eerdmans, 2006), 101. Reinhard Marx, "Sozialethik als hermeneutische Ethik—Bedenkenswerte Aspecte," *Jahrbuch für Christliche Sozialwissenschaften* 43 (2002): 241–47; Bradley R. Munro, "The Universal Declaration of Human Rights, Maritain, and the Universality of Human Rights," in *Philosophical Theory and the Universal Declaration of Human Rights*, ed. William Sweet (Ottawa: University of Ottawa Press, 2003), 109–25; Thomas M. Jeannot, "A Postsecular Exchange: Jacques Maritain, John Dewey, and Karl Marx," in *Philosophical Theory and the Universal Declaration of Human Rights*, ed. William Sweet (Ottawa: University of Ottawa, 2003), 83–98. Johan De Tavernier, "The Historical Roots of Personalism: From Renouvier's *Le Personnalisme*, Mounier's *Manisesto au service du personnalisme* and Maritain's *Humanisme integral* to Janssens's *Personne et Société*," *Ethical Perspectives* 16, no. 3 (2009): 361–92.

88. Louis Janssens, "Personalist Morals," *Louvain Studies* 8 (Spring 1980): 15–16.

89. Ibid., 16.

90. Texts by Louis Janssens, "Particular Goods and Personalist Morals," 55–59; Janssens, "Artificial Insemination: Ethical Considerations," *Louvain Studies* 3 (Spring 1970): 3–29; Janssens, "Personalist Morals," 5–16.

91. Janssens, "Artificial Insemination," 5.

92. Janssens, "Personalist Morals," 7–8.

93. Ibid., 9.

94. Ibid., 9–10.

95. Ibid.

96. Ibid., 10–11.

97. Janssens, "Artificial Insemination," 5.

98. Janssens, "Personalist Morals," 11.

99. Janssens, "Particular Goods," 56.

100. Janssens, "Artificial Insemination," 6.

101. Janssens, "Particular Goods," 56.

102. Janssens, "Personalist Morals," 6.

103. Janssens, "Artificial Insemination," 8.

104. Janssens, "Personalist Morals," 6.

105. Janssens, "Artificial Insemination," 9.

106. Janssens, "Personalist Morals," 6.

107. Ibid., 6–7.

108. Janssens, "Artificial Insemination," 9. Louis Janssens, "Personalism in Moral Theology," in *Moral Theology Challenges for the Future—Essays in Honor of Richard A. McCormick*, ed. Charles E. Curran (New York: Paulist Press, 1990), 98. Janssens "Personalist Morals," 8.

109. Joseph A. Selling, "The Human Person," in *Christian Ethics: An Introduction*, ed. Bernard Hoose (London: Cassel, 1998), 97–98, cited by Kirchhoffer, *Human Dignity*, 175.

110. Janssens, "Artificial Insemination," 10.

111. Ibid., 12.

112. Ibid. Louis Janssens, "Norms and Priorities in Love Ethics," *Louvain Studies* 6 (1977): 207–38.

113. *LS* nos. 138–39.

114. F. Guattari, *As Três Ecologias* (Campinas: Papirus, 1988). I use Leonardo Boff's definitions of ecology because his work influenced *LS* nos. 10, 11, 62, 124, 137, 159, 225, especially 49. See Henry Longbottom, SJ, "Pope Francis's Ecology Encyclical—What Can We Expect?" *Jesuit Post*, December 10, 2014, https://thejesuitpost.org/2014/12/pope-franciss-ecology-encyclical-what-can-we-expect/. Also "Integral Ecology: The Big News of *Laudato Si'*: A Special Interview with Leonardo Boff," by Patricia Fachin and João Vitor Santos (English translation by Rebel Girl), June 23, 2015, http://laudato-see.blogspot.com/2015/06/integral-ecology-focal-point-leonardo.html.

Leonardo Boff and Virgilio Elizondo, "Ecology and Poverty: Cry of the Earth, Cry of the Poor—Editorial," *Concilium* 1995/5 *Ecology and Poverty*, ed. Leonardo Boff and Virgilio Elizondo (Maryknoll, NY: Orbis Books, 1995), ix–xi; Boff, *Ecology and Liberation: A New Paradigm*, trans., John Cumming (Maryknoll, NY: Orbis, 1995); Boff, *Cry of the Earth, Cry of the Poor*, trans. Phillip Berryman (Maryknoll, NY: Orbis Books, 1997), 105; Boff, with Mark Hathaway, *The Tao of Liberation: Exploring the Ecotheology of Transformation* (Maryknoll, NY: Orbis, 2009).

115. Boff, *Cry of the Earth, Cry of the Poor*, 105.

116. Boff and Elizondo, "Ecology and Poverty," para. 2. Also Boff, *Cry of the Earth, Cry of the Poor*, 112.

117. Ibid. Boff and Elizondo, "Ecology and Poverty," para. 4.

118. Boff and Hathaway, *The Tao of Liberation*, 300. See Earth Charter Initiative, "What Is the Earth Charter?," http://earthcharter.org/discover/.

119. Kirchhoffer, *Human Dignity*, 316.

120. Boff, *Cry of the Earth, Cry of the Poor*, 104. Boff and Hathaway, *The Tao of Liberation*, 61.

121. Boff and Hathaway, *The Tao of Liberation*, 292.

122. Mickey, *On the Verge of a Planetary Civilization*, 39n51: "The prefix of the word *integral (in-)* has a negative or privative force (like *un-* in English), and the *-teg-* shares the same derivation as the Latin *tangere* ('to touch'), which is the source of English words like *tact, tangible, tag, tangent,* and *contact* (*Oxford English Dictionary Online*)."

123. Mickey, *On the Verge of a Planetary Civilization*, 17.

124. Ibid., 18–19.

125. *LS* no. 15.

126. *LS* no. 139.

127. Kirchhoffer, *Human Dignity*, 144, cites *Catechism of the Catholic Church*, nos. 1750, 1755, and 1757, http://www.vatican.va/archive/ENG0015/_INDEX. HTM.

128. Kirchhoffer, *Human Dignity*, 144 and 194n61.

129. Ibid.

130. Ibid., 316, 144–49.

131. Global Footprint Network, http://www.footprintnetwork.org/.

132. "About Earth Overshoot Day," http://www.overshootday.org/about-earth-overshoot-day/. Also see Leila Mead, "2019 Earth Overshoot Day Reaches Earliest Date Ever," http://sdg.iisd.org/news/2019-earth-overshoot-day-reaches-earliest-date-ever/, August 1, 2019. Earth Overshoot Day was July 29, 2019.

133. Global Footprint Network, http://www.footprintnetwork.org/.

134. UN Water for Life Decade, https://www.un.org/waterforlifedecade/scarcity.shtml.

135. UN Sustainable Development, Goal 2, http://www.un.org/sustainabledevelopment/hunger/.

136. UN Sustainable Development, Goal 15, http://www.un.org/sustainabledevelopment/biodiversity/.

137. "About Earth Overshoot Day," http://www.overshootday.org/about-earth-overshoot-day/. Also Global Footprint Network, https://www.footprintnetwork.org/.

138. Toolan, *At Home in the Cosmos*, esp. pt. 2, "The Development of Scientific Materialism," 41–74. Toolan cites Donald Worster, *Nature's Economy: A History of Ecological Ideas*, 2nd ed. (Cambridge: Cambridge University Press, 1977), 29.

139. Toolan, *At Home in the Cosmos,* 49.

140. Ibid., 49–50.

141. Ibid., 50. See Descartes, *Discourse on Method*, 6.62.

142. Toolan, *At Home in the Cosmos*, 52.

143. Ibid., 53.

144. *LS* no. 56. Also see *LS* nos. 92, 107, 130, and 193.

145. *LS* nos. 101 to 123.

146. *LS* nos. 105, 108, 115, 204, 219.

147. Joël Molinario, "Ecological Humanism? The Pope Is Calling for a Cultural Revolution," *Global Pulse Magazine*, September 21, 2015, https://international.la-croix.com/news/ecological-humanism/1899 (emphasis added).

148. See *LS* nos. 56, 92, 107, 130, and esp. 193.

149. Tim Kasser, "What Psychology Says about Materialism and the Holidays," *American Psychological Association Newsletter*, December 16, 2014, http://www.apa.org/news/press/releases/2014/12/ materialism-holidays.aspx.

150. Tim Kasser, *The High Price of Materialism* (Cambridge, MA: MIT Press, 2002); Kasser, *Psychology and the Consumer Culture: The Struggle for a Good Life in*

a Materialistic World (Washington, DC: American Psychological Association, 2004); Kasser, *Meeting Environmental Challenges: The Role of Human Identity* (Surrey: Green Books, 2009).

151. An Internet search using term "voices approval of *Laudato Si'*" yielded more than 150,000 hits.

152. "Prologue: A Midrash on Noah," in *To Till and to Tend: A Guide to Jewish Environmental Study and Action* (New York: Coalition on the Environment and Jewish Life, 1995), 3, 6.

153. Holmes Rolston III, "Environmental Ethics: Values in and Duties to the Natural World," in *Ecology, Economics, Ethics: The Broken Circle*, ed. F. Herbert Bormann and Stephen R Kellert (New Haven, CT: Yale University Press, 1991), 81.

nineteen

DIGNITY AND CONFLICT

Religious Peacebuilding

Ellen Ott Marshall

Like every chapter in this book, this one works with multivalent and contested terms. To the complex notion of human dignity, we add religious conflict and religious peacebuilding. I begin with definitions for these terms and then consider the different ways in which human dignity contributes to religious conflict and religious peacebuilding. I focus on two sets of observations, clearly illustrated in current literature: (1) dignity functions as a cause for conflict and also a criterion for the means of conflict; and (2) dignity, informed by the Christian doctrine of *imago Dei*, grounds individual rights and maintains relationship. To these two sets of observations I add a more constructive proposal rooted in my own Wesleyan tradition, namely, that the *imago Dei* is about both process and status. By this I mean that religious conflict and peacebuilding calls one to the ongoing work of recognizing and restoring the image of God in the world. Each of the three main sections of this chapter explores a different topic at the intersection of religious conflict and peacebuilding: nonviolent resistance, reconciliation, and moral injury. After a section of definitions, I first explore the ways in which the *imago Dei* inspires and sustains resistance to physical and structural violence. Second, I argue that the *imago Dei* provides a theological frame that holds rights and responsibilities together and thus keeps justice and reconciliation connected. Third, I turn to descriptions of moral injury to consider the ways in which the image of God is both diminished and restored over time.

DEFINITIONS AND DESCRIPTION

Because the term "conflict" is used for everything from interpersonal disputes to international war, it is important to begin with definitions. Conflict—literally the striking together of different elements as they interact with one another—is a natural and necessary feature of life that includes a spectrum of behaviors from war or revolution all the way to principled nonviolent resistance. (We might also continue the spectrum in another direction to capture behaviors that range from active engagement with conflict to avoidance of conflict.)

Religion has to do with conflict in substantive and procedural ways. Substantively, religious convictions, texts, traditions, and practices generate conflict. Procedurally, religious convictions establish rules for believers' behavior in the midst of conflict. Religion is never the only factor in a dispute, nor are we able to isolate religious influences clearly from political, social, and cultural ones.[1] Yet religion often plays a part in conflict, whether at the level of explicit rhetoric inciting physical violence, or as long-standing practices of exclusion that sustain structural violence, or as implicit assumptions about sin, evil, forgiveness, and salvation that shape a believer's interpretation of historical events and guide her participation in the world.[2] Religion is a contributing cause to conflict and influences the participants' behavior in the midst of conflict. Conflict is religious insofar as the participants' convictions, traditions, sacred texts, and/or ecclesial authorities motivate and guide their striking together.

In many ways, "peacebuilding" has gained usage as a term because of the conviction that conflict is both natural and necessary.[3] Proponents of the term "peacebuilding" see it as a corrective to peacemaking: instead of a superficial effort to "make peace," peacebuilding also addresses underlying causes, deep division, and ongoing harm. In other words, the work of true peace—a peace with justice—requires engaging conflict constructively. For some people, just peace may require the limited and proportionate use of violence (i.e., violence that meets the conditions for just war). For others, just peace may require uncovering the persistent harms in a society and openly challenging those who perpetrate them (i.e., actions of nonviolent resistance). All people share the view that the work of peace is ongoing and requires more than "being nice." Indeed, recent literature on strategic peacebuilding maps a "comprehensive, multidimensional, multifocal, and multidisciplinary process"[4] in which scholars and practitioners from various disciplines and arenas of life work together in the ongoing and dynamic work of just peace. Central to this approach is the argument that "peace is not a static condition," as John Kelsay explains, not one "achieved once and for all." He continues: "Nor ought it be identified as the absence of conflict. Given the dynamics of group life, conflict is a more or less constant factor. The goal is to build relationships that can bear conflict and to forge institutions that sustain those relationships. To endure, the condition we describe as peace must be dynamic. One might say that building and sustaining peace requires constant attention and adjustment to developments in social life."[5] Peace must be built and rebuilt. It is always under construction. The work of peace is dynamic and ongoing and requires constant engagement with conflict, ongoing work of dismantling underlying causes of violence, and building the conditions and relationships for justice.[6] In the words of Jean Zaru, whose insights appear repeatedly in this chapter, peace "consists in consistently being able to deal creatively with inevitable conflict."[7]

As in the case of religious conflict, religion does not enter into the work of peacebuilding in an isolated or monolithic way (isolated from other factors and entering in the same way every time). Rather, peacebuilding can be religious in a variety of ways and to a variety of degrees, and we observe it best in action. That is, rather than speculating about the relationship between religion and peace in abstract terms, we understand the relationship between these two dynamic things—religion and peace—by observing their interaction on the ground, in concrete places, and expressed by people in context.[8] From the ground, we see that religious peacebuilding includes "beliefs, norms, and rituals" expressed and embodied by actors "for whom religion is a significant motivation."[9] These religious actors provide examples of a variety of peacebuilding tasks: "observation and witness, education and formation, advocacy and empowerment, and conciliation and mediation," and speaking to multiple publics at different social levels.[10] Also from the ground, we see that successful peacebuilding involves collaboration among religious actors and "civil society actors, governments, and international institutions."[11] As with conflict, the role and influence of religion in peacebuilding cannot be easily distinguished from other factors; nor is it particularly meaningful to do so. People participate in the work of peacebuilding for a variety of reasons and in a variety of ways; religious convictions, traditions, texts, and authority (among other things) contribute to the substance and shape of their efforts.[12]

Dignity is certainly one religious conviction that informs religious actors in contexts of conflict and peacebuilding. In keeping with the dynamics described thus far, dignity is one concept that interacts with others to influence convictions and actions in a variety of different ways. Before unpacking these, however, I offer one more observation not yet articulated in the religion, conflict, and peacebuilding literature: a religious actor's participation in contexts of conflict and peacebuilding also informs his or her understanding of dignity. The influence from religious conviction to action is not unilateral, rather the believer's experiences in the world also influence his or her understanding of theological concepts. And the Christian concept of dignity, particularly as grounded in the theological doctrine of *imago Dei*, is no exception. Regarding the presence of dignity in contexts of religious conflict and peacebuilding I observe the following. First, dignity functions as a cause for conflict and a criterion for behavior in conflict. Second, dignity grounds rights of individuals and maintains relationship between individuals. We shall see in the final part of the chapter, "Having and Becoming," that our experiences with conflict and peacebuilding enrich our understanding of the *imago Dei*.

CAUSE AND CRITERION

To say that dignity is a cause of conflict sounds odd, but it is true. The affirmation of human dignity inspires religious actors to stand up against the violation of persons and to engage conflict constructively for purposes of social change. Human dignity is a religious conviction that mobilizes believers to challenge the status quo, to resist dehumanizing practices no matter how regularized they have become. The conviction about human dignity motivates the kind of conflict that is an essential part of peacebuilding. We have seen this historically when ecclesial authorities draw on references to human dignity and the *imago Dei* to convey the egregious nature of multiple forms of violence, to denounce those who perpetrate it, and to inspire believers to resist it.

In 1908, the Federal Council of Churches resisted structural violence by calling on Christians to stand "for equal rights and complete justice for all men in all stations of life," for safe working conditions and a living wage, for the abolition of child labor, and for the abatement of poverty.[13] When the National Council of Churches issued its "A 21st Century Social Creed" 100 years later, it underscored the language of human rights with an explicitly theological foundation: "The full humanity of each woman, man, and child, all created in the divine image as individuals of infinite worth."[14] Rather than acquiesce to the forces of industrialization and capitalism, the writers of these statements illuminate the gross inconsistency between human beings as created in the image of God and human beings as exploited in the economic machinery of society. In the rich tradition of Catholic social thought, the dignity of the human person grounds economic, social, and political rights *and also* constitutes the criterion by which one judges policies and practices. The National Conference of Catholic Bishops articulated this criterion in 1986: "Every economic decision and institution must be judged in light of whether it protects or undermines the dignity of the human person."[15] Policies and practices that undermine the dignity of the human person are unjust and must be resisted and dismantled. Dignity emerges here not only as a criterion for just policy but as a just cause for resistance, a morally legitimate reason to engage conflict.

When religious actors draw upon the image of God to ground human dignity, then the just cause and moral legitimacy gain an explicitly theological power. For Christians who hold firm to the *imago Dei* as a core conviction, the violation of human dignity is more than a social transgression—it is sacrilege. From the crucible of such brutality of and resistance to apartheid, Archbishop Desmond Tutu insists that "to treat such persons as if they were less than this, to oppress them, to trample their dignity underfoot, is not just evil as it surely must be; it is not just painful as it frequently must be for the victims of injustice and oppression. It is positively blasphemous, for it is tantamount to spitting in the face of God."[16] Consider the power of this language, particularly in contexts of systematic oppression and violence, contexts where persons are attacked, marginalized, and silenced because of an attribute that renders them "less than." In these places, which of course are all around us, this universal theological affirmation of personhood is, in Tutu's words, both "marvelously exhilarating" and "staggering."[17]

This theological assertion—"We are all, each one of us, created in the image of God"[18]—prophetically denounces perpetrators and systems of dehumanization, inspires resistance, and implicates bystanders near and far. In discourse and action, this assertion has played a crucial role in resistance movements around the globe. In each movement, the universal assertion is applied to particular bodies that are devalued, neglected, or violated—a crucial move if it is to avoid becoming an empty platitude. In addition to a general statement on human dignity, the religious peacebuilder therefore stands outside of a private detention center in south Georgia and insists that the people who have no papers and no status are in fact bearers of the divine image. Similarly, the peacebuilder stands with a woman whose body bears the scars of violence and insists that the violence she has experienced is a desecration of the holy. Human dignity is a universal affirmation, but its power and truthfulness are only truly known when particular, wounded bodies are addressed and defended as holy.

In the United States, we see this clearly in the Black Lives Matter movement. All persons are created in the image of God. But when some bodies are treated as less than, it is crucial to affirm their sacredness explicitly: black lives matter. Leah Gunning Francis captures this point in her study of social activism in Ferguson, Missouri, after the shooting of Michael Brown. She writes:

> For the clergy, standing up for justice on behalf of Michael Brown was about joining the work of God in the world. This was a tipping point in the fight against black lives being deemed as disposable. The people I interviewed, and many more, heeded the call of God to call for justice on behalf of Michael Brown and all black bodies that are deemed less than human. This movement has beckoned all of us to see black people as human beings created in the *imago Dei*—the image of God.[19]

As the Black Lives Matter movement continues across the country, Brian Batnum hears from activists a fundamental demand, "the assertion of their full and unequivocal humanity."[20] This demand does not only echo in the streets as a challenge to police practices, political systems, and judicial proceedings. It should also prompt self-examination in the churches, according to Batnum. "Churches must ask themselves if they reflect an unqualified commitment to the full humanity of one another that is exhibited in Christ's life and work."[21] Christians embody this commitment by joining in a movement that declares that the black body lying in the middle of the street is sacred and the destruction of that body is blasphemy.

Explicitly naming the devalued, violated, and neglected bodies is a theological act of remembering their sacredness and a political act of resisting violence and demanding respect. In the words of Palestinian Quaker Jean Zaru, "resistance is the refusal to be neglected and disregarded."[22] Through resistance, one demands to be seen and treated—or that another be seen and treated—with dignity, as one created in the image of God. When white people hold a sign that says "black lives matter," it is an act of resistance to racism that devalues black bodies. But it is also an act of repentance for the hundreds of thousands of black bodies that white people have violated and continue to violate. Both actions—resistance and repentance—are inspired by the dual awareness that all persons are created in the *image of God*, and yet we do not live that way. Awareness of the image of God calls believers into conflict with systems and practices that treat people as less than. In this sense, dignity—rooted here in the image of God—generates and sustains resistance.

Archbishop Tutu describes the universal affirmation of personhood as marvelously exhilarating and also staggering.[23] Indeed! *All* persons are created in God's image: not only the oppressed, but also the oppressor; not only the victim, but also the perpetrator; not only the advocate for justice, but also the guardian and beneficiary of the status quo. Each and every one of them is also created in the image of God. In these contexts of violence, therefore, human dignity inspires resistance *and* places parameters around it. Religious peacebuilders empowered by a universal affirmation of dignity cannot then violate the dignity of their opponent in the context of conflict. John Paul Lederach captures this paradox perfectly in his discussion of "the dilemma of dignity": "How do I protect my/our dignity and yet recognize and acknowledge the dignity of the other?"[24] In this particular article, Lederach examines the interplay between the "lived internal world [of the religious peacebuilder] that seeks meaning and purpose and the *external life* that seeks safety, understanding and respect." He wonders at the religious peacebuilders' capacity to perceive the sacredness within the enemy-other, precisely in a space that defines their relationships in terms of threat. Lederach asks, "How is it that humanity was noticed and recovered in spite of imminent threat and fear?"[25]

We see this awareness in the writings and work of Zaru, who reminds us that "my enemy, too, is a child of God."[26] In the context of Israeli occupation of the Palestinian territories, Zaru resists nonviolently because she perceives the quality that Quakers refer to as "that of God" in the persons suffering and perpetuating multiple forms of violence. She argues that "a real revolution must concern itself with the triumph of human value and human rights," and she finds "Christian teaching relevant to such a revolution."[27] (She demonstrates the interplay between the internal world and external life that Lederach describes above.) Zaru continues, "Although these teachings are essentially nonviolent, they can never be characterized as encouraging passivity or disengagement in the face of injustice. Rather, Christ's teachings are activist, highly political, and often controversial. They sometimes involve dangerous forms of engagement in social and political conflict."[28] The affirmation of human dignity inspires resistance, but it also shapes it. The form of resistance must continue to recognize "that of God" in the enemy-other, and indeed makes that resistance possible. "It is really only in the light of love that I am liberated to work for peace and freedom," she writes.[29]

To say that human dignity becomes a criterion for the means of resistance codifies something that unfolds in a more wondrous way, as Lederach writes and Zaru demonstrates. And yet, in writings about resistance, we do find this mysterious capacity codified in the pledge and commitments of participants in the movement. Respecting the humanity of the other—or continuing to love the enemy—is a core commitment that shapes the actions of nonviolent resisters. We see this concretely in historical documents from the civil rights movement, which include commitment cards and codes of conduct calling on participants to "walk and talk in the manner of love" and "to refrain from the violence of fist, tongue, or heart."[30]

Zaru articulates a commitment that is core to nonviolent resistance by saying "that means and ends should be consistent."[31] The way in which one engages conflict must be consistent with the goals for social change. Particularly with relationship to human dignity, one cannot create socially just institutions that safeguard and respect human dignity through efforts that violate human dignity. Zaru expresses this in very practical terms as a matter of consistency: "I cannot endorse acts of violence in my day-to-day confrontations and, at the same time, be taken seriously when I speak of an ideal for the future that exalts wisdom, sensitivity, fairness, and compassion as basic requirements for running the world."[32] In an observation parallel to those of Lederach, she conveys the paradoxical power of nonviolent methods of social change: "The offering of respect and concern on the one hand while meeting injustice with non-co-operation and defiance on the other."[33] As war veterans remind us later in this chapter, commitment to human dignity sustains both elements of this paradox: it calls one into conflict with societal forces that violate the person, and it calls one to treat as fully human the violator. The image of God, when taken seriously, muddies our lives, our politics, and our speech.[34] It does not allow us to divide the world neatly between good guys and bad guys. It binds us to people we might rather get away from. If one takes the *imago Dei* seriously, one cannot dismiss anyone as unworthy of care or beyond redemption. In this sense, human dignity grounded in the *imago Dei* is a Christian's greatest affirmation and most challenging truth.

RIGHTS AND RELATIONSHIP

Although commitments to human dignity inform religious peacebuilding, scholars and practitioners working in pluralistic and multidisciplinary contexts more often use the language of human rights. And yet, human rights discourse is by no means settled terrain. Debates abound regarding the meaning of human rights, the assumptions undergirding them, the identification of rights (which claims are rights?), and the foundation for human rights.[35] Here, I simply clarify two points about this. First, Christian theology grounds a notion of human rights for Christians. In other words, there are Christian reasons for holding the view that "certain things ought not to be done to any human being and certain things ought to be done for every human being."[36] Christians affirm this claim not because of its political importance or because of a strong humanistic sentiment. Rather, they hold this assertion to be true because they believe all people to be endowed with dignity by their Creator.[37]

Second, Christian foundations for human rights do more than provide Christian reasoning for an idea that is shareable with non-Christians. They also provide Christians with a certain understanding of human rights, a frame and a foundation. It is especially important to articulate these particularities in pluralistic contexts, despite our impulse to blur all distinctions and create the appearance of common ground. One important element of a Christian understanding of human rights is that it is intrinsically connected to relationship.

To name this as a feature of a Christian understanding of human rights does not mean that only Christians hold it. Indeed, for many, irrespective of religion, one cannot talk meaningfully about rights without also talking about obligations. Rights concern what one is owed as an individual, and this concept has no real content unless the individual is among other individuals.[38] But for Christians, human rights are intrinsically connected to relationship because justice is a relational concept, as Daniel Philpott's recent work on justice after massive injustice illustrates.[39] In *Just and Unjust Peace* and in a recent article in the *Oxford Handbook on Religion, Conflict, and Peacebuilding*, Philpott addresses the argument that reconciliation may be appropriate to interpersonal conflicts but ought not to be pursued in political contexts where justice is required. Philpott challenges the underlying assumption that reconciliation requires bracketing the pursuit of justice by arguing that reconciliation is indeed a form of justice. With right relationship as its "central feature," reconciliation includes "a set of propositions that tells us who ought to do what to whom, for whom, and on behalf of whom and the reasons why."[40] Philpott describes six features of reconciliation as essential to justice after mass injustice. First is the establishment of socially just institutions, which are "based on human rights and the rule of law." He describes human rights as "grounded in the dignity of the person as created in the image of God and in obligations that are grounded in the law of God."[41] Rights are not only about what the individual has, but also about what the individual owes to others. The other five features of reconciliation as justice are acknowledgment of harm, reparations to those violated, apologies, punishment, and forgiveness. In all of these features, Philpott attends to the relationship between victim and perpetrator, individual and society. Reconciliation—justice after mass injustice—is not separate from a notion of individual rights. Instead, "Human rights, the duties and claims that they involve and the dignity of the person that they honor when they are enshrined by law, are themselves a form of right relationship."[42]

We hear a similar argument from Zaru when she writes about the meaning of reconciliation in the context of Israeli occupation of the Palestinian territories. She makes clear that reconciliation is "central to the gospel and those of us who are Christians must be active in reconciling."[43] But she refuses the notion that reconciliation requires bracketing justice or quieting demands for rights and dignity. "I cannot reconcile myself to structures of domination and oppression, covered over with words of peace and reconciliation,"[44] she writes. "Real reconciliation involves a fundamental repair to human lives, especially to those who have suffered. It requires restoring the dignity of the victims of violence."[45] Zaru and Philpott both argue that right relationships—relationships that are also marked by justice, mutual respect, and dignity—are part of the biblical vision of justice. One cannot achieve reconciliation without securing human rights. But, informed by the Christian conception of *imago Dei*, one cannot conceive of human rights outside of the context of relationship. Of course, Christians conceive of the *imago Dei* in different ways. As someone in the Wesleyan tradition, I draw on Wesley's theology of *imago Dei* as a resource for thinking about human dignity as a fundamentally relational concept.

In *The New Creation* (1998), Wesleyan theologian Ted Runyon describes the theology beneath Methodist social witness in the areas of human rights, the environment, and poverty. He highlights a soteriology that "sees the 'great salvation' . . . as nothing less than *a new creation* transforming all dimensions of human existence, both personal and social."[46] Central to this is a particular understanding of the image of God, which reinforces relationality. Runyon explains that Wesley understood "the image more relationally, not so much as something humans possess as the way they relate to God and live out that relation in the world."[47] Wesley described three ways that human beings bear the image of God. First, the "natural image" refers to the endowments that make us "capable of God," or able to enter into relationship with God. These include understanding, will, and freedom. Recognizing that the natural image echoes the more traditional views on capacities, Runyon argues that even here we see that the qualities of the natural image are in the service of relationship. Second, Wesley referred to the political image to articulate the place of human beings in governing the Earth. He argued that human beings are assigned a place of privilege and responsibility, yet this place is nested in a context of relationship to the Creator of all things and requires certain behavior toward others. Runyon explains: "Humanity is the image of God *insofar* as the benevolence of God is reflected in human action toward the rest of creation."[48] Third, in the moral image of God, the human being receives continually from the Creator and mediates to the world that which is received. This is the context of Wesley's proposal for "spiritual respiration"—the ongoing breathing in of the spirit of God and channeling that spirit out into the world. This "unceasing presence of God" underscores our relationship with the Creator; a relationship that we maintain through "a life of service to God, our fellow human beings, and all creation."[49] There is much more to explore historically, theologically, and ethically. Here it is helpful simply to take note of a theological resource that embeds the concept of human dignity in a relational notion. Drawing on this, one need not add a relational argument to the plank of individual human rights; the theological ground for this notion of human rights is inherently relational. To be human is to be in relationship with God and the rest of creation. To be fully human is to live in right relationships of mutuality, dignity, and respect for persons.

HAVING AND BECOMING

So far, I have described a movement from convictions about dignity to actions in contexts of conflict and peacebuilding. However, the vectors of influence also move in the other direction: believers also understand religious convictions differently in light of experience. In this section I explore this dimension of the interaction between dignity and religious conflict and peacebuilding, specifically, the ways in which experiences of violence inform Christian understanding of the *imago Dei*. We understand more fully the profound meaning of *imago Dei* by truly attending to bodies, in their destruction, brokenness, healing, restoration, and transformation.

One of many things I have learned through studying violence is that an act of violence is never an isolated event, but rather always part of a larger story. There are narratives of violence rather than "an act of violence." Similarly, the violation or denial of the image of God is not an isolated and encapsulated event, but, rather, violation and denial are always part of a larger story. The image of God may be violated in a moment, but it is diminished over time through repetition of abuse, systematic discrimination, or a never-ending barrage of humiliation and ridicule. Attending to experiences in specific ways, we see the formation and transformation of personhood over time. We see the ways in which the *imago Dei* gets buried beneath acts of abuse, patterns of neglect, and speech that belittles and betrays. Moreover, we see that this burial occurs in the life of those inflicting violence and of those receiving it.

The literature on moral injury provides a resource for understanding the effect of participation in violence over time.[50] Psychologists and veterans use the term "moral injury" to describe a wound experienced by soldiers when a trusted authority orders them to act in ways contrary to conscience. Jonathan Shay, a psychologist with the U.S. Department of Veteran Affairs who worked with Vietnam veterans, identifies three elements of moral injury: betrayal, legitimate authority, and a situation of great weight.[51] It is a complex dynamic involving personal wrong-doing and also a lack of autonomy, a sense of duty, and a feeling of betrayal. As Iraq veteran Tyler Boudreau makes clear, however, the depth of moral injury does not necessarily correspond with the intensity of violence in which one participated. In his experience, moral injury occurs through ongoing participation in the low-level violence of occupation, during which soldiers repeatedly perform actions that transgress morality. He writes, "What I've found most difficult for people to grasp (and for a while this was hard for me, too) is the full range of 'moral injuries' sustained in Iraq; because it's not always about the killing."[52] Boudreau describes being with veterans of Iraq and Afghanistan as they "described the daily grind of driving in and out of towns, patrolling through streets, searching houses, detaining suspected insurgents, questioning locals, and all the while trying to stay alive."[53] Boudreau very carefully uses the word "occupation" to describe the form of violence that these veterans exacted. He does not deny their role in the atrocities of war, but he focuses on the way occupying a land is also morally injurious, even though the stories and events seem more mundane.

Boudreau's point is powerfully illustrated in a narrative by another veteran named Michael Yandell.[54] Also a veteran of the Iraq War, Yandell tells the story of offering a bottle of water to a young Iraqi boy who had asked for candy. When the boy refuses the water, Yandell becomes angry. He writes,

> I rip the cap off the liter bottle in my hand, dump some of it out on the ground, and throw it at him. An old man, most likely his grandfather, rushes up, grabs the boy, and pulls him away. The old man looks at me, not with anger, hate, or even sadness. His eyes are full of fear. He's afraid of *me*. In that moment, I don't recognize that look, because I don't recognize myself. How can he be afraid of me? I'm one of the good guys, after all.[55]

Yandell will never forget the way that the Iraqi man looked at him; nor will Yandell ever forget that feeling of losing himself, not recognizing the person he had become. Like Boudreau, Yandell felt that his moral center had eroded over time through participation in a system that repeatedly demanded his transgression of moral boundaries—momentous and minor—every day.

Thinking of veterans like Yandell, Boudreau writes, "Through these ostensibly mundane stories, we cried out to the world, 'Our moral fibers have been torn by what we were asked to do and by what we agreed to do.'"[56] After returning home, Boudreau searched for some explanation of why he was hurting in a way that neither a PTSD diagnosis nor a monolithic label of guilt could capture. Moral injury gave language for this experience: "Moral injury is about the damage done to our moral fiber when transgressions occur by our hands, through our orders, or with our connivance. When we accept these transgressions, however pragmatically (for survival, for instance), we sacrifice a piece of our moral integrity. That's what moral injury is all about."[57]

One of the first books to gather stories of veterans who had experienced moral injury was published in 2013 by Rita Nakashima Brock and Gabriella Lettini of the Soul Repair Center at Brite Divinity School.[58] The descriptions, narratives, and poems collected in their book provide rich resources for thinking about human dignity and transformation of persons. For example, in a chapter titled "Killing Changes You," Brock and Lettini include a poem by Camilo "Mac" Bica, a marine veteran of the Vietnam War. The poem, "Warrior's Dance," gives expression to this transformation:

> I fear I am no longer alien to this horror.
> I am, I am, I am the horror.
> I have lost my humanity
> And have embraced the insanity of war.
> The monster and I are one. . . .
> The blood of innocents forever stains my soul!
> The transformation is complete,
> And I can never return.
> *Mea culpa, mea culpa, mea maxima culpa.*[59]

Mac insists that "no one truly 'recovers' from war. No one is ever made whole again." So he strives every "day to forgive and absolve [him]self of guilt and to live with the wounds of war that will never heal."[60]

Those who participate in violence—whether morally justified or not—are also created in the image of God. They do not forfeit human dignity when they participate in violence. And yet, the experiences of veterans suffering moral injury illustrate the ways in which a perpetrator of violence—or participant in an ongoing system of structural violence—loses his or her moral center and comes to feel that she or he has transformed into someone else, and perhaps feels unworthy of love and care. Much as years of abuse and neglect diminish the sense of self, participation in actions contrary to one's sense of morality diminish his or her identity as one created in God's image. Connecting these descriptions with Wesley's threefold understanding of the image of God is illuminating not only for veterans' experiences, but also for our understanding of the *imago Dei* and the relationship between human dignity and transformation. When one violates one's conscience—whether in the performance of duty or in the madness of war—the natural image of God is diminished. Violation of conscience constitutes an attack on understanding, freedom, and will—the very qualities that give us the capacity to connect with God, according to Wesley. In the description from Brock and Lettini, we can hear the diminishment of the political image by which we represent a benevolent God in the world and the diminishment of the moral image by which we receive and channel the grace of God in the world. One of the most powerful features of the narratives of moral injury that veterans are now courageous enough to share is that moral injury accrues over time. It is not so much the result of one dramatic event, but the erosion of one's moral fiber over time as one participates in a system that is both demanding and totalizing.

If violation of the image of God is not an act but a process, the same things must be said of restoration or recovery of the image of God. This too is a process, a narrative of healing or restoration. It is a process of becoming or restoring that which we were created to be. This process is a social process; it involves an interactional dynamic. Another veteran profiled in Brock and Lettini's work gives expression to this. Camilo Ernesto Mejia is a veteran of the Iraq War who describes his preenlistment life as "self-absorbed." He did not see the connections between his problems and the problems of others. But his "experience in Iraq changed that," he says. "Moral injury is painful, yet it has also returned a sense of humanity [to me] that had been missing from my life for longer than I can remember. I have come to believe that the transformative power of moral injury cannot be found in the pursuit of our own moral balance as an end goal, but in the journey of repairing the damage we have done unto others."[61] Repairing the damage we have done to others, in a Wesleyan sense, recovers the moral image of God. Contemporary Wesleyan theology, as Runyon envisions it, involves a call to reflect God's image in the world. Thus, the theological doctrine of *imago Dei* includes moral imperatives. One is not only created in God's image but is also called to recognize the image of God in others and reflect God's image in the world. In this strain of the Christian tradition (though not only here), human dignity is about both being and having. Recognizing and reflecting the image of God in the world is one way to describe the ongoing work of religious peacebuilding.

CONCLUSION

Human dignity carries great authority for Christians and other religious traditions in a variety of contexts. It anchors arguments for human rights, economic rights, civil rights, and cultural rights. It grounds ministries serving the homeless, undocumented migrants, and other marginalized persons. I have reflected on human dignity within three contexts related to religion, conflict, and peacebuilding—nonviolent resistance, reconciliation, and moral injury. We have seen that human dignity mobilizes religious peacebuilders to resist violation of self and others through means that also recognize the dignity of the perpetrator. I have focused on the meaning of dignity when grounded in the Christian doctrine of *imago Dei.* We have observed that belief that all persons are created in the image of God generates and sustains nonviolent resistance.

We have also considered the relationship between rights and relationship, arguing that human dignity grounds human rights and places all people in relationship to one another as equally creatures of God, created in God's image. Finally, we considered the ways that persons continue in processes of diminishing or restoring the image of God in one another and the world. This gives us a way to think about human dignity as a more dynamic feature of human existence.

I return to the point that religious peacebuilding is ongoing and dynamic work. It is ongoing and dynamic not only because violence persists and conflict is necessary. It is also ongoing and dynamic because the interplay between religion and peacebuilding is far from straightforward. Religious peacebuilders do not apply neatly encapsulated convictions in a neutral way to historical developments. Rather, we bring religious convictions to bear on lived experience and gain fresh insights about our convictions in the process. I hope I have demonstrated this dynamic movement between conceptions of the image of God and lived experiences of violation, justice work, peacebuilding, and reconciliation. We also sometimes discover that religious convictions are inhibiting the work of peace by contributing to exclusion, justifying violation of persons, or excusing apathy and quietism in the face of human suffering. The work of religious peacebuilding requires scrutiny of one's convictions in light of our experiences of violence. Although I have explored the connections between the image of God and nonviolent resistance and peacebuilding, I also note that Christian interpretations of *imago Dei* have been used to justify violence and deny care to members of creation. So, this much-celebrated doctrine is certainly not beyond scrutiny and critique. This concept—though certainly subject to misinterpretation and misuse—is far too valuable to be squandered by sloppy thinking, idolatrous interpretation, or self-serving applications.

As one focused on the relationship between religion, conflict (more violent and less violent), and peacebuilding, I write about human dignity with a great sense of urgency because we live in a world that treats bodies like garbage. I think of mangled bodies dumped like refuse, desperate bodies sorting through trash bins, beaten and raped bodies as the receptacles of hatred, neglected bodies treated as a waste of time, depleted bodies used up and discarded, bodies strapped with explosives and detonated. In this world, with so many forms of violence against bodies, the affirmation of human dignity could not be more important and the determination to reflect, recognize, and restore the image of God in all of creation could not be more valuable. And for Christians who believe that the image of God is a process rather than a status, this doctrine calls us to constant work to reflect the image of God in the world through acts of nonviolent resistance, the work of justice and reconciliation, and daily action to respect and affirm the dignity of every person.

NOTES

Portions of this chapter are excerpted from *Introduction to Christian Ethics: Conflict, Faith, and Human Life*. © 2018 Ellen Ott Marshall. Used by permission of Westminster John Knox Press.

1. There is a robust literature debating the relationship between religion and other factors that shape individuals' behavior in contexts of conflict. For a recent account of this literature, see Atalia Omer, R. Scott Appleby, and David Little, eds., *The Oxford Handbook of Religion, Conflict, and Peacebuilding* (Oxford: Oxford University Press, 2015).

2. For a current state of the field of scholarship on religious violence, see Scott Appleby, "Religious Violence: The Strong, the Weak, and the Pathological," in Omer, Appleby, and Little, eds., *The Oxford Handbook of Religion, Violence, and Peacebuilding*.

3. See Robert J. Schreiter, R. Scott Appleby, and Gerard F. Powers, eds., *Peacebuilding: Catholic Theology, Ethics, and Praxis* (Maryknoll, NY: Orbis, 2010).

4. Atalia Omer, "Religious Peacebuilding: The Exotic, the Good, and the Theatrical," in Omer, Appleby, and Little, eds., *The Oxford Handbook of Religion, Conflict, and Peacebuilding*, 16.

5. John Kelsay, "The Comparative Study of Ethics and the Project of the Justpeace," in Omer, Appleby, and Little, eds., *The Oxford Handbook of Religion, Conflict, and Peacebuilding*, 259.

6. See also Ellen Ott Marshall, "Introduction," in *Choosing Peace through Daily Practices*, ed. Ellen Ott Marshall (Cleveland: The Pilgrim Press, 2005), 5–7.

7. Jean Zaru, *Occupied with Nonviolence: A Palestinian Woman Speaks* (Minneapolis: Fortress, 2008), 81.

8. Indeed, this is one of the reasons why Atalia Omer frames her discussion as religious peacebuilding rather than religion and peace: "The concept of peacebuilding entails an active engagement with particular conflicts. It is not a general and decontextualized reflection on religion and peace" (Omer, "Religious Peacebuilding," 15–16).

9. Gerard Powers, "Religion and Peacebuilding," in *Strategies of Peace: Transforming Conflict in a Violent World*, ed. Daniel Philpott and Gerard Powers (Oxford: Oxford University Press, 2010), 322.

10. Ibid.

11. Ibid., 325.

12. Ibid.

13. Federal Council of Churches, "The Social Creed of the Churches," adopted December 4, 1908, http://nationalcouncilofchurches.us/common-witness/1908/social-creed.php.

14. National Council of Churches, "The Social Creed for the 21st Century," issued by the General Assembly of the National Council of Churches, November 7, 2008, http://www.ncccusa.org/news/ga2007.socialcreed.html.

15. National Conference of Catholic Bishops, *Economic Justice for All: Pastoral Letter on Catholic Social Teaching and the U.S. Economy* (Washington, DC: National Conference of Catholic Bishops, 1986), ix.

16. Desmond Tutu, "The First Word: To Be Human Is to Be Free," in *Christianity and Human Rights: An Introduction*, ed. John Witte Jr. and Frank S. Alexander (Cambridge: Cambridge University Press, 2011), 3.

17. Ibid., 1, 2.

18. Ibid., 2.

19. Leah Gunning Francis, *Ferguson and Faith: Sparking Leadership and Awakening Community* (St. Louis: Chalice Press, 2015), 18.

20. Brian Batnum, "Black Lives Matter: Seven Writers Assess the Movement," *Christian Century* 133, no. 6 (2016): 26.

21. Ibid., 27.

22. Zaru, *Occupied with Nonviolence*, 71.

23. Tutu, "The First Word," 1, 2.

24. John Paul Lederach, "Spirituality and Religious Peacebuilding," in Omer, Appleby, and Little, eds., *The Oxford Handbook of Religion, Conflict, and Peacebuilding*, 552.

25. Ibid. (original emphasis).

26. Zaru, *Occupied with Nonviolence*, 74.

27. Ibid., 75.

28. Ibid., 75–76.

29. Ibid., 74.

30. Martin Luther King Jr., *Why We Can't Wait* (New York: Mentor, 1963), 64.

31. Zaru, *Occupied with Nonviolence*, 76.

32. Ibid.

33. Ibid.

34. As I observed in Ellen Ott Marshall, "Affirmation and Accountability: Ethical Dimensions of 'The Blessed Image,'" in *The Vocation of Theology: Inquiry, Dialog, Adoration* (General Board of Higher Education and Ministry, 2017), 106.

35. The language, concept, and assumptions undergirding human rights are also contested territory in the literature of religion, conflict, and peacebuilding. In Omer, Appleby, and Little, eds., *The Oxford Handbook of Religion, Conflict, and Peacebuilding*, see David Little, "Religion, Peace, and the Origins of Nationalism"; Marc Gopin, "Negotiating Secular and Religious Contributions to Social Change and Peacebuilding"; and Atalia Omer, "Religion, Nationalism, and Solidarity Activism."

36. Michael J. Perry, *The Idea of Human Rights: Four Inquiries* (New York: Oxford University Press, 1998), 13, as quoted in Richard Amesbury and George M. Newlands,

Faith and Human Rights: Christianity and the Global Struggle for Human Dignity (Minneapolis: Fortress, 2008), x.

37. This is certainly not the only reason Christians affirm human rights. For example, George M. Newlands develops a Christological foundation for human rights, rooted in the doctrine of incarnation (Amesbury and Newlands, *Faith and Human Rights*, 109–23).

38. Amesbury and Newlands, *Faith and Human Rights*, 25–27.

39. Daniel Philpott, *Just and Unjust Peace: An Ethic of Political Reconciliation* (Oxford: Oxford University Press, 2012).

40. Ibid., 5.

41. Daniel Philpott, "Reconciliation, Politics, and Transitional Justice," in Omer, Appleby, and Little, eds., *The Oxford Handbook of Religion, Conflict, and Peacebuilding*, 343–44.

42. Ibid., 343.

43. Zaru, *Occupied with Nonviolence*, 77.

44. Ibid., 76.

45. Ibid., 77.

46. Theodore Runyon, *The New Creation: John Wesley's Theology Today* (Nashville: Abingdon Press, 1998), 5 (original emphasis).

47. Ibid., 13.

48. Ibid., 17 (original emphasis).

49. Ibid., 18.

50. I explore this connection between moral injury and a Wesleyan understanding of the *imago Dei* in Marshall, "Affirmation and Accountability."

51. Jonathan Shay, "Moral Injury," *Psychoanalytic Psychology* 31, no. 2 (2014): 183.

52. Tyler Boudreau, "The Morally Injured," *The Massachusetts Review* 52, no. 3/4 (2011): 751.

53. Ibid., 752.

54. Michael Yandell, "Hope in the Void: How Veterans with Moral Injury Can Help Us Face Reality," *Plough Quarterly Magazine*, no. 8 (Spring 2016), https://www.plough.com/en/topics/justice/nonviolence/hope-in-the-void.

55. Ibid., paras. 3–4 (original emphasis).

56. Boudreau, "The Morally Injured," 753.

57. Ibid., 749.

58. Rita Nakashima Brock and Gabriella Lettini, *Soul Repair: Recovering from Moral Injury after War* (Boston: Beacon, 2013).

59. Ibid., 20 (original emphasis).

60. Ibid., 75.

61. Ibid., 89.

AFTERWORD

Matthew R. Petrusek and Jonathan Rothchild

In the introduction to this book we asked whether there is any unity to the conception of dignity in different religious and philosophical traditions beyond the appeal to the same word. We can now conclude that the answer is a deeply nuanced, yet nevertheless firm, *yes*: Judaism, Islam, Hinduism, Buddhism, humanism, Protestantism, and Catholicism all affirm that human beings have worth because they are human beings and must be treated accordingly. In other words, to draw on Christopher McCrudden's poignant analogy in *Understanding Human Dignity*, we are singing from the same hymn sheet, after all.

That does not mean, however, that we're all singing in the same language, or that every tradition approves of the particular rendition of the song put forth by other traditions—a fact that makes comparisons complex, particularly when we recognize the difficulty, even impossibility, of individuals standing outside traditions to make "neutral" assessments of their respective understandings of dignity. Yet, as we argued, we can ask certain questions that allow the traditions to have an authentic *conversation*, enabling *different* perspectives to address the *same* topic. Here are the questions again:

1. What sources justify dignity's existence, nature, and purpose?
2. What is the relationship between the divine and human dignity?
3. What is the relationship between dignity and the human body?
4. Is dignity vulnerable or invulnerable to moral harm?
5. Is dignity inherent or attained?
6. Is dignity universal and equal?
7. Is dignity practical?

As we have seen, these questions not only help structure the organization of each tradition's internal conception of dignity; they also provide a framework for comparison. For example, though the traditions differ on the specific nature of the sources of dignity, each tradition appeals to (1) sacred texts, (2) reason, (3) culture, or (4) ecclesial tradition—and in some cases (as we see in Eastern Orthodoxy and Catholicism) a combination of these—to justify their respective understandings of dignity. Likewise, the traditions have vastly different conceptions of the nature of the divine, but the majority examined in this volume—Islam, Protestantism, Hinduism, Judaism, Catholicism, and Eastern Orthodoxy—identify the divine as necessary for human dignity's existence. And even though Buddhism and humanism do not directly derive their understandings of dignity from a conception of God, the divine conceived of as "the transcendent" or "ultimate" is still palpable in their thought and still necessary for giving a full account of how each conceives of dignity. Moreover, though the traditions do not share a unified understanding of the meaning of the body, and less so of the meaning (or existence) of the soul, it is important to note that none of them seeks to locate dignity exclusively within the body—which is another way of recognizing that no tradition embraces strict materialism. Furthermore, the traditions differ on the specific ways they define dignity's vulnerability to moral harm, but all of them recognize that dignity is both *vulnerable* and *invulnerable*, which, in turn, illuminates how the traditions also affirm that dignity is both "inherent" in human beings and "attained" (though their definitions of "inherent" and "attained" and the means by which dignity can be attained differ substantially). This relationship between the inherent and attained, in turn, points to a similar consensus on the question of the universality and equality of dignity: the traditions differ on what constitutes "equality" among all human beings, but all recognize that every individual possesses some basic level of worth, including those who do not share their religious or philosophical beliefs. Finally, each tradition also recognizes that the existence of dignity generates moral imperatives to act, or refrain from acting, in order to protect and nourish dignity itself. In other words, every tradition in this volume recognizes that dignity is practical.

Identifying that these descriptive similarities exist among the traditions—without glossing over their profound and even irreconcilable differences—is an important conclusion in and of itself. Minimally, it helps establish a substantive overlapping consensus. It may indeed be impossible to identify a universal understanding of dignity from an empirical perspective (that is, finding an account that all people do, in fact, embrace); however, finding *widespread* consensus on certain features of dignity, a consensus that can even justifiably be called global, nevertheless marks a major advancement for those seeking to locate an ethical unity within the human family.

Yet the question remains whether these chapters can lead us beyond descriptive conclusions to normative ones. That is, are we ultimately justified in making claims not only about how different traditions *do* understand dignity and its implications but also about how they *should* understand dignity and its implications? The task of determining which view among the different options presented in this volume is most "right" in the sense of "most true" must be left to the work of another book (or set of books!), but we believe that the analysis in these pages authorizes two normative claims about dignity. However we might evaluate the specific content of any tradition's conception of the nature, derivation, and implications of dignity, it is justified to conclude, we believe, that (1) theology should be understood as indispensable for addressing the question of dignity, and (2) dignity should be understood as indispensable for the question of how to do ethics.

The descriptive and comparative components of this book provide, we hope, abundant evidence for the first conclusion. Given the depth and complexity of dignity in the traditions, it is evident that providing a normative account of human dignity—one that adequately addresses the ontological, anthropological, and epistemological meanings of being human—cannot avoid questions that transcend the limits of cultural, psychological, sociological, historical, economic, linguistic, biological, political, environmental, or even philosophical modes of inquiries, as useful as these are to understanding dignity. In other words, precisely because "human dignity" seeks to encompass the *full* meaning of what it means to be human, the answer to the question of dignity should include an accounting of the human experience of, and relationship with, the divine in its manifold forms—including experiences of awe, terror, dependency, emptiness, hunger for permanence, community, joy, unity, brokenness, corruption, abandonment, redemption, and peace, among others. Indeed, it is the turn to theological languages and theological categories—categories such as grace, sin, forgiveness, judgment, heaven, perfection, self-emptying, cosmic order, and sanctification—that not only authorizes the theological dimensions of human dignity in the sense of giving those dimensions a platform for systematic expression and evaluation, but also provides the possibility for adequately addressing some of dignity's most intractable questions, including the following:

- How can we say that dignity uniquely applies to *all* human beings in *absolute* equality if there is no human capacity (e.g., reason, self-awareness, relationality, etc.) that all human beings share absolutely equally?
- How can we say that dignity is both vulnerable and invulnerable at the same time? If moral harm can damage dignity but not destroy it, where do we locate the unassailable dimension of human dignity within the human being?
- If we want to recognize that dignity is not only a static ontological quality of all human beings, but also dynamic in the sense of something to be realized, from where do we derive the normative standard that sets the goal for what it means to live a "fully human" life?
- How do we account for the dignity of those who are near death or severely disabled?
- How do we account for the dignity of human beings who commit evil acts, especially those we cannot attribute to mental illness?

In short, if we ask the question, "What is human dignity?" and we take the most basic expression of that question to mean, "What does it mean to say that every human being created by, and belonging to, the human species has equal worth without exception?," it is myopic—and potentially incoherent—to presume we can arrive at a satisfying answer without addressing the question of God. This is not to say that "human dignity" can somehow provide an indirect proof for the existence of the divine, but it raises the question of whether, in the absence of the divine, we can ultimately establish a justification for the existence of dignity. The question of dignity places all of us, in other words, squarely in theological territory whether we like it or not. That does not mean the theological is where we must begin or even where we must end, but a full accounting of human dignity finally permits no detours around it.

Further, as demonstrated by the case study chapters in part II, we wish to conclude that dignity is an indispensable category for addressing normative questions about conflict and other moral issues. This is not to say that dignity always (or even frequently) offers *unambiguous* clarity on a specific moral problem. As David Gushee observes in his chapter (chapter 7) on dignity from a Protestant perspective, "no one can claim unassailable 'proof' of the rightness, or wrongness, of the principles, rules, and judgments one might derive by making appeal to one's dignity ethic" (191). The chapters in part II make clear, however, that dignity provides an important way of framing and reframing assumptions held with respect to the way we approach conflicts. For example, many approaches to conflict, say, those of liberalism or neoliberalism, view conflict in terms of protecting individual rights and maximizing individual interests, but Hille Haker's (chapter 13) conception of vulnerable agency underscores the intersubjective dimensions of agency and the ways in which dignity is actualized in and through interactions with others. This interactive dimension of dignity engenders what Haker characterizes as the paradox of dignity (in ways similar to the conceptual paradox and social paradox of dignity discussed in William Schweiker's chapter [chapter 11] on dignity and the humanistic traditions): dignity retains its unconditional status even as it is conditional because it remains dependent on and actualized through interaction. This paradoxical character of dignity does not attenuate its normative weight in evaluations of potential courses of action; rather, it upholds the idea that moral deliberations are neither exercises of fully deductive reasoning nor language games but full expressions of human life and thought. Haker reveals a crucial role for dignity, particularly with respect to pervasive problems involving agency, vulnerability, and gendered violence: dignity orients us to how to encounter or not encounter another person with respect and recognition.

Several contributors investigate the deep interconnections between vulnerability and dignity. Zeki Saritoprak (chapter 10), for example, explores Islamic models of humans as the vice-regents of God who are also vulnerable to deception; similar themes are engaged in the respective response chapters by Jonathan Rothchild (chapter 12) (who asserts that the coinherence of responsibility and vulnerability is shared by Islamic and humanistic traditions) and Matthew Petrusek (chapter 9) (who identifies theological distinctions underlying divergent perspectives on vulnerability and moral or spiritual growth in Protestant and Orthodox traditions). Taking as a key point of departure the Buddhist understanding that all things are subject to fluctuation and impermanence (*anitya/anicca*), Kristin Scheible (chapter 2) posits in her chapter on dignity and the Buddhist tradition that a "self-less one who engages in the path of self-cultivation recognizes the vulnerability and value of dignity within herself and recognizes the vulnerability and value of dignity in others" (75).

In his chapter on dignity and immigration, Victor Carmona (chapter 17) similarly connects dignity, respect, and recognition of the other through appeal to the Catholic human rights tradition. Drawing out several of the themes raised in Darlene Weaver's chapter (chapter 1) on dignity in the Catholic tradition, Carmona argues that the mediating character of dignity should inform current immigration policies. In contrast to models that privilege state sovereignty as the primary basis for immigration policies, Carmona holds that dignity requires recognition of individual rights of movement and rights to residency and attention to the global common good and fellowship of humankind. The right to residency is not predicated on a political or legal right; at a basic level, Carmona contends that the right to residency is rooted in membership in the human society. Dawn Nothwehr, in her chapter (chapter 18) on dignity, conflict, and ecology, extends this relationality to include the natural world. Similar to Haker and Carmona, Nothwehr pursues an integrative approach—namely, a "scientific and religious understanding of integral ecology and of the human person integrally and adequately considered" (436)—to uncover a descriptive and normative understanding of human dignity and its implications for environmental ethics. This self-reflexive censure of anthropocentricism becomes manifested, as William Schweiker also observes, as a responsibility for the dignity or intrinsic value of nonhuman life.

Other contributors examine the ways that religion can also create divisions within this membership in human society and threaten dignity. In analyzing current religious and political conflicts in Ukraine, Nicholas Denysenko (chapter 14) unmasks the ways in which religious polemics can generate a sacramental vocabulary that fails to honor the human dignity of the other and exercises power over the other within ecclesial structures (or, as Aristotle Papanikolaou observes about the Russian Orthodox Church in his chapter [chapter 8] on dignity in the Orthodox tradition, it elides the ecclesial and the political in problematic ways). In redressing such polemics through appeal to resources within the Orthodox tradition, Denysenko appropriates the concept of anthropological maximalism, where sacramental identity is rooted in each Christian as a servant of God. Ellen Ott Marshall, in her chapter (chapter 19) on conflict and peacebuilding, likewise recognizes dignity and religion as a cause for conflict. Yet, drawing on her own Wesleyan tradition, Marshall also argues that dignity, informed by the *imago Dei*, grounds individual rights and maintains relationships.

As several of the contributors contend, upholding dignity requires critically assessing structural violence and structural forms of oppression. Haker and Marshall both describe the threats of structural violence, and Terrence Johnson's chapter (chapter 15) on racial violence interrogates structural forms of oppression. In developing a framework for an African American moral humanism and drawing on Delores Williams's concepts of wilderness and Victor Anderson's idea of the grotesque, Johnson attempts to disrupt and dismantle the constructions of blackness in public life. He views dignity as every moral agent's ability to transgress social boundaries. This perspective informs his critique of putatively neutral policies, such as colorblindness, which, despite claims about equality and fairness (that seemingly protect dignity), ignore the ways in which public culture and moral belief construct blacks and their bodies in terms of an absence of innocence (and thereby denigrate dignity) and a humanity in need of subjugation.

William O'Neill (chapter 16) similarly considers the systemic forces within criminal justice that threaten dignity and construct the African American as criminalblackman. In responding to these forces (in ways that have interesting parallels to Karen Enriquez's response chapter [chapter 3] to Buddhist and Catholic traditions that breaks open the label of the barbarian), O'Neill develops a threefold hermeneutic of rights, including a *deconstructive* naming of rights violations, a *constructive* systemic redress of the causal factors contributing to degradation, and a *reconstructive* interpersonal redress and reflection on the policies and institutions that can best support a human rights regime. Similar to Haker, Carmona, and Weaver, O'Neill views dignity as supporting mutual dependency while rejecting collectivism and mediating between retributive politics of rights and the restorative politics of the common good. Furthermore, similar to Johnson's critique of Kantian ideals, such as colorblindness, O'Neill holds that a dignitarian tradition of rights favors a more robust restorative approach to criminal justice.

Several thinkers, including Weaver, Carmona, and Nothwehr, engage the Vatican II document *Gaudium et spes* to establish the general parameters (in terms of basic needs and other opportunities, protections, and rights) for a "genuinely human life." Dignity lies at the center of this genuinely human life, even as the lived expression of such a life may vary greatly and be informed by different moral norms. As Weaver, for example, notes, "Catholic moral theologians disagree regarding moral norms, the relationship between objective and subjective dimensions of morality, and specific moral issues" (38). Similar to Haker's recognition of the paradoxical nature of dignity, such comments should not diminish or disqualify the moral imperatives and nonreductive value commitments generated through recognition of and respect for dignity. Dignity promotes equal and inclusive regard for all persons. Dignity may be expressed differently in diverse legal, cultural, and political contexts, but dignity can supersede cultural differences (e.g., in his chapter on dignity and the Islamic tradition, Saritoprak recounts the story of the Prophet's encouragement to stand up for a funeral procession, regardless of the one who has died) and even divine sanctions (e.g., in their chapter on dignity and the Jewish tradition, Elliot Dorff and Daniel Nevins [chapter 4] write that the Talmud identifies cases where human dignity does, in fact, override rabbinic and even biblical imperatives).

In an increasingly divided world, dignity offers a glimpse at a constructive path for adjudicating human rights claims and deliberating about competing goods. As Chris Chapple notes in his response chapter (chapter 6) on dignity and Hinduism, "the rich textual and narrative traditions of the Hindu faith provide resources for constructive reflection on developing an informed response on how best to foster human dignity even in challenging circumstances" (165). These challenging circumstances in which we foster dignity include seeing and respecting those whose dignity has been violated. Whether framed as Camus's taking the victim's side (O'Neill), affirming the epistemological privilege of the oppressed (Gushee), or "maximiz[ing] the conditions for the possibility of realizing irreducible uniqueness" (Papanikolaou, 209), dignity provides a fundamental baseline against cruelty and marginalization and galvanizes deontological constraints, but it also empowers individuals freely and responsibly to seek authentic relations and pursue shared goods.

In short, the contributions to this book demonstrate that theological perspectives offer timeless and timely insights into the grounds for and implications of a robust conception of dignity that invites interfaith dialogue, interdisciplinary analysis, and interpersonal collaboration in response to common questions and urgent moral problems. Whatever else our moral vocabulary includes, it must embrace dignity as an essential concept.

Contributors

VICTOR CARMONA is assistant professor of theology and religious studies at the University of San Diego.

CHRISTOPHER KEY CHAPPLE is the Navin and Pratima Doshi Professor of Indic and Comparative Theology at Loyola Marymount University.

NICHOLAS DENYSENKO is the Jochum Professor and Chair at Valparaiso University.

ELLIOT N. DORFF is Rector and Sol and Anne Dorff Distinguished Service Professor in Philosophy at American Jewish University.

KAREN B. ENRIQUEZ is assistant professor of theological studies at Loyola Marymount University.

DAVID B. GUSHEE is Distinguished University Professor of Christian Ethics and director of the Center for Theology and Public Life at Mercer University.

HILLE HAKER is the Richard A. McCormick, SJ, Chair of Catholic Moral Theology at Loyola University Chicago.

TERRENCE L. JOHNSON is associate professor of religion and African American studies at Georgetown University.

ELLEN OTT MARSHALL is associate professor of Christian ethics and conflict transformation at Candler School of Theology, Emory University.

DANIEL NEVINS is the Pearl Resnick Dean of the Rabbinical School and dean of the Division of Religious Leadership of the Jewish Theological Seminary.

DAWN M. NOTHWEHR, OSF, is the Erica and Harry John Family Chair of Catholic Theological Ethics at Catholic Theological Union.

WILLIAM O'NEILL is professor emeritus of social ethics at the Jesuit School of Theology at Santa Clara University.

ARISTOTLE PAPANIKOLAOU is professor of theology and Archbishop Demetrios Chair in Orthodox Theology and Culture at Fordham University.

MATTHEW R. PETRUSEK is associate professor of theological studies at Loyola Marymount University.

JONATHAN ROTHCHILD is professor of theological studies and associate dean of the Bellarmine College of Liberal Arts at Loyola Marymount University.

ZEKI SARITOPRAK is professor and Bediuzzaman Said Nursi Chair in Islamic Studies at John Carroll University.

KRISTIN SCHEIBLE is associate professor of religion and humanities at Reed College.

WILLIAM SCHWEIKER is Edward L. Ryerson Distinguished Service Professor of Theological Ethics at the University of Chicago Divinity School.

DARLENE FOZARD WEAVER is professor of theology and associate provost for academic affairs at Duquesne University.

Index

CPSIA information can be obtained
at www.ICGtesting.com
Printed in the USA
LVHW082329230620
658836LV00012B/210

9 780268 106652